# BEYOND ORIENTALISM

*The Work of Wilhelm Halbfass and its Impact on Indian and Cross-Cultural Studies*

# BEYOND ORIENTALISM

*The Work of Wilhelm Halbfass and its Impact on Indian and Cross-Cultural Studies*

*Edited by*

ELI FRANCO
KARIN PREISENDANZ

MOTILAL BANARSIDASS PUBLISHERS
PRIVATE LIMITED • DELHI

*First Indian Edition : Delhi, 2007*



ISBN: 81-208-3110-1

MOTILAL BANARSIDASS
41 U.A. Bungalow Road, Jawahar Nagar, Delhi 110 007
8 Mahalaxmi Chamber, 22 Bhulabhai Desai Road, Mumbai 400 026
203 Royapettah High Road, Mylapore, Chennai 600 004
236, 9th Main III Block, Jayanagar, Bangalore 560 011
Sanas Plaza, 1302 Baji Rao Road, Pune 411 002
8 Camac Street, Kolkata 700 017
Ashok Rajpath, Patna 800 004
Chowk, Varanasi 221 001

PRINTED IN INDIA

BY JAINENDRA PRAKASH JAIN AT SHRI JAINENDRA PRESS,
A-45 NARAINA, PHASE-I, NEW DELHI 110 028
AND PUBLISHED BY NARENDRA PRAKASH JAIN FOR
MOTILAL BANARSIDASS PUBLISHERS PRIVATE LIMITED,
BUNGALOW ROAD, DELHI 110 007

## CONTENTS

## 2. Issues of Comparative Philosophy



## 3. Topics in Classical Indian Philosophy

**4. Developments and Attitudes in Neo-Hinduism**



**5. Indian Religion, Past and Present**

Eli Franco and Karin Preisendanz

# INTRODUCTION AND EDITORIAL ESSAY ON WILHELM HALBFASS

The ground plan for the present volume was conceived by Leszek Nowak, the editor-in-chief of Poznań Studies in the Philosophy of the Sciences and the Humanities and Professor at the Universities of Poznań and Gdańsk, in the academic year of 1989/1990. During this year he, Professor Wilhelm Halbfass of the University of Pennsylvania and one of the editors, Eli Franco, then of La Trobe University, Melbourne, were fellows at the Wissenschaftskolleg zu Berlin/Institute of Advanced Study, Berlin, while the second editor was teaching at the Freie Universität Berlin (Free University of Berlin). Fascinated by the Indological-philosophical personality of Halbfass, Nowak suggested the preparation of a volume containing papers on Halbfass and his work that would be published together with critical responses from the "subject" himself. In the spring of 1993 the editors began to solicit contributions from scholars working in a wide variety of fields such as Indology (especially Indian philosophy and religion), philosophy, religious studies, theology, comparative literature, classical ethnography, folkloristics, anthropology, cross-cultural studies and political studies. The contributors were requested to center their articles on or have them take as their starting point one or more of Halbfass' three major books: *Indien und Europa* (1981) and its English version *India and Europe* (1988) (IE), *Tradition and Reflection* (1991) (TR) and *On Being and What There Is* (1992) (OB). It was also emphasized that the book was not intended as a kind of felicitation volume. Rather, it was made known that the book was envisaged as one that would contain critiques, questions, comments, supplementary observations, different perspectives, etc.

The papers that could finally be included in the present volume originate from twenty-three scholars working in eleven countries spread over three co..tinents; they have been grouped into five broad topical sections by the editors. Halbfass' critical response commences with a long introductory essay in which, among other things, he assesses in a masterly manner the state of Indian studies almost twenty years after the publication of Edward Said's *Orientalism*. Halbfass' responses to the individual contributions follow in altogether four essays after the corresponding sections; because of their brevity the responses to sections four and five are joined in one essay.

It is not a surprise that the largest number of papers centers on or touches upon topics dealt with in *Indien und Europa/India and Europe*, namely, the contributions by Andrew O. Fort (also relating to TR), Yohanan Grinshpon, Klaus Karttunen, Dermot Killingley, Frank J. Korom, Jitendra Nath Mohanty, Srinivasa Rao (also referring to TR), Reena Sen and Sergei D. Serebriany. *Tradition and Reflection* forms the subject and starting point of the second large group of papers, by Johannes Bronkhorst, Stuart Elkman, Minoru Hara, Jan E. M. Houben, Bruce M. Perry (also referring to IE) and John Taber; Albrecht Wezler offers significant supplementary observations on the conception of *karman*. *On Being and What There Is* has caught the attention of three contributors only; Kunio Harikai (who is also inspired by TR) and Viktoria Lysenko both take specific observations in the book as the starting point of their own related investigations and reflections, whereas Joseph S. O'Leary examines in a very broad and substantial manner whether the question of being was at all addressed in Indian philosophy. That only three contributors specifically respond to *On Being and What There Is* may be due to the fact that its impact had not yet been fully realized at the time the editors' invitations to the volume were sent out. However, three other authors respond from their respective viewpoints to *all* three major works of Halbfass: Francis X. Clooney, SJ, Fred Dallmayr and Rada Iveković. Ben-Ami Scharfstein, for his part, presents us with his fundamental reflections on a comparative history of world philosophy, an undertaking in which he feels encouraged by Halbfass' example of joining two intellectual worlds, namely, those of India and the West.

It might be expected that a summary of the contributions would be provided here in the editors' introduction. However, because Halbfass himself presents the gist of the individual contributions in his respective responses, an additional summary would seem to be superfluous, and we rather turn, without further ado, to our "subject."

The editors' personal acquaintance with Professor Wilhelm Halbfass extends back to 1979. During the academic year of 1978/1979 Halbfass temporarily filled the Indological chair left vacant by the retirement of Paul Hacker at the University of Münster in Northern Germany. At a guest lecture that same year at the University of Hamburg's Seminar für Kultur und Geschichte Indiens (Seminary for the Culture and History of India) (now: Institut für Kultur und Geschichte Indiens und Tibets/ Institute for the Culture and History of India and Tibet), he spoke on the correlation of the concepts *darśana* and "philosophy," a topic central to the second part of *Indien und Europa* (which part had mainly been completed at Münster) and one variously taken up by several contributors to the present volume.[1] Among the students listening to this fascinating presentation of Indian materials by a scholar both an Indologist and a philosopher was Karin Preisendanz. In the academic year of 1981/1982 (the monumental *Indien und Europa* had just been published), Halbfass returned to Hamburg, this time to replace Professor Albrecht Wezler during a leave, and she had the privilege to participate in the seminars offered there by him as well as to attend a series of lectures[2]. One of the seminars was entitled "Zur Terminologie und Problematik des Seins" ("On the Terminology and Problematic Issues of Being"), in which key passages from Indian philosophical texts on ontology, which reappeared later on in *On Being and What There Is*, were read and interpreted. Topics connected with *Studies in Kumārila and Śaṅkara* (Halbfass 1983a), the original core of *Tradition and Reflection* on which Halbfass was working during his stay at Hamburg, were treated in a second seminar on Mīmāṃsā and Dharmaśāstra, based on the reading of Medhātithi's extensive commentary on *Manusmṛti* II.6.

The occasion for the next encounter, which would lead to many others over the years, occurred in 1987 when Professor Yehuda Elkana, the long-time director of the Van Leer Jerusalem Institute, asked Eli Franco, then one of the institute's research fellows (the "Indologist in residence"), to invite a scholar of interest to come to the institute. After discussing the matter with Karin Preisendanz, who had moved to Israel in the meantime, he suggested that an invitation be extended to Halbfass.[3] Halbfass was an obvious choice for more than one reason. Most importantly, he is one of the few true specialists in Indian philosophy and intellectual history who appeals in his writings and lectures to open-minded Western philosophers and to the educated general public, the intended audiences of his lectures in Israel. Additionally, despite his research work and manifold obligations at the University of Pennsylvania, he is always amenable to travel, to lecture and to participate in conferences, symposia and various other meetings.[4]

Halbfass was made to pay dearly for this trip. During the twelve days he was in Israel he gave four lectures at three different institutions in Jerusalem and Tel Aviv, a lengthy interview to Kol Israel (Voice of Israel), the Israeli national radio,[5] attended a considerable number of lunches and dinners, and met dozens of people. Somehow he managed, next to all these obligations, to also find some time for leisure and travel. Particularly memorable is a day the editors spent together with Halbfass and Dan Tsalka, one of Israel's leading writers and a close friend of theirs. Halbfass and Tsalka, related to each other through their wide reading and broad intellectual interests and curiosity, enjoyed each other's company immensely. The next day Halbfass stated that he hadn't met such a partner in conversation for fifteen years. Tsalka, in his turn, read *India and Europe*, the revised and expanded English version of *Indien und Europa*, when it was published the following year, and then wrote a short essay inspired by it for the literary supplement of *Ha'ir*, a widely read Israeli weekly newspaper.[6] In the introductory part of this essay, entitled "Thus Spake Kumārila," Tsalka describes Halbfass' scholarly personality with a vivacity that most academics forbid themselves:[7]

"The dogmatist who defends the purity of faith always ignores the yearning that seethes in it: the yearning to extol the ethical, love, equality, self-sacrifice, reason - as if they too are of the absolute; he refuses to understand that this yearning is a necessity that contradicts the absolute and affirms it through that very same contradiction. Without the pathos of this contradiction the wonderful books of faith would never have come into the world: the great poetry, the Psalms, the Prophets, upon which piles upon piles of commentaries were erected by the dogmatist who protects the purity of faith, by his fathers, by his spiritual off-spring.

The dogmatist does not understand this riven sign. 'Love, self-sacrifice, equality, reason?' he says with a slight twist of his thin lips. 'All this may be very well or may not be so very well, but one thing is clear: all this splendour does not abide in the heart of faith unless it is anchored there by heritage, ritual, command, law.'

I always wanted to look into this attitude of the dogmatist outside our spiritual world that is governed by the God of Abraham, Isaac and Jacob or by the God of the philosophers. I read and asked, but a delicate veil of fog always covered the answers, and naturally in these matters one has to be very precise. Suddenly it became possible thanks to three pages, written with great precision, that I found in Wilhelm Halbfass' book *India and Europe*.

A few words on the man. Halbfass is a German who has been lecturing in America for some fifteen years now. The book *India and Europe* was translated into English from German and underwent a sea change (and not only because of the sections and chapters that were added, such as the arresting chapter on Schelling). Perhaps laziness and impatience speak from my throat, but I am glad that what started from a necessity continues – the writing in English of German scholars. Halbfass gave a few lectures here last year; he is a moderate[8] person, with reddish-brown hair and a pleasant manner. There is something in him of the Irish and the Vikings, but he is not as quick-tempered as they. He reminds one of the great Germans of the second half of the last century, the men who read everything, who read what they read without bustle, who fixed what they read in their memory and could join the thanksgiving by Thomas Aquinas: 'Thank you, dear Lord, that I have never read a book without understanding it.' Halbfass excels in a property that is rare nowadays – intellectual tact that is due not to polite manners, but to a multiplicity of angles of contemplation. Thus, when he describes Schopenhauer's attitude towards India, as a matter of course he does not examine the latter's understanding of the Indian concepts from the professional point of view of an Indologist; as a matter of course he is sensitive to Schopenhauer's love for a certain translation and his refusal to abandon it when that translation turned out to be unreliable; as a matter of course he describes the internal and complex movement towards India, the slightly mysterious something that arises from hostility towards his culture, from the aspiration for the imaginary creation of an alternative world, from presentiment and yearning, from a wish for confirmation coming from afar; as a matter of course the smallest oscillations during Schopenhauer's life are examined by him with care and empathy. Halbfass shows the wheels behind the scenery of ideas, but he does not forget the scenery itself, the background colors of the spiritual and intellectual play.

A friend of mine once visited Halbfass at his home and asked him: 'Where do you write?' Halbfass led him to a corner in the bedroom and showed him a little table. 'And where is the card-register?' asked my friend. Halbfass pointed at two copybooks and a pen, which reminds me of the story that Schopenhauer used to tell in order to refute the opinion that a man cannot be a hero in the eyes of his servant: An Englishman came to the cottage of Immanuel Kant, where the philosopher used to retire in order to write. He did not find the great man and asked at least to see his books. 'Books? There are no books here!' replied his servant proudly, 'When we write, we write from memory!'

Well then, how does it look without Leviticus, without Aristotle, without the Midrash, without Maimonides, without the *Summa*, without everything? ..."

Tsalka proceeds to describe Kumārila's ethics with great precision, but this is outside our present purpose.[9] Despite its length, the above quotation is worthwhile not only because of the fair sketch of Halbfass' scholarly personality it includes, but also because it illustrates his inimitable, admirable gift for rendering the seemingly dry and scholastic texts of Indian philosophy fascinating to intellectuals outside the narrow circle of Indologists; as a Swiss reviewer has aptly stated, Halbfass combines European academic thoroughness with the readability of Anglo-Saxon scholarship.[10] For the circle of Indologists, too, his writings have thrown a refreshing new light on many philosophical texts and issues; this may be due to his strong background as a philosopher.

Most of Halbfass' readers are likely not aware of the fact that Indology and Indian philosophy are, so to speak, his second career. His major area of study (*Hauptfach*) at the University of Göttingen was philosophy, that is, Western philosophy, and his very first publication, written while he was still a student, is a review of Sebba's *Bibliographia cartesiana* (Halbfass 1965). His first book (Halbfass 1968a), based on his dissertation written under the supervision of the philosopher Hermann Wein, is entitled *Descartes' Frage nach der Existenz der Welt (Descartes' Query about the Existence of the World)*. He studied Indology only as a minor subject (*Nebenfach*), next to Classics, under the great Buddhologist Ernst Waldschmidt at the Seminar für Indologie und Buddhismuskunde (Seminary for Indology and Buddhist Studies), where he was trained rigorously in Indian philology.[11] Halbfass often enjoys narrating that he is sometimes asked whether he is related to the Descartes specialist Halbfass.

It is indeed surprising that the author of *Indien und Europa* wrote a dissertation on such a purely Western philosophical topic. And yet it is clearly not the work of another person. It is astonishing and fascinating to read today this early work of Halbfass because it has all the characteristics of a mature work of his: in it one meets with his vast erudition; one marvels at his ability to grasp broad issues without losing sight of the minutest details, an ability that brings to mind the image of Halbfass working like a landscape painter who uses a large canvas, but small brushes, slowly and patiently filling the canvas with gentle and well-defined strokes that result in a nuanced, precise and multiple-layered picture; one encounters subtle but clear conceptual analysis, reflexivity of thought,[12] polite but decisive criticism and quiet irony, the narrative skills of a born story-teller; and one sees similarities in the formal and stylistic structuring of the text through the numbering of paragraphs and the announcement, at the end of a paragraph, of the theme of the next. Could it be that Halbfass in his twenties was already the Halbfass we came to know in the middle of his life?

Each one of Halbfass' books enlarges our horizon, impresses us with its novelty and freshness of thought and leaves us breathless from its author's command over primary and secondary sources. Clearly, Halbfass' books could only have been written after many years of diligent work. It is remarkable, however, that not only the broad outlines of his future work, but also its substance can be discerned from early on. Halbfass' most recent book, *On Being and What There Is* (1992), philosophically explores and illuminates the Vaiśeṣika categories, and yet a significant study on Vaiśeṣika ontology was published as early as 1970.[13] His first Indological lecture at the 29th Congrès International des Orientalistes in Paris (1973) was on the conceptualization of being in Vaiśeṣika;[14] the book's title itself is used in print already in 1978 (cf. Halbfass 1978). Also in the case of *Tradition and Reflection* (1991), which examines fundamental issues of traditional Indian self-understanding, one can observe how Halbfass prepared his way with early seminal studies such as the monograph *Zur Theorie der Kastenordnung in der indischen Philosophie* (*On the Theory of the Order of Castes in Indian Philosophy*) (Halbfass 1976a), "Anthropological Problems in Classical Indian Philosophy" (1977), "Karma, *Apūrva* and 'Natural' Causes"

(1980a) and especially *Studies in Kumārila and Śaṅkara* (1983a), a continuation of some investigations begun in *Indien und Europa*.

Similarly, significant portions of *Indien und Europa* were published long before the book appeared. Following his early studies on Vaiśeṣika topics, Halbfass decided to specialize for a while on issues not at the center-stage of scholarship on Indian philosophy or much addressed by the Indian philosophers themselves. Halbfass' articles of this period include "Observations on *darśana*" (Halbfass 1979a) and "Indian Philosophers on the Plurality of Religious Traditions," a paper read at the South Asia Seminar at the University of Pennsylvania in 1980/1981 and published in 1984. Alongside these studies in Indian philosophy Halbfass maintained an active interest in the seemingly unconnected area of the reception of and responses to Indian philosophy by Western philosophers. "Hegel on the Philosophy of the Hindus" was written as early as 1973 and was followed by "Indien und die Geschichtsschreibung der Philosophie" ("India and the Historiography of Philosophy") in 1976 (Halbfass 1976c). In this case, however, the mentioned studies, important as they were, merely could have reflected further, seemingly distinct fields of interest of a versatile scholar. It was only with the publishing (1981) of *Indien und Europa* that they were joined in a larger, common context.

*Indien und Europa* came as an exciting surprise for the scholarly world of Indology, philosophy and religious studies. As one reviewer expressed it, the book brought together in an innovative way Indological research and philosophical research in the history of ideas.[15] This achievement was due, to a great extent, to Halbfass' talent for combining philological perspicacity with regard to particulars with a broad philosophical view with regard to the whole.[16] It was immediately clear then, as it is clear now, that the publication of *Indien und Europa* was a major event in the history of Indology and that the serious study and philosophical appreciation of Indian philosophy past and present would have to change profoundly.

However, despite its consequences for and repercussions on the philosophical study of Indian philosophy, *Indien und Europa,* and equally *India and Europe,* is, paradoxically enough, not about Indian philosophy, that is, not about what usually goes under this title. It does not follow the pattern of histories of Indian philosophy set up by Paul Deussen and continued by Otto Strauss, Erich Frauwallner and others, which commence with the proto-philosophy of the Ṛgvedic and Brāhmaṇa periods or the philosophy of the Upaniṣads, continue with chapters on early Buddhism and the Epic, then move on to classical Sāṅkhya and from there to the other "systems" and later Buddhist developments. Nor does it contain any significant discussion of fundamental areas of Indian philosophy such as epistemology and logic (e.g., *pramāṇa*-doctrines) or ontology (e.g., Vaiśeṣika atomism or Sāṅkhya evolutionism). If *Indien und Europa/India and Europe* had to be described in a few words, one could perhaps say that it is about creative-reflexive misconceptions. The first part of the book is about the misconception, misunderstanding and misrepresentation of India by the West (mainly represented by Europe) in the course of its search for India – whose image often became part of its self-understanding and self-representation: in ten fascinating chapters Halbfass succeeds in covering the entire span from Greek antiquity to the twentieth century. These chapters include remarkable discussions of the medieval Arab travellers, the Christian missionaries, the Enlightenment, the Romantics, Hegel, Schelling and Schopenhauer. The second part is about the misunderstanding of India by the Indians themselves, the misrepresentation of Indian thought (including both philosophy and religion) by the so-called Neo-Hindus, starting with Rammohan Roy, who were increasingly exposed to and heavily influenced by Western ideas, and who projected these ideas back onto Indian antiquity. In this respect, as in many others, the book's title is not intended to convey a symmetrical relation between India and Europe. Neither is it simply concerned with their mutual influences and interactions. Therefore the word order is of significance: "India and Europe," not "Europe and India."[17] The book is primarily about exemplary (mis)perceptions of India by Europeans and by Indians under the complex spell of Europe, not about the (mis)perception of Europe by Indians or about the active impact of India on European culture, be it intellectual or otherwise.[18]

Yet this by itself can hardly explain why *Indien und Europa* and especially *India and Europe* have had such a tremendous impact, not only on Indologists, but also on philosophers, and furthermore on scholars of religion, theologians, political scientists, students of cross-cultural issues, and even on Indian politicians, like D. P. Chattopadhyaya, who – as governor of Rajasthan – convened an impromptu panel on the book in 1991.[19] Why has *India and Europe* become a scholarly bestseller in several editions in the USA and in India[20]? Why was it considered of such importance and interest as to occasion even a recent pirate edition of the American edition from Korea?[21] Why does it appear in numerous bibliographies in introductory texts and collections of essays as well as on reading lists for courses at North American universities in the area of interreligious dialogue, "multi-culturalism," etc.? Why has it already been chosen as the topic of a M.A. thesis? What does it offer in addition, compared with e.g., *Much Maligned Monsters,* a study in which Partha Mitter - in 1977, before the Saidian epidemy broke out - carefully and thoughtfully showed how Indian art and iconography had been repeatedly and systematically misperceived, misunderstood, modified and appropriated by Westerners? Halbfass' purpose is much more ambitious, his scope much wider. It goes without saying that, unlike certain Saidians, he is not merely interested in pointing out misunderstandings with an accusing finger and crying fashionable words of disapproval and contempt such as Orientalism, imperialism, Western domination, etc., paradoxically disparaging and belittling, even denying his own writing self. Rather, he goes beyond that to show us a different way of approaching Indian thought.

What are the characteristics of this way? In his youth Halbfass called for and considered the development of an adequate method for comparative philosophy,[22] but he perceived his own efforts in this direction to be unsuccessful and became increasingly disheartened and pessimistic about the possibility of carrying out such an endeavor.[23] In *Indien und Europa/India and Europe,* he nevertheless proceeded to establish the presuppositions and prerequisites that would make a true dialogue and mutual understanding between Indian and Western intellectual cultures possible, to eventually allow for a mature comparison of Indian and Western thought. It is not without reason that the motto of the book, a quotation taken from an article by Hacker,[24] reads:

> Es müsste ein Philosophieren geben, das auf unmittelbarer Kenntnis von indischen *und* europäischen Quellen gründet. - There ought to be a philosophizing which is based on an immediate knowledge of Indian *and* European sources.

It is indeed a new type of comparative philosophizing that Halbfass inaugurates in *Indien und Europa/India and Europe*. First of all, it exhibits the fundamental requirement of thorough and immediate familiarity with both traditions called for already by Hacker. Its further essential outlines, also with a view to its possible future development, are sketched by Halbfass in the "Epilog" (chapter XX) of *Indien und Europa* and become slightly more defined, in negative and positive terms, in the concluding section of chapter 23 ("India and the Comparative Method") of *India and Europe.*[25] This new type of comparative philosophizing is certainly not the anachronistic analytical approach that lacks hermeneutic depth; Halbfass stresses hermeneutic awareness as a basic prerequisite and ingredient of comparative philosophy and not only demonstrates it throughout the book, but also pays close attention to the hermeneutic situations of those thinkers whose approaches to India he philosophically investigates. Excluding other possible ways of approach in comparative philosophy he writes:

> If "comparative philosophy" is supposed to be *philosophy*, it cannot just be the comparison of *philosophies*. It cannot be the objectifying, juxtaposing, synoptic, comparative investigation of historical, anthropological or doxographic data. Comparative philosophy is philosophy insofar as it aims at self-understanding. It has to be ready to bring its own standpoint, and the conditions and the horizon of comparison itself, into the process of comparison which thus assumes the reflexive, self-referring dimension which constitutes philosophy. ... (IE, p. 433)

Halbfass is far too wise and cautious to design a detailed, programmatic scheme and thus to limit and narrow down future developments or to run the risk of losing himself in over-abstraction and rhetoricalness.[26] And despite a subtle note of doubt that emerges in the above-mentioned section of *India and Europe,*[27] Halbfass provides us later in his scholarly career with two brilliant examples, in the form of *Tradition and Reflection* and *On Being and What There Is*, of how this "method" of comparative philosophizing can be carried out in practice.

Is there a distinctive name to this Halbfassian "method"? Halbfass himself has not termed his "method," but two reemerging words, *Gespräch*/"dialogue" and *Verständnis*/"understanding," could capture what he has in mind. It is quite clear that the usual everyday meanings of these words do not always correspond to the Halbfassian usage; this is indicated already by the fact that "dialogue" appears in inverted commas in the Epilogue (chapter 20) of *India and Europe*. For instance, Halbfass seems to speak of a "dialogue" or "dialogic situation" even when one party is not addressing the other party, but is rather turning to itself in responsive reflection: even when someone like Hacker writes for a European audience, Halbfass considers what he says as part of the ongoing "dialogue" between India and Europe. Also, contrary to what is sometimes presupposed,[28] this "dialogue" is not necessarily a balanced communication between two parties; Halbfass is of course clearly aware of the fact that the "dialogue" has been dominated by Europe so far.[29]

Halbfass' "method" is often said to be Gadamerian.[30] In his use of the crucial concepts of dialogue and understanding[31] Halbfass is clearly indebted to Gadamer. He specifically refers to Gadamer's notions of *hermeneutisches Gespräch* ("hermeneutical dialogue") and *Horizontverschmelzung* ("merging of horizons") and implies (IE, p. 165) that they are relevant to the study of Indian thought. Yet how Gadamerian is he really? Is he simply applying the Gadamerian notion of understanding to a wider "trans-cultural" context?[32] Halbfass accepts Gadamer's view that pre-judgement (*Vorurteil*) is a necessary and important constituent of the process of understanding, that understanding is not "slipping into someone else's skin, as it were," and that the extinction of one's own self is impossible; rather, it is crucial to be aware of one's bias.[33] Halbfass even quotes a passage on the "horizon" from *Truth and Method* which characterizes the "horizon" as something into which we move and which moves with us; according to Halbfass "this statement obviously applies to the general encounter between India and Europe, and to the 'horizon' of Western self-understanding in its relationship with the Indian tradition" (IE, p. 166). Up to this point Halbfass seems to be in agreement with Gadamer. However, once the reader has drawn this conclusion Halbfass begins posing question after question in his unique reflective style, and even before proceeding to the – often implicit – answers[34] to these probing, challenging and enlightening questions the attentive reader will realize that Gadamer has been left behind:[35]

> Is the relationship between India and the West indeed an encounter between two traditions? Is the modern West still a tradition? Are its ways of dealing with other traditions, its methods of objectifying historical and anthropological research, still ways of intercultural communication, interaction or even domination? Is it not their inherent claim to provide something more universal – a global medium and framework of communication, the freedom to approach and "understand" *any* tradition in an "objective," scientific manner? Or does this achievement of universality conceal another, perhaps more fundamental and elusive problem of communication – that between objectifying and detached "research" on the one side and commitment to a living tradition on the other? In other words, is the distance between "tradition" and "modernity" greater than that between any particular traditions? (IE, p. 166)

Here Halbfass parts ways with Gadamer not only in adding complexity and further perspectives to the issue, but also in his presumed answers. Actually, neither Halbfass nor Gadamer answers these questions explicitly: Gadamer did not respond to *Indien und Europa* or *India and Europe* in writing,[36] and Halbfass does not answer his own questions in an expected straightforward manner. Nevertheless, it can be reasonably assumed that Gadamer would reply to the first two questions in the affirmative, while Halbfass would tend to answer in the negative, or would at least modify the use of "tradition" in respect to the modern West. As regards the final question, together with its implication (which appears in the guise of a further question to be reworded as yet another question), Halbfass would certainly tend to answer in the affirmative. This is the Halbfassian "bias," of which he is fully aware. Unlike many of us who share this view, he has the courage to also state its further consequences politely but clearly: With the advance, from the West, of "modernity" and its encounter with and increasing superimposition on "tradition" in Europe and in all other parts of the world, the "Europeanization" of the earth *is* inevitable. In this verdict Halbfass follows Husserl and Heidegger, although, of course, one need not, and Halbfass does not, subscribe to all their partially obsolete interpretations and evaluations of this process. Further, as a result of this "Europeanization," India, or more precisely, modern Indian thinkers and especially those belonging to the Neo-Hindu milieu, perceive themselves to be relegated to an inferior and subordinate position and thus challenged to assert themselves against Europe. Here, too, Halbfass does not mince matters:

> Modern Indian thought finds itself in a historical context created by Europe, and it has difficulties speaking for itself. Even in its self-representation and self-assertion, it speaks to a large extent in a European medium. (IE, p. 375)

Another important influence on Halbfass, although not of a methodological nature in the strict sense of the word, was exercised by the Indologist Paul Hacker, an outstanding figure in the "dialogical" understanding of Indian culture. Halbfass did not study under Hacker. Intellectually, however, he is obviously much closer to Hacker than to Frauwallner.[37] He often refers to Hacker's work, and that at crucial junctions, wrote a major essay on Hacker's concept of inclusivism,[38] and recently edited a collection of Hacker's papers translated into English, complemented by an introductory essay on Hacker's complex scholarly personality.[39] Sometimes it seems that in talking about Hacker, Halbfass is in a way talking about himself. In the concluding remarks of his essay on Hacker's concept of inclusivism he states:

> ... Hacker responds to the Indian tradition, and to Neo-Hinduism in particular. He asserts his own tradition against the Neo-Hindu claims to universality and comprehensive "tolerance." He is not a "pure Indologist," and he does not speak

> solely in the language of "objective" research. He is also a personally and systematically committed participant in the continuing encounter and dialogue between India and Europe. (IE, p. 418)

Neo-Hinduism is the specific object of responsive interest for Hacker as well as for Halbfass. Hacker asserts the superiority of his own Christian tradition against Neo-Hinduism, while Halbfass, in a less confrontational manner, recognizes the domination of the "dialogue" between India and Europe by the West. Like Hacker, Halbfass is not a "pure Indologist." Both scholars are committed participants in the "dialogue" between India and Europe in the sense that their reflections on the Indian tradition are accompanied by reflection on and critical examination of their own traditions. For Halbfass this own tradition is the European philosophical tradition, whereas for Hacker it is mainly the Roman Catholic theological tradition. However, the two differ strikingly in their attitudes: Halbfass writes in a reconciliatory and benevolent mood, while in Hacker's writings, especially those of the later stage of his life, one senses a strong undercurrent of mistrust and aversion in his reaction to Hinduism and Neo-Hinduism. One may even suspect that he saw a danger for Christianity in what he perceived as the cunning passive–aggressive pseudo-tolerance of Hinduism. The role that he allocated to himself was not that of a dialogue participant in the usual, non-Halbfassian sense, but that of a gatekeeper warning unsuspecting and possibly misled Christians of the danger they might fail to recognize, namely, the Neo-Hindu inclusivism, a wolf in the sheep's clothing of tolerance. These remarks, however, are not meant to imply a lack of appreciation for Hacker's towering achievements as an Indologist. On the contrary, mistrust and dislike may sharpen one's sensitivities no less than empathy does. Persons who disliked India and the Hindus played an important role in Indological research, and indeed the field is still indebted to their contributions.[40]

The above reflections lead us back to the novelty of *Indien und Europa/India and Europe*, specifically of its second part. Even though the term "Neo-Hindu" was coined by a Hindu,[41] its use is sometimes felt to be derogatory because it seems to imply that a Neo-Hindu is not a genuine Hindu.[42] Indeed, in the Indological world the Neo-Hindu is generally perceived as – unknowingly – Westernized to a high degree and as somewhat estranged from his own tradition in that he reshapes or even distorts it in response to certain European ideas. Apologetically he tries to show that the latest Western ideas were already present in classical or even Vedic India; such attempts are often subject to ridicule by Western scholars, in part because by the time the Neo-Hindu reaction occurs the relevant ideas may have gone out of fashion in the West and their general appeal faded away. The Neo-Hindu lives in an epistemological limbo: he no longer possesses the traditional learning and approach of the pandits, but he has not yet acquired the philological, methodological and conceptual tools of Western scholarship in order to be able to tackle his own tradition in an alternative way.

Even if there is some truth in this slightly exaggerated characterization, Halbfass has done more than any other Indological scholar to dispel contempt for the Neo-Hindus by Western scholars, a contempt that often leads to general disregard. He has taught us to see how interesting and fascinating the Neo-Hindu writings can be and has impressed on us that the Neo-Hindu interpretation of the classical Sanskrit tradition and its texts should not be judged solely with a view to philological and historical accuracy; in this respect it obviously proves to be rather deficient.[43] Halbfass possesses a strong philological background, and he is no less capable than other philologists to point out the Neo-Hindu distortions and misinterpretations of the Indian tradition in the self-representation *for* and at the same time *against* the West - this he has done, and masterfully, for the key concepts of *dharma* and *darśana*.[44] But Halbfass goes beyond that: he instructs us in the appreciation of these "mistakes" in the light of the hermeneutical situation of the Neo-Hindus and presents those who "commit" them as serious thinkers who try courageously and innovatively to come to grips with the inescapable European modernity without thereby losing their cultural or religious identity. In doing so, Halbfass has profoundly changed our perception of Indian philosophy: Indian philosophy is no longer something that is immovably fixed in the past or, in its present-day "authentic" appearance, a mere fossilized relic from the past.[45] It is alive and "dialogically" creative; it keeps on changing in dynamic encounters, just as the European tradition does.[46] Even though Indian thought is in a rather problematic state at present, is overwhelmed by the West and "has difficulties speaking for itself," Halbfass is quite optimistic - probably more optimistic than most of us - as regards its future:

> This does not mean, however, that the dialogue and debate between India and Europe has been decided in favor of Europe, or that India has been superseded by Europe. The power of the Indian tradition has not exhausted itself in the self-

> representation and self-interpretation of modern India. The dialogic situation is still open. (IE, p. 375)

The much maligned Neo-Hindus - starting with Rammohan Roy, for the investigation of whose thought Halbfass undertook the study of Bengali - and also contemporary Indian philosophers like J. L. Mehta, to whom *India and Europe* is dedicated,[47] are Halbfass' favorite partners-in-dialogue.

The above allows us to understand the particular image of India in *Indien und Europa/India and Europe*, especially in its second part. In the book in general, India appears practically as an India without the Muslims, as has been stressed by Serebriany in his contribution to the present volume. Others have noticed the intriguing fact that it is a largely non-Buddhist India.[48] This general impression arises also in respect to Halbfass' work subsequently assembled in *Tradition and Reflection* and *On Being and What There Is*: Halbfass writes on Kumārila, Śaṅkara, Bhartṛhari, Jayanta and even Mallavādin, but only marginally on Nāgārjuna, Vasubandhu, Dignāga or Dharmakīrti. We can certainly not attribute this to a lack of knowledge of or interest in Buddhism. For instance, the section on Indian philosophy in the *Einführung in die Indologie* contains a masterful brief survey of Buddhist philosophy that shows Halbfass' usual command over and ease with both primary and secondary sources.[49] Rather, the image of India in the "Indian part" of *Indien und Europa/India and Europe* - only to a certain degree, though, the one in TR, and even less so the image in OB which is more of a Heideggerian quest and which is the delayed fulfillment of an early project begun in his youth[50] - is largely determined by the Neo-Hindu point of view and its analysis. Had there been any Neo-Buddhists of significance in India in the last two or three centuries, the image of India responding to the European tradition would certainly have appeared quite differently in *Indien und Europa/India and Europe*. Had Buddhism been alive in the India discovered by the missionaries, deists, etc., or in the India to which the (mis)perceptions of the Romantics, etc., became attached, India's image also in the first part of the book would differ.

What will be the outcome of this continuing encounter between India and Europe? Halbfass does not attempt to predict the future. Nevertheless, *Indien und Europa/India and Europe* seems to tell us that the "Oriental Renaissance" may take place after all. However, it may occur in reverse to the Oriental Renaissance as prophesized by Schopenhauer. It may not be a renaissance of Europe through the Orient, but a renaissance of the Orient through an encounter with Europe. The dormant potential of the extremely self-centered and xenophobic Hindu traditionalism has been awakened and "historically actualized" (IE, p. 369) by the encounter with the West and the subsequent, not yet completed Europeanization, and this encounter may release the universality of the Indian tradition from its extraordinarily elaborated ethnocentric barriers. Furthermore, unlike the European Renaissance which was triggered by the encounter with Greek antiquity that was mediated by Arab and Jewish translators, the "Oriental Renaissance," if it happens, will arise from the encounter of two living traditions capable of a dialogue with each other. Halbfass is clearly a major participant in this dialogue, perhaps the most remarkable participant since Deussen.

We are indeed grateful to Professor Nowak for initiating this project, first of all because the present volume will stand out in the profile of a series usually devoted to Western philosophy and philosophers; the interest in and commitment to Indian philosophy expressed in this way will hopefully awaken the interest of philosophers otherwise not concerned with Indian philosophical issues and cross-cultural understanding. Furthermore, the editorial work was a most exciting, inspiring and rewarding task in many respects. For this we would like to express our sincere gratitude also to the contributors. The present volume brought with it many cross-cultural scholarly friendships.

Special thanks are due to Anne MacDonald, a Ph.D. student in Indian philosophy at the University of Hamburg's Institut für Kultur und Geschichte Indiens und Tibets, who spent many hours editing the papers of some contributors who are not native speakers of English. Her competence and sensitivity helped us, together with the authors, to make these papers that much more accessible to the non-specialist reading audience. She also read through the manuscript of our introduction and made most valuable suggestions and comments. Burkhard Quessel, also a member of the Institut, provided expert advice and patient assistance in all matters of word processing and electronic data management. In addition we are grateful to him for his many suggestions to improve the aesthetic appearance of the volume.

*Institut für Kultur und Geschichte Indiens und Tibets*
*Universität Hamburg*
*Hamburg, Germany*

## NOTES

[1] Cf. the contributions by Houben, Mohanty, Rao, Scharfstein and Serebriany.

[2] The lectures treated the broad issue of *karman* and rebirth, reaching far beyond the observations presented in Halbfass 1980a and its revised version, chapter 9 of TR. It is to be hoped that Halbfass' projected monograph on this topic, first to be published in German, will soon be available to scholars. The gist of it is presented in Halbfass' contribution to the forthcoming *Routledge Encyclopedia of Philosophy* (cf. the list of publications below).

[3] The simplicity of the procedure was typical of Elkana's legendary managerial style. The whole issue was raised and closed in thirty seconds; there were no forms to be filled out, no committees to be convened, no budgets to be discussed.

At this point the editors want to express again their gratitude to Professor Elkana for making Halbfass' visit to Israel possible.

[4] To date Halbfass has given approximately 200 invited lectures and conference papers at locations throughout the world, ranging from the Papal Summer Residence, Castel Gandolfo (cf. Halbfass 1988b and the contribution by Mohanty in the present volume), to the Institute of Advanced Study, Kyoto (cf. Halbfass' contribution to the recently published *B. K. Matilal Memorial Volume*, listed in the list of publications below).

[5] Short extracts from this interview, together with Halbfass' lecture "Europe, India and the Europeanization of the Earth" delivered at the Van Leer Jerusalem Institute, were published in a Hebrew translation by Franco (Franco 1988, p. 80).

[6] *Ha'ir* of December 16th, 1988. The essay was later reprinted in Tsalka's collection of essays *Dapim Mehudakim be'Eṭev* (Tsalka 1993).

[7] The following translation from the Hebrew is by the editors.

[8] The Hebrew word *matun* is difficult to translate; it means "composed," "considerate," "restrained," "cautious," "patient" and "easy-going." All these characteristics fit Halbfass very well.

[9] This topic is discussed by Taber in the present volume.

[10] Cf. Goldschmidt 1981. Goldschmidt's review of *Indien und Europa,* among the first printed notices of the book, is one of those which were also broadcasted (Radio der deutschen und rätoromanischen Schweiz, Studio Zürich, program "Literatur aktuell" of December 23/24, 1981).

[11] The acquired competence in the Sanskrit language was only a natural addition to Halbfass' familiarity with the classical languages of Europe, the prerequisite for his philosophical studies. In this context we may mention Halbfass' short career as an actor in the performances of plays in ancient Greek.

At Göttingen no seminars on Indian philosophy were offered. The only instruction Halbfass ever received in Indian philosophy was during a half-year's stay in Vienna (1961/1962) where he participated in one of Frauwallner's intensive seminars (at that time dedicated to the study of Jayanta's *Nyāyamañjarī).* His fellow students were George Chemparathy, Lambert Schmithausen and Tilmann Vetter; Ernst Steinkellner had already been appointed assistant to Frauwallner.

[12] One of the most conspicuous characteristics of the Halbfassian vocabulary is the extensive use of compounds with self- as first member: self-affirmation, self-alienation, self-articulation, self-assertion, self-awareness, self-centeredness, self-criticism, self-definition, self-demarcation, self-expression, self-identification, self-interpretation, self-questioning, self-representation, self-understanding, etc.

[13] Cf. "Remarks on the Vaiśeṣika concept of *sāmānya"* (Halbfass 1970); cf. also "Conceptualizations of 'Being' in Classical Vaiśeṣika" (Halbfass 1975) and "Zum Begriff der Substanz *(dravya)* im Vaiśeṣika" (Halbfass 1976b).

[14] A considerably expanded version of this lecture was published as Halbfass 1975. In a recent conversation Halbfass gratefully recalled the enthusiastic and encouraging words following his 1973 lecture on being that came from the great Indian scholar and savant Srinivasa Ayya Srinivasan of Hamburg University. Srinivasan's reaction, as well as Steinkellner's response to the lecture, confirmed Halbfass in his decision to venture again into Indian philosophy and Indology, rather than follow up his interests in Western philosophy: although his first appointment, initiated by Waldschmidt who wanted to draw Halbfass into Indology, had been at the University of Göttingen's Seminary for Indology and Buddhist Studies, he had accepted, in 1970, an offer by the Department of Philosophy at Brock University, St. Catherines; this was followed in 1973 by the offer to replace Steinkellner during a leave from the University of Pennsylvania's Departments of Oriental Studies and South Asia Regional Studies. Halbfass' initial appointment there as Visiting Lecturer eventually led him to the position of Professor of Indian Philosophy at the renamed Departments of Asian and Middle Eastern Studies and South Asia Regional Studies.

[15] Cf. Schweer 1990.

[16] Cf. von Hinüber 1983.

[17] The reverse word order in Halbfass 1988b ("Europe, India and the Europeanization of the Earth"; cf. also chapter 24 in IE) is explained by the fact that this paper was prepared for a meeting on "Europa und die Folgen" ("Europe and the Consequences") and therefore takes European self-understanding and claims as its starting point.

[18] Although this should be clear to anyone who has read the book, perhaps the title as such is slightly misleading. It certainly misled Ram Swarup who wrote the longest and most indignant, not to say outraged, review of IE (Swarup 1991). Cf. e.g., pp. 91-92: "But a book named *India and Europe* could as well contain a section named "The European Tradition and the Presence of India", which could discuss Neo-Christianity and Neo-Europe, modifying their idiom under the influence of Indian thought. There is no dearth of data, but there is a reluctance to acknowledge that kind of data under the inertia of an old habit of thinking."

It would go too far to analyze here in detail Swarup's often ignorant criticism (especially as regards areas outside his competence, such as e.g., linguistics, pre-history and archaeology, and Vedic studies). In a kind of intellectual blur, caused by the fatal mixture of a defiant Neo-Hindu attitude with some Saidian ideas, he misses many of the individual and more general points made by Halbfass. His comments become especially slashing and beside the point when he takes up Halbfass' treatment of "experience" and "tolerance" in the appendices to IE, cherished notions in modern Indian self-affirmation. On the whole, one may call Swarup's reaction "exemplary" (in the Halbfassian sense) for the new post-Saidian type of Neo-Hinduism.

[19] As a curiosity one may mention that one Indian reviewer, T. F. Bidari, seems to imply a possible, though unexpected reason for the impact of the book when he writes that the universal message, as he perceives it to be promulgated in *India and Europe,* may help to "ward off dangers of war and inter-state conflicts of serious proportion" (Bidari 1992, p. 49).

IE was the topic of further scholarly panels; however, Halbfass participated personally only in the SACP (Society of Asian and Comparative Philosophy) panel organized by Joseph Prabhu of the California State University, Los Angeles, at the Pacific Division Meeting of the American Philosophical Association in 1989. At this occasion Halbfass presented the main paper, followed by brief responses by Paul Griffiths, John Taber and Joseph Prabhu himself and a general discussion.

[20] The Indian edition of IE, which contains minor corrections, was published in 1990 by Motilal Banarsidass, Delhi.

[21] Unauthorized reprinting of a chapter of *Indien und Europa* in the Netherlands (by the Rijksuniversiteit Groningen) back in 1987 nearly led to legal action on the part of the publisher, Schwabe & Co.

[22] Cf. Halbfass 1968b.

[23] Cf. most recently Halbfass' remarks in his response to chapter 2 (pp. 299-300) in the present volume.

[24] Cf. Hacker 1967/1968, p. 155 (= Hacker 1978, p. 38).

[25] This chapter is based on the article "India and the Comparative Method" (Halbfass 1985).

[26] Cf. already his remarks on "programmes of comparison" and on the reasons for the failure of so many attempts at comparison in Halbfass 1968b, pp. 360-361. Halbfass therefore does not aspire to construe a "serious (philosophical) cross-cultural theory," something that S. N. Balagangadhara implies as a *desideratum* in one of his polemical, mimicking questions while reviewing *India and Europe* (Balagangadhara 1990, p. 394). How much less useful for Halbfass' purpose would be the building of a theory about Western culture itself, an undertaking that Balagangadhara, in his connected remarks on Ronald Inden's *Imagining India* (Inden 1990), claims as necessary for the understanding of the cultural nature of the encounter between India and the West, not to speak of the building of theories of cultures in general (Balagangadhara 1990, pp. 401 and 402).

[27] Cf. the beginning sentence of section 15, chapter 23 (p. 433): "'Comparative philosophy,' *if it is possible at all*, is still in a nascent state ..." [our emphasis]. This note of doubt is not yet found in the corresponding section of "India and the Comparative Method."

[28] Cf. e.g., Dargyay 1989, p. 7.

[29] Cf. e.g, IE, p. 369; cp. also the subtitle of Rainer Kimmig's 1985 review paper on *Indien und Europa*: "Ein ungleicher Dialog" ("An Unequal Dialogue"). The initially unauthorized revision of the subtitle of IE, "An Essay in Understanding," to "An Essay in *Philosophical* Understanding" [our emphasis] for the Indian edition, with the resulting restriction, may similarly reflect considerations of inequality.

A blatant lack of understanding of what Halbfass means by "dialogue" or "dialogic encounter" is reflected by Balagangadhara's sarcastic interpretation of and remarks on a passage in *India and Europe* (p. 208) in which Halbfass summarizes Ram Mohan Roy's contribution to the encounter between India and Europe (Balagangadhara 1990, pp. 391-392). Is it Halbfass' de-mythologization of Roy's role in pre-modern India that irritates the reviewer imprisoned in his *own*, inescapable cultural context (cf. Balagangadhara 1990, especially p. 390)? Interestingly enough, the very same passage of *Indien und Europa* is quoted, in his own English translation, by Harvey Alper in his review of that book, to illustrate the paradigmatic character of Roy's hermeneutical situation as worked out by Halbfass (Alper 1983, pp. 194-195; cf. also the quotation of the original German passage in Kimmig 1985, p. 359, an otherwise highly critical review paper).

[30] Cf. for instance the excellent feature review of *Indien und Europa* by Alper (Alper 1983), p. 192. *India and Europe*, together with *Indien und Europa*, was probably reviewed more often than any other Indological book. Thanks to Halbfass' courtesy, about forty reviews and notices were conveniently made accessible to us; among them Alper's remains our favorite.

[31] The increasing importance of the term "understanding" for Halbfass is reflected in the replacement of the subtitle of *Indien und Europa,* namely, "Perspektiven ihrer geistigen Begegnung" ("Perspectives of their Spiritual/Intellectual Encounter") by "An Essay in Understanding" for *India and Europe* (on the further revised subtitle of the Indian edition cf. above, n. 29). The keyword of the older subtitle, *Begegnung* ("encounter"), remains a significant term for Halbfass; however, it lacks the implication of a continuing dynamic, one of the implications of the term *Gespräch*/"dialogue" which becomes more prominent later in Halbfass' writings.

[32] IE, p. 165: "There is, however, no compelling reason why its [Gadamer's work's] hermeneutical concepts and perspectives should not be applicable in a wider, transcultural context." This is, more or less, where Halbfass' "Ausblick auf weitere Entwicklungen" ("Prospect of Further Developments") (chapter X) ends in *Indien und Europa* (p. 187).

[33] Cf. also Halbfass 1968b, pp. 362-363, on the necessity of adopting a standpoint in comparison and on the deliberate, decided use of one's concepts and viewpoints.

[34] This specific and arresting Halbfassian style is perceived as "simply formulating questions by their hundreds" by Balagangadhara and causes considerable irritation to him inasmuch as he obviously cannot find answers (or "even hints" of answers) to any of them; thus, they possess only a "nuisance value" for him (Balagangadhara 1990, pp. 392-394)!

[35] This represents a significant development in *India and Europe* as compared to *Indien und Europa*; cf. n. 32 above.

[36] He is aware, though, of the impact of his ideas on Halbfass. Dr. Alokeranjan Dasgupta of the South Asia Institute, Heidelberg, who narrated the following little story to Halbfass in 1993, had pointed out relevant portions of IE to Gadamer on an occasion at the beginning of the nineties. Gadamer's reaction was certainly positive; he noticed approvingly how Halbfass had made use of his concepts, left with the book under his arm and had not returned it to date!

[37] Cf. n. 11 above on Halbfass' studies with Frauwallner.

[38] Cf. Halbfass 1983b, which also appeared in a revised translated version as chapter 22 of IE ("'Inclusivism' and 'Tolerance' in the Encounter Between India and the West").

[39] Cf. *Philology and Confrontation: Paul Hacker on Traditional and Modern Vedānta* (Hacker 1995) and Halbfass 1995a.

[40] Especially in Vedic studies in the wider sense pioneer scholars often did not shrink from expressing their deeply felt aversion toward and contempt for their objects of study. Even more recently, the first Sanskrit teacher of one of the editors of this volume was

known to say: "Le sanscrit est une très belle langue. Quel dommage qu'elle n'ait servi que pour dire des bêtises." However, this judgement did not prevent this scholar from spending a life-time with Vedic texts and writing a seminal book on the language of the Brāhmaṇas.

[41] Cf. Halbfass 1995a, p. 11, going beyond the reference to Hacker in *Indien und Europa*, p. 247, and IE, p. 221.

[42] Cf. e.g., Mohanty's contribution to the present volume. In this connection we cannot resist pointing out the misprint (or Freudian slip?) in Kunjunni Raja's notice of the Indian edition of *IE* (Kunjunni Raja 1991), where chapter 13 appears entitled "*Non*-Hinduism, Modern Indian Traditionalism, and the Presence of Europe"! [our emphasis]

Of course, it is beyond the scope of the present essay to even touch upon the problematic issue of whether there are or ever were "genuine Hindus" at all, and if yes, by what criteria they could be determined. For an overview of contemporary positions and a possible solution to this problem within the framework of traditional Indian self-understanding one may refer to chapter 1 of TR ("The Idea of the Veda and the Identity of Hinduism").

[43] Of course, we presuppose that there is an original meaning, which may very well be multifaceted, of a text and a wider intention of its author(s) in his/their historical situation, and that it is possible to arrive at a reasonable degree of understanding of this meaning and intention.

[44] Cf. chapters XV-XVII of *Indien und Europa* and 15-18 of *India and Europe*. These chapters have been singled out by several reviewers with quite different backgrounds; they are said e.g., to be of interest to historians of religion by Inden (cf. Inden 1991) and have evoked also strong theological interest (cf. de Smet 1982, p. 188). On the philosophical side, the Indologist-philosopher Taber has concentrated critically on Halbfass' treatment of the two terms in his review of *India and Europe* (cf. Taber 1991, pp. 230-237), and a reviewer for the *Philosophischer Literaturanzeiger* felt that *darśana* and *dharma* should take a key position in the Indo-European dialogue (cf. Stephenson 1983, p. 36).

[45] Exactly the opposite conclusion has been reached by Kimmig. He is of the opinion that Halbfass devaluates modern Indian thought which is influenced by European ideas, and thus fixes India and its philosophy in the past (cf. Kimmig 1985, p. 359)!

[46] As usual, Baiagangadhara misses the point when he characterizes the chapters on *darśana* and *dharma* as "of narrowly Indological interest" (Balagangadhara 1990, p. 392).

[47] In his foreword to a collection of Mehta's papers (Mehta 1992) Halbfass writes: "When the revised and greatly enlarged American edition [of IE] was published in 1988, it was no difficult choice for me to dedicate it to J. L. Mehta; I could not have asked for

a more serious and sensitive dialogue partner" (Halbfass 1992b, p. XI). Although IE is not explicitly dedicated to Mehta, in the preface it is stated: "Among those from whom I received intellectual and 'hermeneutical' inspiration during my work on both the German and the English versions of this book, I have to mention Jarava Lal Mehta. It would be difficult to imagine a better partner-in-dialogue" (IE, p. XI).

[48] Cf. e.g., Waligora 1984, p. 396. Serebriany, in the present volume, calls for the inclusion of the voice of contemporary Buddhists, as a cultural minority; in the dialogue between India and Europe.

[49] Cf. Halbfass 1979b, pp. 150-155. Cf. also his "Reden des Buddha" in *Kindlers Literatur Lexikon* (Halbfass 1974). In the forthcoming *Festschrift* for Heinz Bechert Halbfass presents us with his observations on *arthakriyā* and *kṣaṇikatva*.

[50] Cf. Halbfass 1968b, pp. 363-364.

# PUBLICATIONS BY WILHELM HALBFASS

## 1. Monographs and Selected Articles

1996

Beobachtungen zur Grundlegung einer interkulturellen Ethik. In: R[am] A. Mall und Notker Schneider (Eds.), *Ethik und Politik aus interkultureller Sicht*. Amsterdam/Atlanta: Editions Rodopi, pp. 31-38. (Studien zur interkulturellen Philosophie/Studies in Intercultural Philosophy 5)

Happiness: A Nyāya–Vaiśeṣika Perspective. In: Purusottama Bilimoria and Jitendra Nath Mohanty (Eds.), *Relativism, Suffering and Beyond: B. K. Matilal Memorial Volume*. Delhi: Oxford University Press, pp. 148-161.

The Eurocentric Approach to India and the Indian Discovery of Europe. In: K. Satchidananda Murty and Amit Dasgupta (Eds.), *The Perennial Tree: Select Papers of the International Symposium on India Studies*. New Delhi, etc.: Indian Council for Cultural Relations and New Age International (P) Limited, pp. 89-107.

Mescaline and Indian Philosophy: Aldous Huxley and the Mythology of Experience. In: Cedric Barfoot (Ed.), *Aldous Huxley Between East and West*. (forthcoming)

Weltbild und Wissenschaft: Beobachtungen am Beispiel Indiens. In: Rolf Kappel (Ed.), *Festschrift der ETH Zürich zum 25jährigen Bestehen des Nachdiplomstudiums für Entwicklungsländer (NADEL)*. (forthcoming)

1995

An Uncommon Orientalist: Paul Hacker's Passage to India. In: Wilhelm Halbfass (Ed.), *Philology and Confrontation: Paul Hacker on Traditional and Modern Vedānta*. Albany: State University of New York Press, pp. 1-23.

Practical Vedānta. In: Vasudha Dalmia and Heinrich von Stietencron (Eds.), *Representing Hinduism: The Construction of Religious Traditions and National Identity*. New Delhi: Sage Publications, pp. 211-223.

Zum Verhältnis von Karma und Tod im indischen Denken. In: Gerhard Oberhammer (Ed.), *Im Tod gewinnt der Mensch sein Selbst: Das*

*Phänomen des Todes in asiatischer und abendländischer Religionstradition*. Wien: Verlag der österreichischen Akademie der Wissenschaften, pp. 75-95. (Österreichische Akademie der Wissenschaften. Philosophisch-historische Klasse. Sitzungsberichte, **624**. Band. Beiträge zur Kultur- und Geistesgeschichte Asiens **14**))

1994

Menschsein und Lebensziele: Beobachtungen zu den *puruṣārthas*. In: Francis X. D'Sa and Roque Mesquita (Eds.), *Hermeneutics of Encounter: Essays in Honour of Gerhard Oberhammer on the Occasion of his 65th Birthday*. Vienna: Institut für Indologie der Universität Wien, pp. 123-135. (Publications of the De Nobili Research Library **20**)

1993

*On Being and What There Is: Classical Vaiśeṣika and the History of Indian Ontology*. Delhi: Indian Books Centre.

Die indische Entdeckung Europas und die "Europäisierung der Erde." In: R[am] A. Mall and D[ieter] Lohmar (Eds.), *Philosophische Grundlagen der Interkulturalität*. Amsterdam/Atlanta: Editions Rodopi, pp. 199-212. (Studien zur interkulturellen Philosophie/Studies in Intercultural Philosophy **1**)

1992

*On Being and What There Is: Classical Vaiśeṣika and the History of Indian Ontology*. Albany: State University of New York Press.[1]

*Tradition and Reflection: Explorations in Indian Thought*. Delhi: Indian Books Centre.

Foreword. In: William J. Jackson (Ed.), *J. L. Mehta on Heidegger, Hermeneutics and Indian Tradition*. Leiden: E. J. Brill, pp. IX-XIII.

Mensch und Selbst im traditionellen indischen Denken. In: Samuel N. Eisenstadt (Ed.), *Kulturen der Achsenzeit II*. Teil 2. *Indien*. Frankfurt

[1] Reviews and notices in: Journal of Asian Studies 52/3, 1993; Religious Studies Review 19/3, 1993; Bulletin d'Etudes Indiennes 11-12, 1993-1994; Revue Philosophique 119, 1994; Indo-Iranian Journal 38/3, 1995; Wiener Zeitschrift für die Kunde Südasiens 39, 1995.

a. M.: Suhrkamp, pp. 129-152. (translated from the English original by Ruth Achlama)

Observations on the Relationship between Vedic Exegesis and Philosophical Reflection. In: K. Kunjunni Raja (Ed.), *S. S. Janaki Felicitation Volume*. Madras: Kuppuswami Sastri Research Institute, pp. 31-40. (*Journal of Oriental Research* **56-62**)

The Buddha and Epicurus. In: Heinz Bechert (Ed.), *The Dating of the Historical Buddha. Die Datierung des historischen Buddha*. Vol. 2. Göttingen: Vandenhoeck & Ruprecht, pp. 105-109. (Abhandlungen der Akademie der Wissenschaften in Göttingen, Philosophisch–historische Klasse. Dritte Folge, **194**. Symposien zur Buddhismusforschung **IV**) (reprinted in Heinz Bechert (Ed.), *When Did the Buddha Live?* Delhi: Indian Books Centre, 1995, pp. 205-209)

1991

*Tradition and Reflection: Explorations in Indian Thought*. Albany: State University of New York Press.[2]

*Anvayavyatireka* und anderes: Zu einem Besprechungsaufsatz von Heidrun Brückner. *Zeitschrift der Deutschen Morgenländischen Gesellschaft*, **141**, *18*-*21*.

Early Indian References to the Greeks and the First Western References to Buddhism. In: Heinz Bechert (Ed.), *The Dating of the Historical Buddha. Die Datierung des historischen Buddha*. Vol. 1. Göttingen: Vandenhoeck & Ruprecht, pp. 197-208. (Abhandlungen der Akademie der Wissenschaften in Göttingen, Philosophisch–historische Klasse. Dritte Folge, **189**. Symposien zur Buddhismusforschung **IV**) (reprinted in Heinz Bechert (Ed.), *When Did the Buddha Live?* Delhi: Indian Books Centre, 1995, pp. 195-205)

The Therapeutic Paradigm and the Search for Identity in Indian Thought. In: V. N. Jha (Ed.), *Kalyāṇa-mitta: Professor Hajime Nakamura Felicitation Volume*. Delhi: Indian Books Centre, pp. 23-34. (Bibliotheca Indo–Buddhica **86**)

---

[2] Reviews and notices in: South Asia in Review 15/2-3, 1991; Journal of Asian History 26, 1992; Journal of the American Oriental Society 112, 1992; Journal of the Asiatic Society, Calcutta 34/1-2, 1992; Pacific Affairs 65/1, 1992; Religious Studies Review 18/2, 1992; Theologische Literaturzeitung 117/3, 1992; Numen 40, 1993; Prajñā 36-38/1-2, 1990-1993; Journal of Indian Council of Philosophical Research, 12/3, 1995.

Tradition und Reflexion: Zur Gegenwart des Veda in der indischen Philosophie. In: Gerhard Oberhammer (Ed.), *Beiträge zur Hermeneutik indischer und abendländischer Religionstraditionen*. Wien: Verlag der österreichischen Akademie der Wissenschaften, pp. 123-146. (Österreichische Akademie der Wissenschaften. Philosophisch-historische Klasse. Sitzungsberichte, **573**. Band. Beiträge zur Kultur- und Geistesgeschichte Asiens 6)

1990

*India and Europe: An Essay in Philosophical Understanding*. Delhi: Motilal Banarsidass.[3]

Deussen and Śaṅkara. In: Gautam Patel (Ed.), *Ādi Śaṅkarācārya (12th Centenary Commemoration Volume)*. Gandhinagar: Government of Gujarat, pp. 37-40.

1989

A Long Road Back to the East. *India International Centre Quarterly*, **16**/2, 29-44. (revised English version of "Europa, Indien und die Europäisierung der Erde")

Observations on *sattāsambandha* and the History of Vaiśeṣika Ontology. *JAOS*, **109**/4, 553-557 (*Ernest Bender Felicitation Volume*)

Śaṅkara, the Yoga of Patañjali, and the So-Called Yogasūtrabhāṣyavivaraṇa. In: R. Balasubramaniam and S. Bhattacharya (Eds.), *Perspectives on Śaṅkara*. Delhi: Government of India, pp. 178-211.

1988

*India and Europe: An Essay in Understanding*. Albany: State University of New York Press.[4]

---

[3] Reviews and notices in: Adyar Library Bulletin 55, 1991; Journal of Indian Council of Philosophical Research 8/2, 1991; Journal of Dharma 16/2, 1992; Path Way to God 26/2, 1992; Archív Orientální 61, 1993.

[4] Reviews and notices in: Annals of the Bhandarkar Oriental Research Institute 70, 1989; Hindu-Christian Studies Bulletin 2, 1989; Religious Studies Review 15/3, 1989; Cultural Dynamics 3/4, 1990; Hinduism Today 12/6, 1990; Toyo Gakuho (Journal of the Research Department of the Toyo Bunko) 71, 1990 (in Japanese); History of Religions 31/1, 1991; Indo-Iranian Journal 34, 1991; Philosophy East and West 41/2, 1991; The Sunday Observer Sept. 1-7, 1991; Annals of the Bhandarkar Oriental Research Institute 74, 1993.

Europa, Indien und die Europäisierung der Erde. In: Krzysztof Michalski (Ed.), *Europa und die Folgen*. Stuttgart: Klett-Cotta, pp. 230-252. (Castelgandolfo-Gespräche) (translated from the English original by S. Marten; translated into Hebrew by Eli Franco in *Proza*, **101/102**, 1988, 80-88, into Polish by A. Szostkiewicz in *Europa i co z tego wynika*, Warszawa: Res Publica 1990, pp. 253-272)

1987

Hegel, Schelling, Schopenhauer und Indien. *Zeitschrift für Kulturaustausch*, **37**/3, 424-433.

Schopenhauer im Gespräch mit der indischen Tradition. In: Volker Spierling (Ed.), *Schopenhauer im Denken der Gegenwart*. München: R. Piper Verlag, pp. 55-70.

Vyomaśiva on *sattāsambandha*. In: G. Ramakrishna et al. (Eds.), *Studies in Indian Culture: A Volume of Essays Presented to Sāhitya Śiromaṇi Professor S. Ramachandra Rao*. Bangalore: Professor S. Ramachandra Felicitation Committee, pp. 65-80.

1986

Mallavādin and Early Vaiśeṣika Ontology. *ALB*, **50**, 271-286. (*Golden Jubilee Volume*)

1985

Hegel on Meditation and Yoga. *Zen Buddhism Today. Annual Report of the Kyoto Zen Symposium*, **3**, 72-84.

India and the Comparative Method. *PEW*, **35**/1, 3-15.

Science and Philosophy in Classical India. In: Peter Gaeffke and David A. Utz (Eds.), *Science and Technology in South Asia (Proceedings of the South Asia Seminar 1981/82)*. Philadelphia: South Asia Regional Studies, pp. 12-14.

1984

Indian Philosophers on the Plurality of Religious Traditions. In: Peter Gaeffke and David A. Utz (Eds.), *Identity and Division in Cults and Sects in South Asia (Proceedings of the South Asia Seminar 1980/81)*. Philadelphia: South Asia Regional Studies, pp. 58-64.

1983

*Studies in Kumārila and Śaṅkara*. Reinbek: Dr. Inge Wezler Verlag für orientalistische Fachpublikationen. (Monographie 9)[5]

"Inklusivismus" und "Toleranz" im Kontext der indo-europäischen Begegnung. In: Gerhard Oberhammer (Ed.), *Inklusivismus: Eine indische Denkform*. Wien: Institut für Indologie der Universität Wien, pp. 29-60. (Publications of the De Nobili Research Library. Occasional Papers 2)

1982

Der Begriff der Erfahrung im Kontext der indisch-europäischen Begegnung. In: Gerhard Oberhammer (Ed.), *Epiphanie des Heils: Zur Heilsgegenwart in indischer und christlicher Religion*. Wien: Institut für Indologie der Universität Wien, pp. 102-128. (Publications of the De Nobili Research Library 9)

1981

*Indien und Europa: Perspektiven ihrer geistigen Begegnung*. Basel/Stuttgart: Schwabe.[6]

---

[5] Reviews and notices in: Journal of the American Oriental Society 105, 1985; Philosophy East and West 35, 1985; Acta Orientalia 47, 1986; Indo-Iranian Journal 30/1, 1987; Toyo Gakuho (Journal of the Research Department of the Toyo Bunko) 68, 1987 (in Japanese); Wiener Zeitschrift für die Kunde Südasiens 33, 1989; Zeitschrift der Deutschen Morgenländischen Gesellschaft 140, 1990 (cf. also the response in 141, 1991).

[6] Reviews and notices in: Die Furche Herbst 1981; Wissenschaftlicher Literaturanzeiger 20/1, 1981; Zürichsee-Zeitung (Stäfa) Nr. 192, 1981; Asien-Bibliographie 117, 1982; Bibliographie de la Philosophie 29/4, 1982; Christ in der Gegenwart Herbst 1982; Indian Theological Studies 19, 1982; Narody Asii i Afriki (Peoples of Asia and Africa) 6, 1982 (in Russian); Referateblätter Philosophie, Reihe E 15, 1982; Theologie und Philosophie 3, 1982; German News (New Delhi) Jan. 20, 1983; Jarman Samācār Jan. 27, 1983 (in Hindi); Philosophischer Literaturanzeiger 36/1, 1983; Philosophy East and West 33, 1983; Zeitschrift der Deutschen Morgenländischen Gesellschaft 133, 1983; Zeitschrift für Missionswissenschaft und Religionswissenschaft 67/3, 1983; Deutsche Zeitschrift für Philosophie 32/4, 1984; Indo-Iranian Journal 27, 1984; Theologische Literaturzeitung 109/3, 1984; Internationales Asienforum 16/3-4, 1985; Orientalistische Literaturzeitung 80/3, 1985; Wiener Zeitschrift für die Kunde Südasiens 29, 1985; Westfalen-Blatt Nr. 161, 44. Jg., 15./16. Juli 1989; Spirita 4/1, 1990.

1980

Karma, *Apūrva*, and "Natural" Causes: Observations on the Growth and Limits of the Theory of Saṃsāra. In: Wendy Doniger O'Flaherty (Ed.), *Karma and Rebirth in Classical Indian Tradition*. Berkeley/Los Angeles/London: University of California Press, pp. 268-302.

The Vaiśeṣika Concept of *guṇa* and the Problem of Universals. *WZKS*, 24, 225-238.

1979

Kulturbeziehungen zum Westen. In: Heinz Bechert und Georg von Simson (Eds.), *Einführung in die Indologie: Stand, Methoden, Aufgaben*. Darmstadt: Wissenschaftliche Buchgesellschaft, pp. 248-255.

Observations on *darśana*. *WZKS*, 23, 195-203.

Paul Hacker (Obituary). *Journal of the Oriental Institute (Baroda)*, 28, 169-170.

Philosophie. In: Heinz Bechert und Georg von Simson (Eds.), *Einführung in die Indologie: Stand, Methoden, Aufgaben*. Darmstadt: Wissenschaftliche Buchgesellschaft, pp. 138-158.

Praśastapāda's Concept of Substance *(dravya)*. In: J. P. Sinha (Ed.), *Ṛtam: Ludwik Sternbach Felicitation Volume*. Part One. Lucknow: Akhila Bharatiya Sanskrit Parishad, pp. 537-544. (published in 1981)

1978

On Being and What There Is: Indian Perspectives on the Question of Being. In: Mervyn Sprung (Ed.), *The Question of Being: East-West Perspectives*. University Park/London: Pennsylvania University Press, pp. 95-109.

1977

Anthropological Problems in Classical Indian Philosophy. In: *Beiträge zur Indienforschung: Ernst Waldschmidt zum 80. Geburtstag gewidmet*. Berlin: Museum für indische Kunst, pp. 225-236.

1976

*Zur Theorie der Kastenordnung in der indischen Philosophie*. Göttingen: Vandenhoeck & Ruprecht. (Nachrichten der Akademie der Wissenschaften in Göttingen. I. Philologisch-historische Klasse, Jahrgang 1975, Nr. 9)

Indien und die Geschichtsschreibung der Philosophie. *Philosophische Rundschau*, **23**, 104-141.

The Study of Indian Philosophy in Germany and Austria: A Survey of Recent Contributions (1965-1972). *Journal of the Oriental Institute (Baroda)*, **25**, 364-375.

Zum Begriff der Substanz *(dravya)* im Vaiśeṣika. *WZKS*, **20**, 141-166.

1975

Conceptualizations of "Being" in Classical Vaiśeṣika. *WZKS*, **19**, 183-198.

Mixed Pickles, statt einer Festgabe dargebracht. In: Jan M. Broekman and Jan Knopf (Eds.), *Konkrete Reflexion: Festschrift für H. Wein zum 60. Geburtstag*. Den Haag: Nijhoff, pp. 115-119.

1973

Hegel on the Philosophy of the Hindus. In: Cultural Department of the Embassy of the Federal Republic of Germany, New Delhi (Ed.), *German Scholars on India: Contributions to Indian Studies*. Vol. 1. Varanasi: Chowkhamba, pp. 107-122.

1971

Anagārika Dharmapāla. In: Karl Deschner (Ed.), *Das Christentum im Urteil seiner Gegner*. Vol 2. Wiesbaden: Limes, pp. 68-81.

1970

Remarks on the Vaiśeṣika Concept of *sāmānya*. In: J. Tilakasiri (Ed.), *Añjali, Papers on Indology and Buddhism: A Felicitation Volume Presented to Oliver Hector de Alwis Wijesekera on his 60th Birthday*. Peradeniya: University of Ceylon, pp. 137-151.

1969

Diderot. In: Karl Deschner (Ed.), *Das Christentum im Urteil seiner Gegner*. Vol 1. Wiesbaden: Limes, pp. 94-107.

Porphyrios. In: Karl Deschner (Ed.), *Das Christentum im Urteil seiner Gegner*. Vol 1. Wiesbaden: Limes, pp. 24-34.

1968

*Descartes' Frage nach der Existenz der Welt: Untersuchungen über die cartesianische Denkpraxis und Metaphysik.* Meisenheim am Glan: A. Hain.

Bemerkungen zur altindischen Staatstheorie. In: Bharatiya Majlis (Indische Gemeinschaft) (Ed.), *Bharati - Festschrift zum 18. Jahrestag der Indischen Republik.* Clausthal: Technische Hochschule Clausthal, pp. 19-24.

Indian and Western Philosophy: Preliminary Remarks on a Method of Comparison. *Journal of the Bihar Research Society (Patna)*, **54**, 359-364.

Plotins Interesse an Heraklit. In: Seminar für klassische Philologie, Universität Göttingen (Ed.), *Festschrift für Karl Deichgräber anlässlich seines 65. Geburtstages*. Göttingen. (private felicitation volume)

1967

In memoriam Rudolf Allers. *Erasmus*, **19**, 193-196.

## 2. Contributions to Encyclopedias, etc.

*Encyclopaedia of Buddhism*. Ed. Gunapala Piyasena Malalasekera. Colombo: Government of Sri Lanka, 1961ff. So far published: vols. 1-5. Article on: Lüders, Heinrich.

*Encyclopedia of Religion*. Ed. Mircea Eliade. New York: Macmillan, 1987. 16 vols. Article on: Indian Religions (History of Study).

*Grosses Werklexikon der Philosophie*. Eds. Franco Volpi and Maria Koettnitz. Stuttgart: A. Kröner Verlag. Article on: Śārīrakamīmāṃsābhāṣya (Śaṅkara).

*Historisches Wörterbuch der Philosophie*. Eds. Joachim Ritter and Karlfried Gründer. Basel: Schwabe, 1971ff. To be completed in 12 vols.; so far published: vols. 1-9. Articles on: Allgemeinbilder; Allgemeinvorstellung; Ansatz; Apriorismus; Bewusstsein, transzendentales; Egoismus (erkenntnistheoretisch); Einsicht; Evidenz; Gewissheit; Idee (Neuzeit); Idee, einfache; Immaterialismus; Inneneinstellung; Intellekt, reiner; Meditation (Indien); Nativismus; Neo-Realismus; Objekt, transzendentales; Phänomenalismus; Philosophie (Indien); Philosophy, Comparative; Realismus vs. Idealismus; Realismus, kritischer; Realismus, naiver; Reflexionsbegriffe; Selbsttäuschung; Selbstverständlichkeit; Subjekt, transzendentales; Täuschung; Tatsache; Topik, transzendentale; Transzendentalismus; Transzendentalphilosophie; Vorstellen (Heidegger); Vorstellung; Vorstellungskreis; Vorstellungsreihe; Vorstellungsvorstellungen; Zweifel; Zweifel, methodischer.

*Kindlers Literatur Lexikon*. Eds. Wolfgang von Einsiedel et al. Zürich: Kindler, 1965-1974. 8 vols. Articles on: Les Passions de l'âme (Descartes); Pensées diverses sur la comète (Bayle); Principia philosophiae (Descartes); Profession de foi du vicaire savoyard (Rousseau); Rāmāyaṇa (Vālmīki); Reden des Buddha; Regulae ad directionem ingenii (Descartes); Ṛgveda; Śārīrakamīmāṃsābhāṣya (Śaṅkara); Tractatus politicus; Tractatus theologico-politicus (Spinoza); Traité de l'amour de Dieu (Malebranche); Traité de l'origine des romans (Huet). Supplementary volume: Ethica ordine geometrico demonstrata (Spinoza). Revised versions and additional article on Śaṅkara, Upadeśasāhasrī in *Kindlers Neues Literatur Lexikon*. München: Kindler, 1989ff. 20 vols.

*Lexikon für Theologie und Kirche*. Ed. Michael Buchberger. 3rd completely revised ed. by Walter Kasper. Vol. 2. Freiburg im Breisgau: Herder, 1994. Articles on: Benares, Bengalen.

*Routledge Encyclopedia of Philosophy*. Ed. Edward Craig. London: Routledge, forthcoming. Article on: Karma and Rebirth (Indian Conceptions).

**Wilhelm Halbfass**

# RESEARCH AND REFLECTION: RESPONSES TO MY RESPONDENTS

## I. Beyond Orientalism? Reflections on a Current Theme

1. The title of this book summons a specter which I might have preferred to keep out of sight: the specter of Orientalism. When I worked on *Indien und Europa* (1981), the German predecessor of *India and Europe* (1988), I was almost completely unaware of the phenomenon and its name. Just prior to the publication of the book, I took casual and passing notice of Edward Said's *Orientalism* (1978). It was obvious that this was a new, rhetorically powerful and polemically charged use of a term which appeared to be on the verge of becoming obsolete. However, I did not see any reason to include an explicit response to this within the context of my own limited project. This decision was made easier by the self-imposed limitations of Said's work, its focus on French and British (as well as American) approaches to Islam and the Middle East, and its relative neglect of Indian studies.

After 1981, it became more and more difficult to disregard or avoid the phenomenon. The number of positive or negative responses to, and reviews of, Said's book increased rapidly, and there were translations into more than a dozen different languages. Moreover, the concept of Orientalism itself, together with the perspectives and polemics attached to it by Said, developed a dynamics of its own, which spread rapidly into other areas of Asian and non-Western studies, including Indian studies. There was an explosion of lectures, discussions, conferences and seminars (including a year-long South Asia Seminar at the University of Pennsylvania in 1988-1989) on the concept of Orientalism and its implications and ramifications. The process was not confined to the arena of theoretical debate; it also affected academic policies and administration, mostly in the United States. In a number of cases, it led to the removal of the word "Oriental" from the names of academic departments and programs. Thus the *Department of Oriental Studies* at the University of Pennsylvania was renamed *Department of Asian and Middle Eastern Studies* in 1992, after a protracted and at times raucous debate of two years. Remarkably, there was much less excitement about the term "Oriental" in Asian countries. Numerous "Oriental" institutes in India, Japan (see Tanaka 1993 on its "Orient," *tōyō*) and elsewhere kept their names intact. In the United States, the American Oriental Society, an explicit target of Said's critique (see Said 1978, p. 294f.), did not change its name. More significantly, the existence and legitimacy of "regional studies" or "area studies" programs, which were also, though less conspicuously, included in Said's great indictment (p. 275ff.), was not seriously questioned in the process. Instead, these programs continue to provide institutional support for the discussion and dissemination of Saidian ideas. In particular, several centers and departments for South Asian studies provide a most hospitable environment for the Orientalism debate. Certainly, this debate is now at least as conspicuous and vigorous in Indian and South Asian Studies as in any other area of Asian studies.

In the meantime, Said's ideas and the Orientalism debate have also become part of a much wider scene of study and debate which deals, in a broad and general sense, with the whole syndrome of "knowledge and power" and the pervasive role of "discourses" in history, culture, and cross-cultural relations. More specifically, we hear about "hegemonic" and "imperial," "colonial," "neo-colonial" and "post-colonial" discourses, about "marginalization" and "multi-culturalism," about the formation of identity and otherness in history and culture, about "construction," "representation," "invention," and "deconstruction." The debate has produced a vast and rapidly growing literature and a distinctive terminology, phraseology and rhetoric of its own, and it has become a major preoccupation in American and British academia and in such large professional organizations as the Modern Language Association of America. It draws inspiration and perspectives from a variety of thinkers, including Karl Marx, Friedrich Nietzsche, Antonio Gramsci, Frantz Fanon, Michel Foucault and, among living authors, Jacques Derrida. I do not want to speculate on the historical meaning and cross-cultural potential of this debate.[1] Instead, I want to return to the more limited problem of how to respond to Said's indictment of Orientalism, i.e., his thesis that the Western study of the so-called Orient, specifically the Islamic world, constitutes a pervasive attempt to deprive it of its identity and sovereignty, and that the academic pursuit of "Oriental" or "Asian" Studies in European and American universities continues to be an extension or reflection of a fundamentally political will to power and domination.

2. Was it possible that I was myself part of the scenario described by Said? Was it possible that my own and anybody else's efforts of understanding Asian traditions were contributing to the formation and stabilization of a discourse of domination? Was understanding itself,[2] or the quest for it, just another manifestation of Orientalism? But what exactly is the meaning of Orientalism, apart from the general connotation of a collusion of knowledge with power, or more specifically, of the "collusion of scholarship with the imperatives of colonial domination" to which Fred Dallmayr refers in his contribution to this volume? How exactly does this collusion work? How does it affect the minds of scholars and the nature of their work? How pervasive is it in Western thought? Is it an exclusively Western phenomenon? What are its symptoms? Is there a cure?

Ronald Inden says that, according to Edward Said, Orientalist discourse "presents itself as a form of knowledge that is both different from, and superior to, the knowledges that the Orientals have of themselves" (Inden 1990, p. 37). This is by no means a mere by-product of colonial domination. It lives on in a wide range of Western attitudes and institutions. In the United States, Inden finds it exemplified by the American Council of Learned Studies (ACLS), the Social Science Research Council (SSRC), the Ford Foundation and the *New York Review of Books*. In a retrospective statement published in 1989, Said himself describes Orientalism as "a structure erected in the thick of an imperial contest whose dominating wing it represented and elaborated not only as scholarship but as a partisan ideology."[3] (In 1976, only two years prior to the publication of *Orientalism*, he had still appreciated "Orientalism as a phenomenon of reception and transmission" and praised its portrayal by Raymond Schwab[4]). For Said, too, there is no doubt that Orientalism, as an ideology and discourse of domination, is by no means confined to the period of colonialism, and that it continues to have an institutional presence in the SSRC or the Ford Foundation (pp. 288, 295).

In the introduction to his *Orientalism* (p. 2f.), Said presents three different, yet (in his view) interrelated and ultimately inseparable meanings of the term: Orientalism is

a) an academic discipline or a field of academic study;

b) "a style of thought based upon an ontological and epistemological distinction made between 'the Orient' ... and 'the Occident'";
c) "the corporate institution for dealing with the Orient – dealing with it by making statements about it, authorizing views of it, describing it, by teaching it, settling it, ruling over it: in short, Orientalism as a Western style for dominating, restructuring, and having authority over the Orient."

While the period around 1800 saw the grand opening of a new phase in the development of the "corporate institution" of Orientalism, and of the academic discipline which is one of its constituents, its roots are much more ancient. In fact, Said pursues them back through the Renaissance and the Middle Ages to the world of classical antiquity. In a sense, the history of Oriental studies is an unfolding of what was there right from the beginning. In spite of the apparent increase in positive Western knowledge, it is ultimately "Western ignorance which becomes more refined and complex" (p. 62). "Orientalism responded more to the culture that produced it than to its putative object, which was also produced by the West" (p. 22). The history of Orientalism is a history of Western self-affirmation and self-elevation through which it asserted and developed "its capacities for encompassing and Orientalizing the Orient" (p. 65).

3. Dennis Porter says that Said was "led to claim a continuity of representation between the Greece of Alexander the Great and the United States of President Jimmy Carter" (Williams and Chrisman 1994, p. 152), a continuity which left no room for internal variation, genuine self-questioning or the conception of alternative approaches to the Orient. In fact, we may go back much further into the Greek past, for instance to the dramatist Aeschylus (525-456 B.C.E.) or even to Homer himself (see, for instance, pp. 11, 20, 56f.). Said associates what he calls "Aeschylus' orchestra" with the "learned envelope of Orientalist scholarship." In Aeschylus' *Persians*, a drama which was written after the battle of Salamis in 480 B.C.E., he finds a programmatic prologue to the history of Orientalism and a summary of some of its central motives: "A line is drawn between the continents. Europe is powerful and articulate; Asia is defeated and distant. Aeschylus *represents* Asia, makes her speak in the person of the aged Persian queen, Xerxes' mother. It is Europe that articulates the Orient; this articulation is the prerogative not of a puppet-master, but of a genuine creator, whose life-giving power

*represents*, animates, constitutes the otherwise silent and dangerous space beyond familiar boundaries" (p. 57).

The word "represent," which appears twice in this quote, is also found in the first motto of the entire book. The motto comes from *The Eighteenth Brumaire of Louis Bonaparte* (German original: 1852) by Karl Marx. Of course, Marx made this statement not about the so-called Orientals, but the peasant proletariat of France, and he made it, moreover, with a touch of irony. The Orientalist's real or alleged claim to represent the Orient is one of the pervasive themes of the book. Said finds it exemplified not only by the colonial ruler and administrator, but also by the philologist, lexicographer, translator, etc., including such a sympathetic scholar of Islam as Louis Massignon: "There is an unmistakable aura of power about the philologist" (p. 132; see also p. 271ff.). Does this mean that products of philologists in general, including dictionaries, etc., are inherently and inevitably prejudicial and pernicious and an expression of the latent imperialism of the scholars? Or does it mean that the collusion with power will interfere with the quality and reliability of such works? Said does not give us a clear answer. Instead, he insists time and again that "all academic knowledge about India and Egypt is somehow tinged and impressed with, violated by, the gross political fact" (p. 11), and that Orientalism as an academic discipline is "a kind of Western projection onto and will to govern over the Orient" (p. 95) or simply, as exemplified by Silvestre de Sacy, a "technology of power" (p. 127). "Can any other than a political master-slave relation produce the Orientalized Orient?" (p. 96).

At the end of his book, Said tries to look beyond Orientalism and toward a state of mind and scholarship which is free from this disease and corruption:

> Orientalizing the Orient ... is to be avoided, with consequences that cannot but refine knowledge and reduce the scholar's conceit. Without 'the Orient', there would be scholars, critics, intellectuals, human beings for whom the racial, ethnic and national distinctions were less important than the common enterprise of promoting human community. (p. 328)

In a sense, the results which Said expects from the abolition of Orientalism are reminiscent of those which Karl Marx expected from the abolition of class and private property: a utopian state in which humans can exist without being confined to roles and identities imposed by others. Just as the proletariat has to liberate itself from the alienating subsumption under categories and conditions created by class society and the ruling classes (see Avineri 1970), Orientals have to liberate themselves from the objectification and essentialization produced by the Western Orientalists and the very structure of the Orientalist discourse.

Unfortunately, however, Orientalism is a contagious disease; it has infected the Orientals themselves. According to Said, "the answer to Orientalism is not Occidentalism." Still, he has to admit that any "former 'Oriental' ... is likely - too likely - to study new 'Orientals' - or 'Occidentals' - of his own making" (Said 1978, p. 328). He does not elaborate on the question whether or to what extent this diagnosis might apply to himself, nor, in a more general sense, on his own identity vis-à-vis "Orient" and "Occident."

There is no need for us to speculate on Said's personal, biographical involvement in the topic of his book. He refers somewhat casually to his "own experiences of these matters" and says that "the life of an Arab Palestinian in the West, particularly in America, is disheartening" (p. 27). He calls Orientalism "a strange, secret sharer of Western anti-Semitism" or even its "Islamic branch"; on the other hand, he has misgivings about the "liberal American identification with Zionism." At any rate, he is dealing with a "dehumanizing ideology" which has to be faced and exposed as such. The word "ideology," though much less frequent and thematic than "discourse," is symptomatic. In his own way, he applies the Marxian concept and critique of ideology as a configuration of ideas produced and upheld by class and group interests and embedded in "false consciousness" ("*falsches Bewusstsein*"). Orientalism, too, is a manifestation of group interests and perspectives; "for a European or American studying the Orient there can be no disclaiming ... that he comes up against the Orient as a European or American first, as an individual second" (p. 11). Said quotes with approval a passage from Anouar (Anwar) Abdel-Malek's article "Orientalism in Crisis" which associates "the hegemonism of possessing minorities unveiled by Marx and Engels" with the attitudes of traditional Orientalists (p. 97; Abdel-Malek 1963, p. 108). Incidentally, this article, which was published in English translation in 1963, is one of the forerunners of the Orientalism debate. Nonetheless, it differs substantially from Said's own work: Its statements are less sweeping and rhetorical; it distinguishes clearly between traditional Orientalism and more recent Western approaches; and its orientation is generally more practical. In particular, it pays very special attention to the work of Joseph Needham, which is completely disregarded by Said.

Of course, the critique of ideologies tends to be ideological itself and may turn out to be more so than its targets. Indeed, the highly ideological nature of Said's critique of Orientalism can hardly be overlooked. Which are the group interests and perspectives represented by this critique? It is immediately evident that neither his *Orientalism* nor any of his other publications can be regarded as an assertion or self-assertion of traditional Islam against its modern Western representations and interpretations. The religious and traditionalistic dimension is completely absent. No reference is made to traditional Muslim sources; apart from Anouar Abdel-Malek, even modern Arab, Muslim or other non-Western writers play no role whatsoever in *Orientalism*.[5] Said never proposes any non-Western alternatives to the Western Orientalist ways of dealing with "self" and "other," "Orient" and "Occident." Said speaks within the Western world, as a Palestinian Arab (*not* a Muslim) living in the West and with a thoroughly Western education. He thinks, writes, and teaches in a Western medium; his audience is primarily Western. His critical impulses and directions are inspired and guided by Western patterns of critique and self-critique. His critique and its object are branches of the same tree. He is very much included in the processes and procedures which he denounces.

4. There is no need for another review of Said's book; nor will I try to survey and assess the numerous reviews which have been written and which cover the entire spectrum from glorification to rejection. Dennis Porter gave one of the more sober and thoughtful assessments (see Williams and Chrisman 1994, pp. 150-161). Bernard Lewis denounced Said in the name of the academic discipline of "Oriental Studies" (Lewis 1982a, 1982b, 1983, 1993), while Jarava Lal Mehta responded in his own uniquely personal fashion.[6] The wide variety of reactions is further exemplified by two responses from different directions and published in radically different journals: the review by Peter Gran in the *Journal of the American Oriental Society* (vol. 100, 1980), a stronghold of that traditional academic Orientalism which was criticized by Said, and the review article "Orientalism and Orientalism in Reverse" by fellow Palestinian Sadik Jalal al-'Azm in the journal *Khamsin*. A comparison of these two responses produces a somewhat ironic result: While al-'Azm's contribution is sharply critical of Said's broad generalizations and counters his references to Western Orientalist essentializations of *the Orient* with citations of a blatant "Ontological Orientalism in Reverse"

from recent Arab thought and literature (see al-'Azm 1981, p. 18ff.), Peter Gran celebrates Said's procedure and summarizes what he considers to be one of his main insights as follows: "European culture resists a scientific study of the world but is content with solipsistic discourse about positive and negative images of itself" (p. 331). Although this piece may be somewhat extreme in its startling lack of critical reflection and historical competence, its basic attitude is by no means unique or even unusual. The article by al-'Azm, on the other hand, provides some welcome correctives and caveats. We are reminded that "the stylist and polemicist in Edward Said very often runs away with the systematic thinker" (p. 6), and that this leads to inconsistencies and confusions. In his polemical zeal against Orientalist constructions and essentializations, he overlooks completely the extent of essentialist constructions in his own presentation. He also overlooks the inconsistencies and confusions in his description of the relations between his three meanings of "Orientalism." More significantly, the causal and conceptual relationship between textual and academic Orientalism and actual political and economic subjugation of the Orient remains unclear and ambiguous. On the one hand, the scholarly enterprise of Orientalism and the formation of images or conceptions of the Orient appears as a reflection and by-product of political and economic interests; on the other hand, it appears as the historical basis of all political, economic and military involvement with the Orient (al-'Azm 1981, p. 8; cf. Said 1978, pp. 91, 203). Finally, Said denounces as typically and specifically Western and Orientalist what appears elsewhere as a most natural or even universal way of cross-cultural encounter and interaction; indeed,

> cultures have always been inclined to impose complete transformations on other cultures, receiving these other cultures not as they are but as, for the benefit of the receiver, they ought to be. (al-'Azm 1981, p. 9; from Said 1978, p. 67)

This leads to gross distortions in Said's critique and leaves it without a clearly identifiable target. In *Tradition and Reflection*, I have described the problem as follows:

> Much of what he says applies only to the European treatment of Islam, but not of other parts of Asia or the non-Western world; other statements, though meant to depict "Orientalism," apply equally to European ways of dealing with Occidental, European phenomena. And finally, a very substantial part of what he says applies by his own admission to the encounter of civilizations and to human group behavior in general, and thus to "Oriental" as well as "Occidental" ways of dealing with "the other" and his otherness. (TR, p. 10f.)

Said fluctuates between unwarranted generalizations and specifications. On the one hand, he disregards internal differences *within* cultures; on the other hand, he overlooks common denominators *between* cultures. He misses, he does not want to see the twists and turns, the unexpected transformations and side-effects in Europe's encounter with Asia, the dynamics of a process which locked, for instance, the Asian activities of the Christian missionaries into the growth of secularism and the critique of Christianity in Europe, and which turned the efforts of such "agents of imperialism" and arch-Orientalists as William Jones or Max Müller into forces which would contribute to the demise of colonialism and imperialism. On the other hand, he does not want to recognize the realm of shared meanings in which even some of the more distorted views of the Orient took place, and without which neither understanding nor misunderstanding would be possible.

In a broad and general sense, he denies the occurrence of understanding itself: What seems to be understanding is, in the end, just another aspect of control.

5. Some symptomatic details exemplify the more general problems associated with Said's critical enterprise and with his conception of Orientalism; at the same time, they illustrate his cavalier attitude toward historical and philological accuracy. In general, attention to such details has been quite rare in the Orientalism debate. I will not enlarge here on some curious statements about Asian and colonial history, for instance, his puzzling references to Japanese history and the "Portuguese experience in the East Indies, China, and Japan" (Said 1978, p. 73). Instead, I want to focus on some interrelated issues which are more directly relevant to our present context.

Said describes the publication of Barthélemy d'Herbelot's *Bibliothèque Orientale* (1697; with a preface by Antoine Galland) as an important event in the history of Orientalism. This is very appropriate; for more than a century, the book was one of the main sources of information and inspiration about the "Orient," especially Muslim culture, in Europe. But this is not Said's point. He views the *Bibliothèque* as a major step in the process of "Orientalizing the Orient" (Said 1978, p. 65). It is an attempt to make the Orient "systematically, even alphabetically, knowable by Western laymen," to turn it "into a rational Oriental panorama, from A to Z" (ibid.) and to represent and domesticate it more thoroughly than in earlier publications. Unfortunately, Said fails to mention that the project of this *Bibliothèque* was inspired and, to a certain extent, guided by a bibliographical dictionary which Galland had found in Istanbul in 1682. It was the work of the great Ottoman scholar and compiler of encyclopedias, Hājjī Khalīfa (or Kātib Celebi, 1609-1657); among Hājjī Khalīfa's other works, we find the famous geographical encyclopedia *Jihānnumā* (*Cihannüma*), an unfinished work which was meant to provide a systematic and, in part, alphabetized survey of the Ottoman empire and the Muslim world, with additional information about Europe. Certainly, the project of making the so-called Orient "systematically, even alphabetically, knowable" was not an exclusively Western idea. For further details concerning the genesis of the *Bibliothèque* and a more balanced assessment of its contents and intellectual orientation, some help is provided by a book which bears the same publication date as Said's *Orientalism* (1978): *Aux Sources de l'orientalisme. La Bibliothèque Orientale de Barthélemi d'Herbelot* by Henry Laurens. Certainly, the statements about Mohammed which Said cites (p. 65ff.) and which were obligatory in those days to get a work of this type published are by no means characteristic of the work in general, nor of the preface by Galland.

Among the readers and users of the *Bibliothèque Orientale*, we find Johann Wolfgang von Goethe (1749-1832), widely recognized as Germany's greatest poet and one of the more universal figures in the history of "world literature" (Goethe's very own concept: "*Weltliteratur*"). In his *West-östlicher Divan* (1819; revised and enlarged, 1827), Goethe presented his poetic vision of a meeting and dialogue between "Occident" and "Orient," Europe and the world of Islam. The poetry itself was supplemented by an enormous, far more voluminous scholarly apparatus which reflects the intensity of Goethe's studies of Muslim culture. From a very early time, not only such popular classics as the *Arabian Nights*, but also the *Koran* itself, Bedouin poetry, etc., were part of his world. His interest and his scholarly and poetic commitment gained new and greater momentum in the period prior to the composition of the *Divan*. The work itself includes not only poems by Goethe himself, but also translations or paraphrases of Arabic and Persian poetry.[7]

In particular, Goethe tries to engage, in a literal sense, in a dialogue with Hafiz, the 14th century Persian poet whom he treats as his poetic and spiritual twin brother, but also respects as a superior predecessor. Indeed, Goethe tries to do exactly what needs to be done according to Said and what the Saidian "Orientalists" failed to do: "to identify with human experience" (Said 1978, p. 328); and this includes, above all, very earthly experiences, such as eating and drinking, love, desire, and death. But Goethe's East-West poetry was also accompanied by intense reflection. He saw the potential pitfalls of what he called "Orientalizing" ("*Orientalisieren*"); and he found an element of escapism in his own fascination with the Orient, or the world of Hafiz.[8] Yet in the end, there was no other choice for him but to commit himself to the whole wide world of shared meanings and common, yet unique human experiences, i.e., to the encounter, dialogue, and interpenetration of cultures. As he says in a posthumous poem, which he wrote at the age of 76 and in appreciation of "Oriental" influences in the second part of his *Faust* (Mommsen 1988, p. 24):

> Wer sich selbst und andre kennt
> Wird auch hier erkennen:
> Orient und Okzident
> Sind nicht mehr zu trennen

["He who knows himself and others will recognize here, too: Orient and Occident can no longer be separated"].

However, for Said, Goethe's work is just another instance of common Orientalist discourse.[9] If there is anything special about it, it is the special (and sinister) role it could play because of the rank and reputation of its author. In particular, Said claims that the *Divan* had a calamitous influence on Karl Marx (see Said 1978, p. 153ff.). According to Said, Marx was originally - "before he was dispatched to Goethe as a source of wisdom on the Orient" (p. 155) - a compassionate humanitarian, full of sympathy for the human miseries in Asia. But the sheer power of Orientalist thought and discourse, as epitomized in Goethe's *Divan*, transformed him into another unfeeling Orientalist. To call this account of Marx's development a "travesty" (al-'Azm 1981, p.15) is almost a euphemism. It is, in fact, as absurd and grotesque as Said's claim that the *Divan* itself was "based ... on a Rhine journey" (Said 1978, p. 19).

Said finds Orientalism in a nutshell in some introductory pieces from the *Divan*, in particular, in the first of the *Talismane* ("talismans"). The first two of its four lines are:

> Gottes ist der Orient!
> Gottes ist der Okzident!

This is a clear and simple statement; it says that both the Orient and the Occident are (in the hands) "of God" ("*Gottes*," genitive), or belong to him. Surprisingly, Said translates this familiar couplet as follows: "God is the Orient! God is the Occident!" (p. 167). He seems to believe that this odd utterance may be associated with such "Orientalist" themes as the "inhuman beauty" and "boundless distance" of the Orient, and with the idea of a "return" to the Orient. The bibliographical note which accompanies the quote informs us that "Sacy's name is invoked with veneration" by Goethe (p. 341, n. 76; Joseph von Hammer-Purgstall was, of course, far more significant for the *Divan*). Another piece of information might have been more appropriate: Goethe's couplet is a quote from the *Koran*, in which he had been interested since his youth (see sura 2, verses 109 and 136). It appears also as a motto in all six volumes of the *Fundgruben des Orients*, edited by Hammer-Purgstall (1809-1818) and one of Goethe's favorite sources.[10]

Of course, Goethe used the words of the *Koran*, especially its words for East (*mashriq*) and West (*maghrib*), in his own way. But what he did had nothing to do with "Orientalizing the Orient" or "Occidentalizing the Occident." On the contrary, it was meant to neutralize and supersede any potential reification and essentialization of Orient and Occident. Certainly, the *Koran* itself can hardly be denounced as a "contribution to Orientalist discourse"; but neither should Goethe's quote from that text.

6. Regardless of the questions and misgivings one may have about Said's *Orientalism*, there can be no doubt that the book addresses highly significant problems. Time and again, we may find the "Orientalism debate" exasperating; nonetheless, we should be grateful that it has been initiated. Even in its excesses and distortions, it is better than no debate at all. There are different ways of reading the book, of responding to its claims and suggestions, of learning from its exaggerations and distortions, and of facing questions which it leaves unanswered. According to Jayant Lele, the most pertinent of these questions can be posed in Said's own words:

> Can one divide human reality, as indeed human reality seems to be genuinely divided, into clearly different cultures, histories, traditions, societies, even races, and survive the consequences humanly? By surviving the consequences humanly, I mean to ask whether there is any way of avoiding the hostility expressed by the division, say of men into "us" (Westerners) and "they" (Orientals). (Lele 1993, p. 66f.; Said 1978, p. 45)

Recent events in different parts of the world provide ample evidence for the validity and urgency of this question, although the example chosen by Said, i.e., the broad division of mankind into "Westerners" and

"Orientals" is not very convincing and may, indeed, be more or less obsolete. In all cases, economic disparities supplement and reinforce the divisions listed by Said. But while I am far from disputing the significance of the question, I do not see it as the central concern or the most fundamental issue in Said's book. His highly confrontational approach and his undisguised essentialization of "others" of his own making would not seem to support such an assessment. I do not even want to speculate on what the deepest concern of the book and the most important among its unanswered questions might be. I want to address just one fundamental problem which I see as a recurrent theme of the book. Although it is often covered by layers of rhetoric and jargon, and although it emerges only rarely in a fully explicit manner, I do believe that it has a distinctive and powerful presence in Said's thought and writing. We may phrase this question as follows: Is there a pervasive mode of thinking and of dealing with others *and* with oneself which is in some special way associated with Europe, and which has accompanied European thought and culture from its Greek beginnings into the modern Westernized and globalized world? Is there something which transforms the other "into an object and thus takes possession of it," which permits "no otherness which is not at the knowing subject's disposal" (Mehta 1985, p. 212), and which may amount to a specifically European affinity between knowledge and power? This question is, of course, an interpretation: It places Said's "Orientalism" in an elusive, but intriguing relationship with Martin Heidegger's notion of the "Europeanization of the earth," which will be one of the recurrent themes in our following discussions. Heidegger postulates a type of pervasive representational thought, of objectification and calculating rationality which is European in its essence and an unfolding of certain events in early Greek thought. Heidegger does not directly associate this with questions of power and, more specifically, with European claims to dominate the world in a political or economic sense. But as his interpretation of Nietzsche shows, he does see the "will to power" as something inseparable from, and implicitly inherent in, the very nature of European representational, calculating thought. The global spread of this way of thinking deprives other cultures of their ability to speak for themselves, and it will distort and discard their own genuine self-understanding. According to Said, the Western, i.e., primarily European, approach to the non-Western world (and the Western conception of knowledge in general) is inseparable from claims of mastery, superiority, and domination. In particular, Europe's exploration and conceptualization of the so-called Orient is presented as a projection of conceptual and epistemic power which reflects and reinforces claims to actual political and economic power. The Western Orientalist attempts to define and understand the "Orient" are in reality ways of depriving it of its identity and autonomy in a political as well as epistemic sense.

There are, of course, enormous and highly conspicuous differences and discrepancies between Heidegger's notion of "Europeanization" and Said's critique of "Orientalism." Yet there are also implicit connections and parallels. Both Heidegger and Said have a penchant for broad and sweeping historical visions and constructions. They tend to see specific episodes in European history as symptoms and manifestations of some deeper structure and to collapse European ways of thinking from classical antiquity to the 20th century into one coherent line of thought and discourse. According to Heidegger, Greek thought opens the "nuclear age"; modern science and technology is a consequence and manifestation of what happened in ancient Greece. Similarly, Said sees one continuous line, one pervasive attitude of representation and epistemic will to power which connects the work and thought of Aeschylus with latter-day Orientalists, imperialists, and administrators.

Neither Heidegger nor Said supplement their statements about Europe with any kind of comparative perspective. For instance, Heidegger insists in presenting the "question of being" as the "destiny of Europe" and the source of science, technology, and Europeanization without considering the possibility that other traditions, such as India, had their own ways of dealing with this question (see below, section III). Said puts the European treatment of Islam at the center of his great indictment of Western Orientalism without considering the Muslim ways of treating other cultures, of conceptualizing otherness, and of creating their own "Orients" (for instance, with reference to India). With good reasons, al-Bīrūnī (973 - *ca.* 1050) has become known as the greatest scholar of India in traditional Islam. If Said had cared to mention him and his views on India, he might have had no choice but to include him in the history of Orientalism. Certainly, his work exhibits some of the characteristic features of Orientalism. Quite apart from his association with the court of Mahmūd of Ghaznī, we may mention his "essentialization" of Indian society in terms of castes, his ideas about Indian irrationalism and traditionalism, his appeals to rationality and disinterested theory, and in general his notion of a fundamental and pervasive Indian otherness. Whether or not we call al-Bīrūnī's brilliant study an "Orientalist construction of India" (using the terminology of Ronald Inden) – it certainly does not offer a genuine alternative to the European and Eurocentric approach.

In 1994, Edward Said added an "Afterword" to his otherwise unchanged *Orientalism.*[11] Looking back at the vast phenomenon of the "Orientalism debate," he finds himself "superseded" as an author, and the book appears to him as a "collective work" (Said 1994, p. 330) which has taken on a life of its own. He provides some welcome clarifications and disclaimers, but does not address the central ambiguity in his notion of "Orientalism," which appears on the one hand as a hostile and hegemonic way of dealing specifically with Islam, but on the other hand as a pervasive feature of the Western treatment of others, or even Western scholarly discourse in general.[12] Apart from his vitriolic outbursts against Bernard Lewis, the self-appointed "spokesman for the guild of Orientalists" (p. 341ff.), Said has misgivings not only about the book's reception by Western Arabists and Islamicists, but also about the responses of Arabs and Muslims, who associate his work with "a systematic defense of Islam and the Arabs" (p. 331), or even with nationalism and fundamentalism. By contrast, he finds the current situation among modern Indian intellectuals as well as Western students of India much more agreeable. Here he sees clear signs for a genuine appreciation and meaningful extrapolation of his work.

7. I will not try to assess and compare the reception and application of Said's critique of Orientalism in the different areas of Asian and non-Western studies. I will limit myself to a few casual and selective observations on developments in the field of Indian studies, which were in some way or other inspired by Said and the Orientalism debate. As my first example, I choose a volume edited by Carol Breckenridge and Peter van der Veer and published under the title *Orientalism and the Postcolonial Predicament* (Philadelphia: University of Pennsylvania Press, 1993). My reasons for this choice are to some extent personal, apart from the fact that the book received an honorable mention from Said himself in the 1994 "Afterword" (p. 343) to his *Orientalism*. The volume is based on the 44th Annual South Asia Seminar at the University of Pennsylvania, which devoted the academic year 1988/1989 to the topic "Orientalism and Beyond." I had some involvement with the organization of this Seminar, but distanced myself from it at a certain point. Two contributions in particular invite comments: "Deep Orientalism? Notes on

Sanskrit and Power Beyond the Raj"[13] by Sheldon Pollock (pp. 76-133) and "Orientalist Empiricism: Transformations of Colonial Knowledge" by David Ludden (pp. 250-278). Both Ludden and Pollock use the concept of Orientalism in a somewhat peculiar, but instructive and symptomatic fashion.

In a statement which seems to be based on a somewhat cursory reading of Said's book, Ludden says that Orientalism "is not the moribund legacy of colonialism that Said makes it out to be" (Ludden 1993, p. 272); it is "much more diverse and vital" (p. 252). In his view, the myths, images, and "icons" created by Western Orientalists have found their way into the minds of the Indian people, especially the nationalists and the political and communal leaders. They served as "weapons in struggles for state power" (p. 273) and came to dominate Indian self-understanding and self-representation. "In nationalism we find the vitality of orientalism today" (p. 271). To challenge the "authority of orientalism," "the nation as a cultural formation of social being and historical becoming" needs to be demolished (p. 274).

From the vantage point of his discovery, Ludden suggests that Said's own "work inhabits a place inside the history of orientalism" (p. 271). Said's concept of Orientalism leaves room for the possibility that the "false, colonial images of the East" might be corrected by the Orientals themselves once they are "free to render images of themselves." But the "implicit promise" of corrigibility and "real truth" is, once again, a symptom of Orientalism. It shows that "Said employs the very positivist logic that gives orientalism life" (p. 271). There is no "truth about the East," not even in the minds of "Easterners." There are only more or less powerful images, myths, or "bodies of knowledge." Knowledge itself is "produced" and "constructed," instead of being derived from valid sources (as traditional Indian philosophers would have told us). If this is so, is there any truth about Orientalism and its role in nationalism, or about myths, images, and their formation? Ludden's presentation seems to take this simply for granted; and while it accuses Orientalism of essentialization and reification it takes great liberty in reifying Orientalism itself.

In conclusion, I want to emphasize that Ludden's general thesis and some of his more specific observations are intriguing and challenging. Unfortunately, their significance is more or less overshadowed by his self-refuting theory of knowledge, and by his unrestrained reification of Orientalism as a "body of knowledge."

In his article on "deep orientalism," Sheldon Pollock wants to widen "the scope of orientalism to include discursively similar phenomena" (Pollock 1993, p. 78) and to open prospects for a "critical Indology" (p. 111ff.). As instances of this wider Orientalism, side by side with colonialist Orientalism, he chooses National Socialist ideology and discourse and, more specifically, the share which German Indologists had in it, as well as the contributions of "high Brahmanism" (as represented by the Mīmāṃsā school) to the "ideological formations of precolonial India" (p. 78). National Socialism practiced the "othering" and "Orientalization," which the French and British colonialists had reserved for foreign and distant cultures, "at home" (p. 77), most conspicuously with regard to the Jews. The Mīmāṃsakas and orthodox Dharmaśāstrins developed an ideology of inequality and a "theodicy of privilege" (p. 110) within traditional India.

All this is meant to uncover a pervasive "morphology of domination" (p. 78) in a wide variety of discourses; it might, indeed, add a whole new dimension to the Orientalism debate. In particular, Pollock reminds us that discourses of domination are not the prerogative of European colonial oppressors. Traditional India has its own rich heritage in this field:

> The self-representation of Indians no more escapes the realm of interests than the representations of their oppressors; and just as there have been other imperialisms than that forming the last stage of capitalism, so there may have been other "orientalisms" to sustain them. (p. 96)

On the other hand, the overt and brutal commitment to power and hegemony in National Socialism may alert us to the inherent, though less visible dangers in other structurally similar ideologies and discourses.

But is it advisable to call all this "orientalism"? Pollock himself poses this question (p. 78), but dismisses it as not very relevant. The potential for this semantic extension, through which metaphorical uses of the term override its primary meaning, was present in Said's own usage. But Pollock goes a step further. All "discourses of power" and their applications to the suppression, exclusion and degradation of others are now expressions and manifestations of one and the same underlying structure of thought and discourse which is called "*deep* Orientalism." Would it not be equally permissible to identify this underlying structure as "deep Nazism" or "deep Mīmāṃsā"? And what will prevent us from calling Kumārila and William Jones "deep Nazis" and Adolf Hitler a "deep Mīmāṃsaka"? Indeed, Pollock draws a direct line from "Justice Sir

William" (Jones) to "SS Obersturmführer Wüst" (p. 111) and postulates an inherent affinity between the hegemonic role of Sanskrit in traditional India (as propagated by the Mīmāṃsakas and others) and the attitudes of its latter-day students among British colonialists or German National Socialists. In accordance with such premises, he sees the "legitimation of genocide" as the "ultimate 'orientalist' project" (p. 96).

Will all this bring us closer to the goal of a "critical," "postmodern" and "postcolonial" Indology, to which Pollock refers in the concluding section of his article? What would such a new Indology be like? Pollock admits that his own ideas are still very tentative. For the time being, they do not offer a potential alternative to the quiet and patient pursuit of understanding ("dialogic understanding"; see below, section II), which is never uncritical, but cannot be iconoclastic either.

8. The most ambitious attempt to apply Said's critique of Orientalism to the field of Indian studies may be found in Ronald Inden's *Imagining India* (1990); in 1989, a collection of essays by Ainslie Embree had been published under the same title.[14] Inden accepts what he calls Said's "bold message" (Inden 1990, p. 38), but wants to go further. In addition to his critique and indictment of traditional Indology, as well as more recent forms of studying India (including "area studies"), he proposes a new epistemological and metaphysical foundation for Indian studies and an entirely new approach to Indian history "from the perspective" of such metaphysics (p. 267). He is convinced that his "shift of presuppositions" and his proposed reform of Indian studies will extend "to the study of other regions of the world - Islam, Africa, China and Japan, pre-Columbian and Latin America, and Eastern Europe" (p. 3), and that his efforts will make it possible to restore true "agency" and epistemic sovereignty to the Indians and all other victims of Orientalism. His proposed new philosophical foundation for the study of India and the non-Western world in general is a somewhat idiosyncratic combination of ideas adopted from Michel Foucault, Edward Said, Antonio Gramsci and, most ostensibly, Robin George Collingwood. According to Inden, the concept of "agency" or "human agency" should replace false essences and essentializations which he sees as a key element of Orientalist discourse (see, for instance, pp. 1ff., 21ff.). In accordance with his central commitment to agency, he also attacks Western scholarly practices of classification, the epistemological belief in knowledge as a "representation" of reality, etc.

The world of Indian studies, as depicted by Inden, is dominated by "hegemonic agents" producing "imperial knowledges" on behalf of the "Anglo-French" and later on the "US-Soviet imperial formation" (p. 36), and various "intellectual architects" (p. 96) who are guided and inspired by such "masterminds" as Hegel (p. 129). Indologists serve as "jungle officers of the Indian mind" (p. 87) or "male managers" of a "female jungle" (p. 85ff.).[15] It has been their collective function to contribute to a comprehensive discourse of domination, a network of inventions and constructs (see, for instance, pp. 93ff., 107f., 128ff.) which has supplanted the epistemic sovereignty of the Indians and their sense of agency with reified essences, most notoriously the castes, and thus deprived them of their capacity "to make their world" (p. 5). They have, moreover, engaged in "wild fabrications" about the nature of the "Indian mind" and tried to "elevate their West by denigrating this Indian Other" (p. 4). Inden wants to liberate the Indians from such degradation and enslavement at the hands of the Indologists:

> I am committed to building on and extending the aspects of the social sciences and history that have been liberating for people and helping them to act as fuller, more knowledgeable agents. (p. 22)

At the same time, so it seems, he wants to liberate Indologists and other Orientalists from their own myths and constructs and turn them into better scholars and more decent human beings.

How should we assess the success or failure of Inden's efforts? How convincing are his attempts to reform Indian studies and to rewrite Indian history? Future developments may tell us more about the inherent potential of his approach. For the time being, the doubts and difficulties which will emerge from a careful and critical reading of Inden's *Imagining India* remain overwhelming. The problems we found with Said's *Orientalism* have not been resolved: some of them may even have become more virulent.

If as Inden says, India and the Indians were "essentialized" by the Indologists, it is certainly no less true and obvious that Indology and Indologists are being essentialized by his own sweeping statements. More than once, the phrase "imagining Indology" may suggest itself to the critical reader of *Imagining India*. Moreover, how does Inden reconcile his sharp critique of the "Orientalist" practice of classification (see, for instance, pp. 16 and 35, with specific reference to Max Müller) with his own habits of classification and essentialist labeling? "Empiricists," "structuralists," "idealists," "Jungians," "Weberians," etc. (defined as such by Inden) are to be found throughout the book.[16] Classification in all its forms was, of course, also practiced in traditional India. The implications of this familiar fact are not addressed by Inden. In general, he makes no attempt to correlate, compare or contrast the "Orientalist discourse" with indigenous Indian forms and levels of discourse. He reprimands Louis Renou for finding a "distortion of reality" in the Brāhmaṇa texts and treating their ritualism as a form of "subjugated knowledge" (p. 39f.); in fact, trying to "subjugate" each other's knowledges and to uncover "distortions of reality" was a most common practice among traditional Indian thinkers. As Sheldon Pollock reminds us, traditional India had its own rich share of discourses of domination; liberating India from such discourses might take a little more than a critique and revision of Western Indology.

I will not try to assess the validity of Inden's attempts to show in more detail "how different the history of India could look from the perspective of a metaphysics that focuses on human agency" (p. 267), i.e., a perspective which does *not* focus on such concepts as caste, culture, or race. However, a few general observations and questions seem to be called for. What precisely is the role of metaphysics - be it Inden's own metaphysics or that of his "Indologists" - in the selection and interpretation of historical documents? How does, how should it guide the work of the historian? Obviously, the way it has guided Inden is not without problems. He cites "Arab travellers" (p. 213ff.) of the ninth and tenth centuries who seem to support his views (by not referring to castes, etc.), but does not mention others, especially the far more knowledgeable al-Bīrūnī, who had a lot to say about castes. And it is somewhat surprising *how* such a critical and philosophically committed scholar as Inden tries to provide evidence for his own ideas about the role of "assemblies" of rural and urban citizenry by citing the declarations and edicts of Rashtrakuta emperors and the "charters" produced by such assemblies (see p. 220ff.). Is it really safe to assume that such documents are free from ideological or hegemonic constructions and distortions?

In *Tradition and Reflection*, I tried to respond to Inden's earlier article, "Orientalist Constructions of India" (1986). I quoted the following statements from this article:

> The capacity to have true knowledge and to act have to be, as it were, returned to the many Others from whom Western practices have taken it. We cannot claim

> to accord independence of action to a sovereign, independent India while still adhering (whether intentionally or not) to presuppositions that deny the very possibility of it. (TR, p. 12)

I suggested that this attempt to liberate India from Western "hegemonic discourses" and to restore its "epistemic and axiological sovereignty" was itself a continuation and extrapolation of Eurocentric practices: "This self-abrogation of Eurocentrism is at the same time its ultimate affirmation." Indeed, the observation still appears valid: The claim to be able to grant sovereignty and "agency" to the Indians and to restore their genuine selfhood is no less presumptuous than the attempt to take it away. Should Gayatri Chakravorty Spivak's observation that "some of the most radical criticism coming out of the West today" reflects a "desire to conserve ... the West as subject" (Spivak 1994, p. 66) apply to this case?

9. I will not try to pursue the "Orientalism debate," the literature on images of, or attitudes toward, the Orient,[17] and the critique of Western "hegemonic discourses" into its further ramifications. Much has been said and written about Western scholars "constructing" or "inventing" non-Western traditions. The following titles of recent publications are exemplary: "The Invention of Caste" (Nicholas Dirks, 1989), *The Invention of Africa* (V. Y. Mudimbe, 1988), or even *Inventing Eastern Europe* (Larry Wolff, 1994). Prior to this, Eric Hobsbawm and Terence Ranger edited their volume *The Invention of Tradition* (1983). Scholars such as David Ludden (see above, section 7), Peter van der Veer ("The Foreign Hand," 1993) or Partha Chatterjee (1986) have tried to demonstrate the role which the Western "constructs" continue to play within non-Western societies, specifically in India. A title like Philip Almond's *The British Discovery of Buddhism* (1988) is somewhat unusual in this climate of debate; however, the phraseology of "construction" is common throughout the book, and Said is one of its authorities (see p. 5).

Other studies, less directly associated with Said's work, explore ways in which non-Western traditions have formed their own "Orients," how this corresponds to or differs from the Western and Eurocentric attitudes, and to what extent they have developed their own modes of Eurocentrism. The case of Japan's intellectual and historiographic treatment of China and the rest of Asia is most instructive in this respect, as Stefan Tanaka has shown in his book *Japan's Orient: Rendering Pasts into History* (1993). There are, of course, numerous recent publications on "xenology," attitudes toward others, and cross-cultural encounters (especially between India and the West) which have little or no connection with the Orientalism debate, for instance Klaus Karttunen's *India in Early Greek Literature* (1989), the thorough and comprehensive survey of early German accounts of India (*Indien im Spiegel deutscher Quellen der Frühen Neuzeit, 1500-1750*), which Gita Dharampal-Frick published in 1994, or *American Transcendentalism and Asian Religions* by Arthur Versluis (1993). For the Indian side, we have, for instance, Aloka Parasher's *Mlecchas in Early India: A Study in Attitudes towards Outsiders up to AD 600* (1991), Tapan Raychaudhuri's *Europe Reconsidered: Perceptions of the West in Nineteenth Century Bengal* (1988) and, in the field of economic history, *Indian Merchants and Eurasian Trade, 1600-1750* by Stephen Dale (1994). There is also much recent work on the role of India in the work of individual writers and thinkers, for instance, Schopenhauer (Meyer 1994).

In my introduction to this chapter, I said that I might have preferred to keep the "specter of Orientalism" out of sight. In practice, this would have been difficult, if not impossible. The "Orientalism debate" is with us and will not go away in the near future. Even disregarding it would count as a statement. But while we have to accept its historical actuality and legitimacy, we should not overestimate its significance. No heroic efforts are called for to defend the dignity of a "discipline" against its detractors; nor is there any need for Bernard Lewis' magisterial wrath. As we have seen, there is a pervasive element of rhetoric and hyperbole in this debate. The concept of Orientalism as such, and apart from its role as a device of rhetoric and polemics, is problematic and elusive. It is "a historical and conceptual hybridization that is no less a construct and projection than the so-called Orient itself" (TR, p. 11). The semantic field of "Orientalism" covers some very specific and some very general traits. Not all of them lie in the path of legitimate and meaningful critique or deconstruction. This implies that the word "beyond" in the phrase "beyond Orientalism" is also problematic and ambiguous. We have to ask: Beyond what? And in what sense?

Certainly, we want to be "beyond" European and Eurocentric claims to higher or absolute authority; we want to be "beyond" the "epistemic subjugation" of non-Western traditions and avoid false essentializations and reifications. We also want to be "beyond" the meaningless proliferation of "objective" information which is one of the ingredients of the "Europeanization of the earth." But do we want to be "beyond" the quiet and patient pursuit of understanding, which has also been part of the history of Indian and "Oriental" studies? And do we want to be "beyond" legitimate generalizations, which are inherent in the process of understanding itself? Once we commit ourselves to the pursuit of understanding, we have to live with the constant presence of misunderstanding and the inevitability of prejudice. But we also have to be aware of the positive potential, the seeds inherent within prejudice, which call for its transcendence and make understanding possible. In this light, we may also be able to find certain positive implications in some of the phenomena criticized by Said or Inden; in 1976, two years before the publication of *Orientalism*, Said himself still recognized the positive potential of "Orientalism as a phenomenon of reception and transmission."[18] Certainly, the commitment to understanding is incompatible with radically iconoclastic attitudes. Understanding itself has been (and needs to be) questioned: Is it something inherently European, and perhaps a secret ally of Eurocentric claims and attitudes? We have to live with this question, while listening to, and trying to understand, the other. There is no other choice. If it commits us to a European, Western identity, it is also our only chance to transcend it, and to open ourselves to other possibilities. Of course, understanding in our modern, global and "multicultural" world is no longer a simple cross-cultural affair. Nor do we know how the ongoing proliferation of information and of channels of communication will affect the meaning of "self," "other," and "understanding." For the time being, the pursuit of understanding has not become obsolete. For those who work in the field of Indian studies, this means listening to the ancient documents as well as the modern representatives of the tradition; it means meeting them, conversing with them, in a realm of shared or shareable meanings and questions.

As we have seen, the critique of Orientalism, as presented by Said and Inden, is a thoroughly Western affair. In a sense, it is no less European and Eurocentric than Orientalism itself. The Indian "others" whom Inden wants to liberate from false European and Western claims do not really emerge as speakers and participants in a dialogue. He speaks about them, not to them; he is the Western authority dealing with their problems and losses. He wants to restore their identity and sovereignty; he never asks himself whether there is anything in the Indian tradition that might affect his own identity or sovereignty. In this sense, we may want to be not only beyond Orientalism, but also beyond the critique of Orientalism.

## NOTES

[1] Excerpts from *Orientalism*, together with texts by Gayatri Chakravorty Spivak, Stuart Hall, Homi Bhabha and many others, appear in two representative "readers": *The Post-Colonial Studies Reader* (Ashcroft et al. 1995) and *Colonial Discourse and Post-Colonial Theory: A Reader* (Williams and Chrisman 1994).

[2] The word "understand" is rare in Said's *Orientalism*; on p. 12, it appears in a loose association with "control," "manipulate," "incorporate."

[3] See Said 1989, p. 211; the paper was originally delivered at the 86th Annual Meeting of the American Anthropological Association in Chicago.

[4] See Said 1976; the article was reprinted with minor additions as the "Foreword" to Schwab 1984.

[5] This changed to a certain extent (though not drastically) after 1980; see Aijaz Ahmad in Williams and Chrisman 1994, p. 170.

[6] Cf. Mehta 1992, p. 237f. Mehta welcomes the reflection of his Indianness in foreign "mirrors" and accepts it as part of his identity. – Further collections of responses are found in the "Review Symposium" published in the *Journal of Asian Studies* (see Kapp 1980) and in Sprinker 1992.

[7] For a comprehensive documentation, see the "Gesamtausgabe" of the *Divan* by Hans-J. Weitz (1972); for an excellent survey and analysis of Goethe's studies of the Muslim and Arabic traditions, see Mommsen 1988.

[8] See Lohner 1971, p. 231 (from an article by Katharina Mommsen); Heinze 1991, p. 161.

[9] See, for instance, Said 1978, p. 199, where Goethe is cited, among many others, for his "contribution to building the Orientalist discourse."

[10] On the work of Hammer-Purgstall (1774-1856) and its significance for Goethe, see Solbrig 1973. Hammer-Purgstall represents aspects of "Orientalism" which find virtually no attention in Said's book. His name is never mentioned by Said; only the *Fundgruben des Orients* appear in a misleading reference on p. 43 (cited as "Fundgraben").

[11] Even the index has not been changed to accomodate the additional pages of the "Afterword"; nor have such blatant errors, as the mistranslation of Goethe's quote from the *Koran* (p. 167) or the inaccurate statements about Japanese history (p. 73) been corrected.

[12] On p. 339 of his "Afterword," Said proudly confesses to "theoretical inconsistencies" in his book and says that it was not meant to be a "theoretical machine."

[13] In an earlier version, which Pollock presented at the University of Pennsylvania in 1989, the phrase "deep Orientalism" was used without question mark. The original title of the seminar on which the book edited by Breckenridge and van der Veer is based was "Orientalism and Beyond."

[14] Inden's initial choice for the title of his book had been "Representing India"; the word "represent" appears now in the title of Dalmia and von Stietencron 1995.

[15] On p. 122, Inden's colleague at the University of Chicago, Wendy Doniger (O'Flaherty), appears as a "retailer of the sacred."

[16] See, for instance, p. 78, for an impressive list of classifying and essentializing labels.

[17] Among recent publications, see, for instance, Lowe 1992 and Melman 1992.

[18] See above, n. 4.

# 1

# Cross-Cultural Encounter and Dialogue

**Francis X. Clooney, SJ**

# WILHELM HALBFASS AND THE OPENNESS OF THE COMPARATIVE PROJECT

Professor Wilhelm Halbfass' scholarly contribution in *India and Europe*, *Tradition and Reflection*, and *On Being and What There Is*, excellent in so many ways, is characterized by three strengths in particular. First, he has offered us a better overview than anyone else of the history of the contacts between Europe and India, and done us the great service of attending to both sides of this contact, not just the European. Second, he has understood better and more fruitfully than most the philosophical issues at stake in such European (mis)appropriation(s) of India, the trivial and substantive reasons for one or another interpretation of India by Europeans. Third, his remedy for the errors that have inevitably marred every correct apprehension has been not the mere pronouncement of some better, higher viewpoint about East and West, etc., but instead a closer, more attentive examination of particular themes in particular traditions of Indian and European thought, so as to restate some of the old questions, discard others, and raise new ones. Together, these three strengths help us to understand much more clearly where we have been and are, and where we might possibly go from here. In this essay I will trace a way of understanding their interconnections, and then chart the direction his work seems to be leading; I will conclude with some suggestions on how it might profitably be complemented by other approaches and perspectives.

## 1. History, Philosophy and Indology

Halbfass' *India and Europe* is a classic which serves to situate as completely as possible (thus far, in a single work) the entire range of relations that have marked the connection of India and Europe over the millennia. Looking into the Greek world's conceptions of its other, missionary encounters (which seem here to be largely in the past), the

Enlightenment and its debates about India's place in the world's intellectual history, and the arena of modern Indology, he establishes a strong sense of the continuities, expectations and fallacies which have marked the encounter; one is left with a strong sense of the development of traditional and contemporary habits of cross-cultural understanding. By his decision to deal with both sides of the encounter and his refined choice of ancient and modern, religious and philosophical instances, Halbfass has successfully mapped many of the most important episodes in the encounter. To praise the book in this way is not to confer on it an omniscience or comprehensiveness - which the author would not claim for it - but rather to commend it for the excellence and provocativeness of what it does achieve: Halbfass has helped us to understand where we stand when we think today about India and the West.

His contribution to our understanding of the history of the European-Indian encounter is greatly enhanced by his reflection on how to think about this material: in the course of studying largely philosophical texts, he philosophizes:

> If "comparative philosophy" is supposed to be *philosophy*, it cannot just be the comparison of *philosophies*. It cannot be the objectifying, juxtaposing, synoptic, comparative investigation of historical, anthropological or doxographical data. Comparative philosophy is philosophy insofar as it aims at self-understanding. It has to be ready to bring its own standpoint, and the conditions and horizon of comparison itself, into the process of comparison which thus assumes the reflexive, self-referring dimension which constitutes philosophy. And, of course, in applying the term and the concept of philosophy cross-culturally and beyond the sphere in which it was created and originally used, we cannot be sure whether we are indeed comparing philosophies, or whether we are comparing the Western tradition of philosophy with other traditions which, in spite of all analogies, are ultimately not philosophical traditions. But this might be a deeper challenge to self-understanding than dealing merely with what is explicitly referred to as philosophy, i.e. with the history of philosophy under the secure and thoughtless guidance of the word "philosophy." (IE, p. 433)

In a highly refined fashion that is philological and philosophical, he appreciates and differentiates the linguistic, epistemological and ontological issues underlying various encounters, understandings and misunderstandings; he discerns kinds and levels of argumentation, gleans what deserves appreciation even from wrong directions and misunderstandings and, in general, locates historical detail in the context of a fruitful apprehension of the main lines of European continental philosophy in the post-Enlightenment period. At the broadest level, he is rightly insisting that the encounter of India and Europe continues to raise issues of self-identity and self-awareness for Indians and Europeans and in today's "Europeanized" world, the issue of the self-understanding of *anyone* in the world.

One of the most interesting chapters in *India and Europe* is an important discussion of the debates among European scholars and lexicographers as to whether to include Indian systems of thought in the category of "philosophy"; characteristically, Halbfass not only details the discussion but elaborates its philosophical ramifications, regarding why someone might think to exclude one or another evidently intellectually serious system, and what such a discussion meant for Europeans. He concludes his consideration of the debate about "Indian philosophy" in this way:

> The question as to whether and in what ways "there is" philosophy in traditional India has, however, not been decisive for the development of the European philosophical interest in Indian thought. From very different angles, and in the name of very divergent philosophies and ideologies, ideas and preconceptions about Indian thought have been enlisted as means of self-understanding, self-affirmation, and self-critique. The interest in, or dismissal of, Indian thought has been associated with the proclamation of one's own identity as well as the search for alternatives. Such crucial motifs as pantheism, quietism, and Stoicism, and questions concerning the "original revelation" and the relationship between philosophy and religion have also been tied to the study of India in a variety of ways. Regardless of the question whether there has been an equivalent to Greek-European "philosophy" and "theory" in India the idea of India has had a significant impact upon the manner in which Europe has articulated, defined, and questioned itself and its fundamental and symptomatic concepts of theory, science, and philosophy. (IE, pp. 158-159)

We must of course be interested throughout in the important theme enunciated here, regarding the uses of India in the self-understanding of Europe; but here we stress the importance of Halbfass' realization that historical relations and interpretations are not merely issues of essence nor of power, but particular situations which can legitimately be invested with philosophical significances (of various sorts) – and understood and learned from. His attention to particular debates is therefore always careful and attentive; he avoids stereotypes and generalizations, and refuses to dismiss any position without giving it due consideration. He is able to discern the importance and effects, long- and short-term, even of ideas that may turn out to be ill-informed or simply mistaken.

Halbfass of course has his list of favored thinkers, valued (in this context at least) mainly on the basis of their contribution to the larger story of Europe's self-understanding in light of its encounter with India; among these three stand forth as most prominent: Hegel (in terms of his influence), Heidegger (in terms of his sober assessment of where the world stands today) and Gadamer (in terms of the conversational model he offers for philosophy today and in the future).

Halbfass is acutely aware of the heritage of Hegel and how this must be dealt with; fortunately, he avoids both adulation of Hegel and a contemptuous dismissal of Hegel as a man who scornfully located India in Europe's past. With customary acuity, Halbfass surveys the breadth of Hegel's earlier and later statements on India - for Hegel's view as to whether there was philosophy in India changed over time - and concludes:

> Hegel tries to comprehend Indian thought as something that is superseded by, and contained in, modern Western thought. This is obviously incompatible with the neutrality and openness which the advocates of the "comparative method" - Comparative Religion, Comparative Philosophy, and so forth - postulate. However, it is also a challenge to some of the unquestioned hermeneutical assumptions of the "comparative" and "coordinating" disciplines: It challenges the very ideas of "comparison" and neutral "understanding." (IE, p. 99)

He also suggests that today's nascent, possibly fruitful comparative method must be understood in the context of Hegelian thought and reactions to it:

> "Comparative philosophy" is still in a nascent state; there is no reason to question its great potential and promise for the future. But once again, we have to be aware that there is a problem concerning the standpoint of the observer. Its neutrality cannot simply be declared. The "comparative method," as an explicit project, has its roots in certain specific constellations of modern Western thought. Although it was frequently associated with anti-Hegelian movements and sentiments and rejected by Hegel himself, its freedom from Hegelian premises and its intercultural neutrality and universality should not be taken for granted. (OB, p. 14)[1]

Halbfass dwells on Martin Heidegger in *India and Europe* in large part because the latter devoted considerable attention to defining concerns of Western civilization and philosophy, and to the limits of the obsession with the question of being. Halbfass values Heidegger's view of the modern predicament, wherein all the sciences - "natural" and "human" - have become "calculating, objectifying, 'representational'" and where this way of thinking for better or worse defines the situation in which any real thinking is occurring in today's world and, even just for its comprehensiveness, which is also definitively undercutting the possibility of a "real" dialogue between "West" and "East."

> Heidegger's thesis concerning the Greek-European origin and essence of philosophy" and "science" is no longer a self-confident proclamation of the uniqueness of Europe as it was for the historians of the nineteenth century and still Husserl. It is, rather, a statement concerning a global predicament. Europeanization "eats away all substance from things." Metaphysics is "one single, but perhaps also the necessary predicament of the Occident, and the condition of its planetary domination."

But this dour assessment is not the end of the story:

> Heidegger refers again and again to the global, universal domination of the Greek-Western "scientific" way of thinking. But he also makes it very clear that this in itself cannot constitute the framework and medium for the future dialogue with the East. The "thinking of the future," which will be ready for this dialogue, can no longer be "philosophy because it thinks on a more fundamental level than metaphysics – a term which means the same." Neither the language of "science," nor that of "metaphysics," nor that of "historical understanding" can provide the proper medium for a dialogue in which all these ideas themselves will have to be questioned. We have to transcend "what is European" ("das Europäische"); we have to reach "beyond Occident and Orient." Yet, neither Orient nor Occident seems capable of opening and establishing a medium and "sphere of their possible dialogue" ("Bereich ihrer möglichen Zwiesprache"). (IE, p. 169)

In his summary reflection at the end of *India and Europe*, Halbfass further insists that we must admit that the world has been "Europeanized" – even as we argue at the same time that the conquest of the world by Western philosophy and technology is only a prelude to further developments:

> Neither the language of "science," nor that of "metaphysics," nor that of "historical understanding," can provide the proper foundation for a dialogue in which all these ideas themselves will have to be questioned. We have to transcend "what is European" ("das Europäische"); we have to reach "beyond Occident and Orient." Yet for the time being there is no escape from the global network of "Europeanization," and no way to avoid the conceptual and technological ways and means of communication and interaction which the European tradition has produced. (IE, pp. 441-442)

Though one must admit the hegemony of the West, it is still true that "ancient Indian thought, in its unassimilable, non-actualizable, yet intensely meaningful distance and otherness, is not obsolete" (IE, p.

442). The very fact of its resistance to easy appropriation – its status as "out of place" today – provides a space over against the hegemony of the West.

In this context Halbfass refers us to the work of Ronald Inden who has applied Edward Said's broader notion of orientalism to the Indian context. Inden highlights the need to uncover and critique the asymmetries in the relationship between Europe and India, the multiple ways in which Europeans have continually manipulated and strategically misconstrued Indian thought.[2] In response to this approach, Halbfass first argues for more careful research on both the European and Indian concepts that are drawn into the orientalist debate, but also cautions us against efforts (such as Inden's) to remedy this past orientalism by means which, however well-intentioned, would merely revise and improve upon the orientalist construction of India yet again:

> The West has imposed its methods of research, its values and modes of orientation, its categories of understanding, its "epistemic absolutism" upon the Indian tradition and alienated the Indians from what they really were and are. It now takes the liberty to remove such superimpositions, to release the Indians into their authentic selfhood, to restore their epistemic and axiological sovereignty. This self-abrogation of Eurocentrism is at the same time its ultimate affirmation. (TR, p. 12)

Here we must notice Halbfass' preference for "dialogue" over "comparison." By "dialogue," "the dialogic" etc., he seems to indicate a more engaged interaction in which both parties learn and both are changed by the encounter (IE, p. 160). He approves of the point made by Raimundo Panikkar (IE, p. 478, note 47), who argued for the virtues of dialogue in preference to "comparison" (IE, p. 402).[3] The situation is therefore essentially a dialogical one, and half the solution lies with India and its counterparts. Europeans have no short-cut to a solution but, indeed, need help from outside their traditional, habitual set of resources. Ironically, as "europeanization" develops and outstrips the West where it began, Europe seems to expect help from places like India: "Europe is turning towards those non-European traditions which it tried to master, supersede, 'understand' and 'explain'; it tries to enlist them as allies against developments initiated by itself. The West is turning towards the East for new inspiration, or even for therapy" (IE, p. 440). And, "In their application within the modern Western world, Indian methods and teachings become parts and manifestations of this world, and the constellation of science and technology. And for the foreseeable future, we may have to live with this tantalizing paradox: The globalization of the world coincides with its parochialization; the meeting and 'dialogue' of the cultures and religions of this world coincides with their trivialization" (IE, p. 441). How things will in fact end up is a drama: there are real possibilities which can be taken advantage of – or lost – in a future that is presented as truly open.

Insofar as the issue of dialogue thus comes to the fore, Halbfass depends heavily on the work of yet a third German philosopher, Hans-Georg Gadamer. In his *Truth and Method*, Gadamer emphasizes conversation and the concomitant apprehension of language as conversational; these views help form Halbfass' understanding of the India-Europe connection, the dynamics of the present situation, and what is possible hereafter. For however the contact between India and Europe has been shaped or mis-shaped, it has had the characteristics of a give-and-take encounter. An inquiry into the contacts must evidently be or become more than a monologue, it too must be a conversation.

It seems, too, that Halbfass has learned from Gadamer how to interpret what he, Halbfass, is doing in his detailed studies of Indian materials: for Halbfass, Indological research itself becomes now a dialogical endeavor. The historical studies of the interrelations of India and the West, and a philosophical assessment of them, serve in turn as background and occasion for a series of particular studies. Having criticized and soberly assessed many viewpoints and turned toward models of conversation and dialogue, Halbfass does not merely add some general evaluations; he proceeds by way of cautious, careful examples, often leaving incomplete his treatment of some large issue that he had opened up. His studies, particularly in Vaiśeṣika and Vedānta,[4] constitute a series of specific meditations as it were, each contributing to the excision of subtle habits of erroneous thinking, including the errors of overemphasizing either the similarities or difference between Indian and Western thought.

His inquiries have a fairly regular style. Ordinarily, he begins by situating historically and theoretically some claim and counter-claim regarding a comparative possibility, and then focuses very closely on certain issues in certain texts. Thus, one study opens with a broad consideration of whether the categories, "reason" and "revelation," "rationality" and "tradition" are applicable in our effort to understand Indian materials; he then problematizes both alternatives – claims that the categories do or don't fit – and embarks upon a masterful and precise analysis of what we learn about this question from the works of one thinker, Śaṅkara.[5] Just as typical of his approach is the posing of a very long set of questions regarding "non-Western ontologies" at the beginning of *On Being and What There Is*. No less than eighteen (unanswered) questions in a row (OB, pp. 12-13) conclude with the disarmingly simple remark, "whatever our answer to these questions may be, it is our first responsibility to understand the Indian statements" (OB, p. 12). Though the closely defined and argued analyses that ensue contribute some modest but substantial insights into the originally posed issue, individual essays often end with only the briefest return to the initial comparative issues: the initial questions have been so problematized that they are no longer pertinent, much less answerable.

His method is strikingly fruitful in a way that leads ultimately to the upset (though not destruction) of the principles by which it proceeds; it leads beyond the very formulations of historical, philosophical and specific thematic inquiries he presupposes as the contours of the general project undertaken in these works. He is showing us how to chart a careful, responsible philosophical path, precisely when the comfortable poles of similarity and difference thus begin to vanish: how to be careful and responsible in our philosophy when there is no longer any unified coherent discourse about what is worth knowing and, indeed, when long-term disagreements and long-held positions of European thought can no longer be taken for granted. To think philosophically is thus to participate in a search for what is worth thinking about, challenging geographical boundaries which had in the past normally and normatively fenced in philosophers' minds.

However one might chart and trace Halbfass' work in these volumes, a key point to be made is that Halbfass is simply arguing in favor of knowledge – factually informed, thoughtfully ordered – over ignorance, in favor of a philosophical reflection and comparative project that is informed by a refined and sophisticated knowledge of the materials that become the subject of comparison: speculation uninformed by an understanding of the subject material under discussion will be pointless, harmful.

We notice too the sobering effect of his analyses; in the course of discovering much that is valuable and useful, they effectively uncover also many of the confusions to which human thinking is liable. Halbfass calls our attention to the innumerable wrong theories, based in wrong information, strewn throughout the history of Europe's encounter with

India. He knows how often Indian materials have been improperly understood, and he is critical of the idea that philosophers might operate at some higher perspective where "mere details" do not matter; misinformed speculation does more harm than good.

## 2. The Openness of the Current Situation

Nevertheless: however meticulous, regular and persistent in his methods, Halbfass is not one to be overconfident about his work, and he does not exempt himself from error and limitation. Indeed, Halbfass' own scholarly triangle – a consciousness of the history of the encounter of India and the West, a philosophical commitment, and a series of specific, clarificatory investigations – is insufficient, at least until its direction and finality are further defined. Once various extrinsic and implausible models of superiority and of equity are stripped away, the self-conscious and critical scholar must articulate (new) reasons for his or her study – if such reasons can be found. In *On Being and What There Is* Halbfass insists on the limits of *every* particular mode of inquiry, and argues against the view that there could be any single, sure method for making comparisons and understanding them:

> At the end, we do not have a well-defined method, and perhaps not even a definite perspective, for our exploration of the Indian texts and teachings. *Our procedure will be eclectic.* We will ask different kinds of questions and borrow our heuristic and exegetic devices from different sources. Whenever it seems appropriate, we will try to derive interpretive perspectives and hermeneutic guidance from the Indian tradition. But, of course, such derivation itself requires understanding and interpretation. Conceptual devices that have been developed by Western philosophical thought will be indispensable tools of translation, interpretation and analysis; *but we will have to use them cautiously*. We have to be constantly aware that our own ontological concepts and premises are problematic ... Using such [Western philosophical] terms does not mean that we know the true and precise meaning of their Indian counterparts; we can only say that we are dealing with comparable areas of thought, debate, and *potential confusion*. Inevitably, exegesis and translation will lead us into these open areas of philosophical reflection and debate. On the other hand, historical and philological problems will often interfere with conceptual problems. Philology, exegesis and philosophical reflection may seem to be inseparable; *we cannot always be sure what we are doing*. This may be frustrating; but it can also be a philosophical challenge. (OB, pp. 15-16; my emphases)[6]

Where does all this lead Halbfass himself? In the introduction to *On Being and What There Is* he admits that even his own philosophical moorings have shifted, to some extent alarmingly, for the compass of his own research has been redirected:

> Over the years, my methodological positions and philosophical allegiances have changed. *The result has been a certain eclecticism and growing doubts concerning the meaning and relevance of the topic itself. We do not know whether the "question of being" is a meaningful question.* But once this question is gone, or reduced to certain linguistic, semantic, or logical technicalities, what else could provide us with a comparable sense of philosophical wonder and perplexity? What would happen to philosophy itself? (OB, p. vii; my emphasis)

Each of the two major sections of *India and Europe* (respectively on the European view of India and the Indian view of Europe) ends with tantalizingly open statements. Part I, which had examined Western attitudes toward India, concludes the observation that non-Western traditions, even if overwhelmed, have been neither obliterated nor accounted for by Europe; indeed,

> [t]hey may, in fact reach far beyond our current capacity of comprehension. They may not be accessible to the very ideas of "research" and "theoretical mastery." We have to detach ourselves from the spell of methodic research and progress. The enigmatic future "dialogue" with the East, to which Heidegger refers, cannot be planned and organized.

The requisite response is an almost mystical openness:

> What we may have to learn above all is "Gelassenheit," a serene willingness to wait, and *not* to plan for this future. (IE, p. 170)

Part II likewise concludes with emphasis on the openness of the situation:

> Modern Indian thought finds itself in a historical context created by Europe, and it has difficulties speaking for itself. Even in its self-representation and self-assertion, it speaks to a large extent in a European idiom. This does not, however, mean that the dialogue and debate between India and Europe has been decided in favor of Europe, or that India has been superseded by Europe. The power of the Indian tradition has not exhausted itself in the self-representation and self-interpretation of modern India. The dialogic situation is still open. (IE, p. 375)

How then are we to proceed in this open situation? We know by now that for Halbfass this openness is not license for visionary generalizations or exotic meta-connections of East and West; there is still no replacement for careful studies (of Vaiśeṣika, Vedānta and other systems) which yield a series of small insights, one after the other.

Yet we must also ask ourselves if even this approach is sufficient; despite its indisputable importance, it may not lead us beyond where, as we have seen, Halbfass himself stood in reviewing his own work in *On Being and What There Is*: "The result has been a certain eclecticism and growing doubts concerning the meaning and relevance of the topic itself. We do not know whether the 'question of being' is a meaningful question" (OB, p. vii). If so, the presupposition that remains implicit in Halbfass' work that careful detailed work will add up to the "big picture" is even less convincing, as is the correlative view that the ongoing dialogue will somehow add up to a satisfactory conclusion. We must therefore seek ways to complement what Halbfass has given us, in charting the way forward.

## 3. Charting the Open Course

I close then with three suggestions regarding where Halbfass - and those of us who have profited from his work and wish to extend it - will do well to direct our attentions: first, toward a more ample appreciation of texts; second, toward a retrieval of religion as a category of understanding that is not to be subsumed by philosophy; third, toward a careful and responsible inscription of the self in Indological study.

First, Halbfass' philosophical, thematic approach, as detailed and faithful to the sources as it is, tends toward a neglect of texts as wholes, preferring instead a series of selective thematic borrowings from texts. Though his studies are impeccable according to the terms of their announced purposes, they inevitably emphasize philosophical over literary concerns, and utilize texts as resources for philosophical inquiry, in terms of the light they shed on one or another selected theme under consideration. Halbfass does not deal with texts as integral works which develop by their own plan, within the margins of their specific beginnings and endings, according to their announced and actual intentions in certain ritual and communal contexts, etc. As texts are made to answer the questions put to them, their literary qualities further recede into the background, and they do not stand forth in their own resistant, complex coherence. The value of perplexing details and turns that whole texts offer, along with their commentaries and other assisting materials, is not very evident in his writing; we are not clearly shown where the particular passages, selected because of their interest to Halbfass, stand in relation to what is of less interest to him, passed over, omitted. Thus, for example, Halbfass' expert analyses of Vedāntic themes tell us almost nothing about the Upaniṣads; his analyses of Advaita, while not misleading us, also do not afford us an overall sense of what the integrated set of issues were for the Advaitins themselves, of how they wrote, where they choose to begin and end, how they commented on one another, etc. Though the thematic approach is extraordinarily fruitful and remains legitimate, unless it is complemented by some other kinds of reading it leaves the reader in the position of having to confront only those questions she or he thinks are important.

Those who, like Halbfass, wish to be partners in dialogue with their "others" will find a particular value in reading whole texts. For these "others" can and do set their own terms and speak according to concerns which may not be those of their interlocutors; "Europeans" who wish to understand India do well to stand (sometimes at least) in the position of having to respond to questions posed by Indians, to follow their ways of arranging knowledge. This possibility is facilitated by attention to whole texts, the questions they pose to us, the ways they have been read and been used in their own traditions, etc.

To complement the thematic approach more strongly by a greater commitment to the demands of whole texts is not merely to spend more time reading. This is a commitment which engages a wider range of philosophical issues and surveys the kinds of available philosophical knowledge, ultimately raising even the question of whether the future of the intellectual discourse can be adequately constrained within the boundaries of philosophical analysis. For example: pointing to the importance of the "writing" tradition of philosophy, which stresses the dynamics of textual interpretation and which thrives on "paradox and style," Harold Coward (1990) has identified Jacques Derrida as a potentially key figure in a new "writing encounter" of India and the West. He has sketched some important ways in which Derrida's work is like that of several important Indian figures, especially Bhartṛhari, Śaṅkara, Aurobindo and Nāgārjuna.[7] Careful reading can take many forms; if Gadamer stands as one of the main inspirations of Halbfass' work, it may take a figure such as Derrida - whose failure to engage Gadamer in an expected conversation turned out to be a highly productive non-event[8] - to extend Halbfass' articulation and assessment of the encounter and chart new paths forward by indicating another way into an appropriation of the texts of the Indian tradition.[9] Then, once questions of textuality and reading and hence of the plurality of perspectives come to the fore, one can take into account still other approaches that are current in cultural studies today as "third world" voices are heard outside of, or in tension with, Europe's classical cultural formulations; feminist perspectives in particular come to mind here.[10]

All the issues we have been discussing thus far - encounter, cross-cultural study, dialogue, textual knowledge - may be highlighted according to their religious themes. My second concluding suggestion then is to suggest that religious discourse, though already a part of Halbfass' work, deserves more attention, if one is to enter forthrightly into the opening Halbfass has cleared.

One aspect of this broader project is for Halbfass simply to enrich the scope and style of his own writing. While he is admirably respectful of religious thought and does not dismiss even excesses which skew the reception of comparative data, he is perhaps too reticent regarding the specific motivations of religious thought, how these operate and what one is supposed to make of them today. Take for instance his references to Ramakrishna, the 19th century priest and mystic of Bengal: Halbfass aptly locates Ramakrishna's system of thought vis à vis other systems in that time period - Keshab Chunder Sen's, for instance - but this location is also a "prosification" of the more poetic and dramatically detailed presentation of a life, experience and thought. One cannot get from Halbfass' dispassionate writing much of a feel for the impulse Ramakrishna brought to religious thinking; the cool, serene eye of Halbfass views a theoretical, intellectualizing Ramakrishna. Not that Halbfass need adopt the guise of the hagiographer or student of religious phenomena; but there is a need, precisely in terms of the dialogic project Halbfass is seeking to rehabilitate, for a style of writing and inquiry that does not so thoroughly filter religious discourse through its philosophical components.[11]

Or, more moderately, in order to broaden his area of inquiry he might simply look at (again, whole) works which deliberately meld religious and philosophical discourse. In the more ancient traditions, for instance, he might consider more than he has the "devotional" schools of Vedānta, such as Rāmānuja's or, in a contemporary setting, a work such as *A Vaiṣṇava Interpretation of the Brahmasūtras, Vedānta and Theism*, by Rampada Chattopadhyay (1992), which combines a close reading of key Vedānta texts with a strong devotional tendency, drawing particularly on the *Bhāgavatapurāṇa* and pious speculations on Ramakrishna.

We noted earlier that Halbfass' observations on the missionaries are limited, locating the missionary project prior to the Enlightenment. Though rightly noting that the missionary contribution to Indology has notably declined (IE, p. 227), he gives almost no sense of how the missionary impulse has continued and taken other forms, even today. Beyond his astute observation that missionaries above all sought to be *understood*, his treatment of them is limited; the intellectual implications of the specifically religious dimension of the encounter of India and Europe gets insufficient attention, as a historical or ongoing phenomenon. He does not tell us what he thinks of evangelization - the missionary impulse to preach the Gospel - as a phenomenon not reducible to other cultural factors, nor to philosophy, nor even to a basis for dialogue. All of this seems pertinent to the open future of which Halbfass speaks, and we cannot afford to overlook it.

Halbfass concedes as much, at least indirectly, in his recent comments on Paul Hacker - comments which echo the Hegelian suspicion, noted earlier, about the pretense to the position of a neutral observer:

> Hacker emphasizes the special affinity between Indian studies and theology (which had become his own major preoccupation by this time [1967/8]): "Today, the proximity of theology is greater than ever before ... But today as ever, India is the classical land for the study of source materials in the history of religion." Such study requires a clear perspective, a sense of direction, a "religious decision" ("religiöse Entscheidung"). A complete absence of preconceptions, a total freedom from any sense of commitment, pure objectivity, would be counterproductive. "Theological thought can open the religious scholar's eyes for realities which would otherwise remain hidden from him."[12]

Though Halbfass is describing the viewpoint of Hacker and does not venture to assume it as his own, neither does he distance himself explicitly from the ideas of a man he admires so greatly (and to whom he dedicated *India and Europe*). How might a more explicit set of theological positions - or positions about theological positions - enable Halbfass to chart more effectively the future of the encounter of India and Europe?

The issue of religious discourse also leads to a set of interesting questions which pertain more directly to the realm of academe in the West today: what is the future of the academic study of religions? is there a scholarly perspective from which to appreciate religion non-reductively? Though Halbfass has not answered these questions, his general sympathies seem to stand in opposition to positions which stress that academic study does, even should, undercut religious perspectives.[13] Halbfass may not wish to be enlisted on one side or the other in this kind of argument, but his scholarly methods and vision open the way to a constructive alternative to reductive approaches to the study of religion and, indeed, provide sound reasons for doing so.

My third concluding suggestion is that we must raise more explicitly the question of the location of the self vis à vis the analysis one undertakes. A commitment to texts and the dynamics of reading, and an analysis of the possibilities of philosophical and religious commitments in the current, open situation of intercultural encounter, together entail a greater concern for the self in general, - but also Halbfass' own self - than has yet been evident in his writings.

As we have seen, his careful and sober approach, marked as it is so clearly by his awareness of the limits of what he can accomplish, emphasizes that knowledge is a reflexive enterprise, in which the presuppositions, methods and purposes of the activity of comparison eventually must come under scrutiny. Halbfass quotes Gadamer favorably on the inevitability of "prejudice":

> Gadamer's hermeneutics teaches us to accept "prejudice" ("Vorurteil") as something indispensable, and to discard the abstract and vacuous ideal of an entirely open and "unprejudiced" understanding. It shows that understanding cannot amount to slipping into somebody else's skin, as it were, and to comprehend or experience the foreign, the other simply in its own identity, or by coinciding with it ... What we need is not sheer "neutrality" and "extinction of one's self," but "the conscious assimilation of one's own fore-meanings and prejudices:" "The important thing is to be aware of one's own bias, so that the text" - and why not an Indian text - "may present itself in all its newness and thus be able to assert its own truth against one's own fore-meanings." Should Gadamer's concepts of "hermeneutical conversation" or "dialogue" ("hermeneutisches Gespräch") and "fusion of horizons" ("Horizontverschmelzung")... not also be pertinent to the interpretation of Indian thought and its literary documents? (IE, pp. 164-165)

But many contemporary writers push the issue farther, insisting on the need to chart all knowledges in terms of their bases in self, and therefore incorporating the implications more deeply in their writings. In *Sexing the Self*, one of the best recent books on this topic, Elspeth Probyn has argued against the (persistent) model that scholarship can be conceived and practiced without the inclusion of the self. Moreover, she persuasively defends the view that one must go beyond the inscription of a generic "self" to the inclusion of a specific, local and gendered self, yet without aggrandizing that self and investing it once again with a higher position: "As a modest proposal, I want to posit the self as a theoretical movement into the text that carries with it the ontological traces of its local origins. This is to say that the self spoken invokes a particular moment of being, but that in its speaking it demands an acknowledgment of the conditions of its possibility, of its existence. Quite simply, the sound of its 'ontologicality' must be met with an analysis of the positivity of its materiality. This is not to 'recognize the self in its otherness,' but always to ask what had to be in place in order for this self to appear at all" (Probyn 1993, p. 80).

The ambiguities Halbfass has encountered and helped bring to our notice in the history and present moment of the encounter of India and Europe tend to make us terribly self-conscious; and if we are to be open in an unpredictable and truly new way, our efforts at the articulation of our selves - precisely in the cross-cultural dialogue - are a resource to be taken positively into account. Who is today's "European"? whence comes the "European" who ventures to think about India?

One hopes that Halbfass will venture to fill out the details of this "prejudice" by locating *himself* on the historical and philosophical maps he composes. Though it is not necessary to expect broad autobiographical accountability, it would be interesting, for instance, to know how the experience of living, teaching and writing in the United States has affected the work of this professor who speaks so frequently of the "Europeanization" of the world, and who so evidently continues to rely on his favorite German thinkers, Hegel, Heidegger and Gadamer. How does "Europeanization" appear when viewed from the United States which, though in many ways still European at its roots, is nevertheless also more and something else? do we still need to talk about "Europe" so much? after several decades in the United States, how does the world look from Philadelphia? and how does the future of Indology appear to a professor who has spent so many years in a "South Asia department"?

These suggestions regarding textuality, religion, and the self, are intended to complement Halbfass' work, to give a more specific frame to the openness he has described. Though of course it would not be fair to expect every scholar to undertake every kind of inquiry - more than most, Halbfass may be justified in staying within the boundaries of the challenges he has already set for himself and continually met so well - nevertheless it is also true that he is the one who sees the future of the relations of India and the wider world to be open and supple, highly important for the self-understandings of all of us – and puzzling enough that the reflective scholar may not be sure of what the questions actually are today. Because Halbfass has excelled, he has fashioned a new place of openness between India and the West, and we hope that he will lead us more boldly into the new, open place.

*Boston College*
*Department of Theology*
*Chestnut Hill, Massachusetts, USA*

## NOTES

[1] On the nascent state of the encounter: "Comparative philosophy, if it is possible at all, is still in a nascent state, and it requires much critical reflection and hermeneutical awareness" (IE, p. 433).

[2] Halbfass refers to Inden's "Orientalist Constructions of India" (1986); since then Inden has expressed his views more thoroughly in his *Imagining India* (1990). Inden criticizes "Orientalist constructions of India" and ways in which Indological discourse has denied to Indians "the power to present themselves," and thus reinforced processes of alienation and subjugation. Indology, too, has projected its objects into a sphere of "otherness," has "reified" and "essentialized" them in its own way, and "has appropriated the power to represent the Oriental, to translate and explain his (and her) thoughts and acts not only to Europeans and Americans but also to the Orientals themselves" (TR, p. 11).

[3] See also reference to East-West dialogue, IE, p. 286.

[4] Further research on "being" in Vedānta is promised by Halbfass.

[5] "Human Reason and Vedic Revelation in Advaita Vedānta," TR, pp. 131-204.

[6] Later in the same volume, in completing an initial survey of the Vaiśeṣika categories and assessing the pros and cons of the use of the categories of modern analytic philosophy to understand Vaiśeṣika, he comments: "To use modern analytical tools as means of clarification is, indeed, very appropriate if it is not based on the premise that there is a state of latest research in ontology that would allow us to assess all previous attempts as more or less successful approximations" (OB, p. 82).

[7] See Coward 1990.

[8] See Michelfelder and Palmer 1989.

[9] Recently, Derrida himself has explored the limits of "the European," in a series of meditations on war and democracy (in *The Other Heading* [1992]) and on death (in *Aporias* [1993]). He fruitfully explores the limits of self-consciousness, self-location and the variety of strategies by which one maps pathways forward, marking out what is possible; he seeks ways to deal with one's "others" that are productive und reaching beyond merely repackaged presentations of oneselves; in *Aporias*, for instance, his meditations on death both undercut much "foolish comparatist predication" (Derrida 1993, p. 58), and take advantage of the fact that "death has no borders," in sketching out a way of thinking "beyond Europe" (my term) while yet wondering if there has even been a "history of death" anywhere but in Europe. As is usually the case with Derrida, this reflection is largely mediated through the reading of specific texts: if one can read differently, one can begin to describe new connections between India and Europe.

[10] One might look, for instance, to the rich, complex critical reflection of Gayatri Chakravorty Spivak on modern Indian fiction by women. For instance, her translation of Mahasweta Devi's short story, "Stanadayini" (Breast-Giver") and analysis of it and of several understandings of it, in her "A Literary Representation of The Subaltern: A Woman's Text from the Third World." See Spivak 1987, "Breast-Giver" (pp. 222-240), and "A Literary Representation of The Subaltern: A Woman's Text from the Third World" (pp. 241-268). The interpretations analyzed include "Western Marxist-Feminist," "Western Liberal Feminist," "French high theory of the Female Body," and that of Devi herself. Spivak's writings chart encounters between "Europe" and "India" which, because largely unaccounted for by Halbfass' research, challenge his work – while yet moving forward some of the fundamental issues of self-understanding and reflection which he highlights. Apropos the tendency of critics to categorize and define neatly what texts are about, she characterizes the problem of cross-cultural categories in an interesting way that in part reflects the concern Halbfass voiced regarding critiques of orientalism: "The lack of fit between this neat narrative and the bewildering cacophony of 'Stanadayini' permits us to ask: why globalize? Why should a sociological study that makes astute generalizations about sex/affective production in the United States feel obliged to produce a 'cross-cultural constant'? Why should a study that exposes gender-mobilization in Britain purport to speak on the relationship between imperialism and motherhood? Why, on the contrary, does 'Stanadayini' invoke the singularity of the gendered subaltern? What is at stake here? How are these stakes different from those of imperialism as such?" (Spivak 1987, p. 252).

[11] E.g., IE, pp. 226-228, 238-239.

[12] Cf. Halbfass 1995a, p. 7. The citations by Halbfass are drawn from Hacker's "Indology between Past and Future" ("Die Indologie zwischen Vergangenheit und Zukunft"); Halbfass' essay is the introduction, "An Uncommon Orientalist: Paul Hacker's Passage to India," to the recently published volume of Hacker's writings, *Philology and Confrontation: Paul Hacker on Traditional and Modern Vedānta* (Hacker 1995).

[13] Consider, for instance, Brian K. Smith's strong position about the possibility of an accommodation between belief and scholarship. After declaring "the particularistic, subjective, intrinsically interested, and always human origins of all claims to 'absolute truth,' 'objective reality,' 'transcendent authority,' 'nature,' and the like" (Smith 1994, p. 323), he goes on to say that the assumptions of the scholar – "that there were human origins, particular class interests, and historical and cultural conditionality at work in religious (and all other) discourse" – "pit the scholar of religion against the religious he or she studies. While some in the profession fervently wish to avoid such a stark drawing of the lines between themselves and the religious they study, I cannot see how such a conclusion can be avoided ... " (p. 324). Smith insists, "There was a time – and for some of us it is surely not yet passed – when such an emphasis served as a necessary corrective to crude ethnocentrism and jingoistic sectarianism and denominationalism. However, *perhaps the time has now come* also to begin to reflect more deeply about the ways in which being religious and being a scholar within that larger tradition called the humanities or the human sciences are often, and perhaps inevitably, fundamentally opposed enterprises" (pp. 323-325, passim; my emphasis). Or is it rather that the time has passed for such disjunctions? In any case, Halbfass' thoughtful and nuanced sense of the range of approaches of Europe to India, and his (albeit underdeveloped) sense of the import and possibilities of religious encounters among cultures surely makes Smith's description seem from the start rather constricted, in debt to an older dichotomy between knowledges and values, knowledges and religions. It would be interesting to see Halbfass take up the range of implied issues more forcefully and show, as I believe he does already implicitly, how the adequate, philosophically nuanced encounter of India and Europe occurs necessarily on multiple levels, only some of which might be described as hostile to or reductive of religious belief, in the short or long term.

**Fred Dallmayr**

# EXIT FROM ORIENTALISM? COMMENTS ON WILHELM HALBFASS

There was a time when cross-cultural understanding was largely a matter of expertise. Study and comprehension of non-Western cultures, including the "Orient," was consigned to an array of area specialists ranging from philologians to historians and cultural anthropologists. Armed with the arsenal of Western philosophical and scientific categories, area studies pursued a somewhat predatory aim: that of incorporating or assimilating non-Western life-forms into pre-established frames of reference (unless they were relegated to a mysterious "otherness" beyond the pale of knowledge). To be sure, incorporation of this kind was not a purely academic exercise, but was buttressed and fueled by concrete political and economic ventures of that time, especially the administrative needs of colonial empires. In Edward Said's formulation, this constellation of factors formed the backdrop of Western "Orientalism," a label highlighting the collusion of scholarship with the imperatives of colonial domination. In its distilled form, this kind of constellation is no longer prevalent today. Our age of postcolonialism has also given rise to forms of "post-Orientalism," that is, endeavors to rupture or transgress the traditional Orientalist paradigm. To the extent that Orientalist discourse was part and parcel of an "Eurocentric" world-view, transgression sometimes heralds a radical anti-Eurocentrism, perhaps even a dismissal of European scholarship as such; to the extent that the latter was tied also to "logocentrism" (or a "foundational" metaphysics), cognitive understanding tends to give way to constructivism, that is, the imaginative invention of traditions and life-forms. All along this trend is corroborated by the ongoing processes of globalization, processes which, in their pervasive effects, undermine the prerogatives of area specialists.

Clearly, the demise of Orientalism cannot be cause for lament. Still, even while welcoming new departures, one may plausibly be concerned about the manner of the demise, that is, the way in which the exit from Orientalism is sought and performed. Is it really possible to move briskly from Eurocentrism to anti-Eurocentrism (and from *logos* to anti-*logos*)? Is it sensible to equate traditional learning - however flawed - simply with colonial oppression? Does the critique of cultural "essences" and stable identities really warrant the claim that traditions and life-forms are "up for grabs" and can be constructed *ad libidum*? In our globalizing context, is there not still room and need for cross-cultural understanding - beyond the confines of Eurocentrism and logocentrism? And does such understanding not involve or presuppose a patient learning process, a sustained effort of reciprocal interrogation - an interrogation which, in turn, can hardly disdain some of the resources (philological, historical, anthropological) of traditional scholarship? As it seems to me, the groundwork for such a post-Orientalist inquiry has already been laid in our time by a group of scholars from the West and the non-West, including such distinguished names as Wilfred Cantwell Smith, J. L. Mehta, and Raimundo Panikkar. A younger member of this group - but by no means "junior" in terms of insights and achievements - is Wilhelm Halbfass whose work is the topic of the present volume. In his outlook and background, Halbfass illustrates and exemplifies some of the important ingredients of the emergent post-Orientalist discourse. Thoroughly trained both in Western philosophy and the specialized research tradition of Indology, Halbfass stands at the crossroads of interacting (sometimes conflicting) life-forms and language games, a position which enables him to act (at least in some respects) as a mediator or honest broker. At the same time, while immersed in academic pursuits, Halbfass is also a clear-headed citizen of the world, completely attentive to the complexities of globalization, and especially to the persisting political and economic asymmetries between West and non-West (asymmetries which render the term "post-Orientalism" intrinsically ambivalent).

As it stands today, Halbfass' opus is already impressive by its range and subtlety; apart from a long string of journal articles, his scholarly reputation is particularly tied to three successive publications: *India and Europe. An Essay in Understanding* of 1988; *Tradition and Reflection: Explorations in Indian Thought* of 1991; and *On Being and What There Is: Classical Vaiśeṣika and the History of Indian Ontology* of 1992. Limitations of space as well as (more crucially) limits of my Indological competence militate against any attempt at surveying this vast field of scholarship. In the following I shall focus my discussion on three issues or topical areas which appear to me particularly salient. First I shall explore Halbfass' approach to cross-cultural understanding and particularly to Indian culture and traditions. Next, I shall shift attention to one of the central concerns of traditional Indian thought: the status and meaning of "being" as articulated in Vedic and post-Vedic texts as well as in philosophical literature. Finally I intend to discuss some political problems besetting the relation of India and the West: in particular the compatibility of "*homo hierarchicus*" with modern democracy and the role and prospects of Indian culture in the context of Western hegemony. These comments will lead me to some concluding remarks on the viability of cross-cultural scholarship, as epitomized by Halbfass' work, in a time of rapid globalization.

## I

In his explorations of Indian culture and traditions, Halbfass is keenly aware of the formidable obstacles and complications besetting such an inquiry. These obstacles are due not only to the temporal distance of classical scriptures and their textual complexity but also – and perhaps chiefly – to the role of Western Indological scholarship itself and its bent to compress Indian culture into Western categorial frameworks (or else to treat it as an essentialized counterimage of the West). In his introductory essay to *Tradition and Reflection*, Halbfass comments specifically on recent discussions surrounding "Orientalism" and Eurocentrism as they have emerged in the wake of Said's famous study. As he notes (TR, pp. 9-11), the basic aim of the assault on Orientalism has been to expose "links between the scholarly exploration and the political subjugation of India and the 'Orient,'" that is, to lay bare the extent to which Western Orientalists have tried to "'represent' the Orient," to "project it as a sphere of 'otherness,'" and in general to "objectify, categorize, and classify it in accordance with European interests of domination." Said's own study, in particular, endeavored to show that Orientalism as an academic discipline has always been "tinged and impressed with, violated by, the gross political fact": namely, its complicity with the "Western projection onto and will to govern over the Orient." While Said himself was primarily concerned with the Western treatment of Islam, his arguments have been extended to India by numerous scholars, including Ronald Inden in his *Imagining India* and other writings. Emulating the deconstructive attacks on Orientalism, Inden charges Indological scholarship with harboring hidden imperialist designs: designs evident in the imposition of "reified" and "essentialized" images on Indian culture and in the attempt to appropriate "the power to represent the Oriental, to translate and explain his (and her) thoughts and acts not only to Europeans and Americans but also to the Orientals themselves."

For Halbfass, deconstructive efforts of this kind cannot be lightly dismissed given the stark background of European colonialism and its pervasive effects. As he writes (TR, pp. 9-12), there can be "no doubt" that the time for a critical reassessment of Oriental scholarship has arrived. Yet, he also cautions against a facile debunking rhetoric which may run afoul of the demands of scholarly integrity. Above all, Said's conception of Orientalism - in Halbfass' view - can itself be seen as a reifying and essentializing construct whose theoretical premises call for critical, perhaps deconstructive scrutiny. One of the main problems of Said's conception is the blending of "highly selective historical observations" with broad philosophical and metaphysical "generalizations," with the latter often riding roughshod over the task of concrete historical interpretation. Resulting from the merger of "very specific and very general traits," Orientalism is in danger of appearing as a "historical and conceptual hybridization that is no less a construct and projection than the so-called Orient itself." Similar considerations apply to the arguments of Inden which, again, are marked by a somewhat indiscriminate fusion of concrete historical observations with "fundamental epistemological and metaphysical" claims regarding the status of knowledge as such. To disentangle this (con-)fusion, more sustained efforts of critical exegesis are again called for, efforts which would address such questions as: "What is the role of essentialization and representation in the critical process itself? What are the standards to expose false constructs and super-impositions?" For Halbfass, one of the chief defects of summary pronouncements is the danger of a surface reversal which leaves untouched perceived abuses. With regard to Eurocentrism, the remedy is sometimes sought in the simple cancellation of Western categories; but in this case the recovery of indigenous authenticity is still ascribed to Western largesse (now in the mode of self-denial):

> The attempt to eliminate all Western constructs and preconceptions and to liberate the Indian tradition from all non-Indian categories of understanding would not only be impractical, but also presumptuous in its own way ... . This self-abrogation of Eurocentrism is at the same time its ultimate affirmation.

The main lesson Halbfass derives from the preceding comments is the need for patient and sustained cross-cultural inquiry which yet remains fully conscious of the pitfalls of Orientalism. Such an approach entails the endeavor to steer clear both of essentialized constructions of India (as Europe's "other") and of a simple deconstructive denial of Indian culture and traditions. Put differently: Halbfass' critique of Eurocentrism consigns him to a path which moves - however cautiously - beyond the Scylla of a homogenized Indian identity (exploitable by colonial administrators and fundamentalist Hindu movements alike) and the Charybdis of a complete lack of cultural distinctiveness (which would leave India at the mercy of Western-style globalization). Several chapters in *Tradition and Reflection* center on possible strands or dimensions of Indian cultural distinctiveness - beyond the pale of a compact essentialism. One such strand running through many centuries and surfacing in varying guises and formulations is the "concept of *dharma.*" Despite the immense diversity of accents among orthodox and heterodox brands of Hinduism, the concept for Halbfass functioned as a broadly shared, though somewhat inchoate frame of reference over long stretches of time. In his words (TR, pp. 14-16): "There is coherence in this variety," one that reflects "the elusive, yet undeniable coherence of Hinduism itself, its peculiar unity-in-diversity." Although there was never "*one* system" of understanding *dharma* but only a tensional network of usages, still the concept provided a kind of "contextuality" which lent coherence to the "luxuriant welter" of traditional Hindu life. From this angle, Hindu life was never the "dogmatic and institutional identity of an 'organized religion'"; but on the other hand, it is "neither an 'Orientalist construction,' nor can it be reduced to a brahminical fiction or projection." This broad contextuality was shared both by "sectarian" movements like Śaivism and Vaiṣṇavism with their specific theistic assumptions and by such "supra-sectarian" thinkers like Bhartṛhari, Kumārila, and Śaṅkara. In all these cases, understanding *dharma* requires a step beyond Orientalism and anti-Orientalism. To quote Halbfass:

> The modern idea of "Hinduism," or of the "Hindu religion," is a reinterpretation of the traditional ideas and, in a sense, a hybridization of the traditional self-understanding. Yet it is by no means a mere adaptation of Western superimpositions. It is also a continuation of the tradition, an expression and transformation of that self-understanding which articulates itself in its commitment to the Vedic revelation.

Another, still more pervasive strand in Indian tradition is the legacy of the Vedas in which *dharma* is one ingredient. Here the contextuality is even more elusive given the factual neglect of the Vedas by broad segments of Hindu life and the distance of Vedic rituals from the popular Hindu pantheon. Even among traditional thinkers formally attached to the Vedas there is wide disparity regarding their status and meaning. Thus, while orthodox spokesmen of the Mīmāṃsā regarded the Vedas as timeless texts without author and beyond the range of error, representatives of theistic traditions viewed the same texts as the word of God, but only as one stage in an open-ended process of revelation. Surveying this field, Halbfass agrees (TR, pp. 1-6) that the Vedas contain "no Hindu dogma, no basis for a 'creed' of Hinduism, no clear guidelines for the Hindu way of life." Yet, reflecting on Louis Renou's notion of "*prolongements réels*," he also sees a discontinuous continuity at the heart of Indian culture. Despite the enormous heterogeneity of that culture, he notes, "an idea and vision of the Veda emerges not only as a focal point of Hindu self-understanding, and a center for the precarious unity and identity of the tradition, but also as a prototype for its inner variety and potential universality." Probing more deeply this prototype, Halbfass presents the Vedas not only as a text but as an "*Ereignis*" of world-disclosure (in the Heideggerian sense) - which implies that Vedic exegesis involves not only a "textual hermeneutics" but a "hermeneutics of the event." In the traditional view, the Veda is the primary or "originary word" (*śabdapradhāna*), signaling a beginning where text and world, language and reality are still unseparated and where the text itself "opens and sustains the 'world.'" Although disseminated, deflected, and corrupted in the tortuous course of Indian history, this Vedic insight was never completely abandoned, remaining active as a trace of the past. In a sense, Halbfass notes (TR, pp. 40-41), "it is this internal multiplicity and variety itself, this challenging and suggestive chaos, that accounts for the significance of the Veda in Hindu philosophy. It provides an elusive and ambiguous guidance, an open, yet authoritative framework, with suggestive hermeneutic patterns and precedents and inherent appeals to human reflectivity." In functioning as a prototype, the Veda harbors an "orientation towards unity and identity" as well as an "inherent tendency to transcend and supersede itself."

In discussing *dharma* and the Vedic tradition, Halbfass also discloses his own preferred approach which can serve as an antidote to Orientalist constructions. Whereas Orientalism objectifies and reifies its target by retaining an external spectator's stance, Halbfass' invocation of hermeneutics implies a dialogical engagement between reader and text, interpreter and *interpretandum* – an engagement through which both partners are potentially transformed (without necessarily entailing an ultimate convergence). As an attentive student of Western, especially Continental, philosophy, Halbfass is thoroughly familiar with the hermeneutical model as developed from Dilthey to Gadamer. Commenting specifically on Gadamer's work, he credits the latter with predicating understanding on the dialogical "recognition of the other, the foreign as such" – beyond the conundrums of total incorporation or expulsion. Objectification in this model is obviated by the participatory involvement of the interpreter who necessarily starts from his own "prejudices" (and not from a clean slate) and for whom the target of interrogation always remains an interpreted "other" (rather than a reified thing in itself). In his own writings, it is true, Gadamer has tended to confine himself to the Western tradition; but, as Halbfass notes (IE, pp. 164-169), there is "no compelling reason" why his perspective should not be "applicable in a wider, trans-cultural context." Gadamer's emphasis on the productive role of prejudice, in particular, can help us realize "that, in approaching Indian thought, we carry with us our Western perspectives and presuppositions not merely as an impediment and aggravation, but as a necessary and positive ingredient of understanding itself." Gadamer's approach has been complemented and radicalized by Heidegger – though with greater attention to the perils of Orientalism (seen as a corollary of the Westernization or "Europeanization" of the world) and its deleterious effects on cultural dialogue. According to Halbfass, Heidegger's thesis regarding the Greek origin of Western philosophy and science was no longer a "self-confident proclamation of the uniqueness of Europe," but rather "a statement concerning a global predicament. Europeanization 'eats away all substance from things.'"

In light of these perceptive hermeneutical insights, the reader is bound to be disoriented by a certain tendency in Halbfass' more recent writings which jeopardizes or calls seriously into question the entire enterprise of cross-cultural understanding. "Over the years," we learn in the Preface to *On Being and What There Is* (OB, p. vii), "my methodological positions and philosophical allegiances have changed. The result has been a certain eclecticism and growing doubts concerning the meaning and relevance of the topic itself. We do not know whether the 'question of being' is a meaningful question." After surveying the history of ontological reflection from Plato to the present, the introductory chapter in the same volume turns to recent Anglo-American analytical philosophy as providing a new slant on age-old quandaries. In the new milieu, Halbfass observes (OB, pp. 7-11), "the focus shifts from the question 'what being is' to the conditions of speaking about it and the confusions in what others have said about it." More specifically, the "methods of modern conceptual and linguistic analysis" and the "tools of symbolic logic" are used "to articulate semantic distinctions, to resolve traditional ontological difficulties by uncovering underlying grammatical and conceptual confusions and to eliminate meaningless questions concerning 'being.'" W. V. Quine is invoked and credited with offering a deft resolution of the "ontological problem" by reducing it to "three Anglo-Saxon monosyllables: 'What is there?'" From the analytical vantage, the role of "being" as a noun and of "being" or "reality" as subjects of statements must be criticized as prime examples of Gilbert Ryle's notion of "systematically misleading expressions" - distortions which can only be corrected through "empirical research in linguistics." Seen against this backdrop, Heideggerian thought now appears in a new, and by no means favorable, light. Heidegger's insistence on the "question of being" is said to have been "stubborn, almost obsessive, and highly idiosyncratic." His later reflections on the history of being are portrayed as largely fruitless, empty speculations: "Such thought is not committed to tangible results and applicable methods"; as a mere reaction against calculative reasoning and conceptual precision, it signals "a withdrawal into poetry, myth, and capricious etymologies. Its aimlessness and futility are deliberate." By indulging freely in "systematically misleading questions," Heidegger's entire work appears dubious and/or misleading: "He seems to represent the consummation of all that is questionable in Western ontology."

Strictures of this kind, in my view, impinge not only on the "ontological problem" and its relevance, but more generally on the role of hermeneutical understanding in Oriental studies. To be sure, Halbfass is not quite ready to dismiss hermeneutics entirely. As he still insists (OB, pp. 12-14), it is "our first responsibility to understand the Indian statements" - which means that we have to be willing to "listen to them as carefully and patiently as possible" and to "be aware of their traditional cultural context and background." Yet, understanding alone is no longer seen as adequate in the absence of critical distantiation and analysis; mere familiarization with Indian culture and traditions is said to be deficient unless it is "supplemented by conceptual analysis and clarification." Such clarification and analysis, however, requires a turn to resources beyond the pale of hermeneutical or dialogical inquiry: "Clarification implies a commitment to objective standards of precision and analysis." Ultimately, this commitment leads to the demand for a neutral and universal standpoint from which all traditions can be objectively assessed without bias (or a Gadamerian "prejudice"). In our century, this demand has been raised most emphatically by logical positivism and the "unified science" movement - some of whose axioms were later continued by analytical philosophy. "Is there," Halbfass asks, "a truly common ground for a comparison of different traditions of thought and a neutral, universal medium through which they can communicate?" And he replies: "One important recent suggestion is that such a common basis is provided by logical and linguistic analysis and exemplified by the methods of modern analytical philosophy of the Anglo-Saxon type." It is in the context of linguistic analysis that the claim has been advanced that analytical methods (especially the use of symbolic logic) are "separated from the restrictions of the various existing languages" and their particular milieux and hence conducive to "a truly universal understanding of the different philosophical traditions."

One of the chief problems of these passages is the return of supposedly banished ghosts. Above all, the invocation of analysis "of the Anglo-Saxon type" tends to jeopardize the exit from Orientalism and Eurocentrism which Halbfass' earlier studies had so diligently pursued. For clearly, the ascent to analytical objectivity implies again the objectification and reification of cultural traditions and their submission to the categorial frames of an external spectator; moreover, the same ascent vindicates the intellectual superiority of the neutral analyst over the array of cultural and historical contingencies. Halbfass is not unaware of these implications; in light of the long-standing association of universalism and Eurocentrism, students of non-Western cultures surely have to be on their guard. Implicitly or explicitly, he writes (OB, pp. 13-15), universalism "entails the idea of a privileged viewpoint, a higher level or more comprehensive horizon of awareness and reflection." While we cannot simply discard this universalizing perspective, we also have to be "aware of its background and historical ramifications." Unable to resolve this tension or dilemma, Halbfass' argument finally ends in compromise or a half-hearted eclecticism. On the one hand, he strongly defends the "merits" of Anglo-American analysis. In the pursuit of objectivity, he notes, we should not underrate "the extraordinary instrumental value of modern formal and analytical models, including symbolic logic, in the interpretation of philosophical texts and traditions"; we should also acknowledge "the potential of orderly scientific progress" and thus be willing to face non-Western phenomena from the vantage point of "latest research." On the other hand, objectivity may well be an elusive and perhaps even deceptive standard; we certainly should not construe the perfection of formal methods as "the implicit telos of Indian philosophy or as the goal and essence of philosophy in general." In fact, analysis and the search for conceptual precision can be obtrusive and "interfere with the task of translating and understanding, and with our obligation to respect the Indian tradition in its own context and dimensions." The upshot of these divergent instructions is a counsel of despair: "At the end, we do not have a well-defined method, and perhaps not even a definite perspective, for our exploration of the Indian texts and teachings. Our procedure will be eclectic."

## II

The ambivalence regarding method cannot fail to have obtrusive effects also on substantive topics of inquiry - although these effects are more noticeable in Halbfass' more recent writings. At this point, I choose for purposes of illustration a topic which is crucial in traditional Indian culture and philosophy and which also plays a prominent role in Halbfass' work: that of the status and meaning of "being." In a way, the topic has always been one of Halbfass' central preoccupations. In the Preface to *On Being* he informs us (OB, p. vii) that the chapters collected in that volume are only fragments of a much larger project: namely, "a comprehensive history of Indian thinking about 'being' and 'what there is.'" The same Preface also promises a future volume on the notion of being in Advaita Vedānta. Reflections on the topic, however, antedate the Vaiśeṣika study by several years. While devoted chiefly to the role of Indian culture in European self-understanding, *India and Europe* contains important chapters on such concepts as *dharma* and *darśana* which bear at least an oblique relation to being. As indicated before, the study also comments on Heidegger's radicalization of hermeneutics, and especially on his critique of the "Europeanization of the earth" under the auspices of Western science and technology. For Heidegger, Halbfass correctly notes (IE, p. 168), this development was also a disturbing ontological happening, by promoting the progressive concealment and oblivion of being in favor of calculative rationality: "Philosophy in this sense, which implies a deep 'forgetfulness of being' ('Seinsvergessenheit'), is the mother of science and technology, and of the Atomic Age."

More sustained soundings of the topic in the context of Indian culture can be found in *Tradition and Reflection*, especially in the chapter on "Human Reason and Vedic Revelation in Advaita Vedānta." Among all the "schools" of classical Indian philosophy, Advaita Vedānta was most closely tied to the Vedic legacy - and this on philosophical and not merely "traditionalist" grounds. While other schools, like Nyāya or Vaiśeṣika, paid lip service to the Vedas, and while proponents of Mīmāṃsā recognized only the ethical (*dharma*) dimension of scriptures, Advaita Vedānta took seriously the character of the Vedas as "originary word" (*śabdapradhāna*), as a world-disclosing event without which human rationality is bound to be left astrand. For Śaṅkara - the foremost spokesman of Advaita Vedānta - human reason was by no means a negligible faculty, but one which was circumscribed by broader contexts (or what one might call ontological conditions of possibility). Left entirely to its own devices, human reason - especially calculative rationality - is bound to lead to oblivion or "forgetfulness of being" in a dual sense: forgetfulness of the being of self (*ātman*) and of being as such (*brahman*). To overcome this oblivion, reason has to remember or recall its own rootedness in the "originary word," that is, in the "revealed" sayings of the Vedas which alone can liberate thought from its egocentrism or anthropocentrism. As Halbfass perceptively elucidates this point (TR, p. 179):

> In claiming its own methods and criteria, human reason displays an anthropocentric attitude of self-confidence and arrogance that is incompatible with that receptivity and openness which is a condition of liberating knowledge. Relying on his own "worldly potential" (*sāmarthyaṃ laukikam*) of intelligence and reasoning alone, man remains attached to that very world from which he seeks final liberation. No effort of "worldly" reflection by the ego upon itself will yield the liberating insight into the reality of the *ātman* as the one absolute witness.

As needs to be stressed again, Śaṅkara's outlook did not imply a simple rejection of reason or a resort to an anti-rational or irrational intuitionism; on the contrary, his writings are in large measure a model of lucid reasoning. As Halbfass observes (TR, p. 180), especially the Upaniṣads - the "knowledge portion" of the Vedas - in Śaṅkara's view "respond to human reason, appeal to it, provide it with a context, goal, and basis"; they also contain "so many hints and implicit patterns of reasoning that they seem to anticipate all merely human intellectual efforts." Yet, reason (*yukti*, *tarka*) for Śaṅkara cannot be entirely self-sufficient; proceeding from an agent "within" the world, reason cannot at the same time survey or thematize the boundaries of that world or the conditions of its own existence. To gain insight on that level, reason has to remember its embeddedness in being - which means it has to be attentive to what is "heard" or disclosed (*śruti*) in the "great sayings" of the Vedas. Unguided by such hearing, reasoning may lead to worldly cleverness, but a cleverness which gets entangled in its own confusions and contradictions. As Śaṅkara repeatedly emphasized - especially in critiquing other schools - unguided reasoning is "dried up" (*śuṣka*), that is, fruitless and groundless. Although useful for certain limited purposes, human reason is inherently unstable and unfounded, and ultimately even liable to refute and supersede itself - thus showing its incapacity to provide a "foundational" metaphysical grounding. To quote a passage from Śaṅkara's *Brahmasūtrabhāṣya* (TR, pp. 146-147): "Conclusions which are based on human reflection alone are unfounded ... . Conclusions at which expert reasoners have arrived with great effort of reflection are viewed as spurious by others, even more expert ones ... . In this way, it is impossible to find a foundation for the conclusions of reasoning, because of the variety of human ways of understanding."

The inherently unstable character of human reasoning is illustrated in *anvayavyatireka* or the method of affirmation and denial ("positive and negative concomitance," "continuity-and-discontinuity") variously practiced by classical Indian schools. As Halbfass elaborates (TR, pp. 162-164), the method was chiefly used for clarifying the meaning of great Vedic sayings, such as the famous *tat tvam asi* (thou art that) - which requires reflection on the self's simultaneous identity with and difference from itself, that is, on the conjunction of presence and absence or the discontinuous continuity of the self with itself (and of *ātman* and *brahman*). According to one interpreter, the method was generally employed in Advaita Vedānta in order "to discriminate between what is and is not the self as well as to show what meanings may be attributed to given terms." This statement, however, is possibly misleading as it seems to reduce *anvayavyatireka* to a simple process of conceptual (perhaps dialectical) definition and determination - a process which might readily be productive of stable identities. This ambiguity is perhaps not entirely avoided in Śaṅkara's writings - or at least in Halbfass' portrayal - where the method often seems to boil down simply to a discrimination between essence and appearance or between the essential and the "accidental" features of an entity. This outcome, however, is foiled by the interpenetration of essence and appearance, and especially by Śaṅkara's association of *anvayavyatireka* with merely human reasoning (*yukti*, *tarka*). As soon as attention is shifted to the great Vedic sayings, the method reveals its self-destabilizing (or deconstructive) quality. To quote Halbfass on this point (TR, p. 175):

> The discriminative knowledge achieved through the method of "continuity and discontinuity" does not anticipate the liberating insight which comes from the Vedic word, nor is there a gradual transition from one to the other. In a sense, reasoning in terms of *anvavavyatireka* produces only an openness which has to be filled, or perhaps even a confusion which has to be eliminated, by the Vedic revelation. To him who has freed himself from false superimpositions by reasoning in this way, who has discarded the whole sphere of objects, who asks in bewilderment (*vīkṣāpanna*) "who am I?" (*ko 'smi*), who may even think that he himself has been discarded (*tyakto 'ham*) in this process: to him the Veda speaks in a meaningful and soteriologically effective manner when it says: *tat tvam asi*.

In Halbfass' study, the discussion of Advaita Vedānta serves a polemical point: namely, to oppose the conjunction of reason/revelation in Śaṅkara's thought to the worldly rationalism espoused by many latter-day spokesmen of Vedānta (or Neo-Vedānta). In a free variation on John Locke's precedent, prominent Indian thinkers in recent times have advocated the basic "reasonableness of Hinduism," mainly in an effort to render the latter more palatable to Western intellectuals. As Halbfass curtly observes (TR, p. 132), such portrayals "should not primarily be seen as contributions to historical and philosophical research"; bent on adjusting Advaita Vedānta to the demands of the modern world, their scholarship is overshadowed by their "apologetic goal." Unfortunately, Halbfass' own position is not very distant from, and often stands in close proximity to, the neo-Vedāntins. Repeatedly he expresses his inability to embrace or share Śaṅkara's conception. "It is obviously impossible for a modern Western reader," he states (TR, p. 180), "to follow Śaṅkara into all the details of his Vedic exegesis." Elsewhere (TR, p. 36) he chides Śaṅkara precisely for his truncated rationalism: "With this radical commitment to Vedic revelation, Śaṅkara withdraws ultimately from the open arena of philosophical debate, which the philosophers of the Pūrvamīmāṃsā, in particular Kumārila, had entered so resolutely." Statements of this kind in a sense anticipate or foreshadow Halbfass' more recent turn to conceptual analysis. As mentioned before, his *On Being* distances itself from classical ontology or at least deprecates the "question of being" as a mode of rational inquiry. There are, no doubt, different ways to account for the more "rationalist" tone of that study. To some extent, the shift may be due to the focus on the Vaiśeṣika school - which respected the authority of the Vedas provided it did not interfere with rational argument. On the other hand, the change can surely also be traced to the noted methodological quandaries. To recall again the gist of these quandaries (OB, p. 15): "Conceptual devices that have been developed by Western philosophical thought will be indispensable tools of translation, interpretation, and analysis; but we will have to use them cautiously."

Despite this methodological shift (I need to stress), *On Being* is by no means devoid of fascinating ontological vistas which entirely transcend the "Anglo-Saxon" paradigm. The chapter on "The Question of Being in India" presents a stunning panorama of classical perspectives, among which Vaiśeṣika is only a late and relatively subordinate position. As Halbfass points out (OB, pp. 24-25, 29-33), being in classical times was thematized in different contexts, including debates on the status of certain entities (such as soul, God, or universals), but also broader ruminations on the origin of the world. In the Vedas and older Upaniṣads, statements on being and non-being were closely linked with reflections on cosmogony and hence often couched in the language of myth or mythological narrative. Whether privileging being over non-being or non-being over being, cosmogony at this point was not simply equivalent to a chain of causation launched by a "prime mover," but was more akin to an opening and disclosure of the world (or in Heideggerian terms, a "worlding of the world"). "What is decisive," Halbfass insists, "is the opening, the separation [of heaven and earth] as such, a separation that implies not only the creation of free space, but also the establishment of firm boundaries, of distinguishability and bipolarity." Hence, the fascination was not simply with an "amorphous primeval substance or substrate as such" but rather with the "open space that is its negation"; using a contemporary phrase, the Vedic sense of the openness of space and world might be called a "primeval metaphysical clearing." What emerges from these considerations is that the popular characterization of classical Indian thought as "fundamentally substantialist and cyclical" is basically mistaken or at least badly misleading or lopsided. According to Halbfass, it may be possible to speak of "two different Vedic 'ontologies'" or, more cautiously, of "different, though perhaps supplementary, perspectives on the reality of the world": whereas the "ontology of substance" plays a more conspicuous role in "later, Indian, specifically Hindu, philosophy" (including the Vaiśeṣika school), the mythology and "ontology of openness" carries a philosophical weight which "should by no means be underestimated." In Vedic-Upaniṣadic texts, being and non-being tend to be inserted in a more primordial "world frame" which is often signified by such terms as *ātman* or *brahman*; *brahman* in particular is often said to transcend both *sat* (what is) and *asat* (what is not). In Halbfass' lucid commentary:

> It would not be appropriate to describe such transcendence of all polarities as the inclusion and disappearance of all distinctions in an undifferentiated primeval substance. We are dealing here with a transcendence of a higher conceptual order; it includes and supersedes the polarity between distinction and nondistinction, differentiation and nondifferentiation itself, and provides important suggestions for later conceptual thought and systematic philosophy.

In post-Vedic Indian thought, the "ontology of substance" gathered momentum chiefly as a consequence of the Buddhist assault on essences and the concomitant ascent of "negative ontology." In reaction against this Buddhist challenge, several philosophical schools – including Vaiśeṣika, Nyāya, and Pūrvamīmāṃsā – rose in defense of a kind of ontological realism (OB, p. 36): "The concept of substance, the doctrine of universals and the assumption of a well-structured universe of durable and identifiable entities, and clearly distinguishable categories, are at the heart of this defense." Halbfass' *On Being* is basically devoted to an explanation of the Vaiśeṣika version of ontological realism. As he shows (OB, pp. 49, 71, 143), the school was centrally concerned with the "horizontal" enumeration and classification of "world constituents" or entities – an effort which seems to concur with Quine's resolution of the "ontological problem" and with Gustav Bergmann's definition of ontology as "an inventory of what exists (is there)." Proceeding along these lines, Vaiśeṣika thinkers listed six fundamental categories or divisions of reality, including substance, quality, motion, and the like; the first rubric was said to comprise nine classes of substances: earth, water, fire, air, ether, space, time, mental organs, and even the soul (*ātman*) – in a veritable orgy of ontological positivism. Being itself (*bhāva/sattā*) was simply viewed as the "common denominator" or the "one universal ingredient of all concrete and particular entities." While offering a sympathetic account of this philosophical system, Halbfass cannot quite refrain from casting a side-glance at other alternatives, especially at the legacy of the "ontology of openness" which continued, in modified form, in Śaṅkara's Advaita Vedānta - which Halbfass characterizes by the fitting term "soteriontology" (liberation in and through *brahman*). The Epilogue to the study (OB, pp. 231-234) broaches themes for which the reader has been scarcely prepared - except through the initial confession of eclecticism. Borrowing a suggestion of J. L. Mehta, Halbfass admits that "representational" or "objectifying" thinking is "fully present in the Vaiśeṣika system of categories." While this may not be a "Cartesian attempt to establish man as the master and owner of nature," it does constitute an effort "to put the world at our intellectual and conceptual disposal, to explain it once and for all through a process of comprehensive enumeration and classification." This admission is followed, in the concluding paragraph, by an even more startling bow to "soteriontology" and even "negative ontology," that is, to the "search for nonrepresentational, nonconceptual, nonpossessive ways of thinking" - although this bow is immediately qualified by endorsement of the "stubborn, though perhaps futile, conceptualization" which is exemplified by Vaiśeṣika ontology.

## III

The final ambivalence marking *On Being* is not simply an ambivalence concerning two ancient schools of thought - about which one might plausibly remain undecided; in its implications, the ambivalence raises again the specter of Orientalism from which these pages began. As indicated earlier, one of the central features of Orientalism was its resort to "objectifying" or "representational" reasoning in an effort to grasp or intellectually conquer alien life-forms from an external (European) spectator's perspective. To the extent that this is the case, an exit from Orientalism in our time seems to accord a certain privilege to an "ontology of openness" over an "ontology of (objectified) substances"; whatever its other corollaries may be, openness implies at least a certain willingness to transcend established categories in favor of a freer recognition of alien life-forms, thus permitting otherness "to be" in a nonpossessive way. The dangers of predatory modes of cognitive incorporation are by no means slighted by Halbfass. As he notes in *India and Europe*, cross-cultural understanding or dialogue today is complicated or tilted by Western hegemony and the ongoing process of Westernization of the globe. "The conditions and perspectives of the two sides of the encounter are fundamentally different," he writes (IE, pp. 369, 375, 340-341); "the relationship is an asymmetrical one." Basically, modern India "finds itself in a historical situation created by Europe [or the West], and it has difficulties speaking for itself." As a result, understanding under present conditions requires a special effort to transcend Eurocentrism or "what is European" ("*das Europäische*") in the direction of greater reciprocal openness. For: "In the modern planetary situation, Eastern and Western 'cultures' can no longer meet one another as equal partners. They meet *in* a Westernized world, under conditions shaped by Western ways of thinking."

Comments of this kind bring into view broader social and political issues – which are the final topic of these pages. Under present conditions of Westernization, cross-cultural understanding is liable to be an intensely agonizing, perhaps agonistic, enterprise. Moreover, Western students of the East are quickly faced with complex questions. How far can openness to the other extend? Are there perhaps (normative) limits to understanding? To put it more provocatively: are there perhaps legitimate aspects of "Europeanization" – beyond the pale of colonial domination and technological or economic supremacy? For present purposes I want to concentrate on an aspect which has tended to dominate or afflict comparisons of East and West: the issue equality and inequality. Ever since the time of Thomas Hobbes, human equality and equal liberty have been the basic premise of Western political philosophy or discourse about politics. Initially formulated only as an axiom (applicable in a hypothetical "state of nature"), the principle of equality and equal liberty in due course came to function as the launching pad for a process of progressive equalization and liberalization of all social conditions – a process which culminated in the establishment of Western democracy. Despite many flawed or contradictory practices, supporters of Western democracy are commonly agreed on the centrality of equal liberty, irrespective of differences of creed, race, color or sex. By contrast, Eastern society has traditionally been charged with harboring despotism (a portrayal persisting from the ancient Greeks to Hegel and beyond). Even if the latter charge can readily be unmasked as a blatant form of Eurocentrism, some concerns are bound to linger. In the case of India, one can hardly ignore the long tradition of social stratification and inequality as manifest in the caste structure and in the elaborative differentiation of forms and stages of life (*varṇāśramadharma*). How is one to assess this age-old legacy?

Is one ultimately forced to choose coldly between Western democracy and Indian culture?

Halbfass' *Tradition and Reflection* contains many suggestive insights on these themes, which can serve as guidepost for further discussion. As it emerges rather quickly, much depends on the meaning and definition of terms like liberty and equality - which cannot simply be left to Eurocentric preferences. In modern Western thought, liberty and equality are commonly treated as qualities of individual agents, that is, of autonomous egos seen as constitutive building blocks of social life; as a corollary, social distinctions or differentiations have to be justified or legitimated against the benchmark of uniformity or equal liberty. Apart from some notable exceptions (like versions of Buddhism), Indian culture on the whole is far removed from this kind of egalitarian individualism; in fact, there is even little corresponding to the Western centerstaging of the human species or "*homo sapiens*" as predestined master of the world. In his chapter on "Man and Self in Traditional Indian Thought," Halbfass elaborates perceptively on this point. As he writes (TR, pp. 266, 272-275), "there is no tradition of explicit and thematic thought about man as man in India, no tradition of trying to define his essence and to distinguish it from other forms of life." Referring to formulas like "*homo sapiens*" or "rational animal," he finds in India "nothing comparable to that tradition in the West which has its roots in ancient Greek as well as Biblical sources and leads through the Renaissance and Enlightenment periods to the growing anthropocentrism of Western thought." As a result, traditional Indian thought in reflecting on "man" (*puruṣa*) or human life places the accent not on a Western-style "species-equality," but rather on something like a fraternal contextuality, that is, the embeddedness of humans in a rich and "luxuriant" fabric of life reaching from the animal kingdom all the way up to the Gods and *brahman*. In Halbfass' words, in the Indian context "the tendency to keep the borderline between men and animals permeable at least to some extent is not surprising. No rigorous anthropocentrism or human self-elevation, even of a soteriological type, can develop in a tradition of thought that takes the idea of *saṃsāra* and the unity of life for granted." While subordinating equality to contextuality, Indian thought also recasts the notion of liberty by severing it from all individualistic, egocentric or anthropocentric designs. Ultimately, especially in Śaṅkara's "soteriontology," freedom means liberation from separation and self-centeredness and hence release into the "world-frame" of *brahman*. To quote Halbfass again:

> The true privilege of man is not to be the master of his world, but to be liberated from it; his mandate is not to employ other creatures as instruments for his own needs and desires, but to use himself, his own human existence, as a vehicle of self-transcendence ... . It is not man as man, as *animal rationale*, who ought to be liberated, but the self in man; and liberation of the self is liberation from being human as well as from any other limiting worldly condition.

Deep in their implications, these comments surely need to be pondered carefully and cautiously. As one should note immediately, phrases like "liberation from the world" or "from being human" cannot and must not be misconstrued as a retreat into a Western-style essentialism or universalism; nor should the expression "unity of life" be misread in the sense of a "melting pot" uniformity. (It may well be that Śaṅkara's opposition to Buddhism was derived from his fear - perhaps a misdirected fear - of such a melting-pot ideology.) In traditional Indian thought, both the notion of fraternal contextuality and the idea of soteriological liberation were closely linked with and even predicated on the assumption of an all-pervasive differentiation and distinctness of world elements. (Liberation, after all, did not signal release of a uniform ego from contexts, but rather liberation from this kind of ego in the midst of context.) This emphasis on differentiation can ultimately be seen as the legitimating underpinning of the Indian caste system and of the theory of *varṇāśramadharma*; in recent time, it has buttressed the formulation of "*homo hierarchicus*" as the character-type marking Indian culture. As Halbfass notes (TR, pp. 273-281), commenting on Indian inegalitarianism (and countering again the democratic claims of Neo-Vedānta): "Traditional Hinduism develops a whole complex system of formalistic and legalistic restrictions, of rules of ritualistic qualification (*adhikāra*), which divide mankind into fundamentally different groups and also determine their access to sacred knowledge and final liberation." In orthodox Hinduism, it is not simply "man as man" who is eligible for liberation; numerous restrictions limit the soteriological privilege "not to man in general, but to specific classes of human beings." This stress on differentiation also marked Advaita Vedānta. For Śaṅkara, human "worldly competence" (*sāmarthyaṃ laukikam*) - which may be equally or inequally distributed - was not sufficient to account for liberating insight. To attain liberation meant "to discover one's own true identity"; but human identity was not the self-constituting ego, but the self-transcending *ātman* (in the direction of *brahman*).

The concluding chapter in *Tradition and Reflection* is specifically devoted to "*homo hierarchicus*" as initially formulated by Louis Dumont; although not narrowly exegetic, the chapter is said to "support in its own way what Dumont calls 'the main idea' of his book." As Halbfass shows (TR, pp. 349, 383-384), *homo hierarchicus* was not an isolated feature but part of a more pervasive rank order or hierarchy of living beings which extended "from Brahma to the tufts of grass." The chapter discusses in detail the various ways in which classical Indian thought justified or legitimated social hierarchy, including the *varṇa* system: ways which ranged from the simple endorsement of Vedic injunctions to biological-hereditary explanations, reliance on character types or inherent "qualities" (*guṇas*), and sometimes even to the invocation of metaphysical "caste universals." There was persistent controversy and contestation among these diverse forms of legitimation - punctuated by occasional attacks on the entire hierarchical system (especially from the side of Buddhism and Jainism). Yet, despite these disagreements, the mainstream Indian view in classical times solidly favored stratification. This was also true of Advaita Vedānta (despite recent liberal construals, which are historically dubious). For Śaṅkara, it is true, all caste barriers and social distinctions were ultimately rooted in *māyā* or *saṃsāra* which the self was meant to transcend; but again, transcendence here did not signal dissolution into sameness, but freedom in the midst of difference. As Halbfass observes (somewhat misleadingly), caste differences here are "irrelevant only in the light of the absolute unity of the absolute, but not with respect to interpersonal relationships," and "there is no suggestion of translating the metaphysical unity into social equality." This reluctance to cancel difference in favor of sameness is exemplified even in the case of the "renouncer" (*saṃnyāsin*) and those "liberated while alive" (*jīvanmukta*) who have transcended *saṃsāra*:

> The freedom conceded to the "renouncer" (*saṃnyāsin*) and even the liberated *jīvanmukta* is carefully channeled. Even in negation and in renunciation, he remains bound to that same order from which he is freeing himself. For the existence and fundamental validity of this order constitutes the precondition for the possibility of liberating oneself from it ... . The *saṃnyāsin* continues to draw his legitimation from that very *dharma* from which he is liberating himself.

What surfaces here are philosophical problems of considerable magnitude which resist easy settlement - and which certainly cannot be adjudicated through the facile invocation of formulas (like Eurocentrism or anti-Eurocentrism). In Indian thought, transcendence of difference (or equality) has itself to be justified in light of a differentiated *dharma* - which is precisely the opposite of modern Western thought where difference or distinction is radically put on the defensive (as in need of justification). What is called Europeanization or Westernization of the world is to a large extent the militant extension of egalitarianism or the principle of equivalence to other parts of the globe (with capital serving as the currency of equivalence). Liberty here is not adverse to equality, because it basically means freedom of choice (where all choices are equivalent or of equal value). Whatever their intrinsic merits may be, the principles of equality and equal liberty are today exported around the globe in a missionary and largely unthinking way, without much reflection on the premises of such principles and how they (and their consequences) might be vindicated. Non-Western societies, on the other hand, which are not readily swayed by these principles, are quickly dismissed as illiberal and undemocratic. India in particular - given the long legacy of *homo hierarchicus* - is likely to be denounced as a major obstacle on the road to world democracy (in a not very subtle resurrection of Orientalism).

As it seems to me, exiting from Orientalism in our time requires more than an exchange of blind charges and counter charges; above all, it requires a serious rethinking of such basic philosophical categories as equality (or sameness) and difference. Perhaps, in reacting against Buddhism, traditional Indian (or rather Hindu) thought has tended to privilege difference too much over sameness (and being over non-being), forgetting the more complex legacy of the "ontology of openness" deriving from the Vedas. But the problems are reciprocal or cross-cultural. As Ernesto Laclau and Chantal Mouffe (in *Hegemony and Socialist Strategy*) have persuasively pointed out, the two principles of equivalence and difference presuppose each other and need to be articulated jointly - but in a way which resists synthesis, yielding only reciprocal destabilization (pp. 182-184). What this points up is an enormous task looming ahead of us in the wake of Orientalism: the task of genuine dialogical learning on the level of basic frameworks, beyond the limits of assimilation and exclusion. By being willing to shoulder this task, Wilhelm Halbfass' work makes an important contribution to cross-cultural understanding which can serve as a guidepost illuminating future endeavors.

*University of Notre Dame*
*Department of Government and International Studies*
*Notre Dame, Indiana, USA*

**Sergei D. Serebriany**

## SOME MARGINAL NOTES ON *INDIA AND EUROPE*

This paper is a kind of *ṭīkā* or a series of *ṭīkās* on Wilhelm Halbfass's *India and Europe*. For me it was both an inspiring and exasperating book to read, and so the paper is a result of my struggles with the text, of my endeavours to understand it from within my own "hermeneutic situation" or – to use another expression from the book – of my attempts at "fusing horizons."

"Fusing horizons," or "fusion of horizons" etc., seems to be the usual rendering into English of the German compound *Horizontverschmelzung* which has been introduced by Hans-Georg Gadamer in his *Wahrheit und Methode* (*Truth and Method*).[1] In *India and Europe* the original German word appears twice (IE, pp. 165, 374), echoed by several appearances of the English equivalent (IE, pp. 161, 165, 439).[2] This German expression, although somewhat ambiguous and never fully and/or explicitly explained,[3] may be considered as one of the key notions in Halbfass's book and, moreover, to be one of the keys to a better understanding of the book itself.

*India and Europe* is subtitled *An Essay in Understanding*. A not less (and probably even more) appropriate subtitle would be *An Essay in Fusing Horizons*.[4] But the simple plural is not fully adequate here, because, to be more exact, one should speak about an attempt to simultaneously "fuse" several pairs of horizons. In terms of traditional European, or Western, scholarly disciplines, Halbfass strives to effect, as he puts it himself, the "cooperation of Indology and philosophy" (IE, p. 286).[5] In more recent terms of "area studies," *India and Europe* is an attempt to "fuse the horizons" of, on the one hand, Indian or South Asian studies and, on the other hand, "European studies" or "studies in Western civilization," more specifically, "studies in the history of Western ideas."

The English, or rather American, version, revised and enlarged, of the original German book may be read and in fact cannot help being read as a rather uneasy synthesis of continental European and American standards. From a slightly different viewpoint, it may be described as a not quite successful synthesis of German traditions of scholarship, thinking and style with the patterns of academic discourse in (American) English. Among other things, one notes a good number of Germanisms in the English language of the book.[6]

This manifold "fusion of horizons" makes *India and Europe* a very special work, a kind of path–breaker. It not only substantially augments our knowledge, but also, and which is probably even more important, opens numerous new perspectives for thought and research: research which is, in more than one sense, both interdisciplinary and intercultural. *India and Europe* demonstrates both the rich possibilities and the considerable difficulties of this style of research.

Certainly, the author himself was fully aware of the inherent difficulties of his task, as well as of the preliminary, provisional, and tentative character of this work.[7] Consequently, from the reader's point of view, the book lacks inner harmony, balance, or what might be called "organic unity," which is of course part of its incisiveness. The book looks not like a Greek temple or a well-designed mosque, but rather like a complex Hindu mandir with myriad dazzling details which do not make, and are not meant to make, at least according to "Mediterranean" standards, a harmonious whole. But probably a more fitting simile, and one more in the spirit of Western civilization, would be that of a construction site where the overall design cannot yet be clearly perceived, except by some superhuman, divine mind, and can only be imagined.

The purpose of this paper is to try to conceive of some more details in this overall design - by analysing some of the key terms in *India and Europe*, which have been left without analysis by the author, and by suggesting further developments of some ideas contained in this book.

*India and Europe* has been addressed primarily to Western and to Westernised Indian readers. In this paper, the questions raised and the remarks offered will inevitably reflect the reactions of a Russian reader of the book and his "hermeneutic situation." Therefore let me try to describe briefly some of the essential features of this "hermeneutic situation," at least as I see it, which are relevant for the theme of this paper.

At the present time Russia is experiencing one of the most serious crises in her whole history. The future is uncertain, but the past is probably even more so. It was a common joke during the "perestroika" years that Russia is a country with a most unpredictable past. Indeed, we cannot help but question and re-valuate the whole of our past, the whole of our cultural tradition. All inherited ideas, notions and words appear suspect; each and every has to stand anew the test of meaningfulness and genuineness. But Russia is hardly unique in this respect. Our predicament is rather just a particular case of today's global "hermeneutic situation," although some universal problems, hermeneutic and otherwise, may be felt more acutely, more urgently in post-Soviet Russia than elsewhere.

We in Russia now feel pressed to test anew all ideas, notions and words, because we are all too painfully aware that the country has been misled by wrong ideas expressed through deceptive words. We virtually have to create a new language which will not lead us astray again, but which will rather provide us a reliable orientation in the world. On the global scale, in view of the many different cultural traditions now coming together, there is a similar need for a new language, a language of global intercultural, or intercivilizational, communications. Since the West has thus far dominated the process of "globalization," the language of Western ideas has been mostly used, more or less effectively, for intercultural communications. Most Westerners have believed that their respectives languages are sufficiently universal to describe all the features and peculiarities of other cultural traditions. Many non-Westerners who received Western education also have come to accept the language of Western ideas as a standard one, though in practice they may have evolved their own "dialects" of this language.

Now, though the language of Western ideas may still remain the most universal one available, there is a growing awareness of its probable inadequacy for describing and analysing other cultural worlds in their entirety. To be sure, there does not exist some ready-made global intercultural language. However, such an all-encompassing language has appeared as a distant ideal and as a topic of discussion.

In *India and Europe*, at the very beginning, Halbfass quotes the seemingly simple and clear words of his teacher Paul Hacker: "There ought to be a philosophizing which is based on an immediate knowledge of Indian and European sources" (Hacker 1978, p. 38; IE, p. XIV). But at the end of chapter 14 (IE, p. 262) there are quoted two paragraphs from Jarava Lal Mehta's book *India and the West* (Mehta 1985) to show that there is no easy way to such a "joint philosophizing," if only because the languages of the two traditions in question are quite different and the contacts between these two languages in the 19th and 20th centuries have, in a way, made the situation even more complicated due to the fact that the two languages were often quite uncritically mixed. Now it is obvious that if we want to undertake a "joint philosophizing" we should first try to judiciously use, side by side, two different languages, with a hope to evolve with time a kind of new synthetic language for this cross-cultural discourse.[8]

Some of the most striking and – to my mind – revealing pages in *India and Europe* may be taken as approaches to evolving such a cross-cultural language for philosophy. I refer first of all to those pages where the author compares and analyses the Western words "philosophy" and "religion," on the one hand, and the Indian, i.e., Sanskrit, words *darśana* and *dharma*, on the other. This analysis of the words, their changing meanings and the cross-cultural interactions of both the words and the meanings is an inspiring exercise not only in the comparative and historical study of ideas, but also, and what is more rare and more difficult, in the comparative-historical study of cultures or civilizations. As in this particular case it is basic terms in both cultures which are taken up, the analysis of the historical interactions between these terms helps to reveal some of the essential differences between the two cultures, as well as some of the most important and sensitive points in the historical interactions between them.

Halbfass makes the point that the Sanskrit word *darśana* originally, i.e., before the intense interaction between India and the West, had meanings that cannot be easily equated with the meanings of the Greek word *philosophia*. It is only as a result of the cross-cultural activities of at least the last two centuries that the word *darśana* in some of the modern Indian languages, including modern Sanskrit, has come to be "loaded" with all the meanings of the Western word *philosophia*; we may call them "loan-meanings" by analogy with the linguistical term "loan-word." Conversely, at least in some texts in English or French etc., dealing with the history of Indian thought, the words "philosophy," *philosophie*, etc., may acquire all or some of the traditional meanings of the word *darśana*.

Of course, philosophers and philologists, as well as scholars in other branches of the humanities, are, or at least should be, always professionally on guard to differentiate between the different meanings of a word and may gain more insights from such an analysis. Besides, this particular cross-cultural situation is not *qualitatively* different from many cases of verbal polysemy within one culture, one tradition. Nevertheless, for many a less sophisticated layman and even sometimes for a quite sophisticated scholar this "overloading" of a word with too many heterogeneous meanings might be indeed too heavy a burden, and one which brings about not insights but rather confusion.

In this respect, the case of the words "religion" and *dharma* seems to be quite an exemplary one, to use one more favourite word of Halbfass. In chapters 17 and 18 of *India and Europe* it is argued, very convincingly, in the first place, though sceptics may claim for more arguments and proofs, that the interpretations of the concept of *dharma* in modern Western "Indology" are often influenced by Neo-Hindu ideas, whereas Neo-Hindu thinkers, in their turn, under the "influence" of the Western concept of "religion," have given the term *dharma* a more universal, more comprehensive meaning than it had in traditional Hindu texts, because *dharma* was put forward as the "native" Indian equivalent of "religion." Thus, the cross-cultural interaction of words and concepts has contributed, in a way, to a cross-cultural misunderstanding, and to the creation, in Western scholarship about India, of a fake notion of *dharma* which has no real "denotate" in traditional Indian culture, being only an intellectual by-product of its "encounter" with the West.

What may be called the purely linguistical interactions between, on the one hand, the words "philosophy" and *darśana* and, on the other hand, "religion" and *dharma*, have been more or less similar, yet the consequences for the larger field of the history of ideas have been, it seems, rather dissimilar, as there must have been different kinds of confusion for different kinds of people.

This line of research and reasoning may be fruitfully extended to other important words or terms of Indian and European culture, and, moreover, to the interactions between other pairs of cultures. For instance, the English word "nation" has been rendered into modern Hindi as *rāṣṭra* and into modern Bengali as *jāti*. This case is an interesting parallel to the cases of "religion" versus *dharma* and "philosophy" versus *darśana*. Among the concepts and terms of the pre-modern Indian tradition there existed no equivalent to the modern European notion and term of nation. Thus in Hindi the Sanskrit word *rāṣṭra,* originally meaning "kingdom" or, roughly, "state," has been loaded with the European (Western?) meanings of "nation," and in Bengali, for the same "load" the word *jāti* has been chosen, whose main previous meaning, which is still current, was that conveyed by the English, originally, of course, Portuguese, word *caste*. The choice of these substitutes has hardly influenced the semantic burden of the English word "nation," but it might easily bring about some confusion for those who think in Bengali and/or Hindi and are not sufficiently aware of the Western concept of nation.

Other similar cases may be those of "history" and *itihāsa*[9] or "literature" and *sāhitya*. These deserve special detailed treatments. As one more case, most topical for the present paper, the pair of words "India" and *Bhārat*(*a*) may be suggested: "India" was initially a European word and concept, some of whose meanings were later, more or less successfully, "loaded" upon the Sanskrit word *Bhārata* which now, in its turn, may influence the meaning(s) of the word "India." But this is part of the further argument of my paper.

Given the analytical nature of the book as a whole and, specifically, the attention accorded to the analysis of words as indicators of cultural interactions, it is all the more strange that in *India and Europe* there have remained utterly unexamined the two title words and notions, that is, "India" and "Europe." It is as hard to imagine that the author was unaware of the problems inherent in these two words and notions as it is futile to guess why he has chosen not to analyse them. Therefore, let me attempt to offer some analytical and comparative considerations on these two words, considerations which are stimulated by *India and Europe* itself, both by what has been stated there and by what has been silently bypassed.

Throughout his book Halbfass treats the words "India" and "Europe" as self-evident and self-explanatory. But very often his treatment of these words reveals, or perhaps one might even say betrays, their ambiguity and inherent complexity. In this respect there are some striking points of similarity between them. Both refer to geographical areas, the two subcontinents of Eurasia, whose limits were and are defined in various ways and may be a matter of controversy. Moreover, both are the names of ideas whose contents have been changing throughout history and which remain matters of controversy. In this sense both "India" and "Europe" may be called "ideologemes," items of ideology, as opposed to factual knowledge.

It would make an interesting comparative and contrastive study to examine the histories of the words, as well as of the ideas, "India" and "Europe."[10] They both first meant only part(s) of the territories to which they came to be applied later; and both, starting as geographical names, only later came to mean "cultural domains."[11]

There is also an important historical difference between the two names: "Europe" is a self-appellation, a name given to the area from the very beginning by its inhabitants; "India," on the contrary, is a name given to the area initially by outsiders and only later, in fact quite late or quite recently, accepted, in one way or another, by the inhabitants of the area themselves. The fact that the name "India" has been given to the subcontinent by Europeans may be interpreted as part of the "Europeanization" of the earth or European "domination" over the world.

But here I am concerned not so much with the whole history of the words "Europe" and "India" as with more recent dimensions of their ambiguity.

"Europe" is of course an old and respected geographical term. But geographers nowadays seem to be in agreement that there are no natural borders which would clearly separate Europe from Asia and that any purely geographical definition of "Europe" can be merely conventional.[12] A topical matter of controversy centres on the meaning of "Europe" as a cultural concept, as the name for a cultural area. "Cultural" of course quite often merges with "political" and even "military." In this sense, there may be narrower and more inclusive interpretations of the name "Europe."

According to the narrower and more traditional understanding, "Europe" is the name for the cultural area in geographical Europe united in the past and, in a way, at present, by Western Christianity. This interpretation implicitly or explicitly excludes from Europe those peoples of geographical Europe who professed or profess Orthodox Christianity, that is, Russians, Ukrainians, Bulgarians, etc., not to speak about those who were, or still are, the followers of Islam, for instance, the Muslims of Bosnia, or the Volga Tartars, or, for that matter, the Turks.

According to broader interpretations of the name "Europe," it should include at least the - formerly - Orthodox Christian peoples of Eastern and Southern Europe and probably even those Muslims who live within the confines of geographical Europe. In particular, the arguments about whether or not Russia and Russians belong to Europe have a long history, which cannot be discussed here.[13] Bulgarians, Rumanians, Serbs,

Ukrainians and other peoples of Eastern and Southern Europe who profess(ed) Orthodox Christianity have their own stories to tell, as do those Muslim peoples who happen to inhabit geographical Europe.

As for the word "India," one of the main dimensions of its present day ambiguity is connected with the events of 1947, that is, with the "transfer of power" from the British Crown to the two new political bodies India and Pakistan. The reader of any book on the history of India is inevitably reminded that what was meant by "India" before 1947 is not what is usually meant by the same word after 1947, even though since 1950 the country in question can be called by what seems to be its official name: the Republic of India. Instead, it is most often just called India.

Historians, especially those who deal with the periods before 1947, for the most part continue to use the word "India" in its broader, pre-1947 sense. Those, however, who focus their studies on more recent events often prefer to employ the term "South Asia" to refer to the whole of the subcontinent. This term sounds "global" and helps to avoid misunderstandings. Among other things, it is "ideology-free."

As far as I know, the comprehensive history of the word "India" has not yet been written. Such a history would include geographical, political, and ideological aspects together with their varying interpretations. It seems that during the 19th century there took place a parallel formation of "India" as a geographical and political notion and of "India" as an "ideologeme," or rather as a number of "ideologemes." I would venture to suggest that the concept of India as a definite geographical area took final shape - in Western consciousness and in the Western science of geography - with the final establishment of the borders of the British Empire there.

For most Britons, and especially for those who administered the Empire, "India" must have been first and foremost just the name for the vast area or the subcontinent, as we now say, which they governed, the name for this important, to say the least, part of the British Empire.[14] In the meantime there developed various other "ideologemes" about India. In this development, from the very beginning of the 19th century onwards, continental Europe, primarily Germany and France, seems to have taken the lead. It is exactly this process, or parts of it, that is studied in *India and Europe*. These European-made "ideologemes" imported into the British Indian Empire contributed to the development of various ideological movements there; parts of this process are also studied in *India and Europe*. In India itself the English word "India," as well as its various counterparts in indigenous Indian languages, could not help becoming a matter of deep ideological concern.

To illustrate the nature of the problems involved, I may refer to but one telling example. The well-known book by Arthur Llewellyn Basham, *The Wonder that was India,* has a characteristic subtitle: *A survey of the* [*history and*] *culture of the Indian sub-continent before the coming of the Muslims* (Basham 1954 and 1967). For Basham himself it must have been just a matter of his specialization: his field being "ancient," pre-Muslim India, he might not have wished to write about later periods. But the title together with the subtitle, and the book as a whole, may be taken to mean that the true India, the one which "was the wonder," was only pre-Muslim and non-Muslim India and that, moreover, Islam and Muslims, though they have been there in India now for more than a millennium, do not belong to India proper and should be treated as non-Indian. This kind of interpretation of Basham's otherwise excellent book may occur and appeal, for instance, to those Hindu chauvinists who now talk about "Indianizing" Indian Muslims. It is worth noting in this connection that the French translation of Basham's book was titled *La civilisation de l'Inde ancienne* (Basham 1976), which helps to avoid such misinterpretations, though the word *ancienne* raises other kinds of questions (see further).

It was, among other things, to combat such kinds of misinterpretations that Saiyid Athar Abbas Rizvi, an Indian Muslim author, published his book titled *The Wonder that was India*, Vol. II, with the subtitle: *A survey of the history and culture of the Indian sub-continent from the coming of the Muslims to the British conquest. 1200-1700* (Rizvi 1993). With full respect for Basham's book, Rizvi now claims that his predecessor's work should be considered as Vol. I of the series. In fact, let me add that a Vol. III of *The Wonder that was India* might as well be written, with the possible subtitle: ... *from the ascendance of European power till the withdrawal of the British. 1700-1950*. Indeed, this period of Indian, or South Asian, history with its own share of tragedies and achievements has been not less wondrous than the earlier ones. It was not, by all means, less authentically "Indian," or, in any case, not less authentically South Asian.

But before going further into these matters, let us return to Halbfass's *India and Europe* and consider in more detail the author's treatment of the word "Europe." By "Europe" Halbfass means almost exclusively

Western Europe, and he uses "the West" and "Western," "Westerners," etc., as virtually synonyms for "Europe."[15] In fact, in some recurrent key formulas found in his book the author evidently prefers "the West" to "Europe." Thus, on p. 53 he refers to "the Western encounter with Indian thought," on p. 65 to "a philosophical 'dialogue' between India and the West," on p. 251 to "the encounter between India and the West," etc. One might suspect here a slight influence of Neo-Hindu writings which usually prefer such dichotomies as "India and the West" or even "the East and the West."

A perspective from India or possibly North America might be responsible also for the fact that the author tries to tell us just one single story about how "Europe," or "the West," "encountered India." But as "Europe" and even more so "the West" are not cultural monoliths, being rather rich mosaics of various cultures and traditions, so the narrative device of telling just one single story looks rather artificial and inadequate. The story obviously consists of a number of different sub-stories and subplots which are certainly deserving of individual narration.

However skilfully Halbfass deploys his unitary narrative rhetoric, his narration cannot avoid revealing the pluralism of European cultural tradition and, consequently, the plurality of European "encounters" with India. Probably one of the most striking stories in this respect is the story of the formation of "Indology" itself. The achievements of French missionaries as well as those of their Italian and German precursors and contemporaries in the 17th and 18th centuries were considerable, but produced only negligible immediate consequences, probably because the official French culture, not to mention Italian and German culture, proved to be too "closed" and self-centered, not ready to "digest" new and exotic information. The British pioneers of "Indology" were thus forced to start practically anew. They could achieve much not only because of their personal talents, but also due to the congenial atmosphere of the British culture of those days which happened to be sufficiently "open" and receptive. Of course, the more practical concerns of administering India were at least as important for the formation of British "Indology." Later, with the consolidation of British power in India and the changing attitudes towards India in Britain and among most Britons, British "Indology" lost its initial momentum. However, by that time, German interest in India, due to certain processes in the German culture, had greatly developed and Germany took over as the leading "Indological power"; indeed, the most important "Indologist" in Britain in the later 19th century, Friedrich Max Müller, was German by birth.

This story, summarised from the pages of *India and Europe*, demonstrates once more - if such a demonstration is needed - the advantages of European cultural pluralism; if the whole of Europe had been like France, or like Britain, or like Germany, its "encounter" with India might have been very different and much less fruitful, both for Europe and for India. On the other hand, the different kinds of "encounters with India" in various European (sub)cultures bring into relief, for an historian, the peculiarities of these (sub)cultures within the common European framework.

Of course, it is largely a matter of scale and style whether the story of "the encounter between India and the West" should be told as one single story or as the sum of several different stories. But given the present stage of our knowledge, it would be, I believe, more fitting and more enlightening to try to tell the separate stories, interconnected as they surely are, before weaving them into one general canvas.

Eastern and Southern European strands ought also be eventually woven into that general canvas. Narrowing the focus to Russia, one may notice that it is not absolutely absent from *India and Europe*, though references to things Russian are mostly cursory and brief.[16]

The Russian merchant Afanasy Nikitin who visited India in the early 1470s is mentioned in a note (p. 459) by way of reference to a doctoral dissertation; his contribution, together with that of others, is dismissed with the following remark:

> We can ignore the few, partly legendary, travel reports on India which reached Europe in the centuries before Vasco da Gama's expedition (1497-1498), since they do not contain new themes or additions to the available information in the field of religion or philosophy. (IE, p. 22)

These words are not quite fair as far as Afanasy Nikitin is concerned. His travel notes, known as *The Journey beyond Three Seas*, may not provide us today with any new information about the state of religion and philosophy in India in the 15th century, but they are, among other things, an interesting document for an historian of religions, their contacts and interactions. Nikitin's notes do belong to the history of "the encounter between India and Europe" or at least to the history of "the encounter between India and Christianity." These notes, written in Russian, end with a peculiar prayer in a mixed Arabic-Persian-Turkic language, transcribed with Cyrillic letters, (Nikitin 1986, pp. 17, 31, 58) which inspired an American scholar to argue that Nikitin had been converted to Islam (Lenhoff 1979). Russian scholars do not agree with this[17], but in any case we may say that Nikitin tried to "fuse the horizon" of his Russian Orthodox Christianity with that of Islam as he encountered it in India and elsewhere. Hinduism apparently did not impress him favourably, though it seems that he mixed with some Hindus on friendly terms.

The name of another Russian traveller to India, prince Alexei Saltykov (1806-1859), has entered *India and Europe* via a quotation from Karl Marx (IE, p. 138). Prince Saltykov made two trips to India: in 1841-43 and in 1845-46. He was an amateur artist and his *Letters from India* were published in Paris, in French, with his own illustrations.[18] His *Letters* and his pictures of India, drawings, water-colours and engravings, were received very favourably both in Russia and in Western Europe.[19]

Almost all of the Russian names to be found in *India and Europe* are mentioned only once. But the name of yet another Russian traveller and adventurer, Elena Petrovna Blavatskaya (1831-1891) or, in the usual English spelling, H. P. Blavatsky, appears as often as three times. She is well known in the West as a co-founder of the Theosophical Society. Once, together with Blavatsky, two other authors from Russia are mentioned, namely, George Gurdjieff (1877?-1949) and Pyotr (Peter) Ouspensky (1878-1947) (IE, p. 399), who are also rather well-known in the West as religio-philosophical "teachers."

The famous Russian anarchist prince Pyotr Kropotkin (1842-1921) is also evoked once because of his alleged personal acquaintance with Vivekananda (IE, p. 233).

There also appear several names of Orientalist scholars from Russia. Fyodor Shcherbatskoy[20] (1866-1942), alias Theodore Stcherbatsky, the eminent scholar of Buddhism, seems to be mildly reproached, and, I believe, justly so, for the fact that his "allegiance to Kantian and Neo-Kantian ideas shaped his interpretation of 'Buddhist Logic'" (IE, p. 135). Nikolai Mironov (1880-1936) is referred to as the editor of the Jain work *Dharmaparīkṣā* by Amitagati (11th century) (IE, p. 321), and Vladimir Minorsky (1877-1966) as the author of a "pioneering work" on encyclopaedic compositions, or compilations, by Muslim authors (IE, p. 459, n. 3).

In the same list two other names may as well be included. Theophilus (Gottlieb) Siegfried Bayer (1694-1738) appears on p. 472, in note 28, as the author of *Historia regni Graecorum Bactriani*, St. Petersburg, 1738.

He was a German scholar who, invited to the St. Petersburg Academy of Sciences, worked from 1726 until his death in the capital of Russia. Bayer is considered as one of the earliest European Sinologists[21], but in Russia he also did some research on India and, in particular, on Sanskrit[22].

In reference to works on Buddhism that were read by Arthur Schopenhauer Halbfass mentions "those of I. J. Schmidt" (IE, p. 107). Isaak Jakob Schmidt (1779-1847), in Russia called Yakov Ivanovich Schmidt, was born in Amsterdam, but lived most of his life in Russia. He was one of the earliest scholars of Buddhism in Europe and is also considered "the founder of Mongolian and Tibetan studies in Russia" (de Jong 1987, p. 21; Babinger 1920).

Last but not least, the theme of Russia emerges in *India and Europe* in connection with Friedrich Nietzsche who called himself "the first perfect European nihilist" (IE, p. 127). The word "nihilist" in this particular sense must have come to Nietzsche from the novels of the Russian writers Ivan Turgenev (1818-1883) and Fyodor Dostoyevsky (1821-1881). Nietzsche's friend Lou Andreas-Salomé (1861-1937), to whom he unsuccessfully proposed and to whom Halbfass refers once, also came from Russia. She was born and grew up in St. Petersburg, a daughter of a Baltic German, allegedly of French Huguenot origins, who was a general in the Russian army (Binion 1968; Peters 1962).

Now this list of Russian names and themes in *India and Europe* invites at least two comments.

First, it seems that no extensive discussion of things European, especially of the 18th-20th centuries, can possibly avoid at least mentioning things Russian.

Second, most names in the list are more or less marginal in Russian culture as a whole, though perhaps very Russian in their very marginality. Indeed, Nikitin was a lonely adventurer, whose remarkable notes were little known even in Russia before they were unearthed by the historian Nikolai Karamzin at the beginning of the 19th century. Prince Saltykov was a kind of voluntary emigrant: he retired from the Russian diplomatic service at the age of 34 and settled in Paris, from where he traveled to India and published his books. Blavatskaya was not able to fit into the Russia of her time either and lived most of her adventurous life abroad. This applies, mutatis mutandis, also to the lives of Gurdjieff[23] and Ouspensky[24]. Prince Kropotkin was arrested in Russia in 1874 and in 1876 had to flee abroad. He returned only in the summer of 1917, to die in 1921. Minorsky and Mironov moved to Western Europe after 1917.[25] Shcherbatskoy remained in Russia, but eventually became what was called "an internal emigrant" and from the early 1920s had his works published almost exclusively in English. Conversely, Bayer and Schmidt were immigrants from Western Europe, i.e., certainly aliens in the Russia of the 18th and the 19th centuries respectively.[26]

On the one hand, the marginality of all these names might not be taken as something peculiar to those who were concerned in Russia, in one way or another, with India or the Orient in general. Actually, some of the greatest figures of Russian culture were, or came to be, marginal, each in his own way, in the Russia of their time. To take just three Russian names, perhaps the best known internationally: Ivan Turgenev lived the larger part of his life in a kind of voluntary exile in Western Europe; Fyodor Dostoyevsky was tried as a state criminal, condemned to death and then spent several years in prison and banishment; Lev Tolstoy, by the end of his life, demonstratively dissociated himself both from the Russian governmental establishment and from the Orthodox Church. Is this peculiar to Russian culture or civilization, or is the marginality of outstanding persons a kind of general law for any culture?

On the other hand, the interest in India does seem to have been veritably and especially marginal in Russian culture, both before the 19th century, i.e., before the rise of modern "Indology," and in the 19th-20th centuries. In this sense the list of Russian names in *India and Europe* is exemplary enough, to use again one of the exemplary words of Halbfass.

Although the history of the "encounter between Russia and India" has not yet been described in any comprehensive and reliable way[27], it can be safely said that in 19th century Russia there neither existed a literary and/or intellectual movement as influenced by India as, say, German Romanticism, nor serious and influential thinkers as responsive to Indian thought, as, for example, Schopenhauer or Paul Deussen.[28] The comparatively "low level" of response to India on behalf of the classical Russian culture of the 19th century[29] emphasizes the peculiar position of Russia in the "concert" of modern European civilization.

Moreover, the history of the "encounter of India with the West" has some interesting parallels in the history of the "encounter of Russia with the West." For instance, the question was and still is discussed regarding the extent to which, if at all, before the "Europeanization" enforced by Peter I, there was anything in Russia worth being called "philosophy" in the Western European sense of the word. After the reforms of Peter I the

Russian language appropriated the word "philosophy," *filosofiya* in Russian, with all of its Western meanings, as well as the idea of philosophy as an academic discipline and as a possible occupation for a person in society. Since then the question has been often discussed, both by Russians and by foreigners, regarding the extent to which that which is called "modern Russian philosophy" is - or should be - actually and consistently what is called "philosophy" in the West. In Russia, very much like in India, there is a tradition of thought which opposes "spiritual Russia" to the "materialistic West."[30]

Such parallels between India and Russia point to the fact that they both were and still are involved in the process of the "Westernization of the world," both being originally non-Western countries or civilizations. Indeed, Russia may be considered part of Europe. But she is not part of the West.

Nevertheless, since the 19th century Russia has been quite actively engaged in the joint European, or Western, venture of exploring India, or South Asia. Probably as the greatest Russian contribution in this field should be considered the well-known *Petersburg Sanskrit Dictionary*, published by the Russian Imperial Academy of Sciences (Böhtlingk and Roth 1855-75; Böhtlingk 1879-89). It is characteristic, and one might say exemplary, that this dictionary is Sanskrit-German, not Sanskrit-Russian, and has been compiled by two Germans: Otto (von) Böhtlingk (1815-1904) and Rudolf (von) Roth (1821-1895). The former, though, was a "Russian German," born in St. Petersburg and a student of the St. Petersburg university.[31]

Another grand Russian project may also be recalled in this context: the *Bibliotheca Buddhica*, a collection of Mahāyāna Buddhist texts, started and edited by Sergei Oldenburg (1863-1934). Russian "Indology" has been always closely connected with "Buddhology," or Buddhist studies, evidently because the Russian Empire had within its borders peoples, namely the Kalmyks and Buryats, who professed Buddhism; thus Buddhism was felt to be the outgrowth of Indian culture closest to Russia and Russians. There is another important point to be mentioned about the *Bibliotheca Buddhica*: it was an international undertaking in which some of the leading scholars of Russia and Europe joined forces. This kind of international and interdisciplinary cooperation was required by the very nature of the task, by the very nature of the phenomenon called Mahāyāna.[32]

Paul Williams, the British scholar of Buddhism, warns against what he calls "essentialist fallacy" in thinking about Mahāyāna, i.e., assuming that one name secures the "oneness," the unitary nature of the phenomenon called by that name (Williams 1989, p. 2). I believe that even with more right and more emphasis one should warn against the "essentialist fallacy" as regards the name "India."

It is almost common place to compare India, or South Asia, with Europe, both in terms of size[33] and diversity[34]. It is probably less common to compare the history of "these two great cultural domains," as Halbfass calls them (IE, p. IX). I suppose that "comparative philosophy" – whatever its future lines of development might happen to be – would benefit significantly from a sister discipline that may be called "comparative history." Here I can offer only some sketchy remarks on the comparative history of India, or South Asia, and Europe.

Halbfass observes that "there can be no symmetry in the historical presentation of the encounter between Europe and India ..." (IE, p. 172). This kind of asymmetry may be related, among other things, to the asymmetry in the histories, i.e., historical developments, of both " cultural domains."

In Europe what is called antiquity, the ancient period, is associated with the growth and spread of empires. The Roman Empire provided Europeans, both Western and Eastern, with basic patterns in various fields of culture. Although the idea and the ideal of the Roman Empire itself survived throughout the European Middle Ages, and even until much later, in reality there emerged a number of separate political bodies, which, during what is called the modern period, that is, since the 15th century, gave rise to the Western European national states.[35] And it is on the basis of these national states that Europe, mostly Western, now strives to achieve a new kind of unity.

In South Asia, during the time which chronologically coincides with European antiquity, there emerged no counterpart of the Roman Empire. The "empire"[36] of Aśoka the Buddhist (3rd century) was rather short-lived, and no "Hindu empire" in the first millennium AD could ever reach comparable limits, which in the case of Aśoka, in fact, had been almost Pan-South Asian.

It is only in the second millennium AD, when in Western Europe national states began to emerge, that successful attempts were made in South Asia to build again pan-subcontinental power structures, or empires. These attempts were undertaken by outside conquerors, the followers of Islam, who came repeatedly from the North-West. The most lasting and the most magnificent was, of course, the empire of the Great Mughals, founded by Babur (1483-1530) at the beginning of the 16th century.

When in the 18th century this empire decayed and fell apart, the British began to build their own Indian empire on and from its ruins. Collected from many pieces, the British Indian Empire was partitioned in 1947 into two large units, which in 1971 became three.

During the second millennium AD in South Asia, like in Europe, regional ethno-cultural identities gradually evolved and regional vernacular languages developed. But these processes did not bring about the formation of anything like durable national states; the imperial trend has prevailed. In today's South Asia, among its larger states, it is only Bangladesh that resembles more or less a European national state. The Republic of India and, to a lesser degree, Pakistan, have inherited the past imperial structures, the British as well as the Mughal. In a way, and in a very meaningful way, it is this composite and comparatively recent imperial legacy, and not any memory of "ancient" South Asian "empires" that may be compared with the legacy of the Roman Empire in Europe. In South Asia all "ancient empires" were practically forgotten by the peoples who later lived on their territories.

It was only in the 19th century, after and due to the advent of Europeans, that historical consciousness – in the Western sense of the word – was introduced into the culture of India.[37] The history of India, or South Asia, as it is known and taught today has been reconstructed during the 19th and 20th centuries through the efforts of Western or Western trained scholars.

As the history of Europe was, and still is, traditionally divided into antiquity, the Middle Ages, and the modern period, the history of India, or South Asia, was, and sometimes still is, also presented as consisting of the three major periods: the "ancient," i.e., "(Buddhist and) Hindu," the "medieval," i.e., "Muslim," and the "modern," marked by the power of Europe over the subcontinent. Such scheming may be called a sort of "historiographical inclusivism," which is quick to include the histories of other cultures or civilizations into one's own habitual historical schemes without allowance for their "otherness."

In particular, the identification of the "Muslim" period in the history of South Asia with the Middle Ages in Europe is very misleading. The gradual establishment of the power of Muslims over the South Asian subcontinent has no full analogy in the history of Europe. Some partial parallels, though, may be drawn: the conquest of Spain by Arabs, the expansion of the Ottoman Empire into South-Eastern Europe and, probably, the rule of the Golden Horde over Russia. For Europe as a whole these were more or less marginal developments, though they had, and continue to have, in different ways, important and lasting influences on European culture. But only had Arabs or Ottoman Turks conquered almost the whole of Europe and ruled over it for several centuries, would we have a possible parallel to what has actually happened in South Asia.

Halbfass writes:

> ... Islam ... penetrated India, established itself there, and developed peculiar traditions of confrontation and disregard, but also coexistence and occasionally symbiosis with Hinduism. (IE, p. 30).

The beginning of the sentence contains obvious understatements. Islam "penetrated India" to stay there for more than a millennium. Of course, different regions of South Asia have been affected by Islam in different ways and degrees: in some regions the majority of the population became Muslim, in some other regions Muslims have never been more than a negligible minority. But on the whole Islam "established itself" in South Asia as a dominant pan-subcontinental political power which lasted from the 13th until well into the 19th century. Islam has also been for many centuries a very forceful and influential cultural power in South Asia. Islam has become part of Indian, or South Asian, culture and civilization.[38]

Therefore the treatment that is accorded to Islam in *India and Europe* must be considered somewhat unfair and inadequate. The pages on Islam in India (IE, pp. 30-35) are included in the chapter on "Islamic Encounters With Indian Philosophy," in which such encounters are treated as antecedents to the encounters of Europe with India. These pages may leave the impression that Islam is considered almost as alien, as foreign, as opposed to India as Europe is. Such an approach would mean that we are ready to concede the word "India" to those Hindu chauvinists who want to equate "Indian" and "Hindu," "India" and "Hinduism." But by whatever name we might call the subcontinent of South Asia, it is obvious that Islam *now* is very much part of its overall cultural inheritance, as is, for that matter, Europe.

Two reasons may be adduced for this unfair treatment of Islam. First, the continental European "Indology" has been traditionally Hinduismcentred.[39] Islam was simply another field of scholarship. There were, and, it seems, still are, few scholars who would include into their field of work, on an equal footing, both Sanskrit and Arabic (and/or Persian), both Hinduism and Islam. The second reason may be that particular angle of vision which Halbfass has chosen for his research: the angle of vision of philosophy, with religion, for the most part, relegated to the background. It is true that there were too few traceable contacts, too little "fusion of horizons" between Hindus and Muslims in those spheres of their respective traditions to which the European word "philosophy" can more or less legitimately be applied. Therefore, from the viewpoint of an historian of philosophy, the Hindu and Muslim traditions in South Asia appear to be two utterly different worlds.

Those spheres of culture that can be called by the English word "religion" yield of course more data on Hindu-Muslim encounters and data even regarding their "symbiosis." But the sources for the study of such encounters are mostly not in Sanskrit but in "vernaculars," and so again belong to another department of Western "Indology," a department which is younger and rather less developed than, for instance, those of Vedic and Sanskrit studies.

All this seems to point to the conclusion that there is a certain risk in studying a different, that is, distant and not one's own, culture from a too specialized point of view, the specialization being conditioned, of course, by the viewer's cultural tradition; there is a risk to overlook or misperceive certain features of the culture under investigation.

Many facts of cultural interactions between Hindus and Muslims in India, or South Asia, lead one to think that had these two cultural traditions been left alone on the subcontinent at least for some more centuries, possibly more interaction might have taken place even in the sphere of "philosophy." But the whole situation was drastically changed with the establishment of the British power and the introduction of the European "ferment" into the world of South Asia.

In the 19th and 20th centuries Hindus and Muslims in South Asia for the most part developed their own separate lines of thought, interacting in different ways with European, or Western, ideas. At least this is how it usually looks in studies on modern thought in South Asia. Studies on Hindu thinkers and/or reformers and on Muslim ones, are, as a rule, separate from each other. But in reality, one supposes, there must have been the love and hate "triangle" of the British, the Hindus, and the Muslims as much in the sphere of thought as in the sphere of politics, though it may be difficult to reveal the actual "workings" of this "triangle." It should become a matter of special research.

As I have already mentioned, Halbfass treats "Islamic encounters with Indian philosophy" as a kind of antecedent to the encounters of Europe and India. Moreover, he writes about "the Islamic mediation of Indian thought to the Occident" (IE, p. 35). "The culmination and at the same time the end" of this mediation is represented by the *Oupnek'hat*, Anquetil Duperron's Latin translation (published in 1801-1802) of the *Sirr-i Akbar* ("The Great Secret"), which, in its turn, was a translation from Sanskrit into Persian of fifty Upaniṣads done, by 1657, under – and perhaps at least partly by – the Mughal prince Dārā Shukōh. The *Oupnek'hat* is known as a source of inspiration for Schopenhauer (cf. IE, pp. 64-67, 106-107).

In the second part of his book, slightly misnamed *The Indian Tradition and the Presence of Europe*, Halbfass chiefly analyses various *Hindu* answers to the challenges of European, or Western, ideas in the spheres of philosophy and religion. Here, to give some symmetry to the two parts of the book, the author could have well considered some "encounters" between Hinduism and Islam as antecedents to the later "encounters" between Hinduism and Europe, or the West. In some specific cases one could probably even speak if not exactly about "the Islamic mediation of European thought to Hindu India" then at least about Islamic ideas and images as catalysts in interactions between Hindu and European, or Christian, traditions.

Let us consider the case of Rammohan Roy (1772-1833), the famous reformer, sometimes called the "father of modern India." Halbfass devotes to him a whole chapter in his *India and Europe* (IE, pp. 197-216) but, in my opinion, says too little about the Islamic dimensions of Rammohan's family background and his own "hermeneutic situation."

To begin with, it should be noted that Bengal, Rammohan's homeland, had been ruled by Muslims since the early 13th century, that is, for more than five hundred years before Rammohan's birth. Hindu and Muslim cultures had interacted in Bengal in many ways and in various spheres. Rammohan's family, in particular, belonged to those Hindus who had served for generations in the administration of the Muslim state in Bengal.[40]

Jawaharlal Nehru, in his *Discovery of India*, described Rammohan as "a product of the mixed Indo-Moslem culture that was then dominant among the cultured classes of India" (Nehru 1964, p. 333).[41] As the language of administration and literary culture under Muslims was Persian, people like Rammohan and his forefathers had to know this language thoroughly. Probably they had to learn some Arabic too. So it is quite natural that the first published work by Rammohan, *Tuhfatu'l-muwahhidin* ("A Gift to Monotheists," 1803 or 1804) was written in Persian and had a preface in Arabic. In this treatise Rammohan claimed that all religions (known to him) have as their basis the idea of one God, though this idea may be expressed in different ways. It is hard to imagine that in a work written in Persian and Arabic and expounding the idea of universal monotheism the influence of Islam was not there. It is almost as natural to suppose that in the later monotheistic and unitarian stance that Rammohan took in his interpretations of Hinduism and Christianity the influence of Islamic unitarian monotheism was also not a negligible factor. We may say that the exposure to Islam was for Rammohan and persons like him a kind of "antecedent" to the later exposure to European, or Christian, ideas, an antecedent which must have conditioned to a certain extent the perception of Christianity of such individuals.[42] A complete description of Rammohan's "hermeneutic situation" (cf. IE, p. 200) cannot possibly neglect this "Islamic horizon."

To some, though probably lesser, extent this must also be true of Rammohan's successor in the leadership of the Brāhmo Samāj, Debendranath Tagore (1817-1905). The Tagore family, like that of Rammohan, belonged to those Hindus who had served under Muslims and therefore, incidentally, degraded themselves in the eyes of the more orthodox Hindus. When the British came it was easier for such people than for their more conservative compatriots to contact the new foreigners and to establish mutually profitable relations with them. As Debendranath's famous son Rabindranath Tagore (1861-1941) wrote in his book *The Religion of Man*:

> I was born in what was once the metropolis of British India. My own ancestors came floating to Calcutta upon the earliest tide of the fluctuating fortune of the East India Company. The unconventional code of life for our family has been a confluence of three cultures, the Hindu, Mohammedan and British. (Tagore 1988, p. 105)

Debendranath Tagore himself knew the Persian language and is reported to have loved the poetry of Hafiz,[43] which might well have been one of the sources of his religious thinking. In other words, his "hermeneutic situation" also had an Islamic dimension.

This dimension was there too, if only by inheritance, in the spiritual and intellectual world of Rabindranath Tagore himself. Of course, Rabindranath was first and foremost a poet. It is misleading to call him a philosopher inasmuch as this word implies systematic and consistent thinking. Nevertheless, he was a thinker too, a very representative - if not always quite original - and, moreover, very influential one, because he was an outstanding and renowned cultural and public figure.

Rabindranath Tagore's life coincided with the final establishment of the British rule in India and the beginning of its gradual withdrawal from the subcontinent. Meeting the challenge of this historical situation, Tagore felt obliged to offer to his fellow Indians, and to himself, a general interpretation of Indian history, of India's past, present and future. And he did articulate quite an elaborate vision of Indian history and culture, expressed in a number of essays and poems, as well as in his most famous novel *Gora*, published in 1910. According to this vision, India was destined to be a meeting ground of various cultures, various traditions - including those of the Islamic world and the West - and her task, indeed her genius, was to evolve out of them a harmonious whole which would be a nucleus of the future global cultural synthesis.[44] On the political plane, Tagore hoped that India (here we must say South Asia) would not follow the Western way of developing separate egotistic "national" states, but would pass straight from being a "non-nation" to what may be called a "post-national" stage.[45]

These visions of Tagore, partly betrayed by actual historical developments in South Asia, are still very topical there. It is also easy to see that the political and social philosophy of Jawaharlal Nehru, as well as the ideology of the Indian National Congress as a whole, had much in common with these visions of Tagore.

Tagore himself may have treated these themes as a poet, a novelist and an essayist, but the problems as such, I believe, deserve to be called "philosophical" and belong to the fields of philosophy of history and socio-political philosophy. The problems were real and even urgent, and it might be an interesting question to consider why in 20th century India they were attended most conspicuously and publicly not by any "academic" philosopher, but by a poet.

Halbfass justly objects to the inflation of the word "philosophy" in many modern Indian writings, to "the tendency ... to use the word 'philosophy' in a broad sense which goes far beyond its academic usage" (IE, p. 291), but Halbfass himself may be charged with going to another extreme, with choosing too narrow a notion of philosophy, which makes him overlook some important aspects of reality.

In particular, it may well be that the direct contribution of Islam to the interaction of traditional Hindu thought and European, or Western, philosophy in the 19th and 20th centuries was not too important. It may well be that Islamic ingredients have a very insignificant place in current interactions between the heirs of Hindu *darśanas* and the ideas of Western philosophy. But if the general theme is called *India and Europe*, we can hardly afford to dispense so easily with the Islamic dimension of India, or South Asia. The "encounter between Indian Islam and Europe," in any case, has been an important part of the "encounter between India and Europe."[46] Consequently, Indian, or South Asian, Islam may remain an important participant in and contributor to "the continuing dialogue between India and Europe" (IE, p. 418).

But the cultural world of India, or South Asia, is not limited to Hinduism and Islam. There are various cultural minorities, such as Parsi-Zoroastrians, Buddhists, Adivasis, etc., whose "experiences" and whose voices must also be included into "the continuing dialogue between India and Europe" conceived in the broadest possible way.

To add some "symmetry" to my paper, one more point may be made. I have noted earlier that the history of "the encounter of Europe, or the West, with India" may be told on the European, or Western, side not as one single story, as Halbfass does it, but as several different, though interconnected, stories: country-wise, or language-wise, or region-wise. The same, mutatis mutandis, may be said about the Indian side of the matter. The story of Indian perceptions of and reactions to European, or Western, culture, i.e., philosophy, religion, etc., may be legitimately told as a complex of different, though more or less interconnected, stories: language-wise and/or region-wise as well as religion-wise.

Halbfass is of course fully aware that "the Indian response [to the West] has many levels and facets," that "it is as complex and differentiated as India itself" and "reflects the linguistic and religious, the social and cultural variety" of the subcontinent (IE, p. 217). Therefore in the second part of the book, which deals with "the Indian response," the author does not even try to tell us "one story," but is openly "selective" and focuses his attention

> on a few important movements and leading individuals who have articulated their xenological positions in an exemplary fashion and who have responded explicitly

and specifically to the European ideas of philosophy, science, and religion (IE, p. 218).

One cannot help noticing that most "leading individuals" described at any length are Bengalis, Bengali Hindus of course.[47] Probably it reflects the real predominance of Bengali Hindus, including Brahmos, in India's "encounter with the West." Or may future research give us a different picture?

We shall hardly expect, as Schopenhauer and Edgar Quinet did, any new Renaissance in Europe or elsewhere from more knowledge about India. But India, or South Asia, will remain a strong *caveat* against any kind of facile europocentrism and europocentric "inclusivism." Halbfass concludes his book with the following words:

> ... ancient Indian thought, in its unassimilable, non-actualizable, yet intensely meaningful distance and otherness, is *not* obsolete. (IE, p. 442)

In my opinion, which has been confirmed by my reading of *India and Europe*, this statement may be legitimately extended *mutatis mutandis* to refer not only to "ancient Indian thought," but to the whole of South Asian culture, from "ancient" to "modern." Moreover, the full extent of South Asia's "otherness" remains yet to be measured and recognised.

*Russian State University for the Humanities*
*Institute for Advanced Studies in the Humanities*
*Moscow, Russia*

## NOTES

[1] Gadamer 1988, p. 273. There is also a second, revised edition of the English translation of *Wahrheit und Methode* (Gadamer 1989), but it is not available to me in full.

[2] It is hardly accidental and, at any rate, very typical for the style of *India and Europe* as a whole, that in most cases Gadamer's expression is part of questions, not always (or not only) rhetorical: "Are the boundaries [between India and the West] finally dissolving? Has there been a genuine 'fusion of horizons'?" (IE, p. 161). "Should Gadamer's concepts of 'hermeneutic conversation' or 'dialogue' ('hermeneutisches Gespräch') and 'fusion of horizons' ('Horizontverschmelzung') which he develops in his controversial classic *Wahrheit und Methode* ('Truth and Method'), not also be pertinent to the

interpretation of Indian thought and its literary documents?" (IE, p. 165). "Will there ever be a 'global philosophy' and a genuine 'fusion of horizons' ('Horizontverschmelzung') ... ?" (IE, p. 374). "Are the boundaries [between Western science and 'Eastern metaphysics of awareness'] finally dissolving? Has there been a genuine 'fusion of horizons?'" (IE, p. 439). In the last quotation there is even a very telling misprint (..."fusion of horizons?"), the question mark as if insisting on being an integral part of the term itself. In *India and Europe* there are some other very suggestive misprints. For instance, on p. 125 there appears a striking phrase "external recurrence," which is, alas, only a misprint for "eternal recurrence" (cf. p. 128).

[3] In the text of *India and Europe* this German word resonates, to my mind and ear, with two other expressions which do not get a detailed analysis either.

First, Halbfass mentions and briefly discusses a book composed by the Mughal prince Dārā Shukōh (1615-1659) and titled *Majma' al-baḥrain*. This book by the ill-fated prince was, as Halbfass puts it, "an attempt to compare and harmonize Hinduism and Islam" (IE, p. 34; cf. p. 416). Now it is the title, if not the book itself, that deserves a closer scrutiny. Halbfass translates the title inaccurately as *Mingling of the Oceans* and leaves it without further comments. But the Arabic word *majma'* (from the verbal root *jama'a* – "to bring together," "to unite," etc.) is, from the viewpoint of grammar, a *nomen loci* and means primarily "a place of union," "a place of gathering," "a meeting place." Abid Husain, the Indian Muslim scholar, translated the title of the book in question as *The Meeting Place of Two Oceans* (Abid Husain 1985, p. 90). Indeed, *baḥrain* is the Arabic dual number from *baḥr* - "a mass of something," "a big river," "a sea," "an ocean." This disregarding of the dual number, this minor linguistic slip in dealing with an Arabic-Persian phrase, is rather symbolic of a more general disregard for Indian Islam in Halbfass's book as a whole (see below).

Moreover, *majma' al-baḥrain* is a phrase from the *Koran*, from the Surah 18 (The Cave: 18:60 and 18:61)). It occurs in the story of Moses narrated in this Surah: "Moses said to his servant: 'I will journey on until I reach the land where the two seas meet, though I may march for ages.' But when at last they came to the land where the two seas met, they forgot their fish, which made its way into the water, swimming at will" (Dawood 1990, pp. 210-211). This phrase, *majma' al-baḥrain*, is one of the most enigmatic in the whole *Koran* and later received various interpretations. In later Muslim scholarship it was traditionally used for the titles of such works that attempted some kind of synthesis, to combine various approaches and viewpoints. Thus, *majma' al-baḥrain* may probably be considered a Muslim "antecedent" of the German term *Horizontverschmelzung*. (I thank my Moscow colleagues Dr. Maxim Kiktiev and Dr. Alexander Kudelin for advising me on this point.)

On another occasion, mentioning Abhinavagupta's *Tantrāloka*, Halbfass quotes from that treatise the Sanskrit phrase *śāstrāṇāṃ melanam* (IE, p. 360), which, I suppose, may be rendered as "the bringing together of [various] fields of knowledge (or: traditions)." Halbfass himself translates the phrase as the "union of the (!?) traditions," but I feel (though I may be wrong) that *melana* as opposed to *milana* must have a causative connotation and is associated not only with *milati* "to meet," "to come together," but also and more so with *melayati* "to cause to meet," "to bring together." Could we consider then Abhinavagupta's *śāstrāṇāṃ melanam* a kind of Sanskrit "antecedent" of Gadamer's *Horizontverschmelzung*?

[4] In a way, according to Gadamer's interpretation, these two variants of the subtitle are almost synonymical. On p. 165 of *India and Europe* Halbfass quotes Gadamer: "Understanding ... is always the fusion of ... horizons ..." (Gadamer 1988, p. 273).

[5] Cf. also: "The following chapters aim at a combination and even integration of Indological and historically oriented philosophical work which may appear unusual and problematic to Indologists as well as to philosophers and historians of philosophy" (IE, p. XIV).

[6] The most conspicuous Germanism is probably the often used word "Indology" (with a capital "I"). As I have gathered from my talks with British scholars, this word (with any "i") is not considered in Britain a proper British usage. In American English the word seems to be used sometimes, but with lower case "i." "Indology" (with capital "I") may be also met in Indian texts in English. Cf. e.g., the posthumous collection of articles by Professor W. Norman Brown, edited by Rosane Rocher from the University of Pennsylvania and published in India (Brown 1978): in introductory contributions by Indian scholars we read "Indologists" and "Indology" (p. X), but the editor in her introduction writes "indology" (p. XVII) and "indologists" (p. XVIII), though she obviously prefers the phrase "Indian (or: Indic) studies." So "Indology" with capital "I" may be considered not only a Germanism but also a kind of "Indianism."

Some passages in *India and Europe* might probably be better understood if read together with the German original. This guess is well substantiated by the two sentences from Dilthey's *Das Wesen der Philosophie* quoted by Halbfass both in the German original and in an English translation (IE, p. 430). The English version is hardly comprehensible without the German original. This shows the common difficulties involved in translating from philosophical German into English. Probably some German philosophical texts are virtually untranslatable into clear English. What is needed in such cases is not a translation, but rather an almost word by word commentary; cf. e.g., the "Translators' Preface" to the revised English translation of Gadamer's *Wahrheit und Methode* (Gadamer 1989, pp. XI-XIX).

[7] Cf. e.g., the very first words of the preface: "*India and Europe: An Essay in Understanding* is, indeed, nothing but an essay, a preliminary attempt, an introduction" (IE, p. IX).

[8] As Mehta put it in a rhetorical question: "... Shall we begin to understand both [traditions] in their mutual otherness, to learn the language of each and so to evolve ways of thinking and talking which will be truly appropriate to our membership of both worlds, striving in such fashion to transform it into one?" (Mehta 1985, p. 163; IE, p. 262).

[9] Cf. below, n. 37.

[10] On "Europe" cf. e.g., Hay 1968 and the literature mentioned there. On "India" one could hardly refer to a similar study.

[11] On "Europe" cf. Seignobos 1939, p. 13: "The name Europe, originated by the Greeks, has changed its significance with each succeeding age. It was first applied to the south-eastern region adjoining Asia, next extended to the lands on the northern shore of the Mediterranean, then to those bordering on the Atlantic, and lastly to those of the centre and east as they gradually came in touch with the Mediterranean world. It was a geographical term, implying no idea of any community between the inhabitants. It is only in modern times that a comparison of the European population with that of the other continents has led to the recognition of a common stock of feelings and customs proper to the European peoples, and given them a consciousness of solidarity, which is, however, somewhat vague."

On "India" cf. Masson-Oursel et al. 1934, p. 1: "The name *India* has been used in different periods for very different regions. In its original Persian sense it meant the Sindhu river, the *Indos* of the Greeks, and so, by derivation, all the land lying beyond the Indus for a man entering the country from the west ... "; Moreland and Chatterjee 1953, p. 1: "We must begin by defining our subject, for the name 'India' has in the past meant different things to different people, sometimes merely a narrow strip of coast, at others the greater portion of southern Asia"; Wink 1991, p. 5: "... the Arabs, in contrast to the medieval Christians, developed their conception of India in direct and prolonged contact with it. In a political-geographical sense, 'India' or *al-Hind*, throughout the medieval period, was an Arab or Muslim conception. The Arabs, like the Greeks, adopted a pre-existing Persian term, but they were the first to extend its application to the entire Indianized region from Sind and Makran to the Indonesian Archipelago and mainland Southeast Asia. It therefore appears to us as if the Indians or Hindus acquired a collective identity in interaction with Islam."

[12] Cf. e.g., Parker 1960.

[13] Cf. e.g., Hay 1968, pp. 124-127 and Walicki 1979, passim.

[14] Cf. the characteristic definition of India in the *EB* (vol. 12, p. 150): "India, a great country and empire of Asia under British rule, inhabited by a congeries of different races, speaking upwards of 200 different languages."

[15] It is only rarely that such contexts occur where "the West" and its derivatives do not mean Europe proper. For instance: "At first, the initiative in the transmission [to Indians] of European - and Western - knowledge and thought lay in the hands of the missionaries" (IE, p. 256). In the next paragraph Thomas Paine and his *The Age of Reason* are mentioned.

[16] It is interesting to note that in *India and Europe* Russia is included, in a way, in the list of European countries by being not listed in the index, though mentioned at least once in the book itself (p. 160); no European country except Greece is listed in the index.

America, however, is listed.

[17] Cf. e.g., the paper by Yakov Lurye in Nikitin 1986, p. 75ff.

[18] The Soviet *Bibliography of India* lists the following publications by Saltykov in French: 1) [Saltikoff, A.D. ] Lettres sur l'Inde. Paris, 1848; 2) Soltykoff, A. Voyages dans l'Inde. 2 éd. Paris, 1851; 3 éd. Paris, 1858; 3) Soltykoff, A. Habitants de l'Inde dessinés d'après nature par le prince A. Soltykoff. Paris, 1853 (Kotovsky and Sosina 1976, p. 84).

[19] Cf. the preface by L. B. Ąlayev to the latest Russian edition of Saltykov's *Letters* (Saltykov 1985, pp. 3-8).

[20] In Russian the stress is on the last syllable, rhyming with "toy."

[21] The biography of Bayer written by Knud Lundbaek (Lundbaek 1986) contains an analysis of his Sinological research.

[22] Cf. Kotovsky and Sosina 1976, p. 541.

[23] Gurdjieff was born in Transcaucasia as a subject of the Russian Empire, but ethnically was of mixed Armenian and Greek descent. He left Russia, not to return, sometime after 1917 and died in Paris in 1949. Cf. e.g., Bennett 1976.

[24] Ouspensky was born in Moscow in 1878, left Russia sometime after 1917 and died in exile in 1947.

[25] On Minorsky cf. e.g., Bosworth 1971. I have not been able to find any literature on Mironov. My colleague Dr. Alexei Vigasin has kindly let me know the years of Mironov's birth and death, which information he could procure only from archives.

[26] Andreas-Salomé may be considered as a very special case of a bi-cultural person. Though she chose to become a German rather than Russian writer and lived most of her adult life in Germany, she apparently never forgot her Russian "roots." Among other things, she was a mediator between Russia and Rainer Maria Rilke, with whom she traveled twice to her native country (Binion 1968; Peters 1962).

[27] Even the history of "Indology" – Indian or South Asian studies – in Russia has not yet been properly written. In English I may refer to the article by George Roerich (Roerich 1945), which is informative but very dated, and to the book by Grigory Bongard-Levin and Alexei Vigasin (Bongard-Levin and Vigasin 1984) which, written before "perestroika," unfortunately combines solid scholarship with propagandistic cliches. The history of the "encounter between Russia and India" is treated in a more general way in a book by an American scholar, Robert H. Stacy's *India in Russian Literature* (Stacy 1985). Literature in Russian is richer, but rarely very satisfying.

[28] The name of Lev Tolstoy may be recalled, of course, in this respect, but the response of Tolstoy to India (as well as India's response to Tolstoy) is often misrepresented and misinterpreted. On the Russian, or Soviet, side this theme was very much part of the politics of "Indo-Soviet friendship." The kind of scholarship produced for the sake of this "friendship" is well represented by the book *Tolstoy and India* written by a Soviet author and published by the Sahitya Akademi in New Delhi (Shifman 1978). The book leaves much to be desired, and the theme still awaits earnest research. To put it briefly, it may be said that Tolstoy's knowledge about India was very inadequate, very mediated; he responded not so much to India proper as to some particular Western projections of things Indian. I have tried to make this point by analysing the particular case of Tolstoy's interest in the sayings of Ramakrishna (Serebriany 1987).

[29] I may refer in this connection to one more specific case-study of my own (Serebriany 1993a).

[30] Cf. e.g., Walicki 1979, passim.

[31] Like Andreas-Salomé, Böhtlingk chose in the end to live and die in Germany. However, in Russia he was and still is considered a Russian scholar. It may be noted in this connection that in St. Petersburg, up to the 20th century, there remained a small community of local Germans. One of the architects of the Soviet rocket power, Boris V. Rauschenbach, came from this community.

[32] The original *Bibliotheca Buddhica* died in the late 1930s. In the early 1960s attempts were undertaken, in Moscow, to revive the series. Since the mid 1980s the attempts have been renewed. Several books have been published. However, now it is not an international, but only Russian endeavour.

[33] Cf. e.g.: "The size of India is enormous. The country is almost as large as the whole of the continent of Europe without Russia ..." (Majumdar et al. 1946, p. 6). "A history of India is equivalent in range to the history of Europe excluding Russia ..." (Dunbar 1939, p. V).

[34] Cf. e.g.: "The Indian Empire is the abode of a vast collection of peoples who differ from one another in physical characteristics, in language, and in culture more widely than the peoples of Europe" (Rapson 1922, p. 37). "It is historically incorrect to think of 'Indians' as we think of French or Portuguese: it is not less incorrect to think of them as we think of Europeans. The truth lies somewhere between these contrasted views" (Moreland and Chatterjee 1953, p. 6).

[35] In Eastern and even Central Europe imperial structures lasted longer and crumbled only in the 20th century.

[36] Using the Western word "empire" in this and similar cases, do we not make the same kind of risky cross-cultural leap as when we uncritically use "philosophy" for *darśana* and "religion" for *dharma*?

[37] Of course, Muslims, in India too, had their traditions of historiography. But they were interested almost exclusively in the history of Islam and Islamic peoples. They did not take interest in the history of pre-Muslim India. The Hindus had almost no precedents in their traditions for the Western idea of history and historiography. In modern Indian languages, e.g., in Hindi, the old Sanskrit word *itihāsa* has been made to mean "history." This lexical development is similar to the cases of *darśana* versus "philosophy" and *dharma* versus "religion."

[38] Cf.: "It is a fact of immense significance that whereas in the making of Europe the conquests of Islam played the role of a powerfully effective but mostly external factor, in the East the expansion of Islam went on for more than a millennium and here, in South and large parts of Southeast Asia the association with Islam became so intimate that, as a result, we find an *Indo-Islamic* pattern of society and culture" (Wink 1991, p. 1). Cf. also e.g., the book by S. Abid Husain (Abid Husain 1985). It is the earnest attempt of a modern Indian, Western educated Muslim to interpret the whole of Indian history and culture in such a way that Islam would be included as an integral part of this whole.

[39] Halbfass quotes and approves the following statement by the late Jan Gonda: "The Muslims [in India], whose religious beliefs and social institutions sharply contrast with those of the Hindus, resisted the process of absorption (?), without in turn being able to leave their own imprint (?) on India" (IE, p. 31). The inadequacy of this statement is rather striking. Cf. the statement of André Wink in the previous note.

[40] The family name of Rammohan, in Bengali *Rāy*, is derived from the title *rāy-e-rāyān* ("the prince of princes") that had been granted to the great-grandfather of Rammohan by the Muslim Nawab of Bengal (Collet 1962, p. 2). This title itself is a peculiar cross-cultural and cross-lingual mixture: the form is Persian, but the word *rāy* is evidently derived from the Sanskrit *rājan* (probably through the vernacular *rāya*).

[41] The statement about "the cultured classes of India" is evidently too sweeping. Probably it reflects how Nehru wished to see and interpret Indian history. The traditions of his family also combined Hindu and Muslim, and later Western, elements. The case of the Nehrus is one more indication of the importance of Islam and its "imprint" on India.

[42] Halbfass is somewhat ambiguous in his statements about Rammohan and Islam. On page 35 we read: "The Persian language and Islam are also of significance for the work of Rammohan Roy, the Bengali pioneer of Hindu revivalism (?) at the beginning of the nineteenth century." On page 202, after discussing the *Tuhfatu'l-muwahhidin* (which title is rather inaccurately, to my mind, translated as "Gift to Deists"), Halbfass asserts that "in Rammohan's later publications, Islam and the Persian language do not play any noticeable role," although "some remarkable quotes in Arabic in the *Second Appeal to*

*the Christian Public* still indicate his familiarity with the Koran." But on page 200, "Islamic thought" as a source "of Rammohan's inspiration" is put under a strong suspicion, as it is listed together with "Freemasonry."

[43] I have failed to find any textual proof for this information, but my source is quite reliable: it is Krishna Kripalani, Rabindranath Tagore's close associate and grandson-in-law, the author of the poet's biography (Kripalani 1962). I had a chance to talk to Krishna Kripalani in Moscow, in 1983.

[44] Cf. e.g., the collection of Tagore's essays in English titled *Towards Universal Man* (Tagore 1969).

[45] Tagore developed these ideas in his book *Nationalism* (Tagore 1917).

[46] No history of this "encounter" can be considered complete without such names as (to list only the most important ones) Syed Ahmad Khan (1817-1898), Muhammad Iqbal (1873-1938), and Maulana Abul Kalam Azad (1888-1958).

[47] Rammohan Roy, Debendranath Tagore, Keshab Chandra Sen, Ramakrishna, Vivekananda, Bankim Chandra Chatterji, Aurobindo Ghose are all Bengalis. The list of non-Bengalis, to whom comparable attention is given in *India and Europe*, is much shorter and may be actually exhausted by three names: Dayananda Sarasvati, Sarvepalli Radhakrishnan and Ananda Coomaraswamy.

**Reena Sen (née Mookerjee)**

# SOME REFLECTIONS ON *INDIA AND EUROPE: AN ESSAY IN UNDERSTANDING*

In the following, I shall be presenting a few points which constitute my reflections or responses vis-à-vis the absorbing and important work of Wilhelm Halbfass, *India and Europe: An Essay in Understanding*. What draws me to the book is chiefly the subject-matter. However, two more factors make it rather irresistible for me to respond to this particular work of his. These are: (a) my belonging to India and (b) my exposure, however limited it may be, to the European tradition, culture and philosophy, which dates back to the 1960's.

## I

The publication of the original German version of *India and Europe* (*Indien und Europa*, 1981) had already made known the worth of the contribution, at least to a limited audience. The English version of the same (1988) made it accessible to a much wider readers' forum and further established the reputation of the book. Writing for the present volume provides me with the opportunity to congratulate Halbfass for the vast task undertaken and accomplished in the form of a single book. Further debate and controversy are evoked by the variety of issues addressed in this book. But it is precisely this variety which primarily accounts for its vitality. In his candid approach Halbfass never hides his identity, i.e., his belonging to the European tradition, and makes in his interpretative move an attempt to present things as they are[1]; thus, he maintains the spirit of dialogue.[2]

*India and Europe* covers at once several points of view, namely, the historiographical, Indological and, of course, the philosophical. The work brings to focus the encounters between the East and the West or Europe, and thereby attempts to "describe and clarify some of the historical pre-suppositions of their mutual understanding." Halbfass tells us in clear terms that "This is not a book on the current situation or the most recent developments in the 'East-West dialogue.'" Such being the orientation, a survey is undertaken from antiquity to the very threshold of the twentieth century, vis-à-vis an essay in understanding between India and Europe.

The title of the book is quite telling, since it does not only to a large extent shield the author from possible misunderstanding, but most importantly reveals the hermeneutical perspective to which the author remains basically committed. In his interpretation and discussion Halbfass moves with unsurpassable ease from one tradition to the other, one of which is usually "alien" or "foreign." Thus *India and Europe*, which is also highly instructive and builds a step towards one's self-understanding, is a book of absorbing interest.

The command over the different languages which Halbfass wields is impressive. The book stands out, by all standards, as an instance of high scholarship and academic excellènce, and is not a mere compilation or juxtaposition of points of view. Its method of posing questions makes the difference. Also, the sober moderation of Halbfass' critical effort comes to expression throughout the text.[3]

At the outset the author is successful in historically analysing the beginnings of Indological research and describing the motivations and presuppositions of leading Indologists.[4] Chapters on Hegel, Schelling and Schopenhauer follow. Chapters 9 and 10 discuss issues of significance; chapter 9 especially (the exclusion of India) deals with a hard fact. Chapters 6 and 10, however, raise serious concerns as to the furtherance of any future thoughtful encounter between India and Europe.[5] Chapter 12 (on Rammohan Roy) and the rest of the chapters which follow remain of fundamental interest.

Halbfass has sufficiently discussed various claims as to the origin of philosophy, and specifically the claims as to the respective priority of Greek and Indian philosophy. Now, it cannot be denied that India, along with its tradition and "philosophy," is one of the oldest civilizations of the world. Even within the European tradition Voltaire was "convinced of the priority of the Indian achievements in the area of secular learning and worldly culture." He considered the Indians to be the people "to whom we owe our numbers, our backgammon, our chess, our first principles of geometry, and the fables which have become our own."[6] With Jones, Wilkins and Colebrooke one finds similar views. Halbfass points out that "they too were advocates of the view that the mythological, religious and philosophical tradition of India was especially ancient and pristine."[7] And in view of the "basic similarities," Sanskrit, Greek, and Latin were believed "to have sprung from some common source, which perhaps no longer exists."[8] It has been maintained by Indian scholars on the subject that the earliest literature, the Vedas, dates back to 1000 B.C. and that the earliest Upaniṣads were written between 700 B.C. and 600 B.C.[9] One cannot but recall the views of Dayananda, to whom Halbfass refers more than once.

> Dayananda recommends that the Indians learn from the virtues and achievements of the Europeans: ultimately, however, all of humanity must learn from those ancient and sacred sources which anticipate in principle all future developments and whose original guardians were the Indians. (IE, p. 245)

II

As Halbfass proceeds with his hermeneutical exercise, he refers to points of view which cannot be accepted. But let us move with the spirit of openness and readiness for further understanding and dialogue. In fact, it would be too hasty to take certain statements at face-value: e.g., that Indian philosophy is something obsolete,[10] that it belongs to the past, and that it has been superseded by the European; or further, that "expulsion of India" at one stage shows, among other things, that India had no "concept of philosophy" to offer. Other views of that ilk include the ideas that in India there has been mixing up of philosophy and religion, that it is after all purpose *(prayojana)* which remains the motivating factor at the back of whatever quest for philosophy India may claim to uphold, and that reference to the Divine ultimately constitutes the basic trait of Indian tradition in philosophy. Finally, it has been claimed that philosophy worth the name is the outcome of "hard work" accomplished by the Europeans, and the "Europeanization of all foreign parts of mankind is the destiny of the earth."[11]

These contentions need not be viewed either with a defeatist or with a scornful attitude. They are in fact expressions of a certain kind of experience and should be viewed accordingly, i.e., from the point of view of the hermeneutic situation, to understand issues and dispel misunderstanding, however marginal that may be for the rehabilitation of Indian philosophy and tradition. Let it be noted that Halbfass makes some valuable observations of his own[12] which give a positive dimension to Indian philosophical thought. Nevertheless, we too shall refer to a few points here, as well as in the following section, in the form of a rejoinder while trying to correctly understand the context of the Indian philosophical endeavour.

One cannot but question the familiar European contentions about Indian philosophy mentioned above and pose counter-questions, in order to seek clarification and to obtain meaningful conclusions. Thus: Are Indian thought and philosophy really obsolete with all their difficult and "alien" character? How can this be so when we consider the Indian context? Moreover, the ancient thought and tradition itself - as Halbfass has shown - did undergo a process of adjustment in the face of innumerable encounters and experiences. Is it not that in the face of such exposures Indian thought and tradition retain their identity, e.g., in the form of "Neo-Hinduism," in the philosophical perspectives of Aurobindo and Vivekananda for example? In fact, there is a kind of ongoing continuity in the Indian tradition and philosophy which extends from classical antiquity to the present, and which shows itself in the philosophical endeavours and perspectives of K. C. Bhattacharya, Gopīnāth Kavirāj, Radhakrishnan and Aurobindo.

One indeed does come across philosophy proper in the Indian tradition. The wonder that is at the root of all genuine philosophy finds its magnificent expression in the question as to the origin of the world, as in the hymn of *Ṛgveda* X.129.[13] And then, not to mention the Upaniṣads, there are systems like Nyāya-Vaiśeṣika, which can be said to represent true philosophizing. In addition, Indian philosophy too can be "scientific"[14] in the true sense of the term, as one witnesses with Nyāya-Vaiśeṣika physics.[15]

Thus, Indian philosophy is not something obsolete and true philosophy only found in Europe. As to the contention regarding the mixing up of philosophy and religion, it too cannot be sustained. First of all, it is important to note that the term "religion" is not without an element of ambiguity. It is not clear why the term should necessarily come to relate to some deity or god. In other words, religion may be viewed as indicating a search for ultimate reality, i.e., as pointing towards some kind of metaphysics, as, for example, the Upaniṣads bear witness.

Further, the expression "religion" does not necessarily posit or imply performance of rituals. Had that been so, it would have been almost impossible to attribute some sort of religion to personalities like Vivekananda or Gandhi. In fact, there are ethical implications to the term "religion," which is why we find both Vivekananda and Gandhi expressing their respective religiosity in terms of ethics. Vivekananda speaks of work and action, and Gandhi speaks of truth; for Gandhi it is truth which actually amounts to religion.

Also, there is an atheistic philosophical school in India, namely, the Cārvāka school.

In conclusion, let it be reiterated that at one point the two, philosophy and religion, do converge or meet, and that both philosophy and religion in their own way seek truth. What it is that constitutes truth is, of course, debatable.

To turn to the other allied contention, viz., that Indian thought does not originate in wonder and is not guided by the desire to know, and that it is purpose (*prayojana*)[16] which is the motivating factor. In other words, it is purpose which matters for the philosophical quest, the primary objective being to achieve liberation or salvation.

Now, first of all, there may be some misunderstanding here, since this purpose does not seem to be equivalent to the pragmatic attitude or to the egoistic approach which is presumed by the Western interpretation. Further, it is true that references to liberation (*mokṣa)* feature prominently in Indian thought and philosophy. But one has to bear in mind that this fact alone does not nullify the provision for true concern for philosophy. On the contrary, it is the desire for knowledge that brings one to speak at one stage of possible liberation. In fact, to speak in terms of this purpose is expressive of the innermost unrest and a serious quest for true knowledge. Such knowledge can be nothing but knowledge pertaining to the soul (*ātman*). It is thus knowledge or truth relating to the soul which is revealed to the seeker in and through meditation and *yoga*, i.e., *sādhana*,[17] and which takes one to the path of self-realization, self-understanding, or liberation/emancipation,[18] namely, the knowledge that *ātman* is *brahman*, *brahman* is *ātman*. The questioning self, asking the question: "Who am I?", ultimately comes to realize its identity[19] with *brahman* and attains the luminous state, i.e., the state of bliss (*ānanda*). This is referred to in the well-known passage "From darkness unto light," i.e., truth. Perhaps one is asked to embark on a difficult path, but that alone can neither stop the quest itself, nor deny the possibility of eventual fruition of one's endeavour.

With the above words it is perhaps also clear in what sense Indian thought or philosophy may be deemed as meaningful in relation to the Divine. The Divine by itself is nothing extraneous; and the move on the part of the seeker remains a thoroughly immanent one: the seeker needs basically to look "within."

To conclude the discussion of the issue we cannot but look for an historical grounding of this special nature of Indian philosophy. Reference could be made to a story recorded in the *Kaṭhopaniṣad*, the story of Naciketas, the son of Gautama. Naciketas was moved by the spirit of wonder which set him on the path of self-knowledge, to gain insight into the mystery of life and death and consequent rebirth. In his discourse with Yama, the lord of death, Naciketas was nôt allured by the dazzling prospects of enjoyment on this earth offered to him by Yama in the form of boons, and thus obtained the grace of Yama and became enlightened.[20]

## III

In the previous section we referred to some issues as they feature in the work under discussion. It has been stated that philosophy worth the name is the "hard work" accomplished by the Europeans, and that the "Europeanization of all foreign parts of mankind is the destiny of the earth." In the concluding section of the text, "In Lieu of a Summary and Conclusion," Halbfass envisions an amicable hermeneutical procedure, from which both the Orient and the Occident could possibly gain significantly:

> The West is turning towards the East for new inspiration, or even for therapy. Can it expect help from those ways of orientation ...? Can it retrieve and adopt for its own future what it once tried to supersede and relegate to the past? (IE, p. 440)

But further he observes:

> No calculated importation and application of Eastern ways of thinking, or methods of meditation, will enable us to reverse history or change the basic conditions of a world which is dominated by science and technology ... The recent history of Indian spiritual movements in the West illustrates this simple truth: In their application within the modern Western world, the Indian methods and teachings become parts and manifestations of this world, and the constellation of science and technology. (IE, p. 441)

And the conclusion follows that for the time being, for Indians as well as Europeans, "'Europeanization of the earth' continues to be inescapable and irreversible" (IE, p. 442). This notion of the Europeanization of the earth and mankind hovers around two basic points. First, it refers to the "pure theory" or philosophy which we owe to the Europeans[21]; second, it refers to advanced science and technology which dominates the world of the Europeans, i.e., the global scenario. The above two perspectives, viewed as historically relevant truths, generate the thesis of "Europeanization of the earth."

At this point, we would like to make a few points of some relevance.

1. Let it be noted that "pure theory" and the assigning of importance to it are quite pertinent. However, the issue of "pure theory" needs to be viewed in relation to a possible limit. And at one stage or another, "pure theory" has to make room for praxis.[22] For a theory to be of worth it must relate to the world.[23] It is interesting to note that Husserl's philosophy itself undergoes such a shift insofar as Husserl accommodates the notion of "lived experience" (*Lebenswelt*) and attaches great value to it.[24]

2. Further, the above thesis of "pure theory" has been in a way superseded by the theories of eminent philosophers within the European tradition itself. This one notes initially in Hêgel, who succeeded in projecting dynamism (as against Kant), unleashing the notion of dialectical movement. The follow-up is in evidence to a great measure in the philosophical writings of Heidegger and Gadamer. Heidegger's analysis of being (*Sein*) proceeds through an analysis of the facticity or factuality[25] of *Sein*, the being there of *Sein*, its being-in-the-world (*Dasein*). The understanding of *Sein* in terms of its factuality is accomplished in relation to the horizon, namely, time or temporality. From Gadamer we learn that "history precedes me and my reflection, I belong to history before belonging to myself." As Paul Ricoeur rightly observes: "At this point Gadamer is heir to Heidegger."[26]

3. In addition, how exactly does the notion of "pure theory" achieved by the Europeans stand in relation to all that goes under the title of the "constellation of science and technology"? How do the two influence each other? In which direction do they influence each other? In other words: Does "pure theory" vouch for the latter? Or is it that "pure theory" and the "constellation of science and technology" stand side by side in stark isolation, just like two opposite "poles," which thereby suggests a possible hiatus within the European tradition or model itself? With this we turn to take a close look at the other issue of relevance, namely, the current progressive move of science and technology in relation to the question of the Europeanization of the earth and mankind.[27]

4. Here also the question of a limit need be borne in mind. For whom are science and technology? Obviously for us, the human beings; their purpose is to meet the big, lofty, or even small needs and requirements

of mankind. Nevertheless, even though it may sound simplistic and possibly naïve, it remains that science and technology should not be allowed to overpower man or to shape his destiny, because man, gifted as he is, finds his self-expression in varied spheres, e.g., arts,[28] music, sculpture, etc. With this in view, science and technology should be channeled so that provision is made for the appropriate expression of the more subtle aspects of man.

5. It is, moreover, important to consider certain implications or even hazards associated with the acceptance of a certain domination by science and technology. Such implications or hazards may be, for example, of the following order: *political*, where the unfortunate polarization of the world may assume disproportionate dimensions; *financial*, where large amounts of finances may be expended toward the goal of achieving superior scientific and technological skills, leading to the possible neglect of the advancement or even maintenance of other human dimensions; *military*, where there may be pressure to maintain a top-level efficient military unit in terms of the latest scientific and technological equipment, which thereby pushes other aspects which require attention into the background; *environmental*, relating to ecology, where there may be pollution due to the dumping of excess toxic wastes or radiation, emanating as a result of the diffusion of bombs on a large scale.

Such problems or hazards as outlined above are not unknown to us. But they are so acute that mere awareness will not suffice. They need be pointed out and emphasized when we – whether Indians or Europeans – yield to the possibility of our destiny being shaped by the modern technological apparatus or nexus.[29]

6. Accordingly, it is most urgent to be mindful of the need to maintain a balance or equilibrium and to make it a priority. After all, science is for man, not the other way around,[30] and it should not engulf him to create an absurd situation in which man is blindfolded as the vanquished and not the victor. In other words, to tolerate a free, random spree of science would mean to let it eat out the humanity in man.[31]

7. What has been pointed out above does not, however, amount to a denial of the importance of science and technology in our lives in the world. On the contrary, science and technology need be given their due. However, fear of having reached a dead end is expressed when one is led to speak, for example, of the "Europeanization of the earth." Could one look beyond it? Moreover, what happens to the hermeneutical venture on the part of Halbfass, to whose pursuit he otherwise remains very much

committed? What happens to the possible "fusion of horizons" of which he, like Gadamer, speaks? Or is it that the question of a possible "fusion of horizons" retains its prospect within the given European traditions alone? It may be, given the context, that one confronts a "blockade" in respect to a true hermeneutical venture or exercise.

8. Further, it is a fact that we cannot wipe out our past. But is it that history or historicality lets itself be understood only in terms of predictability? The question is: Can history be planned?[32] Does history proceed in terms of rational, scientific calculation and programming? Or could one, alternatively, entertain the view that history, displaying marks of unpredictability, unfolds itself in more than one way or on more than one track? Perhaps the movement of history is not just one-dimensional, but cyclic as well.

9. Although one may agree with Halbfass and thus admit that in the context of the recent move vis-à-vis the Western world the Indian methods and teaching also become parts of the Western world, the "constellation of science and technology," the question remains: Does any such move or involvement lead one to be necessarily in favour of the thesis of "Europeanization of the earth"? Or is it that the above situation just constitutes a sort of "in-between" stage for the Indians, in which one remains aware of one's heritage as well? It may be that there remains a gap in argumentation.

10. One point, however, should not go unnoticed. It relates to the simple yet very difficult question as to what and how much is understood when one refers to or speaks of "science." (i) As per common-sense norm, anything may go under the name of science or be termed scientific which is seen to be "rational," for example, systematic studies relating to any issue or department of knowledge. (ii) But to be more sophisticated and technical, one has to accommodate a notion of science or scientific which relates to the effort to understand nature and to unravel its mysteries. (iii) Also, the recent developments of science indicate a move towards a notion of science as technology and technocracy.

It is of interest to note that if we mean by science that which falls under (i) and (ii), then we all look forward to it and value it, perhaps with the hope to capture the mysteries of nature and deepen one's self-understanding. In that case, the merely negative notion of the Europeanization of the earth and mankind has to undergo substantial modification. Insofar as science is taken in sense (iii) (technology and technocracy), however, the one who accepts science as such must be on guard that his self-identity does not become immersed in the whirlpool of rapid change. One need not hesitate to face this change with an attitude of readiness to accept - within certain limits - whatever technological developments occur in one's socio-cultural setting. But amidst that turbulent rush the question of self-identity has to be kept in mind, while the possibility of acknowledging one's self-identity in terms of an "identity-in-difference" has to be accepted.

11. It is Heidegger who, like Husserl, foretells the near-future destiny of the earth, but nevertheless expresses reservations. *Techné*[33] (technology) may not contain the whole story. Toward what direction, then, could man look? As Halbfass points out, Heidegger speaks of going beyond both the Occident and the Orient. Does Heidegger, with his poetic insight, envision a possible silent dialectical evolution or revolution after all, which involves the Occident and the Orient as well, and even goes beyond? Are we to understand the situation accordingly when Heidegger speaks of *Gelassenheit*, the patient waiting for the truth to unfold itself?[34]

12. Or could we, by accepting a priority-thesis where the emphasis or priority falls on man as part of his environment, undertake a "dialogue" involving the East and the West in terms of a humanization of the earth? In other words, this would lead us to ponder, for our meaningful survival, the necessity to keep science or technology and technocracy within a certain limiting framework[35] or bounds, whereby man would not be made subordinate to the achievements of science; the latter should be geared to the former instead. Man would not in such a case be viewed as one more article to negotiate with, one more object among the other objects of the world. It is the dignity of man, his humanity, his confrontation with tradition and modernity, his effort to live up to the measure of cultural integrity and the respective value-structure, which should come to matter and direct the course of our dialogue decisively.

The above situation remains surcharged with ethical overtones, which suggests that any hermeneutical excursion entails an ethical orientation[36]; this orientation makes it what it is, namely, a possible meaningful exercise in understanding. Could we look forward to such a yardstick or parameter in our effort to understand cross-cultural issues and encounters? That would, however, demand of us a significant amount of tolerance marked by confidence and self-respect, accompanied by an attitude of reciprocity, the readiness to share and understand that what is considered to be "alien."[37] Hopefully, one may thus experience progress in laying the foundation for realizing one's identity, i.e., identity-in-difference, keeping the prospect of a "fusion of horizons" wide open.

*Calcutta University*
*Department of Philosophy*
*Calcutta, India*

## NOTES

[1] See e.g., the treatment of Hegel and Husserl.

[2] Cf. IE, p. 286.

[3] Cf. e.g., IE, p. xiii: "Modern Indian thought finds itself in a historical context created by Europe, and it has difficulties speaking for itself. Even in its self-representation and self-assertion, it speaks to a large extent in a European idiom. This does not, however, mean that the dialogue and debate between India and Europe has been decided in favor of Europe, or that India has been superseded by Europe. The power of the Indian tradition has not exhausted itself in the self-representation and self-interpretation of modern India. The dialogic situation is still open." It is also to be noted that Halbfass quotes Anquetil in the following way: "'Let us study the Indians as we study the Greeks and Romans' ... – critically, but respectfully, and without ridiculing them" (IE, p. 66; see also p. 375).

[4] IE, pp. 1-83.

[5] Halbfass has been alert to the possibility of misunderstanding in the process of encounter as well.

[6] Cf. IE, p. 59. Halbfass also acknowledges that the presence of India is felt in other spheres too, e.g., in art, literature, music, etc.

[7] Cf. IE, pp. 62-63.

[8] Cf. IE, p. 63.

[9] Cf. Dasgupta 1922, pp. 6, 28.

[10] Halbfass concludes his book with the words that "ancient Indian thought, in its unassimilable, non-actualizable, yet intensely meaningful distance and otherness, is *not* obsolete" (IE, p. 442).

[11] IE, p. 167; cf. also p. 442.

[12] Cf. IE, p. 286.

[13] "There was not the non-existent nor the existent then; there was not the air nor the heaven which is beyond. What did it contain? Where? In whose protection? Was there water, unfathomable, profound?"(Macdonell 1960, p. 207).

[14] P. R. Roy speaks about Indian philosophy and its scientific stance. He refers to the theory of five elements and the theory of atoms as held in the Indian tradition, comparing them to the theories of ancient Greek philosophers, e.g., Empedocles and Democritus. He, however, argues to the effect that the Greek philosophers are rather indebted to their Indian counterparts, in view of the antiquity of the Āraṇyakas and the Upaniṣads. Incidentally, Roy also strives to show how the theory of *māyā* can be scientifically explained. See Roy 1978, pp. 1-19.

[15] Cf. Dasgupta 1922, p. 326: "The four kinds of atoms are earth, water, fire and air atoms ... Ākāśa (space) is absolutely inert and structureless ... Atomic combination is only possible with the four elements. Atoms cannot exist in an uncombined condition ... Two atoms combine to form a binary molecule (*dvyaṇuka*). Two, three, four, five dvyaṇukas form themselves into grosser molecules of tryaṇuka, caturaṇuka etc." Dasgupta further refers to the view of B. N. Seal, according to whom the "atoms have also a tendency to unite" etc. (pp. 326-327).

[16] IE, p. 269.

[17] Cf. Madhusūdana Sarasvatī's *Gūḍhārthadīpikā* ch. II, pp. 48-49, 54, 56, 70, 72, in Gupta 1977.

[18] Cf. Dasgupta 1922, p. 58-59: "Emancipation thus is not a new acquisition, product, an effect, or result of any action, but it always exists as the Truth of our nature ... It is the realization of our nature that is called emancipation."

[19] Cf. Radhakrishnan 1948, p. 103.

[20] Cf. Dasgupta 1922, pp. 58-61. See also Radhakrishnan 1948, p. 170, who refers to Plato (*Phaedo*, 85): "A man should persevere till he has achieved one of two things: either he should discover the truth about them for himself or learn it from some one else; or if this is impossible he should take the best and most irrefragable of human theories and make it the raft on which he sails through life," and Plotinus (*Enneads*, VI, 9, 4): "Out of discussion we call to vision, to those desiring to see we point the path, our

teaching is a guiding in the way, the seeing must be the very act of him who has made the choice."

[21] Cf. IE, p. 167. The sort of contribution one encounters vis-à-vis the Indian tradition and philosophy has been noted in section II of this article.

[22] See Vázquez 1977, pp. 1-33.

[23] See Sen (née Mookerjee) 1992.

[24] Cf. Edwards 1972, p. 98: "One ... major change in the conception of phenomenology had occurred. ... Now Husserl distinguished sharply between the world as known to science and the world in which we live, the *Lebenswelt*. Scientific knowledge, he now believed, can be understood only if we first understand the *Lebenswelt*." See also Husserl 1981, p. 258: "Like me every human being ... has his fellow men and always counting himself, civilization in general, in which he knows himself to be living. ... Thus men as men, fellow men, world ... and ... language, are inseparably intertwined; and one is always certain of their inseparable relational unity, though usually only implicitly, in the manner of a horizon."

[25] Cf. Heidegger 1963. Also note that as being in-the-world, *Dasein*, in and through "concernful dealings," relates oneself to the given environment (*Umwelt*), viz., with entities (*Zeug*), equipments, whose equipmentality consists in its in-order-to ... Thus ultimately the notion of serviceability comes in, positing along with it the notion of work. Cf. also Sukale 1976, p. 121f.

[26] Ricoeur 1978, p. 158.

[27] One has to recall here also that what goes by the name of science the world owes, to some extent, to the ancient Indian tradition; see Roy 1978, pp. 1-19.

[28] Cf. Gadamer 1988, pp. xii-xiii: "That truth is experienced through a work of art that we cannot attain in any other way constitutes the philosophic importance of art, which asserts itself against all reasoning. Hence together with the experience of philosophy, the experience of art issues the most pressing challenge to the scientific consciousness to acknowledge its own limits."

[29] It is a fact that man looks forward to science to meet his daily needs through the latest gadgets, to achieve quick success with the help of computers and super-computers, to wield command in the field of military strategy. But how can one overlook the task of taking lessons from the two world-wars, which we believe to be now a matter of the past, as if it were a "dead past"?

[30] Cf. Russell 1966, p. 25f. Note that Russell makes interesting references, viz., to Burtt's *Metaphysical Foundations of Modern Science* (1924) and Whitehead's *Science and the Modern World* (1926).

[31] Heidegger speaks in the same vein. Europeanization "eats away all substance from things ..."; see IE, p. 169.

[32] Cf. de Crespigny 1975, p. 49f.

[33] Cf. Murray 1978, p. ix: "While technology is a mode of uncovering in its own right, its relentless drive to dominate the whole of Being, man included, poses a momentous danger to Western society. Heidegger calls this the dominating Framework (*Gestell*) of modern technology."

[34] See Heidegger 1988.

[35] See Russell 1966, pp. 69-75.

[36] The phrase "ethical orientation" does not suggest anything relating to "prescriptions." If, however, ethical or moral implications come close to the notion of "practical," that by itself does not imply the notion of "pragmatic." We recall here the name of Vivekananda and his ideal of a "practical Vedānta." See also IE, p. 241.

[37] Rabindranath Tagore pictured India as a shore, a meeting point of millions of people, coming from a great variety of cultural traditions and nationalities, for whom he then visualized mutual understanding leading to a profound fusion. See Tagore 1912.

**Klaus Karttunen**

## GREEKS AND INDIAN WISDOM

For ancient Greeks, the distant and exotic Indians were also a somewhat admirable people. They were, for varying reasons, generally held in high esteem. It is not a new idea to emphasize the importance of Alexander's campaign as a boundary line in the Greek awareness of India; this has already been pointed out by scholars such as Halbfass in *India and Europe*. Nevertheless, since the situation proper to the Hellenistic period has often been assumed to apply to the early sources, a renewed discussion of these documents may not be entirely superfluous.

The Greek concept of Oriental Wisdom stemmed originally not from ideas about India, but rather about Egypt and the Near East. In the early period the supposed source of wisdom was especially perceived to be in Egypt. It was later located to be in Mesopotamia, and was determined to be in India only with Alexander the Great. Later too were Jews and Iranians included in the idea of Oriental wisdom. It is important to note that in these cases the wisdom apprehended was always connected with tradition and philosophy, with civilization.

The concept of primitive wisdom, too, is important in the early Greek sources. It is within this context that we encounter the "vegetarians" of Herodotus and and the just Indians of Ctesias. Let us first consider Herodotus:

> There is another tribe which behaves very differently: they will not take life in any form; they sow no seed, and have no houses and live on a vegetable diet. There is a plant which grows wild in their country, and has seeds in a pod about the size of millet seeds; they gather this, and boil and eat it, pod and all. In this tribe, a sick man will leave his friends and go away to some deserted spot to die – and nobody gives a thought either to his illness or death.
>
> All the Indian tribes I have mentioned copulate in the open like cattle; their skins are all of the same colour, much like the Ethiopians'. Their semen is not white like other peoples', but black like their own skins – the same peculiarity is to be found in the Ethiopians. Their country is a long way from Persia towards

the south, and they were never subject to Darius. (*Hist.* 3, 100f., transl. A. de Sélincourt, rev. A. R. Burn)

It has been generally accepted that a specific and "real" Indian religious group served as the basis for the above description. Lassen's suggestion of Brahman forest dwellers (*vānaprastha*) (Lassen 1852, p. 635ff.) has been widely followed[1]. Charpentier (1909, p. 158) has suggested Śaiva ascetics, Rawlinson (1926, p. 22f.) Buddhist monks, and Puskás (1983, p. 205) Jainas as the models of our Herodotean account.

Studies of Greek ethnography, however, present a different interpretation of this passage. Reese (1914, p. 66f.), though still dependent on Lassen's interpretation, found the latter part of the account (3,101) difficult to combine with a religious sect and saw, using the terminology of his time, a case of "*ein schwarzes Urvolk.*" Rossellini and Saïd (1978), myself (Karttunen 1988 and 1989, p. 125), and Romm (1992) are quite doubtful regarding even this interpretation. Not commenting directly on the passage in question, Halbfass (IE, p. 11) goes only so far as to state that ideas, such as vegetarianism, later associated with Indian religion, may be found in early Greek sources.

On several occasions I have emphasized that to some extent Indian sources could be at the basis of early classical accounts (see e.g., Karttunen 1989, p. 121ff.). In this case, however, any link with Indian ascetics, be they Brahmans, Śaivas, or Jainas, seems to be so thin that it hardly deserves serious consideration. A further ground for the rejection of this claim is that the description closely parallels the Herodotean description of other distant and primitive[2] peoples. But before going into detail we must also consider Ctesias. The great justness of Indians (or of various Indian tribes) is mentioned no less than five times in the excerpt of Photius (Jacoby's F 45):

He says of Indians that they are very just, and of their customs and laws. (F 45, 16)
They (the Pygmies) are very just and follow the laws just like other Indians. (F 45, 23)
And he says much about their (Indians') justness, their devotion to their king and their contempt of death. (F 45, 30)
They (the dog-heads) are black and very just, just like other Indians, with whom they are trading. (F 45, 37)
They (the dog-heads) copulate with their women on all four like dogs, and they held it shameful to do it in another way. They are just and most long-living among all men as they live 170 years and some of them even 200. (F 45, 43)

As in the previous instance, an Indian model has been suggested, most recently by Vofchuk (1982b, p. 68ff.) and, at least to some extent, by Arora (allows some extent of idealization, but does not mention any of the close parallels; 1982, p. 481, and 1983, p. 97). Part of the idealizing approach (Romm's "inverted ethnocentrism"), however, was to attribute great justness to the primitive peoples living in the most distant parts of the Oikumene. Our best examples of the idealizing style are furnished by Herodotus, whose *Histories* are the earliest extant comprehensive ethnographic account, although parallels could be drawn even from the imperial period (Strabo and Tacitus). In the ethnographic part of Herodotus' work we find frugal life, high morality, justness and wisdom in every distant corner of the earth, often with emphasis on the opposition of these to the laxness in the central parts. The happy Hyperboreans living beyond Scythia in the far north, the Long-living Ethiopians in the south, the nomadic Massagetae in the northeast and several other distant peoples can well be put on the side of our Indians. These notions were of course not invented by Herodotus; they are found as early as the Homeric description of Scheria.

However, these peoples were not only just and wise. For the Greeks they were primitive, devoid of civilization. Most of them, not knowing agriculture, lived from the spontaneous fruits of the earth which they often did not even bother to cook. If they were not cannibals themselves, they often lived close to them. They had no fixed abodes, and while they were called wise they were also simple. Their customs and religion lacked the complexity and subtlety of those of the Greeks, their sexual practices were different. Many of their customs were clearly considered unnatural, although this verdict was occasionally tempered by the notion of ethnic relativity. And this was the case in every distant region, so that if we discard some minor details, which sometimes may well have been founded on real evidence, there is little room left for real Brahmans in the accounts of ascetic and just Indians.

A perusal of Herodotus' histories furnishes plenty of additional examples. Cannibalism (like in India in 3,99) is customary among the Massagetae (1,216), the Issedones (4,26), and a Scythian tribe (4,106), vegetarianism among a Libyan tribe (4,184). Agriculture seems to be unknown among the Ethiopians (3,22), the Massagetae, who do not sow (1,216; like Indians in 3,100), the Scythians, who do not till the land (4,2; 4,46), and among a part of the Libyans (e.g., 4,191). Simple religion and customs are emphasized in the case of Persians (1,131f.),

Scythians (4,59ff.), and Libyans (4,184; 4,188). Sex is had in public in Caucasia (1,203; like in India in 3,101),[3] and more or less promiscuously among the Massagetae (1,216) and the Nasamones (4,172) and other Libyan tribes (4,176; 4,180). Like Indians in Ctesias, the Ethiopians are long-living and just (3,21ff.), and exceptional health is ascribed to Libyans (4,187), great justness to the cannibal Issedones (4,26). All these peoples are found living in the middle of various miracles of nature, e.g., in Ethiopia (3,18; 3,23), in Arabia (3,107ff.), in the far north (3,116; 4,13; 4,23ff.), and in Libya (4,168ff., especially 4,191f.).

As was stated previously, Alexander's campaigns radically changed the Greek conception of India. The components of the early ethnographic conception were not dismissed. Ancient ethnography was, to a great extent, entertainment, and the stories about just Indians and Indian marvels never lost their popularity.[4] But now there was much more to tell. Real Indian ascetics were met in Taxila; Onesicritus apparently conversed with them, and soon they became famous. Later these ascetics were given the name Gymnosophists, the naked philosophers. In the Hellenistic and Roman periods they, or more generally the Indian Brahmans described in Alexander histories and by Megasthenes, were seen to represent the paragon of Indian wisdom, a wisdom which was itself a new kind. The Brahmans were now freely given the status of philosophers who used intellectual arguments and who had attained their admired saintliness by deliberate choice but whose frugal way of life was even more admired. Rather little was said, or known, of their philosophy.

It has been pointed out, however, that Onesicritus' account of the exposition of their doctrine that he claimed to have obtained through interpreters in Taxila curiously resembles the teachings of his own master, the Cynic Diogenes (Brown 1949, p. 38ff.). And that it probably was. The naked ascetics were real and probably they even gave an account of their tenets, but what they said was first interpreted by the interpreters, and then even twice more by Onesicritus, intellectually to himself as he heard the translation, and again for the benefit of his readers when he was writing his book. Furthermore, he is known to have related in his book much material that he thought might be interesting and entertaining, if not strictly exact to truth.

This new conception of Indian wisdom, too, was thus to a great extent a Greek phenomenon. There was a demand for Indian sages, and their wisdom was provided according to this demand on the basis of real contact which was, however, freely interpreted. The intellectual barriers between the two civilizations were too high, and the Greeks were not able to overcome them to gain an accurate understanding of Indian thinking.

The campaigns of Alexander were considered to be a major turning point by Greeks themselves, and in their wake literature on Alexander became very popular. What was told of Indian philosophy, veritable or not, much agreed with the ideas within the then fashionable schools of thought of the Cynics and the Sceptics, and later of the Stoics. To a great extent the Western tradition of Indian philosophy was kept alive and popular by the Cynics and Stoics. The ascetic Gymnosophists became a model for true philosophic life, and as such remained known even in the Middle Ages. But this depiction is something entirely different from the old ethnographic view of Indians as keepers of primitive wisdom and righteousness.

*University of Helsinki*
*Department of Asian and African Studies*
*Helsinki, Finland*

## NOTES

[1] Rawlinson 1862, p. 407; How and Wells 1964, p. 288; Vofchuk 1982a, p. 93ff.

[2] The term primitive is here used to describe the way the Greeks, with their well-known sense of their own superiority, considered them.

[3] It is curious to note that in F 27 B Jacoby Megasthenes mentions public sex and cannibalism in the Caucasus, though here the Indian Caucasus (the Hindukush) might be meant. Cannibalism – of old people as often found in Herodotus – and vegetarianism are later met in Strabo's account (4,5,5) of Ireland, another corner of the Oikumene.

[4] It is interesting to see that in a rather late – and markedly entertaining – form of literature on Alexander, viz. in the Alexander Romance and especially in Alexander's Letter to Aristoteles, the early ethnography has again achieved a more central position. See Gunderson 1980 and Romm 1992, p. 109ff.

**Dermot Killingley**

# *MLECCHAS*, YAVANAS AND HEATHENS: INTERACTING XENOLOGIES IN EARLY NINETEENTH-CENTURY CALCUTTA[1]

> Electricity and steam-power are placing the different parts of the world in inter-communication with each other, and, as a result, we Hindus no longer say that every country beyond our own land is peopled with demons and hobgoblins, nor do the people of Christian countries say that India is only peopled by cannibals and savages.
>
> Vivekananda (1984, p. 240)

Any cultural tradition has a view of those outside it, which is closely related to its view of itself. The outsider may be regarded indiscriminately as inferior, hostile or dangerous, or may be differentiated into dangerous and beneficent categories. A culture's view of the outsider is an important variable to which Wilhelm Halbfass, in his study of the encounter between India and Europe, has given the name xenology (IE, p. 173). While xenology may recognise different classes of foreigners and may regard them favourably or unfavourably, it is always ethnocentric in that it regards them all primarily as foreigners. Indeed, it is by regarding them as foreigners that it is able to treat them as objects to be differentiated.

Halbfass's book raises many important issues about Indian thought, the reception of it by European intellectuals, and the ways in which Indian thinkers in the nineteenth and twentieth centuries have adapted traditional ideas. This paper is a response to one of these issues, and is much indebted to Halbfass's treatment of the subject. It attempts to sketch the various currents of xenological thought which met in early nineteenth-century Calcutta, and to examine their interplay in the debates surrounding Rammohun Roy.

## Xenology in the Sanskrit Tradition

From the time of the *Ṛgveda*, the Āryans defined themselves in opposition to outsiders, whom they referred to as *anārya*, *dāsa* or *dasyu*. The picture is complicated by the inclusion of a non-Āryan class within the society dominated by the Āryans, reflecting the subjugation of a non-Āryan people. It is in a verse of one of the later hymns within the oldest collection of hymns (in *ṚV* X.90.12) that we first find the subjugated people given the general name *śūdra*, which is frequent in later literature. In that verse, the *śūdra* is treated as part of the same social body as the Āryans, the body being represented as a man and the *śūdra* as his feet (cf. Killingley 1991, p. 11). There are thus two kinds of non-Āryan: one, the *śūdra*, who is regarded as servile, and another who is regarded as hostile. From the time of the Brāhmaṇas onwards, the word *mleccha* gradually becomes the preferred term for these enemies of the Āryans.

A myth in the *Śatapathabrāhmaṇa* allies the *mlecchas* with the *asuras*, the enemies of the gods. This myth is one of many episodes in the perennial struggle between the gods (*deva*) and the demons (*asura*), in which the gods defeat the demons through their knowledge of ritual. In this case they do so by appropriating *Vāc* ("speech"), which represents not language in general but the language used in ritual, which later came to be known as Sanskrit. The demons were left with the language of the *mlecchas*. A brahmin therefore should not speak the language of the *mlecchas* (*Śatapathabrāhmaṇa* 3.2.1.24). This myth sets a pattern which is followed in later uses of the word *mleccha*: the *mleccha* is defined in terms of language, is excluded from Āryan ritual, and represents that which must be avoided in order to be a true Āryan.

The self-identification of brahminical writers is closely linked to the idea of *dharma*. *dharma* is "the framework and context in which the Aryan is an Aryan, and from which the *mleccha* is by definition excluded" (IE, p. 320). In a well-known passage on the general theory of *dharma*, the Veda is said to be the ultimate source of *dharma*, and the tradition and customs of those who know the Veda (*smṛtiśīle ca tadvidām*) are said to be a secondary source - to be used, it is understood, where our knowledge of the Veda is deficient, it being unthinkable that the Veda itself should be deficient. The third source is the practice of the good (*ācāraś caiva sādhūnām*), and the last is one's own satisfaction - to be appealed to when reference to the previous authorities still leaves a choice (*Manu* 2.6). While these four sources are mentioned in descending order of authority, the most effective ones, and the ones relied on most by the *Manusmṛti*, are the second and third. This necessitates a definition of who are the knowers of the Veda. Knowledge of the Veda is restricted to the three twice-born *varṇas* (i.e., the brahmins, *kṣatriyas* and *vaiśyas*), the *śūdra* being explicitly excluded from it (*Manu* 4.99; cf. 3.156; 10.127). It also necessitates a definition of the people referred to as the good, and this is provided not in terms of behaviour, but in terms of birth and geography. The land between the rivers Sarasvatī and Dṛṣadvatī (to the south-east of the Sutlej) is called Brahmāvarta (the territory of Brahman or the holy land), and its customs are identified as the practice of the good (*Manu* 2.16f.). The following verses, perhaps reflecting a later stage in the expansion of Āryan hegemony, say that the authority for the behaviour of all people on earth is a brahmin born in a region ranking next to Brahmāvarta, named as Brahmarṣideśa (the country of the divine sages), and defined as the country of the Kurus, Matsyas, Pañcālas and Śūrasenas (*Manu* 2.19f.). This indicates a territory including the country of the rivers Ganges and Jumna, roughly from Delhi to Mathura, and extending westwards to around Ajmer in Rajasthan.

As a corollary to this geographical location of the people who are authorities on *dharma*, the *Manusmṛti* (2.23) designates the area which is the natural habitat of the black antelope as suitable for Vedic ritual, and the land outside it as *mleccha* country. It is not clear what area this refers to. However, the preceding verse (*Manu* 2.22) defines Āryāvarta, "the territory of the Āryans," as the land bounded by the Himālayas, the Vindhyas, and the eastern and western oceans - that is, the Indo-Gangetic plain as opposed to peninsular India, and including the previously-mentioned Brahmāvarta and Brahmarṣideśa. The passage ends with a general statement that the twice-born should live in the territories mentioned. The *Manusmṛti* therefore reflects an ancient view, or is compiled from verses reflecting several views, that some part of northern India is the proper place for Āryans to live. Although the area in which the twice-born - which in effect usually means brahmins - may live has since been extended to include peninsular India, the same principle of avoiding migration to foreign countries is embodied in the prohibition against sea travel which prevailed in the nineteenth century. The attitude to foreigners authorized by the *dharma* literature is therefore one of avoidance.

This is not to say that Indians did not voyage to foreign countries; they settled in several parts of South-East Asia (Coedès 1948), or brought back reports of them, even though the accounts which appear in the Purāṇas (especially *Vāyupurāṇa*, ch. 48) and in the *kathā* literature are too fantastic to have been of much use to the ancient navigator, and present puzzles to the modern historical geographer (Wheatley 1961). The people who went to South-East Asia included brahmins, and traces of brahminical culture can still be seen there, especially in the languages of the region, in literature, notably in the many versions of the Rāma story, in ritual, and even in the community of brahmins which conducts royal rituals in Thailand. South-East Asian kings sought to legitimate their status through brahminical rituals, initiating a process of sanskritization similar to that which occurred in India itself.

The brahmins who lived in South-East Asia and performed rituals there appear to be in breach of *Manu* 2.23f., which restricts the twice-born and their rituals to northern India; but then, so do the brahmins of peninsular India. The ninth-century commentator Medhātithi resolves the apparent conflict between the text and current practice by explaining that any territory can become suitable for Vedic rituals if a righteous king conquers the *mlecchas* and establishes the system of four *varṇas* there (IE, p. 178). Medhātithi does not say whether the king who establishes such an outpost of Āryāvarta may himself be of *mleccha* origin. However, it is reasonable to think that he may, since it is generally recognized that in the Kali age all kings are non-Āryan, even in Āryāvarta. Nor does Medhāthiti state that such a country becomes Āryāvarta, but he gives it an equivalent status. This status is similar to that of *dār al-islām* in Islamic legal theory: a land in which Islamic law is protected.

There is thus some differentiation in the brahminical view of foreigners. Such differentiation is found already in the *Manusmṛti*, where certain peoples are said to be nations (*jāti*) of *kṣatriyas* who have neglected ritual and disregarded the brahmins, and have therefore sunk to the position of *śūdras* (*Manu* 10.43f.). These include Draviḍas (Tamils), Yavanas (Greeks), Śakas (Scythians), Pahlavas (Parthians) and Cīnas (Chinese); the text must have been composed at a time when these peoples were known in India, and when Tamil Nādu was still regarded as foreign, as it is in the passage on the geography of *dharma* referred to above. The inclusion of these peoples as fallen *kṣatriyas* expresses a recognition of the power which they held in neighbouring regions or in India itself, and also an aspiration that they may be restored to the position of *kṣatriyas* and so become patrons of Vedic ritual and of brahminical learning. Indeed, according to the myth of the struggle between the brahmin Vasiṣṭha and the *kṣatriya* sage Viśvāmitra, these powerful peoples were created by Vasiṣṭha expressly to protect his wish-granting cow - a symbol of brahminical values - from his rival.[2] The fallen *kṣatriya* is also a potential *kṣatriya*, who can become an actual *kṣatriya* by accepting the brahminical norms which were abandoned by his ancestors. Since many men of non-*kṣatriya* origin did in fact found dynasties which patronized brahmins and took part in brahminical rituals, the passage may be a legitimation of this practice. There is an interesting parallel here with the early twentieth-century Śuddhi ("purification") movement, in which the Ārya Samāj converted Muslims to its own form of Hinduism through a purificatory ritual. The theory which legitimated this movement was that these Muslims were descendents of Hindus, and were being restored to the position of their ancestors. This appeal to the hereditary principle is no less interesting for being unnecessary according to the teachings of Dayānanda, the founder of the Ārya Samāj: he held that status should depend on quality, not birth, and that all humankind were originally Āryas.

Among these terms for foreigners who are regarded as fallen *kṣatriyas* and thus as more than ordinary *mlecchas*, *yavana* has a complex history. It is derived, through an Iranian language, from the name of the eastern Greeks, the Ionians, and was extended to refer to Greeks in general. In the Pali story of the dialogue of the Buddhist monk Nāgasena and the Indo-Greek king Menander, the *Questions of Milinda* (*Milindapañha*), it refers to the Indo-Greeks who ruled in North-West India in the second century BCE, and it is these Yavanas who are referred to in the *Manusmṛti*. The *Milindapañha* represents the king not as a representative of Greek culture, but as a patron of brahmins. He thus fulfils the role of the *kṣatriya* which, as we have seen, was proper to rulers of foreign origin. But later, the term *yavana* is especially associated with the sciences of the Greeks, particularly mathematics and astronomy.

While *mleccha* is a generic term for all outsiders, or all who do not have a particular claim to respect, *yavana* is used as a specific term for specific peoples, though not always for the same people. In the eighteenth and nineteenth centuries it referred most often to the Muslims, who had replaced the Greeks as invaders from the West who brought with them a wide range of practical skills as well as a literary and scientific culture. In the nineteenth century it could also refer to another such nation of invaders, the British. The use of the term *yavana* to denote different peoples in different periods is an example of a tendency in the Sanskrit tradition to use existing terms rather than introduce new ones, and to see new knowledge through the framework of earlier concepts.[3] This tendency helps to maintain the view that all knowledge is to be found in the Veda. Change is accounted for by making it inherent in the source, so that the tradition appears impervious to outside influence. We can see this in the use of the ancient caste-name *caṇḍāla* for castes which were not known when the use of this name in Sanskrit was first established. But the practice of fitting new knowledge into old conceptual frames is not unique to the Sanskrit tradition; in the field of xenology, we find it in the use of the names "Indies" and "Indian" in English, which we shall discuss in the next section.

## Xenology in the European tradition

"Indies" and "Indian" were applied to newly-discovered lands and peoples in South-East Asia and the Americas, in addition to their older use with reference to South Asia. The reason for giving them these names (and corresponding words in other European languages) is usually said to be that they were discovered by European navigators in the course of their search for new routes to India, and at first mistaken by them for India itself.[4] But there is also a symbolic appropriateness in the names. The newly-found Indies and Indians were placed in the same category as India and its inhabitants because they were perceived as potential objects of mercantile or colonial exploitation, this perception being an important part of European xenology. In Britain, knowledge of India and attitudes to it were closely connected with the activities of the East India Company, founded in 1600. But during the late eighteenth and early nineteenth centuries the Company was transformed, in a gradual and sometimes haphazard way, from a trading company to a colonial government, and this change affected the way in which the British viewed Indians.

So long as the British operated in India by the permission of Indian powers, they were not averse to showing deference to Indian rulers when their client position required it, although they "thought of Mohammedans as profligate and of Hindus as superstitious, and of both as quite incomprehensible" (Spear 1963, p. 128). As the Company's status and role changed, the number of British in India increased, and so did their functions, their reasons for choosing an Indian career, and their backgrounds: men came to India as soldiers, as administrators, as traders, and later as teachers, without necessarily having any previous contact with the country. "The result was to set in motion a double current, of increasing contact and knowledge of Indian life, and of increasing contempt of everything Indian as irrational, superstitious, barbaric and typical of an inferior civilization" (Spear 1963, p. 129). Among the examples whom Spear mentions are two who came to India as lawyers, and were also distinguished men of letters. Sir William Jones came as a judge in 1783, imbued with Enlightenment ideas about Indian culture, and eager to see it at first hand. He drew up a list of topics for research on Indian culture on the voyage out (Mukherjee 1968, p. 74), and in January 1784, within four months of his arrival, he founded the Asiatic Society of Bengal. On the other hand Thomas Babington Macaulay, who came to Calcutta in 1834 to take up the newly-established post of Law-Member of the legislative council, expressed complete contempt for Asian culture, and while others read Sanskrit with pandits before breakfast, he read ancient Greek for pleasure at a prodigious rate. The difference does not result from the interval of half a century between them, so much as from the choice of attitudes and pursuits which were available to a scholarly Briton in Calcutta.

"What's that black man doing here?" is the reported remark of a former officer of the Indian army on finding Rammohun Roy in an English drawing-room. "Black," as a term for Indians, went out of favour in the course of the nineteenth century;[5] but in the eighteenth century it was regularly used, as shown by the term "Black Town" discussed below. "Black," in British xenological discourse of the eighteenth and nineteenth centuries, implies more than simply ethnic identity. The people referred to as "blacks" are regarded as naturally subordinate, and as potential if not actual slaves.[6] This view was backed by what at the time was respectable scientific evidence. Linnaeus regarded African blacks (whom he classified as Afer niger, one of four human varieties) as natural slaves (Poliakov 1974, p. 161). The French zoologist Georges-Louis Buffon regarded their black colour as a mark of degeneracy.

Although Indians were popularly referred to as "blacks," they were placed in a different category from Africans. The speculations of the eighteenth century on the differences of races said much about Africans (especially Hottentots) and Laplanders, but little about Indians. On the other hand, India became the centre of attention for those who sought to construct an account of the origin of culture, religion and language, and sometimes of humanity itself, either discarding the Biblical story of Eden, the Flood, and the Tower of Babel, or transforming it to fit new ideas. Linnaeus' theory of the origin of all life on a mountain which gradually emerged from the water, a rationalized version of the story of the Ark on Mount Ararat (Poliakov 1974, p. 184), led such thinkers to look to mountainous regions of Asia: first the Caucasus, and then the Himalayas. In time India became "the birthplace of all races and of religions, *the womb of the world*."[7]

Theories of the origin of life may seem to us to have little to do with theories of the origin of political, literary and philosophical culture, because we are used to the idea that such cultural features evolved slowly long after the appearance of *homo sapiens*. But the eighteenth-century thinkers had not got rid of the idea that wisdom is learnt from the ancients (though this idea had been ridiculed by Bacon and others), and readily supposed that the most ancient race was also the wisest. The highly influential writers Zephaniah Holwell and Alexander Dow presented India as the home of a rational, deistic religion which had since become degenerate; and this idea was taken up by continental deists who were anxious to demote ancient Israel from its position as the origin of monotheism. Voltaire's *Essai sur les moeurs et l'esprit des nations* exalted India as the source of religion in its original, rational form (IE, p. 56f.). On the other hand, he treated Negroes as a different race from whites, sprung from a different origin, and far inferior; he also put the notion that they are naturally servile to practical effect by investing profitably in the slave trade.[8] Johann Gottfried Herder presented India as the birthplace of civilization, making use of Linnaeus' theory of the mountain of creation as well as Dow and Holwell (Poliakov 1974, p. 186f.; IE, pp. 69-72).

The set of assumptions associated with the word "black" conflicts with another trend in British xenology: the belief in the unity of humankind, which was held by many, though not all, Enlightenment thinkers. This belief was consistent with the Biblical account in which all humankind originated from Adam and Eve, and that all inherited the effects of the Fall. Belief in the inferiority of blacks could be squared with the Biblical account either through the old theory of a pre-Adamite people (Poliakov 1974, pp. 131-134) or else by reference to Noah's curse in *Genesis* 9.25-27 (which was actually directed against Ham's son Canaan, but was often associated with the name of Ham, and in turn with Africans).

Those who regarded blacks as inherently different from Europeans, either because they were of a different origin or because their ancestors had degenerated, were generally secular thinkers. The contrary belief was summed up in the anti-slavery slogan "Am I not a man and a brother?". This slogan, with its accompanying picture of a black man, does not remove the foreignness of the black, but it at least transforms him (or her) from a potential slave to a potential object of philanthropic endeav-our. It also makes him or her a potential object of missionary endeavour; anti-slavery was linked in England with Evangelicalism.

From the Evangelical point of view, humankind is divided into Christians and heathens. But this division is complicated by the long-established use of the word "Christian" to mean "decent, normal, human, fit for human beings."[9] We may also note a tendency to use the same names as both ethnic and religious labels. The names "Moor" and "Turk," which referred originally to ethnic groups in North-West Africa and Asia Minor respectively, were both used to refer to Muslims in general.[10] "Hindu," in origin a geographical name, was similarly used both as an ethnic name (which could be used in the collocation "Hindu Christian") and in phrases like "the Hindu system of religion," and, from the early nineteenth century, in the new and increasingly used word "Hinduism." "Gentoo," from Portuguese *gentio* "gentile; heathen," was used in India both in the same sense as "Hindu," and with reference to the Telugu people and their language (Yule and Burnell 1903, p. 367).

The sudden increase in missionary activity in Britain at the end of the eighteenth century was promoted by the rise of Evangelicalism as a movement affecting Anglicans as well as Dissenters, and by the decline of Calvinism among the Baptists. It contradicted the Enlightenment attempt to displace the Bible as a unique revelation, and the ideas of Herder and others that the Indians possessed a superior culture that had no need of help from Europe. The missionary enterprise also implied a denial that Indians were inherently inferior; they appeared so only as a result of circumstances. As the Evangelical spokesman Charles Grant put it, "The Hindus err, because they are ignorant; and their errors have never been fully laid before them."[11] It thus rejected both the theology of Calvinism, in which depravity could not be remedied by human effort, and the secular belief that some races were incapable of cultural improvement.

Yet another way in which Europeans regarded foreigners was as potential critics of European culture. The exotic civilizations which were variously held up by different Enlightenment writers as examples, such as the Chinese, the Amerindians and the Polynesians (Hampson 1968, p. 153) were based on travellers' reports interpreted through the assumptions of those who used them, and were thus in effect fictitious. Some, indeed, were overtly fictitious. A stock motif in the fiction of the period is the foreign visitor who observes European society, or the European traveller's encounter with a foreigner who presents a novel response to the European's account of his own culture; the modern equivalent is the man from Mars. Montesquieu's *Lettres Persanes* (1721) uses two Persians in Paris as mouthpieces for the author's views on government and on universal human nature (Hampson 1968, pp. 110-112). Swift's *Gulliver's Travels* (1726) is another and more obviously fictitious example. These encounters with fictitious foreigners express the realization that European culture is no longer to be considered the only or the central culture. The existence of other cultures, and especially of the undoubtedly ancient and reputedly highly orderly and rational culture of China, was disturbing to European assumptions (Hampson 1968, pp. 25-27).

## Calcutta

Early nineteenth-century Calcutta is a particularly fruitful field in which to study the interaction of Western and Indian xenologies. Calcutta was a city of foreigners: a xenopolis. Several groups of its inhabitants came from different parts of North India: Khattri and Agarwal traders from the upper Ganges basin and the Punjab, Marwari bankers from Rajasthan, Parsi and other traders from Gujarat. These made Calcutta into a node in the network of trading settlements which stretched across northern India (Marshall 1987, p. 15). Others came as migrant workers: Bhojpuris from Behar in the west as domestic servants, and Oriyas from Orissa in the south as domestic servants and palanquin-bearers (Sinha 1978, pp. 33-61, 249-264). Besides these, there were Jewish, Armenian, Greek, Persian and Arab traders from the west, Burmese cooks and Chinese shoemakers from the east, and the complex, internally stratified class known collectively as East Indians or Eurasians, or in the eighteenth century as *Callah Feringhee* (Urdu *kālā farangī*) - "black Europeans" (Sinha 1978, p. 44f.). These were partly descendants of Portuguese settlers, but included also "men and women who ceased to be considered as Hindoos and Muhammedans because they live amongst Christians and eat and drink as they do and the women kept as concubines by Englishmen of which there are many." Ethnic identity in this case, as often, was a matter of culture rather than of descent, and the cultural criterion was in some cases a negative one: some of this class "are called Christian mainly because they are made to eat all kinds of meat and to do such kind of business as neither Muhammedans nor Hindoos will do."[12] While this class included domestic servants, its preferred occupation was clerical (Sinha 1978, p. 47).

The original inhabitants of Calcutta, who lived mainly by agriculture and fishing, were marginalized and pushed out in the course of the eighteenth century by the growth of the xenopolis (Sinha 1978, p. 33). The Bengali Hindus, who were a little over half the inhabitants of Calcutta,[13] were themselves incomers, starting in the sixteenth century with the Setts and Basaks, who were pious Vaiṣṇavas. They, and those who followed them, were meticulous in caste practices and lavish in patronage (Killingley 1993, pp. 27-29), none more so than the legendary financier and patron Nabakrishna Deb of Sobhabazar.

The British in Calcutta numbered three thousand or more. While "British" is the term commonly used today, they commonly referred to themselves as the English. But their view of themselves as English depended not on any positive notion of English identity, so much as on their shared consciousness of not being natives. There was a high proportion of Scots, Irish, Huguenot and Dutch names among them, and it was perhaps to avoid the discrepancy between this fact and their self-identification as English that they also referred to themselves as Europeans. They included the Company's servants, military men of all ranks, independent merchants (whom the Company regarded as interlopers), teachers, clergy, tradesmen and artisans; the lower classes among them tended to live in the intermediate town and to merge with the East Indians. The British, like the Bengali Hindus, had access to a long literary, cultural and religious tradition, and tended to legitimate themselves by reference to that tradition. By reference to its own tradition, each of these two groups considered itself superior to the other, but at the same time they collaborated with each other closely.

The term "black" was applied to all Indians by the British in Calcutta, who saw the city (as also Bombay and Madras) as divided between the "White Town" or "European Town" which they inhabited and the "Black Town" (Sinha 1978, p. xvii). This division was only partly a geographical one; it was also a conceptual one which simplified the geographical facts. Between the "White Town" and the "Black Town" was the part inhabited by the Portuguese Eurasians, Greeks, Armenians and others, which has been termed the "grey town" or "intermediate town" (Sinha 1978, pp. 7f.; 12). Moreover, the European Town itself was interspersed with bustees inhabited by the milkmen, washermen, domestic servants and others who served it. "The phenomenon of dualism, in its origin derived from the pre-colonial trading settlement pattern, reflected the concern of the Europeans with defence and security, manifested in the fort and the fence, and the concern of the 'natives' about maintaining their own mode of social and economic organisation" (Sinha 1978, p. 7). In the nineteenth century the separation was for social rather than strategic reasons, and it was also part of a conceptual dualism which went beyond geography. To the British in India it was a dualism not of two entities of equal status, but of self and other, the European Town being regarded not only as the rightful place of the British, but as the locus of the identity of Calcutta itself; for their lyrical descriptions of Calcutta as a city of palaces refer to the European Town, silently excluding the Black Town.

## Rammohun Roy

From 1815 to 1830, Rammohun Roy was one of the best-known inhabitants of the xenopolis. He bought two houses in 1814, one in Simla (Similiyā) in the northern part of the town, a quarter inhabited by wealthy Bengali Hindus, and one in Chowringhee, where the European Town and the intermediate town meet. Some time later he built a garden-house at Maniktala and furnished it in European style (Biswas and Ganguli 1962, p. 96f.). In this house he received European as well as Indian visitors with lavish hospitality. The mutual avoidance which characterized the social geography of Calcutta does not seem to have prevented him from forming cordial social relations with Europeans, although he seems to have avoided eating with them. Together with other prominent Hindu residents of Calcutta, he cooperated with Europeans in public ventures such as the Calcutta School Book Society and the Calcutta School Society. He also collaborated with the Sanskritist Horace Hayman Wilson in research on the date of Śaṅkara. The two letters on this subject from Rammohun to Wilson which survive, together with Wilson's mention of Rammohun's work in the preface to his dictionary, show a relationship of friendly respect (Wilson 1819, p. xvif.; Biswas

1973; Killingley 1978, p. 96). He was not, however, a member of the Asiatic Society founded by Sir William Jones. This society had no Indian members until 1829, when five Bengalis, including two of Rammohun's associates, Prasanna Kumar Thakur and Dwarkanath Thakur, were elected to membership. The absence of Indian members was not a matter of principle; Jones himself had suggested the possibility of "learned natives" as members. But it seems that until 1829 no Indians had applied – the wealthy being insufficiently scholarly, and the pandits being too conscious of their subordinate position (Kejariwal 1988, p. 152f.).[14]

Contact with Europeans was not unusual in Calcutta, both at work and in social life. With the decline of traditional sources of patronage, many pandits had taken employment in the law-courts, in Fort William College, which trained the East India Company's British recruits, in missionary establishments and as private teachers. Such contact had a different significance for Rammohun from other prominent Bengali Hindus. For them, with their insistence on rules of purity, it was a polluting contact, requiring a bath before they could eat (Chatterji 1972, p. 19; Killingley 1993, p. 28). In his controversies with Hindu opponents, Rammohun was able to point out the inconsistency between his opponents' claim to orthodoxy and their eagerness to collaborate with Europeans. In his earliest Bengali publication, he asks:

> What ancient *dharma* allows brahmins to become servants of Yavanas or the like, to study Yavana sciences, and teach Yavanas? (*RG* 1, p. 5; Killingley 1982, p. 10)

Several of the pandits who wrote attacks on his work did in fact work for Europeans. He points out various ways in which they expose themselves to pollution by doing so.

> What *śāstra*, or what ancient tradition, tells them to teach the English, whom they call *mlecchas*? What *śāstra* tells them to touch paper, which is really the Yavanas' food, and write books on it, or what tradition authorizes it? In what ancient tradition do we find that they should eagerly take in their hands letters fastened with wafers moistened with the spittle of Englishmen? And what ancient tradition authorizes them to invite the people they call *mlecchas* to *pūjās* of the gods in their houses? (*RG* 1, p. 200f.)

This satirical passage makes use of some fundamental assumptions about *dharma*. The authorities for *dharma* are, as we have seen, the ancient texts and respected customs; any behaviour not authorized by these is reprehensible. Letters that have been sealed by licking, in the European manner, are polluting; Rammohun's Bengali phrase means literally "letters fastened with wafers that are moist by being made into the Englishmen's left-over food." The same idea that left-over food is polluting is probably referred to in the previous sentence, together with a satirical implication that the English bureaucrats nourish themselves with paper. The English are referred to both as *mlecchas* and as Yavanas.

The accusation of contact with Yavanas, or of acceptance of Yavana influence, was frequently leveled against Rammohun and his associates. The opponent referred to as the Poet (*kabitākār*) accused him of going to receptions dressed as a Yavana, which in this case must mean a Muslim, since Rammohun frequently dressed in Mughal style. He answers:

> Though it is shameful to answer such petty remarks ... I shall do so. Firstly, *dharma* and *adharma* are entirely activities of the mind; what have they to do with dress or the like? Secondly, if tailored clothes are Yavana dress, I ask whether the Poet and his relations, and many idolaters, go to receptions dressed in tailored clothes. If the Poet says that it is not wrong for brahmins who worship idols to wear tailored clothes, but that it is wrong for worshippers of God, or that it is right at this time of day but not at that time of day, I shall certainly investigate the matter when he cites his authority for it. (*RG* 2, p. 75f.)

Here, Rammohun is making several points. Firstly, that dress is irrelevant to *dharma*. Secondly, that tailored clothes (*śilpavastra*) are not peculiar to Muslims, since they are also worn by Hindus on formal occasions instead of their traditional simple unsewn dress of upper and lower cloth. Thirdly, that any rules on the matter should be authorized by the literature of *dharma*. But the main thrust of the argument is that he is not alone in choosing a non-traditional style of dress, and that this choice has nothing to do with his religion. He thus rejects the assumption that *dharma* depends on avoidance of the foreign (further Killingley 1993, p. 66f.).

But Rammohun goes further: he claims that Hindus can learn from foreigners, not only in fields in which they had clearly done so, such as mathematics and astronomy, but in the worship of the one true Brahman. The main theme of his works on religion is that monotheism is "real Hindooism, as that religion was practised by our ancestors, and as it is well-known even at the present age to many learned brahmans" (*EW*, p. 90). But an important secondary theme is that this monotheism is also to be found in other cultures. Among the objections to monotheism which he discusses in his first Bengali work, is that it is a novel doctrine which is taught only by one or two people. In the course of his answer, he claims that it has ancient authority within the Sanskrit tradition in the *Vedāntasūtras* and in Śaṅkara. He also points to monotheistic sects using vernacular languages, such as the followers of Nānak and Dādū. But first, he points to monotheism outside India, suggesting that it is foolish to base one's ideas on those current in one's own country:

> Hindustan is not so much as one twentieth of the world whose boundaries we have ascertained and over which we travel ... Outside Hindustan, the people of more than half the world worship one pure supreme God.

He concludes:

> If the people of this country [Bengal] would enquire and travel, they would never believe those allegations that this doctrine is different from that of the whole world and of all pandits. (*RG* 1, p. 11; Killingley 1982, p. 13; cf. *RG* 2, p. 72)

In the same book he writes:

> To hold an opinion merely on the grounds that it is the opinion of one's own people, is to behave like animals, which always imitate the actions of their own kind. (*RG* 1, p. 5; Killingley 1982, p. 9)

Although Rammohun based his religious teaching largely on Sanskrit texts, his view of the foreigner was that of the Enlightenment rather than that of the brahminical tradition. The value which he put on travel is clear from the opening of his first work, the *Tuhfat al-Muwaḥḥidīn*:

> I travelled in the remotest places of the world, in plains as well as in hilly lands, and found the inhabitants thereof agreeing generally in believing in one being who is the source and governor of all that exists, and disagreeing in giving peculiar attributes to that Being. (*EW*, p. 943)

It also appears in his own voyage to England, and in his protest to the French ambassador Talleyrand at restrictions on travel:

> Enlightened men in all countries must feel a wish to encourage and facilitate human intercourse in every manner. (Biswas and Ganguli 1962, p. 502)

He also used the literary device of the fictitious foreigner, though not in a critique of Bengali culture but of Christianity. In his *Dialogue between a Missionary and Three Chinese Converts* of 1823, he uses the three fictitious converts as representatives of a rational culture to whom the doctrine of the Trinity is absurd. He makes the same point in the fourth number of his *Brahmunical Magazine*, and though there he writes in the name of an actual Hindu pandit, Śivaprasād Śarmā, the knowledge of Christian theology which he attributes to him makes him almost a fictitious figure.[15]

To his Christian critics, Rammohun appeared either as a deist or as a heathen. The term "deist" may have been suggested partly by the notion that had been current since Dow and Holwell, that the ancient Indian religion was deism. Already in 1807, the Baptist missionary William Carey wrote that "India swarms with deists" (Kopf 1969, p. 139). This was before Rammohun was known to Carey or had written in English; so the word could not have reference to Rammohun's followers as it later did. Carey was unlikely to have come across any Hindu who could readily be called a deist, so he may either have been influenced by the above notion, or have been referring not to Hindus but to Europeans.

The term "Heathen" was applied to Rammohun by the Baptist missionary Joshua Marshman, in his critique of Rammohun's compilation *The Precepts of Jesus*. Rammohun immediately objected, arguing that as a believer in one God he could not be so described. But Marshman replied that an Indian is either a Christian, a Heathen or a Mussulman, and "no one can be a real Christian without believing the Divinity and Atonement of Jesus Christ" (Marshman 1822, p. 6; Killingley 1993, p. 143). Marshman's use of the term was both xenological and theological.

The attitudes to foreigners which were available in early nineteenth-century Calcutta were varied, being based on the brahminical tradition, the attitudes developed within the East India Company's service, the scholarship of those who formed the Asiatic Society, the philosophy of the Enlightenment, and Evangelicalism. To some extent it was possible to choose between these attitudes, or to combine them. Evangelical aversion to heathen ideas did not prevent Carey from devoting himself to Sanskrit studies (Kopf 1969, p. 80), any more than it prevented Macaulay from devouring the Greek classics. Attitudes of mutual avoidance coexisted with cooperation and mutual dependence.

*University of Newcastle upon Tyne*
*Department of Religious Studies*
*Newcastle upon Tyne, England*

## NOTES

[1] This paper was first presented at the annual seminar on the Sanskrit Tradition in the Modern World, Newcastle upon Tyne, 1994. I am grateful to participants at the seminar for discussing the paper and making valuable suggestions.

[2] The story appears in *R* 1.31-64, and *MBh* 1.165; I am grateful to Dr John Brockington for these references. Both passages use the term *mleccha* itself as an item in the list of peoples; but the peoples who are regarded as fallen *kṣatriyas* are usually distinguished from *mlecchas* in general.

[3] See further Killingley 1991, p. 13f.

[4] The use of the words "discover" and "discovery" has often been criticized as Eurocentric, especially when Columbus' voyage was commemorated in 1992. However, if we remember that they are relative terms, referring to the acquisition of knowledge by a particular group of people, we do not need be worried by the fact that the same knowledge was already possessed by other groups.

[5] "Old-fashioned, and heard, if still heard, only from the lower class of Europeans; even in the last generation its habitual use was chiefly confined to these, and to old officers of the Queen's Army" (Yule and Burnell 1902, p. 97). This remark appeared in the first edition of 1882; "the Queen's Army" refers to the regiments of the British Army serving in India as distinct from the army of British India, formerly the East India Company's army.

[6] This is apparent not only in phrases such as "work like a black," but in the curious euphemism "white slavery," which implies that black slavery is natural.

[7] Jules Michelet, 1831, quoted in Poliakov 1974, p. 199. "The womb of the world" is in English in the original, perhaps quoted from an English source.

[8] I am grateful to the editors for pointing this out.

[9] The *OED* (s.v. *Christian* B 3) quotes a remark on this usage from the first Earl of Shaftesbury, *Characteristicks of Men, Manners, Opinions, Times* (1732) III, p. 88: "The very word Christian is, in common Language, us'd for Man, in opposition to Brute-beast, without leaving so much as a middle place for the poor Heathen or Pagan."

[10] The *OED* gives quotations for both names from the sixteenth to the eighteenth centuries. "Moor" continued into the twentieth century with reference to the Muslim population of Sri Lanka. The third Collect for Good Friday in the *Book of Common Prayer* refers to "all Jews, Turks, Infidels, and Hereticks," evidently as comprising all

categories outside the "remnant of the true Israelites," i.e., the Christian church.

[11] Charles Grant, *Observations on the State of Society among the Asiatic Subjects of Great Britain*, quoted in Ghosh 1926, p. 28.

[12] Mr Justice Hyde, notes written in 1777, quoted in Sinha 1978, p. 45. Sinha also notes, citing H. A. Stark, *Calcutta in Slavery Days*, Calcutta 1917, that some members of this group were of partly African descent. The Police Census of 1837 gives 4,746 "East Indians" and 3,181 "Portuguese" (Sinha 1978, p. 43), although in many other sources these are treated as a single category. Perhaps "Portuguese" refers here to those with more claim to Portuguese ancestry, and "East Indian" to those of English ancestry; but elsewhere people with Portuguese names are called "East Indians."

[13] The 1837 census quoted in the previous note gives 123,318 "Bengali Hindus" in a total population of 229,714.

[14] Kejariwal (1988, p. 225f.) usefully criticizes the "Orientalist" thesis, according to which Orientalism is "a Western style for dominating, restructuring, and having authority over the Orient" (Said 1978, p. 3). The concept of Orientalism is best known through Said's work, where it refers mainly to European interest in the Islamic world; but the term was similarly applied by Kopf to the study of India. Kejariwal shows that, far from being used as a means of personal advancement (as claimed by Kopf 1969), Asian studies received little encouragement from the Government. The Orientalist thesis is often a device to enable modern scholars to dominate, restructure and have authority over their predecessors, without the need to understand their work.

[15] Rammohun's attack on the Trinity in the fourth number of the *Brahmunical Magazine* is discussed in Killingley 1995.

Wilhelm Halbfass

# RESEARCH AND REFLECTION: RESPONSES TO MY RESPONDENTS

## II. Cross-Cultural Encounter and Dialogue (Responses to Chapter 1)

1. The words "encounter" and "dialogue," which the editors have chosen as title-words for the first part of this book, are central, but elusive terms in *India and Europe* (and its German predecessor, *Indien und Europa*). Just as the words "India" and "Europe" themselves do not appear in the index, neither do they. There is no definition, no theory, no explicit thematic treatment of "encounter" and "dialogue." Yet their presence is pervasive. In a sense, the entire book was meant to fill these concepts with content, to exemplify and illustrate them through concrete historical and hermeneutic processes. In *Indien und Europa*, the German word for encounter appears in the subtitle: *Perspektiven ihrer geistigen Begegnung*. The English subtitle refers, instead, to "understanding" (but the term "encounter" emerges again in the title of two of the four appendices which were added to the English version).

Unlike "encounter" and "dialogue," "understanding" does appear in the index, and it receives a certain amount of thematic treatment. But again, its primary role is not that of an explicit topic of theoretical discussion. Understanding, too, is something the book was meant to exemplify and illustrate. Always dogged by its shadow or counterpart, misunderstanding, it emerges and gains momentum in the attitudes and references of Europeans and Indians to each other. Likewise, it can be exemplified and actualized in our own retrospective review of, and reflection on, these mutual responses. In the following, I will try to briefly reexamine and clarify my usage of the three terms. This will serve as an introduction to the debate with my respondents.

In a series of recent publications, Gerhard Oberhammer has proposed "encounter" ("*Begegnung*") as a central category of religious hermeneutics and has tried to demonstrate and exemplify its significance for the interpretation of the Indian religious and philosophical tradition (Oberhammer 1987, 1989, 1991; see also D'Sa 1994). My own use does not carry any comparable terminological weight. It is, in its cross-cultural application, not much more than a convenient label for a variety of processes through which individuals or groups of different cultural, linguistic or religious backgrounds take notice of each other and their mutual otherness, and through which they start (in a positive or negative fashion) responding to each other, and, at least potentially, questioning or redefining their own identity.

"Dialogue" is more problematic. More often than "encounter," it appears in quotation marks (see, for instance, IE, pp. 160, 368, 439); this indicates that I am referring to current cross-cultural and interreligious usages of the term which require caution and scrutiny. But in spite of the frequency of such questionable, thoughtless and merely rhetorical usages, I do not see any alternative. Consequently, the last paragraph of my "Epilogue" uses the word without quotation marks (IE, p. 375). There is no alternative to speaking and listening to one another, but we must not be naive about it. What is the language in which Indians today speak about themselves and their tradition? Do they still speak for the tradition? How does this tradition itself speak to me? What is my ability to listen? How can I understand the tradition on the one hand, and the broken identity of its modern representatives on the other? Do I understand myself in the process? Could it be that understanding itself is not just a European, but a Eurocentric notion? With all these questions in mind, I still have to listen and to speak to the other. Whatever the problems with "dialogue" and "understanding" may be – these are channels that have to be kept open.

Speaking of understanding may seem almost obsolete at a time when the debate is dominated by terms such as "representing," "imagining," "construction," "deconstruction," etc. Is there any room left for understanding? Is "understanding" nothing but another name for construction or representation, and just another expression of the European and Eurocentric claim to power and domination? Indeed, there is an undeniable element of intellectual mastery and domination, of being able to speak for the other, in the very idea of understanding. But then, there is also the element of openness, the readiness to hear and to receive and to question one's own premises and identity. And if understanding involves construction, it is also, and in an equally significant sense, deconstruction. Understanding and dialogue are inseparable. Understanding itself is of the nature of a dialogue, and implies the presence of and the movement towards a realm of shared meanings. No participant in the encounter between India and the West has developed these ideas more eloquently and described the problems and prospects of understanding more clearly than J. L. Mehta: "The whole enterprise of 'understanding,' it would seem, is a characteristically Western one. It must be added, however, that it is also a recent one, even in Western history." Yet the emergence of "understanding," at a time when the West tried to dominate, master and objectify other traditions (and, perhaps, to overcome the sense of tradition altogether), may nonetheless herald "a new mode of thinking without objectifying, more appropriate to this new venture in mutuality." Understanding a text can only take place in a world of shared or shareable meanings. We must recognize that it deals with questions which are still our questions, however remote and distorted the answers may appear at first sight. "And we understand the text not by transposing ourselves into the mind of the author but by sharing the meaning of what he says and allowing for the possibility of its being true" (Mehta 1985, p. 130). Understanding proceeds from a standpoint, through prejudice and misunderstanding, but it also entails the readiness to return to oneself and one's prejudicial standpoint, and to be changed in the process; "all understanding, therefore, changes us and presupposes readiness for that" (p. 131). "The two partners in the dialogue of thought that is understanding are not so much the agents of this as themselves taken up in it and carried by this movement" (p. 132).

I will now turn to the individual contributions and relate, if appropriate, the questions which they raise to these introductory observations on "encounter," "dialogue," and "understanding."

2. Klaus Karttunen reminds us of the elusiveness of the earliest Western (i.e., Greek) references to India, and of the difficulty, if not impossibility of correlating such references with the "realities" of Indian life, or with actual experiences Greek or other Western travelers may have had in India. Certainly, as Karttunen himself has shown in his earlier publications, for instance in his careful analysis of the Greek traditions about India's "fabulous races" (see Karttunen 1989, with references to earlier studies), the possibility of actual Indian sources and

connections for such legendary and mythical notions cannot and should not be disregarded. But his present contribution suggests that the search for anything specifically and factually Indian in the early ethnographic ideas (as recorded by Herodotus and Ctesias) about "primitive" Indians, their sexual and dietary habits, etc., might be futile. This is, above all, a projection of "otherness" in far-off lands, and it does not matter much whether it is India or Ireland. But these beginnings are by no means typical of the Greek approach in general. There was, as Karttunen emphasizes, change, radical change, brought about by Alexander's campaign and the actual contacts and encounters it made possible. There were timid and elusive beginnings of a dialogue, although for many centuries these beginnings were once again relegated to myths and stereotypes about a far-off and inaccessible realm.

The contrast between the earliest Greek references and the xenological situation in early 19th century Calcutta, as described by Dermot Killingley, could hardly be more drastic. There is not much sheer "otherness" left at this time and place. Calcutta is a "xenopolis" (Killingley, p. 132), with much interaction between different religious, ethnic or cultural groups, but also between individuals with mixed or broken identities. There are, so we may say, obvious beginnings of a "fusion" (as well as confusion) of horizons. The examples provided by Dr. Killingley (see p. 134ff.) illustrate the complexity of the situation. Calcutta was a place of encounter not only for different groups of people, but also for different and to some extent competing forms of conceptualization and assessment of otherness. Moreover, we find the beginnings of a situation in which a sense of identity needs to be preserved not just against others, but against a potential merger or evaporation of traditions and traditional identities. This was the atmosphere in which Rammohan Roy, the so-called father of modern Indian thought, grew up. Rammohan's complex position between India and Europe, tradition and modernity, reflects this xenological potential of early 19th century Calcutta.[1]

From here, a further historical and hermeneutical step takes us to the reflections of Reena Sen of the University of Calcutta, a representative of present-day intellectual life in Calcutta, who teaches such subjects as the philosophy of Hume, Kant, and Heidegger. She focuses on the meaning and implications of the "Europeanization of the earth," the problematic relation between the European claims to "pure theory" and the "constellation of science and technology" (see p. 109, § 3), and the prospects and problems of a "fusion of horizons." What happens to the "hermeneutical venture" if it should turn out that such fusion is itself a projection of European thought and perhaps one of the manifestations of the "Europeanization of the earth"? How can we deal with the continuing imbalance of the encounter which jeopardizes the very idea of a genuine "fusion of horizons"? Certainly, such questions, which seem to be implied in Professor Sen's reflections, cannot be taken lightly.

In various ways, questions concerning "Europeanization," "fusion of horizons," "dialogue," etc., as well as the meaning and identity of India and Europe in these processes, are addressed in the contributions of Francis Clooney, Fred Dallmayr and Sergei Serebriany. Their observations refer more specifically and explicitly to my views and statements. I have to deal with them in greater detail.

3. In his thoughtful, sympathetic and overly generous contribution, Francis Clooney raises numerous significant issues. It is impossible to discuss all of them. I will focus on the three "suggestions" for my future work with which he concludes his article (under the title "Charting the open course"). He recommends greater attention

> first, toward a more ample appreciation of texts; second, toward a retrieval of religion as a category of understanding that is not to be subsumed by philosophy; third, toward a careful and responsible inscription of the self in Indological study. (p. 39)

All three suggestions have an undeniable bearing on the basic themes of this chapter, and they have, moreover, potentially far-reaching implications for Indian and cross-cultural studies in general.

I fully recognize what is perhaps the most significant implication in Professor Clooney's first suggestion: the danger of imposing one's own interests and perspectives, which is inherent in any thematic and inevitably selective treatment of Indian texts. More than once, I have expressed my worries and concerns in writing and distanced myself from any attempt to demonstrate the philosophical relevance of Indian texts by simply correlating them with "terms and methods which are currently in use or fashion in certain American or European philosophy departments" (Halbfass 1980b, p. 48). I have also rejected the notion of a "philosophical reconstruction" of Advaita Vedānta (as proposed by Eliot Deutsch), which would disregard the exegetic dimension (see TR, pp. 133 and 183, n. 11). Against this, I have tried to demonstrate the central historical *and* philosophical significance of exegesis in Vedānta, specifically in Śaṅkara. I have also tried to adopt the hermeneutic principle that any selection of themes should not just be a reflection of my interests, but take its clues from the tradition itself, and that the themes as such should then be pursued through a broad spectrum of interrelated texts and commentaries. Of course, I am fully aware that my textual research may not always do justice to my own theoretical postulates. I certainly agree that a more complete consideration of "whole texts" would be desirable for those who want to be "partners in dialogue with their 'others'" (p. 40). In the end, consideration of practicality and feasibility will have to play a role, and a balance will have to be struck between the demands of "whole texts" and the pursuit of themes and problems.

However, I am not entirely sure whether I understand what Dr. Clooney means by "a more ample appreciation of texts." On the one hand, he speaks about literary qualities, criteria of composition, the internal structure of texts; on the other hand, he refers to their "ritual and communal contexts" (p. 39). What is the connection? Also: What is a "whole text"? Quite obviously, this concept poses some special problems when applied to the ancient Indian tradition. Here, we have a gradual transition from a highly developed orality to a culture of writing. We have, moreover, a long history of incorporating, arranging and rearranging pieces of the tradition (both oral or written) in a variety of texts and contexts (for instance, in the Purāṇas, the *Manusmṛti* and other *dharma* texts, but also in many Upaniṣads). Where in these processes does "wholeness" have its proper place? Whatever we do with "whole texts," we should make sure that we are not misled by the notion itself, and that our concepts and theories of "text" and "textuality" do not interfere with our readiness to read and to listen. I find it difficult to believe that there are as many different forms of "careful reading" (p. 40) as Clooney seems to think. I am not sure whether I would want to count Jacques Derrida among the "careful readers"; and I am quite unable to expect much help and guidance from the superficial comparisons of Harold Coward (ibid.).

My notes on the second "suggestion" can be shorter. Although I do not have the benefit of a religious faith or affiliation, I am convinced that there is still a realm of religious meaning for me which I may share with those who do have such faith. I know that religions are intensely committed and indispensable ways of dealing with questions which continue to be my own questions, and which no science can even comprehend as questions. In this sense, "losing" a religion or the commitment to a particular religious tradition does not have to mean losing one's sense of religion; and it certainly does not have to amount to positivism or the relegation of religions to mere objects of research. However, I have been unable to receive much guidance and inspiration from what I have learned about contemporary "interreligious dialogue"; and I do not feel qualified to make any significant contribution to "a retrieval of religion as a category of understanding."

The third suggestion, concerning the "inscription" of one's own self in one's research (or "the location of the self vis à vis the analysis," p. 43), is perhaps the most intriguing and challenging one. The Indian texts which I have studied over the years, and which I continue to love and admire, are for the most part in the impersonal *śāstra* style. Bhartṛhari, Śaṅkara or Udayana do not speak about themselves. Moreover, the person who convinced me to pursue Indian studies professionally, Ernst Waldschmidt (1897-1985), exemplified a kind of learning and research from which personal statements or any "inscription of the self" were by definition excluded. Looking at myself in this light, I have at times felt ashamed for exposing my personal interest in what I was doing. Now I am told that I should bring more of my personal identity into my work. Why? How?

I am, of course, ready to admit that for anybody who wants to engage in cross-cultural dialogue a sense of identity, as well as a willingness to make it part of the dialogue, is significant. But how far should we go? What is relevant for the dialogue as a meaningful process, and what is only of anecdotal interest and ultimately distracting from the dialogic process? And how can I avoid turning myself into an object of analysis while trying to locate myself in the dialogue, and to determine my social, cultural or psychological identity? This, too, would distract from the dialogue. I am convinced that engaging in a dialogue requires a certain amount of self-oblivion. Nonetheless, I have no problem accepting the "personal" questions asked by Professor Clooney as legitimate (see p. 44), and I will try to respond to some of them, though very briefly.

How has the experience of living, teaching and writing in the United States affected my work? I can only make some guesses. It has certainly facilitated the transition and fluctuation between Indian studies and philosophy. It has fostered my commitment to combining classical Indian studies with an interest in modern India. It has sharpened my awareness of the vicissitudes of globalization and multiculturalism, of cultural merger and attrition, and of the rediscovery and reaffirmation of cultural identities. It has, above all, provided me with perspectives on Europe and on the "Europeanization of the earth," which I might not have had otherwise. Clooney wonders about my use of "Europeanization," and whether we still need to talk about "Europe" so much. In fact, it is not in spite of, but rather because of my life and work in America that I continue speaking of Europe and Europeanization. As a matter of fact, references to "Europeanization" were first introduced in the American edition of IE. It is never mentioned in the German edition (Halbfass 1981). Nothing in my view expresses the fundamental ambiguity of our pluralistic, globalized, seemingly cosmopolitan world so well as the expression "Europeanization of the earth." It may be a somewhat hyperbolic phrase, and its precise historical implications may be questionable. Nonetheless, it is a legitimate and effective reminder of the fact that much of what we consider to be universal and global today has very parochial roots, and it suggests the possibility that the openness and universality of our modern world remains caught in a globalized parochialism.

One final note in response to Clooney's "personal" questions. More than once, he refers to my "favorite German thinkers, Hegel, Heidegger and Gadamer" (p. 44; p. 32f.). There is no doubt that I have quoted these thinkers many times (although Heidegger emerges only in the American edition of IE and is virtually absent from its German predecessor), and that they have provided important perspectives for my work. But I would be reluctant to call them my "favorite German thinkers." This title belongs, and has always belonged, to Arthur Schopenhauer.

4. Fred Dallmayr uses the word "Orientalism" more frequently than any other respondent, and he addresses the issues associated with it more directly. Much of what I have to say on the entire syndrome of "Orientalism" has been said earlier, so I will not repeat it here (see above, "Research and Reflection: Responses to my Respondents," I).

Professor Dallmayr's initial diagnosis is clear and convincing. If we take "Orientalism" as a "label highlighting the collusion of scholarship with the imperatives of colonial domination" its demise "cannot be cause for lament." Yet, one may still be "concerned about the manner of the demise." While colonialist Orientalism may have lost its momentum, forms of "post-Orientalism" are on the rise which seem to be no less troublesome. The rejection of colonialist Orientalism has in recent years been combined or confounded with far more radical and sweeping denunciations and rejections of the whole tradition of European knowledge, or even the "cognitive enterprise" per se. Evidently, this implies a rejection of the entire framework in which not only Orientalism itself, but also the critique of Orientalism could originate.

"Is it really possible to move briskly from Eurocentrism to anti-Eurocentrism (and from *logos* to anti-*logos*)?" (p. 50). Our answer to this question has to be clear and simple: No. The various recent forms of "anti-Eurocentrism" cannot lead us beyond the Eurocentric constellation of our modern world. Instead, they may prevent us from facing the problem, or perhaps even reinforce it. We cannot simply replace "Eurocentrism" (or "logocentrism") with its opposite. There is no room for such "opposites." Any discourse of rejection is inevitably futile as long as it is unable to face the extent to which it is permeated by what it rejects. Modern "Eurocentrism" which coincides with the "Europeanization of the earth," is, of course, no longer a particular kind of ethnocentrism, which would coexist with or might be replaced by other "centrisms," or culturally and geographically bound views of the world. In the universality of its cognitive claims, it suppresses and anticipates its own rejections and opposites. For the time being, we have no choice but to accept the historical predicament of Europeanization, and to try to understand it from within, patiently, ready to ask questions without expecting immediate answers. Trying to discard or replace it would be an act of self-deception.

Does the European tradition itself, does the global constellation of Europeanization and Westernization provide us with perspectives which would help us to recognize its own limits and its inherent parochialism? Are there internal signs which point toward what is not within these limits? Are there signs of an impending historical conclusion and consummation of the process of Europeanization, and of the entire syndrome of science, technology, progress, objectification, research, historical understanding, etc.? Are there channels within this globalized and hegemonic, yet constantly self-alienating Western "tradition" which keep it open for a deeper otherness, an otherness beyond the reach of research, objectification, scientific explanation or historical understanding? Could understanding itself be one of these channels? Are we perhaps ready for alternatives without even knowing it? Is the search for otherness and alternatives in itself misleading, and has it concealed from us what has always been with us?

These are grand and dramatic questions. It is, no doubt, important to ask such questions which concern the very nature and possibility of "cross-cultural dialogues." Yet in the end it may be more important to simply engage in such dialogues and to pursue the work of understanding through careful and patient reading and listening. Certainly, we should not be naive in this pursuit; we have to think about the meaning and the conditions of the possibility of what we are doing. On the other hand, we should make sure that we do not end up in an abyss of reflexivity. We do not know when or whether our grand questions can be answered. In the meantime, however, there is interesting work to do. It is time now to move on to another, more specific issue.

In his reflections on my treatment of the "question of being" in *On Being and What There Is*, Dallmayr expresses concern that I may be shifting away from an earlier hermeneutic openness, and that I have adopted in this later work methodologies and philosophical allegiances which might jeopardize "the entire enterprise of cross-cultural understanding" (p. 55), or "the exit from Orientalism and Eurocentrism which Halbfass' earlier studies had so diligently pursued" (p. 57). In particular, Dallmayr refers to what he sees as a rather unfavorable presentation of Heidegger's thought and as unwarranted concessions to "the methods of modern analytical philosophy of the Anglo-Saxon type" (p. 57; quote from OB). He states:

> For clearly, the ascent to analytical objectivity implies again the objectification and reification of cultural traditions and their submission to the categorial frames of an external spectator; moreover, the same ascent vindicates the intellectual superiority of the neutral analyst over the array of cultural and historical contingencies. (ibid.)

Subsequently, he cites my own doubts concerning the meaning and legitimacy of any kind of philosophical universalism, or of a privileged and all-encompassing viewpoint. Nonetheless, he is convinced that my attempts to accommodate analytical thought in my approach to Indian ontology have gone too far, and that I have, at least temporarily, abandoned my hermeneutic position of understanding, and my role as a participant in a dialogue.

The problems associated with Dallmayr's observations are complex and elusive. My response will be tentative and incomplete.

First of all, my own statements concerning the "achievements" of modern analytical thought may not have been entirely clear, and there seems to have been a certain misunderstanding on Dallmayr's part. My references to the analytical "achievements" in exposing and resolving conceptual and linguistic confusions are certainly not without a sense of ironic distance. On the other hand, my statements concerning the utter questionability of the question of being, which I find in Heidegger, or the puzzlement about being in Plato, should not be read as a pejorative or "unfavorable" diagnosis. Certainly, I would not want to exchange such questionability and puzzlement for Quine's (or J. S. Mill's) deceptive clarity and precision:

> We do not know whether the "question of being" is a meaningful question. But once this question is gone, or reduced to certain linguistic, semantic, or logical technicalities, what else could provide us with a comparable sense of philosophical wonder and perplexity: What would happen to philosophy itself? (OB, p. vii)

Nonetheless, I have argued for a – limited and cautious – application of modern analytical tools (as tools of clarification) in the interpretation of Indian concepts and doctrines, and I have, moreover, distinguished between familiarization and assimilation on the one hand and analysis and clarification on the other (p. 12). Is this a contradiction? Does it imply an abandonment of the hermeneutic path? I don't think so. Anyone who wants to understand Indian thought will have to recognize

> the extent to which the formal and analytical dimension is actually present within the Indian tradition; in its own way, this tradition calls for such instruments of interpretation. In a sense, analysis itself is a hermeneutic response to Indian thought and a manner of fulfilling its own inherent aspirations. (p. 14)

Of course, we should never forget the limits of this approach. Precision and analysis can become obtrusive, and they can interfere with the task of understanding. Above all, we should not construe the refinement of analytic tools as the inherent telos of philosophical thought, be it Indian *or* Western; and we should always be aware that in India the "tradition of transcending analysis, differentiation, and conceptualization" has ultimately been more powerful (p. 15).

Finally, I want to add a note on the concept of universalism itself. Dallmayr is right: "in light of the long-standing association of universalism and Eurocentrism, students of non-Western cultures surely have to be on their guard" against universalistic claims (p. 57). However, we should not present universalism in general as some kind of evil spirit that has to be exorcised at any cost and in all its manifestations. Some kind of universalism, some claim to a privileged viewpoint seems to be inherent in the formation of culture itself. It is certainly present in traditional Indian thought, where it appears, for instance, in the form of inclusivism. Recognizing this, and trying to understand and correlate different types and levels of universalism, is simply part of the cross-cultural hermeneutic enterprise. Cross-cultural dialogue does not take place in the mode of a simple I-Thou relationship. We may expect both sides to bring some kind of "third" or external standpoint into the relationship and the dialogue, a standpoint from which not only the other, but also the dialogic relationship itself can be faced and assessed. Likewise, they will have certain claims and preconceptions concerning the space and framework in which the encounter and dialogue take place. There are, of course, more or less pervasive, more or less obtrusive universalisms, and they may be more or less detrimental to the dialogic process. It is neither possible nor desirable to eliminate all of them. There is at least one kind of universalism, one fundamental universalistic assumption without which dialogue and understanding themselves would be impossible: the assumption that we and our "others," partners in the hermeneutic process, are living in a world of shared or shareable meanings.

5. On the first page of his "Marginal Notes on *India and Europe*," Sergei Serebriany suggests that *An Essay in Fusing Horizons* might be an equally, if not more appropriate subtitle of my book. I must admit that I still prefer the less pretentious *An Essay in Understanding*. But I don't want to argue about this. Instead, I want to turn immediately to the central questions raised by Dr. Serebriany, i.e., questions concerning the meaning and identity of "India" and "Europe," as referred to in my book (including the role of Russia on the European side, and that of Islam on the Indian side).

> Given the analytical nature of the book as a whole and, specifically, the attention accorded to the analysis of words as indicators of cultural interactions, it is all the more strange that in *India and Europe* there have remained utterly unexamined the two title words and notions, that is, "India" and "Europe." It is as hard to imagine that the author was unaware of the problems inherent in these two words and notions as it is futile to guess why he has chosen not to analyse them. (Serebriany, p. 76)

In the following, Serebriany offers "some analytical and comparative considerations on these two words, considerations which are stimulated by *India and Europe* itself."

Indeed, the author of *India and Europe* was not unaware of the problems inherent in his title words. So why did he not discuss them in an explicit fashion? Why did he not define his understanding of "India" and "Europe"? I feel tempted to quote here what I said earlier about "encounter" and "dialogue," two other pervasive terms which remain virtually undefined and unexplained: "In a sense, the entire book was meant to fill these concepts with content, to exemplify and illustrate them through concrete historical and hermeneutic processes" (see above § 1). But this would be too simple and potentially misleading. Serebriany's "considerations" provide, indeed, a welcome opportunity to offer my own retrospective reflections on the "self-appellation" "Europe" and the foreign, imposed name "India," and to clarify my usage and understanding of these two words (something I might or should have done earlier, perhaps in the form of an "appendix").

First of all, I am not dealing with India and Europe per se, i.e., as geographical realities or cultural "essences" that might be described and defined by some outside observer, apart from the ways in which they understood themselves and each other. My book is about "horizons of self-understanding and perspectives of mutual understanding," and it "deals primarily with images, projections, theoretical responses and reflections" (IE, p. ix).

I have tried to record and understand how people who called themselves *ārya* and identified themselves as guardians of the Veda and legitimate residents of *bhārata* (or, earlier, *āryāvarta*) responded to others, outsiders, both within "South Asia" and abroad, how this ancient sense of identity and otherness was transformed and yet reaffirmed through the vast array of interacting traditions which we call Hinduism, and how it lives on even in the radical reinterpretations of modern Hindu thought. Whether we like it or not, the Muslims were never fully included in this dynamic, far-reaching and otherwise very flexible tradition of self-understanding and self-definition. On the other hand, I have tried to show how these people and their traditions were understood, labeled and defined by others who identified themselves as Greeks (Hellenes), etc., as Christians, or later on as Europeans, and how these processes affected the identity of the participants in the encounter. In doing so I have dealt with a variety of self-appellations and imposed names (apart from *ārya*, for instance, *hindu/hindū*, *yavana*, etc.). This attention to names was, in fact, one of the reasons why I decided to deal with the Muslims in the "European" or "Western" part of my book (after much hesitation). The outlook on India in early Islam comes from west of the river Sindhu/Indus. Like the Greeks whose philosophical heritage they shared, the Muslims derive the name for the country and its inhabitants (al-Hind, Hindu) from the name of the river, and their sense of a fundamental Indian otherness is by no means less pronounced than that of other Westerners. On the other hand, the Indians ("Hindus") classify them, together with the Greeks and other invaders from the west or northwest, as *yavanas*. It would be absurd to claim that I have avoided all geographical connotations in my presentation of the encounter between India and Europe. Still, it should be clear that I have tried to avoid a "regional studies" approach. I have not dealt with the question regarding what those people who happened to live in the area between the Atlantic Ocean and Ural Mountains on the one hand, and those who happened to reside between the Himalayas and Cape Comorin on the other, have said or thought about each other in the course of history. Instead, I have dealt with a series of encounters between two pervasive traditions, or rather clusters of traditions, which I have tried to understand in terms of their own conceptions of identity, otherness, continuity and change.

*India and Europe* begins with a chapter on Greece and Rome. For this, it is not essential whether or not the concept of Europe had any significance for the Greeks themselves. It is enough that once the idea of Europe began gaining momentum, Greece, the Greek language, Greek thought, etc., were inseparable from it. This includes, of course, the Latin adaptations and reinterpretations of Greek thought, its uses and transformations in Christianity (which for many centuries provided the strongest factor of coherence and identity for what we call Europe), and finally, its contribution to the genesis of modern scientific and secular thought. Through these developments, Europe itself appears as a dynamic process of "Europeanization" and an expanding horizon, with layers of meaning being added to its identity in the course of history. It remains to be seen whether what we have called the "Europeanization of the earth" is a further expansion of this identity or its evaporation.

At this point, some brief notes on the use of the expression "the West" (or "the Western world") and its semantic relation to "Europe" may be in place. Serebriany observes correctly that Indians often prefer to speak of "the West" instead of "Europe," for instance, in such phrases as "India and the West" or "the East and the West." But talking about East and West in general is also very familiar in "the West"; we don't need Kipling's famous couplet to remind us of that. There is certainly no reason to suspect, as Serebriany does, "Neo-Hindu" influence in my use of "West" or "Western." Nor is it true that I use "the West" or "Western" simply as synonyms of "Europe" and "European," certainly not in a geographical sense. For instance, in my presentation of Vivekananda (IE, pp. 228-242), "West" and "Western" are used deliberately and consistently to indicate the inclusion of America, which provided such an important experience for Vivekananda. There is, of course, a great deal of overlap. This may simply be in accordance with common usage or relate more specifically to an Indian perspective for which, up to the early 20th century, Europeans, especially the British, were the Westerners par excellence. It may, of course, also be associated with the "Europeanization of the earth."

Quite naturally, Serebriany takes a special interest in the role of Russia within Europe and its encounter with India. Of course, after my preceding statements, I cannot propose an answer to the familiar question whether Russia *is* European or Asian. I can only comment on the way in which it has participated in the cultural dynamics and the processes of self-identification and self-demarcation which we may call the "Europeanization of Europe" (see Bartlett 1993, p. 269ff.). Serebriany believes that the casual references to Russian authors and scholars I have given throughout my book are sufficiently representative. They indicate that Russia did, in fact, participate in the encounter, but that its response was rather subdued and marginal. I can, however, not agree with Serebriany's suggestion that this "low level" of Russia's response to India highlights its generally marginal role in Europe (p. 84). What then about Spain, which has virtually no tradition of Indian studies?

Much has been said about Russia's ambivalent attitude toward Europe (so conspicuously different from that of Poland) on the one hand, and the ambivalence of its acceptance by the rest of Europe on the other. Its geographical configuration has, of course, contributed to this ambivalent and peripheral position, which has been described as that of an internal European "Orient." We don't have to add to these debates.[2] At any rate, the Russian exploration of Indian and Buddhist thought has been part of the general European scene, and it has closely interacted with it.

No reasonable person can possibly disagree with Serebriany's assertion that "Europe and even more so the West are not cultural monoliths" (p. 80). But I have to disagree strongly with some of the conclusions he draws from this truism. He suggests that before venturing on a "single story" about "India and Europe" we should tell "separate stories" which might then be woven together at a later time (p. 81). His examples show that by "separate stories" he means, above all, encounters of different European countries with India. As "one of the most striking examples" meant to support his suggestion he refers to the "story of the formation of 'Indology' itself" (p. 80). Unfortunately, his brief summary of this "story" is quite inaccurate. It misrepresents the general level of receptivity for Indian materials and disregards the international nature of the missionary enterprise, the Enlightenment and other developments which helped pave the way for modern Indian studies, as well as the international reception of the works of the British pioneers, such as William Jones. If it is true that Europe is not a "cultural monolith," can we really say that France or Germany (which was not even a political entity in those days) are such monoliths? I don't think that it is necessary or advisable to first produce a whole set of "separate stories" and then try to weave them together at some later time. There are already enough clearly recognizable common threads in that rich and complex tapestry which we call Europe.

Of course, once the framework, the European context is there, there is always room for additional details, as well as for revisions and corrections. I am fully aware that my presentation is neither balanced nor in any way complete. I have dealt, above all, with philosophical or at least theoretical and conceptualized interpretations. I have, within the limits of my expertise, preferred some languages and literatures over others. But the attempt had to be made.

On a slightly more humorous note: Serebriany finds "a good number of Germanisms in the English language of the book" (p. 72) and calls the word "Indology" the "most conspicuous" one (p. 96, n. 6). He states that this word "is not considered in Britain a proper British usage." In American English, if used at all, it should be spelled "indology." Apart from my own usage, he finds "Indology" only in some articles by Indian authors. He concludes: "So 'Indology' with capital 'I' may be considered not only a Germanism but also a kind of 'Indianism.'" Indeed, the word "Indology" is not as common as "Sinology." But the English language is a huge living and growing organism which is no longer bound by the sensitivities of British users. My numerous American readers, reviewers and collaborators have neither found a Germanism nor an Indianism in "Indology." And quite apart from my own use of the word, I could easily identify dozens, even hundreds of occurrences of the word in recent American publications. Even Rosane Rocher, whom Serebriany cites in support of "indology," has in the meantime adopted the spelling "Indology."[3]

I would not have referred to this trivial matter if it were not connected with more serious questions which Serebriany raises with regard to the word "India," and which he affiliates with his suggestion that there might be a potentially dangerous "essentialist fallacy" (p. 86) associated with this name. Serebriany states correctly that "the comprehensive history of the word 'India' has not yet been written" (p. 78). He adds: "Such a history would include geographical, political and ideological aspects together with their varying interpretations." He also suggests (with specific reference to the 19th century) that "India" as a geographical and political notion ought to be distinguished from "India" as an "ideologeme." I am not quite sure what he means by "ideological" and "ideologeme." I presume it has to do with ideas about India's cultural and religious identity.

It is the use of "India" as an "ideologeme" which Serebriany associates with an "essentialist fallacy" and with divisive and exclusivistic tendencies, specifically with regard to the treatment of Indian Islam. To exorcise these unwholesome tendencies, he wants to substitute the regional term "South Asia," which "sounds global" and is "ideology-free," for "India" (p. 78). I have already dealt with the problems of the "regional studies" approach. Its apparent freedom from "essentialist" cultural, religious, or nationalistic implications is deceptive. The very "objectivity" and "neutrality" of regional notions may well conceal deep-rooted claims to control and domination. If the expression "Neo-Colonialism" has any meaning at all, it may, indeed, be exemplified and illustrated by the "regional studies" approach. More specifically, substituting "South Asia" for "India" would leave its neighbors, such as Pakistan and Sri Lanka, in a somewhat precarious situation. Finally, I have already noted that this substitution would have been completely inappropriate for my own hermeneutic approach.

Again and again, Serebriany worries about the treatment of Indian Islam. He fears that the title of A. L. Basham's book, *The Wonder That Was India* (together with its subtitle, *A Survey of the Culture of the Indian Sub-Continent before the Coming of the Muslims*) might suggest that the Muslims "do not belong to India proper," and that this might appeal to "Hindu chauvinists" (p. 79f.). He sees a similar danger in my treatment of the encounter between India and Europe, and even in my use of the word "India." In fact, he refers to the "Hindu chauvinists" again in connection with *India and Europe* (p. 88) and assures us once more "that Islam *now* is very much part" of the "overall cultural inheritance" of South Asia. There is no need to argue about this. But I want to emphasize once again that *India and Europe* is neither a book on the "overall cultural inheritance" of South Asia, nor on modern Indian politics; above all, it is not meant to be a contribution to "area studies."

To conclude this discussion, I have to respond briefly to a lengthy note on my treatment of Dārā Shukōh's *Majma' al-baḥrain* (p. 95, n. 3), which Serebriany finds "symbolic of a more general disregard for Indian Islam." He does not say anything about my summary of the contents of the book and focuses entirely on its title. He complains that I have not paid enough attention to the fact that *baḥrain* is a dual form. In fact, the context makes it clear that we are dealing with the "two oceans" Hinduism and Islam. However, Dārā Shukōh's ideas about concordance were by no means limited to Islam and Hinduism. If he had not found the phrase *majma' al-baḥrain* in the Koran itself, he might actually have preferred some plural form. Serebriany also finds fault with my rendering of *majma'* as "mingling" (which is not my own translation, but borrowed from Mahfuz al-Haq). He insists that this is a *nomen loci*, and that it might be translated as "a meeting place," etc. Fortunately, we have a document from Dārā Shukōh's own time, produced for him and perhaps to some extent by him, which shows that the connotation of a *nomen loci* in *majma'* was of no significance for him. I am referring to a Sanskrit translation of his work which bears the title *Samudrasaṃgamagrantha*. Quite obviously, the word *saṃgama* refers to a "coming together," "meeting" or "mingling" as such, and not to its location. One could, of course, argue about further details (as well as about Serebriany's curious notes on the *śāstrāṇāṃ melanam* in Abhinavagupta's *Tantrāloka*); but this would not lead us anywhere. My main point is that there is absolutely nothing "symbolic" in my treatment of Dārā Shukōh's *Majma' al-baḥrain*.[4]

Nonetheless, I want to emphasize that I am by no means satisfied with my treatment of Islam in *India and Europe*. Including a chapter on Islam in the "Western" section of the book was justified because of the initial Muslim perspective. But for the sake of balance, I might have done well to include another chapter in the Indian part. Once Muslims, like other "Westerners," had viewed India as a foreign land in the East. But then they established themselves as residents of that country, many of them being of native Indian stock, and became part of the Indian xenological scene. They shared some of the Hindu perspectives on Europe and differed in other respects. To some extent, their presence prepared the

Hindu encounter with Europe. All this deserves a separate presentation and analysis.

## NOTES

[1] I want to emphasize again that I borrowed the term "xenology" ("Xenologie") from Munasu Duala-M'bedy; see IE, p. 507, n. 2.

[2] See Wolff 1994; see also the texts by Joseph de Maistre, Franz von Baader and Joseph Görres in Lützeler 1982. In 1987, the identity of Europe and the problems associated with it were discussed at the Papal Summer Residence (Castel Gandolfo); for the proceedings of this meeting see Michalski 1988 (including my own presentation, Halbfass 1988b).

[3] See Breckenridge and van der Veer 1993, p. 215f. (as well as the index).

[4] On the *Samudrasaṃgamagrantha* see Raghavan 1945-46; Schimmel 1973, p. 40, renders *majma'* as "merging." IE, p. 463, n. 5, quotes the full title with "two oceans."

# 2

# Issues of Comparative Philosophy

**Jitendra Nath Mohanty**

# BETWEEN INDOLOGY AND INDIAN PHILOSOPHY

Wilhelm Halbfass was originally trained as a philosopher, and then chose to be, at least to begin with, an Indologist. So he knows better than most the tension between the two disciplines. His work is characterized by excellent philological research and also by genuine philosophical understanding. Thus he remains a model for Indologists who want to work in the field of Indian philosophy. In this essay, I intend to reflect on the tension he articulates so well in his article "Europa, Indien und die Europäisierung der Erde" (Halbfass 1988b). For the questions that I shall raise, examples could be drawn from his other works. But I will, for the sake of brevity, focus on this short but remarkable piece.

## 1. "Indology" and "Indian Philosophy"

Let me begin with a few general remarks. "Indology," like "Sinology," is a strange discipline whose subject matter is an entire country – its history, language, religion, culture, civilization. So it also includes study of India's philosophies. But is it not remarkable that there is no such discipline whose subject matter is one of the European countries - no *Deutschologie*, no *Frankologie*. Only the non-European, or rather the Oriental countries were made themes of such global disciplines. There is something like *Germanistik*, but that is concerned with the German language and literature. There is no comprehensive unitary discipline about the entire German culture. Is this a historical accident? Or, has it something to do with what Halbfass calls "objectification"? I do not think that objectification of another culture *eo ipso* results in violence to that culture. But one cannot but be suspicious of a certain kind of selective objectification.

Within the tradition of Indology, scholars have passed judgments on Indian philosophy. It is like a scholar in *Germanistik* using available philological methodologies for judging the philosophical content of Kant's

*Kritik der reinen Vernunft*. It has been good for European philosophy that no such "Occidentalism" laid claims to judge matters philosophical. Classical philologists did not decide upon questions of Aristotelian logic unless they happened, like Günther Patzig, to be philosophically trained.[1] Should it not be the same with regard to Indian philosophy? There have been, to be sure, philosophers such as Schopenhauer and Deussen and Hegel who have passed judgments about Indian philosophy. But either their enthusiasm or attention did not match their knowledge of the philosophical literature or, as in Deussen's case, they remain minor figures in the history of Western philosophy.

But is there something that can properly be called "Indian Philosophy"? Or, is Indian philosophy a creation of neo-Hinduism?

## 2. Traditional Hinduism and Neo-Hinduism

How significant is this distinction taken over by Halbfass from Hacker?[2] The distinction would be significant if it were a special feature of the history of Indian - more specifically, of Hindu - civilization. But is it? Can one not, in a similar vein, distinguish between "*fortlebendem tradionellem Christentum*" and "*Neu-Christentum*"? Is not there a noteworthy difference between the new self-understanding of (Protestant) Christianity and the classical Christian self-understanding? In general, can one not always find a distinction between "traditional X" and "neo-X" - the neo-X exhibiting new attempts to interpret, apply, modify X? One good example is available, if we replace X by "Kant" (or, "Kantianism"). If a culture's self-understanding is always, as a rule, caught up in a process of historical development, in response to historically confronted challenges, the response of neo-Hinduism is what it should be (despite minor aberrations, exaggerations and/or enthusiasms). What is more, if no cultural phenomenon, religion including, remains tied to the original formulations and the classical statements, then it is not Hinduism alone that is guilty of evolving into a "neo-form." To the contrary, that such varieties of response to the new challenges (from the West) were forthcoming, demonstrates the resilience of Hinduism.

One of the accomplishments of neo-Hinduism is taken to have given new interpretations of the traditional Hindu idea of *dharma* and *darśana*. The former is taken to mean "religion," and the latter is construed as "philosophy." This brings us to the critical question, are the *darśanas* philosophies? Also, is *dharma* religion?

### 3. *darśana* and "Philosophy"

The neo-Hindus started writing in English. (Is that the original sin?) So they had to have English renderings of the Sanskrit words. From Quine, we have learnt that there is no radical translation. Is the translation of *darśana* into "philosophy" good enough, despite differences in context and content? Or, should we try a better translation? Would "a view," "a sight" (from √*dṛś* = to see) have been better? But why? May not a purist object that here the English word "seeing" is being used in a rather unusual sense? Halbfass, to be sure, does not himself desist from translating *darśana* into "philosophy." As a matter of fact, he always uses the locution "Indian Philosophy," and in my view rightly so. But is that a concession to neo-Hinduism? I do not think so. I believe, the traditional *darśanas* are philosophies, and the difference between Carnap and Heidegger is no lesser than that between Heidegger and Gadādhara. It is only a myth of a particular brand of historiography of philosophy that there was a root idea underlying Western philosophy, of which all subsequent philosophies (and sciences and technology) are developments.[3] There is no such root idea, no such primal *Urstiftung*. There have been questions, one leading to the other, modes of argumentation, disputation, paradoxes and puzzles, various ways of thinking, attempts to free oneself from myths and achieving pure theoretical knowledge. If one follows the questionings made in the *darśanas*, the argumentations and disputations that take place amongst the various schools, the critical spirit that pervades them, then one would have to admit that they are philosophies – they belong to the same genre and are different from literary works, scientific treatises and religious scriptures. The *darśanas* are *philosophies. The question is, how is *philosophy related to philosophy?

If the neo-Hindus, in their eagerness to emphasize the superiority of the *darśanas*, especially of the Vedānta, ascribed to them superior spiritual power, that is no more an exaggeration than Husserl's claim that transcendental phenomenology can save the European civilization from its crises, no more edifying than Heidegger's claim that Western metaphysics alone could make science and technology possible (without asking, how science and technology could have been possible in India and China).

## 4. Theory and Practice

But was there pure theoretical thinking in India? Husserl did not want to ascribe philosophy to Indians on the ground that their thinking was mythical-practical. I do not know on what grounds Heidegger held that philosophy was Western in origin, but he does seem to have agreed with Husserl in this respect. This attitude goes back to Hegel who held that Indians had not been able to raise their intuitions to concepts. In "Europa, Indien und die Europäisierung der Erde," Halbfass states these views, but does not critically evaluate them save recognizing - and rightly so - that in this respect Hegel's example has been decisive for historians of philosophy. The lesson has been: exclude Indian philosophy from that history, and regard philosophy as "pure theory" as far as the Greeks were concerned. However, Halbfass knows more Indian philosophy than all three - Hegel, Husserl and Heidegger - combined, and should know that their views were determined as much by their preconceptions as by their ignorance. Apart from referring to my essay "Theory and Practice in Indian Thought,"[4] I will here assert (no more dogmatically than any of the three) the following: for one thing, Greek thinking at the beginning, certainly through Socrates and Plato, was not free from myths, nor was it free from both the mythical and the practical. For another, many Western writers tend to elevate Biblical stories to the level of revelation, while regarding similar stories elsewhere to be mythical - a distinction which makes sense from within the Judeo-Christian tradition, to be sure, but not outside it. Thirdly, there is no paradigm for theoretical thinking, no one way of drawing the distinction between theory and practice, and to limit philosophy to the sort of theory that emerged in Aristotle, would be too restrictive: it would not even include the concept of theory that emerged with Bacon, not to speak of modern science and mathematics (as Hans Jonas has so elegantly shown)[5]. Gradually, liberated from the mythical-practical, Indian thinking, in the *darśanas*, became theoretical - maintaining by way of memory, and also theoretically justifying, the practical goal of *mokṣa*. Philosophy need not, even within the Western tradition, be completely sundered from practice.

## 5. History and Historicity

Halbfass writes: "Hegel sah keinen Anlass, die Ursprünge und früheren Stadien zu glorifizieren."[6] However, this is not quite so. It is well-known how much Hegel glorified Greek thought, especially Aristotle. The Greek world remained for him the model of *Sittlichkeit*, despite its substantial immediacy which on his view was destroyed from within.[7] Likewise, in a clearer way he was enamoured of Christianity (as contrasted with Judaism), by the way of spirit's becoming flesh, of God-man, which appears in a secularized form in the self-reconciled spirit. Halbfass is right when he writes: for Hegel,

> [d]as europäische Denken muss der Rahmen sein und die Kategorien stellen für die Betrachtung von jedweder Tradition des Denkens. (Halbfass 1988b, p. 235)

What Hegel should have said: Philosophy should be able to do that, and that philosophy is neither European nor Oriental in the long run.

It is remarkable that the analytical philosophers - who are not contaminated by Hegelian historicism or Heidegger's *Seinsgeschichte* - have no problem in ascribing "philosophy" to the Indian tradition. It is the "continental" philosophers who find here something which goes against their deeply held prejudices. Quine, Strawson and Dummett - to name three distinguished analytical philosophers - not only have no *a priori* doubt (how could there be philosophy outside of the Western tradition?) on this matter, but have admitted (to this author) that they were convinced that good (and bad) philosophy knew no geographical limits.

Historicism may have, in many ways, a liberating influence, but unless carefully thought through it may provide a subtle way of justifying one's deeply held prejudices. For one's use of history can be selective, and you can concoct a story, by clever selection and juxtaposition, which would seem to have a moral. There is therefore a point in the post-modernist rejection of a grand narrative and pluralization of histories.

This past summer, in Freiburg, a young Heideggerean (who has authored two books on Heidegger) said: "'History' is an European accomplishment." I asked him: "How did you know that?" "We have learnt this from Heidegger," he said. "Have you ever wondered," I asked, "how did Heidegger make this discovery?" Making an assertion is the least important part of doing philosophy, the really important thing is to ground your assertion. Did Heidegger arrive at such a conclusion by historical, textual, ethnological research? Or, is it an *a priori* claim? Like many similar claims, this too needs to be questioned. For my present purpose, I will press the following points:

i. If "history" is Judeo-Christian in origin, Judeo-Christianity is Asian, "Oriental" in its roots, not Western, not European.

ii. The Greeks were no better historians than Indians, and had a circular view of time, more distinctively than the Indians.

iii. Looking at the concept of time (which is one component of one's view of history), we have to say: (a) not all Indian philosophies regarded time as unreal; (b) not all Indian philosophies regarded time as cyclic;[8] (c) a sense of the unreality of time characterized much of early Christianity; (d) Western understanding of time itself oscillated between a cyclic and a linear view of time (as Gould has shown[9]); (e) a culture may have a sense of history without that sense being articulated in the philosophies; (f) one must distinguish between an awareness of history and a recognition of the historicity of human existence.

If we keep all these in mind, some of the global assertions philosophers are apt to make will seem to be poorly legitimized.

Freed from these global historicist prejudices, Husserl's phenomenology, Heidegger's *Daseinsanalytik* and Hegel's *Logic* would still remain major philosophical accomplishments.

## 6. "Europeanization of the Earth"

If the idea of pure theory is not typically Western, and if Western philosophy and science are not pure theories in Husserl's sense, then Husserl's thesis about Europeanization of the Earth becomes empty. What Husserl means by "Europeanization" is not borrowing Western science and technology, or European life-style, but accepting, as the norm of thinking, the Idea of Pure Theory which, according to him, defines the Idea of Europe. But Europe itself has abandoned that illusory ideal, and to suppose that mankind will be transformed by that Ideal is another example of that naïvety which is often to be found in the most sophisticated and self-critical of thinkers.

But "Europeanization" may mean accepting, and being transformed by that acceptance of, European, i.e., Western, science and technology. In that case, "Europeanization of the Earth" may very well indicate the trend of the times. But it would be a significant historical judgment only if it is taken together with the other allied phenomena: only then would it be possible to pass a satisfactory judgment on the overall history of mankind (if there is any such). These other phenomena, to be taken into consideration, are, to mention only a few of them:

(a) the non-Western (Indian, Arabic and Egyptian) origin of a large part of classical mathematics;

(b) the development of science and technology in India and in China;[10]

(c) the contribution of the Middle East, i.e., of the Arabs, to the material civilization of Europe after the Crusades;

(d) influence of China on Europe;

(e) the impact of Oriental religions and thought on the West.

Placed in the larger context, it would most likely turn out that there is more give and take than a one way track, that (Western) science and technology as such are not Western, and that "Europeanization of the Earth" also means transformation of Europe itself. Add to this the consideration that the so-called "Europeanization" came about not by virtue of the superior theoretical accomplishments of the West, but as a spin-off of the political hegemony, and now of economic power.

Would not the consequence be, as Hannah Arendt wrote to Karl Jaspers, a "deprovincialization of western philosophy"?[11]

## 7. Beyond the Occident and the Orient

Halbfass remarks, rightly I believe, that we must transcend "the European," that we must reach beyond the Occident and the Orient (1988b, p. 251). But for this one does not have to wait for an unforeseeable future - for the present, succumbing to the unavoidable Europeanization. For me there is more hope than that. Europeanization of mankind is a myth. Good philosophical thinking - despite the thinker's self-understanding to the contrary - is *always* "beyond the Occident and the Orient." Philosophy cannot rest satisfied with these mythical concepts of "Orient" and the "Occident," which need to be "deconstructed" into infinite systems of differences. All great thinkers transcend that distinction. Only some of them misconstrue their accomplishments in narrowly historicist terms.

Indian philosophy never understood itself in such historicist terms. A *darśana* was not regarded as a *cultural* phenomenon, but as science which claimed to give knowledge of things as they are. Consequently, many familiar relativistic positions do not show up in the Indian tradition. Hence its seeming a-historicality, as of any science. However, what was relativized to epochs was the distribution of moral values.

*Temple University*
*Department of Philosophy*
*Philadelphia, Pennsylvania, USA*

## NOTES

[1] Cf. Patzig 1969.

[2] Cf. Hacker 1978, pp. 386, 480–482.

[3] Examples of such historiographies are to be found in Hegel and Heidegger.

[4] Cf. Mohanty 1994, ch. 1.

[5] Cf. Jonas 1959.

[6] Cf. Halbfass 1988b, p. 234.

[7] See Hegel 1966, pp. 464-482.

[8] For the variety of Indian views on time, see, amongst others, Balslev 1983.

[9] Gould 1987.

[10] Cf. Ray 1956, Seal 1958 and Needham 1954-85.

[11] Cf. Kohler and Sauer 1992, p. 157.

Joseph S. O'Leary

# HEIDEGGER AND INDIAN PHILOSOPHY

## I: Is the Question of Being Unique to the West?

Inspired by Heidegger's ontological questioning of Western tradition, Wilhelm Halbfass attempts to retrieve comparable ontological dimensions of Indian thought, which have been neglected by other scholars. He sees "no good reason to adopt Heidegger's own exclusion of his ideas from the interpretation of non-Western traditions" (OB, p. 25). If, for Heidegger, the being-question is present in a latent or repressed way in Descartes, Kant, Nietzsche and the early Husserl, although they do not formally discuss being *qua* being, why should it not be equally present in Indian thought?

Using Heideggerian phenomenology to apprehend what is afoot in Indian tradition in a discreet, suggestive and non-dogmatic way, Halbfass shows a sophisticated awareness of the problematic aspects of Heidegger's enterprise. The "history of being" which Heidegger distilled out of a selective focus on the ontological implications of past philosophical debates tends, though powerfully illuminating, to a determinism or fatalism which is implausible and paralyzing. Halbfass calls this construction into question by insisting that being is a universal concern, not a distinctively Western one, and that "being is one of the central and pervasive themes of Indian thought" (OB, p. 21).

If my comments here take the form of doubts and misgivings - most of which have surely occurred to Halbfass itself - , the reason is not only my hesitancy to make positive statements about Indian philosophy, of which I know so little, but also a sense that, given the promise of Halbfass's approach for the mutual clarification of Indian and Western thought, such misgivings need to be aired as fully as possible lest the process be short-circuited by hasty identifications. This merely dubitative posture may not save me from mistakes, but I am happy to think that Professor Halbfass's corrections will provide the surest of safety-nets.

My principal misgiving concerns Halbfass's scepticism about the Heideggerian question of being, a scepticism which facilitates his claim that ontology is a universal enterprise, but at the same time risks robbing this enterprise of any major philosophical interest. Certainly, Heidegger's view of Western thought needs to be demystified to some extent. In part, his construal of the meaning of being is a modern, idiosyncratic reflection, and this may relativize his claim to retrieve the buried truth of the entire philosophical tradition. The word "being" itself may be incapable of sustaining the edifices of systematic metaphysics or even a unitary reflection on the meaning of being pursued in phenomenological style. Heidegger's attempt to gather things together in the *Ereignis* may be incompatible with the intrinsic pluralism of language, and the *Ereignis* may reflect a Greco-Germanic sense of being which is but one historical possibility among others, even within Western culture. His effort to step back from Western philosophical tradition to uncover its fundamental bearings, by a phenomenological bringing into view of matters that this tradition occludes, may suffer from a narrow purism in its focus on the being-question. Perhaps the Heideggerian path of questioning has no future unless opened out fully to historical pluralism and relativity (see O'Leary 1992). Just as one may take over Hegel's dialectical negativity without adopting his system, so one may best do justice to the Heideggerian path of thinking by giving it such a pluralist inflection. Just as orthodox Hegelians have been an almost insignificant strand in the *Wirkungsgeschichte* of Hegel in comparison with heretics such as Marx or Kierkegaard, so the future impact of Heidegger may have little to do with orthodox Heideggerians, perhaps already an anachronistic species.

The being-question may not be as monolithic or as absolutely central as Heidegger supposes. Yet if one sees his concern with it as misguided, and surrenders to "growing doubts concerning the meaning and relevance of the topic itself" (OB, p. vii), the evident richness of Heidegger's thought is left untapped. If the language of being turns out to be an inadequate vehicle for this richness, then a better one needs to be constructed. Despite my doubts about particular features of Heidegger's construction of the "history of Being," I consider that the basic thrust of his thought - the step back from rationalism to the phenomenality of being - opens the most fundamental perspective now available for the assessment of Western philosophy. As sunlight falling on old stone carvings brings out their forms with a startling warmth of presence, so Heidegger's reading lights up the most intimate concern of Western philosophy. His analysis of metaphysics as onto-theology applies squarely to the definition of that science in Aristotle, Aquinas, and Suarez (see Marion 1994, p. 574), but it also sheds light on the ontological depth of German idealism, as the *Erkenntnistheorie* of Heidegger's academic elders had failed to do (see *GA* 42, pp. 156-163). The Western philosophers *respond* to Heidegger's reading as the pages of Beethoven or Chopin to the fingers of a great if sometimes eccentric pianist, and his reading of the history of philosophy will retain its authority until those who query it come up with a more illuminating story. However, - and this is my second misgiving about Halbfass's enterprise - it seems that Indian philosophy does not respond comparably to Heideggerian readings; the question of being has no thrilling resonance for it; its harmonies are not fully awakened by the Western touch.

(a) The Question of Being

The title *On Being and What There Is* sounds as Greek as Greek can be. Is it appropriate for a work on Indian ontology? The legitimacy of this transference becomes doubtful if we recall how rare and strange the question of being is, even in Greece:

> Le problème de l'être - au sens de la question *Qu'est-ce que l'être*? - est le moins naturel de tous les problèmes, celui que le sens commun ne se pose jamais, celui que ni la philosophie pré-aristotélicienne, ni la tradition immédiatement postérieure ne s'est posé en tant que tel, celui que les traditions autres qu'occidentales n'ont jamais pressenti ou effleuré. [The problem of being - in the sense of the question *What is being?* - is the least natural of all problems, one which common sense never poses, one which neither pre-Aristotelian philosophy nor the immediately posterior tradition posed as such, one which is never sensed or glimpsed in non-Western traditions.] (Aubenque 1991, pp. 13-14)

It may be excessive to say that the question of being is not even glimpsed in non-Western traditions. Yet unless it is brought into sustained, explicit focus, it is a question that tends to evaporate. Indian reflection on the logic of being-words seems not to have attained this focus, not being firmly anchored in Parmenidean wonder at the fact that beings *are*.

For Heidegger, this wonder is the founding event of Western thought: "ἔστι γὰρ εἶναι 'Es ist nämlich Sein.' In diesem Wort verbirgt sich das anfängliche Geheimnis für alles Denken" ["'For there is being.' In this saying lies hidden the initial mystery for all thinking"] (*GA* 9, p. 334). As early as 1922 he found here "the historical paradigm for the immediacy of the encounter with Being":

> Whatever is encountered *is*. *Dasein* is *the* basic trait of its look [*eidos*]. The overriding experience here, which has a way of obtruding upon what a being is, is *that* it is. It is in this sense that any being in its look of be-ing is simply one. Parmenides' thesis is the expression of an original encounter with being itself. The force, simplicity, directness, and so the underivability of this encounter of an entity from itself and for itself correspond to the latent difficulty of illuminating and exposing such a Being. (Kisiel 1993, pp. 245-246)

Aristotle, unlike Parmenides, is a thinker of form, but as Heidegger shows in *Vom Wesen und Begriff der φύσις* (*GA* 9, pp. 239-301) form is not mere stuff or shape, but the concentrated actuality of being. Dismissing Antiphon's conception of nature as underlying matter (e.g., wood as the nature of the bed), Aristotle defined *φύσις* as "*τῶν ἐχόντων ἐν αὐτοῖς κινήσεως ἀρχήν ἡ μορφὴ καὶ τὸ εἶδος*" ["the shape or form of things which have in themselves the source of their motion"] (*Physics* 193b,3-4). Only when *φύσις* is grasped in terms of form is it "*zureichend als οὐσία, als Art der Anwesung begriffen*" ["adequately grasped as *οὐσία*, as a species of coming to presence"] (*GA* 9, p. 274). Aristotelian form (*μορφή*, *εἶδος*) is not a mere attribute but a mode of being. Form and matter are in a relation of actuality and potency, and each of these terms is defined ontologically. When being is interpreted phenomenologically as coming to presence, form or *ἐντελέχεια* is grasped as the event of the coming to presence of an entity. Form as an ontological idea (in Plato) answers the question,

> Wie sieht das Seiende als Seiendes aus? Als was zeigt sich das Seiende selbst, wenn ich es nicht hinsichtlich einer bestimmten Eigenschaft, sondern nur als Seiendes betrachte? [How does the entity *qua* entity look? As what does the entity itself show itself, when I contemplate it not in view of a given quality but only as an entity?] (*GA* 22, p. 252)

To grasp forms in a merely logical, objectifying way is to be blind to what is nearest to hand:

> Entsprechend den Farbenblinden gibt es auch *φύσις*-Blinde. Und bedenken wir, dass die *φύσις* als eine Weise der *οὐσία* (der Seiendheit) bestimmt wurde, dann sind die *φύσις*-Blinden nur eine Art der Seinsblinden. [Corresponding to the colour-blind there are also people who are blind to *φύσις*. And when we consider that *φύσις* is qualified as a mode of *οὐσία* (beingness), then the *φύσις*-blind are but a variety of the blind to being.] (*GA* 9, p. 264)

Banal conceptions of stuff and shape, matter and form, are the "*Allerweltstrasse*" of Western thinking (*GA* 9, p. 274); Heidegger presents these as a decline from originary Greek insight, but they may well belong to the ordinary stock of notions latent in the grammar of Indo-European languages.

The question "*τί τὸ ὄν*?" (*Metaphysics* 1028b,4) - "what is a being *qua* being in its being?" - invites two sorts of reply. The first reply, a rational, speculative one, analyses the characteristics of being as such, and founds being in its ultimate cause, the supreme being. This reply constitutes onto-theo-logy, the distinguishing structure of Western metaphysics, fully explicit in Descartes and Leibniz (*GA* 40, p. 88; Heidegger 1957b, pp. 44-53). What is wrong with onto-theo-logy is that, as onto-logy, it flattens out the phenomenological apprehension of the being of beings, eventually reducing it to an abstract and colourless *ens commune*. Concomitantly, as theo-logy, in grounding being in a supreme first cause it subjects being to the principle of sufficient reason; beings are now explained, in a rationalistic way, and are not allowed to flourish "without why" like the rose of Angelus Silesius (Heidegger 1957a). Just as Voltaire's Pangloss, caught up in the Lisbon earthquake, has only one question: "*Quelle peut être la raison suffisante de ce phénomène?*," so one might imagine a caricatural ontotheologist examining a rose: "Aha! A being! And its ground? Why, being as such, being in general, *ens commune* (onto-logy). But is this sufficient? Must we not pose a supreme being which is the source of its being and the unifying ground of beings-as-a-whole? And this we call God (theo-logy)." In this construction is lost not only the fragrance of the rose, but the phenomenality of being and the authentic otherness of God.

Heidegger overcomes onto-theology by his retrieval of the Aristotelian question as a hermeneutical and phenomenological interrogation of the coming to presence of beings. He himself interrogates the experience of being (our everyday understanding of isness; our search for authentic existence; our wonder at the fact that there are beings rather than nothing) and the language of being (the everyday uses of "is"; the languages of philosophical and poetic tradition) in order to discover the meaning of being or the truth of being, which he ultimately names the *Ereignis* - the "event" which grants the being of beings, which enables "the worlding of world" and "the thinging of things." This is not a metaphysical foundation but the phenomenological essence of the givenness of beings. The vocabulary of being is inadequate, a culture-bound Western product, to what is emerging here, so that Heidegger has to develop his own style of quasi-metaphorical saying.

The basic step in ontology is to distinguish "being" from "beings" so as to clarify their relationship. Halbfass accepts Quine's question "what is there?" as "the fundamental ontological question" (OB, p. 70), thus reducing ontology to a merely ontic "inventory of what exists" (OB, p. 49). Such an inventory will, to be sure, carry an implicit ontological commitment (a notion of what being is). But if this commitment is not thematized, or if its thematization is seen as impossible, then we do not have ontology in Aristotle's or Heidegger's sense. Crude thematizations – e.g., "what exist are just physical things" – lack a sense of the *question* of being. Even loftier thematizations – e.g., "all that exists is Brahman" – may not have glimpsed the question of being. The issue may have been decided in an ontic contest between different descriptions of what there is, rather than in an ontological clarification of what it means to be. Even if, with Nietzsche, one dismisses inquiry into being as a mist, it does seem to be a distinctively Western mist.

Analytical philosophers may deplore Heidegger's "use and misuse of 'systematically misleading expressions'" (OB, p. 11), yet have they produced critical studies of Heidegger's language and thought-patterns that could measure the strength and limits of his revival of the being-question? That would require some basic sympathy with his concern for the authentic phenomenality of beings. Full-blooded positivists dismiss the entire ontological tradition as based on systematically misleading expressions. They could be answered by a logical clarification which retrieves and justifies the discourse on being or, in Heideggerian style, by a study of the phenomenological content of being-language. It can happen that a philosophical classic reveals weaknesses when approached in the logical way, while retaining its power in the phenomenological perspective. Thus Parmenides confuses different senses of the word "is," and the logical reading shows him at best as forming the notion of a pure existence without qualities, which replaces Thales's water or Heraclitus's fire in the role of ultimate explanatory principle. The phenomenological approach, on the other hand retrieves coherence and depth in his thought by reading him as a thinker of the event or phenomenon of being.

Heidegger is aware that the term "being" is a tricky one. He envisages its multivocity as a weave or skein, a *Geflecht*, translating the Aristotelian "*τὸ ὄν λέγεται πολλαχῶς*" (*Metaphysics* 1003a,33; 1028a, 10) in phenomenological terms as "*Das seiend-Sein kommt vielfältig zum Scheinen*" ["The coming to manifestation of being is manifold"] (Heidegger 1956, p. 46). His own use of the vocabulary of being acquires its coherence from its rigorously phenomenological character. The precise bearing of his explorations can be measured only in terms of the matter with which they are concerned - not the logic or conceptuality of "being" but the concrete modes of the presence or givenness of beings in their being. However, it is misleading to say that the later Heidegger withdrew "into poetry, myth, and capricious etymologies" and "does not even attempt that kind of historical and systematic clarification that we find in Heidegger's earlier statements" (OB, p. 10). The critiques of Leibniz and Hegel in the mid-fifties (Heidegger 1957a, 1957b) show that he kept up his quest for a clear overview of the history of the being-question.

### (b) A Distinctively Greek Question

The Greek question of being is foreign even to Western ears. It points to what is nearest at hand yet farthest from our reflective grasp. The question is doubly foreign to Indian ears. The Parmenidean wonder at being was not a foundational event in Indian thought, and so the subsequent Aristotelian question "What is being?" was never posed in the same sense, nor did India produce a metaphysics in the sense of a science of being *qua* being. There is a fit between the being-question and the history of Western metaphysics which makes its illumination central and foundational; the light it can shed on Indian thought may introduce distorting emphases. To ask what destiny of being lies behind Indian thought, as J. L. Mehta does (Mohanty 1992, p. 289), is to risk forcing it into shapes suggested by the Western story (while drawing on questionable reaches of Heidegger's thought).

Heidegger would probably agree that blindness to being is universal - and not only because of the Westernization of the earth through technology. Attention to being must then be equally universal. But it is only in the West that such attention has been thematized as a central concern, by a rare handful of powerful thinkers. The other traditions have different languages for awakening to the reality of the things themselves. As a distinctive thematization of a universally latent problematic - a thematization which in its concrete elaboration has of course many parochial, non-universal features - Western philosophy has an irreducible identity. Thus Heidegger writes, as early as 1939:

> Philosophie heisst *abendländische* Philosophie; - es gibt keine andere als die abendländische, sofern das Wesen dessen, was Abendland und abendländische

> Geschichte ist, durch das bestimmt wird, was überhaupt Philosophie heisst. Darunter haben wir, unter Absehung von jedem Schulbegriff und jeder historischen Deutung der Philosophie als einer Kulturerscheinung, zu verstehen: die Besinnung auf das Seiende als solches im Ganzen, kurz - aber auch wieder unbestimmt, weil mehrdeutig - *das Fragen der Seinsfrage*. "*Sein*" ist das *Grundwort* der Philosophie. [Philosophy is *Western* philosophy; there is no other, for the essence of the West and Western history has been determined through what is called philosophy. Ignoring all academic notions and historical accounts of philosophy as a cultural phenomenon, we should understand it as: reflection on what there is as such as a whole; in short - though this too is indeterminate because polyvalent - *asking the question of being*. "Being" is the *ground-word* of philosophy.] (*GA* 68, p. 9)

It could not be said that "being" is the *Grundwort* of any Indian philosophy. Some of Heidegger's strongest pronouncements on the specificity of metaphysics date from the mid-fifties:

> Der Stil der gesamten abendländisch-europäischen Philosophie - es gibt keine andere, weder eine chinesische noch eine indische - ist von der Zwiefalt "Seiendes-seiend" her bestimmt. Ihr Vorgehen im Bereich dieser Zwiefalt ist massgeblich von der Auslegung geprägt, die Platon dieser Zwiefalt gegeben hat. [The style of all Western/European philosophy - there is no other, neither a Chinese nor an Indian - is determined from the twofold, "beings-being." Its dealings with this twofold take their normative shape from the Platonic account of this twofold.] (Heidegger 1954, p. 136)

The word "style" here suggests that there is a contingency to the development of philosophical and religious traditions comparable to that of artistic styles (see O'Leary 1994), so that what seems normative and natural within one culture may remain unthought of in another. The concept of being is a cultural construction just as much as is that of *mokṣa* or *karman*. Our present insight into cultural pluralism (as Dilthey understood) forces us to renounce the illusion that these great words are transparent namings of the real.

Metaphysics, for Heidegger, is not a system but "*jenes Wissen, darin das abendländische geschichtliche Menschentum die Wahrheit der Bezüge zum Seienden i. G. und die Wahrheit über dieses verwahrt*" ["that knowing in which Western historical humanity preserves the truth of the relation to beings-as-a-whole and the truth about beings-as-a-whole"] (*GA* 9, p. 241). Western philosophy is "*einzigartig*" and "*eindeutig*" (Heidegger 1956, p. 14) because of the unusual question that guides it, the question of the being of beings: "*Die Philosophie ist unterwegs zum Sein des Seienden, d. h. zum Seienden hinsichtlich des Seins*" ["Philosophy is underway to the being of the entity, that is, to the entity in regard to being"] (Heidegger 1956, p. 25). This very simple, but also quite confusing question about beings in their being is one that occurred to the Greeks and that only they pursued in depth:

> Gerade dies, dass das Seiende im Sein versammelt bleibt, dass im Scheinen von Sein das Seiende erscheint, dies setzte die Griechen, und sie zuerst und allein, in das Erstaunen. [Just this, that the entity remains gathered in being, that in the manifesting of being the entity appears, this plunged the Greeks, and them first and only, in amazement.] (Heidegger 1956, p. 22)

It is in this sense that the question, "What is that?" is "*eine ursprünglich griechische Frage*" ["an originally Greek question"] (Heidegger 1956, p. 17), for it is pushed back to its ontological basis: "What is this being *qua* being?"

If Heidegger had embarked on a dialogue with India, he might have been as unwilling to talk about being as he was when in dialogue with theology, or with Japan. This is perhaps less an "exclusion" (OB, p. 25) than a sense that, however fruitful inquiry into the ontological aspect of Indian thought may be, we need to go beyond this if the Indian "great beginning" is to put us in question in light of its own foremost concerns. Even in the case of Western sources which use the Greek language of being correlations with Greek ontology can be treacherous. I am thinking of the Johannine vocabulary of *λόγος*, *εἶναι*, *ἀλήθεια*, *πνεῦμα* and how entirely it would be falsified if one tried to bring it into direct connection with metaphysical or Heideggerian concerns (see O'Leary 1980). Via Philo of Alexandria, John inherited Platonic vocabulary, yet the remarkable thing is how he frees this vocabulary of any associations with the demiurge of the *Timaeus* or any other theme of philosophical ontology.

The claim that the question of being is uniquely Greek does not imply ignorance of the fact that there have been Indian debates about "being," with logical procedures similar to those of the West. "His assertion that the 'question of being' is the one and only question of philosophy seems as excessive as his stubborn insistence that not only ontology, but philosophy in general, is a uniquely Greek-European phenomenon" (OB, p. 11). But in Heidegger's defence it should be noted that he is reducing Western philosophy to a local, historical tradition with a specific question, the question of being; there is no suggestion that India lacked logical analysis and speculative penetration. While Greek thought, at its most distinctive, bathes in the light of being, in other traditions it is not under the aegis of the being-question that logic, ethics, causally based cosmology, theories of truth and of beauty are developed, but in light of some other distinctive opening for thought, such as the question of spiritual liberation. Though much of Indian thought is oblivious of spiritual liberation just as much of Western thought is oblivious of the being-question, the topic of liberation exerted on some of India's greatest thinkers a magnetic attraction comparable to that which being has had at high points of Western philosophy. It is not on the question "what is being *qua* being?" that Indian philosophical radicality converges, and India has largely been spared the intellectual headaches this question has always caused.

Heidegger is the opposite of a Eurocentric imperialist, for his awareness of the historical contingency of Western ontology clears the path to a radical pluralism of what he calls the "great beginnings," though to be sure there is a certain essentialism in the way the tries to cleanly differentiate these traditions (notably the Hellenic and Semitic traditions in the West). His discovery that Greek ontology is but a province of thought makes him a pluralistic thinker in principle, not a provincial one. To stress the commonalities between India and Europe to the point where these differentiations are flattened out is to regress from this dialogal openness. J. N. Mohanty, whose criticism of Heidegger's view of history resembles Halbfass's, seems to court this danger:

> To hold that, since the specific question about the meaning of Being (raised by Heidegger) was not asked in the Indian tradition that tradition's concern with Being cannot yield ontology, would be misleading, for not all those who thought about metaphysics and ontology in the Western tradition asked the Heideggerian question about the meaning of Being ... Metaphysical or ontological thinking is not Greek in origin: a certain variety of it is. (Mohanty 1992, p. 152)

But it is precisely the generic similarity between Indian and Greek philosophy that Heidegger wants to get beyond. The Greek "variety" is not one among others. It is a grasp of being (subjective and objective genitive) which did not come to pass in this insistent, determining way in other traditions, despite their random and tentative broodings on the sense of the word 'being.'

Mohanty thinks that the importance of the subject-object distinction in Indian thought confutes Heidegger's view that it belongs to the Western destiny of being (Mohanty 1992, p. 289); but Heidegger sights Cartesian subjectivity and objectivity in terms of their ontological upshot within Western thought; he does not deny that analogous distinctions may have been made in other traditions, but there they do not play a role in the unfolding of the question of being. How little Mohanty appreciates the strength of Heidegger's reading of the Western metaphysical adventure can be gauged from his misunderstanding of the term "onto-theology": "Heidegger continued to look upon the Kantian Transcendental unity of apperception, the Hegelian *Geist*, the Fichtean Ego as but secularized versions of deeply theological notions. Not surprisingly, Heidegger characterized Western metaphysics as onto-theological" (Mohanty 1992, p. 297).

## II: Ontological Themes in Indian Thought

### (a) The Analysis of "Being" is not Central

The intense logico-linguistic discussion about the words "*as/asti* (corresponding to the Latin *est*, Greek *esti*, English *is*, etc.) and *bhū/bhavati* (which has an intriguing etymological kinship with Greek *phýō/phýsis*)" (OB, p. 22) does not necessarily amount to focussing the question of being as a basic one, in the manner of metaphysics. Still less does it amount to attending to the phenomenon of being, as the Greeks did in their "wonder" at the enigma of being and as Heidegger attempts to do more explicitly by means of phenomenological hermeneutics or poetic thinking. (Poetic thinking could be seen as a more refined and rigorous version of phenomenological hermeneutics, in that it is less encumbered with metaphysical conceptuality and more attuned to the thing itself.) Even if the *darśanas* intensively discuss being and substance (*bhāva, sattā, astitva, dravya*), this may be no more than a scholastic clarification of abstract concepts, of which "being" may be just one among others. The distinction between *sattā* (being) and the second-order concept of *astitva* - "is-ness," "irreducible identity, identifiability" (OB, p. 144), which can apply even to non-existence - is a lucid clarification of ideas, but does it reflect an experience of being? Has the notion of being sufficient valency in Indian thought to be invoked as a solution to the problem of evil, as in the Augustinian teaching that evil is nothing substantial, but a mere defect of being? Never more than a pallid universal - whether conceived as an abstraction or as a primal stuff -, it cannot serve to name the concrete actuality of entities in their analogous diversity.

The verbs for "to be" in Sanskrit are "commonly treated as verbs expressing a peculiar kind of process or action" (OB, p. 22). So is the verb *sein* in Heidegger. But the process or action in question is exclusively the presencing of beings in their being, and confusion with any other kind of process or action is scrupulously avoided; hence the difficulty of Heidegger's language, which is at the service of a basic simplicity. Does the Indian discussion of "to be" bring into view the phenomenon of being in a comparable way? Such topics as occurrence, durable presence, genesis, change, manifestation, actuality/potentiality are ontic rather than ontological unless their specifically ontological import is isolated. Heidegger's exegeses of Aristotle go one step further, descrying the phenomenological core of the ontological statements. Similarly, the logic and semantics of nonbeing and negation do not necessarily amount to a metaphysical question ("why are there beings rather than nothing?") or, still less, to a thoughtful grasp of the phenomenon of nothingness.

The "horizon concepts" or "mythical projections under which being itself is subsumed" (OB, p. 23) suggest that the question of being never acquired autonomy and primacy in Indian thought. It could easily be treated lightly and subordinated to other concerns. When Frauwallner finds parallels between the movement in India from myth, to home-made "scientific" explanations of natural phenomena, to the introduction of a doctrine of categories, and the Greek progress from myth, to Pre-Socratic "science," to Platonic-Aristotelian categoriology, these parallels throw into relief what is missing at every stage: the ontological interest which prevails in the greatest Greek thinkers. As cosmologists, logicians, category-analysts, the Indians are close to the Greeks; but the elusive question of being remains the distinctive trait of the latter. Moreover, the proto-scientific dimension of Indian thought never flourished, for lack of empirical observation; "*die indische Philosophie erreicht auf diesem Gebiet auch nicht annähernd die Leistung der griechischen*" ["in this domain Indian philosophy doesn't even come near the attainments of Greek philosophy"] (Frauwallner 1956, p. 7). Could there be a connection between the non-emergence of the question of being and this lack of empirical curiosity about bodily substances? The Greek wonder at being inspired the interrogation of beings; the Indian readiness to treat the external as secondary or illusory leads to a volatilization of the being-question in favour of issues of spiritual release.

No doubt Sanskrit, just as much as Greek, lends itself to a speculative development and precise analysis of being-language. But isn't there an extra twist in the Greek fascination with being that has no equivalent in the Indian world? Systems of thinking of different cultures may freely intermingle at their lower reaches - in logical or ethical discussion - but when one traces them back to their fundamental motives their difference appears. As the *Seinsfrage* loses its specifically Greek contours it can blend with a more general commonsense puzzling about the logic of "to be" found also in Indian tradition.

Greece is more worthy of question than India on the topic of being:

> As Indo-European, Sanskrit also is in some measure "metaphysical," as distinct from the languages of the Far East, with the notions of Being embedded in it, grammatically and conceptually. It is metaphysical in being representational, concept-generating, and in being productive of ontological speculation about Being as the ground of all that is ... Since *this* possibility of thinking has been fulfilled in its amplest and purest form in the Greek tradition, Heidegger is not interested in how Sanskrit speaks. (Mehta 1987, p. 27; see OB, p. 230)

On other topics, however, India may be the privileged dialogue-partner. Sanskrit shares with Greek "a common stock of philosophical problems, insights, and confusions" (OB, p. 129) in the discussion of universals. Such logical topics were perhaps only imperfectly integrated with the ontological question in the West, and ontological presuppositions may have been a barrier to the development of logic.

Again, Indian epistemological discussions were often in advance of the West, perhaps because they were not clogged by Western commitments to substantial being. In the West, it is only with Kant that epistemology and logic are foregrounded to supplant ontology in the manner of Udayana's (11th century) definition of *astitva* as "being the object of affirmative awareness" or "ascertainability without reference to a counter-entity" (OB, pp. 156-157), or his definition of *dravya* as "what is not the locus of the utter absence of qualities" or "the substrate of three layers of inherence" (OB, p. 93). The Vaiśeṣika thinkers know that "objectivity and cognizability as such cannot establish the distinction between being and nonbeing" (OB, p. 157), but this again sights the reality of being only in a logical perspective and offers no distinct positive conception of its nature.

In the treatment of perception (see Matilal 1986), the rival claims of phenomenalism, representationalism and direct realism could be discussed all the more lucidly in that the ontology of substance was not hovering over them as a daunting enigma. Heidegger is a direct realist; he would say: "I see the tree in the garden, not the representation of the tree," but with an ontological, Aristotelian twist, quite absent in India - "I apprehend the tree in its being, either letting it be in poetic, meditative thinking, or cramping its being in technological, calculative objectifications." Merely epistemological clarification of perception cannot fulfil the Western philosopher's thirst for being, to which Heidegger recalls the tradition, and which he retrieves beneath the epistemological burrowings of Descartes and Kant. A parallel argument that Indian epistemology is led by the tacit question of being would be less persuasive.

Again, many themes in the philosophy of mind as developed in the West seem to have been explored more radically in India, so that here one cannot afford to neglect "how Sanskrit speaks." Conversely, it would be hard to discuss Yogācāra, for example, without drawing on the resources of a Hegelian or Husserlian phenomenology of consciousness. Yet the "selective affinities" (Larson and Bhattacharya 1987, p. 641) between parts of both traditions do not amount to identical problematics. In any case they do not concern Heidegger's question; he uses the term "consciousness" only for the modern medium of the apprehension of being, which, since Descartes, entails an occlusion of the authentic phenomenality of being. On the theme of consciousness, India may challenge Europe, whereas on the theme of being, it is Europe's force that challenges India.

Reference to India certainly introduces a broader horizon, bringing our own puzzling ontological legacy into a fuller perspective. But it may be instructive above all as showing how a great intellectual tradition can get on *without* the question of being. Analogously, what makes Buddhism instructive to Christianity is the way it gets on without the question of God. The "relativistic detachment" (OB, p. 12) such comparison induces may weaken our commitment to the frameworks of our own tradition, but it is likely also to confirm that our tradition is local and idiosyncratic – that monotheism is characteristically Jewish and that ontology is characteristically Greek, even if one does find notions of God and of being in other traditions.

### (b) Being as Stuff and as Abstraction

The Indian notion of being wavers between reification and conceptualism, both of which occlude at base the phenomenon of being. There is no higher understanding of being whereby a critique of these notions could be carried out, though they may be transcended towards an absolute beyond being. Some Sāṅkhya statements look like universal ontological theses, e.g.: "There is no origination for what is not, nor destruction for what is" (OB, p. 59). But these may amount to no more than a principle of conservation of the material universe. Thinkers who see *sat*, pure being, as "the universal substrate" (OB, p. 59) may likewise think of being only as a stuff; the *Chāndogya Upaniṣad*'s teaching that "In the beginning my dear, this world was just Being" (OB, p. 26) glides swiftly into an evolutional unfolding, of which being is no more than the undifferentiated point of departure.

Prabhākara (Mīmāṃsā) rejected the general concept of existence on the ground that "we do not in fact perceive things as merely existing. The true sense of existence is merely the individuality of things (*svarūpa-sattā*); it is not a true class character" (Keith 1978, p. 58; see OB, p. 156). The apperception of being *qua* being, in its transcendental, analogous character – which is neither an empirical datum nor an abstract concept – is again missed here.

In Vaiśeṣika, ontological thought was arrested by a fundamental option for ontological realism (Frauwallner 1956, p. 119) and especially by the treatment of *sattā* as a "reified universal" (OB, p. 150). For Halbfass, the notion of inherence (*samavāya*) has ontological status as "the one pervasive structure of our universe that constitutes the condition of the possibility of concrete, qualified entities and of contingent existence" (OB, p. 148). A faint suspicion: do the refinements sighted here depend on a Kantian lens? Others view this notion of inherence as another reified abstraction. But if we see inherence as a pervasive ontological structure, comparable to Buddhist dependent origination or Vedāntic *māyā*, we may still ask whether these structures which govern the emergence and relations of beings ever bring into focus their being *qua* being. A causal and logical ordering of things may trace their origins without interrogating their being, as happens in the sciences for example. The extra step which raises the question of being may be a step back or away from sensible logical or causal thinking. It is doubtful if Western discourse on being is a harmonious continuation of logical and causal investigation; it seems rather to introduce a troubling cloudiness; and even when being is finally tamed to logic and grounds it seems unhappy in its onto-theological abode, as if itching to break out again. In India the analysis of being never clouds over in this way. Buddhism and Vedānta also take a step into realms irreducible to logic or common sense, but led by other issues than the question of being. The energy of fundamental questioning is captured by these issues, and being as such is not what becomes problematic.

Again, defences of stable identity against Buddhist doctrines of universal momentariness and flux (OB, p. 151) are not properly ontological. The concept of "practical efficiency" (*arthakriyā*) as a criterion of being focusses on the problem of distinguishing reality from appearance (OB, p. 152) rather than on the question of what being as such is. If the Buddhists used it to give a reductive account of being-language, this again is not ontology but a discrediting of ontology. On the Buddhist side, being had only conventional reality, and did not become a subject of contemplation for its own sake; on the other side, the defence of robust ontological realism against Buddhist subversion left little leisure for disinterested musing on the enigmatic character of being. Such musing remains a peculiarly Greek pastime and to pursue it today one has to think as a Greek rather than as an Indian.

Vyomaśiva (c. 800-850 CE) expresses the Vaiśeṣika ambition thus: "I shall enumerate everything in the world that has the character of being" (OB, p. 69). Does this mean that an ontological understanding - "one comprehensive horizon of being" (OB, p. 70) - underlies the task of categorization? The idea of being (*bhāva*) at work here may be an unexamined one, just an everyday commonsense notion of what is real. If one proceeds from it to the listing, never returning back to thematize the enigmatic aspects of the notion itself, one has not embarked on ontology in the sense of a questioning of being. The explicit discussion of *bhāva* in Vaiśeṣika resorts to abstract universals immediately; "existence is a universal only" (*sūtra* I.2.4, quoted OB, p. 140), "that genus which is not a species lying under any superior genus" (Potter 1977, p. 140). "'Reality' (*sattā*) constitutes the 'ultimate universal' or 'supreme generality.' It is all-inclusive and pervades all substances, qualities, and motions" (OB, p. 117). "Being is one, because of the uniformity of its mark 'is,' and because of the absence of any mark of differentiation" (Potter 1977, p. 213).

> Being is not a substance, because it possesses one substance. It is neither a motion nor a quality, because it exists in qualities and motions. Also because of the absence of genus and species in it, Being is known to be different from substance, quality, and motion. For the same reasons, substanceness, qualityhood, and motionhood are known to be different from substance, quality, and motion. (Potter 1977, pp. 213-214)

Being here is a pure abstraction, comparable to substanceness or motionhood. Aristotle, in contrast, rejects the interpretation of being as supreme genus (OB, pp. 2, 140); only in doing so can he keep open the question of being in its multivocity, and glimpse the irreducibility of being as the *transcendens schlechthin* (*GA* 2, p. 51; *GA* 9, pp. 336-337), in its qualitative difference from entities (the ontological difference). Phenomenologically, existence is not a universal, a predicate universally applied, but in each case the distinctive act or event of existing – *ἐνέργεια*. Here Vaiśeṣika finds nothing worthy of thought. The readiness to identify *bhāva* as the supreme genus cuts off the question of being at its roots. In the West, when being is thought of in this abstract way it represents a forgetfulness of the question; in India it represents a failure of the question to emerge. We have at best an undetermined sense that "as the supreme universal it is also something over and above, and different from, the particular and perishable entities in which it occurs" and "imperishable and permanent" (OB, p. 140; see also p. 144).

(c) Shared Themes

1. *Form*. There is a wonder at form in Indian thought. But again it is not clear that this carried the charge of a wonder at being. Is there any Indian notion of form that plays the specifically ontological role that *εἶδος* has in Plato and Aristotle? Even the "form itself is emptiness" of the *Heart Sūtra* grasps phenomena in their phenomenality, not specifically in their being. A phenomenology of the empirical world in view of emptiness is quite a different matter from one in view of being. Though one might find in Plotinus, Spinoza, Berkeley, Bradley, or Bergson some rough analogies to Madhyamaka and Advaita notions that the objective world with its differentiations has a merely conventional reality, or that all empirical objects are merely superimpositions on the pure undifferentiated ultimate reality, nonetheless such ideas are still, after two centuries of Western exposure to Vedānta, experienced as foreign and unsettling. The Western concern with being and form seems to have worked against a radicalization of the question of appearance and reality. This concern was reinforced by the Christian metaphysics of creation which stressed the distinct existence of finite created substance, and by the doctrine of Chalcedon (451) which, by insisting on the integrity of Christ's human nature, formed a bulwark against emanationist or absorptionist accounts of the relation of human and divine (see von Balthasar 1988, pp. 35-41;

he refers sweepingly to "*asiatische Auflösung*," p. 122). To Western thinkers, Indian reflection on *māyā* and emptiness initially seems but an inchoate groping toward their own mastery of logical determinations. But if these Indian worlds of thought could be tucked neatly away in the folds of Hegel's *Logic*, they would not be worth our study. Their cultural and historical roots make them more than mere intellectual contructions. As living paths of thought they elude our mastery and summon us to open dialogue.

2. *Causality*. In Indian thought a fascination with causality has given rise to theories at least as subtle as those of the West. However, this causal reasoning was not applied to being *qua* being, but only to entities - cosmic or psychological - in their arising and passing way. Cause, in India, is not the Aristotelian *aition*, namely "*jenes, was verschuldet, dass ein Seiendes* das *ist, was es ist*" ["that which is responsible for the fact that a being is *that* which it is"] (*GA* 9, p. 246). We do not find in India "Parmenides's persistence in holding fast to the purity and simplicity of the experience contained in the single Greek word *Esti* ('it is'), by the sharp repulsion of the obtrusive tendency to address being in terms of *doxa*, as coming to be and passing away" (Kisiel 1993, p. 246). Descending from the Eleatic acropolis one may indeed retrieve the world of coming to be and passing away as a worthy theme of specifically ontological thought; but this was not the Indian perspective.

In the West, causal arguments for the existence of God quickly become ontological. The arguments from motion or design can be reduced to the argument that finite or participated being requires to be grounded in Being itself. The arguments of Udayana in the *Nyāyakusumāñjali* sometimes have a familiar feel to Western readers, for instance the temporal argument against self-causation: "Nor can things be self-caused, since a thing cannot both originate at a certain time and yet exist prior to that time, and the causal relation involves temporal succession" (Potter 1977, p. 559); compare Aquinas: "*nihil est causa semetipsius; esset enim prius seipso, quod est impossibile*" (*Contra Gentiles* I 18). Yet as he develops his causal reasoning, it is striking how rarely he alights on the ontological notions that would immediately suggest themselves to the Western mind. "Causation just means regular connection between something prior to the effect and the appearance of that effect" (Potter 1977, p. 560). There is a touch of Humean refinement to this, but no sense of the production of an effect as an ontological (rather than merely ontic) event - no glimpse of the cause as bringing the effect from potency to act in virtue of its own actuality. This might give Udayana a modern cast, prompting comparison of his arguments with Western discussions of causality since Leibniz. Most of his arguments are epistemological: "we need the hypothesis of God to justify the initial acceptance of the Vedas by reasonable men" (Potter 1977, p. 574). Epistemological acuity seems to crowd out talk of being. Again, when Udayana plays with the notions of "latent causality, potentiality, and manifestation" (OB, p. 58) in his dialectical refutation of the sheer actualism of the Buddhist doctrine of momentariness, it does not appear that these acquire any properly ontological consistency for him.

Earlier, Vyomaśiva had defined the production of objects as "connection with their own causes and reality" rather than merely "(coming into) existence after prior nonexistence" (OB, p. 193); this had some ontological bite. Udayana regresses to the view that "'Being an effect' is simply the state of being of something that did not exist before" (OB, p. 195). His disregard of the earlier stress on *sattāsambandha*, "connection with reality," may reflect a major ontological reorientation as Halbfass suggests. But *sattāsambandha*, as originally used by Praśastapāda (6th century), "does not answer or even address the question what being, reality, or existence is." It has the merely logical, classificatory sense of "having reality as a predicate" (OB, pp. 170, 174). It seems that discussion of causality never made the breakthrough to a radically ontological treatment.

3. *Act and potency*. Halbfass claims that the debate between Sāṅkhya *satkāryavāda* and Vaiśeṣika *asatkāryavāda* - between "actualization of the nonactual" and "production of new actualities out of preexisting underlying actualities" (OB, p. 186) - is not merely about causation but is "a genuinely ontological debate," albeit marked by "a certain refusal to address each other's basic premises concerning the nature of being and the different meanings in which the words *sat* and *asat* are used" (OB, p. 58). The "being" from which things originate in Sāṅkhya is a kind of being that Vaiśeṣika does not recognize at all, characterized by "potency, potentiality, latency, indefiniteness, and subtleness" (OB, p. 185). There is a contrast in ontology here, but if the two *darśanas* did not join battle on this topic, then the specifically ontological question was eluded.

Even if the Vaiśeṣika *sattā* could be seen, in the light of the Sāṅkhya *pradhāna*, as "a mere storehouse of potentialities or as potentiality par excellence" (OB, p. 177), the potentiality in question is not purely ontological δύναμις but the concrete evolutional substrate, the "indefinite, nonmanifest, nonactualized ground" of the cosmos (OB, p. 185). Criticizing the language of modern Sāṅkhya scholars who talk of effects as "specifications of the inherent generativity of primordial materiality" (Larson and Bhattacharya 1987, p. 68), Halbfass says such language "does not address the fundamental ontological issue" (OB, p. 59); but it may be an Aristotelian lens that enables him to sharpen the ontological focus. If the Sāṅkhya sources did not in fact get beyond a material image of evolutionary transformation, we must not read back into them Aristotelian conceptions of δύναμις, ἐντελεχεία and final causality. These notions can be applied to Sāṅkhya from outside, but they have a transcendental generality that the Sāṅkhya notions lack. Since they capture aspects of being *qua* being, they apply to any being whatsoever, from God to the abstractions of mathematics or logic. True, a general concept of potency, applicable to everything, is found in Vaiśeṣika; but its ontological foundation is not securely grasped. To stress Udayana's concern with "potentiality" (OB, pp. 58, 65) is to underline the fact that he does not reflect on potentiality as a state of *being*. To conceive of the potential and the actual in a general commonsense way, or merely as abstract logical categories, is not to attain the Aristotelian insight into potential being and actual being.

In Yoga, "Transition from potentiality (*śakti*) to actuality (*abhivyakti*) in the mental sphere means change from an unconscious, 'unnoticed' (*aparidṛṣṭa*) state to a conscious, 'noticed' (*paridṛṣṭa*) one" (OB, pp. 60-61): here there is no reference to being. "Present phenomena are manifest, that is, actual; past and future phenomena are subtle, that is, potential ... The concepts of actuality and potentiality are thus used in an attempt to clarify the nature of time" (OB, p. 61). Again, the contrast between subtle and manifest is not the equivalent of the Aristotelian focus on being in potency and in act. It seems misleading to see here an insight into "the enigmatic relationship between being and time" (OB, p. 62). Nor do Bhartṛhari's questions - "How does the verb *be* (*bhū*), how does the noun *reality* (*sattā*) refer to time? ... How can 'being' itself in its verbal sense, as an act or process, be there?" (OB, p. 207) - rise from the logico-ontic to the ontological level. Again, Bhartṛhari's thesis that time (conceived as a substance) activates "those powers and potentialities (*śakti*) that constitute the condition of the possibility of all actual, particularized existence," or that "reality itself (*sattā*), the highest universal, is unleashed and manifested in those lower universals (*jāti*) which are the eternal prototypes and potentialities of all particulars" (OB, pp. 205-206), is a speculative construction that does not entail a phenomenological meditation on the interplay of being and time.

4. *Time*. The closest one comes to such a phenomenology in India is in the Buddhist tendency to "an increasingly radical and explicit fusion of being and time or temporality" (OB, p. 221). But even here Nāgārjuna uses the mutual dependence of past, present and future to prove that none of them has real existence; this demonstration of emptiness shows little puzzling over the phenomenon of time for its own sake. For Advaita, "time appears as fundamentally incompatible with reality in the true sense" (OB, p. 221), whereas Western thought, even in Neo-Platonism, has dwelt attentively on the being, or half-being, of time. The Greek way of posing the question "What is time?" or any other "What is" question is honed by a focus on essence or being. Indian definition, in contrast

> n'a pas de rapport avec ce que nous appelerions l'essence d'une chose ... Parce que je lis l'universel dans le concret, au niveau même du concret, je suis dispensé de penser cet universel, de le conceptualiser, d'en définir l'essence [has no relation with what we would call the essence of a thing. ... Because I read the universal in the concrete, at the very level of the concrete, I am dispensed from thinking that universal, from conceptualizing it, from defining its essence]. (Biardeau 1957, pp. 373, 375)

Indian analysis was not answerable to a strict, authoritative regime of essence (as even Christian theology has been); its starting points and its goals were of varied religious or speculative kinds, each determining a style of analysis only rarely coincident with the "scientific" and "philosophical" attitudes central in the West. Heidegger is the heir of Aristotle (and Augustine) whose aporetic interrogation of the most salient phenomenological features of time set the agenda for Western thought on the subject. Rather than dissolve time in true Being he focusses more sharply the phenomenon of being by bringing into view the inevitable temporality of its play of presence and absence.

## (d) Categories

Halbfass's account of the Vaiśeṣika categories confirms the impression that categories in Indian thought do not carry the same ontological intention as in Aristotle. Aristotle's categories are rooted in a full apprehension of substances in their being; there are few of them and they lend themselves to empirical, phenomenological exposition and interrogation (as in the *Physics*); Vaiśeṣika categories are abstract and multiply, to fill out a system, more by logical distinction than by reference to phenomenological aspects of observed entities; if they map out "what there is," they do so with little attention to the being of what there is. Udayana's attempt to derive and justify the Vaiśeṣika categories (OB, p. 79) stresses the primacy of substance (*dravya*) in a commonsense way, but does not attempt to order them in terms of being.

Heidegger was aware of the categorical genius of the Sanskrit language:

> Eine *κατηγορία* ist ein Wort, durch das eine Sache in dem "belangt" wird, was sie ist. Diese vorphilosophische Bedeutung von *κατηγορία* bleibt weit entfernt von derjenigen, die dem lässigen und oberflächlichen Fremdwort "Kategorie" in unserer Sprache noch verblieben ist. Der erwähnte Aristotelische Sprachgebrauch entspricht vielmehr ganz dem griechischen Sprachgeist, der allerdings ein unausgesprochen philosophisch-metaphysischer ist und daher die griechische Sprache zusammen mit dem Sanskrit und der gutverwahrten deutschen Sprache vor allen anderen Sprachen auszeichnet. (Heidegger 1961, II, p. 73) [A *katēgoria* is a word in which a thing is "indicted" as what it is. This prephilosophical meaning of *katēgoria* is far removed from that which the casual and superficial foreign word *category* still retains in our language. The Aristotelian usage just cited corresponds much rather to the spirit of the Greek language which, as tacitly philosophical and metaphysical, distinguishes Greek, along with Sanskrit and cultivated German, above all other languages.] (Heidegger 1982, p. 37; modified)

But the "special affinity between ontology and categoriality" (OB, p. 139) does not mean that a developed system of categories necessarily implies a profound ontology; indeed the question of being can throw one's categories into confusion, whereas dexterity in handling categories can go hand in hand with forgetfulness of being.

Kaṇāda's six categories do not include "isness"; neither do Aristotle's ten, but *οὐσία* is related to *εἶναι*, *ὄν*, whereas *dravya* (substance) is not related to *sat* or *astitva*. To be sure, among the six, substance, quality, and activity are singled out as connected to being (*sattā*). In the list of ten we find *śakti* and *aśakti*, potentiality and nonpotentiality. There is confusion as to whether the universal, *sattā*, applies to all positive categories or to the first three only. In any case since the three following categories (universal, particularity, inherence) inhere in the first three, and since quality and activity inhere in substance as their substrate, there is a strong identification of substance with being, as in Aristotle. So in this sense "explicit conceptualization of being" does indeed "emerge out of the enumeration and classification of what there is" (OB, p. 139). But does it emerge as just a formal abstraction? Is it an especially thought-provoking concept, a source of wonder - or is it merely an occasion for logical clarifications? "Is the Vaiśeṣika ontology an epiphenomenon of its categoriology? Is there an understanding of being which is prior to, and the condition of, its project of categorial analysis and enumeration?" (OB, p. 139). "A sense of 'being' that implies, above all, enumerability and identifiability" (OB, p. 220) is a very undeveloped notion of the meaning of being - and one that is "internally inconsistent, theoretically unfeasible" and "soteriologically irrelevant or counterproductive" (OB, p. 70). Even if other Indian thinkers formulated such negative evaluations of the ontological upshot of enumerability, they did not necessarily do so from an ontological concern of the sort that we are likely to import into the Indian framework. Neither the positive nor the negative implications of Vaiśeṣika ontology bring it into the neighbourhood of the highest Western thematization of being.

Even if Indian thought lends itself to Heideggerian exegesis in a way that biblical thought, for example, does not, what the exegesis yields is much less rich than in the case of Western sources and also much less illuminating as regards the internal dynamic of Indian thought. In Western thinking led by the question of being the categoriology is a fleshing out of the prior understanding of being (even in philosophers such as Hegel who have "forgotten" being as the Greeks saw it). The tendency to enumeration, so tiresome in Abhidharma, Sāṅkhya and Vaiśeṣika, never took hold among the Greeks, because their overriding philosophical interest was not the multiplicity of beings but their unity in being. Vaiśeṣika enumeration aims to be an exhaustive catalogue of the many; some Vedāntin critics insisted that "an understanding of Being cannot be gained through an enumeration and classification of different entities. True, absolute being transcends and precedes all distinctions, including the distinction between being and nonbeing" (OB, p. 159). But do even the Vedāntins linger in meditation on the *ἕν πάντα* in terms of the being of beings? Does their quest for unity get beyond an ontic totalization? Having identified the principle of cosmic unity, do they go on to interrogate it, and to dwell on the enigmatic interplay of the one universal reality of being and the many distinct individual entities? Their monism is the obverse of Vaiśeṣika enumeration, and equally argues a forgetfulness of being: they "argue against the very possibility of defining entities, of establishing them in their individual identity, and of defining and establishing being itself in its distinction from nonbeing" (OB, p. 232). The failure to focus being as being is in both cases due to an overriding concern with spiritual liberation. Multiplicity, for the Abhidharma or Vaiśeṣika, is of interest primarily as a map of the obstacles or aids to liberation, while the Vedāntins' stress on unity also has a primarily soteriological purpose; whether controlled by categorization or totalized and dissolved in some form of monism the many ceases to obstruct liberation.

When Western metaphysics declines into representational thinking, used as a means of technological mastery of the earth, an expression of the will to power, this should not be equiparated with vaguely similar features in Indian thought:

> "Representational," "objectifying" thought is fully present in the Vaiśeṣika system of categories, in its enterprise of enumerating and classifying whatever there is, and above all, in its conceptualizations of being. To be sure, it is not a Cartesian attempt to establish man as the master and owner of nature; but it is an attempt to put the world at our intellectual and conceptual disposal, to explain it once and for all through a process of comprehensive enumeration and classification. Being itself is either objectified and appears as an entity among entities or it accompanies the process of enumeration as its receding horizon or expanding shadow. (OB, p. 231)

Here a Heideggerian lens allows one to find a phenomenon of rationalistic decadence in Indian scholasticism, and at the same time this casts doubt on Heidegger's claim to explain such phenomena in the West exclusively in terms of the destiny of the thinking of being. But what also emerges is that the Indian phenomenon lacks the distinctive ontological import that it has in Western rationalism; it even appears to suffer a certain aimlessness in comparison with the intense determination of the Western rational project. The fixational character of Vaiśeṣika categorizations, criticized by Śaṅkara (OB, p. 231), contrasts with the dynamic thrust of Western rationalism precisely in this: that the West is haunted by the quest for Being (however narrowly conceived) whereas Vaiśeṣika is trapped in the enumeration of beings. In short, Vaiśeṣika thinking is ontic, not ontological. Or if it has an ontological upshot, this is clarified by reference to the Greek tradition, just as the relevancy of Western philosophy to the attainment of *mokṣa* could be clarified only by reference to the Indian tradition.

### (e) The Absence of the Question of Being in Nāgārjuna and Śaṅkara

The Indian style of thought which effects a "simultaneous de-objectification of the objectified" may make Indian philosophy "a treasure house of direct promise to the Heideggerian quest" (Mehta 1987, p. 44). But to conflate it with the Heideggerian tension between calculative and meditative thinking is to slur over the basic difference between the thought of being and the nondual apprehension of Brahman or *śūnyatā*. Nāgārjuna and Śaṅkara, in their overcoming of the conventional in the name of a different kind of thinking or apperception which reaches highest truth, recall Heidegger's overcoming of metaphysical and technological reason in the name of the thinking of being. In both cases what is to be overcome is allowed validity in its proper sphere; though in both cases there is a certain ambivalence towards the realm of the conventional that is never quite resolved. But the ultimate truth aimed at in the Indian thinkers is of a loftier order than the contemplative apprehension of beings in their being, and they do not have any time to linger on the latter occupation. Advaita overshoots the thought of being to affirm instead "the nondual state of *ātman/brahman* that is prior to, and the condition of, all apparent dichotomies and alternatives, including those between being and nonbeing" (OB, p. 233), and the same may be said of the Madhyamaka affirmation of emptiness. The contemplative nonduality both cultivate cannot be equated with Heidegger's goal, the togetherness of being and thinking in the *Ereignis*.

Halbfass claims that in addition to the negative ontology - "beyond being and non-being" - Indian thought also apprehends the character of being in a positive way in a kind of "soteriontology." Śaṅkara's concept of liberation and Nāgārjuna's emptiness have "an undeniably ontological dimension" (OB, p. 39). The trouble is that any transcending of beings to their ground or to their true identity has an *implicit* ontological dimension, but its explicit thematization is likely to remain vague or inadequate unless the question of being has been elaborated beforehand. To what extent is Halbfass's focus on the ontological upshot of Śaṅkara's or Nāgārjuna's language the product of his schooling in Western ontology?

Unlike earlier Buddhist analysis, which stopped at the identification of *dharmas* as its end-point (OB, p. 54), Nāgārjuna's question about the ultimate reality of these *dharmas* and his diagnosis that it is emptiness offers a semblance of the Western question of being. But is the doctrine of emptiness established by ontological inquiry into the being of *dharmas* and is it presented as an answer to such inquiry? There is a dialectical dissolution of the *dharmas*' claim to substantial identity, so that they are no longer obstacles to the vision of emptiness, but the topic of the being of these entities does not emerge prominently. When Nāgārjuna treats objective categorizations as "part of the conventional world of *saṃvṛti* and *vyavahāra*" to be surpassed in "the transcendence of *is* and *is not* ..., the disappearance of our preoccupation with being and nonbeing" (OB, p. 233), he takes conventional notions of being and non-being as they stand, and then transcends them towards a condition to which ontological language does not apply; he does not interrogate them for their own sake; the idea of being is undone not by a leap back to its origin (the *Ereignis*) but by a leap forward to *nirvāṇa*.

The transcendence of both *sat* and *asat* was typical of higher Indian speculation from Vedic times (OB, p. 32) and prevented a focus on beings in their beingness. "The sense of transcending the entire 'ontic' realm, which we find not only in Vedic-Upaniṣadic thought, but also, though in a radically different style, in Buddhism (most notably in Nāgārjuna's *Śūnyavāda*)," (OB, p. 43) is not something distinctively ontological: it overleaps the phenomenon of beingness in favour of Brahman or emptiness. To say that "radical critique of worldly notions of being and identity may, indeed, be reflections and expressions of an intense search for, and commitment to, being and identity" (OB, p. 233) is an impossibly vague statement that only confirms that Nāgārjuna never embarked on the discourse of the question of being; Heidegger's critique of worldly notions of being is indeed ontologically motivated, but Nāgārjuna's motivation is radically different, however one describes it. David Loy believes that "Buddhism includes a strong ontotheological element" which Nāgārjuna seeks to deconstruct. He explains the Madhyamaka distinction between conventional and ultimate truth in Derridian terms: ultimate truth "points beyond language and therefore beyond truth, raising the question of 'the truth of truth' and the very possibility of truth in philosophy" - "the 'higher truth' ... is that there is no truth" (Loy 1992, pp. 227, 241, 244). Such loose analogies blur the specific contours of what Nāgārjuna was doing in the second century and what Heidegger and Derrida are doing in the twentieth. The Indian "'tension and balance' between objectification and its transcendence" follows a spiritual dynamic as remote from Greek ontology as it is from Christian mysticism. The Indian "meaningful silence about being" (OB, p. 234) is a silence that is not really about being but about that of which the language of being cannot speak. Heidegger never gives up the effort to bring being to speech, even if the names he finally comes up with are no longer ontological ones. Indian categorization lacks ontological bite, and its move to silence is a further move away from the being-question.

## III: Quasi-Heideggerian Overcoming in Indian Tradition

(a) Can Heidegger's quest for a regrounding of thinking in a contemplative presence to being and beings, world and things, be extended, *mutatis mutandis*, to Indian philosophy? Analogous extensions of Heideggerian overcoming to Christian theology, favoured by Heidegger himself in his dialogue with theologians, have had a twofold character. The first stage has been an overcoming of the metaphysics in Christian tradition, implementing the Heideggerian critique not for the sake of the "truth of being" but for the sake of the biblical revelation, compromised by its ontological explication (O'Leary 1985). The intra-Christian differentiation of original, authentic Christianity from the various forms of occlusion or forgetfulness which it has fallen into is not a distinctively Heideggerian path of overcoming, but a structural similarity allows us to call it "quasi-Heideggerian." The movement from occluding secondariness back to the primary and originary, whether in Heidegger, in Christianity, or in Indian thought, can become too sweeping. But whatever demystification or deconstruction is required need not entail an invalidation of its basic concern. If deconstruction makes of the ontological difference only one difference among others, in a general play of *différence*, "weaving the ontological difference's traits into the quasi-synthetic arrangement of differance" (Gasché 1994, p. 105), or if it treats the quest for a more faithful phenomenological grasp of the event of being or the event of revelation as the product of a delusive metaphysics of presence, then deconstruction itself becomes a rationalism sunk in forgetfulness of being.

Since Indian philosophy was not affected by Greek thought, Heidegger's critique of metaphysics has no direct application to it, apart from inspiring a general attentiveness to the alienating character of abstract formalism and suggesting a method of historical genealogy. An intra-Indian differentiation of the authentic depths of Indian thought from alienated traditions does not have to wrestle with the Western fate of rationalism and technology, but with whatever fate hangs heavily on

Indian history. (Of course India has to struggle with the modern West as well, and may appropriate the Heideggerian critique.)

Halbfass evokes "the Vedic sense of the openness of space and what we may call a primeval metaphysical *clearing*" and "a sense of wonder and amazement about that which appears in this extended openness, the spatial and temporal things that emerge in it ... experienced in the sheer amazing presence and inexplicable contingency of their existence" (OB, pp. 30-31). As Heidegger finds traces of a primordial unhiddenness in the Pre-Socratics, the Vedas reveal in its first immediacy the Indian experience of the "worlding of world." Yet the topics of wonder, contingency, and the clearing (*Lichtung*) are perhaps still too Heideggerian to match the intrinsic phenomenological lineaments of the Vedic world. One remembers Heidegger's comment on Bultmann's existential interpretation of New Testament categories: "That's too Heideggerian for me!" Again, how serviceable are the Heideggerian elements in this statement?: "One may say that *Brahman* and *Atman* are the ground-words of the Indian tradition, not just words or concepts, but the very embodiment of that primordial unhiddenness in the light of which the Indian mind thenceforth breathed and thought" (Mehta 1970, p. 305). "Primordial unhiddenness" has a specific phenomenological thrust in Heidegger, as a description of the originary truth (*ἀ-λήθεια*) of being, but it is devalued when used indiscriminately to describe the other "great beginnings." Similar applications of Heideggerian language in Christian theology have the same doubly falsifying effect. The central Indian phenomena are the depths of the mind or the supreme simplicity of emptiness, themes remote from Heidegger as the otherworldliness of Neo-Platonism is.

The Indian love of concept and speculation is too close to what Heidegger was fleeing from, and does not offer the refreshing contrast of the Chinese use of characters and aphorisms to name things in their concreteness. It is with Daoism, and the Daoist element in Zen Buddhism, that his thought finds the most vibrant affinities. His recall to living in the present world, to letting things be in a wise passivity, and his use of paradoxical language to awaken to here-and-now reality, are quickly understood by Asian readers. The vast spaces of Chinese paintings are conjoined with an intensively this-worldly sense of mortals in their finitude and of the thereness of things, and thus invite Heideggerian attention. Regrettably, his dealings with the East were thwarted by the language-barrier: "The greatest difficulty in this enterprise always lies, as far as I can see, in the fact that with few exceptions there is no command of the Eastern languages either in Europe or the United States" (quoted, Nagley 1970).

Both Christianity and Indian thought can learn from the Heideggerian quest for the phenomenal, worldly reality which grounds Western metaphysical language. The overcoming of metaphysics puts in question its basic frameworks, such as the distinction between being and becoming, and questions back to what underlies these frameworks and is occluded by them. In Indian thought, the distinction between the world of *karman* and transmigration and the salvific goal of release constitutes a basic framework that has perhaps been grasped in ways that occlude its original significance. To bring to light the unthought of this tradition, an overcoming should focus not on "forgetfulness of being" but on "forgetfulness of release" - in this respect Buddhism and Vedānta play a quasi-Heideggerian role.

If Buddhism, in its concern with liberation, neglects the being of the beings it analyses as "empty of self-nature," it may be that Heidegger, conversely, in his fascination with the "thinging of things" neglects the realm of transmundane spiritual freedom. Each tradition is pursuing its own overcoming from within, in an irreducible variety of ways - Heidegger, Wittgenstein, Derrida on the one hand; different forms of Vedānta and Buddhism on the other. When the Eastern and Western styles of overcoming meet, the resulting hybrids may be superficial academic constructions or a convincing new departure. The gesture of overcoming has on both sides to be released from its doctrinaire sheath - Buddhist, Vedāntic, and Heideggerian orthodoxies are relativized as they are brought to bear on traditions remote from their original field of application.

(b) Heidegger's reading of the history of metaphysics digs beneath homonyms to discover the quite different ontological horizons presiding over, say, the principle of contradiction in Aristotle, Leibniz, Hegel, and Nietzsche:

> Der Satz sagt jeweils Wesentliches nicht nur über den "Widerspruch," sondern über das Seiende als solches und über die Art der Wahrheit, in der das Seiende als solches erfahren und entworfen ist. (Heidegger 1961, II, p. 159) [The principle says something essential not only about "contradiction" but about the being as such and about the kind of truth in which the being as such is experienced and projected.] (Heidegger 1982, p. 112)

Can we bring the tired doxography of histories of Indian philosophy into such an enlightening perspective, by differentiating the horizons within which theses and principles are generated? An obstacle to this is the relative stability of Indian intellectual history. Heidegger overcomes metaphysics as a history that has run its course; only the completion of this history allows us to step back to what could not be thought by any system within the tradition. Has Indian thought also completed a historical trajectory that now opens up a space for more radical questioning? Whereas Heidegger's many targets – the Platonic dualism between soul and body, literal and figurative, medieval creationism, the onto-theological constitution of metaphysics, the increasing hegemony of the principle of sufficient reason, the objectivation of beings and the dominance of narrowly defined Cartesian subjectivity, the technological reduction of being to the functional, the latent nihilism of metaphysics – are united under a single rubric: the story of being's self-concealment in the various formations of metaphysics, it is hard to tell a similar overarching story of Indian thought. The major systems persist with little change from the time of their consolidation. Even if Śaṅkara or Rāmānuja represent a transformation in the essence of Vedānta or the Mahāyāna sūtras and philosophies are a revolution within Buddhism, these developments are not matched by contemporaneous events in the other traditions.

Heidegger's story of how metaphysics moves through various transformations of its essence, as destined by being, belongs to a tradition of such stories (Hegel, Dilthey, Nietzsche). The composition of the tale is helped by its narrow setting – philosophical Europe, dwindling after Descartes to Germany alone – and by the cult of progress and sense of historicity that have increasingly marked Europe. India is too big, and the social distances between its schools and religions too wide, for a tidy story to be told, nor does it help the teller by any innate sense of its own historicity. Indian thinkers laboured at an eternal tradition, rather than worrying, with Hegel, that their works would be sold off at the next bookfair. In the age of the Cathedrals, as the scholastics unrolled their commentaries on Aristotle and the *Sentences*, Europe may have briefly enjoyed that boundless intellectual peace which was the Indian norm. Perhaps one of the results of exposure to India will be that history will lose the hegemonic status it enjoys in Hegel and Heidegger (and in theology in its relation of mutual influence to these thinkers).

(c) The foundational Indian texts – the Vedas, the Upaniṣads, the Buddhist Sūtras, the *Bhagavadgītā* – raised questions about being only incidentally to cosmological, psychological and soteriological debates. In the *darśanas*, there is inverse proportion between scholastic analysis of the concept of being and existential concern with deliverance. In Vedānta and Mahāyāna the soteriological reflection on the status of the saṃsāric world generates a functional ontology, but this is not developed for its own sake. When Greek philosophy came under the sway of soteriological concern, in Neo-Platonism, its ontological heritage was simplified: the question of being yielded to an ordering of being in terms of transcendence – strongly oriented to the One beyond being. Something similar happened in India, except that the ontological basis was overshadowed from the start.

Biblical theism also generated a special sense of being: the conviction that things are sustained in being by God at every moment, that in their finitude they reflect God's glory. This is a large component in the ontological interpretation of causality in the West, along with Neo-Platonic interpretations of Aristotle. Heidegger does little justice to the power of this biblically-inspired ontology when he denounces Christian philosophy as a square circle, on the grounds that faith is qualitatively different from philosophical questioning (*GA* 40, p. 9; *GA* 9, p. 379). He might have similar misgivings about the Indian philosophies that appeal to Vedic authority, though it would be hard to apply his purist ideal of the autonomy of philosophy and his rigid notion of faith and its authority to the looser relations prevailing between the Vedas and Indian philosophy. Philosophy always has contingent cultural matrices in which it is embedded, though it aims to free itself from them; these generally include a dialogue with religion. Heidegger half-freed himself from Christianity only to hitch his thought to a Neo-Hellenic religious tradition refracted by Hölderlin.

Heidegger saw theism as occasioning an arrest of the ontological quest: the question of being is curtailed when one immediately answers the question, "Why are there beings rather than nothing?" by referring to God the creator, the source of all being (see *GA* 40, pp. 8-9). He would probably see the Naiyāyika arguments for the existence of God (see Potter 1977, pp. 100-111) as reducing the world to a thing made, thus closing access to its being. Brahman in Vedānta is Being (*sat*) as is God in medieval theology (*ipsum esse subsistens*): the theologically radical character of this thought may be at the expense of ontological questioning. When Bhāsarvajña (c. 860-920) invokes "divine cognition" as "a framework and receptacle of reality in the widest sense - wider than the highest universal, *sattā*, and encompassing also *astitva*, the common denominator of all six categories" (OB, p. 219), he may seem to transcend the abstractness of the Vaiśeṣika concept of being, but the concreteness he introduces is a theological rather than an ontological one; the truth of being is more remote than ever.

The thirst for the Absolute, both in Christianity and in India, has been in tension with the consideration of being, for the being of beings - whether approached phenomenologically or in speculative reflection - is not something absolute; neither is it relative; it simply is - "*Es 'ist' Es selbst*" (*GA* 9, p. 331). Vaiśeṣika began as a pure natural philosophy, yet already Praśastapāda presents understanding of the six categories of the *Vaiśeṣikasūtras*, their similarities and dissimilarities as a condition of release (Potter 1977, p. 283), and attempts to explain cosmic process in karmic terms, and with reference to an omnipresent invisible soul, increasingly drew this school into the soteriological drift characteristic of Indian philosophy (Frauwallner 1956, pp. 90-105). The connection between knowledge and salvation here is external, paying lip-service to the general Indian ideal of philosophy as salvific. Classical Nyāya, in contrast, is a doctrine of salvation; its twelve objects of knowledge are soteriological key themes (Frauwallner 1956, pp. 27-28, 73-76); "body," for instance, is focussed not as an objective, physical datum but as an element of personhood, mistaken for the self because of the delusion of "mineness" (Oberhammer 1992, p. 245).

Philosophical salvation was a feature of the Greek philosophies - Stoicism, Epicureanism, Neo-Platonism and some aspects of Plato's own teaching - but after Judaism, Christianity and Islam drafted philosophy in their service, an autonomous philosophical doctrine of salvation was not recovered until Spinoza; even the German idealists could not draft a philosophical path of salvation independent of Christianity. Schopenhauer replaced Christianity in this role with Indian doctrines of salvation. Since then, Nietzsche and Heidegger come closest to creating an autonomous philosophical soteriology. Heidegger's message of a right relation to being can be a bridge to the soteriological philosophies of India, permitting a demystified access to them which should also shed light on the problems of interreligious dialogue.

(A special word of thanks to Eli Franco and Karin Preisendanz for their valuable comments.)

*Sophia University*
*Department of English Literature*
*Tokyo, Japan*

Srinivasa Rao

# "SUBORDINATE" OR "SUPREME"? THE NATURE OF REASON IN INDIA AND THE WEST

1. Continuing in the illustrious German Indological tradition, Professor Wilhelm Halbfass has shed light on many a dark corner in the vast, complex area of Indian philosophy. His exposition on "Darśana, Ānvīkṣikī, Philosophy"[1] clearly brings forth in vivid detail how in classical India attempts were made, albeit with no ultimate success, to develop and use the concept of an autonomous reason in the field of philosophical thought. The high status accorded to scriptural authority (*śruti*) in Indian thought also receives a sympathetic exposition in his writings. The fact that wherever *śruti* is accorded primacy, reason is systematically relegated to a secondary place is also depicted by him in admirable detail. As a direct consequence of the facts of according primacy to revelation and also subordinating reason to revelation, successive generations of historians of philosophy in the West came to conclude that there was no "philosophy" in India. How this was done is also very graphically sketched by Professor Halbfass.[2] Since the act of assigning a subordinate role to reason in one's philosophizing seems so manifestly "unphilosophical" to a typical Westerner or even to a westernized Indian, the role assigned to reason vis-à-vis revelation or any kind of authority in some of the schools of Indian thought requires deeper investigation. Since the Indian philosophical classics themselves contain very little information on this issue, and since Professor Halbfass' work appears to have prepared the necessary ground for a more detailed investigation of this issue, the nature and role of reason in the context of classical Indian thinking will be the main focus of this exposition.

2. It is a fairly strongly held belief among some modern writers on classical India that the concept of "reason," insofar as that concept is usually understood and adopted in Western philosophy, has been generally absent among several Indian philosophical schools. While the

primacy given to "authority" in many of the Indian schools of philosophical thought, be it scriptural authority or the authority of a great teacher of a school, has made almost every early European historian of philosophy declare that India had no "philosophy" at all, it has also made some recent Indian thinkers defend the subordination of reason to revelation on grounds of the ultimacy "of a transrational 'experience,' which includes and fulfills, but does not contradict, the aspirations of human reasoning."[3] Since "reason" is the acknowledged king in the modern world-views dominated by science, a good number of writers on Indian philosophy have chosen to address themselves to the "problem" of scriptural authority versus reason. This modern, extensive debate concerning the relative merit or superiority of revelation over reason or, of reason over revelation, or even the debate about the relationship between the two, has no equally extensive parallel in the philosophical writings of classical India. This problem of *reconciling* revelation with reason seems to be a very serious problem only for the modern writers on India, and in particular for those who have been influenced by Western thought.

3. If the nature and function of reason as understood by most of the classical Indian philosophers happens to be radically different from the Western ways of understanding the same, there will be a serious problem. On the understanding that the modern Western conception of reason and its function (or role) is the correct one, virtually the whole of the classical Indian tradition of philosophy stands rejected as unphilosophical. If, in the past, many Western writers on India and on philosophy did maintain that Indian philosophy was really no philosophy at all, they all did so by treating the Western conception of reason and philosophy as paradigmatic. Though this early attitude has undergone a transformation in later years with the subtleties of the Indian ways of thinking coming to be increasingly recognized, one can still come across a stray writer like A. K. Warder who does not recognize Śaṅkara as a genuine philosopher and hence devotes only two sentences to him while writing a 200 page book called an *Outline of Indian Philosophy*.[4]

Therefore, one has to be reasonably clear about the meaning of terms like "reason," "revelation," and "philosophy" when they are used in the classical Indian context. The Vedas and the Upanisads are certainly regarded as scriptural in character, but they are not regarded as scriptures in the same way *The Bible* and *The Koran* are regarded as scriptures. The common meaning shared by the Western term "philosophy" and the supposed Indian equivalent of that term viz. *darśana* is not very considerable. Likewise, the Indian terms *tarka* and *yukti* stand for notions that represent only some aspects of the pervasive concept of "reason" in the West.

It must also be emphasized here that it is very important, and also necessary, to distinguish between a people's *ability* to use reason and their *knowledge* concerning the nature of reason. The first is entirely independent of the second in the sense that it is not at all necessary to possess any kind of theoretical knowledge concerning the nature of "reason" in order to be able to effectively *use* reason to achieve one's purposes. The ability to use reason is exactly like our ability to use language without any kind of knowledge of the theory of linguistics. This fact should be able to explain adequately the sense of wonder in anyone as to how the civilizations of the past (including the so-called "high cultures") were able to make so many achievements in science and technology although they never bothered to investigate deeply into the question of what exactly is the nature of human reason. Therefore, the complete absence of any theoretical discussions concerning human reason in any culture cannot be looked upon as a serious deficiency. Hence, one cannot also look upon the presence of any such discussion in any culture as a great merit. It will be easy to appreciate this vital point if we see that people belonging to cultures possessing detailed knowledge concerning the nature of human reason have not necessarily behaved more rationally than others belonging to cultures where such theoretical knowledge concerning human reason has been conspicuous by its absence.

4. Persistent and extensive investigations into the nature of human reason and rationality are generally peculiar to Western thought. Reason as a distinctive faculty clearly emerges for the first time in Greek thought, in Parmenides, when he distinguishes between "the way of seeming" and "the way of truth." The autonomy and superiority of reason gets firmly established through the work of Zeno. His paradoxes succeeded in making men accept that it is no more reasonable to believe even in what is clearly perceived. This success was so far-reaching that Plato also came to adopt it in the formulation of his metaphysics as well as epistemology. Later, the followers of his pupil Aristotle went on to define man as a "rational animal." The influence of Plato, Aristotle and

their followers has been so great on all subsequent thinking in the West that it is hardly possible to overestimate its extent.

While Parmenides distinguished only between the faculties of perception and reason and held the latter to be superior, Plato went further in making reason an integral and the most important part of man himself. The "rational part" of man's soul ought to be in control of the other parts and if good is to be achieved in the Republic, men of reason ought to be in ultimate control of everything. The Philosopher-King of Plato is someone who has clearly and willingly subordinated his feelings and will to his reason. Since Plato regarded the sensible world as a sort of very poor imitation of the world of Forms and did not also show interest in any rational understanding of the world, it is clear that for him only the world of Forms was rationally comprehensible and not the world of our everyday experience.

If Aristotle, in contrast to Plato, believed that the sensible world was rationally comprehensible, it was because he believed that the Forms of things - which alone are rationally comprehended - were "parts" of the things themselves and not part of a separate world of Forms. We must also take special note of the efforts of the Pythagorean philosophers who attempted to demonstrate that the universe was built up of numbers. Since natural numbers are rational quantities, any attempt to show that the things of the world are "made up of numbers" is an attempt at demonstrating the rational constitution of the world. Only through mastering mathematics can one achieve an understanding of the nature of the world. It is noteworthy that in the Pythagorean conception of the world there is no supernatural agency endowed with reason (like a creator God) that is responsible for the rational constitution of the world. Since we are ourselves rational beings, we are able to understand the world that is also rationally constituted. The idea that whatever any rational being can comprehend should itself be rationally constituted becomes more explicit only in later Western thought.

In later Western thought, the world's rational comprehensibility is grounded in the rationality of its creator viz. God. Galileo declared that "the great book of Nature" was written in the language of mathematics and thus paved the way for the pervasive belief that the method of mathematics was the method of natural philosophy as well. There was also the transition from the idea of a *rationally constituted* Nature to the idea of a *mechanically constructed* Nature. Thus, there was a vigorous building up of rigid systems of mechanics, astronomy and metaphysics.

The scientific materialism that arose in the nineteenth century can also be seen as a direct consequence of this. Although the recent revolutions in the natural sciences - specially physics and biology - have upset the notion of a rigid, mechanical Nature, yet they have never undermined the time-honoured notion of a *rationally comprehensible* Nature.

5. Since the notions of reason and rationality remained the pivotal notions of Western world-views for several centuries, repeated discussions concerning the nature, scope, power and limitations of reason naturally assumed a great deal of importance. Virtually every major movement in Western philosophy can be viewed as resulting from a reappraisal of the role of reason in arriving at an authentic understanding of the nature of man and the world. Free exercise of reason has led to the development of many kinds of world-views and the whole of the Western intellectual tradition may perhaps rightly be characterized as the "adventure of reason." In this tradition, reason is the hero. Here reason is not an accessory to anything else; it does not subserve any other entity or purpose. It is autonomous. When reason is autonomous, one goes wherever reason takes one and the resulting thought-structures are what are called "pure" disciplines. Pure mathematics and pure sciences are thus the clearest evidence of reason reigning supreme in the realm of human thought. If the West has largely been the leader in these areas of human thought, it is because of the pre-eminence given to reason in the development of conceptual structures.

This development of the Western intellectual tradition where reason enjoys a pivotal role does not seem accidental. There are several good reasons for it, but one very important reason for this line of development seems to lie in the absence, in the Western tradition, of a sharp distinction between mind and the Self. At least to the extent to which I am aware of the Western tradition, I have failed to discover any sharp distinction between the mind and the Self while this distinction is very characteristic of almost the whole of Indian tradition. In the Western tradition, reason constitutes an essential aspect of man's being. Man is a physical organism endowed with reason and man's rational being has primacy over his physical being. Only a rational being is capable of discrimination and as a rational being, Man in the West ended up discriminating himself sharply from Nature. Man also came to occupy the centre stage of Nature by virtue of the rationality that was supposed to be unique to him. The anthropocentric phases of Western thought thus appear to be the very natural consequences of conceding the essentially rational being of Man. This anthropocentricity had its advantages as well as limitations and one of its most beneficial effects was the resultant "adventure of reason." Had there been no such "adventure of reason," we would surely have missed a great heritage – the heritage of Western scientific thinking – that has justly become a part of the heritage of the whole of mankind.

6. In the Indian tradition there is no similar great "adventure of reason" on a similar grand scale. What is there is rather more aptly characterizable as the "adventure of the Self." Disinterested reason is not independently at work to a significant extent in the Indian systems – philosophical or nonphilosophical. Nor is reason the pre-eminent constituent of the human person. Generally, in most Indian systems of philosophy, Man is a "Self." He is identified with consciousness as such, or he is regarded as possessing consciousness pre-eminently. This consciousness is neither mind itself nor is it even an essential characteristic of mind. Reason is a characteristic feature of the mind rather than of the Self itself. Man is capable of freely exercising this reason and when he is doing so, he is said to be engaged in "discrimination." Man *ought to* discriminate, and all men do end up discriminating some time or other, and some schools treat this discrimination *(viveka)* as a characteristic feature and function of the mind or the intellect *(buddhi)*. There has been a long debate in Indian philosophy as to whether the mind (*manas*) is to be counted among the sense organs (*indriya*), but the Indian philosophers have never been in doubt – with the exception of the materialists – about mind being distinct from the Self.

The Indian systems are also perfectly familiar with the concept of "rational investigation" or "rational inquiry" and the term in Sanskrit which denotes these concepts is *jijñāsā* or *mīmāṃsā*. But such rational inquiry is always the function of the intellect and never of the Self. Any such rational inquiry always has a pre-determined purpose and is always goal-oriented. It is never undertaken "for its own sake." The Indian thinkers in general have hardly felt the need of rationally inquiring into anything just for the sake of inquiring. They have almost never resorted to an adventure of reason with the intention of just going wherever reason took them. That is how, probably, the ancient Indians did not develop any of the "pure" sciences although they had the necessary raw material as well as the intellectual equipment to develop them. For example, a good deal of geometric knowledge existed in ancient India; but still a work like Euclid's *Elements* never came to be written. The ancient Indians were very much capable of building up axiomatic systems. The grammatical work of Pāṇini exhibits great axiomatic sophistication, but such skill was not applied to develop any axiomatic system of geometry. The construction of elaborate and intricate sacrificial pits of exactly specified complex shapes and dimensions was very common in ancient India. Such construction was impossible in the absence of an advanced level of knowledge of plane and solid geometry. But no one axiomatized this knowledge as Euclid did in ancient Greece. Another example could be the movements of the planets. These movements were known with great accuracy and precision to ancient Indians and they even knew the methods by which the orbits of the planets could be correctly calculated, but yet anything like Kepler's laws of planetary motion was not formulated by them. Even today there are hundreds of pandits in India who construct almanacs that correctly portray all planetary motions and positions; but they are totally unaware of any modern astronomy and have never even heard the name of Kepler or his laws.

The ancient Indians had very extensive knowledge concerning thousands of plants of medicinal value and such knowledge could be built up only after a systematic study and analysis of all available plants, shrubs and trees. This sophisticated body of knowledge which may be named the "science of medicinal plants" *(vanauṣadhiśāstra)* is not identifiable with the modern, theoretical science of botany because it is not a study of plants in general. The ancient Indians had very accurate and minute knowledge concerning horses and elephants, but without in any way being systematic zoologists. Examples of this kind can be shown in many other fields.

The investigation into the nature of things has always been done by Indians, but it has always been done only with a purpose and this purpose has usually been other than obtaining the knowledge of those objects for its own sake. No kind of activity was encouraged or recognized as legitimate unless its purpose was known and was also acceptable. Whenever a technical treatise (*śāstragrantha*) is composed by any Indian author (in classical times or even today, in the classical tradition), the purpose of that work is always stated in the beginning. This purpose may sometimes be just as ordinary and superficial as "for the enjoyment of the learned" (*vidvajjanamanorañjanārtham*), but there *has to be a purpose* for composing a work. For example, Jīvanātha Miśra, the author of a treatise on astrology called *Bhāvakutūhala* says in the first stanza of his work that he is publishing it for the benefit of the learned men (*vidāṃ hitāya prakāśyate Bhāvakutūhalam*). Even activities that constitute artistic expression like singing or dancing are not for their own sake, nor are they supposed to be indulged in exclusively for the sake of human enjoyment. Sāgara Nandin, the author of a treatise on dance and drama called *Nāṭakalakṣaṇaratnakośa* says that dance is the means of realizing *dharma* etc. (*dharmādisādhanaṃ nāṭyam* ...). Even human enjoyment has to have an acceptable goal and cannot be pursued for its own sake. In Indian culture, the broad goals of any form of human action have been considered to be fourfold: material well-being (*artha*), fulfillment of legitimate desires (*kāma*), duty (*dharma*) and final liberation (*mokṣa*). The pursuit of material well-being and satisfaction of desires has to be carried on within a framework laid down by the principles of *dharma* and cannot be pursued in any way one likes. All actions must be done in a manner that is conducive to the ultimate and supreme goal of final liberation. Thus, there is a hierarchy of mutually consistent human goals (*puruṣārtha*) and all human action must be properly coordinated within this broad framework, for the ultimate good of oneself and of one's fellowmen.

7. In the above scheme, the knowledge of things as they are is never rejected as unnecessary in principle. In so far as the knowledge of objects as they are is invariably required to achieve certain human ends, disinterested rational investigations are necessarily undertaken to attain such knowledge. Objects are noticed essentially in relation to the other purposes they are expected to serve. A plant is of no intrinsic interest in itself; it is of interest only in so far as it is of some possible use for man. Even the relations among objects is not of any intrinsic interest except when such relations are directly relevant to the ends pursued by men. For example, the science of astronomy never exclusively developed in India as an independent branch of knowledge that was intrinsically interesting in itself, but was largely developed and used as contributory to the practice of astrology - a branch of knowledge that was directly concerned with human ends. The ancient Indians were in possession of the kind of data concerning planetary movements which Tycho Brahe had compiled with extraordinary skill; they also had the extraordinary acuity which Kepler possessed. Yet, while Kepler could perceive the "laws"

that the planets obeyed in their systematic movements, the Indians failed to perceive them. While Kepler could "look for a pattern" in planetary motions, and also find it, the ancient Indians never found such a pattern since that was not what they were looking for when they were observing and recording planetary motions. In other words, while it was some kind of a disinterested observation that suggested the laws of planetary motion to Kepler, there was no similar disinterested observation on the part of the ancient Indians. Therefore they never saw the "patterns" in the heavens which Kepler unmistakably saw.

8. It must also be noted that the differences in the role assigned to reason in India and the West are also rooted in their peculiar religious traditions. In the West, rationality constituted the inner core or the very stuff of Man. In pre-Platonic thinking reason was what was essentially responsible for the proportion or order observed in Nature. For them, the order found in Nature was similar to the order found in mathematics. For the Pythagoreans natural order and mathematical order were identical. Nature was the very embodiment of mathematics for them. When the interest shifted from nature to Man as in Socrates and Plato, the principle of order still retained its hold on them. They now spoke of the ordering of the "inner man" that was to be achieved through putting the rational part of the human soul in control of its other parts. This ordering of the parts of the human soul had its analogue in the outer human society where order and balance were supposed to be achieved through putting the Philosopher-Kings in control of all affairs.

But the real revolution in the West comes when investigations into Nature get seriously linked up with theological thinking associated with *The Bible*. The two important ideas of this period are: (1) Nature as a creation of God, and (2) Man as a being created by God "in his own image." In this new scheme, Man comes to share with God his rationality and consequently the world ceases to be a total mystery insofar as it can be grasped in rational terms. In this scheme only Man is endowed with mind or consciousness. Nature is not conscious. The whole of Nature came to be looked upon as a kind of giant, complex machine. Though the natural world was wholly mechanical in character, it was constructed perfectly rationally by its Creator and in so far as Man possessed reason, he could comprehend the world and the nature of things. Being rational consists in being able to see the original "designs" (of the great Creator God) that lie at the root of things. God is the ideal reasoner who has written the "Book of Nature" in the language of mathematics. He is also the great "watchmaker" who has designed this wonderful mechanism of Nature. Therefore this "book" or "clock" of Nature can be understood only through reason. And Man is inherently capable of understanding Nature precisely because God has made him "in His own image." God's creation has no "purpose." He just wills the existence of the world and it comes into existence immediately. Man's understanding of this world also has no "purpose." Man understands Nature only to marvel at it as God's great handiwork. Thus, the autonomy of disinterested reason which is characteristic of the Western intellectual tradition is also very much rooted in the classical religious tradition based on *The Bible*.

9. The role assigned to reason is rooted in a very different kind of religious tradition in India and therefore its role is very different. The world is not a creation of God according to most of the classical schools of Indian philosophy. In fact, the Indian milieu is very peculiar in that although thousands of different gods and goddesses have been worshipped by the common people throughout the history of Indian civilization, the god of the popular religion was not transformed in a big way into the god of the philosophers at least until the advent of the theistic schools of Vedānta beginning with Rāmānuja around the twelfth century A.D. It must be noted here that none of the heterodox (*nāstika*) schools believed in God; nor did any of the orthodox (*āstika*) schools give God any significant position except later Nyāya. The ancient Indian philosophers are noted for constructing world-views in which a Creator-God is *not* a necessary component. The world is virtually beginningless (*anādi*) according to most of the ancient Indian philosophers.

The world, although uncreated by any rational Creator-God, is yet orderly and the Vedic thinkers emphasized a certain kind of "order" (*rta*) in the world. But this notion of primordial order does not retain great importance in later times and an entirely different kind of order comes to rule the universe of our experience - the order created by the law of *karman*. This law of *karman* is conceived so powerfully that it enables the Indian philosophers to fully explain the being as well as the affairs of man in this world in a rational manner without invoking any divine principle. It is this law of *karman* that is responsible for man's being-in-the-world and such being-in-the-world is considered some kind of "bondage" for the human Self. The primary goal of all schools of Indian philosophy whether "*āstika*" or "*nāstika*" (with the sole exception of the materialists) is to point out a way out of this "bondage." Discriminative knowledge is considered essential to achieving such freedom from bondage. According to all these schools such knowledge comes only from a discriminative knowledge of the true nature of the Self. It is not at all the original nature of the Self to be bound although it is normally found in a state of such bondage.

Liberation is therefore achieved through a knowledge of the true nature of the human Self and of the bondage it is subjected to. Such knowledge is attained through discrimination or rational inquiry. A comprehensive knowledge of the nature of things may be attained through rational inquiry, but such knowledge has no intrinsic worth. It has value only as an aid to final liberation. For example, in Advaita school, one has to ascertain the true nature of the world only in order to know what the true nature of the Self is. In the Sāṅkhya school one has to investigate into the nature of the world only in order to achieve the aloofness of pure consciousness from everything material. In the Vijñānavāda school, an analysis of the nature of things and of human experience is merely an aid to realizing the ultimate nature of reality as being mere pure consciousness (*vijñaptimātratā*). These are some of the most transparent cases. The idea that liberation - variously termed as *mokṣa*, *kaivalya* or *nirvāṇa* in the different schools of Indian thought - is some kind of "transcendence" of man's normal being-in-the-world, is unmistakably the dominant and recurring theme throughout the centuries and it still forms the basis of the thinking of even ordinary Indians who are not philosophers. In such a world-view, knowledge for its own sake has little significance and therefore it cannot play a central role in, or dominate, the thought-structures.

10. If it is accepted that knowledge for its own sake had little appeal for ancient Indians, one may voice a difficulty in that it comes in the way of explaining how ancient India gave rise to a considerable amount of scientific knowledge since such knowledge is not normally considered possible unless reason is exercised freely with the sole objective of knowing what things are in themselves. It would indeed be quite surprising that a people solely concerned with liberating themselves from a bondage to this world also ended up with so much authentic knowledge about the world itself - a knowledge that is impossible to attain without

an intrinsic interest in the world itself. But there is a satisfactory explanation for this.

It must be noted that although liberation is the supreme end, it is not the sole end of man in India. Although supreme, liberation is one among the four accepted ends of human life. The three others are *dharma*, *artha* and *kāma*. *kāma*, usually rendered as "desire," and *artha*, usually rendered as "material wealth," are to be pursued within the framework of *dharma* or "duty." *dharma* ensures that a man does not lose sight of the supreme end "*mokṣa*" in his pursuit of the lower ends of desire and of material wealth. The attainment of desires as well as of the material well-being of man necessarily require the production of various kinds of goods and services out of the things that naturally exist in this world. Such production not only requires the development of certain tools, techniques and skills but also requires a clear understanding of the nature of the things as they really are.

For example, it is necessary to have an image of a god of one's choice in order to be engaged in the daily activity of worshipping. This requires the idol to be sculpted out of some material. Let us suppose it is a stone sculpture. In that case, it is evident that a stone idol cannot be produced without fully understanding the nature of the stone out of which it is to be produced. Therefore, an understanding of the characteristics of various kinds of stones becomes a necessary prerequisite for the practice of sculpture or architecture (*śilpaśāstra*). Similarly, health cannot be ensured unless the nourishing or toxic properties of various kinds of food stuff and plants is systematically understood. These properties can be systematically understood only through studying what the characteristics of foods and plants really are. These types of understanding are possible only through an objective study of things and such a study is possible only through the employment of reason with the sole objective of understanding what those things really are. *Neither a sense of wonder nor any curiosity is at the root of such investigations*. Therefore reason is here merely a tool to accomplish certain pre-determined human ends. There is a free exercise of reason, but it is not an exercise for its own sake. There is a broad framework of individual and social good within which human reason is allowed to function freely. If this point is kept in view, one can understand why the ancient Indians attained a high level of scientific knowledge about many kinds of things without, at the same time, developing any of the pure sciences to a considerable degree as the Westerners did.

11. From the above exposition, it is probably clear that reason has been differently conceived in the Western and the Indian traditions. While reason, or mind, has been conceived as being of the very essence of man in the West, not reason but the Self has been conceived as the essence of man in India. Reason is but a tool to be used by the Self or the self-conscious being for its own purposes, and in particular, for the attainment of liberation. While reason is autonomous - because man himself is autonomous - in the Western tradition, reason is essentially subservient to human ends in India. These differing conceptions of the role and nature of reason have also led to the development of two distinct traditions - the scientific, intellectual tradition of the West and the spiritual, *darśana* tradition of India. We must note at this point that there is an organic connection between the way reason was conceived in the West and the way a scientific tradition was also developed there. The scientific tradition of the West that has become a universal heritage is a direct consequence of conceiving the role and nature of reason in a particular way. If a similar or parallel heritage of science did not take root in the Indian soil, it is because of a very different conception of the nature and role of reason entertained in Indian culture which was not conducive to such a development. On the other hand, there is a distinct connection between the different spiritualistic traditions of India and the role assigned to reason in Indian culture. While science had to break away from religion and theology to develop by itself in the West, no such circumstance arose in the Indian tradition. This is the reason why while there is no sharp break between religion and philosophy in India, the two have clearly parted ways in the West. While the pervasive influence of scientific discoveries and developments has brought about changes in the philosophic thinking in the West, the introduction of science has not transformed the religio-philosophical scene in India in any fundamental way.

12. Against the above background, it is not very difficult to see why the attempts made in classical India to institute an autonomous reason as central to philosophy did not meet with permanent success. The *tārkikas* and others, who tried to rely entirely on reason and did not wish to acknowledge any other source of authentic knowledge except an autonomous reason, were naturally and inevitably sidelined in the highly pragmatic, goal-oriented milieu of classical India. Halbfass' brief and accurate narration of the development and the subsequent eclipse of

*ānvīkṣikī* as an autonomous discipline or method in classical India[5] will be very illuminating if the general milieu in which such eclipse took place is kept in view.

13. Since reason was never conceded any autonomy and was always looked upon as a tool in classical India by most of the philosophers, its subordination to *śruti* or Upaniṣadic revelation in Śaṅkara is natural and is also consistent with the existing general tradition of looking upon any kind of reasoning as essentially a tool that subserves some purpose. The irreconcilable disagreements among the mutually opposed schools of philosophy like Sāṅkhya, Nyāya, Vijñānavāda, etc., which relied chiefly on reason and treated reason as sacrosanct, served only to highlight the limits of autonomous reason when it came to addressing a fundamental question like what is the nature of ultimate reality. Since these schools relied heavily on *tarka* and *yukti* to establish their basic tenets, they were subjected to a detailed, devastating criticism by Śaṅkara. Śaṅkara's practice of subordinating reason to the authority of *śruti* is part of the general practice in classical India of looking upon reason as essentially a tool of accomplishing predefined human ends. The purpose of the employment of reason has tc lie outside of that reason and the purpose of starting an enquiry has to be other than that enquiry itself.

14. Therefore, only when the Western conception of an autonomous reason is adopted as basic to any kind of philosophizing, one is faced with the "problem" of reconciling reason with authority or revelation. While accepting such autonomy of reason, if one also concedes that whatever is knowable is knowable through reason alone, the problem becomes compounded. That is because the realm of what is knowable is not coextensive with the realm of what is knowable through reason. Following the path of reason, Descartes came to the conclusion that the only thing he could be certain about was of himself as a thinking being, and after conceding the autonomy of pure reason, Kant had to conclude that this autonomous pure reason did not allow him to believe in the Self. If reason deals with possibilities, then, since possibilities are always infinite, different routes taken by reason end up in the justification of different possibilities. This was very distinctly realized in classical India. In the method of *pūrvapakṣa-siddhānta* which is adopted by classical Indian philosophers, though the statement of the *pūrvapakṣa* begins with some actual stand taken by a rival school, as the argumentation proceeds, even merely possible stands that the rival school could have taken are

also formulated and refuted. In some of the classical Indian philosophical works, the range of such rival possibilities taken up for consideration and refutation is indeed astonishing. Even while reason is employed merely as an auxiliary tool in the service of revelation, the range allowed for the free operation of reason by the *pūrvapakṣa-siddhānta* method is often comparable to the range available in any purely rationalistic school of thought. This is why, though most of the important Indian philosophical classics are only commentaries on other works, they are still creative works in their own right. The commentators, while relying on the fundamental premises made available to them on the authority of the original authors, think up newer possibilities viz. newer objections that might be made against their school and also newer ways of defending their own position. The potentialities of free reason are utilized to a great extent in such exercises.

Reason is like a bird which flies freely in the sky all day, but returns to its nest at dusk. Just because the bird has a pre-determined final destination, i.e., its own nest which it reaches at dusk, it cannot be said that the bird did not fly freely at all. Similarly, reason employed with a pre-determined goal can still be free. Reasoning done just for the sake of reasoning is like a bird that is just flying. A bird that is just flying may rest on a tree when it becomes dark, but it will not be there when the day breaks. It will be on its flight again. Likewise, a position adopted purely on the basis of reasoning may be held for a while, but it will be abandoned when better reasoning becomes possible. Even this new reasoning will stay only until even better reasoning does not become available. Logically, totally free reason cannot reach any final conclusion; it cannot rest or nest anywhere. Nothing can be certain for such reason because anything is possible. Since possibilities constitute an ever-receding horizon, reason has to go on and on indefinitely. Autonomous reason finds itself between infinite regress and infinite "progress" and this progress is merely regression in the reverse.

This characteristic limitation of autonomous reason was clearly perceived in classical India by many thinkers including philosophers. Therefore, they always tied reason to a determinate human purpose. Since most of the early schools of Indian philosophical thought originated out of a perceived need for attaining permanent freedom from evil, bondage and suffering, any free exercise of reason had little utility in such a specific practical context. If anything, reason could only serve as a useful tool in achieving the desired end. Reasoning that did not accomplish this task was regarded as wasteful and empty. Therefore, the best thing for reason to do is to remain subordinate to human experience - empirical or transcendental.

*Bangalore University*
*Department of Philosophy*
*Bangalore, India*

## NOTES

[1] IE, ch. 15.

[2] IE, ch. 9.

[3] TR, p. 131.

[4] Warder 1971, p. 194.

[5] IE, pp. 263-286.

Rada Iveković

## THE POLITICS OF COMPARATIVE PHILOSOPHY

After a lifetime of dealing with Indian philosophy and particularly with Indian philosophy in its relationship to Western philosophy I can testify to the fact that we also have to deal with some sort of misunderstanding between the two philosophical traditions. Indian philosophy has often been studied by Indologists in the West, yet philosophers have seldom approached it. Working on Indian philosophy as a philosopher requires that one be an Indologist and a Western philosopher in one. Luckily, some very brilliant minds have been both. Yet they too encounter the difficulty of approaching a different tradition. This difficulty appears both as a methodological one as well as one of subject-matter, as is acknowledged in the work of Wilhelm Halbfass. We all deal with comparative philosophy, while the concept of comparative philosophy is in itself vague, ill-defined and, moreover, clearly a Western one. Comparative philosophy has so far covered both unfair and prejudiced treatments of the Indian tradition as well as positive attitudes to it. I have myself attempted to call my activity, which necessarily involves some degree of asymmetrical approach, "contrastive philosophy," or, in French, "*philosophie comparante*" (comparing philosophy) instead of the usual "*philosophie comparée*" (compared philosophy).[1] I felt uneasy with the term "comparative philosophy," because I was aiming at investigating a common ground for both Western and Indian philosophy, a ground which was *not* available beforehand but had to be created.[2] I tend to think now that the term ("comparative philosophy") does not necessarily have to be avoided, but rather has to be better defined through concrete work on a given material.

India and Europe have represented two diverse *civilizational choices*. It seems to be as yet difficult, or early, to give a final assessment as to what the philosophical relationships between the two might have been or might lead to. My first teacher of Indian philosophy and of philosophy *tout court*, Čedomil Veljačić alias Bhikkhu Ñāṇajīvako (Ñāṇajīvako 1983, 1992), spent a lifetime on it and gave generations of Indologists in the country then known as Yugoslavia who concerned themselves with philosophy a fair understanding of it. Wilhelm Halbfass probably comes closest to an understanding of this when he writes:

> India has not reached out for Europe, has not searched for it, has not historically prepared the encounter with it. It has been the object of European interests of political domination, economic exploitation, religious proselytism, scientific research and historical understanding, but also the goal and referent of Utopian projections, of searching for the identity and the origins of Europe, of European self-questioning and self-criticism. The conditions and perspectives on the two sides of the encounter are fundamentally different; the relationship is an asymmetrical one. Europe has brought about the historical situation within which India and Europe came to face each other, and to speak and listen to one another. This is a basic condition of modern Indian self-understanding and self-articulation. Even in their rejection of, or their self-affirmation against, European ideas and orientations, modern Indian thinkers are not free from such ideas. Explicit or implicit reference to the West, and membership in a Westernized world, is an irreversible premise of modern Indian thought.
>
> Does this mean that Europe simply dominates the "dialogue" with India, that it has once and for all determined its medium and conditions, and that it has thus deprived India of the possibility to speak for itself? Does it mean that the horizon of the encounter is simply a European one?
>
> India has been surprised and overpowered by the encounter with Europe: and yet in its own way, it has been ready and prepared for it. The Hindu tradition has disregarded the non-Indian world, has enclosed and isolated itself in its own immanent structures; yet within this framework, it has produced an extremely rich heritage of forms of spiritual interaction, of dealing with religious plurality and the divergence of human orientations; through its self-centered and xenophobic traditionalism, it has created a remarkable potential of openness and universality. In a sense, this dormant potential was awakened and historically actualized by the encounter ... . (IE, p. 369)

It is indeed Europe or the West – the "West" being the universalistic claim of Europe – that is providing the framework for the encounter and for an (im)possible dialogue. This situation of asymmetry amounts to the one described by Jean-François Lyotard as intrinsically unfair to one of the two sides concerned: it is the situation of a *différend* where the discourse of the complaining party has no sense in the language of the dominant party, because the dialogue is made in the latter's language only (Lyotard 1983). It seems that India would not have sought for the dialogue of its own.

The question which therefore arises, and Halbfass puts it very clearly, is whether this necessarily implies a permanent and inevitable European, or Western, domination, since the cultural-political asymmetry is taken for granted. Does the "Westernization" of India irreversibly imply a loss of some specificities and values inherent in her culture or philosophy? We could furthermore ask if the mode of the *différend* is at all an appropriate way to deal with the divergences of India and Europe.

Let us start with the overall picture. The West has globalized its civilization by enforcing it on the rest of the planet. In order to be able to do so – because this constitutes a move of appropriation used both in history and in philosophy – it had to proclaim its civilization neutral and universal. This universality may be largely false, since it is but an imposed particularity. It is nevertheless accepted either tacitly or with resistance; in any case it has become a fact. This globalization of the Western model is a globalization much for the worse, and the more remote it is from the model-giver, the more degenerate it is. However, it is also a blind spot in the sense that the West does not seem prepared to acknowledge the cultural dissymmetry, or the arbitrariness of its universalistic claim. Not only does the political West refuse to do so in the evidence of the economic and political breakdown of the world-order at the end of the 20th century and of a generalized bloodbath largely as the result of its past colonial involvement. It seems further to be unable to face this fact theoretically. The "theoretical West" envisages such a possibility only when compared to the Other. But the concept of the Other, indispensable in this process, is itself a Western construct and obsession.

It is not that the Indians do not have the expression or the concept of the Other. They do, and it is *anya*, and also *dvaita*. However, in the European tradition the concept of the Other is linked to the metaphysics of the subject, or agent, which is clearly not an Indian preoccupation in philosophy. The idea of the Other is heavily exploited in different wakes of philosophy in the West, as the flip-side of the subject, and especially so in the various post-modern and the like "philosophies of the difference."

The Other understood in this sense would rather be something to be overcome in the main currents of the Indian orthodox tradition or of Buddhism, since it would be considered a possible source, or result, of illusion or of apparent multiplicity. But this is certainly not a concept of the Other that could contribute, as in the European version, to the globalization of one dominant point of view. On the contrary, one has the feeling that avoiding it, avoiding or overcoming the split subject/object in the Brahmanical tradition or pursuing the *advaya* in Buddhism, is a willing effort to prevent any such globalization. This is an example of what I called a "choice of civilization." Furthermore, the subject and its Other bear testimony to the Western ontological concern, weak if not absent in the case of India.

Whereas the orthodox Brahmanical position may vary from hostility or indifference to ontology all the way to basing it on *ātman*, the Buddhist position, starting with cognitive nihilism (or should we say relativism?), may safely be assumed to be the most radical of nihilisms in the sense of an at least intended indifference to any ontology. Naturally, these basic philosophical attitudes affect philosophical thinking as a whole. Thus, although Indian culture as a whole found itself playing the role of the "Other" for the West, much as other areas of colonization did, it did not produce the big divide of its own. Integration rather than separation would cover the area of that which in the West relates to ontology. (Whether this produces another, secondary and derived type of ontological issues is another matter.) Ontology will be subtly avoided, at least officially, especially in the Buddhist interpretation. In India there is no clear-cut opposition between "materialism" and "idealism." The two are rather discarded. In the words of Bhikkhu Ñāṇajīvako:

> Nothingness, nullity, and consequently authentic (viz. not dialectically sophisticated, as it sometimes happens also in mahayanic speculation) nihilism excludes the logical possibility of destructive action (*ucchedo*) as the primordial metaphysical error of illusion (*avijjā*). This follows from the anti-ontological standpoint of *nihilation* (the term opposite to "*an*-nihilation" as used for materialistic destructiveness) of both the world as object "in itself" (*attena*) and the cognizing subject "for itself" (*attaniyena*). (Ñāṇajīvako 1992, p. 273)

The choice of understanding *anya*, the other, as something that should be reached for and included rather than excluded, though not in a universalizing gesture, and the divergence from it as a gap to be bridged in harmony, constitutes a civilizational choice implying all the other differences.

As regards the East and the West, not to speak of other directions, there seems to be but one historical "subject," and that is the West self-legitimized by placing itself face to face with the Other it is giving itself. This Other, a historical and social construct as much as the subject, is defined through its relationship to the Same, or the subject, but is not supposed to self-define itself. India, among others, has found herself in the role of an Other for Europe, particularly since the 17th century. It is also the position of a mirror for the West. (The fact that the event can be more or less dated could add some fruitful reflection to the comparison of the "Orient" with other types of the "Other" for the West, for example the feminine. The feminine as a figure of the Other is much older than the Orient.[3])

It seems useful to examine different approaches to these problems as they take shape with different scholars. We shall immediately see that the figures of the Other vary with the Western authors who write about them. What interests us here is indeed the principle, and not always the chosen identity of the particular Other.

For Čedomil Veljačić alias Bhikkhu Ñāṇajīvako[4], a Western promoter of comparative philosophy, the problem does not seem to pose itself in an acute manner. He practices a kind of "affirmative action" in philosophy, dealing with otherwise neglected traditions which are perfectly familiar to him. He solves the methodological problem by overcoming it in anticipation. Western philosophy is generally guilty of incomprehension and misinterpretation of the Oriental traditions. Yet justice can be restored through Western philosophy itself, once it is reformed. A fair symmetry can easily be achieved; nothing intrinsic in Western thinking may prevent it. As an anti-Eurocentrist Veljačić proposes the dialogue, considers it to be immediately viable, and also enacts it through his own effort. Veljačić is less concerned with the West not actually hearing what other philosophers have to say. He is not concerned with analysing the elements of Western thinking which impede openness to the Other as a matter of principle. He will also not obstruct his own work by methodological preliminaries. In some important way he is but right. He makes Nāgārjuna, Husserl, Yājñavalkya or Kant converse by playing the role of the intermediary himself, in his personal capacity. He rejects the question "Is there such a thing as philosophy in Asia?" as absurd and biased, the obvious answer for him being yes. His work has the merit, as very often is the case for comparative philosophy in general, of launching us directly towards topics of Indian philosophy as much as towards those of Western philosophy. Yet Veljačić does not theorize the relationship between the two, or the character of the philosophical space within which this takes place. It is as if his own comparative method does not really raise methodological problems. Differences are taken as granted but subject to overcoming. Although he elaborates on the basic divergence regarding ontology, he does not seem to translate this into an asymmetry of a *différend*, by which the "dialogue" would be but vainly and injustly attempted within the conceptual apparatus, or within the language, of one side, namely, the dominant one.

This sort of critique is the one which is brought within sight of philosophy by contemporaries such as Derrida, Irigaray, Lyotard, Serres, Sloterdijk, Axelos, Deleuze and others, although *not* on any material from other cultures, but as a matter of principle.

Halbfass has noticed the subtler discrepancy between the two philosophical traditions, Western and Indian. The one is interested in the Other for the better and the worse, without there being a reciprocity. It is as if the system of the Same had won in a general framework, even though it may be a bad universalism. Halbfass is not moralizing. He is trying to figure out how to proceed in philosophy *under these conditions of asymmetry* that Veljačić didn't care much about. For Halbfass, the asymmetry has to be accepted in some way, which would also be Veljačić's tacit position, and worked through. He elaborates and analyses the different facets of the problem of asymmetry between the two traditions, the conditions of incommensurability so to say, through a principally methodological concern. Yet Halbfass is wary of proposing solutions. He also notes another important fact:

> And for the foreseeable future, we may have to live with this tantalizing paradox: The globalization of the world coincides with its parochialization; the meeting and "dialogue" of the cultures and religions of this world coincides with their trivialization. (IE, p. 441)

Instead of a conclusion he prudently quotes the words of an Indian philosopher, J. L. Mehta. I imagine that both Halbfass and Mehta propose to assume and recognize the ruling dissymmetry between the cultures. And Mehta adds, according to Halbfass:

> ... there is no other way open to us, in the East, but to go along with this Europeanization and *to go through it*. Only through this voyage into the foreign and the strange can we win back our own self-hood; here as elsewhere, the way to what is closest to us takes us the longest way back. (IE, p. 442)

And, continues Halbfass,

> For Indians as well as Europeans, the "Europeanization of the earth" continues to be inescapable and irreversible. For this very reason, ancient Indian thought, in its unassimilable, non actualizable, yet intensely meaningful distance and otherness, is *not* obsolete. (IE, p. 442)

What seems to be important after the first stage of recognition of the asymmetry by the non-European scholar is its articulation which amounts to giving one's self, as the Other's Other, an identity as well as a historic, collective subjectivity. I assume that this is a subjectivity which would aspire to become another co-subject. At the end of the process the Other would not any more be included in the economy of the Same as it is now. The Same and the Other would then change their meanings; they would amount to a *relationship*. Everyone within the relationship would be at the same time equally the Same and/or the Other, depending on the perspective. The question then arises: Would we imperceptibly have passed from an asymmetrical situation to a symmetrical one, and is this at all thinkable? Or need this be thought of as symmetry at all? How does one get away from the asymmetry? And should one strive for it?

Halbfass's answer doesn't seem unambiguous here. As usual, he is careful in passing judgements. It would seem on the one hand that, given the already achieved globalization of the West, there is no possibility or no need to get away. If that is so, it would seem necessary to construct equity within asymmetry. Is that likely? As yet we have no answer to that, however doubtful it may seem. It is the same as asking whether "difference" is thinkable without discrimination.

The philosophers of the difference in the West have all pondered over this asymmetry, although very few of them are versed in non-European philosophical traditions. They are mainly conscious of thinking that asymmetry, while at the same time starting from it, thus reduplicating it somehow, in a gesture that would set it "right" but that would also change the meaning and the direction of reflection itself. Thinking would now be caught in the self-referential. This self-referentiality weakens the initial position and claim. It produces self-irony as well as a humility of thinking that accepts being relativized and welcomes the insecurity of the absence of foundations. Thus the philosophers of difference approach the problem as a topic, but they approach it also through the philosophical move and mode as well as through the new rejection of ontology, and it is necessary to discern these levels. They all know that "everything" has been decided in principle before language itself, ever since and within the symbolic order, and that thinking encounters almost unfathomable obstacles when it endeavours to think that which permits it. That is indeed the asymmetry, especially when the "Other" is the feminine whose exclusion, as opposed to that of the Orient, does not seem to be datable in history. (But the main figures of the Other, such as "the woman," the "Orient," and "God," remain in post-modernity the same as they had been in modernity; they still have the same structure and they still obey the same description and valorization; post-modern thinking once again bears thereby testimony to its despising of the historicity of which, on the other hand, it has not managed to liberate itself.) It is in this skepticism regarding the limits of language and thinking that some of them become akin to Buddhists. The philosophers of the difference, in the critique of the West they have partly, though not unambiguously undertaken as their task, proceed now mainly to re-evaluate the figure of the Other through tracing it and recognizing it down to its origins, which means into the symbolic, the prelinguistic, the unconscious, the maternal, the different (or the *différend*, *la différance*), the inhuman(e), the sublime, etc.; their terminologies vary. And not only the origin of the Other is of concern here: it is really the subject's own origin which is being traced from the Other (Sloterdijk 1988, 1989). The initial asymmetry is reversed in this way, but it is also pushed beyond the threshold of consciousness and of language, beyond the split subject-object; yet it goes without saying that the asymmetry, though under control, remains. That is, the "reversing" of the asymmetry does not take place in the same reality, since no other symbolic order is proposed or seems possible. This effort to "gynecologize" philosophy (the term is Sloterdijk's) is also a gesture of reappropriation of the origin of the Same much more radical than in the philosophical past: an effort not to have to go through the Other on this earth, to get rid of it, or to get one's own origin from beyond, from that other dimension. It is necessary to pass through the Other not so much to rehabilitate it, but rather in order to exceed it or overcome it towards that place where it is not yet and where the partition has not yet occurred, the safe haven of the not-yet-divided. The valorization of the Other is but an additional aspect not essential to its evolving. It is a deconstruction through the negative. It is a regression towards the "place of birth," towards the unconscious, towards the presymbolic, towards the undecidable, the indiscernible.

Are we moving towards a dead end? Can we expect a dialogue with the Other in such asymmetry? And why does the "place of the Other" always seem to remain empty? This is so not only and simply because of the blind spot. It is also not so because of the *différend*, which is why the discourse of the Other cannot be reduced to that of the Same, and this not only because a consensus would not be possible or would be insufficient and wouldn't resolve the problem. This is so because the same move of universalization and of domination on the part of the same philosophical, political Western and modern subject has been maintained even in the declaration of abdication of the latter in contemporary Continental philosophy. This is where the post-modern move to rehabilitate the Other shows its modern origin and reveals itself not to be a radical turn from it.

The process passes through several stages: first, the recognition of the asymmetry as a situation of domination; second, the push backwards in order to attain that which allows the asymmetry; third, proceeding as if a lasting symmetry between the Same and the Other had been attained. However, here we encounter the illusion. This "as if," this mimesis, cannot be indifferent or give the same results regardless of the fact of who is practising it, whether it be the one who had been defined as the Same within the former setup or the Other; for the two do not have the same historical support. One of the two, "the Same," has been globally confirmed through history; the other, "the Other," hasn't. What is at stake here is the subject. Namely, the former "weak ones" and the former "strong ones" cannot renounce their "subjects" with equal enthusiasm and in the same manner. In other words, the subject will not be able to simply quit; it will be dethroned and will also have to understand it. This is where we stand. Discovering the blind spot doesn't guarantee emerging from it.

Indeed, perhaps we shall be guided, helped to come out, born of the Other and of ourselves at the same time. Perhaps a symmetry and equity, too, has to be constructed from the "outside," perhaps more than anything else. Halbfass's move of recognizing the asymmetry of the different civilizational choices would in that case be necessary, but may not be altogether sufficient. He undoubtedly deserves credit for being vigilant regarding the blind spot. Within philosophy for us here in the West what he proposes might as well be the only practicable way.

However, something could come to us from somewhere else some day, and we ought to be ready, although we cannot predict which way should be followed. It is something that has to be thought of in the long run. However, in the long run, and maybe in the short run too, we must also think about the end of our world. Maybe that is what we are waiting for? This humility of thinking, and even of theory, has always been more congenial to Indian philosophy than to the Western one.

We discover that the philosophical balance between India and the West presupposes a political balance or rather, the politics of the philosophical discourse. This is where we come to the problem of *reception*, an untreatable problem in and by philosophy.

Why is it necessary to go through the politics of discourse? (Let us be reminded of this universe where the Other is an invention of the Same.) We have to make our way through that because the split between "I" and the Other, between the subject and its other, is set into words and works through language even before we can think it. The Same becomes self-established by entering being, while it relegates the Other to "being" or to an "as-if" of being. Or non-being is assigned to the Other, in spite of, or *because of*, the Other's origin in being. The Other is reduced to mimesis. Yet the Other attempts to escape, thereby tearing apart the Same and opening it to multiplicity. This is how difference is produced. By tearing apart the Same its Other tears apart the monolithic and monological discourse as well. When the Other autonomizes and positions itself in order to give some sense to its own language, it disturbs and violates the one-and-only language declared to be universal, while at the same time it lacks words to express its own truth. We are confronted with a situation of asymmetry where the truth of the one has no sense in the language of the other.

Going towards the Other, meeting it even when it presumably is our own invention materialized, destabilizes us and questions first of all our own identity. The Other and the Orient remain the directly unthought here, or perhaps that which remains thought of sideways, or differently. Yet at the same time, we can never tell where the imperceptible limit between "I" and the "Other" lies: it has no space of its own. How to present, translate or call the Other without being untrue to it and to oneself? While speaking of French and American philosophy, Lyotard writes:

> This inconsistency proceeds from an ethnocentrism that I would call maniacal because it is obsessed by the exact partition of what belongs to the ones and what to the others. As if no uncertainty could be tolerated regarding cultural propriety of a thought. It is easy to discern, in the formulation of such a symptom, an anxiousness regarding identity. (Lyotard 1991, p. 10)[5]

There is no clear-cut decision within the accepted context. By cutting short we accept a postmodern difference lacking in depth. A consensus is not possible. However, a *dissensus* is likewise improbable. The *dissensus* is after all operating everywhere where the failure of the Western model meets the unspeakable and the inaudible, unspeakable and inaudible for us, of the Others, of the other civilizational choices.

I call a civilizational choice the whole of cultural vectors, all linguistic, symbolic as well as thought configurations, manners, beliefs, specific networks of power, all the enunciations and/or the pre-suppositions which underline a specific *Weltanschauung* insofar as they are implicit in philosophy and insofar as they cause certain enunciations to be recognized as its parts according to its inherent logic. It goes without saying that the same enunciation can appear in different choices of civilization, or contexts, but it will find itself each time at different historical crossings and/or divergent problems. It will represent very different positions in each of them.

Everything holds logically within a choice of civilization. In the Indian tradition, for example, there is no ego, if not mainly in a negative sense, no subject, no constitution of an identity which would be projected towards the Other, creating it thereby, in order to appropriate it. All the historical, political differences follow from there, not always at our advantage, for the Indian civilizational choice does not seem to have produced the mechanism of appropriation of the world, of the Other. Not having produced an Other is not a failure, but a *choice*. Thus India has not or has only hesitantly represented the Other for itself. Indeed, the "others," women, low castes, animals, deities, etc., seem to suffer less from misrepresentation. This unfortunately doesn't seem to eliminate the violence against the Other. The figure of representation seems to be less compelling, but the figure of universalization exists, as well as that of abstraction, and they are not less elaborate than in the West. Or as Halbfass has it:

> We may agree with J. L. Mehta's statement that the Indian tradition has produced a unique "tension and balance" between representational and nonrepresentational thought or between objectification and its transcendence. (OB, p. 234)

Halbfass points out the tendency, especially in Advaita and in Buddhism, to transcend dual states, or to return to a transcendent unity of being and non-being which precedes and transcends objectification through thinking, enumeration, nomination, classification, etc. This transcendence presupposes and does not ignore dichotomies and representation themselves. However, India has not chosen to elaborate these. The rejection of ontological conceptualization, he thinks, nevertheless has ontological implications (OB, p. 233).

However, India has also known the discourse of the Same in the imperative mode; that is what the Veda had come to stand for with the

Brahmanical domination and counter-reformation - mainly as a response to Buddhism, although it was not its meaning from the beginning. If there is transcendence in Brahmanism or Hinduism, as well as in other religions, it is transcendence towards the undifferentiated which is "neutral" and thus masculine; lost in it is that which is irreducible in this difference, its depth, and this in spite of the other possibility, present yet not developed, which would have been to articulate the sexual difference all the way into the "divine." Had that been pursued historically, transcendence could then really have been the concrete Other, and not the abstract deity, in philosophical thought, because the Other remains irreducible to the Same.[6]

There is no elaborate figure of the Other in the Indian tradition, as much as there is a disliking for ontological preoccupations. This is a choice. However, as Halbfass suggests,

> any transcendence of, or withdrawal from, ontological conceptualization and objectification presupposes and requires that kind of honest and stubborn, though perhaps futile, conceptualization which we found exemplified by the Vaiśeṣika ontology and categoriology. There can be no meaningful silence about being without such efforts of speaking about it. (TR, p. 234)

India, the Orient, is the Other we have given ourselves, as Halbfass puts it. By which words should one call this Other to a dialogue, a dialogue that has no status in its tradition? And why should one do it? Isn't dialogue also a Western setting? How is it possible not to pressure the Other with violence while proposing the dialogue? This is a problem of the politics of discourse. The problem of reception of which one clue resides at the side of the Other is invisible and unsolvable from "this side." We would have to de-center ourselves. Identity is caught up in a paradox. It is the impossible position between "I" or "we" and the "Other," never accountable.

How could one break with the arrogance of one's own cultural identity without necessarily renouncing it - when this arrogance seems to be constitutive of it? Jacques Derrida would confirm the paradox here: we must be true within treason itself (Derrida 1991). But is it sufficient to take note of the de facto asymmetry in order to be exonerated? Instead of giving some space for the Other to speak, space that will remain empty, shouldn't we try to go one step further and listen to the Other, to that other language, and try to understand it? That would produce a world of multiple co-subjects. However, it would be uncontrollable. Why should Europe, the West, always be that inexhaustible source of universality? How could one insure collaboration between multiple subjects?

In order to come to this sort of *advaita* from the Western position we certainly have to start by doing what Wilhelm Halbfass does when he lets the Other speak. The most radical moves in these matters seem to be the moderate ones.

*Université de Paris* – 8
*Département de Philosophie*
*Vincennes à St. Denis, France*

## NOTES

[1] I hold this last distinction from Roger-Pol Droit 1986, and from discussions with him.

[2] That is what I attempted in Iveković 1992.

[3] In Iveković 1992 I have compared the Orient and the feminine as figures of the Other, as they are treated by some Western philosophers.

[4] See, besides the books already mentioned, Ñānajīvako 1965, 1972, 1973 and 1987. For a complete bibliography (Serbocroat and foreign) until 1985, see the journal *Kulture Istoka* 6 (1985) (Belgrade).

[5] See also Michel Serres, who thinks about these problems in his own way (Serres 1991, pp. 81-84).

[6] This is a reference to the excellent elaboration by Luce Irigaray in her seminar at the CIPh in 1991, an elaboration which unfortunately doesn't get much confirmation from Indian philosophy, but points at a possibility.

Ben-Ami Scharfstein

# THE THREE PHILOSOPHICAL TRADITIONS*

I take pleasure in beginning with a word of appreciation to Wilhelm Halbfass. He is not a philosopher merely preaching the advantages of hermeneutics but a scholar-philosopher who has made the intellectual effort to master Western and Indian philosophy well enough to join them convincingly in the same intellectual world. Encouraged in part by his example, I am writing a book to be called *From Uddālaka to Kant: A Short Comparative History of World Philosophy*. It seems to me important to use direct, untechnical language as much as possible and to avoid elaborate detail, so that the history should be open to interested laymen and students as well as to philosophers. The desire to have non-professional readers explains why I have taken so little for granted, sometimes inserting definitions that are quite unnecessary to philosophers, and why some of my bibliographies are introductory and rather full, though very far from complete. I hope that my work will help to spare beginners in philosophy from the prejudices that still blind so many of their elders.

What follows is, with minor variations, the still tentative introductory chapter to my history. If any of its present readers advise me how to improve it, I will be very grateful because such work is, at bottom, a collective no less than individual enterprise.

## What, in This Essay, Is Considered to Be Philosophical?

There are three great philosophical traditions, the Indian, the Chinese, and the European. Before I describe them, I want to ask and answer, very briefly, what philosophical traditions are, why I say that there are only three, and why it is best to study them together, as they are studied here, rather than separately or successively.

What is a philosophical tradition? A chain of persons who relate their thought to that of their predecessors and in this way form a continuous transmission from one generation to the next, from teacher to disciple to disciple's disciple. Or rather, because a whole tradition is made up of many subtraditions, it is one and the same tradition because all of its subtraditions share common sources and modes of thought and develop by reaction to one another. A tradition is philosophical to the extent that its members articulate it in the form of principles - if only principles of interpretation - and of conclusions reasonably drawn from them, and it is philosophical to the extent that its adherents defend and attack by means of reasonable arguments - even those that deny reason - and understand and explain how they try to be reasonable. As history demonstrates again and again, no philosophy is purely rational, pure rationality being an unreasonable, impossible ideal. Matters of religion, communal loyalty, reverence for teachers, and cultural habits, not to mention individual psychology, have always limited rationality, so that subtraditions or philosophical schools are rational by tendency rather than in any absolute way.[1]

I go on to my second question: Why say that there are only three great philosophical traditions? To claim this, one must put aside the correct but, for our purpose, misleading definitions of philosophy as wisdom or as the group of principles, either stated or implied, by which any person or community views life. In keeping with the original meaning of the term "philosophy," "love of wisdom," philosophers, one supposes, have wanted to be wise, yet experience has taught that there is no good reason to think that they are necessarily so except, circularly, by their own definitions, and no good reason to think that non-philosophers cannot be equally wise - perceptive, farsighted, sagacious - in the ways that their particular lives have made natural. Nor is there any good reason to suppose that traditions that are not philosophical by the definition I have adopted have not had their own depth of sophistication and practical intelligence (which is implicitly also theoretical).

Let me pause briefly to give a few examples of what I mean by this last statement. The definition I require here implies that ancient Mesopotamia and Egypt had no philosophical tradition. This implication holds true even though the Mesopotamians' religious texts show that they were trying to imagine, that is, to discover the universal and permanent principles below the surface of things. On the basis of these principles they erected often fantastic hypotheses from which they could extrapolate what could or should happen. A different, more modest kind of understanding can be extrapolated from the Mesopotamian epic of Gilgamesh:

like Greek drama, the epic warns against the attempt to overcome the nature of things. In the end, the hero gets, though maybe refuses, the advice (accepted by Voltaire's Candide) to relax his heroics, accept the unheroic pleasures of life, and submit to the fate of all humans. The quite dissimilar *Dialogue of Pessimism* is a debate of a man with himself in which he makes contrary judgments on how he should act. It ends, it seems, with a skeptical, gloomy, yet humorous acceptance of all the contradictory positions - what is good is bad and what is useful is harmful. As in *Ecclesiastes*, the reason appears to be that a human being understands too little to know what is best to do. Like the wisdom literature of the Egyptians and Hebrews, that of the Mesopotamians teaches the lesson of a temperate acceptance of life and life's duties.[2]

All this suggests the intellectual accomplishment of the Mesopotamians, which is matched by that of the other great, equally ancient civilization, the Egyptian. To give one of many examples, the Egyptians explain the world with the help of the cosmic goddess Maat, who unites in her person the values of order, equilibrium, truth, and wisdom, and so keeps the world tolerable to the human beings who tenant it. Yet god as conceived by the Egyptians remains ambiguous in number: except for the twenty years during which the pharaoh Akhenaten tried to force monotheism on the Egyptians, god for them remained both one and many, always being discovered in new manifestations. In this way, the Egyptians expressed their tacit conviction that nature has its unity but cannot be summed up in a fixed number of gods or forces.[3]

All this, I repeat, is not philosophy as I mean it here. If we think of philosophy in its more general sense as wisdom in the face of the difficulties of life, we discover that "primitives," as we have miscalled them, can be our equals. This holds true of the answer given by an Eskimo shaman to the explorer Knud Rasmussen when Rasmussen pressed him to justify his religion. Taking Rasmussen outside, the Eskimo asked him why the blizzard was so cruel and then showed him a sick woman and asked why the innocent must suffer. Rasmussen hesitated and the Eskimo said, "You see, you are equally unable to give any reason why we ask why life is as it is. All our customs come from life and turn towards life; we explain nothing, we believe in nothing, but in what I have shown you lies our answer to all you ask."[4]

This Eskimo shows that a cold climate and apparently simple life can produce wisdom, but so can a hot climate, as is proved by African proverbial thought, at times as pointed as anything in La Rochefoucauld or Nietzsche. "Those who are absent are always wrong," says an African proverb; and "Wisdom is like mushrooms that come after you have finished eating (too late!)"; and "A healthy ear can stand hearing sick words."[5]

Such proverbs are akin to African dilemma tales, which put arguable, humorous problems to a group of listeners. Take the example of the Nigerian tale in which a blind man accompanied by his blind wife, blind mother, and blind mother-in-law, finds seven eyes. Two he gives to his wife, two he takes for himself, one he gives to his mother, and one to his mother-in-law. He is left with a single eye in his hand. If he gives the remaining eye to his own mother, his wife - who is there looking at him - will make him feel ashamed, but if he gives it to his wife's mother, he will be afraid, because a mother is not to be trifled with. The teller of the tale challenges the audience to make and justify the choice, which is not unlike the choices we try to work out in philosophical ethics or, more practically, in the medical dilemmas now discussed by philosophers and hospital committees.[6]

Why are such profound myths, clever proverbs, and dilemma tales not philosophy in the sense intended here? The myths are not because, relying on traditional narratives and on imagination, they do not usually make their meaning explicit and never justify it by careful reasoning - the meaning remains basically implicit. The *Dialogue of Pessimism* is not philosophy as meant here because the speaker does no more than state the opposing views between which he is caught, the Eskimo's insight because it is not developed, and the African proverbs and dilemma tales are not, for the same reason, and also because they are not related with enough care to explicit principles - at least to principles by which situations may be analyzed.

Yet mythology, debate against oneself, existential emotion, proverbial sharpness, and exercise in hard choices all join philosophy in the sense used here when, in keeping with the definition adopted, they are argued out reasonably; when the principles on which they rest are distinguished from the conclusions built on them, or when it is reasonably argued that there are no such principles; when the methods of argument are themselves justified; or when the story, emotion, cleverness, or confrontation with oneself or others is put in a relatively unbroken sequence of reasonings. Such intellectualizing is not always to the good because the tendency of reason to devalue what it has not succeeded in making verbally explicit and logically consistent makes it apt to miss a great deal to which imagination has given the form of religion and art.

## Why Are There Only Three Philosophical Traditions?

I have still not answered the question why I have said that there are only three philosophical traditions, the Indian, the Chinese, and the European. What about such others as the Jewish, Muslim, Japanese, and Tibetan? Well, yes and no, as philosophers say, they are and are not separate traditions - the matter is more complicated than it seems at first. It is possible to argue that even the Indians, Chinese, and Europeans never arrived at points of view unified enough to justify classifying them as distinct traditions. In all three, there are obvious and unobvious points of cleavage. To mention only the most obvious, in India, the Indians who regarded themselves as orthodox tried to delegitimize, that is, read out of tradition the philosophies they classified as unbelieving; in China, the Taoists mocked the tradition that Confucians revered, and during China's later history, orthodox Confucians saw Buddhism as deeply foreign to Chinese tradition; and in Europe, it is not hard to distinguish the different national traditions - philosophy that is by tradition either French, English, German, Italian, or other.

To justify classifying each of the three great traditions as distinct, one therefore has to show that it has a unity that prevails over all the internal differences it exhibits. Or if the attempt to show that unity prevails seems tenuous or subjective, one has to show that each of the three has pervasive habits of thought and a history of self-reference - of person to person, intellectual group to group, group to authoritative person, tradition, or text, and so on. This would be unity in two separable senses, that of continuity and that of self-reference. Continuity makes everything subsequent in the tradition lead back to the same beginnings in time, place, or attitude. Self-reference is the quality that makes any isolated statement or philosophy difficult to understand without setting it in the contextual web that determines what is internal to the tradition and what is external to it, belongs to another world of thought and action.

Even China, which alone of the three traditions has had a single government for much of its history, has undergone dramatic changes of dynasty and probably of the character we identify as Chinese; and, like India and Europe, it has always contained a great variety of territories, people, languages, and cultural traditions. All the same, most Chinese thinkers have shared the same classical language, same historical reference points, and (in imperial China) same education, which was essential to their prestige and to their usual competition for government office.

The unity of India and Europe has been more tenuous. However, the great old classics of the one were Sanskrit and of the other were Greek and Latin, and just as classical Chinese was the learned language of educated Chinese, Sanskrit remained that of learned Hindus and Latin of learned Europeans, so that, in each tradition, reference to the past would normally be to the same classical literature. As for Japanese thought, philosophically it depends mainly on the Chinese, as the Tibetan depends mainly on the Indian, that is, Buddhist, while the Jewish and Muslim, though each has its own history and dogmas, draw their philosophy proper from the same Greek and Roman sources and, in this limited but real sense, are part of the European tradition.

Philosophy had just three territorial origins, three beginning languages, three historical pasts, and three webs of self-reference. That there have been just three major philosophical traditions is, therefore, a fact, a brute fact, I would say. Whoever is so minded can emphasize the breaks in each and the vagueness at times of the borders between them, borders like those of diffuse clouds; but the notions themselves of breaks and borders imply that there are some things single enough to be broken and separate enough to have borders of some kind.[7]

## In What Way a History of the Three Traditions Is Better than that of Any One Alone

As the unity of the human world grows obvious, it grows obvious that interest in one's native culture alone is an intellectual limitation, a sad one, I think. Anyone who believes that philosophy – taken in the rather technical sense adopted here – is confined to a single tradition is demonstrating ignorance or prejudice. So far as I know, the opinion (voiced by distinguished but in this matter ignorant Westerners) that only Europe has had philosophy in any demanding sense of the word is never shared by those who have studied Indian or Chinese thought carefully.

Granted that there are three philosophical traditions and that interest in them all is justified, why claim, as I do, that is it best to begin by studying them together, or – to diminish the claim somewhat – to begin by comparing and contrasting them in revealing detail? One reason is that each of them is endless in extent and depth, so that if it seizes one's interest, one sinks into it and the chances of studying another seriously are greatly diminished; and if, nevertheless, one does study another, it is likely to be as a subject that is minor in interest and importance. How can one hope to make a just comparison of traditions if one begins by prejudging, in act or thought, the relative importance of any one of them?

A second reason for learning the three together is that the variety of positions one becomes aware of becomes greater, so that each philosophy is seen in the light of a larger number of contrasts, and so that non-Western modes of reasoning can be seen to be plausible or at least stimulating. And if one learns the three together, there is a better chance to explore the possibility that there are philosophical positions, arguments, or matters of concern that are truly universal. This possibility is one in favor of which, on pragmatic, biological, and personal grounds, I myself incline. But the opposite, I should say, more romantic inclination, makes things even more interesting: by changing your eyes, you see things - meanings, relationships, and values - to which you have been blind. A perceptive traveller in philosophy learns to grasp what has been invisible because too familiar or, on the contrary, too distant, and learns to make new, more varied discriminations. The Chinese philosopher Hsün Tzu, of the third century B.C., says, "The nature of man is evil; his goodness is the result of his activity." The German philosopher Kant, of the eighteenth century, says, "The question here is: whether man is good by nature, or evil by nature, or whether he is by nature equally receptive to good and evil, according as one or another hand happens to mould him." Anyone curious enough to explore the likeness between both statements must learn their contexts before considering if the two philosophers' problems are as similar as they appear. To begin with, one must ask what both mean by good, evil, and nature? And one must ask how much of the similarity is the result of translation from, respectively, Chinese and German, into the same standard English? The questions are not trivial nor the answers simple.[8]

Yet even if what I have been contending is true, there remains a practical objection, which is that no one knows enough to teach the three traditions together except very superficially. In answer, I admit that no person can know all three in genuine depth - I certainly do not pretend to. Yet those who make this objection ought to think further and take into account that much the same argument applies to the history of even a single tradition. It is easy to show that no one, however industrious, has nearly enough time to make a more than superficial study of the works of all the philosophers and schools considered important in either the Indian, the Chinese, or the European tradition. Our human limitations are such that it is an accomplishment to learn even a single philosopher really well - how difficult it is to bend one's understanding to fit that of someone else, especially someone different in culture and experience, someone who may have written thousands of pages and made acknowledged and unacknowledged shifts of position and shown all the coherence, incoherence, and quirkiness of which a thinker is capable! If a really adequate knowledge of the sources were demanded, it would be extremely unlikely that anyone could write a history of modern European philosophy or, for that matter, write any history of any kind of any extended period or large area. I have heard a specialist in Hellenistic philosophy say that it is now impossible for anyone to know even Greek philosophy; scholarship has grown too detailed. But since we have and need general histories, it stands to reason that they can be written only because their authors are ready to contend with their relative ignorance. Unless they were willing to do so, in history as in other fields of learning, we would be left with the work of specialists too narrow to see anything whole and would lose the ability unable to see in a wide yet relatively informed perspective. To study or write the history of philosophy of any tradition or period, one must be ready to omit very much, to take more than a little on the authority of others, and to try to make clear to oneself what is of great and what of less importance. The total number of philosophical works that can possibly be studied by a historian who takes all three traditions together is no greater than the number that can possibly be studied by a historian of any one of them, so that the selectivity of the comparative historian must be greater, as must surely be the dependence on other scholars - the mere linguistic competence demanded grows almost beyond human possibilities. I am confident, however, that once the philosophical classics of the three traditions are more widely known and their initial strangeness in a different tradition has worn off, the easier texts will be as accessible as the easier native ones; the highly technical ones, foreign and native, will always require elaborate commentaries.[9]

## A Distant, Preliminary View of the Three Traditions

This first view of the three traditions begins with the chronological chart of the philosophers to be discussed here. In choosing just these philosophers, I may have been influenced by their suitability for comparison. But this influence, conscious or not, can only have been marginal because most of the philosophers listed are indispensable to the traditions to which they belong and which they largely define; and it is the part their ideas play in creating their respective traditions that I intend to emphasize. That is, I have ordinarily adopted each tradition's retrospective view of its own development and of the contribution that each of its philosophers made to it. I must concede that a few of the persons who appear in the chart - Confucius is the most conspicuous example - are not philosophers by the definition I have given, but they belong here because they are the fathers of their respective philosophical traditions. I must also concede that, to write a coherent history of a practical size, I feel compelled to leave out more than a few great philosophers. The philosophers that do appear are not invariably great, and a number of them, chosen to represent certain points of view, might have been exchanged for others.

The italicized names on the chart are those of philosophers I should have taken up if I had I wanted to make this history more nearly complete and, especially, if I had continued this history up to our own times. In spite of their relatively early date, I do not deal with the Buddhists Hui-neng, Fa-tsang, and Dogen. This is because Fa-tsang and Dogen, who are, respectively, Chinese and Japanese Ch'an (Zen) thinkers, are best compared with Europeans such as Kierkegaard and Nietzsche, these four comprising a group, as I see it, of post-metaphysical irrationalists. And Fa-tsang, with his philosophy of all-in-all, would make a particularly interesting pair with Hegel.

Now, to begin with, look not at the names of the particular philosophers but at the way in which the names cluster at some points and are absent at others, leaving the chart blank:

## CHRONOLOGY OF GREAT PHILOSOPHERS*

| INDIA | CHINA, JAPAN | EUROPE |
|---|---|---|
| B.C.E. | | |
| **Uddālaka** (? 9th c.) | | |
| **Yājñavalkya** (? 9th c.) | | |
| | | **Heraclitus** (fl. 500) |
| **Mahāvīra** (599-527) | | **Parmenides** (b. 515) |
| **Buddha** (563-483) | **Confucius** (551-479) | **Socrates** (470-399) |
| | *Mo-tzu (480-390)* | **Democritus** (460-370) |
| | | **Plato** (428-348) |
| | **Chuang-tzu** (4th c.) | **Aristotle** (384-322) |
| | **Mencius** (371-298) | **Pyrrho** (365-270) |
| | | **Epicurus** (341-270) |
| | | **Arcesilaus** (315-241) |
| | **Hsün-tzu** (298-238) | |
| | *Han Fei-tzu (280-233)* | |
| | | **Carneades** (214-129) |
| | | **Lucretius** (99-55) |
| C.E. | | |
| **Nāgārjuna** (fl. 200) | | **Plotinus** (205-270) |
| | | **Sextus Empiricus** (3rd c.) |

* A good many of these dates are doubtful, and some, especially of the Indian philosophers, are known only vaguely – all that is really known of the dates of Uddālaka and Yājñavalkya is that they precede the Buddha. As for the Buddha, there are scholars who go beyond minor adjustments of his dates and situate him a full hundred years later. In this chart, which aims at maximal simplicity, I have not allowed myself more than two question marks nor used the abbreviation c. or ca. to indicate approximation. Vasubandhu may represent two philosophers rather than one, but this is not the place to divide him. While a number of undoubtedly great philosophers do not appear in this chronology, some of the philosophers I do write about are absent here because I could not stretch the notion of a great philosopher enough to include them. As explained in the text, Alfarabi, Avicenna, and Maimonides are considered to belong to the European tradition. Finally, for the sake of a no doubt quixotic and merely relative neutrality, in this chronology, though not elsewhere, I use the abbreviations B.C.E. and C.E.

| | | |
|---|---|---|
| **Asaṅga** (fl. 450) | | **Proclus** (410-485) |
| **Vasubandhu** (fl. 450) | | |
| | | |
| **Bhartṛhari** (450-510) | | |
| **Dignāga** (480-540) | | |
| | *Hui-neng (638-713)/ Shen-hui (670-762)* | |
| **Dharmakīrti** (600-660) | *Fa-tsang (643-712)* | |
| **Śaṅkara** (fl. 700) | | |
| | | |
| **Jayarāśi** (fl. 800) | | |
| | | **Alfarabi** (870-950) |
| **Udayana** (fl. 1050) | | **Avicenna** (980-1037) |
| **Śrīharṣa** (fl. 1150) | **Chu Hsi** (1138-1200) | **Maimonides** (1135-1204) |
| | *Dogen (1200-1253)* | **Aquinas** (1225-1274) |
| | | ***Duns Scotus (1266-1308)*** |
| **Gaṅgeśa** (fl. 1320) | | ***William of Ockham (1285-1347)*** |
| | | |
| *Raghunātha (fl. 1500)* | *Wang Yang-ming (1472-1529)* | |
| | | **Descartes** (1596-1650) |
| | | **Spinoza** (1632-1677) |
| *Gadādhara (fl. 1650)* | | **Locke** (1632-1704) |
| | | **Leibniz** (1646-1716) |
| | | **Berkeley** (1685-1753) |
| | | **Hume** (1711-1776) |
| | | **Kant** (1724-1804) |
| | | ***Hegel (1770-1831)*** |
| | | ***Kierkegaard (1813-1855)*** |
| | | ***Nietzsche (1844-1900)*** |
| | | ***Peirce (1839-1914)*** |
| | | ***James (1842-1910)*** |
| | | ***Dewey (1859-1952)*** |
| | | ***Husserl (1859-1938)*** |
| | *Nishida (1878-1945)* | ***Russell (1872-1970)*** |
| | | ***Wittgenstein (1889-1951)*** |
| | | ***Heidegger (1889-1976)*** |

The names we see clustered at the top of the three columns express the fact that all three traditions went through an early period in which there was enough conflict and enough freedom to encourage the simultaneous appearance of many quite different points of view. Competition between these points of view stimulated the intellectual self-assertion that constitutes philosophy. In all three traditions, this was a time of the breaking and building of social structures that encouraged adventurous intellectuals to think aloud, to play, pray, and dream in the mode of reasoning. In response to their own ambition or the urging of their disciples or rulers, they duelled with neighbors of like philosophical or other ambitions, neighbors who varied, to use distinctions then already made, from hidebound conservatives to wild radicals and damnable sophists.

It is not chance that in the geographical areas of each of the three traditions there were then many small states rubbing shoulders in amity or, often, enmity. In some of these states – in Europe, Athens is the example – the habit of freedom was strong enough for it to be possible to argue almost anything, though Anaxagoras, Socrates, and maybe others paid for the freedom they exercised. The upshot was that in all three traditions there were sages or intellectuals, typically with entourages of followers, to argue for or against the already existing tradition of a golden age, for or against this-worldliness, and for or against altruism or egoism. However religious or traditional India and China may appear to later eyes, everything sacred and everything profane could then be mocked by those of a turn for mockery or debated by those of a mind to debate. These wars waged with reasons led to the development of thought about thought, by which I mean about the hows and whys of reasons and reasoning. Not only do we find the beginnings of an almost formal logic but, along with it, a conscious playing about with paradoxes – the players happy as children with glittering new intellectual toys – and a readiness to demonstrate virtuosity as such in the logic or rhetoric of debate.

The philosopher Karl Jaspers calls this period the axial age because so much on which human thought turned was originated in its course – ours, he says, is another such age, the first in which history ceases to be a collection of local histories and becomes world history.[10] Jaspers takes as his starting point the eighth century B.C., but if we restrict ourselves to the sixth and fifth centuries alone, we find not only the sages and philosophers listed in our chart, but writers, artists, and scientists who were equal creators of the three traditions, and, beyond the three, creators of other traditions, such as the prophets Ezekiel and Second Isaiah, who also helped to extend basic human thought, philosophy taken in its broader, more simply human sense.[11]

I go on to the relative emptiness of the chart, except for India, during the period beginning with the first century A.D. and ending in the eleventh or twelfth. It should not be supposed that there are no names to fill the gap, which reflects the judgment that these are not the names of the great creators of the philosophical traditions (for Europe, I have probably been unjust in omitting the leading Stoics). As the chart implies, there was a great change in Chinese philosophy that took place when Buddhism became acclimatized to its Chinese home and when Confucianism had to reconstruct itself in competition with Buddhism. But this intermediate period – intermediate from our position in time – is just that of the flourishing of Buddhist philosophy in India, as well as of its philosophical opponents, all of them sharpening one another's philosophical wits by means of their rivalry. It was through the now sophisticated Buddhist philosophy that India made the thought of China, Japan, and Tibet far more varied and subtle than before.

As compared with the crowded column of European philosophers, the near-emptiness of the Indian and Sino-Japanese columns from the seventeenth century and on has an involved explanation, not all of which I am sure. At least some of it is likely to be the result of Western ignorance in general and my own ignorance in particular. I mean that the Indian and Chinese thinkers of this time have been studied in the West far less than their predecessors. To the best of my knowledge – I have confessed my ignorance – the only classical Indian school that continued to be obviously creative, as opposed to just increasingly intricate, was that of logic, in this period called, with reason, the New Logic (Navya-Nyāya). The school of Vedānta may, more hesitantly, be added. But other classical schools also remained alive, and the verdict that their later work was uncreative may be the result of our inattentiveness to distinctions that they perceived and that we, too, may sometime come to perceive as of genuine interest. Or perhaps we already perceive them so but are unaware that others have preceded us in recognizing their interest.

An example of possibly unjust omission is that of the Chinese "searchers for evidence." They were the members of a seventeenth- and eighteenth-century group of reform-minded thinkers. Using philology as their instrument, they hoped to recover ancient truths, purify them of later metaphysical dross, and, with these truths, go about reforming society. The "searchers for evidence" (*k'ao-cheng*) advocated the use of empirical criteria such as stone and bronze inscriptions, genealogies, and chronologically precise biographies; and they discussed Chinese astronomy and mathematics in relation to the European. Some of them (such as Tai Chen (1724-1777)) tried to legitimize this European science by assigning it a Chinese origin. By and large, the skeptical and empirical tendencies of these thinkers served the purpose of reconstructing the antiquity they revered. Their closest European analogues were the Renaissance scholars whose passion was to recover and relive Greco-Roman antiquity. But for all his courage and importance, Tai Chen seems to me not to show an intellectual intensity great enough to be classed as a great philosopher. But my verdict may be the result of insufficient knowledge.

This whole late period, during which European philosophy flourished and non-European philosophy appears, rightly or wrongly, to have lessened its creative intensity is also the period that experienced foreign rule. Such rule may well have sapped the life of the Indian and then the Chinese philosophical tradition by weakening their social power and by impelling them in the direction of an at first necessarily crude encounter with Western thought. In India, Muslim raiders and conquerors exercised an increasing influence from the early eleventh century. Some Muslim rulers were simply intolerant, while others were tolerant either out of conviction or for merely pragmatic reasons – the extraordinarily tolerant emperor Akbar created a monotheism based on Hinduism and Christianity as much as on his native Muslim religion. In wartime, Muslim rulers often demonstrated their piety by desecrating or destroying Hindu temples, which in the villages were centers of social life and of potential resistance. In retaliation, a Hindu rebellion was likely to result in the same treatment of mosques. The clash was not between peoples who felt themselves to be equals because, to the intolerant on either side, the other was composed of the uncivilized or dangerous, of infidels, as the Muslims saw the Hindus, or of barbarians, as the Hindus saw the Muslims. The fact that the center of the school of New Logic was in Northeast India, which had remained untroubled by the earlier, more fanatical Muslims, may help explain the school's continued creativity.

It is not a priori unlikely, as modern Indian Muslims have claimed, that the Hindus who willingly converted to Islam were those who had felt themselves most victimized by the caste system; and the mystical sects of Islam might pull at already mystically inclined Hindus. But for Hindus generally, the contact with the Muslims was external because the Muslim religion was imageless, ruled by dogma, and relatively egalitarian, while they, the Hindus, worshipped images and belonged to hereditary groupings, *jātis*, into which they were born and in which they lived, worshipped, worked, and died. To leave or be expelled from such a group was to become culturally naked and humanly isolated.

I have been speaking of the Hindus in relation to the Muslims, but when the British became dominant, as happened in the later eighteenth century, the results were just as complicated and hard to summarize as those of Muslim dominance. I allow myself to avoid any detail here and to say only that, in the long run, European thought proved to be a dangerous, sometimes demoralizing rival to the traditional thought of India.[12]

In China, unlike India, the first great outside influence, which came from India in the form of Buddhism, was quite peaceful. By about the fourth century A.D., Buddhism had been transformed from a foreign into a native, Chinese religion. However, in the eyes of orthodox Confucians it was offensive and even dangerous because, they argued, a Buddhist was encouraged as such to transfer allegiance from the family and from the Confucian hierarchy of teachers and officials to the Buddhist monastery, and was encouraged, at least in principle, to renounce marriage and even the most usual and innocent animal pleasures - all the goals that most ordinary humans pursue without question. But, as lived, Buddhism proved far more pliant than such orthodox complainants could admit, and many individuals were Confucian and Buddhist (or Taoist) at once, with a feeling, attested to by poets and artists, of inward wealth rather than inward contradiction.

As a result of the different form of life it encouraged, of the shift in allegiance it demanded of those deeply faithful to it, and of its heavy involvement in court politics, Buddhism aroused strenuous opposition and was subjected to persecution, though not of the most drastic kinds practiced in Europe. The monasteries' wealth was confiscated and their monks were dispersed, causing the decline of all but two sects, Ch'an (Zen) and Pure Land.[13]

The Europeans who first influenced the Chinese were the missionaries. Their influence was mostly on the scholars or court officials who were intrigued by their foreign learning or the clocks and other devices they brought with them. However, the missionaries were eventually expelled and their converts subjected to persecution. It was not until the middle of the nineteenth century that a serious contest began between the Chinese who favored tradition and those who wanted to introduce

Western learning or practices. The contest, like the contests elsewhere between traditionalists and Westernized reformers, was fierce and bred great fears and hopes.

But we have to leave such political contests and go back to philosophy proper and to the causes for its real or apparent loss of creativity in India and China. In both traditions, threats from the outside have led to repeated retreats inward. The kind of retreat I mean is to an orthodoxy that demonstrates its faithfulness to tradition by insisting on remaining fixed, that is, by ignoring or pretending to ignore the worth of everything that is foreign to it. Such a retreat was possible because the Indian and Chinese traditionalists were unable to conceive that there could be languages equal in refinement and exactness to Sanskrit – taken to be utterly sacred and beautiful – or, in the case of China, to classical Chinese – taken to be incomparably superior in every way – or conceive that there could be philosophical cultures that might at all approach the richness and rightness of their own. As the Indians and Chinese understood it, their thought had undergone a process that began in inspired wisdom and continued by way of the differentiation, refinement, and expansion that made each culture inexpressibly right and deep, so that those who had formed themselves by its means could retire into its depths without feeling any sense of narrowness, that is, of provinciality or loss of universal truth. Both the Chinese and Indian traditions of philosophy have functioned as "a sophisticated theoretical structure of self-universalization and self-isolation."[14] The European tradition, too, has usually exhibited this narcissistic attention to itself alone. But this should not lead us to forget the obvious, that a community preserves itself by excluding from power any foreigners and foreignness that endanger its unity, such as it may be.

History shows that in India the Buddhists looked outward more than the Hindus. But Buddhism proved unable to survive there, and deeply Hindu or Confucian philosophers were alienated from Buddhism and rarely acknowledged any need to consider a foreign tradition as if it could teach them anything of intellectual or spiritual value. By the twentieth century, of course, such a view became implausible to an increasing and finally dominant number of intellectuals.

Despite what I have said, it should not be assumed that the Hindus isolated themselves completely from Muslim thought; there were all kinds of mutual influences, but none of great importance to classical philosophy. Finally, however, whether earlier or later, Western thought, along with Western commerce and Western arms, became a subversive influence everywhere. The effect of the West became so dominant that a Hindu or Chinese was (and is) likely to accept Western values while insisting that his native tradition developed their equivalents earlier or at least by itself: everything Western worth anything was already there in the Upaniṣads or *The Book of Changes*. To give a more subtle though more doubtful example, researchers into the intellectual life of the seventeenth century China point out, as I have implied, that it resembles European thought in being oriented - ironic word here - toward the critical, empirical, and even material. It is true that the Chinese have always had an interest in history, philology, and archeology, all of them needed to subject documents and ideas to a critical analysis. But perhaps the researchers were tempted by the desire to show how far the Chinese tradition could go toward an educated empiricism by means of its own resources alone. The play of pride and shame in one's tradition never disappears. And of course, both Indian and Chinese nationalists have responded to humiliation by outsiders by stressing the essential superiority of their native thought.[15]

## Is the Conception of Philosophy the Same in the Three Traditions?

We are still not clear of initial problems. This is because in speaking of philosophy I have been making the perhaps mistaken assumption that such an enterprise or profession in fact exists in India and China. One interesting though much too simple way of testing the assumption is to ask whether terms for "philosophy" exist in Sanskrit and Chinese, and if they appear to exist, whether their meanings are close enough to the European to justify including them in the same history. Although I am committed to saying yes, this answer is not self-evident. The moment of word-investigation that follows gives a useful reminder of the kind of difficulties that comparative philosophy faces.

It soon becomes evident that the Sanskrit or Chinese terms that Westerners have perhaps thoughtlessly used to translate "philosophy" and "school of philosophy" do not mean just what is meant by the terms in European languages.[16] This mismatching has sometimes been a source of both pride and shame, and it has made it easy to claim that not only the terms but also the subject-matter and the institutions of the European tradition, such as its schools of philosophy, are unique to Europe.

It is true that, by a philologist's careful standards, the terms themselves for "philosophy" are different in meaning, but this difference is not in itself crucial. It might be so if each tradition had permanently fixed the technical meanings of its philosophical terms. Equivalents were sometime stabilized by the need for exactness in translation. In China – notably in the seventh century under Hsüan-tsang's direction – Sanskrit originals were translated by large groups of specialists. In Tibet, the meanings of Sanskrit terms came to be fixed either by usage or official decree: according to the late eighth-century *Word-Combination* (*Mahāvyutpatti*) misleading translations were revised and terms whose meaning "had to be fixed in accord with an interpretation" were given official equivalents.[17] All the same, the meanings of general philosophical terms have varied a good deal in all three traditions, so even though the terms' webs of relationship vary, there is a good deal of overlapping. As long as the likelihood of similarity-in-difference is understood and it is taken for granted that philosophically important terms are clarified when studied in context, no great misunderstanding need arise from the equation of a term like "philosophy" with the terms in translates. It can be just as misleading to be overexact, by insisting on distinctions finer than the context makes necessary, as to be careless; and the level of abstraction - of distance of terms from their local associations - should be appropriate to the translator's particular aim.

Let me spell out what I have just said in enough detail to make the point convincing. I begin with Greece, where the term was invented.[18] There, in Greece, the word "wisdom" (*sophia*) could be used, as it was by Plato, to distinguish between true wisdom and the false wisdom taught, he complained, by the sophists. Aristotle used the word for the highest intellectual virtue, which he contrasted with practical wisdom. As for *philosophia*, "the love of wisdom," Socrates explains in the *Apology* that what he does is to persuade young and old to care less for body or money than for excellence of soul. When, later, in the *Phaedo* he speaks of his impending execution by the Athenians, he explains that God has laid on him the duty of living a life of philosophy and examining both himself and others, and that because he believes that he has spent his life in this way, he is confident that he will be greatly blessed after death. For this reason, he goes on, all those rightly engaged in philosophy are training themselves for dying – philosophy is the proper training for death! But Plato himself also uses *philosophia* to name the search for true knowledge in the sense of the discovery of the unchanging principles of knowledge. Afterwards, the Greek concept of philosophy becomes whatever the history of Western philosophy had made it become – there are very many variations.

Perhaps to the astonishment of Westerners, we find no term in traditional India for "philosopher" as distinguished from sage, saint, or the like (for "logician" there is the rough equivalent *tarkika*). But there are two old terms, *ānvīkṣikī* and *darśana*, that can be equated with "philosophy."[19] The first of these, still sometimes translated by "philosophy," appears to have meant a method of reasoning or science of investigation. Considered to be "a source of light for all sciences, an instrument for all activities, a foundation for all religious and social duties," it was appropriated by the Logic School (Nyāya) as a self-description; but it continued to be used in the neutral sense of "logical reasoning."[20] Since it was associated with logic, the term could also be associated with sophistry and with secular, anti-traditional points of view – the nuances were sometimes unfavorable. The more orthodox or believing philosophers kept such analytic reasoning in its place by insisting that it could always be corrected or refuted and therefore could not reach the absolute truth, which only the authority of scripture or intuition could establish. It appears to me that, except for the Logic School, orthodox Indian philosophers were more likely to use logic in order to bare contradictions in their opponents' views than to establish their own positive doctrines. In the usual ways of metaphysicians, these doctrines were simply proclaimed at the start or were accepted as the revealed truth, the Veda intuited by the sages who founded their respective schools. The doctrines were then defended by logical counterattacks on those who had attacked them logically. To interject my own opinion, I think that it was sensible of these philosophers to use logic to attack and refute rather than to prove, because logic finds flaws in reasoning but cannot build philosophies by its own power alone.

Whether that dictum is accepted or not, we come to the second Sanskrit term, *darśana*, equated with "philosophy." Taken etymologically as meaning "(act of) seeing" and extended to mean "realization," it has been used to strengthen the presumption of Indians that their tradition is superior to the analytic, wholly theoretical interests they (mistakenly) attribute to Western philosophy in general.[21] Some Westerners, however, have claimed that the difference between the Indian and Western terms shows that the Indian tradition has lacked the very concept of philosophy as the West has understood it.

In time, especially in classifying their philosophies, most Indians came to prefer the term *darśana* to designate an Indian "view," "doctrine," or "system." In the nineteenth century, when the Indians began to study European philosophy, they used *darśana* to translate the concept. But not all of them have been happy with the translation. Sometimes they have complained that it deprives Indian thought of its native difference from Western ways of thought. Sometimes, too, they have proclaimed that all philosophy should be understood in the light of the spiritual doctrine of India, which defines philosophy more profoundly than philosophy itself is able to – the true (more than) philosopher is the seer.

What of China?[22] It turns out that China, too, lacked an exact equivalent to "philosophy." The invention of a new term for it, by a Japanese, makes another illuminating footnote to comparative philosophy. The story of the term begins in 1862, when a young Japanese named Nishi Amane was sent to study in Leiden, from where he brought books by Comte, Mill, Montesquieu, Hegel, and other philosophers, along with the ambition to reform Japanese thought in their light. The group of Illuminists he joined were dedicated to encouraging Western liberalism in Japan. One of the group said, sarcastically, that all that Japan had to be proud of was its scenery. Another favored Western science on the grounds that it was not Western but universal; and he said that only Western-style, constitutional government conformed with human nature. As always, such sentiments provoked a conservative reaction.

Nishi himself, who favored and translated Mill's *Utilitarianism*, created much of the Japanese philosophical terminology. Long before, when preparing to lecture on Greek and European philosophy at the Center for the Investigation of Barbarian Books, he had tried to approximate the Greek meaning of "philosophy" by abbreviating the Japanese words "science of questing wisdom" into the term *kitetsugaku*. But he had then applied the word only to philosophy in the Western sense. Now he decided to coin a more general word. To this end, he analyzed the Western concept of "philosophy" and found a possible Chinese analogue, an old word composed of a character of two hands and an axe (meaning, perhaps, "to break open," as with an axe) and another character, one for mouth (meaning "by using thought or speech"). As a whole, the word means, roughly, "to speak with deliberation" or "to conceive." Now, having discovered the concept of philosophy, as he thought, in classical Chinese, Nishi felt justified in abbreviating his earlier term to *tetsugaku*, to be applied to philosophical thought universally, Sino-

Japanese (Confucian, Taoist, Buddhist, etc.) and Western alike. Invented in 1874, the term proved very successful and was widely adopted in East Asia, including China, though only in its ideographic, pictorial form, of course – the Chinese sound being transliterated *zhe-xüe*.[23]

Not only "philosophy" but also "school" (of philosophy) creates a problem. In Chinese, the nearest old term is *chia*, literally "family," used in the sense of "scholarly lineage," which implies that the task, like the task assumed by an Indian school, is to keep an intellectual and spiritual heritage. The Indian schools kept their heritage by a method that made their philosophies grow, like trees, in concentric rings of argument and counter-argument. That is, although they supposed that their respective positions expressed a truth that was timeless, they kept investigating it in increasing detail, mostly, it seems, to defend their versions of it against the always renewed objections of their rivals. Indian philosophers were likely to conceal their originality, much as did medieval Jewish, Muslim, and Christian philosophers, who had committed themselves to preserve rather than renew the truth – Maimonides and Aquinas and their followers are good examples. The view that one should concentrate on preserving an already revealed truth must have lowered interest in the philosophical changes brought about by individuals. If so, the fact that the present history concentrates on individual philosophers reflects a Western rather than old Indian point of view. But this statement, too, has to be qualified because the story of Indian (including Buddhist and Jain) philosophy, as the Indians themselves tell it, is filled with incredibly able heroes. The Chinese accounts are historicized, though they, too, begin with mythically improved or invented ancestors. Such comments on Indian, European medieval, and Chinese philosophers are not meant to imply that the present account can escape the modern Western bias I try to moderate. If – as I doubt – the desire to understand those different from oneself and the desire to go beyond stereotypes are predominantly Western, then I do not really want to escape completely. In any case, the idea of a complete escape is an illusion that retains something of the disappointment or anger that – will we or nill we – we cannot escape being what we have become.[24]

What I have told of the relation between the Indian, Chinese, and European terms for "philosophy" and "school of philosophy" implies that an exact correspondence of such concepts is impossible but that a working correspondence is not hard to reach. This is because, as I noted earlier, the old terms have been subjected to such a variety of interpretations that if one wants to be as exact as possible, the meaning of every use, Indian, Chinese, and European, has to be worked out in detail. Such understanding profits by conscious analysis, but the more usual and subtle learning is by way of the tacit understanding that comes with the actual study of particular texts.

## Telltale Sign of Philosophy: Logic

Reason, I have said, is the test of philosophy, and the clearest overt sign of reason is the conscious use of logic. The ability to use an explicitly logical method can therefore be used as a criterion by which to judge whether or not a tradition is truly philosophical.[25] Now if the basis of explicitly logical thinking is the law of contradiction (of a pair of contradictory statements, one is true and the other false) then all three traditions are philosophical because they all implicitly recognize the law and use it at times in different conscious variants. In ancient India an at least semi-technical use of the term "mutual prohibition" or "contradiction" (*vipratiṣedha*) began some time between the fifth and third centuries B.C.[26] The philosophers of the Logic School (Nyāya) assume the law of contradiction in their discussions and give it practical expression in their arguments. Indian philosophers who qualify the law of contradiction for their own doctrinal reasons argue that there is a kind of negation that, not being exclusive, does not give rise to self-contradiction.[27] Occasionally the law of contradiction or the companion law of excluded middle are stated explicitly. Both occur together in the following eleventh-century text:

> There is no other sort, when there is mutual opposition. The opposed cannot be [in] one and the same, since the very utterance would be contradictory. A kind other than the positive and the negative is not possible, for they are of the nature of mutual affirmation and negation. By merely denying the positive, the negative is affirmed.[28]

The ancient Chinese have a different cast of mind.[29] Because their language is analytic rather than inflected, they at first conceived of their sentences as only a succession of "names," that is, words. The earliest explicit recognition of the importance of word order in sentences or, rather, strings of words, occurs in a text of the third century B.C. When referring to the logical relation between a pair of words, the ancient Chinese of a logical cast of mind may say that the words follow from one another or "dismiss" (are inconsistent with) one another, or that if one is inadmissible, so is the other. In one text, the law of excluded middle takes the form of the statement that when two men contradict each another in a disputation and one opinion is right ("fits the fact"), the other is necessarily wrong (does not "fit the fact"). Use is made of the term *pei* to state that something is inconsistent, illogical, or self-falsifying. To give an example, an ancient, logically inclined Chinese, unhappy with Chuang Tzu's statement that to accept a proposition from one point of view is to reject it from another, retorts, "To deem all saying self-falsifying is self-falsifying" - as Chuang Tzu, always logically brazen, shows he understands.[30]

Unlike either the Europeans or the Indians, the Chinese have no formal logic; and they neither theorize about the truth as such nor are tempted to hypostatize it.* But they of course have the verbal means to agree with what we speak of as a true statement and disagree with a false one. The Chuang Tzu book complains that "the disputers of this world all say: 'The finest substance has no form. The greatest thing cannot be

---

* Chad Hansen and Angus Graham are prominent among those concerned with the status of logic in Chinese philosophy. Hansen says, quite rightly, that classical Chinese philosophy "does not generate any theory of something resembling the Euclidean process." He goes on, "Thus it has no basis for using a concept strongly similar to the core concept of reason." Taken together, the words "no basis," "strongly similar," and "core" make his words both hard to refute and possibly misleading. But Hansen's conclusion that "Chinese thinking is non-contrastively rational" in that "no classical Chinese theorist is either a rationalist or an anti-rationalist" seems closer to the elusive truth; only the unyielding "no" is not quite plausible. If Hansen would modify the sentence and say that no classical Chinese philosopher "is either a *complete* rationalist or an anti-rationalist" - a verdict that, on close analysis, fits all Indian and all European philosophers - he would be right. If he modified the sentence and said "is *ever* a rationalist or an anti-rationalist," he would be wrong. Chinese philosophers do have rationalistic impulses at times. See Hansen 1991, p. 192.

Graham gives an answer that seems to me just (1991, pp. 291-297). He finds more analytic sharpness in his heart and in Chinese philosophy than Hansen does. Where Graham hardens contrasts, Hansen softens them. Hansen's views are applied to the whole of ancient Chinese philosophy in *A Daoist Theory of Chinese Thought*. On the controversy surrounding Hansen's views, see the essays in Lenk and Paul 1993. See also the criticism of Hansen in Peerenboom 1993, pp. 57-61. Peerenboom (p. 60) is sure that the author of the *Huan-Lao Boshu* (Silk Manuscripts of Huang-Lao), written in the fourth or third century B.C., "is adamant that language corresponds to reality" and "is concerned ... with the truth of the matter in the old fashioned sense of 'fitting the facts.'"

encompassed.'" The answer is the rhetorical question, "Is that the reliably real state of affairs?"[31] Naturally, the ancient Chinese use a variety of terms to express their sense of what is true, right, or real. Tones omitted, the terms include: *shih*, meaning "be this," "be it," "be right," which pairs with its opposite, *fei*, meaning "not be this," "not be it," "be wrong"; *shih*, meaning "be solid," "be real," the opposite of which is *hsü*, meaning "be empty," "be tenuous," "be unreal"; *jan*, meaning "be so," "be the case," the opposite of which is *fou*, meaning "be not so," "not be the case"; and so on.[32]

Though the Chinese had no developed formal logic, interpreted understandingly, their arguments seem as logically consistent as ours do; and it is not difficult to recast the more explicitly logical (Later Mohist) writing in European logical forms and – risking cultural distance – to recast them in syllogisms.[33] Some of the Chinese were logically playful or logically serious enough to act the sophist and defend paradoxes. The following two paradoxes are reminiscent of Zeno: "No matter how swift the barbed arrow, there are times when it is neither moving nor at rest"; and "Take a pole one foot long, cut away half of it every day, and at the end of ten thousand generations there will still be some left."[34] The most famous of the Chinese sophists, Kung-sun Lung, was "a man of Chao who enjoyed hair-splitting and paradoxical talk." He wrote essays on themes such as "a white horse is not a horse," "ice is not cold," and "coals are not hot."[35] His notorious exclusion of a white horse from among horses inspired an anecdote about an attempt at tax evasion: a man argued with a customs inspector that he did not have to pay the tax on horses because the horse he was riding was not a horse but a white horse. Kung-sun Lung is right only if one assumes that "white horse" is conceptually excluded from "horse," the "proof" being that the one term cannot always be substituted for the other. Perhaps the sophist's trick was no more than to shift when under attack from one to another of the two possible meanings of the Chinese sentence, from "a white horse is not a horse" to "(the meaning of) 'white horse' is not (the meaning of) 'horse.'" But, even if right, this solution is too easy to satisfy for long and Kung-sun Lung's paradox, as developed in his simply worded but enigmatic essay, has proved an irresistible challenge to exegetes.[36]

It is true that the early exploration of logical problems and paradoxes soon died out, to be revived, in a different spirit, when Buddhism took root. However, from the start, Chinese thought takes on the logic implicit in the structure of the Chinese language. The extreme brevity and extreme ambiguity of the classical language are countered by context, to be sure, but also by fixed rules for word order, and by a pervasive parallelism, supplemented by antithesis, of words, phrases, longer passages, and topics.[37] The lack of interest of later (non-Buddhist) Chinese philosophers in logic as such is compensated for by their concentration on the lessons that history teaches for social and political thought. This concentration, natural to persons who are themselves most probably in government service, is used to exercise persuasion on others like themselves and, not infrequently, high officials or rulers, men of a kind likely to be attuned to case histories and other historical evidence. In Europe too, historical evidence, which is not demanded for epistemology or metaphysics, finds its natural place in social and political theory and is drawn on, in the form of precedent, for legal purposes.

It is typical of Greek and most later European philosophers to make a sharp distinction between inductive reasoning - the accumulation of particulars in order to arrive at a necessarily uncertain generalization - and deductive reasoning - at its most effective, the derivation of true particular conclusions from a true generalization or a universal. In contrast, Indian philosophers never make this sharp distinction. Deduction is to them incidental to the process of accurate induction. The explicit distinctions the Indians make are between contradictory, inconclusive, or certain reasons, the certainty being established by the absence of the counterexamples that would prove the induction to be doubtful. To formalize the process of induction, the Indians use their traditional reasoning procedure, usually, though misleadingly, considered to be a syllogism. It is natural enough to use the name "syllogism" because the Indian form has an appearance like that of a European syllogism. Furthermore, although in its complete guise, including a non-syllogistic example, it has five rather than three members, it is easy - too easy - to translate the Indian form into a European syllogism with the usual two propositions followed by a conclusion*. Certainly, the name "syllogism"

---

* In its complete form, used for debating mostly epistemological issues, the Indian "syllogism" has five members:

(1) Hypothesis: The mountain possesses fire.
(2) Reason: because (it possesses) the state of having smoke.
(3) Example: Whatever possesses smoke possesses fire, such as a kitchen.
(4) Application: So does this (particular mountain possess fire).
(5) Conclusion: Therefore, it does so (possesses fire).

is applicable if we adopt Aristotle's very general definition of a syllogism as "a discourse in which, certain things being stated, something other than what is stated follows of necessity from their being so."[38] However, the Greek problem is not the Indian one. The problem of the Greek syllogism is whether or not the middle term (the humanity of "all men are mortal" and "Socrates is a man") relates the mortality common to all men with the mortality of Socrates in particular. In contrast, the problem of the Indian form is whether or not one property (of "possessing fire," for example), occurrences of which have been reliably observed, pervades or encompasses another property (of "possessing smoke"), instances of which have also been observed. How, in our cognitive acts, do we infer this? the Indian asks. When we look at smoke, is our awareness of the cognitive structure, the "universal," of smokiness pervaded or encompassed by awareness of the cognitive structure of fieriness? Or: If we see smoke on a mountain and know from other evidence - like the positive evidence of a kitchen stove and the negative evidence of a lake - that wherever and only wherever there is fire there is also smoke, then we know that the instance of smoke we see is, like smoke in general, accompanied by fire: the "proving property" of smokiness ensures that the property of fieriness, which overlaps and contains the property of smokiness, is really possessed by the subject, the mountain that is the "property-possessor."

Note how the extensional and intensional senses of smoke and fire coincide. The extensional sense, that of the inclusion of meaning-location in meaning-location, is apparent in such a sentence as "Whatever is a locus of smoke is also a locus of fire." This can be translated into

---

In practice, in "inferring for oneself," the Indian "syllogism" is usually abbreviated to: "The mountain possesses fire, because of smoke. "Stated in a three-member form like that of the European syllogism, this Indian "syllogism" becomes:

(1) This mountain is a locus of smoke.

(2) Every locus of smoke (instance of smoke-possession) is a locus of fire.

(3) Therefore this mountain is a locus of fire.

Whatever pervades - fills, encompasses - something else occurs in all or more than all the loci of that which it pervades.

Nyāya philosophers are much preoccupied with the attempt to give pervasion (*vyāpti*) a detailed, fully satisfactory definition. Because the Indian form expresses the pervasion of one property by another, there is no need for the middle term of the Aristotelian syllogism (Ingalls 1951, pp. 32-33; Goekoop 1967, pp. 11-12; Potter 1977, pp. 180-206; Wada 1990, pp. 32-36).

the statement that any instance of the class of smoke-loci is included among the instances of the class of fire-loci. But the Indian speaks of the locus as smoke-possessing or fire-possessing, that is, as having a certain quality or property. He refers to cognitions and uses the language not of class and class-membership but of occurrence and possession.[39] I have spoken of awareness as pervaded or encompassed. To pervade, which is literally to pass through, means, to penetrate or permeate. It conveys the sense that the terms - the smoke and fire - are related to each other by their meanings. To encompass, to include by surrounding, conveys the terms' extensional relationship.

To the Indian thinker, the main, inductive function of logic is to ascertain with formal care if a certain property really belongs to a certain subject or if the connection is only accidental, imaginary, or illusory. His most difficult question is whether or not we can discover the conditions of pervasion for making an inference free of error. The insistence on an example agreed to by all, rules out of discussion premisses that are not accepted by all as true. It is reminiscent of Kant's insistence that a geometrical proof must involve the actual construction of a geometrical figure.[40]

The Indian process of "reasoning for others" obviously merges logic as pure, formal reasoning with a theory of perception or cognition, the theory being clear enough to be represented as an abstract rule.* This makes the rules of logic into rules of perception as well.[41] The Indian insistence on an acceptable example fits the style of Indian debating and introduces into logic what in the West is theory of knowledge. Given the factors that the Indians consider relevant to logic, it is not surprising that the Indian form is structurally so different from the European that it is can reasonably be denied the name of "syllogism"; but the convenience of the name has so far prevailed over the demand for terminological strictness.[42]

There is some justification for considering the induction-oriented logic of the Indian philosophers to be a kind of deduction - in a not very

---

* Put as such a rule, the elementary Indian logic of induction is this: "For any knower *S*, if *S* has a perceptual cognition, *Fx*, and then remembers the rule 'Wherever there is *F*, there is *G*' as instantiated in the uncontroversial case *O*, and then perceives in *x* the same *F* as before but this time as figuring in the remembered rule 'Wherever there is *F*, there is *G*,' then *S* will experience an inferential cognition of the form *Gx*, provided that there is no relevant hindrance" (Mohanty 1992, p. 111).

helpful way, Aristotle himself claims that induction is based on deduction.[43] One of the usual form of Indian logic *(tarka)*, regarded as an aid to inductive generalization, is rigorous formal implication that begins from an if-then premise. But inductive logic, too, becomes rigorous. This happens in the philosophy of the Buddhist philosopher Dignāga, of the fifth or sixth century A.D., who recognizes that the validity of reasoning as such depends - as Aristotle recognizes it to depend - on the rightness of its form, not the truth or falsity of its premises. As in Aristotle's logic, formal reasoning is taken by Dignāga to compel assent only when carried out in an ideal way. His logic tests whether or not the chosen property of one class of individuals is incompatible with (disjoined from), in part compatible with (is "erratic" with respect to, only overlaps), or fully compatible with (completely fills or pervades) the property being considered of another class of individuals.[44] Dignāga's logic is an attempt, conveniently represented by Venn diagrams, to match classes by their intensions. It confirms the absence of error in the inference by which the "arguable property" is shown to pervade the class of individuals with which the inference is concerned.

It must in candor be added that Dignāga's logic, though an impressive achievement, is not very satisfactory and that the tests he sets for induction are so difficult that they have aroused the suspicion that they are designed to show that no actual human procedure could meet them with complete success, that is, make an unquestionable induction. The suspicion makes it possible to guess that Dignāga's logic is akin to a Buddhist's intellectual variety of meditation, that it is, in other words, an exercise meant not for empirical assurance but for a stringent, dispassionate insight into the illusoriness of human judgment.[45]

My description of Dignāga's logic is too quick and vague to do more than indicate that it has a formal structure. In any case, by the time the New Logic School (Navya-Nyāya) flourished, in the fourteenth century, Indian logic was already abstract enough to be translatable into contemporary symbolic logic. But once it has undergone the translation, it loses interesting subtleties.[46] To the Nyāya philosophers, unlike (probably) the Buddhist, Dignāga, the point of complicating and formalizing the logic of induction is to show that freedom from error or, to put it in their term, the determination of "invariable concomitance," is an achievable ideal for practical life. The Nyāya philosopher believes he can create a logical freedom-from-error formula, one that tells how to forestall the danger of a deviation (the logical contradictory of a pervasion) and so to make counter-examples - even future counter-examples - extremely improbable, even impossible, the philosopher may hope. But a theoretical formula can be difficult to apply, and if one hopes to apply it perfectly, too difficult. As the Indian philosopher is well aware, a deviation from an inductive conclusion is not self-contradictory and so always remains logically possible. Therefore the induction-oriented necessity of Indian thought is weaker than necessity as conceptualized in the West.[47]

As long as we see that Indian logic is meant to define the logical conditions for eliminating inductive errors, it seems unimportant if we classify it as inductive or deductive, or, for that matter, extensional or intensional. This issue of classification should not obscure the fact that the logic is an explicitly formal one.

One logical characteristic does stand out as unique to European philosophy. It is the parallel between philosophical reasoning and Euclidean geometry, by which I mean, the adoption of the idea that to prove something one must begin with definitions and axioms and continue, in principle without error, by way of a chain of demonstrated proofs to a conclusion that cannot logically be denied. This method, historically most familiar in Spinoza's philosophy, goes back, of course, to the Greeks, especially Aristotle, and it came into some vogue during the sixteenth and seventeenth centuries.[48] But although European philosophers have often accepted the method as an ideal, it has been more effective in stimulating the metaphysical imagination - witness Spinoza again - than in attaining its goal. Judged by its aim to attain certainty, it has always failed. The truth, I believe, is that philosophers, although often very careful in their reasoning, do most of it by the same informal and fallible methods as laymen. Even if a philosopher agrees to accept the verdicts of logic, arguments can be restated in arguably defensible forms. Despite the deductive ideal they have often held, European philosophers, including Aristotle himself, have rarely tried and have nowhere ever succeeded in composing genuinely deductive philosophies; even in science, Newton's *Optics* is quite exceptional.[49] The philosophers' difference from laymen lies less in the formal consistency of their reasoning than in their dependence on philosophical tradition with its legacy of analyses and technical terms, which can give philosophies such a formidable appearance to outsiders. Seen from the inside, the philosophies are always vulnerable.

## Telltale Sign of Philosophy: Disputation

The subject of logic, which so often distinguishes philosophy in its professional aspect, is related to a social form that has often sustained philosophy as a profession. I am referring to philosophical debates conducted in accord with a set of rules. The object of such rules has been to ensure the contestants an equal opportunity, to define what kinds of reasoning are acceptable or unacceptable, and to provide a method for deciding the winner. Such formal debates were held in all three traditions.

I begin with philosophical debating in China.[50] We know that in the late fourth century B.C., philosophical disputes (*pien*) emphasizing logic and paradox were held, at least sometimes for no more serious reason than sport. As mentioned earlier, the interest in logic as such died out. In a later age, in the third century A.D., a more literary kind of discussion or debate came into vogue. The obvious reason was the politics of the time. Intellectuals had been taught by their tradition that they were responsible for the morality of the government, but conditions were so difficult for them that many became disillusioned with politics. Making what might be an anguished choice, not a few of them rejected traditional morality in favor of one or another kind of mysticism. One of these intellectuals writes in a poem that, having left riches and honor behind, his heart is ashes in a withered, immaterial, mystic house. Now, at last, he is able to forget his troubles; but can he be sure, he asks, that he can leave his social self and humanity behind and live in the mystic void alone.[51]

Such intellectuals practiced what the Chinese called "pure talk." The term refers to the conversations in which the disillusioned intellectuals met to think and banter "purely," free of the yoke of now corrupted social obligations. They took pleasure in the cleverness and irreverence of their banter, and they drank, took drugs (to prolong their lives), speculated on transcending moral doctrines by means of spontaneity, practiced unconfucian naturalness by going nude, mocked the heroes of Confucianism, and talked anarchistically and Taoistically against despotism. What matters here is that some of their talk was in the form of debates, with a formal thesis, refutation, and rebuttal, and some was concerned with abstract subjects such as speculative cosmology, Taoistic or Buddhistic "nothingness," the existence of immortals, the identity and equality of all beings, and the like. The echoes of such talk and debates helped make the third century a memorable one in Chinese intellectual history.

What of Greek and later European debates?[52] By the classical age of Greece there were already teachers and handbooks for disputation. Aristotle, who elaborates on both the proper and the deceptive strategies of debate, tells us of public disputes in which one person maintains a thesis that another tries to destroy by showing that it has consequences either false or absurd. Later, in medieval Europe, there were university disputations on set subjects in which a student answered a question the presiding master had put and then answered objections to the answer he had given. The "free questions" kind of disputation had no questions announced in advance, was open to everyone, and gave the opportunity to show off one's logical dexterity or play out one's personal rivalries. All disputations were supposed to be based, as Aristotle had recommended, on commonly agreed presuppositions and - as the medievals agreed - on authoritative quotations, the arguments being developed by means of syllogistic or like reasoning. But formal disputation lost its vitality in the later fourteenth century, and it had no consistent parallel in the rough-and-tumble of European philosophy after the Middle Ages.

For debate, India was the most developed of the traditions.[53] The rules were more elaborately worked out and the practice of debating had a much greater social impact. To give some sense of the types and rules of debate, I follow the Logic School, which is nothing if not systematic. It divides debates into three basic types, those of "discussion," "disputation," and "wrangling." In the first of these, discussion, the persons engaged are set on attaining the truth rather than on winning. To attain the truth, thesis is set against thesis, proof is based, point by point, on a combination of evidence and argument, and no argument known to be untrue is used - what kind is true and what untrue is clearly specified. In contrast to Western philosophy, though not Western law, the rules of evidence include a carefully assessment of the verbal testimony relied on. The defeated side is said to harbor no anger.

Indian "disputation" is different in that it consciously aims at victory. For this reason, even though it holds to the same standards of reasoning as "discussion," it allows the use of "quibbles" - ways of assigning argument-destroying meanings to the opponent's words - as well as other tricks meant to demolish the opponent's case (tricks of the kind Aristotle deals with in his *Sophistical Refutations*). Finally, in "wrangling," a debater does nothing to establish his own position but only criticizes and condemns his opponent's arguments. Because no thesis need be defended, this is the form of debate a thorough skeptic would have to choose.

Held in a monastery or a royal court, a debate between eminent philosophers was a great public entertainment. There are many well-known stories according to which the losers of a debate and his disciples became followers of the winner. It seems that a victory could determine the allegiance of a king - maybe he had political motives the stories tell us nothing of - and the dominance of the winning side throughout his realm. As an example we may take the surely mythical story of the debating skills of the seventh century Buddhist philosopher Dharmakīrti, which shows that a philosopher was expected to prove his greatness by overcoming and converting opponents.

The story tells that, to develop his skill against Hindus, Dharmakīrti concealed his identity and studied with their teachers. The most eminent of these was the great Mīmāṃsā master, Kumārila. From him Dharmakīrti learned the art of refutation so well that in a three-month series of debates he, one by one, defeated and converted to Buddhism the five hundred experts in the six Hindu systems of philosophy. Furious, Kumārila insisted that Dharmakīrti debate him and demanded that, if he lost, he should be killed. However, Dharmakīrti refuted each of Kumārila's five hundred theses with a hundred arguments. After further victories over other philosophers, Dharmakīrti went to Dravalī, a center of Hindu learning, where he rang a bell and publicly challenged anyone there to debate him. The local Hindu philosophers either kept silent out of fear or ran away. Then the great Vedānta philosopher Śaṅkara sent a message offering to debate, on condition that if he, Śaṅkara, won, Dharmakīrti would either convert to Vedānta or be drowned. According to the wish-fulfilling Buddhist story, Śaṅkara was repeatedly defeated, in the end had nothing more to say, and in spite of Dharmakīrti's urging, jumped into the Ganges and died. Dharmakīrti then converted many of Śaṅkara's followers, while others ran away. When Śaṅkara was reborn with a sharper intellect and greater debating skill, Dharmakīrti defeated him again, with the same results.[54]

Not everyone, however, approved of public debates. Buddha himself, whose manner was that of calm, authoritative reason, had stressed how cruel it was to attack opponents in debate and how useless it was to debate metaphysical questions. Metaphysical debate was useless to him because, on one interpretation, it dealt with insoluble problems, and on another, perhaps better one, because it prevented people from accepting the solution to existential pain that he was teaching. And besides, why debate the questions with non-Buddhist philosophers, who had never learned the Buddhist truth? Such is the moral of the famous Buddhist parable of the blind men and the elephant, which tells of the king who assembled all the men blind from birth and let them feel an elephant. The blind men who had felt the elephant's head said he was like a water-pot, those who had felt his ears said he was like a winnowing-basket, those who had felt his tusks said he was like a plowshare, those who had felt his trunk said he was like a plow-pole, and so on. The blind men fell to arguing and fighting with their fists, a sight that delighted the king. The moral of the parable is: "The heretics who do not know good from evil or right from wrong, brawl, wrangle, and strike one another with the daggers of their tongues."[55]

## The Three Traditions in Themselves: Unique, Alike, and Neither

Having adopted a moderately stringent definition of philosophy, we have seen that philosophy did exist in all three traditions and that, in all three, philosophers were consciously aware of logic and engaged in formal disputations. We have also seen that Chinese logic, though it developed for a brief period, remained mostly implicit and that Indian logic was never detached from epistemology. As for disputations, in China, it seems, they were relatively infrequent and of indecisive importance; in medieval Europe they were frequent and important; and in ancient and later India they were frequent and sometimes of great social and even political importance.

On the surface, then, we find both general similarities between the traditions and particular differences. The natural question that follows is how deep the similarities and differences may go. In answer, some scholars tend to stress similarities, others, differences, though most, I think, try to strike a balance between the two. My own answer is that both the similarities and the differences run very deep and are of extraordinary interest, and that, to confound the simplifiers, there is no similarity not tinged with difference nor difference not tinged with similarity.

To begin with differences: It is possible to take an extreme position and claim that each of the traditions is incommensurable with the others, that is, that no tradition can be grasped by means of the categories and habits of thought of the others. This extreme is empirically implausible and the attempt to argue in its favor entails its own denial: Whoever goes beyond the mere assertion and undertakes to explain how and why traditional Indians, Chinese, and Europeans were - and, to later interpreters, remain - impenetrable worlds apart, is most probably assuming the ability to enter into each of the worlds so as to show that they are closed to one another. The explanation explains what, it is claimed, is impossible to explain.

Therefore the belief in total incommensurability, if any one really holds it, seems to me implausible and I will not deal with it any further here.[56] Besides, the relations between the traditions have not justified it. Yet there are claims that the differences are so pervasive that every cross-cultural comparison of philosophies is necessarily a reductive one. One of the direct implications of such a claim is that each of the philosophic terms involved in a comparison has a meaning or group of meanings that a substitute in another philosophic language necessarily distorts; and, so it is implied, the successive distortions end in a basic misunderstanding of the philosophy as a whole. Possible examples are easy to point out. We have already mentioned the misrepresentation of the Indian "syllogism" by the Greek syllogism, the losses that occur in the translation of later Indian logic into symbolic logic, and the misleading attribution to the ancient Chinese of an understanding of propositions in the sense given them by Western logic.

The charge of misunderstanding can be illustrated with the help of some current interpretations of Chinese philosophy. Earlier, I suggested a comparison between the statements of Hsün Tzu and Kant that human beings are by nature evil. But Hsün Tzu's mode of argument, with its stress on ethical precedent and the exact application of terms, is not at all Kantian. Nor is Hsün Tzu at all Kantian when he recommends a way out of pressing ethical situations for which there are no accepted rules of conduct. In such situations, he advises, one should guide oneself by the indirect means the Chinese term for which, *t'ui-lei*, has been translated "analogical projection." To make such a projection, one must pay careful attention both to the issues involved and to the terms with which to characterize them, and then, having found the most appropriate traditional analogy, one must apply it to the situation in question. By projecting the analogy with such care, the situation is put into the measured, rational context that tradition has created. "Each analogical projection is basically an attempt to specify the concrete significance of *tao*, and it thus represents a temporal mediation between the ideal of *tao* and the actual world."[57]

In keeping with such an analysis, it is stressed that in the Chinese tradition problems are solved not by abstract reasoning but by the considered extension of old, historically fixed norms. Since everyone who denies the norms is taken to be unreasonable, rationality is measured by obedience to the norms.[58] It is therefore the goal of all the most ancient Chinese philosophers to teach how language should be used to guide action effectively. They therefore see their task as the identification of a constant *tao*, that is, "a form of discourse that *reliably* guides behavior."[59] Western philosophy, it is argued, bases itself on the ideal of a Euclidean kind of proof, and on the ideal of the individual whose self-rule requires free rational choices, not tradition. In contrast, Chinese philosophy is based on the belief that language, which is created by convention, must be used to reinforce the social good. When thinkers such as the Taoists diverge from this model, they move not toward the "argumentative theater" of other philosophers but toward poetry and painting.[60]

Suppose that for the moment we assume that between the philosophical traditions there are great intellectual gaps expressed by differences of the kind that have already been stated: the particular differences between Indian, Chinese, and Western logic, and the general differences between India, its interest focussed on strategies of living and redemption, China, its interest focussed on concrete ethical problems, and Europe, its interest focussed on abstract proofs, theories, and entities. Does our assumption separate the three traditions so widely that any direct comparison, guided, to begin with, by surface likenesses, must prove illusory?

I think not. My counter-assumption is that, at a deep level, the traditions must be substantially alike. I say this for the simplest of reasons: the biological likeness between human beings, the similarity of their social needs, and their similar ways of fulfilling themselves, intellectually and otherwise. Philosophies everywhere have been strenuously intellectual counterparts of the opposition between modes of compliance and modes of revolt - often simultaneously of both. In this sense, philosophies are alike and their comparison, if not simplistic, can be rewarding. It is still a great challenge to demonstrate the universality of logic, or that of the basic mechanisms of philosophical argument, which seem to me few, or of basic elements of political thought or esthetic response. But whatever the challenge, the crudeness of the initial comparisons is the inevitable condition for learning how to refine them. The moral is only that the beginnings of understanding should not be mistaken for its final conclusions.

While the initial similarities between traditions may have a false simplicity, so may the initial contrasts. The (non-Buddhist) Indian philosophers are true to the Vedic tradition, one repeats; but they invariably interpret the tradition in favor of the school to which they belong, so that their faithfulness to tradition is not much more than the faith that tradition must verify what their group has made of it. Of all the Indian schools, only the *Mīmāṃsā*, meaning "(School of) Investigation" (to interpret the ritual intention of sacred texts) is seriously and literally faithful to the Veda. One may repeat that the Chinese philosophers, as well, are faithful to tradition. Yet in the relatively brief period, from the sixth to the third centuries B.C., when indigenous Chinese philosophy is at its most creative, only the Confucians, in no way then dominant, are seriously faithful to tradition. All the schools appeal or at least refer to history, but invariably interpret it to support the particular positions they have arrived at. And European philosophers are not necessarily opposed to tradition. There were organized groups of philosophers faithful to Plato, Aristotle, and Epicurus. Medieval philosophers were, of course faithful, to their respective traditions of Judaism, Christianity, and Islam. Later, there were considerable if relatively short-lived subtraditions of Cartesians, Kantians, and Hegelians. All told, if there is a great divide between East and West, it is not faithfulness to tradition as opposed to neglect of it.

Nor is the great divide the use on the Chinese side of analogy, projected or not. Analogy has been essential to the thought of everyone everywhere. The analogical projection of traditional moral judgments is the instrument by which tradition has developed as such, as witness, among others, the Talmudists and the thinkers of medieval Europe and Islam; and it has at all times been essential to ethics, political theory, and the practice of law.[61]

Nor is the European faithfulness to abstract entities and deductive ideals as great a divide as it may seem in a stereotypical polarization. Aristotle himself, the inventor of formal logic and a rationalistic proof of god's existence, does not fit the stereotype. Instead, he emphasizes that the "philosophy of human life," by which he means the ruling art of politics (including ethics) is no exact, demonstrable science. This philosophy depends on practical wisdom and on the early inculcation of good habits. "The end aimed at is not knowledge but action."[62] Furthermore, as I have pointed out, very few of the European philosophers who adopted the ideal of consistent deduction tried seriously to achieve it in their own philosophies. To be sure, syllogistic reasoning was very influential during the Middle Ages, but it disciplined the form of philosophy more often than it determined its substance. And so, for all the differences between the three traditions, it is difficult to distinguish between them in terms of sweeping global abstractions.

I supplement this protest against excessively polarized differences with a few examples of interesting similarities: The ladderlike structure of nature that Aristotle describes is unmistakeably like that of Hsün Tzu. Both the Greek and Indian atomists defend their belief that matter cannot be infinitely divided by arguing that unless matter is composed of atoms in some sense finite in size, the infinitely continued division of matter would end in the total disappearance of matter. Greek and Indian skeptics often hit on the same intellectual mechanisms for refuting certainty of any kind. Sophists and materialists appear in all three traditions.[63] The standard Buddhist arguments against substance and, especially, a metaphysical self are essentially the same as those of Hume. A Buddhist philosopher and Kant both argue for a critical philosophy (in the Kantian sense) with essentially the same attack on the ability of consciousness to give an objective representation of what is taken to be the external reality.

But even if such examples are granted, they are fragments isolated from unique traditions. Does the uniqueness of each tradition not determine the uniqueness of everything that belongs to it? My answer is this: The practitioners of any one philosophical tradition are attuned to its subtleties and dismayed by a comparatist's possibly careless "It's all the same!" The philosophers' disputes - with themselves and their opponents - are in and through the tradition (or subtradition) that comes to constitute their intellectual substance. Because of its emotive, intellectual, and perhaps social effect, the difference over which a philosopher disputes with a near philosophical neighbor is likely to be of great immediate importance to both; but for an outsider it is likely to be no more than a negligible quibble. As the person within a certain tradition sees it, to try to compare its philosophy with that of another tradition is like trying to play two discordant games at the same time. However, the comparatist is neither the practitioner of any one philosophy nor the participant in any one game but the philosopher - the theme-and-variation philosopher - whose interest is in the varieties of philosophies or games. Among other questions, such a philosopher asks, what is the activity of which these philosophies or games are the varieties? The natural answer is that a common name implies some untrivial congruity. But in what, and why? And if philosophies and games prove to be incongruous with others of their respective designated kinds, why has language accorded them a misleading verbal congruity? Depending on how it is practiced, the comparatist's pursuit may or may not be predominantly philosophical - the history of philosophy and the sociology of knowledge may be seductive, and neither is in itself philosophy. But if the pursuit is philosophical, it is so in a special way.

My conclusion is that the philosophical traditions are either unique or alike depending on one's position in relation to them - inside or outside - and the standard of judgment one adopts, that is, the kind and degree of abstraction one allows oneself in order to deny or justify comparison. Both sides are right, if one wishes, or neither, if one insists.

If we turn from these issues to the usual ones of metaphysics, we find certain striking differences between traditions. One of these concerns the belief in god. The later European philosophical tradition generally assumes an all-powerful creator god, the Indian tradition often opposes it, and the Chinese tradition puts natural forces and Heaven in god's place. To begin with Europe, from the Middle Ages on, most European philosophers have depended for their moral and metaphysical arguments on the belief in god, who creates and rules the universe. In the popular religion of India and China, reward and punishment by gods is usual, but in both traditions taken philosophically, there is an often impersonal attitude according to which reward and punishment are akin to what Europeans take to be natural law. More exactly, in some Indian philosophical systems the powers and person of God are like those usual in Europe. In other Indian systems, God creates in that he rearranges matter, but matter exists as absolutely as he does; and in still other systems, the world-creator, the personal god who is the object of human devotion, is an emanation of (and identical with) the unqualified, featureless, unknowable reality that is god in the final sense. Though unknowable, he is of a nature much discussed by European philosophers and theologians. So classical Indian and Chinese philosophy can be atheistic in the sense that it leaves human fate mainly to impersonal forces that are intrinsic to the universe, that is, to matter, *karman*, *tao*, Heaven, or the Supreme Ultimate, and to the understanding, intuition, yogic exercises, or meditations supposed to affect, attain, abolish, detach, or surpass them.

From a Western standpoint, what is most strange about the Indian conception of god or gods is that some of the most devout groups have been totally atheistic - the gods they acknowledge are part of nature and subject to its laws. Much of Buddhism has been of this sort, though not consistently, and so has Jainism, and so has the orthodox, ritualistic school of Mīmāṃsā.

To experience the energy a Mīmāṃsa philosopher might put into the refutation of the belief in a creator-god, consider the following summary of arguments against such a god: In order to create the world, god would have to have the desire to create it; to have to have any desire at all, including the desire to create, he would need a body; if he had a body, the body would have to have been created by a preceding creator; if his body were eternal, the matter of which it was made would have to be as eternal as he; if it were possible for him to have no body, it would be impossible for him to influence matter, that is, the atoms of the world. Furthermore, if he had no body, he could not know anything, because to know something, just like to desire something, one needs sense organs, but sense organs, knowledge, and desire are all material; and so on. And if god created the world out of compassion, there was no one to be compassionate to before living persons were created; and if he created them out of compassion, then why did he not create only happy beings; and if he could not create only happy beings, he is not all-powerful. And if it is argued that we know he created the world because he said that he did, he may have said this only to emphasize how powerful he is; and so on. As for the holy words of the Vedas, the truth of which is self-evident and uncontradicted by experience, they need no author or guarantor other than themselves. Besides, no witness was present to see god create them; and so on. While later adherents of Mīmāṃsā thought of god as the supervisor of the law of *karman* that is, of rewards and punishments, it is clear that, to the Mīmāṃsā philosopher whose views I have repeated, belief in a creator-god could only weaken and denature religion.[64]

India and all Buddhist countries are also distinguished from Europe by their belief in the law of *karman*, according to which every act committed with either a good or evil purpose is rewarded or punished, by the very nature of the universe, in either the present life or a future one, so that each person's fate is the accumulated result of previous acts going back indefinitely far. It is widely believed that a god or a Buddha of mercy may intervene to change one's fate, and believed that in certain circumstances *karman* can be transferred, like money, from one person to another. But in principle, *karman* is understood as Europeans understand natural law. Philosophers worked out its theory in some detail.[65]

Yet despite the endless life and the possibility of accumulating the rewards granted by virtue of good *karman*, the ideal of the Indian philosophical systems - materialism and related skepticism excepted - is to break out of the cycle of birth and death. The Indians seem to fear not only the endlessly returning pains but also the exhausting pointlessness of cosmic circulation. The way out as the orthodox systems, Buddhism, and Jainism agree, is to end the cycle by getting rid of the ideas, emotions, and desires - the worldly elements - that perpetuate it, and then to remain in a transcendent state of rapture, if that is the right word, or, as others believe, of total neutrality or higher indifference. The analogous ideas of Western religious philosophy are not developed with the same persistent attention to detail.

China differs both in its religion and its metaphysics (or protoscience). Its lasting native theories do not postulate a god but only natural forces and the equilibria between them, which, if disturbed, have to be restored; otherwise, humans suffer disaster. The extreme Chinese reverence for ancestors is cultic, although in Western eyes such reverence is only weakly religious. This reverence is supported, especially among the Confucians, by an impersonal, politicized cosmology. For the Confucians come to be deeply concerned with the fate of the prevailing dynasty, because, they believe, its rise and fall are critical to the fate of all the Chinese; and this rise and fall are determined by Heaven, which works according to infallible rules of justice. Sooner or later, the Chinese know, the dynasty will grow unrighteous, its vitality will be sapped, and Heaven will decree that it be replaced.[66]

This whole Chinese mode of thought, from which an omnipotent creator and lawgiver is excluded, construes nature, including humankind, as a web of forces in the changing rhythms of which everything moves and flourishes or decays; in addition, the parallel between microcosm and macrocosm is widely accepted. Chinese thought can therefore be classified as a species (or group of species) of organicism. The result is that, unlike Westerners and many Indians, the ancient Chinese do not believe they are directed by a transcendent god who gives them orders from above; instead, they see themselves as natural organisms pervaded by the nature that comprises them. One consequence of this attitude is that they have little if any of the idea of natural laws, in the sense of definite rules that God imposes on nature as he does on human beings. There is no full Chinese equivalent to "And God said, 'Let there be lights in the firmament of the heavens to separate the day from the night; and let them be for signs and for seasons and for days and nights, and let them be lights in the firmament of the heavens to give light upon the earth.'"[67]

But once again, one should avoid exaggerated polarization. "Heaven," which is the Chinese equivalent of "providence" and the "supreme principle of nature," is like the Western god in that it issues decrees, those, already mentioned, that determine the fate of dynasties. Though never regarded as a creator, Heaven was worshipped by the Chinese emperors and often somewhat personalized, like the earlier Shang Ti, the God on High - this is the term for "god" in Protestant translations of the Bible. Surprisingly, the philosopher Mo-tzu, of the late 4th or early 3rd century B.C., expresses himself like a European philosopher who is justifying god's ways. Mo-tzu writes:

> Moreover there is a basis for my knowing how generously Heaven loves the people. It is the fact that it [Heaven] has orbited the sun, moon and stars in order to illumine and lead [the people]. It has instituted the four seasons of spring, autumn, winter and summer in order to guide and untangle them. It sends down snow, frost, rain and dew to grow the five grains, hemp and [mulberry leaves] for silk, thereby enabling the people to gain and be benefitted by them ... It has created kings, dukes, marquises and earls, causing them to reward the worthy and punish the violent.[68]

Not only does early Chinese philosophy contain occasional passages implying that there is an organizer or ruler of the universe, but there are two known occurrences of the phrase "laws of Heaven" (*t'ien fa*), which in the one instance, relating to human affairs, can be translated "natural law," and in the other, relating to the human body, the state, and the physical universe, can be translated "laws of nature."[69] The general conclusion is that the absence in China of the idea of a lawgiving god and of laws of nature is not absolute and not reason enough for an unyielding contrast between the thought of China and Europe. Furthermore, it is clearly not true that organicism is Chinese rather than European. To sharpen the contrast is to forget that organicism of a kind is not unknown to Plato, that Aristotle is strongly influenced by (non-reductive) biology, that the Stoics' universe is a form of organicism, that Leibniz believes profoundly in it, and that Kant makes philosophical use of it. It is Kant who states that "pure speculative reason has a structure wherein everything is an organ, the whole being for the sake of every part, and every part for the sake of all the others."[70] There is no reason to go on to Schiller, Goethe, Schelling, Hegel, and a host of aestheticians and biologists in order to show that organicism, although always rivalled by analytic or reductive philosophies, had a great influence on the history of European thought.[71]

## The Three Traditions in Themselves: Spiritual Transcendence against Positivistic Curiosity?

The distinctions I have just made between the three traditions are of great importance to both religion and philosophy. Now I feel it necessary to warn against the most common distinction made between India or China and Europe, or, more comprehensively, between East and West. As mentioned earlier in relation to India, the distinction is as follows: Eastern philosophy is spiritual and integral with life, while Western philosophy is abstract, materialistic or positivistic, and split off from life. In one exposition of this view, it is said that Greek philosophy studies society and man, which are the outer reality of human life, while Indian philosophy denies outer things in favor of an undeniable, ultimate, inner reality. Modern Western philosophy, it is said, represents the triumph of the objective or outward attitude, which, however helpful morally and politically, must be balanced by truly religious consciousness, which is the deeper, inward, Indian one.[72]

The view is seriously misleading. To see this, recall that in all three traditions, especially in the Indian and European, philosophy in the more technical sense came to be the province of specialists whose doctrines were usually unintelligible or pointless to most people, just as they are today. In each of the traditions, the tie between philosophy and religion remained strong - although even in the medieval universities of Europe there was a clear distinction, often accompanied by a struggle for influence, between the faculties of theology and philosophy. Typically, philosophers in all three traditions have claimed that their doctrines give those who studied them a better understanding of what was true and worthwhile and how this desired goal can be attained. This holds even of the positivists or materialists, well-known exponents of which are found in each of the traditions, and even of the philosophical skeptics in each of them, though not necessarily of the combative or playful reasoners we name sophists.

If we think of the Western philosophers listed in the chronology toward the beginning, the opinion that they are concerned mostly with outward matters, meaning material, social, and political ones, can be plausibly held of only a few of the thirty-four, most clearly of two Greeks, Democritus and Epicurus, one Roman, Lucretius, and one Englishman, Hume, to whom Russell may possibly be added; and it can be made of the various kinds of positivism that were widely though far from exclusively accepted by Western intellectuals from about the time of the French Revolution, but not ever of Western philosophy as a whole. This is the fact.

The fact is also that, East and West, most philosophy has been concerned with salvation, whether this-worldly or other-worldly. However, the interest of Hindu and Buddhist philosophers in salvation is different because it is so often tied up with the belief that to live is basically to suffer. This attitude is not characteristic of Indian philosophy at the start but begins at about the time of the origin of Buddhism – did conditions then make it especially easy to draw attention to suffering? – and remains prominent in most of the classical philosophies of India, to which reason appears valuable mostly because it helps humans to escape suffering. Take, for example, the basic text of the classical school of *Sāṃkhya* (meaning, roughly, "enumeration" of the categories of existence and, extended to refer to a school, "the school that analyzes by means of enumeration of these categories"). The text begins by stating that because human beings are tormented by the three kinds of suffering, they want to know how to get rid of it, something that can be permanently accomplished not by material or by revealed, Scriptural means, but only by a discriminating understanding.

Each Indian school having adopted different means for such a purpose, Indian philosophy can be understood, almost as a whole, as a kind of transcendent utilitarianism, one that does not exhibit curiosity for its own sake and seeks transcendent experience. Yet transcendent experience and intellectual conviction are not really separated by the Indians but (very often) supposed to support one another and, finally and in effect, to be the same – Spinoza uses a different machinery of thought, but was he so different in this particular conviction? European philosophy does not ordinarily lay so great an emphasis on suffering – the Stoics, the Neoplatonists, and thinkers like Pascal and Schopenhauer are among the not infrequent exceptions – but European philosophical thought, like the Indian, has usually expressed the hope for transcendence. And in thinking of the emphasis of Indian philosophy on suffering, we should remember that the suffering or, better, the negative quality it attributes to life is not suffering in its merely ordinary sense but in that meant by Spinoza, having to do with the objective nature of the universe and the philosopher's ability to distinguish between the transient, on the one hand, and the eternal on the other.

This need to be objective and renounce the suffering that results from the painful impermanence of everything worldly is the moral of the Buddhist parable about Kisa Gotamī. When her young son died, she took his body on her hip and went from door to door asking for medicine to cure him but was met only with derision. When she asked the Buddha for the medicine, he, in his compassion, told her to make a round of the whole city and bring him tiny mustard seeds from any house in which no one had ever died. When she failed to find even one such house, she understood that not only her boy had been overtaken by death, but that all things are impermanent and death is a law common to all mankind. Seeing this, she became reconciled to death and cast her boy into the burning-ground.[73]

It is doubly deceiving to make the distinction between philosophy as pure inquiry for the Europeans and as the science of liberation for the Indians or, for the Chinese, of morally differentiated action, moral merger with humanity, or intuitive unity with nature. Consider again the view that that Chinese philosophy is interested in "erecting, initiating, motivating, and insinuating actions and action-oriented attitudes, not in describing a transcendent world independent of actions and consciousness."[74] Even if we take this description to be accurate, it remains true that the Chinese philosopher is at times motivated by curiosity and always by the desire to express himself and to create a body of interesting thought. It also remains true, I am sure, that the philosophies of India and Europe, use their descriptions of transcendent worlds, etc., to insinuate actions and action-oriented attitudes. No philosophy is without its social dimension and effect.

I say this not because I suppose that Indian or Chinese thinkers agree with the Europeans who agree with Aristotle that the contemplation of the truth, the theoretical life, is the best of all lives. But Indian philosophy exhibits structures and refinements that, inspired or not by the need for liberation or defense against rival schools, lead to an analytical sharpness the exercise of which is its own reward; and the public victories it may bring have an additional, this-worldly sweetness. Sharp and detailed as contemporary philosophers may be, it does not take much reading in the sources to learn that many of their Indian (and medieval European) predecessors were their matches. This equality cannot be tested by resurrecting medieval Europeans, but it is still possible to question traditional Indian philosophers. Accordingly, not long ago, an experimental five-day dialogue was held, in Sanskrit and English, between a group of Indian pandits of the Navya-Nyāya school and a group of contemporary, Western-oriented Indian philosophers. The participants were at first disconcerted to discover that "there were so to speak, no philosophically uncommitted or neutral words in Sanskrit which could serve as even rough equivalents of what was sought to be conveyed through the English terms."[75*] Challenged to depart from the mere defense and exegesis of their traditional positions, some of the pandits suggested how Nyāya might be developed in new directions. Some of the pandits were later introduced to modern Western logic and some of the Western-oriented philosophers studied Navya-Nyāya logic. Each side is said to have developed a profound respect for the other and to have discovered philosophically exhilarating differences. The moral drawn is that

> a contrasting analysis which leads in a different direction and gradually builds an imposing structure of philosophical construction over millennia is something

---

[*] For the subject of the dialogue, the experimenters chose Russell's doctrine of propositions - propositions, technically speaking, are ignored by Indian philosophy - as explained in the *Principles of Mathematics*. Russell's main points were summarized, a Sanskrit translation was made for the pandits who knew no English and translators into and from Sanskrit were provided. Given the pandits' habitual defense of their philosophy, it is not surprising that (with the exception I note below) there was no obvious change in their position; changes in the positions of the modern philosophers are not recorded. But each side in the dialogue appears to have had an at least fairly clear understanding of the other, and the discussion is detailed, analytical, and pertinent. The pandit who, at the end, summarizes the Nyāya response holds that "the postulation of a separate kind of entity called 'proposition' is groundless" and adds that, if he understands Russell correctly, "such a theory does not deserve to go unattacked." Russell's temperament was such that, had he been available, he would not have foregone an answer, supplemented, no doubt, with a biting witticism. (Quotations from Krishna et al. 1991, pp. 212-213.)

> whose possibility one can not even conceive of if one is confined to one philosophical tradition alone, which one inevitably treats as the only possible tradition and hence as universally paradigmatic in character.[76]

I am convinced that the analytical sharpness and constructive complexities of Indian philosophy show the operation of curiosity working for its own, non-doctrinal, non-salvational reasons, trying to build reality as it can and solving the intellectual difficulties it has revealed in the process. When intense, philosophy is a habit of thought, a calling, and a passion, the stubborn search for either a detailed rational objectivity or a philosophical escape from it.

Not suprisingly, therefore, a sharp distinction between Indian salvational and Western non-salvational philosophy is deceptive. Even recent European philosophy, whether of the Existentialistic or Wittgensteinian kind, has searched for escape from unnecessary pain (to Wittgenstein himself the pain that results from philosophical bewitchment by words). Or it has searched for salvation of a sort by means of the acceptance of one's own finiteness and death, or by means of the renewed illumination of Being in a world darkened by objectivity, utility, and science (the first aim is that of the early Heidegger, the second, of the late one).

## How the Constraints of Orthodoxy Can Intensify Philosophical Reasoning

These last words are a reminder that both Wittgenstein and Heidegger come close to repudiating the whole of philosophy. But as was said in the beginning, their repudiation is considered philosophical when philosophy is defined to include reasonable arguments that deny reason, whether in general or in its philosophical guise. Wittgenstein remains a philosopher even when he tries to dissolve away the content of philosophy and leave only a critical method of examining what is said, especially by philosophers, and Heidegger remains a philosopher even when he turns to poetry to reveal Being or, for the sake of that revelation, turns back to pre-Platonic thought. Chuang Tzu, Ch'an (Zen) monks, and Kierkegaard find their truths not by means of philosophical solutions but philosophically intractable paradoxes – the reasoning more often implied than stated in Ch'an Buddhism is that articulated in earlier, more explicit Buddhist philosophy.

I have been making essentially the same defense for studying the orthodox philosophical theologies of Hinduism, late Buddhism, Judaism,

Islam, and Christianity as forms of philosophy. But there is not only their religious orientation to consider, but their orthodoxy as such. By definition, religious orthodoxy and, for that matter, any orthodoxy, is opposed to the free use of reason and, in this sense, inhibits the pursuit of philosophy. A skeptic, disbeliever, or believer in reason alone is therefore apt to claim that religious orthodoxy is the antithesis of any philosophy worthy of the name. But as I have said in different ways, the ideal of reason alone has never been fulfilled. The problems with which philosophers have dealt have always been so far beyond a provable solution (as their critics have shown) that *any* stand a philosopher takes must incorporate assumptions, explicit or implicit, that are neither proved nor, it has so far appeared, provable. Therefore whatever stand one takes (including the one now being taken) is incompletely reasonable or, to someone unsympathetic to it, arbitrary or foolish. Except for the rules or technical arguments whose power to convince is independent of any system – the law of contradiction is the simplest example – a philosophy must reflect not reason as such but reason in accord with one's social heritage and individual experience. In this sense, a philosophy is the intellectually formulated projection of a tradition or personality, or, to be more exact, of both at once.

Given the power to do so, orthodoxy suppresses any reasoning that conflicts with its dogmatically held tenets. But the human intellect is never wholly servile for long. The person who is orthodox and, at the same time, philosophical is like a musician or painter who creates within the confines of an accepted style. Particular dogmas and methods of thought being inescapable, the person's self-expression is limited to variations on the accepted position. Since nothing else is allowed, the creative impulse is confined to the exploration of this position in increasing detail or intensity, by which I mean an intensively, even microscopically directed attention. The individual thinker then uses the permitted style of thought in order to express the most intensive variations allowed, often different enough in their variety or intensity to be fiercely resisted by unintensive or differently intensive thinkers. The restriction itself can act as a powerful stimulus. In the long run, therefore, even the most restricted style allows original thought to live and, not infrequently, to flourish.

Of course, orthodoxy is not confined to religion. If we think of philosophical orthodoxy as, minimally, the commitment to remain faithful to a particular standpoint, then there have been many truly or ostensibly orthodox exponents of many great philosophers, the list of which ends for the while with Heidegger and Wittgenstein. What is lost by orthodoxy is compensated for, more or less, by what is gained. Considering the history of thought in the light of human limitations, philosophers impoverish themselves excessively if they insist that philosophy should exclude thought that is dominated by traditional religion or by orthodoxy of any particular kind. One ought not to forget that philosophical attacks on orthodoxy are deeply indebted to it; the more truly independent the line of thought, the more likely it is to be primitive. In all three traditions, the attacks owe their structure and technical resources to the dogmatically developed thought that they intend to undermine. In the heat of battle against an orthodoxy, the intellectual debt owed it by its opponents is not easy for them to acknowledge. Of course, the orthodoxy increases its ability to survive by making use of the resources its unorthodox opponents put at its disposal.

## The Three Traditions in Themselves: Their Uniqueness of Style

Is it possible to grasp the differences between the three philosophical traditions in a summary way? Not really. And, really, it is a mistake to trust any formula designed to sum up any one of the three. To venture such a formula is to undertake an exercise in the disclosure of a non-existent essence, to confuse the intricate variations within variations of intellectual history with the possible formulaic brevity of mathematics or the magical compactness of *mantras*. How could an aphoristic sentence or two capture any tradition that has grown over thousands of years and has engaged persons of so many degrees of philosophical creativity and so many types - wise, sharp, scholarly, bibliomaniacal, confrontational, conciliatory, narcissistic, rebellious, compulsive, and just plain weird? True, many of these philosophers were in the service of teachers the contradiction of whom was a sin against reverence and loyalty. But the human lust to think as an individual is not easily denied, and so what one could not say against tradition or in one's own name was attributed to an old sage or put down as a mere elucidation of the accepted text, until sub rosa change after change made the tradition something it has never been before.

But in spite of the necessary failure of the brief formulas I have ridiculed, only a coward of a comparatist would evade the effort to characterize the different traditions, to see them summarily, if only as a beginning on which to elaborate. After all, each of the three has its individuality, which can be recognized though not put into quite satisfactory words. One recognizes a fragment of Indian, Chinese, or European philosophy as one recognizes a face or voice in a sea of different faces or voices, without any hesitation. The identifying characteristic may be the particular abstract message, but I think it is less usually the abstraction in itself, which is likely to have counterparts in the other traditions, as its style, which includes its manner of approach to the subject, the rhythm, emphasis, and style of compression or expansion in which it progresses from idea to idea to conclusion. For the same reason that mathematicians recognize one another's styles in mathematics, there must also be something in the nature – the principles and the organization - of the logic per se by which to identify the philosophical tradition and perhaps the subtradition and even the individual philosopher.

All that is quite vague. Can I describe, briefly and simply, some of the individual characteristics of the Indian, Chinese, and European styles of philosophizing? To make an answer more nearly possible, I confine myself to the standard or classical doctrines. Well, then (very inadequately), an Indian philosophic system is likely to depend on a source – which opens and closes with an invocation to the patron sage or god – so abbreviated that, taken by itself, it is near impenetrable. It is so brief probably because it is meant for memorizing in a predominantly oral culture and certainly because it is meant for elucidation by teacher and commentary.

In a typical Indian discussion of a philosophical problem there is a systematic, if only formal fairness in that the text repeats and responds to the views of all the rival schools. The frequent compression of the text is likely to face the interpreter with the problem of deciding whether a statement represents the opinion of the writer or of the view the writer means to refute – a mistake in understanding that is as serious as confusing yes with no. The to and fro of argument is signalled by an armature of phrases such as:

> But what is the proof?; but in this case; well, then (how would you respond) if (we say)?; if it were so, exactly this should also be the case; this is not right, because; but would this not be similar?; no (this is not so) because; others, however, say; this is also incorrect; well, then (how do you respond) if?; but how can there be?; this is not so; well then, let us admit that; that (dilemma); and it is not so; but then, if; and one should not say; if one assumes that; well, then (let

us say that); with this (argumentation); well, then (let us say that); that may be enough.[77]

It is Indian style, as well, for the philosopher to put arguments in verse, accompanied by a commentary written either by himself, a follower, or, sometimes, a member of a rival school. The commentaries and subcommentaries are technical and often ambiguous because they are meant for teachers and students who are used to the issues and the style in which they have traditionally been put. Like the Indian philosophical treatises, they are, at their best, dry, direct, sharply reasoned, pious, and acidulous - a laborious pleasure to those who have acquired the Indian taste. In accord with the Indian taste, philosophical texts are given an imaginative punctuation by means of stock analogies such as the rope mistaken for a snake, the shell mistaken for silver, the mirage of water, the hare's (non-existent) horns and the (impossible) son of the barren woman.

Because I cannot do so briefly enough, I refrain from reviewing the characteristic assumptions and modes of analysis of Indian philosophers, who, not unlike the Chinese, love to work with numbered categories.[78] But they have shown an ability far beyond any of the Chinese (except the Buddhists) or Europeans to go explicitly inward and make an inventory of the objects, conditions, and functions of perception and conception - of perceptions that are preverbal, postverbal, normal, abnormal, illusory, supernormal, and divine, and of each separate sense and all the senses together; and of self-perceptions and perceptions of space, time, universals, and cognitions - cognitions of dreams, memories, recollections, recognitions, imaginations, reveries, and trances; and of desires, aversions, and emotions - emotions of attachment, clinging, yearning, lust, detachment, love, joy, anger, resentment, dejection, fear, greed, longing, conceit, hatred, forbearance, contentment, equanimity, tranquillity, endurance, wonder, and *rasa*; and of subliminal consciousness, supraliminal consciousness, supraliminal supernormal consciousness, and transcendental consciousness.[79]

There was much that was artificial in this inward analysis, yet, all told, it shows how intensely the Indians could concentrate on these very elusive processes. It is not surprising that the Indians' fascination with inward life is related to their interest in transcendence. Their earliest philosophy already shows intense appreciation of the ability to dream whole rich worlds, a sign to them that the ego can, by itself, both create and identify itself with everything it experiences, which is to say, with all perceptible reality, which is (often) to say, with a cosmic ego in nature identical with the personal one. When a person is asleep, Indians explain, he is like a king, who moves everywhere as he likes; the dreamer is everything that his self invents. This view of the power of the dreaming self made it natural for the mystical Indians to believe that deep, dreamless sleep, which they took to be the highest level, was a way of attaining certainty and peace by going beyond the lower, dreaming consciousness - which still differentiates things - and by leaving the individual unlimited by anything or anyone else, his borders having vanished in the undifferentiated common reality.

What of the style of classical Chinese thought? It is equally if not more compressed than the Indian, besides which it lacks many of the grammatical indications that are considered essential for clarity in Sanskrit or in Greek, Latin, and other European languages. Let me give as an example a short passage in which Hsün Tzu, in the course of his attack on the view that human beings are by nature good, defines what is meant by good and evil:

> All men in the world, past and present, agree in defining goodness as that which is upright, reasonable, and orderly, and evil as that which is prejudiced, irresponsible, and chaotic.

This passage is, on its face, fully intelligible; but try to understand the following approximately literal substitution of English words for Chinese characters. Needless to say, the Chinese is more compact and, in the orginal, unedited text lacks punctuation.

> Everybody past-present Heaven-below's
> that-which called good-ones:
> alignment pattern equableness good-order are;
> that-which called evil-ones:
> One-sidedness irregularity turbulence disorder are.[80]

Such clarity as is inherent in the Chinese language comes largely, as I have said, from the way the characters are organized. The characters march across the page in their fixed and parallel order and unchanging (uninflected) shape, like so many logical/esthetic symbols - each symbol's meaning to be chosen from among a variety of possibilities in accord with the immediate context, the general context of which is the whole of classical literature. The reader sees the phrases echo and enchain one another into rhythms and meanings such as these taken from Lao Tzu:

> The whole world recognizes the beautiful as the beautiful, yet this is only the ugly; the whole world recognizes the good as the good, yet this is only the bad.
>
> Thus Something and Nothing produce each other;
> The difficult and the easy complement each other;
> The long and the short off-set each other;
> The high and the low incline towards each other;
> Before and after follow each other.
>
> Therefore the sage keeps to the deed that consists in taking no action and practises the teaching that uses no words.[81]

To those who have not learned a classical text in the classical way, the text contains a set of riddles to be solved by finding the most probable combination of meanings and intended associations. The process is not unlike solving subtle crossword puzzles, because the texts, compiled by thinkers each of whose memories held a great part of the classical literature, are quite certain to quote, paraphrase, or hint at other, unnamed texts the reader is assumed to know; if the assumption proves false, the thinker - the thinker's text - abandons the reader as unworthy of any subtle understanding.[82] But there are also comparisons, stories, conversations, and historical instances to lighten the way.

As shown by the passage from Lao Tzu, the correlative style of Chinese writing and thought, with one thing or idea set alongside or against another, creates a rhythm like that of the changing correspondences by which, the Chinese believe, the universe functions. Subtlety rules even their frequent stereotypes. Take, as an example, the Confucian notion that human nature is good but requires considerable education, and that a family-like harmony, achieved by unequal but faithful reciprocity, is the social and the universal ideal. But the Chinese are very sensitive to the nuances of these deceptively modifiable stereotypes. The obtuse will miss the subtlety concealed within the platitude that allows it to enter another's mind without jarring it. As classical Chinese philosophers say, the correct application of language is the key to ethical behavior, because the mind - the heart - acts according to the distinctions of the words it uses. Is this a hypersimple or hypersubtle view? Something of both, maybe. Taken as a whole and at its best, the Chinese view expresses an ideal of actively personal and impersonal harmonizing like that achieved by the calligrapher who infuses the poem he writes - sometimes on the painting he himself has made - with the forces whose entangled contrariety catches and inspires an intensive quality of life.

I've forgotten Chinese queerness, crudeness, heartbreak, hatred, and other traits, which come to expression in philosophy as in other media; but I cannot say it all. Nor can I show in adequate detail that most of the indigenous Chinese philosophy was written not in a special philosophical language, but in the usual literary style, as essays, letters, conversations, and expansions of a master's words. I mention this, as I earlier mentioned the Indian style of commentaries and treatises, one intended for technical precision, because European philosophy seems to me to have been extraordinarily varied - often, like the Chinese, merging indistinguishably with literature in general, but often written, like the Indian, in learned styles impenetrable to laymen.

Given the brevity I must observe, I can only hint at the great variety of European styles. At the very beginning there is the style of epic poetry chosen by Parmenides and, later and differently, by Lucretius. Also at the beginning, there is the contrary, aphoristic style, of Heraclitus, and, later, there are the aphoristic styles of Francis Bacon - an aphorism, he said, is a seed of thought - and of Pascal, Nietzsche, and Wittgenstein. Toward the beginning, there are the drama-style of Plato and the contrary style of (the surviving) Aristotle, who is always analyzing and always discovering systematic connections but always correcting himself, so that he never gets to a finished system. There are the dialogue-treatises of Cicero, the discourses of Epictetus, and the meditations of Marcus Aurelius; and the style of free, imaginative, often eloquent composition of Plotinus and the copious commentary-style of Proclus, carried over into the commentary-style of the Middle Ages. But Proclus also has a Euclidean style, which Descartes uses for a sketch and Spinoza elaborates in his *Ethics*. This Euclidean style is parallelled in later philosophers who, like Wolff, Hegel and, in one book, Wittgenstein, stress formal structure. Then there is the style of the free essay, which we find in Plutarch, in the quotation-patchwork intimacy of Montaigne, and in many others. The detailed treatise cannot, of course, be forgotten. In Kant and those who follow him, it is often made up of convoluted sentences, furnished with special technical terms, that go from one deep difficulty to another. And now, to make the barest mention of the present, many write and think like the academic professionals they are, whether in the style of Wittgenstein, Heidegger, or some other philosophical mentor; but they nearly all aspire to the clear victory by argument that none of them ever wins.

Everything I have said up until now is by way of introduction, by way, that is, of reflection on the kind of work to be done, but it is not the work itself. If, as a result of the work, we will come to see that the philosophy of the other traditions shares a good deal with ours, the discovery will make clear what is common to philosophically thinking humans but is unlikely to invigorate philosophy as such. This is because the philosopher is far less interested in recovering variations of old thoughts than in thinking ahead, as far and as exactly as possible, into unknown territory. What can push thought ahead in comparative philosophy is not the similarity one finds or misses but the strain one undergoes in the finding or missing, and, when a similarity is found, the strain in showing it for what it is and marking out its limits.

*University of Tel Aviv*
*Department of Philosophy*
*Tel Aviv, Israel*

## NOTES

* For their help in writing this essay, I want to express my gratitude to Yehuda Landa, a specialist in Greek philosophy; to the editors of this volume and Shlomo Biderman, all three specialists in Indian philosophy; to Ornan Rotem, a specialist in Buddhism; to Yoav Ariel and Irene Iber, the first a specialist in Chinese philosophy and the second, in Chinese culture generally; to Ruth Manor, a logician; and to Tsvi Tauber, a particularly open and attentive philosopher.

[1] Scharfstein 1978, chaps. 1, 2 ("Three Philosophical Civilizations: A Preliminary Comparison," "Scriptures, Revelation, and Reason").

[2] *Mesopotamian thought:* Bottéro 1992 (esp. for *The Dialogue of Pessimism*); Dalley 1989, p. 150 (esp. for the probable moral of the Gilgamesh epic); Garelli 1969; Jacobsen 1976, chaps. 7 and 8, and epilogue; McCall (1990); Pritchard 1955, pp. 600-601 (*The Dialogue of Pessimism*).

[3] *Egyptian thought:* Assmann 1989; Brunner 1970; Hornung 1983, esp. "Conclusion"; Yoyotte 1969.

[4] *Eskimo thought:* Rasmussen 1929, vol. 7 (1), pp. 54-56. See also Rasmussen's other books.

[5] Leslau and Leslau 1962, pp. 8, 9, 19, 48, 51.

[6] *African thought:* Bascom 1972, pp. 148-149. For a fairly detailed attempt to formulate a particular traditional African philosophy see Gyekye 1987. Contemporary African thinkers have been preoccupied with the question of whether or not indigenous African thought may be considered to be philosophy. See, e.g., Mudimbe 1988.

[7] *Indian philosophy:* Dasgupta 1933 (a series of lucid, relatively concentrated lectures); Frauwallner 1973 (a not particularly elegant but generally reliable translation of the German original, an unfinished work of original scholarship that tempts fate by trying to work out the historical development of early Indian philosophy); Matilal 1982, 1985, 1986, 1990 (Matilal was a noteworthy mediator between Indian and Western, especially analytical, philosophy); Mohanty 1992; Potter 1965; Tiwari 1986 (especially the essays by K.H. Potter, B.K. Matilal, and A. Sharma).

*Relations between Indian and European philosophy:* Glasenapp 1960; Halbfass 1988a (= IE, a clear-minded, very knowledgeable account of the intellectual relationship); Pappu and Puligandla 1983 (contemporary Indian philosophers assessing the present status of their tradition); Sharpe 1985; Sommerfeld 1943.

*Chinese philosophy:* Allinson 1989; Fung 1952, 1953 (a standard work that, unlike the other histories of Chinese philosophy mentioned here, continues up to the twentieth century), 1948; Qi 1991; Graham 1989 (philosophically sharp); Lenk and Paul 1993; Mote 1989 (brief, clear, and intelligent); Schwartz 1985 (in particular, alert to the relation between Chinese and world culture).

*Relations between Chinese and European philosophy:* Ching and Oxtoby 1992; Gernet 1982; Mungello 1989.

*Japanese philosophy:* Brüll 1989.

*European philosophy:* I include Europe for the sake of the symmetry I am trying to preserve, but to keep the bibliography manageable, confine it to a few recent books on the history of the history of Western philosophy. Braun 1973; Geldsetzer 1968; Lavine and Tejera 1989; Rorty et al. 1981; Schneider 1990.

[8] Chan 1963, p. 128; Kant 1974, p. 184.

[9] *Comparative philosophy and "interpreting across boundaries":* Deutsch 1991; Larson and Deutsch 1988; Lewis et al. 1985; B.-A. Scharfstein, chap. 1 ("Cultures, Contexts, and Comparisons") in Scharfstein 1978.

[10] Jaspers 1949a, pp. 91ff.

[11] Eisenstadt 1986; Jaspers 1949b; Fohrer 1972.

[12] *India and the Muslim and British conquests:* Ahmad 1964 (especially Part 2, chaps. 1, 2); Basham 1975 (parts 3 and 4); Thapar 1966, chaps. 12-14; Hay 1988; Jones 1989; Sharma 1988.

By implication, I deny the basic *philosophical* creativity of the new or renewed theistic cults, but the Kashmiri Abhinavagupta (c. A.D. 1000) is an impressive figure and, at the least, a great esthetician. On his thought see Muller-Ortega 1989. For the continued development of Navya-Nyāya see Ingalls 1951, pp. 4-27 (a clear, sympathetic description of the main personalities of the school). For a fuller account, see Potter and Bhattacharyya 1993.

[13] *China and Buddhism:* Ch'en 1964, 1973; Wright 1959; Zürcher 1972.

[14] The quoted words, used to describe Hinduism alone, are from IE, p. 187.

[15] *Recent Chinese philosophy under Western influence:* Brière 1965; Chan 1963, chaps. 36-44; de Bary et al. 1960, chaps. 22-29; Elman 1984; Fairbank 1992, esp. chaps. 9-13; Gernet 1982; Levenson 1968.

*On recent Japanese thought under Western influence:* Gluck 1986; Nakamoto 1990; Tsunoda et al. 1958, chaps. 15-29.

*Recent Indian thought under Western influence:* Bharati 1970, 1978, 1982; Lipsey 1977 (the same editor and publisher have put out two volumes of Coomarawamy's selected papers); Organ 1989; Pappu and Puligandla 1983 (essays by contemporary Indian philosophers); Sharma 1988.

[16] Nakamura 1988.

[17] Snellgrove 1987, vol. 2, p. 442.

[18] Peters 1967.

[19] IE, chaps. 15 ("*Darśana, Ānvīkṣikī*, Philosophy"), 16 ("The Adoption of the Concept Philosophy in Modern Hinduism"), 21 ("The Concept of Experience in the Encounter Between India and the West").

[20] IE, pp. 273-286 (p. 275 quoted).

[21] IE, pp. 263-273.

[22] *China and Japan:* Grimm 1981; Hamada 94; Lao 1989; Piovesana 1968; Sivin 1992.

[23] On Nishi, see Hamada 1994, pp. 17-22, and Piovesana 1968, pp. 5-18.

[24] On the need to escape and its difficulty see Scharfstein 1989. See also: Dasgupta 1922, chap. 4 ("General Observations on the Systems of Indian Philosophy"); Sivin 1992.

[25] *Competing philosophical conceptions of rationality:* Biderman and Scharfstein 1989. See also *Philosophy East and West* 52/4 (October 1992), an issue largely devoted to the subject of "culture and rationality."

[26] *Logic in India:* Bagchi 1933; Bhattacharyya 1990 (vol. 1, a general introduction to Navya-Nyāya concepts, relates them carefully to symbolic logic); Goekoop 1967 (consistently translates Navya-Nyāya logic into symbolic logic); Hayes 1988; Ingalls 1951; Matilal 1968; Potter 1977; Potter and Bhattacharyya 1993; Staal 1988 (for the use of *vipratiṣedha* see p. 110); Wada 1990.

[27] Staal 1988, pp. 110, 125-126. There is relevant material in all of the first five chapters of the book.

[28] Mohanty 1992, pp. 120-121. Mohanty quotes Udayana's *Nyāyakusumāñjali* 3.8.

[29] *Chinese logic (or its absence):* Bodde 1991; Graham 1989, 1986, 1978; Hansen 1993, 1991, 1989, 1983, 1992 chaps. 1, 2; Harbsmeier 1993, 1989; Reding 1993; Peerenboom 1993.

[30] Graham 1978, pp. 25, 38-39, 199-200 (quoted). For further examples see Graham's index under "contradiction." Despite the difficulty of conceiving abstractly of a sentence, the ancient Chinese have a near equivalent, *tz'u*, which refers to a deliberately composed verbal utterance (pp. 208-209). The exceptional text I mention is interpreted as using *tz'u*, the usual meaning of which is "phrase," as having the meaning "sentence"; and it conceives of the sentence as having a parallel structure and, perhaps, an organic unity (pp. 480-483). Graham later repented of having considered the *tz'u* to be the equivalent of a proposition. Hansen, who rejects the meaning of "sentence," prefers that of a string or unit of words made up of functional parts. See Hansen 1992, p. 45.

[31] Harbsmeier 1989, p. 132. The quotation is from *Chuang Tzu* 17.21.

[32] Harbsmeier 1989, pp. 126-130. Harbsmeier's essay is a rebuttal of Chad Hansen and others who make sweeping statements such as that "Chinese philosophy has no concept of truth" (Hansen 1983, p. 492).

[33] Paul 1993. See also Reding 1993.

[34] Chuang Tzu, in Watson 1968, p. 376 (*Chuang Tzu* 33).

[35] Graham 1978, pp. 174-175.

[36] The anecdote is from Harbsmeier 1989, p. 152. Chad Hansen uses the white-horse paradox to exemplify his thesis that the Chinese language uses mass nouns. Graham agrees, but with qualifications, while Harbsmeier resists in what seems to me convincing detail – see Harbsmeier 1991. To follow the white-horse controversy as reflected in the work of a single scholar, see Graham's three articles written at different times and reaching different conclusions in Graham 1986. The last of the articles contains a complete translation of Kung-sun Lung's authentic essays.

[37] Bodde 1991, chap. 2, "The Dynamics of Written Chinese," gives a fair description of the factors that make for ambiguity as against those that make for clarity. He quotes opinions (pp. 91-96) of those who think that any idea at all can be well enough expressed in Chinese. To this view he objects, as he does to the opposite, that the influence of the language on ideas is all-encompassing.

[38] Aristotle, in Barnes 1984, vol. 1, p. 48 (*Anal. Pr.* 29b).

[39] Matilal 1985, pp. 166-170; and Mohanty 1992, pp. 125-131.

[40] Mohanty 1992, pp. 113-115, 117-118, 46-47.

[41] Mohanty 1992, pp. 112-15.

[42] See Bhattacharyya 1990, vol. 1, pp. 47-49, Mohanty 1992, pp. 122-125, and Staal, 1988, chap. 7.

[43] Guthrie 1981, pp. 187-190. E.g., in *Prior Analytics* 68b, Aristotle speaks of "the syllogism that originates an induction," taking "induction" here in the sense of "perfect induction."

[44] The following characterization of Dignāga's logic is based on Hayes 1988, chap. 4.

[45] Hayes 1988, pp. 161-167.

[46] Goekoop 1967 (contains extensive translations of Navya-Nyāya logic into symbolic logic); Ingalls 1951; Matilal 1985, chaps. 1-3, and 1968; Staal 1988, chaps. 2, 3. My statement on the subtleties that remain untranslated echoes Ingalls as quoted in Matilal 1985, p. 155. See also Bhattacharyya 1990, vol. 1, which makes both a formal and philosophical comparison of Nyāya with Aristotelian logic.

[47] Potter and Bhattacharyya 1993, p. 71-75, 79-81; Mohanty 1992, 118-122, 125-131.

[48] *History of logic in Europe:* Kneale and Kneale 1962. See also Hamblin 1970, chaps. 2, 3 (on Aristotle and the Aristotelians), 5 (on the Indian tradition).

*On the early history of the axiomatic method in Europe:* O'Meara 1989; Schüling 1969.

*Spinoza's logical method:* Bennett 1984, esp. chap. 1; Curley 1988; Parkinson 1954; Wolfson 1934, esp. vol. 1, chaps. 1, 2.

[49] See Hintikka 1989 for an attempt to rehabilitate the importance of logic and deduction in philosophical and scientific argument. He believes in the dovetailing of deductive and interrogative strategies.

[50] *Debate in China:* Balazs 1964, chap. 14 (on pure talk); Demiéville 1986, esp. pp. 828-846; Graham 1978, introduction, part 1.1; Henricks 1983, a translation of debates in essay form between the poet, musician, and essayist, Hsi K'ang and others; I have paraphrased from it.

[51] Holzman 1976, pp. 170-171.

[52] *Debate in Europe:* Leff 1968, pp. 137-184; Lloyd 1979 (chap. 2, on dialectic and demonstration in Greece).

[53] *Debate in India:* Matilal 1985, chap. 1, pp. 9-29, 1986, chap. 3; Solomon 1976, 1978.

[54] Chimpa and Chattopadhyaya 1970, pp. 230-233.

[55] The parable of the blind men and the elephant is from Burlingame 1991, pp. 75-77.

[56] *On cultural relativism:* For a refutation of extreme cultural relativism see Scharfstein 1989. There are relevant essays in Lewis et al. 1985. Dascal (1991) suggests philosophic ways of reacting to relativism. On relativism with respect to comparative philosophy, see Deutsch 1991 and Larson and Deutsch 1988.

[57] Cua 1985, p. 85.

[58] Hall and Ames 1987, pp. 324-325.

[59] Hansen 1992, p. 3.

[60] Hansen 1992, p. 53.

[61] For Talmudic thinking, characterized as "the non-propositional logic of fixed association" and dialectical argument – argument developed by means of questions and answers – see Neusner 1994, chaps. 1, 3, 4.

[62] Aristotle, *Nichomachean Ethics* 1181b (quoted), 1094b, 1095a 5-6 (quoted) (quotations from Barnes 1984, vol. 2, pp. 1866, 1730). See the account in Guthrie 1981, chap. 15.

[63] See, e.g., Basham 1951; Chattopadhyaya and Gangopadhyaya 1990; Reding 1985.

[64] Embree 1988, pp. 80-82 (a Jain argument against a creator-god); Lott 1950; Radhakrishnan and Moore 1957, pp. 498-505 (Mīmāṃsā arguments against god as creator); Sinha 1956 (see entries under "Īśvara (God)" in index).

[65] O'Flaherty 1980; Reichenbach 1990.

[66] The complex origins of the belief in Heaven, T'ien, are described in Eno 1990. For early times, see also Loewe 1986.

[67] Genesis 1.14, in May and Metzger 1973. For a detailed characterization of Chinese thought as organicistic and lacking the idea of natural laws, see Needham 1956, chap. 18.

[68] Mo-tzu 27, as translated in Bodde 1991, p. 335.

[69] Bodde 1991, pp. 342-343.

[70] Kant 1933, p. 33 (B xxvii-xxviii).

[71] In the last paragraph I draw on the article "Organicism," by G. N. G. Orsini, in Wiener 1973. Apart from Needham 1956 and Bodde 1991, pp. 332-355, see Peerenboom 1993, pp. 81-84. Like Bodde, Peerenboom thinks that Needham's discussion of laws of nature is too strongly polarized. To this I add that the organicism discussed is limited in early Chinese thought and fully developed only in Neo-Confucianism.

[72] This kind of statement has been repeated too often to document, but one can find a variant in Radhakrishnan 1923, 1927b (see the introductory pages of vol. 1). My representation of the view I think mistaken is paraphrased in part from Raju 1983, pp. 69-71, 79.

[73] Burlingame 1991, pp. 92-94.

[74] H. Lenk, introduction to Lenk and Paul 1993, p. 6.

[75] Krishna et al. 1991. For a broader description see Krishna 1993. The quotation is from p. 73.

[76] Krishna 1993, p. 75.

[77] OB, pp. 248-255. The translation is of a passage from the commentary of Vyomaśiva, of perhaps the ninth century A.D. on the standard Vaiśeṣika treatise written by Praśastapāda, of perhaps the sixth century A.D.

[78] See the attempts made by J.N. Mohanty in his *Reason and Tradition in Indian Thought* (1992) or those made by a variety of Indian philosophers in Pappu and Puligandla 1983.

[79] This list has been mostly drawn from the tables of contents of Sinha 1958, 1961.

[80] The passage is from Hsün Tzu 23, as translated word for word in Bodde 1991, p. 51, and normally in Watson 1963, p. 162.

[81] Lao Tzu, *Tao Te Ching* 1.2, trans. Lau 1982, p. 5 (the same translation - under the same name - was published by Penguin Books in 1963).

[82] Bodde 1991, pp. 74-80.

**Wilhelm Halbfass**

# RESEARCH AND REFLECTION: RESPONSES TO MY RESPONDENTS

## III. Issues of Comparative Philosophy (Responses to Chapter 2)

1. The transition from encounter, dialogue and understanding to comparative philosophy and comparison in general is not without problems. Comparison implies objectification and, ideally, a standpoint apart and equally distant from the objects of comparison. To some extent, juxtaposition and comparison are, of course, ingredients of understanding itself; and as long as they accompany the hermeneutic process in a casual and subordinate fashion, they cannot be cause for concern. As we have noted earlier, cross-cultural understanding does not occur in the mode of a simple and direct I-Thou relationship; there is also the accompanying and mostly implicit phenomenon of a "third standpoint" which faces not just the other, but also the relationship as such and one's own position in it. This becomes a (potentially virulent) problem only when comparison is promoted to a deliberate method or pursued as the systematic principle and inherent goal of cross-cultural and historical understanding in general. This has been stated by Hans-Georg Gadamer in *Truth and Method*:

> The essence of comparison presupposes the freedom of the knowing subjectivity, which is in control of both members of the comparison. It makes things contemporary as a matter of course. Hence we must doubt whether the method of comparison really satisfies the idea of historical knowledge. Is it not the case that a procedure – adopted in some areas of the natural sciences and very successful in many fields of the human sciences, e.g., linguistics, law, art history – is promoted from being a subordinate tool to central importance for the essence of historical knowledge, and which often gives false support to superficial and uncommitted reflection? We must agree with Yorck von Wartenburg here when he writes: "Comparison is always aesthetic, it is always concerned with the

form;" and we shall recall that before him Hegel brilliantly criticized the comparative method.[1]

If raised to the level of a central and dominating principle, comparison would certainly be incompatible with the dialogic approach which is committed to listening as well as speaking and which does not claim a superior standpoint or an objectifying distance from these processes. The surge of the comparative disciplines in the 19th century was indeed preceded by a propagation of comparison in the natural, especially biological, physiological and anatomical sciences. It remains generally committed to a morphological viewpoint, which aims at the discovery of pervasive structures and general, objectifiable laws in any field to which it is applied. Some brief historical reminders would seem to be in place at this point.

In some sense or other, and certainly in the subordinate role which was just mentioned, comparison has, of course, accompanied cultural processes since ancient times, and it is obviously contained in the experience of cross-cultural encounter itself, in the awareness of identity and otherness. But beginning in the 17th and more forcefully, in the late 18th century, it is placed in a new role and raised to a new level: It is proclaimed as a method, an objectified procedure, a strategy of cognitive mastery. This begins with the studies of "comparative anatomy" by Nehemiah Grew in the late 17th century; more than a century later, we have the more famous and influential works on comparative anatomy, embryology and physiology by Georges Cuvier and others. Since the early 19th century, this was followed (often in connection with Indian materials) by a large number of comparisons and projects of comparison in the humanities, for instance, comparative mythology, grammar, linguistics, and anthropology. Wilhelm Dilthey, the target of Gadamer's criticism, propagates "comparative psychology." In 1874 Max Müller, who published widely on the "comparative science of religion," "comparative theology" and "comparative mythology," could say: "The comparative spirit is the truly scientific spirit of our age, nay of all ages."[2]

In 1804 the first "comparative history" of philosophy was published (J. M. Degérando, *Histoire Comparée des systèmes de philosophie*), but the expression "comparative philosophy" emerges only toward the end of the 19th century. It seems that it was first used in India by two scholars from different parts of the country, i.e., Virchand Raghavji Gandhi (1864-1901), a contemporary of Vivekananda and the representative of Jainism at the World Parliament of Religions in Chicago (1893), and Brajendra Nath Seal (1864-1938) at the University of Calcutta, one of the leading academic philosophers in modern India. Around 1850, the great reformist Sanskrit scholar Vidyāsāgar (i.e. Īśvarcandra Śarmā, 1820-1891) had developed curriculum proposals for the Calcutta Sanskrit College which aimed at the study of Indian and Western philosophy in an explicitly comparative fashion. Gandhi's use of the expression "comparative philosophy," which he applies to traditional Indian doxographic literature, is casual and does not imply any specific program for future studies; it just testifies to his belief in the comparative potential of the Indian tradition.[3] Seal's use is far more deliberate, significant, and programmatic. It proposes the systematic study of comparative philosophy and other comparative disciplines, with the goal of furnishing "new and comprehensive material for more correct generalisations" and "for the discovery of general laws of the social organism." Such phrases clearly indicate an affiliation with Auguste Comte's positivism which had numerous followers in 19th century Bengal (including Seal's father). There is a clear affinity and perhaps even historical connection between the statements of B. N. Seal and the work of Paul Masson-Oursel, whose *La philosophie comparée* (1923; English translation: *Comparative Philosophy*, 1926) is an application of the positivist project and an attempt to utilize philosophical traditions as data for a universal anthropology. In Seal himself, there is, however, an important second motive which we may call apologetic: His use of the "historico-comparative method" is meant to combat Eurocentrism and the Hegelian manner of subordinating non-Western tradition to European thought: "Historical comparison ... implies that the objects compared are of co-ordinate rank" (IE, p. 423).

The positivist affiliation, or the combination of positivist elements with an explicitly or implicitly apologetic motivation, has not lost its significance in the field of "comparative philosophy." One of its goals is still to rectify and balance the Eurocentric perspective and to replace subordination with coordination. The affiliation of such coordination with positivism (and, at least indirectly, with anthropocentrism and Europeanization) is, however, often overlooked.

My own learning process in matters of comparative philosophy has been long and tedious. It can be described as the slow erosion of an initially very strong commitment and enthusiasm. In some of my earliest lectures and publications, I tried to develop a "method" for the systematic comparison of Indian and Western philosophy, or to establish "comparative philosophy" itself as a special method for the historiography of philosophy. During the following decade, my enthusiasm cooled down, but did not evaporate entirely. In a statement first made in 1973 and revised and published in 1978, I said, with regard to a comparative treatment of the question of being:

> Rather different possibilities of cross-examining the Western theme of being seem to be suggested by what is called - *faute de mieux* - "comparative philosophy," a discipline which still has difficulties in establishing itself as a discipline, and which has not yet produced any "story of success." Its reputation is still rather questionable, and among its more characteristic features is the discrepancy between its pretensions and its actual results. ... What comparative philosophy needs is courage, modesty, and patience; not the accumulation of more and more juxtaposable data, not the rash jumping to general conclusions concerning "essential" differences and "ultimate" identities, but the courage and patience to develop gradually its own hermeneutics, to adjust its means, methods, and expectations to its subject matter, and to grow into its own context of understanding and of being understood. (Halbfass 1978, p. 96)

My subsequent references are basically historical and retrospective, and they show that I had abandoned my initial hope to develop and utilize a special *method* of comparative philosophy. I expressed doubt whether "it is possible at all." I also questioned its "allegedly neutral, purely theoretical, and objective approach" and suggested that the apparent openness of comparative research might be "conditioned by an implicit European parochialism, by one peculiar, almost idiosyncratic manner of understanding reality" (IE, p. 433). Whatever the *future* meanings and uses of comparative philosophy may be - I certainly do not see any promise in returning to its positivistic and apologetic past.[4]

2. To my great relief, none of my respondents really propagates or advocates "comparative philosophy" as a special *method* of philosophy or cross-cultural understanding.

Ben-Ami Scharfstein's beautiful essay on the "three philosophical traditions" (i.e., those of India, China, and Europe) is, as he tells us, "the still tentative introductory chapter" to his work in progress, *From Uddālaka to Kant: A Short Comparative History of World Philosophy*. It is obvious that this will not be a book on "comparative philosophy" in Masson-Oursel's sense. It has no agenda above and beyond widening the horizon of philosophy students. It does not try to translate philosophy into anthropology. It remains committed to the philosophical questions which were asked, answered and debated in the three great traditions, and it uses the non-Western (i.e., Indian and Chinese) approaches as vantage points for a reconsideration of Western notions. If it is "comparison," it is "dialogic comparison" which remains committed to the idea of understanding. I am convinced that the book will prove its value in the classroom. Its pedagogic qualities are obvious, and I look forward to trying it out in my own classes.

In his introductory remarks, Scharfstein tries to clarify the concept of tradition and asks the question: "Why say that there are only three great philosophical traditions?" This is, indeed, a question which needs to be asked, and which has become increasingly controversial in recent years. What should be done with Tibet, Japan, the Muslim and Jewish traditions, as well as numerous forms of oral and tribal wisdom, which also deserve to be recognized as legitimate interpretations of the world and of human existence in particular? As one conspicuous example, we may mention recent discussions on what has been called "ethnophilosophy" and "sage philosophy" in Africa. The increasing attention paid to these phenomena not only by African authors (for instance, H. Odera Oruka), but also by Western academic teachers of philosophy (such as Heinz Kimmerle of the University of Rotterdam), and the growing readiness to recognize them as manifestations of philosophy, cannot be denied. On the other hand, African authors themselves have criticized the notions of "sage philosophy" and "ethnophilosophy" (for instance, P. J. Hountondji) or emphasized the necessity of an African participation in the *Western* enterprise of philosophy (for instance, Kwasi Wiredu). We may have to wait for future developments in this and related areas of debate.[5]

For the time being, Scharfstein's approach seems to be reasonable as well as practicable. Traditions which do not exhibit certain criteria of conceptualization, argumentation and reflexivity are, without any judgment as to their own inherent value and validity, excluded from the historical domain of philosophy. Other traditions, such as those of the Muslims, Jews, Tibetans or Japanese, are affiliated with, or even subsumed under, the three main traditions. This avoids the pitfalls of Eurocentrism on the one hand, and of a thoughtless and indiscriminate pluralism on the other.

After this basic decision, Scharfstein discusses the reasons for, and the practical and didactic feasibility of, studying the three philosophical traditions *together* (p. 240ff.). He asks whether the concept of philosophy is the same in all three traditions and focuses on a number of exemplary issues as they arise within these traditions. Cross-cultural correlations are chosen carefully; familiar generalizations are supplied with some less familiar, but necessary caveats (see, for instance, p. 276ff.).

Of course, we do not yet know what the book which will follow this introduction will be like. If I were to write a similar work of "dialogic comparison," it would perhaps include some imaginary dialogues between representatives of the three traditions, for instance, between Śaṅkara and Descartes on the foundations of knowledge (i.e., the Veda and the Cogito), Aristotle and Nāgārjuna on arguments, debate, and the "two truths," or even such modern figures as the Neo-Vedantin Vivekananda and the Indologist Paul Hacker on the role of the person in ethics and the possibility of "Practical Vedānta." I might also try to correlate some of the guiding patterns and underling premises of Indian philosophy and culture, such as the dichotomy of action and inaction (*pravṛtti* and *nivṛtti*), the doctrine of karma and rebirth, and the scheme of the four goals of life (*puruṣārtha*) with issues of contemporary philosophical and public debate.

The "three traditions" approach has been taken repeatedly in the course of this century. We find it, for instance, in Paul Masson-Oursel's positivistic *La philosophie comparée* (1923) and again in P. T. Raju's *Introduction to Comparative Philosophy* (1962). Raju's book has a "brief comment on the view of Georg Misch" (p. 306ff.). I take this opportunity to call attention to the work of this pioneer of cross-cultural philosophical studies. Misch, who was born in Berlin in 1878 and died in Göttingen in 1965, was one of the very few professors of philosophy in Europe who did not restrict their academic teaching to Western materials. His *Der Weg in die Philosophie* (1926), which appeared in a greatly enlarged second edition in 1950 (and an English translation under the title *The Dawn of Philosophy*, also in 1950), is a spirited and personally committed attempt to retrieve those creative impulses and guiding questions which account for the origin and early unfolding of philosophical thought in ancient Greece, India, and China. Misch, who knew India and China from personal experience, was Wilhelm Dilthey's disciple and son-in-law. In a sense, he tried to put his teacher's "philosophy of life" to cross-cultural use. Dilthey himself had done very little in that direction.

3. Rada Iveković uses the expression "comparative philosophy" in the title of her contribution. But she proceeds immediately to questioning the meaning and legitimacy of the term and the corresponding idea. She calls

the concept "vague, ill-defined and, moreover, clearly a Western one." Her own idea of a *philosophie comparante* ("comparing philosophy") aims "at investigating a common ground for both Western and Indian philosophy, a ground which was *not* available beforehand but had to be created" (p. 221). However, I do not want discuss the potential questions and problems relating to this enterprise. Instead, I want to focus on what is evidently one of the central themes of her contribution - a theme which also happens to be a central issue in my presentation of the encounter between India and Europe. I am referring here to the asymmetry of this encounter and dialogue. The asymmetry, which goes along with the "Europeanization of the earth," concerns, above all, the language of the encounter and dialogue, the conceptual tools of articulating selfhood and otherness which are available to the participants in the encounter. It may be good at this point to recall that Heidegger's own notion of Europeanization is, unlike that of Husserl, about the language which is available in current cross-cultural dialogue, and the encroachment of European modes of thought and speech upon the non-Western speaker, not a crude representation of the other by the European, but a subtle undermining of his ability to speak for himself. Heidegger, of course, presents his concept of "Europeanization" in a dialogue on language ("Aus einem Gespräch von der Sprache") between a Japanese and himself. Iveković reminds us that the problem has been faced by a diverse group of thinkers, especially in France, although usually without any reference to Indian materials or even cross-cultural encounters in general. "This sort of critique is the one which is brought within sight of philosophy by contemporaries such as Derrida, Irigaray, Lyotard, Serres, Sloterdijk, Axelos, Deleuze and others, although *not* on any material from other cultures, but as a matter of principle" (p. 226). More specifically, she refers to Jean-François Lyotard's description of the situation: "it is the situation of a différend where the discourse of the complaining party has no sense in the language of the dominant party, because the dialogue is made in the latter's language only" (p. 222).

Recent efforts to explore the actual feasibility of balancing the situation of the encounter and perhaps reversing the asymmetry of the dialogue deserve our attention. But are they really more than isolated curiosities? In a series of conferences initiated by Daya Krishna on behalf of the Indian Council of Philosophical Research, attempts have been made to test whether (and, if possible, to demonstrate that) traditional Sanskrit pandits can deal, in Sanskrit, not only with their own tradition, but also with problems of modern Western philosophy and science in a manner which would not be fundamentally different from the way modern Western terms and concepts are used to deal not only with the Western, but also the Indian tradition (see Krishna et al., 1991). Can such efforts produce convincing answers to questions such as the following ones, which I raised in *India and Europe* with regard to the inherited hermeneutic resources of traditional or traditionalistic Sanskrit pandits:

> Do they possess traditional means of understanding which are sufficient to respond to and interpret the modern world? Does the tradition itself provide such a framework of understanding? (IE, p. 261)

The setup of Daya Krishna's meetings is, of course, somewhat artificial and remains embedded in a thoroughly Western or Westernized context.[6] Such experiments ought to be encouraged, but we can hardly expect any significant hermeneutic reversal from them. In general, there seems to be little we can *do*, in terms of organized, methodic procedures, to bring about a fundamental change. The urge to act, to organize, to initiate change may, in fact be counterproductive. For the time being, there seems to be little choice but to continue the (admittedly asymmetrical) dialogue, the careful reading and listening, the patient work of understanding the other, but also understanding our own conditions and limits. We have to be ready for a certain amount of "*Gelassenheit*."

This seems to be in accordance with the view of Iveković when she suggests that "something could come to us from somewhere else," and that we have to have the patience and the "humility of thought" to wait for it. We cannot predict what it will be; we cannot know for sure what we are waiting for. Maybe it is (in a literal or perhaps not so literal sense) simply "the end of our world" (p. 229).

4. Srinivasa Rao's contribution on "the nature of reason in India and the West" reminds us of important divergences concerning the role of reason and the nature of man in the two great traditions of thought. He does so in a cautious, non-confrontational manner, without essentialization, but emphasizing predominant trends. We hear about the early elevation of reason in Greek thought, its identification with the highest level of the soul in Plato, and its association with ideas of human autonomy and the free pursuit of knowledge for its own sake throughout the history of Western thought. In India, on the other hand, it is associated with the fundamentally instrumental capacity of the mind (*manas*)

and generally subordinated to the self (*ātman*), the supreme principle in man. Indeed, recovering the identity of the *ātman* means, most distinctively in Śaṅkara's Advaita Vedānta, transcending the instrumentality, the nexus of means and ends (*sādhyasādhanabhāva*) which constitutes our ordinary worldly reality. These basic observations are then illustrated and expanded by statements on the rather different courses which science and the critique of tradition, especially religious tradition, have taken in India and Europe.

There is little to disagree with in this presentation. I just want to offer two supplementary observations.

a) Professor Rao's conciliatory and balanced presentation should not let us forget the extent to which the concept of reason has served as an instrument of European self-assertion, even as an emblem of superiority and uniqueness, and as a device to deny equal status and the capacity for science and philosophy to the so-called Orient. On the other hand, Indian responses to such claims often display a somewhat hasty and helpless apologetics.

b) I would warn against overrating the actual role of pure theory in the West, and the extent to which the ideal of a self-sufficient, autonomous reason has really been present and effective in Western thought and history. No doubt, the "adventure of reason" in the West, the readiness to go wherever one might be taken by it (p. 210) has no equivalent in India. Yet there is also a deep and pervasive association of reason with mere instrumentality in European thought, and its inability to lead and show ultimate goals has been recognized more than once, for instance by David Hume, Arthur Schopenhauer or Max Weber. Here, of course, we do not have the metaphysical safety net of the self (*ātman*), and reason itself may appear as a slave of the emotions (as in Hume) or the blind will (as in Schopenhauer). In more recent thought, the instrumental nature of reason and rationality has often been emphasized, as, for instance, in Jonathan Baron's definition of rationality as "a property of the methods used, or rules followed (or not followed), not of the outcome of the process" (Baron 1985, p. 5). Others have denounced the systematic development of the inherently instrumental powers of reason as a process of alienation and degradation. Instead of establishing the human subject in its autonomy and sovereignty vis-à-vis the external world, it has brought about an increasing submission of this subject to the dynamics of instrumentalization, and ultimately to the instrumentalization of human existence itself. Herbert Marcuse's idiosyncratic synthesis of Marx and Heidegger exemplifies this critique.

5. With remarkable clarity and simplicity, Jitendra Nath Mohanty presents a series of pertinent questions and observations concerning the study of Indian philosophy, the encounter between Indian and Western thought and, most specifically, the relation between Indology and Indian philosophy. I will try to respond, more or less explicitly, to his queries in the order in which they are presented.

If there is "Indologie" ("Indology"), why is there no "Deutschologie" ("Germanology"), but only something like "Germanistik," which deals not with "the entire German culture," but only with "the German language and literature"? Does this imply a "selective objectification" of a non-Western culture? Classical Indology, with which I grew up, is, of course, not fundamentally different from other branches of philology, such as "Germanistik" in the sense of "German philology" or, more specifically, classics or "classical philology," i.e., the study of the languages and literatures of Greece and Rome. Indology in this sense is Indian philology, the study of India's *classical* languages and literatures, above all, Sanskrit. In fact, Ernst Waldschmidt, who was Professor Mohanty's and my own teacher at the University of Göttingen, was a professor of Indian philology ("Indische Philologie"). Of course, there may still be a lot of objectification in Indian philology, but I don't think that it was selective in the sense that it was applied to "Oriental" traditions only. In practice, European, especially German, Indology, was never a "global discipline" whose subject matter was an "entire country" or region. This distinction belongs to the "regional studies" (or "area studies") programs which have been created in more recent times. I am far from trying to denigrate my own Department of South Asia Regional Studies and its members (which would, of course, imply some self-denigration). I only want to suggest that it would not be difficult for anybody with the appropriate mindset (i.e., with a desire to uncover hidden agendas and potential collusions between power and knowledge) to convert some of the arguments against traditional "Indology" and "Oriental Studies" into arguments against "South Asia Regional Studies." These final remarks are, of course, not part of my response to Mohanty, with whose diagnosis of the treatment of *Indian philosophy* within traditional European universities I agree completely.

What is the significance and legitimacy of the "Neo" in expressions like "Neo-Hinduism" and "Neo-Vedānta"? Could we speak of "Neo-Christianity" as well? In fact, I have used this term in *India and Europe* (p. 373), and not all of my Christian readers and reviewers were entirely happy about the term. Concerning the expression "Neo-Hinduism": I have, over the years, distanced myself increasingly from Paul Hacker's somewhat simplistic use, most explicitly in the introduction to my recent collection of Hacker's Vedānta studies (Halbfass 1995a). Still, I believe that "Neo-Vedānta" and "Neo-Hinduism" are useful and legitimate as convenient labels. They are simply abbreviations for important developments and changes which took place in Indian thought since the period around 1800, i.e., the relatively unprepared opening to foreign, Western influences, the adoption of Western concepts and standards and the readiness to reinterpret traditional ideas in light of these new, imported and imposed modes of thought. We have, however, to emphasize that the demarcation of these modernist trends against "surviving traditional Hinduism" is more problematic than it appears in Hacker's dichotomy. Incidentally, we should not forget the extent to which "Neo-Vedānta" and "Neo-Hinduism" were used in India and by Indians. Hacker himself borrowed the term "Neo-Hinduism" from the Jesuit scholar and long-time resident in India, Robert Antoine, who may have adopted it from the Bengali Brajendra Nath Seal, whom we already mentioned as an early champion of comparative philosophy. It seems likely that Seal (1864-1938) was the inventor of this term, which he used to characterize the literary work of Bankim Chandra Chatterjee. "Neo-Vedānta" (or Bengali *abhinava vedānta*) was used by Indians as well as Europeans in 19th century Bengal.

Concerning the semantic relation of *darśana* and "philosophy" and the applicability of the European word "philosophy" to the Indian tradition of thought, I agree completely with Mohanty that there is no justification for a puristic and Eurocentric restriction of the scope of philosophy and for an exclusion of India from the historiography of philosophy. In fact, I have argued about this in great length and detail in several chapters of *India and Europe*. The problem of the correlation between *darśana* and "philosophy" is, in my view, more complex. In my earlier publications, I have tried repeatedly to analyze and interpret the historical and hermeneutical processes and the continuing problems pertaining to this correlation: it is not necessary to repeat my arguments here (see IE, chs. 15, 16 and 19). The idea of a Greek "root idea" or *Urstiftung* of philosophy, which Mohanty rejects, emerges as a central issue in the article by Joseph O'Leary, whose approach is diametrically opposed to that of Mohanty. I will have to refer to it again in my response to O'Leary.

Next Mohanty moves on to the issue of "theory and practice" in the Indian and European traditions. Inevitably, this has to be one of the central issues for anybody trying to come to a cross-cultural understanding of these traditions. In *India and Europe*, I have tried to distinguish substance from hyperbole and ideology in the Greek and later Western claims to "pure theory":

> The ideas of "pure theory" and "knowledge for its own sake" can hardly be considered as definitive and self-evident achievements of the European tradition; nor are they unquestionable standards for assessing or disqualifying non-European traditions. (p. 270)

Numerous authors have discussed the intricate relations between "knowledge" and "human interests" (J. Habermas) in Western thought. On the other hand, the Indian tradition has developed its own modes of transcending all practical and goal-oriented interests, and the means-ends-relationship itself. Simple disjunctions in this area are entirely inappropriate.

> There are various, often implicit forms of interaction and confrontation between theory and practice on both sides. We certainly can compare and contrast these, and the different historical directions which the relationship between theory and practice, or knowledge and its goals and uses, has taken in India and in Europe. (IE, p. 271).

Concerning Mohanty's remarks on "history and historicity" in India and Europe, I would be reluctant to correlate notions of time and history in the manner he proposes. It may be true that the Greeks, too, "had a circular view of time." Yet it seems undeniable that they paid much greater attention to the documentation and chronological and narrative retrieval of such sequences of temporal events and human actions which are commonly known as history. This was at the same time a manner of retrieving and asserting their cultural and ethnic identity and of demarcating it against the otherness of others. It is well-known that the oldest extant "histories" in Greek, most notably the work of Herodotus, are much closer to comparative ethnographic accounts than to historiography in the modern sense. Stating this special role of ethnography and history in Greek literature, as compared with Indian literature, should, of course, not suggest any kind of metaphysical ranking.

The next query concerns Edmund Husserl's conception and proclamation of "Europeanization," which means for him the inevitable conversion of the globe to a Greek-European sense of "pure theory." My preceding observations on "theory" and "practice" show that I find such claims and proclamations concerning "pure theory" as questionable as Mohanty himself does. However, that kind of Europeanization which Heidegger describes as an encroachment of European modes of thought and speech upon non-European speakers and their submission to the European syndrome of science and technology (which implies objectification, calculation, and "progress") continues to be an intriguing and disturbing phenomenon. I do not believe that the citation of non-Western contributions to "Western" science and the postulate that "good philosophical thinking ... is always 'beyond the Orient and the Occident'" (p. 169) constitute an adequate response to this global phenomenon. Nor is this a mere spin-off of Western political hegemony and economic power. Indeed, we can easily agree with Mohanty's suggestion that Europeanization "also means transformation of Europe itself" (ibid.).

6. I am grateful to Joseph O'Leary for his intense and eloquent contribution which addresses and pursues central, though not entirely explicit questions in, or perhaps behind, my study *On Being and What There Is*. It is the kind of response I hoped for, but did not really expect to see after I had finished this idiosyncratic mix of specialized Indological research and timid reflections on fundamental philosophical questions. O'Leary is right in suspecting that his "doubts and misgivings" did, at least in part, occur to me, too. But I did not proceed to pursue them, and I would hardly have been able to articulate them in the same eloquent and persuasive fashion. However, while I was facing these doubts and questions concerning my approach, and while I was considering some of the basic alternatives suggested by O'Leary, I also saw them as temptations of thought and potential distractions which had to be resisted and avoided. I am still not entirely sure of my decision. But at any rate, I am convinced that without it I would not have been able to continue my work in Indian philosophy as a hermeneutically committed combination of philological research and philosophical reflection. I might also say: I was simply not ready to abandon that world of shared meanings and questions (not just "hasty identifications" or "generic similarities") in which I was finding myself.

What I am saying is basically a confession. I have not provided any additional arguments or empirical, textual, evidence to support what I decided to do. But my faith in arguments and evidence in areas of disagreement like the current one is somewhat limited. Therefore, I will neither attempt to prove that my decision was the right one, nor will I try to refute O'Leary's views. I suspect that anything I might say or quote could once again be relegated to the level of "generic similarities" (p. 180), or the "lower reaches" (p. 183) of culture, and that some higher or more profound level of authenticity or exclusivity might be invoked against it, which I might once again be unable to recognize. How can I argue against Heideggerian pronouncements such as those quoted on page 178, which assert in the mode of a tautology that philosophy is nothing but Western philosophy and *cannot* be anything else? How can I argue and cite evidence against someone who is bound to assure me once again that this would be "precisely the generic similarity between Indian and Greek philosophy that Heidegger wants to get beyond" (p. 180)? But how could Heidegger attempt to "get beyond" what he never even tried to know or understand? How can I even *disagree* in a meaningful dialogic manner with someone who seems to be intuitively certain, through some kind of "phenomenology" which is inaccessible to me, that the "grasp of being (subjective and objective genitive)" in Greece and Europe, and with it Greek and European philosophy as such, is not "one among others," and that all other traditions may at best have "random and tentative broodings on the sense of the word 'being'"? At this point, I cannot help presenting another confession: I find it easier to relate to such statements of exclusivity and uniqueness when they are expressions of religious faith and not accompanied by references to phenomenology.

I want to repeat here that I am not entirely sure of my position; I just want to present it as openly as possible. I also want to say again that in dealing with Indian texts about being I do not have a sense of "random broodings," nor do I have, while reading Plato's or Aristotle's casual statements on "wonder," a sense of any "great beginning." Why can these not be called "random and tentative broodings"? Are they really expressions of a "grasp of being" and of the "metaphysical" question, "why are there beings rather than nothing" (p. 182)? O'Leary misses this question in Indian thought; but I cannot find it in Greek thought either. On the other hand, I do find a sense of wonder about the very existence of the world, the presence of distinctive entities, the openness of space and the ability to move in it in the Veda. But once again, O'Leary may tell us (and has, in fact told us) that this is merely a "generic similarity" with Greek thought, and that it does not do justice to "the intrinsic phenomenological lineaments of the Vedic world" (p. 198), nor to the "great beginning" (pp. 180f. and 198) of India's commitment to the core theme of "spiritual release." Once again, a fundamental or perhaps merely programmatic and emblematic notion is raised to a level of higher (or deeper) authenticity which removes it *eo ipso* from the realm of shared or shareable meanings and questions. Would it not be advisable to permit some sense of doubt and deal more cautiously with the allegedly unique sense of wonder among the Greeks (which was, of course, part of the Greeks' own self-understanding, self-definition and, perhaps, self-mystification)? What is wrong with granting the Vedic people an authentic sense of wonder of their own? And what is wrong with granting the Buddha a sense of wonder which he experienced when he discovered (according to legendary accounts) the phenomena of pain, temporality and death? Can these phenomena not be objects or causes of genuine and authentic wonder? Certainly, Schopenhauer (who was, of course, dismissed by Heidegger) found the truly philosophical sense of wonder not in regard to the sheer existence of the world, but in regard to its misery and inadequacy.[7]

To say it once again: all this is not meant as a refutation of O'Leary's approach (which is by no means simply identical with that of Heidegger). I only want to state very clearly (and at the same time reassure myself) that this approach does not and cannot work for me in my philological reflective and hermeneutical interaction with Indian thought. And it is simply incompatible with my experience of, and commitment to, shared meanings. Could it be that I miss something fundamental, a fundamental opportunity of understanding the Indian as well as the Western traditions according to their own inherent measures of achievement and greatness, as grounded in their own unique and incomparable "great beginnings"? Am I still unable to open myself to the dawn of a new, more radical pluralism that might shine upon us after we have gone through the radical exclusivity of the "great beginnings"? Could it be that I exclude myself from a new and greater openness by *not* excluding India from the scope of philosophy and the question of being? I cannot be sure. But for the time being, I find the specter of false exclusivity more threatening.

I have said that O'Leary's approach does not work for me. Does it really work for him? I will not presume to answer this question. But I want to suggest that it has left some deep ambiguities and unresolved tensions in his presentation.

On the one hand, Heidegger and O'Leary with him seem to suggest that there was absolutely *no* philosophy in India or China, because there was simply *no* "grasp of being (subjective and objective genitive)" (p. 180) and because their "great beginnings" were not beginnings of philosophy, but of something else. But then, within the very same context, O'Leary states that this does *not* amount to an absence of philosophy or the "grasp of being" in India and elsewhere; it only "did not come to pass in this insistent, determining way" (ibid.) While Greek and European thought "bathed in the light of being" (ibid.) and were "haunted by the quest for Being" (p. 194), the "question of being" played *less* of a role in India. It was *less* thematic, *less* problematic in India; it was not treated with the same focused intensity and the same "transcendental generality" (p. 190). "Yet unless it is brought into sustained, explicit focus, it tends to evaporate" (p. 173). If it could evaporate, it must have been there in the first place, and it must have had some role and presence in the "great beginning" of Indian thought.

But did the Greek-European tradition really bring the "question of being" into "sustained, explicit focus"? Does not Heidegger himself tell us that its history in the West is primarily a history of oblivion, that its role was by no means a matter of thematic and explicit focus, and that he had to retrieve it from underneath other thematic issues, as the "unthought" in Western thinking? O'Leary would not (and could not) disagree with this, but could and does reply that such neglect is still entirely different from the neglect of the question in India. It is Europe's own authentic oblivion and neglect of its very own question, while India may have other great questions or "distinctive openings" which it can authentically neglect and forget, such as "spiritual liberation" or "release" (see pp. 180 and 199).

In the introduction to his article, O'Leary declares his "hesitancy" to make statements about Indian philosophy of which, as he claims, he knows "so little" (p. 171). As a matter of fact, his references to details of Indian thought are generally very sensitive and pertinent. By and large, I see little need to elaborate on specifics. Certainly, I could not have hoped for a more thoughtful and conscientious reader of *On Being and What There Is*. But this is not the point. The central issue is and remains the notion of "great beginnings," of hermeneutical and historical keys which might help us unlock, consummate and "overcome" (see p.

197ff.) the Indian and Western traditions. In a general sense, this notion does seem to hold the promise of a new and more radical pluralism (p. 180), a true dialogue between partners who recognize each other's spheres of authenticity and greatness. But the scheme is too grand and simple; and there is too much closure and exclusiveness on the way to the promised land of true openness. The damage it could inflict might be irreparable. But then again, I am not entirely sure of myself. I am also not completely sure of my own reading of O'Leary's reading of Heidegger. Could it be that the statements about "great beginnings" are just a peculiar way of speaking about much more ordinary and commonly accepted assumptions concerning "cultural constructions" and "cultural pluralism" (p. 178)? But why then would we need the intimidating terminology?

Professor O'Leary should take the sharpness of my response as a compliment. It reflects a grateful recognition of the pertinence of his comments, a commitment to understanding, and an attempt to come to the rescue of understanding itself. In the end, I am convinced that we are moving on common ground, and that we *have been* meeting in a realm of shared meanings and questions.

## NOTES

[1] Gadamer 1988, p. 206 (with revisions and corrections); for Hegel's critique of comparison see IE, p. 424f.

[2] For more detailed information and bibliographical references relating to this and the following paragraph, see IE, pp. 419-433 and 576-578.

[3] See Gandhi 1964, p. 19; Gandhi refers to Haribhadra's *Ṣaḍdarśanasamuccaya* and its commentary by Guṇaratna. I was not aware of this reference when I wrote the chapter on "India and the Comparative Method" (IE, pp. 419-433).

[4] See, for instance, IE, p. 432f., OB, p. 13f., and the survey article Halbfass 1989. My earliest published statements on "comparative philosophy" appear in Halbfass 1968b (a contribution marred by misprints).

[5] On the debate about African "sage philosophy," "ethnophilosophy," etc., see Kimmerle 1993.

[6] See Krishna et al., 1991; the volume presents, for instace, statements in Sanskrit on philosophical issues raised by Bertrand Russell.

[7] Schopenhauer's reflections on "wonder" ("Staunen," "Verwunderung") are quoted and discussed in Misch 1950a, p. 89ff.; Misch also deals with Plato's and Aristotle's sense of wonder.

# 3

# Topics in Classical Indian Philosophy

Jan E. M. Houben

# BHARTṚHARI'S PERSPECTIVISM (1): The *Vṛtti* and Bhartṛhari's Perspectivism in the First *kāṇḍa* of the *Vākyapadīya**

Es giebt nur ein perspektivisches Sehen, nur ein perspektivisches "Erkennen"; und je mehr Affekte wir über eine Sache zu Worte kommen lassen, je mehr Augen, verschiedne Augen wir uns für dieselbe Sache einzusetzen wissen, um so vollständiger wird unser "Begriff" dieser Sache, unsre "Objektivität" sein.

Friedrich W. Nietzsche

*ekasminn api dṛśye 'rthe darśanaṃ bhidyate pṛthak/*
*kālāntareṇa caiko 'pi taṃ paśyaty anyathā punaḥ//*

...

*prajñā vivekaṃ labhate bhinnair āgamadarśanaiḥ/*

Bhartṛhari

## 1. Introduction: Bhartṛhari's Perspectivism

1.0 There is a simple principle which pervades the whole of the *Vākyapadīya* (short: *VP*, which will usually mean in this article: the *Vākyapadīya-kārikās*, or *VP-kārikās*). It is reflected in its structure from beginning to end, and finds sometimes more explicit expression in specific *kārikās*. The principle is that, in a very fundamental way, the validity of different perspectives is accepted. Throughout the *Vākyapadīya*, different viewpoints are discussed in their mutual opposition and complementariness. Sometimes the viewpoints are simply enumerated.[1] Sometimes Bhartṛhari adds a statement of what would be acceptable from two opposed points of view.[2] Sometimes he has an undeniable preference for one view or the other.[3] And sometimes he seems to develop "his own" view by integrating the opposed views of other thinkers.[4] But even if he prefers one view or develops a new synthesis, others are not totally discarded. His preferences are generally pronounced against the background of a relativizing attitude.[5] With this approach Bhartṛhari differs from the familiar, more openly polemic approach in Indian philosophical works in which other systems are unequivocally refuted and one's own system is defended.[6]

One could give this principle in Bhartṛhari's approach the name of "conceptual relativism," or "perspectivism," the latter term mainly in accordance with some observations made by Wilhelm Halbfass[7] (see quotation below, in section 1.2). In simple words, this would mean that it is beforehand assumed that things appear differently from different points of view, or in different conceptual frameworks. This may be contrasted with the assumption that it is possible to make complete and universally true statements about a thing. The principle would explain, at least provisionally, why it is so difficult to find a systematic exposition of a certain well-defined philosophy in the *VP-kārikās*, if one does not want to accept in advance the interpretations of commentaries and later authors. There is a certain aloofness towards the different theories discussed by Bhartṛhari, even towards those theories which seem to be his own construction, or those which are presented by the commentaries as "the author's own view."[8]

1.1 In one form or the other, the principle has been acknowledged by several scholars. They were confronted with it, had to recognize it, and struggled with it in search of Bhartṛhari's "own view" and his own philosophical system. Thus, according to the Herzbergers, Bhartṛhari is "studiously non-committal" (Herzberger and Herzberger 1981a, p. 1). According to Krishnamoorthy, Bhartṛhari "was familiar with a relativist and rationalistic approach"; his *VP* "steers a middle course between the Buddhist stance of extreme subjectivism or nihilism and the Vedantic peak of Absolutism, and adopts a uniquely relativistic perspective, accommodating equally Nyāya realism and Mīmāṃsā positivism" (Krishnamoorthy 1983, p. 1). Biardeau recognized that Bhartṛhari "wants to rise at once above all controversies by showing the conditions of possibility of any system of interpretation, rather than to prove the truth of a certain particular system."[9] The desire to discover a well-defined philosophical system in the *VP*, and the difficulties experienced in finding or constructing it, are reflected in Iyer's remark that "Though Bhartṛhari has arranged the material gathered from the Munitraya in some kind of sequence, one cannot say that it is all made up into a complete system" (Iyer 1969, p. 404).

1.2 Halbfass (IE, pp. 268-269) referred to Bhartṛhari's recognition of the validity of different "perspectives," or, without directly using the term, to his "perspectivism," in the context of the development of the doxographic literature in India:

> Quite obviously, the Jaina tradition provided a natural setting for the development of doxographic literature, as we find it represented by Haribhadra's *Ṣaḍdarśana-samuccaya*. ... In choosing *darśana* as his doxographic titleword, Haribhadra did not simply continue or resume the old usage of *darisaṇa*, but he also referred to a usage which had gained momentum outside of Jainism, and which had prepared the word *darśana* for its special doxographic role. The greatest representative of the Śabdādvaita tradition, Bhartṛhari (who lived most probably during the second half of the fifth century), provides early and informative testimony for this usage. ... In his *Vākyapadīya*, as well as in his commentary on Patañjali's *Mahābhāṣya*, Bhartṛhari uses *darśana* in the sense of "view" and "perspective," and then also of "way of thinking" and "doctrine." ... We find different perspectives, different ways of seeing the same reality in many areas. There is the "perspective of unity" (*ekatvadarśana*) as well as the "perspective of aggregation" (*saṃsargadarśana*); in such and similar compounds, *darśana* is used in a way which recalls the Jaina concept of *naya*. In his commentary on the *Mahābhāṣya* Bhartṛhari also uses the more specifically doxographic expressions *vaiśeṣikadarśana* and *mīmāṃsādarśana*.

Halbfass also refers to the end of the second *kāṇḍa* of the *VP*, where it is said that "insight gains distinctness from (the study of) different traditional views," (IE, p. 268, translation of *prajñā vivekaṃ labhate bhinnair āgamadarśanaiḥ*, *VP* 2.489ab[10]). He adds that "This statement sounds almost like a motto and a programmatic justification of the future doxographies, in particular if we consider the perspectivistic approach of the Jainas" (IE, p. 268).

1.3 The precise role and importance of "perspectivism" in Bhartṛhari's philosophy are yet to be determined. According to Halbfass, the doxographic usage of the word *darśana*, "perspective," in the *VP* stands in a "peculiar affiliation with the philosophy of the absolute 'word'" (IE, p. 268). For, although the *VP* abounds in perspectivistic passages, there are places where Bhartṛhari does seem to commit himself to a well-defined "own view." Sometimes, his (seeming) commitment to one view (e.g., the famous semantic theory of Metaphorical Existence in the *Saṃbandhasamuddeśa*), is strongly relativized if the larger context of the *VP* is taken into consideration (cf. my study of the *VP*, Houben 1992b, Part 2 and 3, esp. discussion of *kārikās* 39-51). In other instances, however, no "alternative commitment" can be found on a certain issue.

This is especially true for the beginning of the *VP*, which starts with a group of *kārikās* which read like a series of established tenets which the author accepts and is planning to elaborate and defend in the rest of his work. The wish to interpret the whole of the *VP* in the light of the first few *kārikās* (cf. Peri Sarveswara 1981, p. 75) is understandable, but, as we have seen above, leaves us with a number of problems. Instead of attempting to reconstruct a closed philosophical system, it may be more useful to ask a few questions: What is the relation between Bhartṛhari's "perspectivism" and his commitments to an "own" philosophy? Should we understand Bhartṛhari's "doctrinal tolerance" as an offshoot of an underlying "inclusivism,"[11] thus, as a method to promote the own ideas, and as a more hidden way to be just as polemical as other philosophers in the Indian tradition? If yes, on what level should we look for the ideas Bhartṛhari is seeking to promote? Do they concern, e.g., the validity of the Veda, the acceptance of ontological doctrines, or the status of grammar, or a combination of these?

Halbfass, referring to "Jaina perspectivism and the Vedāntic form of treating other doctrines," observed that

> In no case, however, does a presentation of the opinions of others imply a relativizing or abandoning of one's own position. Instead, the own position is explicated and justified precisely through the discussion of other positions – by demarcating one's own teachings against them, or by claiming to encompass and transcend them. (IE, p. 355)

Does this apply to Bhartṛhari's perspectivism as well?[12] And is his perspectivism more like the Vedāntist's "vertical" or "hierarchical" inclusivistic model, like the Mādhyamika's subordination of other viewpoints to the own view (or "non-view") of "emptiness" (*śūnyatā*),[13] or rather like the Jaina's "horizontal" inclusivistic model (cf. IE, p. 414)? Attempts to answer these important questions have to wait till we have a better picture of the scope and function of perspectivism in Bhartṛhari's own work. Relatively simple instances of Bhartṛhari's perspectivism have been mentioned in note 1. In the present article, I will focus on three more complex and partly problematic cases in the first *kāṇḍa* of Bhartṛhari's *VP*.

## 2. Bhartṛhari's Perspectivism and the Ancient *Vṛtti* on the *Vākyapadīya*

2.0 In the *Vṛtti* too, we find the tendency to enumerate different views and to point out oppositions between possible perspectives which are valid in their own theoretical contexts. As in the *VP-kārikās*, certain "preferred views" come to the fore against this background of the different views discussed. Are the perspectivist and relativizing attitude and the preferences in the *Vṛtti* similar to those in the *VP-kārikās*? Differences in ideas and theoretical preferences were sought and found earlier, especially by Biardeau (1964b, pp. 1-21).[14] Bronkhorst, too, has argued that the *VP-kārikās* and *Vṛtti* sometimes espouse different ideas (Bronkhorst 1988, pp. 112-114; also 1991a).

2.1 Because it is so important for our understanding of the first *kāṇḍa* of the *VP*, and for the *VP* as a whole, we will have to study the *kārikās* along with the *Vṛtti*. In another article (Houben, forthcoming: "Bhartṛhari's *Vākyapadīya* and the Ancient *Vṛtti*"), I discuss the two competing main views on the identity of the author of the *Vṛtti*: according to some it is written by Bhartṛhari, the author of the *kārikās*; according to others it is written by someone else. In that article I show how some (often very subtle) evidence can be adduced for either view. There, I concentrate on arguments used in the discussion till now, such as the evidence of the colophons, references to the *VP* and *Vṛtti* by later authors, etc. I also show that some of the alleged differences in doctrine and philosophical position in the *VP* and *Vṛtti*, as formulated mainly by Biardeau and Bronkhorst, were based on an inaccurate understanding of the difficult passages of the *Vṛtti* and of the extremely concise *kārikās*. I want to add here that some of the misunderstandings arose possibly because of a certain lack of appreciation of the importance of the perspectivist attitude of Bhartṛhari, which is also reflected in the *Vṛtti*, when attempting to pinpoint theoretical differences between the two.

2.2 Nevertheless, if we study the three cases in which Bhartṛhari's perspectivism is manifest, we will see that there are sometimes (subtle) differences between the *VP-kārikās* and the *Vṛtti* in their doctrinal or theoretical choices and preferences. At the end of this article we will have to ask: Is there any regularity in the differences (and possible differences) between *VP* and *Vṛtti*? Can we make an attempt to formulate how the *VP* and *Vṛtti* differ systematically, even though it was till now not possible to reconstruct a complete system on the basis of the *VP* and *Vṛtti* together?

## 3. Bhartṛhari's Approach to Knowledge and Truth: the *pramāṇas*

3.1 Before we start to discuss the three cases, it is expedient to study a passage which is not strictly or strikingly perspectivistic in outlook, but which provides useful background information about Bhartṛhari's approach to knowledge and truth. This may be helpful if we try to understand his attitude to alternative systems of knowledge and alternative truth claims. In this passage, *VP* 1.29-43,[15] Bhartṛhari discusses the relative value of the *pramāṇas*, i.e., means of gaining reliable knowledge. The subject is taken up again in other passages which will be incidentally referred to, but we will focus on this passage. This and other relevant passages have been discussed in Aklujkar's "The number of *pramāṇas* according to Bhartṛhari" (Aklujkar 1989a; cf. Aklujkar 1989b). (Earlier discussions are found in e.g., Biardeau 1964a, pp. 332-348, and Iyer 1969, pp. 83-97.) Aklujkar argues that

> whereas most other traditions of Indian philosophy, knowingly or unknowingly, emphasized the separability of the means of cognition (*pratyakṣa* "perception", *anumāna* "inference", etc.), the Grammarian-philosophers like Bhartṛhari ... played down the separability of the means and looked upon them as functioning conjointly; (Aklujkar 1989a, p. 151)

moreover, while

> thinkers like Dignāga avoid such overlapping of *pramāṇas* by restricting the object of *pratyakṣa* (to *svalakṣaṇa*, i.e., by redefining *pratyakṣa*), the Grammarians accept the overlapping as an unavoidable fact of life and view the operations of (so-called separate) *pramāṇas* as basically complex. (Aklujkar 1989a, p. 151, note 1)[16]

The question that remains is

> Which *pramāṇa*-s does the Grammarian have in mind when he puts forward his view? His *pramāṇa*-s may not be as separable as those of others and he may not be interested in so defining them as to make their domains mutually exclusive, but how many common sense definitions precede his view or are presupposed when he takes his stance? (Aklujkar 1989a, p. 152)

That the *pramāṇas* which Bhartṛhari is willing to accept are only perception (*pratyakṣa*), inference (*anumāna*), and traditional knowledge (*āgama*); and, specifically, that he did not look upon intuition (*pratibhā*) as another means of cognition, is what is defended in the mentioned article (Aklujkar 1989a).[17] Iyer, however, was of the opinion that *pratibhā* was a *pramāṇa* for Bhartṛhari, and even the most important one: "*Pratibhā* has been declared to be the most reliable source of it [sc. of valid knowledge, JH]" (Iyer 1969, p. 187). That *pratibhā* was the most important source of gaining knowledge was also Biardeau's conclusion (1964a, pp. 317, 320).[18]

However, as has been pointed out by Aklujkar (1989a, pp. 155-156), in the most important passage discussing *pratibhā*, 2.143-152, *pratibhā* may be considered to be "knowledge itself looked at from a specific point of view" (Aklujkar 1989a, p. 155). The fact that Bhartṛhari states that people look upon it as a *pramāṇa* (2.147) means, according to Aklujkar, not that it is a *pramāṇa* in the sense that *pratyakṣa* etc., are *pramāṇas*, but rather that "the knowledge that *pratibhā* is, is viewed as reliable and becomes a basis or means for action" (*ibid.*).[19] In any case, it cannot be accepted as an independent means of gaining knowledge, because its intimate relation with *āgama* is emphasized in 2.151. In our passage (*VP* 1.29-43), *pratibhā* is not referred to at all.

3.2 Against this background, *kārikās* 1.29-43 make some statements about the relative value of the three *pramāṇas*, viz. perception (*pratyakṣa*), inference (*anumāna*), and traditional knowledge (*āgama*). The context, as shown by the first and last *kārikā* of our passage, 1.29 and 43, is the validity and value of the traditional texts (*smṛti*) of grammar. This will come under the heading of traditional knowledge (*āgama*) which may include revealed texts (*śruti*) as well as composed texts (*smṛti*).[20]

*kārikā* 30 emphasizes the importance of *āgama* and the weakness of *anumāna* if it is without *āgama*. The following *kārikās*, 31-34, continue to play down the value of *anumāna*.[21] *kārikā* 35 mentions a special perceptual knowledge (based on the "trained eye" of specialists of gems and coins) which is not directly communicable to others and which results from practice. *kārikā* 36 points out that powers of supernatural beings are beyond perception (*pratyakṣa*) and inference (*anumāna*) , and that they are only the results of *karman*, i.e., action or ritual. Though it is not spelled out, this no doubt means that these too are ultimately based on *āgama* (traditional knowledge), which teaches (ritual) acts and the results to be expected from these acts. Next, *kārikās* 37-39 are devoted to the validity of cognitions derived from that specific kind of direct perception which is the privilege of "those whose (inner) light is manifest and whose mind is not obscured," in other words of *ṛṣis* and *yogins*.[22]

3.3 The *kārikā* which follows those discussing extraordinary perception (37-39) is 40, according to which people have little use of scriptural teaching (*śāstra*) to know what is good or bad:

> With regard to these two topics, [namely] "This [is] meritorious" and "This [is] demeritorious," there is little use of traditional texts for human beings down to the *caṇḍāla*.

By saying that people have little use of traditional texts it is not yet clear what source of knowledge does guide them in their decisions concerning *dharma*. According to the interpretation in the *Vṛtti*, they follow the statements of those having extraordinary perception. Another theoretical possibility would be that they follow their own intuition. The problem with *kārikā* 40 is that it was attributed to Vyāsa (Pārāśarya), the author of the *Mahābhārata*, by Kumārila and later on by Jayanta Bhaṭṭa. Abhinavagupta mentioned it as a saying of Ādimuni (Vyāsa) incorporated in the *VP* (Abhyankar-Limaye 1965, Appendix III, p. 204). What is more, also according to the criteria formulated by Iyer and Aklujkar, *kārikā* 40 does not belong to the main text but to the *Vṛtti* (Iyer 1966, p. x; Aklujkar 1971a, pp. 510-511: To be a *kārikā* of the main text, a verse should not be introduced by the *Vṛtti* as a citation; and it should have its own explanatory comments). Nevertheless, the *kārikā* in both interpretations referred to above does fit well into the argument of the *kārikā*-passage.[23] If the *Vṛttikāra* is not identical with Bhartṛhari, the criteria of Iyer and Aklujkar should be applied with care because it is possible that the *Vṛttikāra* assigned the status of "illustrative statement" to a *kārikā* or *kārikās* which he did find in the text he was commenting on. Although the status of 1.40 in Bhartṛhari's *kārikā*-text is indeed doubtful, it seems too early to relegate it with certainty to the *Vṛtti*.[24]

In the *kārikās* which follow, finally, traditional knowledge (*āgama*) is compared with the continuum of consciousness, and the limited value of mere inference (*anumāna*) is once again emphasized (41-42) before the author returns to the traditional, composed texts (*smṛti*) of grammar (43).

3.4 While in this passage Bhartṛhari makes a case for the acceptance of *āgama* as an important *pramāṇa*, he also points out the importance of direct perception. It may be recalled that some thinkers (especially the Mīmāṃsakas) tended to emphasize *āgama* as the most important *pramāṇa* and played down the role of direct perception (of *yogins* and *ṛṣis*)[25]; but others (e.g., Vaiśeṣikas, Naiyāyikas, Yoga-Sāṅkhyists; also Buddhists) recognized and emphasized the validity and importance of direct (including supra-natural) perception as a means of reliable knowledge.[26] According to the latter, the validity of the scriptures is based on the reliable knowledge gained by reliable persons through direct (supra-natural) perception.

3.5 What is Bhartṛhari's stand in this controversy? As pointed out above, the initial and concluding *kārikās* of the passage, 1.29 and 43, show that it should support the validity and value of traditional texts (*smṛti*) of grammar; and *kārikās* such as 30 and 41 suggest that among the three *pramāṇas*, *āgama* is unequivocally accepted as prior and basic to the others. In the controversy between those accepting direct perception as primary and those accepting *āgama* as primary Bhartṛhari could then be placed without much difficulty on the side of the latter.[27] This one could further corroborate by pointing to a later *kārikā* in the first *kāṇḍa*, 1.150. The *kārikā* is as follows:

> *jñāne svābhāvike nārthaḥ śāstraiḥ kaś ca na vidyate/*
> *dharmo jñānasya hetuś cet tasyāmnāyo nibandhanam//*

This may be translated as follows:

> If knowledge were spontaneous,[28] there would be no use of the traditional texts. (But) if dharma is the cause of knowledge, the tradition (of revealed texts) is the basis of that (*dharma*).

Here I translate the words *jñāne svābhāvike* as they are apparently interpreted by the *Vṛttikāra* (*VP* I, pp. 204.7-205.3). However, as will become clear below, Bhartṛhari does not deny that knowledge can be/is in fact spontaneous.

3.6 There are two passages in the second book which seem particularly relevant in this respect. First, *kārikā* 2.233-234:

> *śāstreṣu prakriyābhedair avidyaivopavarṇyate/*
> *anāgamavikalpā tu svayaṃ vidyopavartate//* (233)
> *anibaddhaṃ nimitteṣu nirupākhyaṃ phalaṃ yathā/*
> *tathā vidyāpy anākhyeyā śāstropāyeva lakṣyate//* (234)

> In the traditional texts, it is only nescience (*avidyā*) that is described through different derivations/procedures. But knowledge approaches by itself, without the conceptualizations[29] of traditional texts.[30] (233).

Just as the undefined (because not yet existing) result is not connected with its causes, like that also knowledge is inexplicable and (only) seems to have the traditional texts as its means of access. (234)

The immediate context of these *kārikās* is a discussion of the variability of grammatical explanation. The traditional texts are therefore in the first place grammatical texts, the nescience in the first place ignorance exhibited in incorrect speech, and the knowledge that approaches by itself in the first place the knowledge of correct speech, which arises not as a direct result of the analyses and derivations of grammatical treatises. Yet the *kārikā* is stated in such a manner that it is not difficult to read in it a more general statement which stresses that knowledge arises spontaneously, not as a mechanical result of the study of traditional texts. Also the *Vṛtti* interprets it as a very general statement. *kārikā* 233 is explained as the view which the *trayyantavādins* (early Vedāntins?) have "with regard to each and every traditional text" (*sarveṣv eva śāstreṣu*); *kārikā* 234 as a statement open to an interpretation according to the "view of origination" (*utpattipakṣa*) and the "view of the real" (*satyapakṣa*), i.e., the view of those accepting that causal processes lead to results which were formerly inexistent (*asatkāryavāda*), and the view of those who think in terms of manifestations of pre-existing effects.[31]

3.7 The second relevant passage is the one on intuition (*pratibhā*), 2.143-152. Here there is little doubt that Bhartṛhari assigns considerable value to this intuition, which extends from verbal understanding (*VP* 2.143-145) and human intuitions "how to act" (*itikartavyatā* in *VP* 2.146, cf. *VP* 1.40!), to the intuition or instinct of animals such as the male cuckoo if it changes its melody in spring[32] (2.145-150). In the final *kārikā* of this passage, several kinds of intuition are enumerated, and the first kind is precisely intuition that is *svabhāva-upapādita*, "brought about spontaneously" or "on the basis of one's own nature." Interestingly, the immediately preceding *kārikā* connects this intuition with *bhāvanānugata āgama*, probably to be interpreted as "internalized traditional knowledge"[33]. One is led to believe that for Bhartṛhari intuition (including even instinct) and traditional knowledge are not contradictory, but rather the two sides of one coin, or the two extremes of a single continuum.[34] In the light of this passage, it has become difficult to defend that the *svābhāvikaṃ jñānam* of *VP* 1.150 is entirely rejected by Bhartṛhari. Rather, we have to say that he accepts that one may indeed have valid spontaneous knowledge, but that having this knowledge is made possible by following the tradition of revealed texts.

The passage on *pratibhā* in the second *kāṇḍa* has therefore unexpected consequences for the passages on the *pramāṇas* in the first *kāṇḍa*, especially because it shows that the term *āgama* has for Bhartṛhari dimensions which were not yet obvious from the outset. That Bhartṛhari gives a very abstract meaning to *āgama* (to accept this is in any case unavoidable in the *pratibhā*-passage), a term which had more concrete and well-defined meanings for other thinkers, need not surprise us if we think for instance of Bhartṛhari's abstract interpretations of a term like *śabda* (sound, word) if it refers not to the audible word but to the unitary signifier expressed by it (cf. Houben 1990) - not to speak of a few passages where *śabda* is associated with *brahman* and *ātman*.

3.8 If we now cast another glance at the controversy referred to above, we see that we have to reconsider our interpretation of Bhartṛhari's position in it. If the more abstract meaning of *āgama* and the acceptability of spontaneous knowledge are taken into account, *kārikās* 29-43 may be read as an attempt on Bhartṛhari's side to take into account or integrate two contradictory standpoints. It has now become difficult to place Bhartṛhari with certainty on either side of the dividing line between the two parties. Whether or to what extent the thinkers belonging to these parties would accept Bhartṛhari's integration is of course a different point which need not be discussed at this place.

Although the passage cannot be considered a strong example of "perspectivism," the interpetation at which we have arrived suggests an underlying tendency in Bhartṛhari to approach different, even opposing viewpoints in a positive way. Moreover, the passage provides us with a basis to study and evaluate the following partly problematic examples where Bhartṛhari evinces his "perspectivistic" approach in a clearer way, although this is not always properly reflected in the *Vṛtti*.

## 4. Three Cases of Perspectivism in the First *kāṇḍa*

### 4.1 First Case: Bhartṛhari on the Results of the Use of Words

*kārikās* 155-157 form the first passage to be considered. They discuss the effects which one may expect from the use of words. The *kārikās*, especially 157, are rather obscure if one tries to interpret them in accordance with the *Vṛtti*. They are as follows:

*rūpādayo yathā dṛṣṭāḥ pratyartham yataśaktayaḥ/*
*śabdās tathaiva dṛśyante viṣāpaharaṇādiṣu//* (155)
*yathaiṣāṃ tatra sāmarthyaṃ dharme 'py evaṃ pratīyatām/*
*sādhūnāṃ sādhubhis tasmād vācyam abhyudayārthinām//* (156)
*sarvo 'dṛṣṭaphalān arthān āgamāt pratipadyate/*
*viparītaṃ ca sarvatra śakyate vaktum āgame//* (157)

The *Vṛtti* on these *kārikās* may be paraphrased as follows: First, it is said that just as in daily life colour, taste, smell and touch may have perceptible (*dṛṣṭa*) and imperceptible (*adṛṣṭa*) results, in the same way words may have perceptible and imperceptible results. Perceptible results of words would be e.g., the removing of snake poison on account of the pronounciation of certain words[35] (Vṛṣabha explains: the *mantras* from the *Atharvaveda*), and imperceptible results would be e.g., a specific imperceptible result from the repeated recitation of certain *sūktas*. The *Vṛtti* on the next *kārikā* explains that, just as there is a tradition that words have perceptible results, it should be understood that correct words may also lead to merit (*dharma*). And, finally, the *Vṛtti* on 157 says the following. First a possible objection is stated: On the basis of the fact that words have the capacity to remove snake poison, one could just as well conclude that words would lead to demerit (*adharma*). According to the *Vṛtti* the answer should be: In all traditional texts there is with regard to obtainments which have perceptible and imperceptible results (*dṛṣṭādṛṣṭaphalāsu pratipattiṣu*), a possibility that opposite results are obtained (*viparītaphalaprāptiḥ*). Therefore, once a certain traditional text is accepted as authoritative, if a demonstration is given with regard to that well-established text, it is accepted as something that strengthens the understanding of it.[36]

We note first that the *Vṛtti* on 155 speaks of perceptible and imperceptible results of colour etc., and that it says that words too may have perceptible and imperceptible results. According to the *kārikā*, however, colour etc., are observed (*dṛṣṭāḥ*) to have certain capacities, and words are similarly observed (*dṛśyante*) to lead to the removal of snake poison etc. It seems that the *kārikā* refers only to perceptible results. Perhaps the *Vṛttikāra* admits this in the commentary on the next *kārikā*, where he states as the first step of the argument that words have perceptible results, and as the second step that on that basis it should be understood that correct words may lead to merit (*dharma*). This *dharma* is no doubt considered as an imperceptible result. *kārikā* 155, however, did not go beyond the conclusion that words may have at least perceptible results.

The introduction of imperceptible results in the explanation of 155 does not really contribute to a proper understanding of the argument. The two *kārikās* may now be translated as follows:

> Just as it is observed that colours etc., have well-defined capacities with regard to certain things, in the same way one observes that words [have well-defined capacities] to remove snake poison etc. (155)
> Just as they have a capacity to do this (i.e., to remove snake poison etc.) it should be understood that they also [have a capacity] to [produce] merit. Therefore, good people desiring elevation (*abhyudaya*), should use correct words. (156)

The problems with the *Vṛtti* on 157 seem to be more serious. First, we do not see any reflection in it of the first line, *sarvo 'dṛṣṭaphalān arthān āgamāt pratipadyate*. The *Vṛtti* connects the second line, which says that opposite results may be stated, directly with the argument in the previous *kārikās*: on the basis of the fact that words have a capacity to remove snake poison, why not conclude that demerit (*adharma*) is obtained? It is possible, perhaps even likely, that the *Vṛttikāra* read *sarvo dṛṣṭaphalān* instead of *sarvo 'dṛṣṭaphalān* of the editions (the latter also being Vṛṣabha's way of reading the text), because he refers only to perceptible results in the first part of the argument of the objector. But then the connection between the first line of 157, which would reflect the first step of the argument as stated in *kārikās* 155 and 156a, and the second line of 157 would remain problematic.[37]

The second problem is that the *Vṛttikāra* interprets "the opposite" (*viparītam*) in the second line of 157 as the opposite of *dharma*, which occurs in the first line of the previous *kārikā* 156. Of course, one would like to interpret it as a reference to something in the immediately preceding line, especially because there is no reference to *āgama* in the preceding *kārikās*. (The expression *śabdāḥ* in 155 cannot be interpreted as a reference to *āgama* or *āgamas*, because it refers to the "correct words" of the language.) But whether one reads *dṛṣṭaphalān* or *'dṛṣṭaphalān*, one arrives at the interpretation *adharma* only by a very roundabout way. One could connect *viparītam* with *sarvatra*. This is what Iyer does: "In regard to everything mentioned in it, it would be possible to postulate the opposite" (Iyer 1965, p. 124). But then the problem with the explanation in the *Vṛtti* is still that the *kārikā* does not directly recall the preceding argument.

The third problem is that the most important point in the *Vṛtti* is not even hinted at in the *kārikā* under discussion. The *Vṛtti* gives an answer to the so-called objection in the second line of the *kārikā*. This answer consists in a methodological principle: Once a certain text or system of thought is accepted as the starting point, arguments should be accepted in accordance with the accepted system. The principle does not seem unsound, and it may have been acceptable to Bhartṛhari. But we do not find any trace of it in the *kārikā*.

One of the ways to save the *Vṛttikāra* which I can think of is to assume that he read the *kārikā* in the opposite sequence: first the second line as the statement of the objection in connection with the preceding argument, and next the first line as the rejoinder: if a traditional text mentions imperceptible (or perceptible) results, this should be accepted. I do not think that this is a very attractive solution, as such an inverted order of the two lines is nowhere recorded.[38]

But what would be the most simple and straightforward translation of the *kārikā*? The first line does not present many problems: "Everybody obtains things leading to imperceptible results on the basis of *āgama*." Whether this *āgama* should be interpreted in a very abstract way as traditional knowledge, or in a more concrete way as a traditional text and the specific system expressed in it, is not clear. As for the *Vṛtti*, from the fact that it has *āgama* in the plural it may be inferred that the word was taken in the more concrete way. The second line may be translated as follows: "With regard to each *āgama*, it is possible to state the opposite."

While I agree with Bhartṛhari that it is dangerous to assign too much value to isolated argumentation, I think that the problems with regard to the *Vṛtti*-interpretation are such that they permit attempts to arrive at a better interpretation of the *kārikā*. What would it mean if the opposite can be stated with regard to each *āgama*? In the light of the immediately preceding line this could very well mean that everyone obtains *āgama* on the basis of things leading to imperceptible results. The problem referred to here would be closely related to what was said in 1.30cd and 1.150. The purport of the *kārikā* could then be paraphrased as follows: Just as it can be said that one obtains knowledge of means to obtain imperceptible results[39] (i.e., *dharma*) on the basis of *āgama*, in the same way it can be said that one obtains knowledge of *āgama* on the basis of one's means to obtain imperceptible results (i.e., *dharma*).[40] The connection with the preceding two *kārikās* would be that the fact that the use of certain words has certain effects, and specifically that the use of grammatically correct words leads to elevation (*abhyudaya*), has to be accepted or believed on the basis of *āgama*. The additional point made in the second line of 157 would be that it can be said that each *āgama* was once acquired on the basis of someone's "means to obtain imperceptible results."

Of course nothing can be proved. But the above interpretation seems to be a reasonable alternative for the not very satisfactory interpretation of the *Vṛtti*, an alternative, moreover, which goes well with what has been expressed in other, less problematical *kārikās*. It should be noted, moreover, that the *Vṛtti* gives a polemical interpretation to the passage, which, as I have shown, may also be understood in accordance with the format which is so common in the *VP*: the enumeration of two contrasting or complementary viewpoints (see note 1).

### 4.2. Second Case: Bhartṛhari on the Eternality of the Universe and Revealed Texts (*śruti*)

The next case I want to consider is Bhartṛhari's attitude towards two competing views with regard to the eternality of the universe and revealed texts (*śruti*). A crucial passage is *VP* 1.172-173:

> *anādim anavacchinnāṃ śrutim āhur akartṛkām/*
> *śiṣṭair nibadhyamānā tu na vyavacchidyate smṛtiḥ//* (172)
> *avibhāgād vivṛttānām abhikhyā svapnavac chrutau/*
> *bhāvatattvaṃ tu vijñāya liṅgebhyo vihitā smṛtiḥ//* (173)

It is said that the authorless revealed text ( *śruti)* is beginningless and uninterrupted; as for the composed text ( *smṛti*), being written by the well-educated, it is (only) not interrupted. (172)
Those evolved from the undivided (i.e., the primeval *ṛṣis* evolved from *brahman*), [had] a perception with regard to the revealed text (*śruti)* as in a dream. And having understood the nature of things, [authors] have created the composed text (*smṛti*) on the basis of indications (in the *śruti*). (173)

According to the view referred to in *kārikā* 1.172, the revealed texts are eternal and without author. The *Vṛtti* (on this and the next *kārikā*) explains that on this view the revealed texts are eternal in their diversified state,[41] and that the world too is eternal, without interruption.[42] The opposite view, expressed in *kārikā* 1.173, is that at the beginning of a cosmic cycle the primeval *ṛṣis* have a cognition "in" or "with regard to" the revealed text. The *Vṛtti* explains that on this view the revealed text is thought to be undivided in the beginning.[43]

On the first view, the universe and the revealed texts are eternal in their diversified state, on the second view, they evolve from a unified to a diversified state and vice versa. (I will not go into the way both views deal with *smṛti* or composed texts, as this is not directly relevant in our present discussion.) The first view may be provisionally identified as the view of the Mīmāṃsakas, who do not believe in cosmic cycles (explicit pronouncements of this view, however, are found only in later texts; cf. Helārāja's *na kadācid anīdṛśaṃ jagat* as a reference to Mīmāṃsakas in *VP* IIIa, pp. 49.1, 51.21). There may have been also other thinkers and schools of thought working with a "continuous universe." The other view is held by those who accept that the universe is time and again created from a unified basis, and dissolves back into that basis at the end of each period. What Bhartṛhari seems to do is that he simply juxtaposes the two views without an exclusive commitment to the one or the other.

In a different context the two views are again referred to. In the *Jāti-samuddeśa* the view is explained that what is expressed by words is the universal. With regard to the permanence of the universals, Bhartṛhari mentions the view of some, according to which each universal will always have some basis to reside in, because there is never a dissolution of all objects at the same time.[44] In the opposite view, the universals are absorbed in their ultimate cause at the time of cosmic dissolution.[45] Here the cosmic cycles do not concern the revealed texts directly, but the entire universe which would necessarily include the revealed texts.

While Bhartṛhari states the two without making a clear commitment, some scholars are convinced that it is the second view which is Bhartṛhari's own view. Thus, Aklujkar explains without any hesitation:

> According to Bhartṛhari, after the dissolution of the universe, the *Veda* remains in a unitary, subtle form which is not different from the language-principle, *śabda-tattva-brahman*. It again appears as a diversity with main and subsidiary divisions after the creation of the universe. (Aklujkar 1971b, pp. 173-174)

Iyer explains as Bhartṛhari's view:

> The *Veda*, then, is One at the time of Creation, is later diversified due to the incapacity of man and again becomes One at the time of Dissolution (*Pralaya*). (Iyer 1969, p. 95)

How do these scholars know that this is Bhartṛhari's view when the *kārikās* simply juxtapose the two views?

Iyer says openly that it is "According to the *Vṛtti*," that "Bhartṛhari believed in the cyclic view of creation and dissolution" (Iyer 1969, p.

94). From the support mentioned by Aklujkar (1971b, p. 174, note 39) it is evident that it is again mainly the *Vṛtti* which according to him may lead one to this conclusion. Aklujkar mentions also *kārikās* 1.9, 10a and 11a[46] as supportive evidence, but they may easily be interpreted in the light of the Mīmāṃsā view as well. *VP* 1.124,[47] also mentioned by Aklujkar, seems to combine or juxtapose two interpretations of *pariṇāma* and *vivarta*, and cannot be taken as an indication that Bhartṛhari would have been unfavourably disposed towards the view of the continuous universe. Aklujkar expresses the same opinion in "Bhartṛhari's concept of the Veda":

> Unlike the Mīmāṃsakas, however, he [i.e., Bhartṛhari, JH] does not view the Vedic texts ... as ultimately eternal (i.e. beyond cyclicity) or as something realized without human involvement. (Aklujkar 1991, pp. 5-6, § 3.2)

It may be true that Bhartṛhari did not *defend*, in the way the Mīmāṃsakas did, that the Vedic texts themselves are eternal. But he did not refute this either. There are no indications that a non-cyclical view would be unacceptable to him. Again, the reasons mentioned by Aklujkar why it should be accepted that Bhartṛhari preferred the cyclical view are mainly based on the *Vṛtti* (Aklujkar 1991, p. 15, note 40c), and if the *Vṛtti* is bracketed off, nothing compels one to conclude Bhartṛhari's non-acceptance of the Mīmāṃsā-view on this specific topic.[48]

In fact, however, the *Vṛtti* on the two most important *kārikās* in this context, 1.172 and 173, simply explains the two different views and attributes them to different groups of thinkers. It distinguishes moreover some subgroups. But it does not express a strong commitment to one of the groups of thinkers. Here, it remains as non-committal as the author of the *kārikās* himself. When Iyer concludes that Bhartṛhari "believed in the cyclic view of creation and dissolution" (Iyer 1969, p. 94) this is probably on the basis of the way the *Vṛtti* commented on earlier *kārikās*, for instance 1.5.[49] At this place, the *Vṛttikāra* gives a paraphrase (*VP* I, p. 24.2-4) and next a long citation from *Nirukta* 1.20 according to which "seers" who "had direct insight into *dharma*" handed down *mantras* by way of instruction to those who did not have such direct insight into *dharma*; next, later generations (*avare*), losing their capacity for instruction, transmitted the texts, Vedas and Vedāṅgas, in order to grasp [at least] a reflection (? *bilma*, explained as *bhilma* or *bhāsana*).[50] The idea of primeval *ṛṣis* who instruct, on the basis of direct perception of *dharma*, later generations with lesser mental capacities, suits the cosmic cycle view very well.

Yet *kārikā* 1.5 itself need not necessarily be interpreted in such a way that there would be one Veda at a certain point in history, and that this one Veda is next divided. As explained in the *Vṛtti* under a view attributed to *apara*, the *kārikā* is also compatible with the view that the oneness of the Veda co-exists with its plurality:

> Someone else says: Just as speech which is differentiated with differences in region, continues to be the basis of a single meaning even if there is difference in the specific (phonetic) forms (of the words); and that very (speech) (becomes) the cause for postulating and establishing differences in region etc.; in the same way, although there is difference in Vedic schools, the expressions of the revealed texts continue to be the basis of a single meaning; only the difference in the specific (phonetic) form is the cause for postulating and establishing differences between Vedic schools.[51]

In this passage, I translate *apara* as "someone else," although, according to Aklujkar,

> One can show with unmistakable evidence that *apara* does not always mean simply "someone else" or "different"; it is often connotative of approval, as if it is intended to be dissolved as *na vidyate paro yasmāt*. (Aklujkar 1972, p. 186)

Whatever the derivation and precise connotations of the word, it is very clear that it refers to a certain author and that a distinction is maintained with other authors. I therefore prefer to stick to the simple and neutral translation "someone else" for *apara*, even if the view attributed to this "other" author was considered acceptable by the author of the *Vṛtti*. The citation from the *Vṛtti* translated above is followed by an entirely different view: There really was a time in which the Veda was one, although now in the Kali-era it has become manifold. This view is introduced by "others are of the opinion" (*apare manyante*, *VP* I, p. 26.3-5). It is again a "cosmic cycle" view, going well with the elaborate reference to the primeval *ṛṣis* of *Nirukta* 1.20: The Veda and its many branches is like the eightfold Āyurveda which was one and undivided in the remote past (*purākalpe*), but became diversified with the advent of Kali-yuga, the present bad era (*VP* I, p. 26.3-5). Since the *Vṛttikāra*, after the short reference to the alternative view of the Veda's unity which co-exists with its plurality, returns to the "cosmic cycle" view after having first paid so much attention to it, he creates the strong impression that the "cosmic cycle" view is preferred.

Finally, we may also refer to the *Vṛtti* on *kārikā* 1.1, where the *Vṛttikāra* suggests cosmic cycles by contrasting development (*vivarta*) with *saṃvarta* (dissolution),[52] while the *kārikā* has only the verb *vivartate*, which may also be interpreted as a continuous, beginningless process ("behaves in various ways"), not interrupted by periods of *saṃvarta*. The cosmic cycles concern here the entire universe, but this would obviously imply similar cycles for the traditional revealed texts.

Why should the possibility for a non-cyclical interpretation of 1.1 be left open? For one thing, even before the notion of time is introduced in 1.3 (time as a capacity of *brahman*), it is said (in 1.2) that the One behaves as (*iva vartate*) different from its capacities although it is not different (*apṛthaktve 'pi śaktibhyaḥ pṛthaktveneva vartate*). Moreover, if we assume that only a cyclical worldview would be acceptable to Bhartṛhari, we run into problems at places where he analyzes "time" and "sequence," and concludes that they cannot be applied in a simple and straightforward way to an existent or to reality (e.g., *VP* 3.3.69; 3.9.85-86). Next, whatever Bhartṛhari's commitment to it, he speaks positively of the idea that the universe itself (not *brahman* or some abstract entity) is something essentially sequenceless (e.g., 3.9.46). But language permits us to express things only with reference to time and some of its divisions (e.g., 3.9.58). All this makes an exclusive cyclical interpretation of 1.1 problematic, if not unacceptable.

Another point is that some early authors seem to have interpreted the first *kārikā* not only in terms of an "illusionistic" *vivartavāda*, but also in terms of *pariṇāma*.[53] The notion of *pariṇāma* was not only a crucial term in cosmological accounts of Sāṅkhya-thinkers,[54] but it was also used in Buddhist works such as Vasubandhu's *Vijñaptimātratāsiddhi*, which has been mentioned as a work of which Bhartṛhari must have had some knowledge.[55] In the Sāṅkhya ontological account which involved the term *pariṇāma*, cyclicity of the world was not a necessary element.[56]

It is not that Bhartṛhari would have rejected the cosmological *vivarta-saṃvarta* interpretation of the *Vṛtti*, but if we remain open for an alternative, non-cyclical interpretation we will see that the introductory *kārikās* of the *VP* are suddenly much closer to the viewpoint of Sāṅkhya's *YD* or even of Vasubandhu: With the word *vivartate*, interpreted non-cyclically as "behaves in various ways," *VP* 1.1 becomes more closely parallel to Vasubandhu's *kārikā* 1 of his *Triṃśikā Vijñaptimātratāsiddhi*, the *kārikā* which explains how the varying (*vividhaḥ*) deceptive references (*upacāra*) to self (*ātman*) and elements of the world (*dharmas*) proceed (*pravartate*) in a transformation (*pariṇāma*) of consciousness. This deceptive reference to the transformation of consciousness is a beginningless (*anādikālika*) process according to Sthiramati's commentary (*ViS*, pp. 15.22-23, 16.6). The parallellism is, of course, not complete and may imply not more than that Bhartṛhari was in dialogue also with the ideas of Vasubandhu or related thinkers.

I will refrain here from considering the possibility of a non-cyclical interpretation of *VP* 1.1 in more detail and refer instead to my discussion of other aspects of the problem in my thesis (Houben 1992b, part 3, under *VP* 3.3.81), where I have also discussed the *Yuktidīpikā*-definition of *pariṇāma* as a continuous process (*YD*, p. 75.6-7). What is important in the present context is that the cyclical interpretation which the *Vṛtti* seems to suggest need not be accepted as the one exclusively intended. For Bhartṛhari there seem to be two acceptable theoretical alternatives (cyclical and non-cyclical view of the universe and revealed texts) to which some *kārikās* explicitly refer (1.172-173; 3.1.42-43).

### 4.3 Third Case: Bhartṛhari on the Relation between Correct and Incorrect Words (*śabda* and *apabhraṃśa*)

The last passage to be discussed is 175-183 (especially 181-183), the subject of which is the grammatically correct word (*śabda*) and the incorrect word (*apabhraṃśa*), the latter being not only a mispronunciation of the former (*VP* 1.175-180), but also a linguistic form which, though incorrect according to Sanskrit grammar, has gained currency in certain circles (*VP* 1.181). Further things about *śabda* and *apabhraṃśa* are said in the next two *kārikās* (182-183) which conclude both this passage and the first *kāṇḍa*. *kārikās* 181-183 are as follows:

*pāraṃparyād apabhraṃśā viguṇeṣv abhidhātṛṣu/*
*prasiddhim āgatā yena teṣāṃ sādhur avācakaḥ//* (181)
*daivī vāg vyatikīrṇeyam aśaktair abhidhātṛbhiḥ/*
*anityadarśināṃ tv asmin vāde buddhiviparyayaḥ//* (182)
*ubhayeṣām avicchedād anyaśabdavivakṣayā/*
*yo 'nyaḥ prayujyate śabdo na so 'rthasyābhidhāyakaḥ//* (183)

A straightforward translation would be:

Among those who do not speak correctly, the incorrect words have by force of tradition gained general acceptance, so that for them the correct word is not expressive. (181)

> Divine speech is nowadays (*iyam*) mixed up by incompetent speakers. But the upholders of non-permanence have with regard to this doctrine the opposite view. (182)
> Because there is no interruption for both groups, if one word is used with the intention to use another, then this word does not express the (intended) meaning. (183)

The usual interpretation, as explained for instance in Iyer's "Bhartṛhari on *apabhraṃśa*" (Iyer 1964; cf. Iyer 1969, pp. 59-60), is that in this passage Bhartṛhari sets forth his view of the "divine speech" which has become corrupted and that he refutes an opposite view according to which the corrupt forms precede the correct forms which are the work of grammarians (cf. also Tripathi 1986, pp. 86-88; Sharma 1977, pp. 236-237). Moreover, even if a period in which the "divine speech" is not corrupted is not accepted, it is to be admitted that only the correct word is directly expressive of a meaning (Iyer 1964, p. 246).

It may be doubted, however, that such an interpretation reflects Bhartṛhari's intentions correctly. That *kārikā* 182 refers to two opposite views is rather obvious. However, that only one of these would be acceptable to Bhartṛhari and that the other is only mentioned to be refuted (Iyer 1964, p. 244, note 8, and 246) is less obvious.[57] Similarly, that *kārikā* 183 would imply that only correct words are (really or directly) expressive of their meaning is not very clear either.

There need not be much doubt about the first view referred to in 182: It apparently implies that there was a time, long, long ago, that people only employed correct (Sanskrit) speech. In the course of time, this pure and correct speech became more and more corrupted. This corresponds to the explanation in the *Vṛtti*.

More difficult it is to get an accurate idea of the other view. For this we may cautiously invoke the help of the *Vṛtti* on 1.182, which says with regard to the other view:[58]

> But those who propound the impermanent, who do not accept that correct words lead to merit (*dharma*), (and who) consider the established fixity of correct forms to be similar to the conventions among wrestlers, say that the collection of correct (namely, Prakrit) words is *prākṛta* in the sense of "being in the *prakṛti*." But later on a changed form (namely, Sanskrit) has been established, which was arrived at through accentuation and phonological and morphological modification[59] by persons with impaired understanding.

The second view would therefore be that the grammatically "correct" (Sanskrit) forms cannot claim to be really "correct" as they are in fact derived from more original (Prakrit) forms. The latter are the forms which are correct according to this second view. Such a view would also suit a brief reference in *MBhD* 1, p. 16.28-29, and a passage in the work of the 11th-century Jaina-scholar Namisādhu (commentary on Rudraṭa's *Kāvyālaṃkāra* 2.12 which enumerates different languages and language varieties) (cf. Houben 1994a, pp. 3-7; Bronkhorst 1993). The explanation of *prākṛtam* as *prakṛtau bhavam* (also in *MBhD* 1, p. 16.28-29; and in the form *tatra bhavam ... prākṛtam* in Namisādhu's commentary on *Kāvyālaṅkāra* 2.12) implies a reference to *P* 4.3.53 (cf. Kahrs 1992 and Houben 1994b).

With this we have an idea which two views are referred to in 182. While the reference to the second view is very laconic, there has been till now no reason to say it was referred to only to be refuted. We may therefore now take a closer look at 183, the last *kārikā* of the passage. An important problem in this *kārikā* is: What is exactly meant with *ubhayeṣām avicchedād* (which I translated above as "Because there is no interruption for both groups"?). The two groups could refer to the two groups of words, the "correct" ones and the "incorrect" ones. This is the interpretation adopted by Iyer in his translation (Iyer 1965, p. 155), and in his explanation in the article referred to above (Iyer 1964). It could also be a reference to the upholders of non-permanence (*anityadarśinām* in the previous *kārikā*) and the upholders of permanence (who hold that there was an originally pure, divine language). This is apparently the interpretation adopted by Biardeau (Biardeau 1964b), who translates "dans les deux hypothèses" ("according to the two hypotheses").

However, in both interpretations of *ubhayeṣām* it seems that the absence of interruption (*aviccheda*) should refer to the absence of interruption in the tradition of words. This would refer in the first place to the tradition of "correct" Sanskrit words, a tradition to which Bhartṛhari referred explicitly at several places (*VP* 1.29, 43, 178). The next phrase in the *kārikā*, "if one word is used with the intention to use another, then this word does not express the (intended) meaning," would then refer to someone who wants to pronounce a correct Sanskrit word, but pronounces it wrongly. As in the earlier *kārikās* 1.175 and 180, Bhartṛhari would stress here that the intention of the speaker (*vivakṣā*) should be taken into account if one is to decide whether a word expresses a meaning correctly or not.

In the light of the wording of 183, in the light of the preceding *kārikās*, and especially in the light of the second view referred to in 182

- which was probably not preferred by Bhartṛhari but neither refuted - there is, however, no reason to stop here: the general statement in 183 applies equally to the complementary situation of the tradition of Prakrit words and of those having an "opposite view." Taking into account that in some circles in Bhartṛhari's time the "incorrect" Prakrit forms were cultivated, and taking into account 181, which seems to refer to this situation, *kārikā* 183 would then also refer to someone who wanted to pronounce a Prakrit word (with which he was not familiar, for instance because his mother-tongue was a different Prakrit or a non-Āryan language), but knew only the corresponding Sanskrit word. It should not be forgotten that the forms which are correct and original according to one view, are incorrect or derived according to the other. As the *kārikā* speaks of *anyaśabda- ... anyaḥ ... śabdaḥ*, the two forms (which we may call Sanskrit and Prakrit) seem to be on the same level in the context of the statement. It seems, therefore, that 183 contains a statement which applies to both views referred to in 182, of which one is probably preferred, but neither of which is refuted.

The picture changes somewhat if the *Vṛtti* on 183 is taken into account. According to the *Vṛtti*, 183 refers to a third view, in which no cosmic cycles are accepted. If we are to associate this view with thinkers in Bhartṛhari's time, we should probably think again of the Mīmāṃsakas, because they do deny cosmic cycles (cf. above under 4.2), and because they did express ideas according to which there are parallel traditions of Sanskrit and non-Sanskrit words (which they call *mleccha*-words). This is clear from some passages in the *Śābarabhāṣya* (*ŚBh* on *MīS* 1.3.10, 24-29). Whether these Mīmāṃsā-passages or other ones were known to and intended by Bhartṛhari, has to remain, unfortunately, problematic (cf. Bronkhorst 1989). In any case, the *Vṛtti* on 183 starts as follows[60]:

> Even for those for whom there was no previous cosmic cycle (*kalpa*) nor ever a divine, pure speech, for them too this established distinction between correct and incorrect words, is always transmitted without interruption by the well-educated, much like the established distinction between women that may and those that may not be approached.

After having clarified the context, the *Vṛtti* continues to explain the statement in the *kārikā*[61]:

> Here, the generally accepted (*rūḍhaḥ*) word and the not generally accepted (*na rūḍhaḥ*) word which is applied to meanings while another word is intended, as into account. According to the *Vṛtti*, 183 refers to a third view, in which no

> cosmic cycles are accepted. If we are to associate this view with thinkers in Bhartṛhari's time, we should probably think again of the Mīmāṃsakas, bium of the (corresponding) correct word, or there arises merely an idea (of the intention) on account of the habit of careless people like from the winking of the eye etc.

Here it is not clear to what extent the author of the *Vṛtti* made use of a third source (concerning the view of "those for whom there was no previous cosmic cycle"). Otherwise, however, the strong denial of the *Vṛtti* that generally accepted "incorrect" words can ever be directly expressive of meaning (*vācaka*), has certainly no support in the *kārikā*, and is in disaccord with 181 as well as with 1.27cd and 3.3.30cd[62], in which Bhartṛhari accepts that incorrect words may be *vācaka*. The last-mentioned place, 3.3.30cd, says even literally that there is no difference between the correct and incorrect word in being *vācaka* (*vācakatvāviśeṣe*). Also in the *MBhD* it is accepted that as far as the expression of meaning is concerned, the incorrect word is not different from the correct word, the only difference being that the latter leads in addition to elevation (*abhyudaya*).[63] It is true that this denial of direct expressiveness of "incorrect" words is in the *Vṛtti* a continuation of the view of the third group of thinkers. It is very easy, however, to read these statements at the same time as the final view of Bhartṛhari, something which not only Iyer apparently did (e.g., Iyer 1964, p. 246), but also, among others, Helārāja several centuries before him (cf. his comments on *VP* 3.3.30 and the discussion in Houben 1992b, Part 3, under *kārikā* 30).

While the view that incorrect words are inexpressive of meaning should therefore not be attributed to Bhartṛhari (or identified as the one preferred by him), it remains unclear whether 183 should be seen as the third view of another group of thinkers, or as an observation of Bhartṛhari with regard to two opposed views with which he was confronted in his time. However, if 183 is interpreted as a view with which Bhartṛhari has special sympathy, whether it is his own contribution to the discussion or a reflection of a view propounded by others, the latter half of the interpretation in the *Vṛtti* becomes very unlikely.

Nevertheless, with all these options of interpretation, the last two *kārikās* remain a good example of "perspectivism" as defined in the introductory sections of this article. They refer to either two or three views, and though one may be more preferrable than the other, there is no sign that a view is mentioned only to be refuted later (as was the opinion of Iyer, see reference above). Even the view that grammatical (Sanskrit) words are derived from more original (Prakrit) words is mentioned not in order to be refuted later, but, apparently, only in order to be mentioned. The effect of this "mentioning without refuting" of an opposite view is no doubt a relativization of the own view.

What is remarkable in the *Vṛtti* is the stubborn unwillingness to recognize the direct expressiveness of *apabhraṃśa*, although Bhartṛhari clearly recognizes it elsewhere (see references above), at least as an acceptable theoretical possibility, and at least under certain circumstances (when incorrect words have become current: 1.181). The same unwillingness, incidentally, may be recognized in the *Vṛtti* on 181, where the understanding through incorrect words by those who do not know the correct ones is described as a process of inference (*anumāna*), although the view of direct expression would no doubt be more acceptable here in the light of 1.27 and 3.3.30; and in the *Vṛtti* on 1.27, where no reflection is found of the phrase in the *kārikā* that there is no difference between correct and incorrect words (*sādhu* and *asādhu* words) with regard to their expression of a meaning.

## 5. Discussion and Conclusion

We have thus seen several instances of Bhartṛhari's perspectivism and relatively non-committal attitude with regard to controversies with which he must have been confronted in his own time and environment. In the first case discussed, concerning the results to be expected from the use of certain words, there seems to have been a juxtaposition of two complementary viewpoints (*dharma* is the basis for obtaining *āgama*; *āgama* is the basis for knowledge of *dharma*). In the second case Bhartṛhari juxtaposed two views concerning the eternality of the universe and of revealed texts, without showing a strong commitment to either view. In the third case, Bhartṛhari referred to two or three alternative views concerning the relation between *śabda* and *apaśabda*, grammatically correct and incorrect words.

What is perhaps most remarkable, is not that Bhartṛhari enumerates different views, but that he seems to avoid attempts to establish the superiority of one view over the other, even if one would expect Bhartṛhari to have a "natural" preference for one of two opposed view. For instance, the view which accords a superior status to Sanskrit (1.182) suits the whole enterprise of Bhartṛhari's *VP* obviously much better than the opposite view. Even here, there are no arguments to establish the own tradition against the other. It is at this point that the passage on means of gaining knowledge becomes relevant (1.29-43 discussed in section 3 above), because it can make us understand why Bhartṛhari has no recourse to arguments at this place, but simply juxtaposes different traditions. For, if the passage on *pramāṇas* made one thing clear, it is that the role of argumentation and logical inference (*anumāna*) is secondary to both traditional knowledge (*āgama*) and direct perception (*pratyakṣa*). In that light, an argumentation to defend a traditional position would be entirely out of place. In addition, the passage gave us an example of how two opposing views on the *pramāṇas* have been taken into account by Bhartṛhari.

Another unavoidable theme of this article was the difference between *Vṛtti* and *VP*. Looking back, it can be said that the differences observed between the *Vṛtti* and what seems to be the most straightforward interpretation of the *kārikās*, consist mainly in differences in emphasis and differences in the degree of commitment to a certain view. This is clear in the second and third case discussed above. In the second case, the *Vṛtti* seems to emphasize more than the *VP* the view of cosmic cycles and the periodical reappearance and diversification of the Veda. In the third case, the *Vṛtti* is unwilling to accept that incorrect words may under certain circumstances (when they have become current) express their meaning directly. In the first case the interpretation of the *Vṛtti* seems less satisfactory than a straightforward interpretation of the *kārikās*.

Differences are there, but it is not easy to define exactly in what sense the *Vṛtti* deviates from the *VP-kārikās*. Of course, if it was difficult to reconstruct a well-defined philosophy on the basis of *kārikās* and *Vṛtti* together (for those emphasizing the continuity of these two texts), we should not expect to find a well-defined philosophy in the isolated *Vṛtti*. Rather, we should be alert for differences in attitudes, valuation of and familiarity with different schools, etc., differences which are perhaps manifest in only some passages (where the *Vṛttikāra* feels free to follow his own inclination) and not in others (where the *kārikās* do not offer enough scope for this). We can start very carefully and say that the *VP-kārikās* breathe more an atmosphere of creative encounters between different groups of thinkers. Can we also say that the *Vṛtti* follows and continues Bhartṛhari's perspectivism to a considerable extent, but evinces the traces of a more seclusive attitude when emphasizing and defending the ideas and ideals of one's own group against those of outsiders?

This brings us to an important problem to which we have only indirectly referred. We have seen that Bhartṛhari (unlike the Mīmāṃsakas) keeps the door open for those accepting the direct perception of extraordinary individuals as a valid means of gaining knowledge. The minimal implication of this acceptance is that a cyclical view of universe and revealed texts, time and again cognized by the *ṛṣis* at the beginning of a new cosmic era, becomes possible. One may wonder, however, whether this acceptance should perhaps accommodate even the followers of Buddhism and Jainism (two movements based on the teachings of persons allegedly having an extraordinary perception and knowledge)? It is perhaps possible to read this in the *kārikās*, but definitely not so in the *Vṛtti*.

Above (end of section 4.2), we have noticed that there are some possible points of contact between the *VP* and a Buddhist work, the *Vijñaptimātratāsiddhi*. With regard to the revealed texts, however, Bhartṛhari (in the *kārikās*) takes only two perspectives into account: either they are eternal in their diversified state; or they become unified and diversified in the course of cosmic cycles of evolution and involution. The full rejection of the Vedic texts (as generally advocated by Jainas and Buddhists) is not a perspective acknowledged by Bhartṛhari. He does recognize "spontaneous knowledge," but this is ultimately again traceable to traditional knowledge (*āgama*). Did he perhaps accommodate the Buddhists and Jainas in a way about which they themselves would not be all that enthusiastic?[64]

Whatever our answer should be to these questions – which deserve a more elaborate discussion than is possible in this article – there seems to be another difference here between the *VP* and the *Vṛtti*.[65] While the *VP*, just as the *MBhD*[66] and the commentaries by Puṇyarāja and Helārāja, refers now and then to Buddhists and Jainas, such references are conspicuous by their absence in the *Vṛtti* on the first *kāṇḍa*.[67] In another article I have drawn the attention to two places in the first *kāṇḍa*

> where Bhartṛhari seems to refer without much doubt to Buddhists and/or Jainas, and the *Vṛtti*, most probably making use of material derived from Jaina sources, avoids an explicit reference to them.[68]

In the light of these, admittedly subtle, differences between *VP* and *Vṛtti*, we may have to rethink some of the evaluations of Bhartṛhari's *VP* by Halbfass (who wants to attribute, with Aklujkar, *VP* and *Vṛtti* to a single author: TR, pp. 65, 81, note 62). In the *VP kārikās* of the first *kāṇḍa*, there is indeed "an irreducible gradation or hierarchy, to be measured in terms of distance of the Vedic word" (TR, p. 65) inasmuch as Bhartṛhari distinguishes between the revealed texts (*śruti*) and the composed texts (*smṛti*) based, at least partly, on these revealed texts. But to what extent can we say that for Bhartṛhari "the Veda assigns standpoints and conditions of legitimacy" (*ibid.*), and that he uses the Veda as "criterion of legitimacy and 'orthodoxy'"[69] (TR, p. 64), if we follow Bhartṛhari in his acceptance of the authoritativeness of the direct perception of "those whose (inner) light is manifest and whose mind is not obscured" and of those having the "vision of a *ṛṣi*"? Can we speak at all of the Veda as "criterion of legitimacy and 'orthodoxy,'" if it legitimates (or threatens to legitimate) not only the intuitions of, for instance, Kaṇāda, the founder of the Vaiśeṣika-system, but also those of the Buddha and the Mahāvīra, and even, through the notion of *pratibhā*, the instinct of the male cuckoo in spring? Is the function of the Veda in the *kārikās* proper perhaps even more universalistic and inclusivistic (or rather perspectivistic) than recognized by Halbfass when he wrote that

> Bhartṛhari's understanding of religious and philosophical plurality may appear ambiguous and evasive in its combination of restrictive and universalistic implications, of inclusivism and exclusivism (TR, p. 65)?

Is some of the ambiguity perhaps the result of reading Bhartṛhari through the glasses of the *Vṛtti*-author, who tended to a more restrictive and exclusivistic attitude?

All these questions will be on our way if we try to improve our picture of the scope and function of perspectivism in Bhartṛhari's work. But the credit for bringing the important feature of "perspectivism" into sharp focus and placing it in the dynamic context of different schools in Bhartṛhari's time (such as Jainism, Madhyamaka Buddhism and early Vedānta) developing each their own perspectivistic or inclusivistic models, goes to Wilhelm Halbfass and the books which lay at the basis of this and the other articles of this volume.

*International Institute of Asian Studies*
*Leiden, The Netherlands*

## NOTES

In this paper I elaborate some observations on Bhartṛhari's philosophy of language, made during my study of the *Saṃbandhasamuddeśa* (cf. Houben 1992b, Introduction, section 2) as a Ph.D. student at the University of Utrecht (1988-1992). The study at the University of Vancouver was made possible by the Government of Canada through a Government of Canada Award (1988-1989). Thanks are due to the Netherlands Organization for Scientific Research for financial assistance on several occasions, and to the International Institute for Asian Studies (Leiden), which enabled me to finalize this paper. I am greatly indebted to Professor A. Aklujkar and Professor J. Bronkhorst, with whom I could discuss problems of interpretation in Bhartṛhari's work for several years. I thank Pt. V. B. Bhagavat (Pune) for the discussions which I could have with him on difficult passages in the *VP*. Earlier versions of this paper were read by Professor A. Aklujkar, Professor J. Bronkhorst, Dr. E. Franco, Dr. H. Isaacson, Dr. K. Preisendanz, and Professor T. Vetter. I am very grateful for their critical and stimulating comments and suggestions. I am especially indebted to Dr. E. Franco and Dr. K. Preisendanz, whose detailed criticism on some aspects of my argument inspired me to revise the overall presentation and organization of several sections.

[1] A few examples: *VP* 1.71 refers to four views (two doctrines, the doctrine of unity and the doctrine of multiplicity, combined with two hypotheses, one postulating language as something produced, one postulating it as something given); *VP* 1.110 enumerates three views on the "material" which is transformed into sound; the first two *kārikā*s of the second *kāṇḍa* enumerate at least eight different views on the nature of the sentence; *VP* 2.117-142 discuss different ways of viewing the word and its meaning; 3.1.1 enumerates three ways of dividing words into categories; 3.2.1 lists synonyms and different ways of understanding "substance" (*dravya*); according to Helārāja's explanation of this *kārikā* the different synonyms are linked with different schools of thought.

[2] E.g., *VP* 3.3.64-65.

[3] As in the second *kāṇḍa*, where a long and intricate discussion suggests that eventually the view that the sentence is primary is preferred. This position tallies with the one adopted explicitly at a few places in the third *kāṇḍa* (e.g., *VP* 3.1.1, 3.4.1-2).

[4] As in *VP* 1.44-59, which I discussed in my thesis (Houben 1992b, Part 1, section 4.2), and to which I hope to return on a future occasion.

[5] This applies to Bhartṛhari's basic attitude towards the major viewpoints and philosophical schools of his time. Cf. e.g., *VP* 1.75ab: *tatra yan mukhyam ekeṣāṃ tatrānyeṣāṃ viparyayaḥ*. "With regard to what is primary in this matter according to some, others hold the opposite." Nevertheless, Bhartṛhari rejects certain views, theories and statements without reservation. For instance, the Vaiśeṣika statement that there is no relation at all between word and thing-meant (*VS* 7.2.19) is thoroughly refuted in the first half of the

*Saṃbandhasamuddeśa* (*VP* 3.3.1-28). Also in the *MBhD* we find places where Bhartṛhari disagrees with certain views without compromise (even with Patañjali's view in the discussion on *P* 1.1.41 starting in *MBhD* 6b, p. 20.4). Very often, however, if Bhartṛhari seems to have refuted a certain view (and if commentators confirm that Bhartṛhari did so), the same view reappears later in a renewed form. A single example from the intricate second *kāṇḍa* may suffice at this place: the *abhihitānvaya*-view on the sentence meaning is according to Puṇyarāja refuted in *kārikās* 2.15 and 16 (*VP* II, p. 10.10: *tad dūṣayitum āha*, 11.6: *abhihitānvayavādī nirastaḥ*). In 2.44-46, however, and in 2.441-442, a similar *abhihitānvaya*-view reappears in more refined formulations.

[6] It is easy to find good examples of authors adopting an openly polemical style after Bhartṛhari (e.g., Kumārila Bhaṭṭa, Jayanta Bhaṭṭa, the author of the *Yuktidīpikā*). As for the period before Bhartṛhari, one may think of Nāgārjuna as a master in attacking and refuting other systems, but who did not claim to have a system of his own.

That not just a few exceptional authors in India's philosophical tradition have adopted a not directly polemical framework for their expositions occurred also to Hacker (cf. Hacker 1983). In his perception, the central characteristic of these authors (especially Advaita Vedānta authors) was their "inclusivism." The term as employed by Hacker implies a strong commitment to one's own philosophical system which one seeks to promote, and which one does not wish to relativize. Because I am not sure that this applies to Bhartṛhari, I have not adopted the term "inclusivism" as the central concept of this paper, although I do not deny that in some respects Bhartṛhari's work may be understood in an "inclusivistic" sense.

[7] My use of the term, however, is more comprehensive than Halbfass', who tends to recognize "perspectivism" in the full sense only in Jainism, where it is equivalent to a "'horizontal' model of inclusivism," although the Jainas, like the Vedāntins with their "vertical" model of inclusivism, do "claim a superior vantage point, and a higher level of reflection" than the others (IE, p. 414). In Bhartṛhari's works, Halbfass finds the doxographic usage of "perspective" (*darśana*) "in preliminary stages of development" (IE, p. 268). In all these cases where the (limited) validity of divergent perspectives is positively recognized, and where this recognition seems to form part and parcel of the "own view," I will speak of "perspectivism."

To what extent there are similarities with Western and modern philosophies which have been directly or indirectly linked with the name "perspectivism" (e.g., the work of Leibniz, Nietzsche, Ortega y Gasset, Goodman, Putnam) is a problem which cannot be discussed here, both for reasons of space, and because too much remains unclear with regard to Bhartṛhari's thought, his intentions and his intellectual and social environment. Only in order to indicate that there is perhaps more than just a very superficial similarity with these Western "perspectivists," I would like to make the following very preliminary observation: If we compare Bhartṛhari as a philosopher with e.g., Friedrich Nietzsche, we see that, apart from an enormous amount of differences, the two are similar in attributing a very limited value to logic and inference, in criticizing and "undermining" comprehensive rational philosophical systems (Nietzsche more openly than Bhartṛhari), and in being highly sensitive to "different points of view." For the way Bhartṛhari criticizes and "undermines" the Vaiśeṣika program of "enumerating all existents of the universe," cf. his discussion of the notion of "relation" in the *Saṃbandhasamuddeśa* (see Houben 1992b, Part 3, especially under *kārikā* 19). For the role of "perspectivism" in Western philosophy, theory of science, in psychology, the humanities and natural sciences, cf. König 1989.

[8] For instance, Bhartṛhari is less committed to the view that Sanskrit was originally a divine, pure and ideal language than the *Vṛtti*, and Helārāja on 3.3.30, suggest. Helārāja discusses 3.3.72 and 3.3.83 as if they represent the ultimate viewpoint of Bhartṛhari, whereas Bhartṛhari keeps in fact some distance. See my discussion of *kārikās* 30, 72 and 83 in my thesis (Houben 1992b).

[9] Biardeau 1964a, p. 263: "B. ... entend d'un seul coup s'élever au-dessus de toutes les polémiques en montrant les conditions de possibilité de tout système d'interprétation, plutôt que de donner les preuves de la vérité de tel ou tel système particulier."

[10] This verse belongs to the concluding section of the second *kāṇḍa* (2.481-490), which was possibly written by a student or commentator of Bhartṛhari; cf. note 21.

[11] Cf. Hacker 1957, Oberhammer 1983, and IE, p. 404. Hacker, who introduced the concept of "inclusivism," considered it to be an exclusively Indian "form of thinking." This, however, can hardly be maintained. Halbfass has demonstrated how it was also present in several periods and contexts in the Western tradition (Halbfass 1983b; IE, pp. 415-418). Of interest for the study and development of the theme of "inclusivism" and related concepts (including "perspectivism") is also the "case-study" in W. Slaje's article "On 'Tolerance' and 'Syncretism' in the Yogavāsiṣṭha" (Slaje 1992).

[12] There are places where Bhartṛhari relativizes in advance a certain opposition in viewpoint, before showing his own preference for one of the two positions. In *VP* 2.57 and 58, for instance, the opposition between *vākyavāda* and *padadarśana*, and the related opposition between considering the *saṃhitā*-version and the *pada*-version of Vedic texts as more original, are relativized before the grammarian's preference for viewing the *saṃhitā* as more original is supported in 2.59 (cf. also Houben 1993). In my view, this implies a relativization of the own position, but it may also be argued that the relativization is just a matter of presentation. I will not pursue this point further at this place, but in the first case, Bhartṛhari would be even more "perspectivistic" and less "inclusivistic" than suggested by Halbfass.

[13] Like the Vedāntists and the Mādhyamikas, Bhartṛhari seems to work with two "levels of truth" (conventional and absolute); cf., for instance, OB, p. 91, where it is observed that Bhartṛhari's "functional and empirical concept of substance is superseded by the idea of an absolute substance, which coincides with the nondual brahman, the ultimate ground of language and the world."

[14] Biardeau's arguments are critically discussed in Houben, forthcoming.

*nānarthikām imāṃ kaś cid vyavasthāṃ kartum arhati/*
*tasmān nibadhyate śiṣṭaiḥ sādhutvaviṣayā smṛtiḥ//* (29)
*na cāgamād ṛte dharmas tarkeṇa vyavatiṣṭhate/*
*ṛṣīṇām api yaj jñānaṃ tad apy āgamapūrvakam//* (30)
*dharmasya cāvyavacchinnāḥ panthāno ye vyavasthitāḥ/*
*na tāṃl lokaprasiddhatvāt kaś cit tarkeṇa bādhate//* (31)
*avasthādeśakālānāṃ bhedād bhinnāsu śaktiṣu/*
*bhāvānām anumānena prasiddhir atidurlabhā//* (32)
*nirjñātaśakter dravyasya tāṃ tām arthakriyāṃ prati/*
*viśiṣṭadravyasaṃbandhe sā śaktiḥ pratibadhyate//* (33)
*yatnenānumito 'py arthaḥ kuśalair anumātṛbhiḥ/*
*abhiyuktatarair anyair anyathaivopapādyate//* (34)
*pareṣām asamākhyeyam abhyāsād eva jāyate/*
*maṇirūpyādivijñānaṃ tadvidāṃ nānumānikam//* (35)
*pratyakṣam anumānaṃ ca vyatikramya vyavasthitāḥ/*
*pitṛrakṣaḥpiśācānāṃ karmajā eva siddhayaḥ//* (36)
*āvirbhūtaprakāśānām anupaplutacetasām/*
*atītānāgatajñānaṃ pratyakṣān na viśiṣyate//* (37)
*atīndriyān asaṃvedyān paśyanty ārṣeṇa cakṣuṣā/*
*ye bhāvān vacanaṃ teṣāṃ nānumānena bādhyate//* (38)
*yo yasya svam iva jñānaṃ darśanaṃ nātiśaṅkate/*
*sthitaṃ pratyakṣapakṣe taṃ katham anyo nivartayet//* (39)
*idaṃ puṇyam idaṃ pāpam ity etasmin padadvaye/*
*ācaṇḍālamanuṣyāṇām alpaṃ śāstraprayojanam//* (40)
*caitanyam iva yaś cāyam avicchedena vartate/*
*āgamas, tam upāsīno hetuvādair na bādhyate//* (41)
*hastasparśād ivāndhena viṣame pathi dhāvatā/*
*anumānapradhānena vinipāto na durlabhaḥ//* (42)
*tasmād akṛtakaṃ śāstraṃ smṛtiṃ ca sanibandhanām/*
*āśrityārabhyate śiṣṭaiḥ sādhutvaviṣayā smṛtiḥ//* (43)

[16] (a) Note that Aklujkar's "overlapping" implies not just that two separate *pramāṇas* may work with regard to one object, but that there is overlapping even in the operation itself of a *pramāṇa* (in the sense, for instance, that even a simple, direct perception of an external object would beforehand be to some extent shaped by language and concepts). In contrast, the Naiyāyikas, for instance, can easily accept different *pramāṇas* working with regard to the same object (cf. their *pramāṇasaṃplava*, *NBh* on 1.1.3), but they nevertheless want to make a clear distinction between the individual functioning of each *pramāṇa*. This sometimes proves to be a very difficult thing to do, e.g., when they want to exclude from perceptual judgments those having verbal origins: cf. Potter 1977, pp. 162-165.

(b) Cf. Frauwallner 1959, p. 115 [791]: "Ferner haben wir gesehen, dass in den logischen Werken Dignāga's die Unterscheidung zwischen Wahrnehmung und Vorstellung eine entscheidende Rolle spielt ... Bhartṛhari dagegen, für den jede Erkenntnis von Worten begleitet ist, kennt einen solchen Unterschied nicht. Für ihn stehen Wahrnehmung und Vorstellung sowohl der Erkenntnis wie auch dem Objekt nach vollkommen auf gleicher Stufe." If we accept Aklujkar's observations, the fact that Bhartṛhari does not sharply demarcate the *pramāṇas* in their operations cannot be considered a form of naïvety, nor can Dignāga's sharp distinction in his logical works between pure perception and knowledge in which inference plays a role be considered an indisputable "step forward" in logic. Their stance is simply different. Because Bhartṛhari may very well have known earlier Sāṅkhya-philosophers (especially Vindhyavāsin: Frauwallner 1958, p. 114 [253] and 1959, p. 99 [775]) who did distinguish sharply between pure perception and perception accompanied by thinking, a minor qualification to Frauwallner's formulation should be proposed: "Bhartṛhari ... *macht* (instead of: *kennt*) einen solchen Unterschied nicht." As regards the possibility to separate the *pramāṇas*, it may be noted that the Mīmāṃsakas considered the relation between language and meaning (of Vedic texts) a *pramāṇa*, precisely because they considered it independent (*MīS* 1.1.5: ... *tat pramāṇam ... anapekṣatvāt*); according to Śabara it is independent from other people and from other cognitions (Frauwallner 1968, pp. 24.12-13 and 48.13). As far as I can see, this necessarily implies that it is also independent from other *pramāṇas*.

[17] Bhartṛhari's way of dealing with three *pramāṇas* which are fundamentally interrelated would therefore correspond to the position adopted in the *Yuktidīpikā* (especially *YD*, pp. 29.26-34.26). The *YD* (the author of which was clearly familiar with Bhartṛhari's work) accepts three *pramāṇas* and insists that they are not independent; cf. e.g., *YD*, p. 30.30-31: *na tu ... iha ... svatantrāṇi trīṇi pramāṇāni syuḥ* ("But here (in our system) the three *pramāṇas* would not be independent"). According to the Sāṅkhya-volume of the *Encyclopedia of Indian Philosophy*, those accepting independent *pramāṇas* were the Naiyāyikas (Larson and Bhattacharya 1987, p. 240). The point of the interdependence of the three *pramāṇas* (see also Larson and Bhattacharya 1987, p. 98) may well go back to pre-Bhartṛhari Sāṅkhya but it is not easy to prove this with references to available texts or passages.

[18] Biardeau 1964a, p. 317: "c'est cette intuition intérieure, ce jaillissement de l'idée en son point d'émergence que les êtres vivants suivent comme autorité ultime, moyen de connaissance droite -*pramāṇa*-." In close connection with her literal interpretation of *VP* 1.132 (on p. 318 she translates *vāgrūpatā ced utkramet ... na prakāśaḥ prakāśeta* as "Si la connaissance perdait sa forme éternelle de parole, la lumière n'éclairait plus"; cf. discussion in Houben 1992b, part 3, under *kārikā* 87), Biardeau arrives at the conclusion that perception and all other *pramāṇas* are subordinate to *pratibhā*, cf.: "Bhartṛhari ne nous dit-il pas que si la connaissance n'avait pas éternellement la forme de la parole, la lumière n'éclairerait plus?" (Biardeau 1964a, p. 319); "Elle est donc l'unique moyen de connaissance droite et tout autre moyen de connaissance droite lui est subordonné, y compris la perception" (Biardeau 1964a, p. 320).

[19] The way *pratibhā* is said to function as a *pramāṇa* without being one of the generally accepted *pramāṇas* (*VP* 2.147: *pramāṇatvena tāṃ lokaḥ sarvaḥ samanugacchati*), can perhaps be compared with the way Pāṇini (in *Mahābhāṣya* (*A*) I, p. 39.10) and the Buddha (first verse of Diṅnāga's *Pramāṇasamuccaya*) are said to be *pramāṇabhūta*. On

the latter expression, cf. Ruegg 1994. On *pratibhā* see further note 34 below and the references at its end. That there is some parallelism between Diṅnāga's and Patañjali's statements was also pointed out by A. Wezler (referring to earlier remarks by E. Steinkellner) in note 30A to Thieme 1982-83.

[20] Cf. *MBhD* 1, p. 7.16-17: *pāramparyeṇāvicchinna upadeśa āgamaḥ. śrutilakṣaṇaḥ smṛtilakṣaṇaś ca.* "Traditional knowledge (*āgama*) is teaching (handed down) uninterruptedly in a tradition (from teacher to pupil); it is in the form of revealed texts (*śruti*) and in the form of composed texts (*smṛti*)." Cf. Iyer 1969, p. 92; Aklujkar 1971b, pp. 169-170; Bronkhorst in *MBhD* 1, pp. 116-117, note 33; Bühler 1882. In *VP* 1.148, however, *āgama* apparently does not include *śruti*, nor even *smṛti* but seems to refer to philosophical treatises of different schools (cf. 1.149).

[21] Bhartṛhari does not simply reject inference, as was suggested by Frauwallner (1959, p. 94: "Bhartṛhari ... der die Schlussfolgerung als Mittel richtiger Erkenntnis glatt verwirft"), but points out its limitations, if it is used in isolation, without reference to traditional knowledge (*āgama*). Cf. Iyer 1969, pp. 83-84; and *VP* 1.151-153; 2.151; also, though perhaps written by a student or commentator (or the *Vṛttikāra*) of Bhartṛhari (cf. Aklujkar 1978; Bronkhorst 1988): 2.484, 489-490. Bhartṛhari's stance may be compared with that of modern philosophers of science according to whom there are in each field of science authoritative paradigms (disciplinary matrices, or research programs) beyond which one cannot go without becoming "unscientific" (Kuhn 1970, 1977; Lakatos 1978; Morin 1991, p. 213). The authoritative paradigms or research programs are somewhat like Bhartṛhari's *āgama* in its most abstract sense. Aklujkar compared *āgama* with Quine's "conceptual scheme" (Aklujkar 1989b, pp. 18-21). For *āgama* in the concrete sense of revealed text (*śruti*) and composed text (*smṛti*) (claimed to be) directly dependent on *śruti*, however, there seems to be no good place in a framework of modern philosophy of science.

The Buddhists who accept only perception and inference as means of gaining valid knowledge (e.g., Diṅnāga; the *prāmāṇya* of other means, e.g., *āgama*, can be derived from these; cf. Hattori 1968, pp. 24-25, 73) cannot work with absolutely valid revealed texts either, and they have to derive even the authoritativeness of the Buddhist Scripture from perception and inference. For the Mādhyamika Bhavya, however, *āgama* (i.e., Buddhist Scripture) occupied a much more important position; according to Lindtner it was for him even "the most fundamental *pramāṇa*, provided, naturally, that one does not forget to practice yoga" (Lindtner 1993, p. 211). For the importance of inference in Nyāya and Vaiśeṣika, cf. Potter 1977, pp. 179-207; in Sāṅkhya, cf. Larson and Bhattacharya 1987, pp. 94-103.

[22] The term *yogin* in the sense of "practicioner of *yoga* or meditative practices" is not found in the *VP*. There have been attempts to reconstruct "Bhartṛhari's philosophy of *yoga*" (e.g., Iyer 1969, pp. 141-145), but if we maintain a distinction between *Vṛtti* and *kārikās*, the latter contain hardly any basis for this (Houben 1992b, Part 3, under *kārikā* 56-57). Nevertheless, it is not unlikely that *kārikā* 37 and 38 refer not only to the "vision of a *ṛṣi*" (*ārṣaṃ cakṣus*) but also to what is in other texts known as *yogipratyakṣa* (cf.

Isaacson 1993). Especially 37 reminds one of *YS* 3.16 (for *atītānāgatajñānam*), and *YS* 2.18 and 52 (for *prakāśa*, and the idea that the covering under which it is hidden in normal circumstances may disappear). Perhaps, one can infer on the basis of the word *abhyāsa* in *VP* 3.1.46 (*jñānaṃ tv asmadviśiṣṭānāṃ tāsu* [sc. *jātiṣu*] *sarvendriyaṃ viduḥ/ abhyāsān maṇirūpyādiviśeṣeṣv iva tadvidām//*) that Bhartṛhari accepts that through practice one can develop a supernormal perception (for *asmadviśiṣṭānām* in *VP* 3.1.46a cf. *VS* 2.1.18). The *Vṛtti* on 37 and 38 identifies those having the extraordinary perception as *śiṣṭas* (the "well-educated," or "elite"; cf. Deshpande 1993).

[23] Cf. Biardeau 1964b, p. 82, note 1: "dans le texte du *VP*, la *kārikā* contribue au développement de la pensée de l'auteur." In the sequel of this note, which continues on pp. 84-85 of the same work, Biardeau makes much work of elaborating the second interpretation referred to above, viz. that of people following (to some extent) their own conscience.

[24] Cf. also my remark on *VP* 1.111-116 in Houben 1994a, p. 8, note 17.

[25] For the Mīmāṃsā view on the *pramāṇas*, see Biardeau 1964a, pp. 68-100; Frauwallner 1968; Bhatt 1989. The *Śābarabhāṣya* on *MīS* 1.1.4 accepts perception only in the domain of "something (actually) present," thus leaving no room for the perception of "past and future things" (e.g., Frauwallner 1968, pp. 22-30).

[26] Cf. Isaacson 1993, and above, notes 21-22. For the Buddhists: Hattori 1968.

[27] This was done for instance by H. Nakamura in his article "Bhartṛhari the scholar" (1960), which was severely criticized by Aklujkar (1971b).

[28] These two words may also be translated as: "Since knowledge is spontaneous ... ." The conclusion of this premiss may then be taken as a statement that is rejected in the next line. In the *Vṛttikāra*'s interpretation, it seems, the *kārikā* contains two mutually exclusive statements, and the entire first line, both premiss and conclusion, is to be rejected.

[29] The element *vi-* in *vikalpa* (an important term in the *VP*, cf. e.g., 1.8, 2.116, 3.3.82) may indicate either the differentation within a conceptualization or the divergence between different conceptualizations. Thus: "dichotomizing conceptualizations" or "diverging conceptualizations."

[30] I interpret *āgama* here not in the abstract sense of "traditional knowledge" but in the sense of "treatise" or "traditional text" (cf. 1.148 and the epilogue verses of the second book, 2.486-487, 489-490).

[31] Is the use of the term *satyapakṣa* (also interpretable as "the true view") instead of *satkāryavāda*, perhaps another indication of the *Vṛttikāra*'s preference for it?

[32] Cf. *VP* 2.149:

*svaravṛttiṃ vikurute madhau puṃskokilasya kaḥ/*
*jantvādayaḥ kulāyādikaraṇe śikṣitāḥ katham//*

"Who changes the melody of the male cuckoo in spring? How are small animals etc., taught to make a cobweb etc.?"

The answer suggested in the context is that the melody changes on account of the cuckoo's *pratibhā*, and that the small animal such as the spider knows how to build a cobweb also by *pratibhā*. It is a kind of *pratibhā* which will come under the category mentioned in 150 as *svabhāva-upapādita* (see below) and seems to be equivalent to what we would call not "intuition" but "instinct."

[33] Cf. Iyer's discussion 1969, pp. 90-92 and his notes 31-35.

[34] An unexpected clarification of the notion of *pratibhā* can be found in the *Padārtha-dharmasaṅgraha*-passage on *ārṣaṃ jñānam* to which Dr. Isaacson kindly drew my attention (*PDhS(J)* § 288): *āmnāyavidhātṝṇām atītānāgatavartamāneṣv atīndriyeṣv granthopanibaddheṣv anupanibaddheṣu cātmamanasoḥ saṃyogād dharmaviśeṣāc ca yat prātibhaṃ yathārthanivedanaṃ* [*PDhS(J)*: *yathātmanivedanaṃ*] *jñānam utpadyate tad ārṣam ity ācakṣate. tat tu prastāreṇa devarṣīṇāṃ kadācid eva laukikānāṃ yathā kanyakā bravīti śvo me bhrātāganteti hṛdayaṃ me kathayatīti.*

*pratibhā* would thus be at the basis of the composition of the sacred texts by the *ṛṣis*, but it would occasionally also occur among normal people. According to the *pratibhā*-passage in the *VP*, *pratibhā* would also be involved in the understanding of sentences in everyday communication. And the notion is even further developed to include the instinct of animals. This creates a direct connection between everyone's linguistic understanding and intuitions, and the inspired composition of sacred texts by *ṛṣis*. It also creates a direct connection between "spontaneous knowledge" and the "sacred texts." On the notion of *pratibhā* see further Kaviraj 1924; Gonda 1963 (chapter 15); Tola and Dragonetti 1990; Houben 1992a, pp. 229-230.

[35] Bhartṛhari denies that this provides a reason to assume a relation between *śabda* and *artha* in *VP* 3.3.35-36. The argument of concrete effects of *mantras* is used in a different way by the Naiyāyikas (cf. *NBh* on 2.1.68 and my discussion of *VP* 3.3.35-36 in Houben 1992b Part 3). Another reference to "healing *mantras*" in the *VP* is in 2.323.

[36] Although I tried my best to explain the argument of the *Vṛtti* in as simple and straightforward a way as possible, it may be that the reader feels a bit confused at this point. A similar feeling after reading the *Vṛtti* several times made me search for a different explanation of the *kārikās*.

[37] The statement *sarvo dṛṣṭaphalān arthān āgamāt pratipadyate* (perhaps the *Vṛttikāra*'s interpretation, although Vṛṣabha and modern editors interpret *adṛṣṭaphalān arthān*) is not very convincing taken by itself: Usually it is claimed that only *adṛṣṭaphala arthas* are to be derived exclusively from traditional texts. One would expect that at least for some *dṛṣṭaphala arthas* observation and inference are also acceptable sources. And if someone

wants to derive his *dṛṣṭaphala arthas* only from traditional texts, it can still not be claimed that everybody does so.

[38] There is, perhaps, another way out if one wants to defend the author of the *Vṛtti*: He may have had a concept of how to write a *Vṛtti* which differs from the one I am implicitly employing. Even then, however, it may be argued that the divergence which I noticed above is considerable compared with other *VP-kārikās* and corresponding *Vṛtti*-passages. The *Vṛtti* does bring in its own, new points in the discussion, but usually there is a closer connection with the statement in the *kārikā* and often some crucial expressions are repeated or paraphrased before the own contribution begins. A more definitive judgment can only be passed after a comprehensive study of different *sūtra*- and *kārikā*-texts with their *Vṛttis* and other commentaries (see Bronkhorst 1990 and 1991b for some important preparatory steps in the direction of such a study).

[39] Vṛṣabha explains the *adṛṣṭaphalān arthān* as "liberality, non-violence etc." (*VP* I, p. 211.24, reading *dānāhiṃsādīni* instead of *dānahiṃsādīni*).

[40] To mention just one traditional example of persons obtaining detailed knowledge after practicing a specific "means to obtain imperceptible results": In the introductory passage of the *Carakasaṃhitā* (1.1-29), a group of meditating saints (*atha te śaraṇaṃ śakraṃ dadṛśur dhyānacakṣuṣā*, *Carakasaṃhitā* 1.17) delegated Bharadvāja to acquire Āyurveda (medical science) from Indra (*Carakasaṃhitā* 1.25: *so 'nantapāraṃ triskhandam āyurvedaṃ mahāmatiḥ/ yathāvad acirāt sarvaṃ bubudhe tanmanā muniḥ//*).

[41] *VP* I, pp. 223.6-224.3: *ye śabdapramāṇakā eva kevalaṃ sarvam eva śāstrapratyayam adṛṣṭaphaleṣv artheṣu[ṣv?] abhiśaṅkanīyatvād apramāṇaṃ puruṣasya darśanam iti manyante teṣāṃ śrutismṛtyor avicchedāviśeṣe tulye cobhayor arthasya nityatve śrutir avyabhicaritasvaravarṇānū[nu?]pūrvyadeśakālaniyamā na kena cit kartrā prakārāntareṇā[a vā?]vasthāpitapūrvā sarvakālaṃ sarvadeśeṣu praticaraṇaṃ vibhāgena vyavasthāpitā.*

[42] *VP* I, p. 226.1-3: *yeṣāṃ tāvad iyaṃ nityaiva lokasya vibhāgena pravṛttir naiva kā cid yugamanvantaravyavasthā, nāpi brahmaṇo 'sādhāraṇaḥ kaś cid ahorātravibhāgo vidyata iti darśanaṃ teṣām uktaḥ śrutismṛtipravṛttidharmaḥ purastād anantare śloke.*

[43] *VP* I, p. 227.6-7: *śrutiṃ tu yathādarśanam avyabhicaritaśabdām eva prathamam avibhaktāṃ punaḥ saṅgṛhītacaraṇavibhāgāṃ samāmanantīti āgamaḥ.*

[44] *VP* 3.1.42:

*anucchedyāśrayām eke sarvāṃ jātiṃ pracakṣate/*
*na yaugapadyaṃ pralaye sarvasyeti vyavasthitāḥ//*

"Some say that each universal has a substratum which cannot be destroyed. Everything is not simultaneously in destruction: so [universals] are well-established (on their substrata)."

[45] *VP* 3.1.43:

*prakṛtau pravilīneṣu bhedeṣv ekatvadarśinām/*
*dravyasattvaṃ prapadyante svāśrayā eva jātayaḥ//*

"According to those adopting the perspective of unity, when the differences are dissolved in the basis or ultimate cause (*prakṛti*), the universals, having themselves as substratum, acquire existence as the (ultimate) substance."

[46] *satyā viśuddhis tatroktā vidyaivaikapadāgamā/*
*yuktā praṇavarūpeṇa sarvavādāvirodhinā//* (9)
*vidhātus tasya lokānām aṅgopāṅganibandhanāḥ/*
*vidyābhedāḥ pratāyante jñānasaṃskārahetavaḥ//* (10)
*āsannaṃ brahmaṇas tasya tapasām uttamaṃ tapaḥ/*
*prathamaṃ chandasām aṅgam āhur vyākaraṇaṃ budhāḥ//* (11)

[47] *śabdasya pariṇāmo 'yam ity āmnāyavido viduḥ/*
*chandobhya eva prathamam etad viśvaṃ pravartate//*

[48] Aklujkar was no doubt right when he objected to Nakamura's remark that "Bhartṛhari's position on the eternality of the *Vedas* is 'precisely the same as' that of the Mīmāṃsakas" (Aklujkar 1971b, p. 173, referring to Nakamura 1960, p. 283). However, there is no good basis to identify the alternative view explained in the *Vṛtti* as the one to which Bhartṛhari would be committed to the exclusion of the Mīmāṃsā view and all other views not accepting world cycles. In note 40c of his 1991 article on "Bhartṛhari's concept of the Veda," Aklujkar cites first a sentence from the *Vṛtti* on *VP* 1.6 as a statement of the cyclical view, and gives next the following - not very convincing - argument for attributing the cyclical view to Bhartṛhari: "As B[hartṛhari] accepts a stage of *saṃhṛtakrama vāc* or *sūkṣma śabda*, as he cites, apparently with approval, passages expressing a cyclical view of things, and as he speaks of cyclicity in the operation of *vāc* at the level of ordinary experience, it follows that the *sarga-sthiti-laya* way of looking at the existence of Vedic *śākhās* is the way he approves." There is, of course, lack of implication between the premisses and the conclusion. The presupposition seems to be that one of the specific viewpoints on the issue is "Bhartṛhari's own view," but this cannot be taken for granted.

[49] This belongs also to the *Vṛtti*-evidence referred to by Aklujkar 1971b, p. 174, note 39. *VP* 1.1-5 form a syntactic whole and are as follows:

*anādinidhanaṃ brahma śabdatattvaṃ yad akṣaram/*
*vivartate 'rthabhāvena prakriyā jagato yataḥ//* (1)
*ekam eva yad āmnātaṃ bhinnaśaktivyapāśrayāt/*
*apṛthaktve 'pi śaktibhyaḥ pṛthaktveneva vartate//* 2)
*adhyāhitakalāṃ yasya kālaśaktim upāśritāḥ/*
*janmādayo vikārāḥ ṣaḍ bhāvabhedasya yonayaḥ//* (3)
*ekasya sarvabījasya yasya ceyam anekadhā/*
*bhoktṛbhoktavyarūpeṇa bhogarūpeṇa ca sthitiḥ//* (4)
*prāptyupāyo 'nukāraś ca tasya vedo maharṣibhiḥ/*

*eko 'py anekavartmeva samāmnātaḥ pṛthak pṛthak//* (5)

[50] *Nirukta*, Sanskrit-section, pp. 41-42: *sākṣātkṛtadharmāṇa ṛṣayo babhūvuḥ. te 'varebhyo 'sākṣātkṛtadharmabhya upadeśena mantrān samprāduḥ. upadeśāya glāyanto 'vare bilmagrahaṇāyemaṃ granthaṃ samāmnāsiṣuḥ, vedaṃ ca vedāṅgāni ca, bilmaṃ bhilmaṃ bhāsanam iti vā* (almost identical, *VP* I, pp. 24.5-25.1). On *sākṣātkṛtadharman* cf. also Ruegg 1994, pp. 307-308.

[51] *VP* I, pp. 25.5-26.3: *apara āha – yathā vāg deśabhedena bhinnā saty api svarūpabhede ekābhidheyanibandhanatvam avyatikrāntā, saiva ca deśādibhedaprakalpanavyavasthāhetuḥ, evaṃ caraṇabhede 'py ekārthanibandhanatvam avyatikrāntāni śrutivākyāni. svarūpabheda eva caraṇabhedaprakalpanavyavasthāhetur iti.*

[52] *VP* I, p. 10.1-2: *sarvavikārapratyastamaye saṃvartād anākṛtāt pūrvaṃ vikāragranthirūpatvenāvyapadeśyāj jagadākhyā vikārāḥ prakriyante*; cf. Vṛṣabha on *sarva* in *sarvavikārapratyastamaye: sarvaśabdena mahāpralayam āha, tatra na kācin mātrāpi śiṣyata iti* (*VP* I, p. 10.9). Cf. Hacker 1953, p. 19: "Der Kommentator sieht im Vivarta keinen Gegensatz zum Pariṇāma oder Vikāra. Er stellt ihm wie wir sehen werden dem Saṃvarta gegenüber."

[53] Cf. Jayanta Bhaṭṭa in *NM* II, p. 484: *vivartavādo 'pi na samañjasaḥ. tathā hi – vivartate 'rthabhāvena iti ko 'rthaḥ? na tāvad arthātmanā śabdaḥ pariṇāmam upayāti.* In a footnote the editor explains why Jayanta suddenly introduces the notion of *pariṇāma* at this stage: *vākyapadīye hi "vivartate 'rthabhāvena" "yat tasya (śabdasya?) pariṇāmo 'yam" iti vivartapariṇāmaśabdau paryāyatayā bahulaṃ prayuktau.* It should be added that not the *Vṛtti* but only the *VP-kārikās* give occasion for inferring that the terms were used as synonyms: the *Vṛtti* uses the term *vivarta* in a well-defined sense and distinguishes it from *pariṇāma*. For the interpretation of "Śabdabrahmavāda" in terms of both *vivarta* and *pariṇāma*, see also Vācaspati Miśra's *Nyāyakaṇikā* on Maṇḍana Miśra's *Vidhiviveka* (*NKaṇ*, p. 293.8-10, *NKaṇ(G)*, pp. 208.31-209.9), Śāntarakṣita and Kamalaśīla (*TSaṅ*, p. 67, *kārikā* 128; p. 72, *kārikā* 144). Cf. also Gaurinath Sastri 1959, p. 57, and 1991, p. 46.

[54] Cf. Larson and Bhattacharya 1987, pp. 10, 23, 65-73; cf. also the *Yuktidīpikā*-definition of *pariṇāma* as a continuous process (*YD*, p. 75.6-7).

[55] E.g., Lindtner 1993, pp. 195-198, whose rather impressionistic argument is valuable for the references it contains to Buddhist sources which are possibly relevant for Bhartṛhari's use of the terms *vivarta* and *pariṇāma*. For different Buddhist (Sarvāstivāda) theories of *pariṇāma* see also Chatterjee 1980, pp. 139-143 (note 7).

[56] Accounts of the periodic manifestation and dissolution of the world in later Sāṅkhya texts are, according to Larson and Bhattacharya, "more reminiscent of epic and Purāṇic cosmologies than of the older Sāṃkhya traditions" which "focussed largely on epistemology, psychology/physiology, and ethics" (Larson and Bhattacharya 1987, pp. 33, 37).

The *Yuktidīpikā* rejects the possibility of a complete cessation of the world in the following statement: *pradhānapuruṣayorhi bhoktṛbhogyabhāvāpekṣanimitto 'yaṃ tattvasargo mahadādiḥ, bhāvasargaś ca dharmādiḥ, bhūtasargaś ca brāhmādiḥ pravartate. sā cāpekṣā puruṣānantyān na nivartata ity ato 'rthavatīnāṃ hi prakṛtīnāṃ tadaparisamāpter na nivṛttir asti* (*YD*, p. 90.15-17). Cf. also the *YD* on *Sāṅkhyakārikā* 68 and 69 (*YD*, pp. 143-144). If the myth on the creation of the world referred to in *YD*, p. 127.7-13, is taken literally, the *YD* would accept a beginning of the world. There are, however, reasons to doubt that we are permitted to assume an easy literal interpretion as the intended one, cf. Larson and Bhattacharya 1987, p. 634, note 30: "The Sāṃkhya conceptualization of *mūlaprakṛti* as *triguṇa* and *guṇapariṇāma* obviates the need for separate treatments of such traditional philosophical notions as time, space, or God. Put another way, these latter categories have no place in the Sāṃkhya philosophical analysis, since *mūlaprakṛti* as *triguṇa* represents the functional equivalent. Space and time are derived correlates of a beginningless process of combination (*saṃghāta*) and change (*pariṇāma*)."

[57] Note that in the *VP viparyaya* means usually simply "opposite," "alteration," without negative connotation (in the sense "wrong"). Cf. e.g., *VP* 1.75, 2.436, 3.9.105, 3.10.7. Cf. also Monier-Williams 1899, p. 974, s.v. *viparyaya*, where *buddhi-viparyaya* ("opposite opinion") illustrates the meaning "opposite" of *viparyaya* at the end of a compound.

[58] *VP* I, p. 234.2-5: *anityavādinas tu ye sādhūnāṃ dharmahetutvaṃ na pratipadyante, mallasamayādisadṛśīṃ sādhuvyavasthāṃ manyante, te prakṛtau bhavaṃ prākṛtaṃ sādhūnāṃ śabdānāṃ samūham ācakṣate. vikāras tu paścād vyavasthāpitaḥ, yaḥ saṃbhinnabuddhibhiḥ puruṣaiḥ svarasaṃskārādibhir nirṇīyate iti.*

[59] For the expression *svarasaṃskārau* cf. *Śuklayajuḥprātiśākhya* 1.1; Yāska's *Nirukta*, 1.12, 14, 15; 2.1; Cardona 1988, p. 654: "Yāska uses *svarasaṃskārau* with reference to accents (*svara*) and the derivational formation of words from bases and so on."

[60] *VP* I, p. 235.1-2: *yeṣām api ca naiva purākalpo na ca daivī vāg asaṅkīrṇā kadācid āsīt teṣām api gamyāgamyādivyavasthāvad iyaṃ sādhvasādhuvyavasthā nityam avicchedena śiṣṭaiḥ smaryate.*

[61] *VP* I, p. 235.3-5: *tatrānyaśabdavivakṣayā bālapralāpavad artheṣu prayujyamāno yaḥ śabdo rūḍho yaś ca na rūḍhas tāv ubhāv apy arthasya na vācakau bhavataḥ. tatra tu sādhuvyavahitā vā bhavaty arthapratipattir abhyāsād vā pramattānām akṣinikocādivat saṃpratyayamātraṃ jāyate.*

[62] *VP* 1.27cd: *arthapratyāyanābhede viparītās tv asādhavaḥ*. "While there is no difference (between correct and incorrect words) in expressing the meaning, incorrect words are the opposite (i.e., not a means towards merit (*dharma*))." *VP* 3.3.20cd: *vācakatvāviśeṣe vā niyamaḥ puṇyapāpayoḥ*. "Or, while there is no difference (between correct and incorrect words) in being expressive, there is a restriction concerning merit

and demerit." Cf. also *Mahābhāṣya* (*A*) I, p. 8.21: *samānāyām arthagatau śabdena cāpaśabdena ca dharmaniyamaḥ kriyate*. Cf. the discussion in Houben 1992b, Part 3, under *kārikā* 30.

[63] Cf. *MBhD* 1, pp. 26.13-14, 27.4-6. At the same time, the *MBhD* mentions a view according to which incorrect words do not express their meaning (*MBhD* 1, p. 10.14-15).

[64] Aklujkar gave a few considerations why Bhartṛhari's notion of *āgama* would probably have included not only the various Brahmanical texts, but also the Buddhist and Jaina traditional texts (Aklujkar 1991, pp. 2-3). He also suggested that Bhartṛhari could do so by assuming lost parts of the Veda as the seed of non-Brahmanical *āgamas*, and by requiring only a remote and indirect relation with *arthavāda* and *arthavāda*-like statements in the Veda (Aklujkar 1991, pp. 3, and 13, note 20). On Kumārila's restricted use of the hypothesis of the "lost Veda" see TR, pp. 60-62.

[65] Note that I do not consider the differences in emphasis and attitude noticed here and in the preceding as a strong and independent reason to consider the *Vṛtti* as written by a different author than the *kārikās* (one could think of a single author undergoing a certain development in his thinking and attitudes, or a single author addressing a different public in *kārikās* and *Vṛtti*, etc.). Yet, once we have started to doubt single authorship of *kārikās* and *Vṛtti* because of other reasons (cf. Houben, forthcoming), the easiest way to account for the whole situation would be to accept different authors (perhaps related to each other as teacher and pupil) with a largely similar background, but with differences in character and attitude.

[66] In the *MBhD* (1, pp. 19.11 and 23.24) established notions and expressions in the Pāṇinian tradition are interpreted in terms of Jaina and Buddhist doctrines.

[67] The first explicit reference I can find to the Buddhists is in the second *kāṇḍa*, the *Vṛtti* on 2.22 (reference to *kṣaṇikavādins* who are contrasted with *trayyantavids*). The reference to Candra in the concluding section of the second *kāṇḍa* (*VP* 2.486) highlights only his contribution to the grammatical tradition, but does not identify him in any way as a Buddhist. The *Vṛtti* on 1.182 probably makes direct or indirect use of Jaina sources. It is not clear, however, whether the *Vṛttikāra* wanted to present the ideas which are reminiscent of the Jaina-attitude towards Sanskritic culture explicitly as Jaina-ideas (he attributes them to the *anityadarśins* of the *kārikā*, and *anityadarśana* does not seem a very good characterization of the Jaina-doctrine) (Houben 1994a, pp. 6-7; Bronkhorst 1993, pp. 406-408). The *Vṛtti* contains numerous quotations but none from Buddhist sources. Helārāja, commenting on the third *kāṇḍa*, however, finds several occasions to cite Buddhist authors. For Vṛṣabha the Buddhists are an extreme case, but they are still within his horizon (cf. the way he refers to them in *VP* I, pp. 61.8, 86.13, 88.9).

[68] Houben 1994a, p. 11, note 21 (c) (on *VP* 1.110, 113-114) and pp. 6-7 (on *VP* 1.182 with *Vṛtti*); on a third relevant place in the second *kāṇḍa*: pp. 17-18 (on *VP* 2.444 and *Vṛtti*); the *Vṛtti* on 2.40, however, probably does refer to a technicality in *Jainendravyā*-

*karaṇa* (Houben 1994a, pp. 16-17).

[69] This "use of the Veda as criterion of legitimacy and 'orthodoxy,'" however, is "less conspicuous and overshadowed by its all-comprehensive metaphysical status" (TR, p. 64).

Johannes Bronkhorst

# PHILOSOPHY AND VEDIC EXEGESIS IN THE MĪMĀṂSĀ

In *Tradition and Reflection* (p. 31) Professor Halbfass makes the important observation that the Mīmāṃsā school of Vedic exegesis is not, not even in its own self-understanding, an expression or manifestation of Vedic thought and life. He then goes on to ask a number of questions, among them the following: What is the relationship between philosophy and Vedic exegesis and apologetics in the Mīmāṃsā? The remarkable fact is, as Halbfass observes on p. 30, that Śabara, Kumārila, and Prabhākara, the most important thinkers of the school, do not try to derive their teachings on epistemology, ontology, categoriology, and the philosophy of language from the Veda. Apologetics plays therefore a major role in the formulation of many philosophical positions. This is true of the theory of *svataḥprāmāṇya*, the "self-sufficient validity," "self-validating authority" of valid, specifically Vedic, cognition, which, in Halbfass' opinion (p. 32), is obviously motivated by apologetic concerns. Yet Halbfass makes a point of stressing that this and other school positions make an important contribution to the philosophical debate of its time and beyond, especially in the hands of Kumārila, "the most important representative of classical Mīmāṃsā thought and apologetics."

The present article takes up once again the question of the relationship between philosophy and Vedic exegesis in the Mīmāṃsā. It seems possible to go further than Halbfass in this respect, and to show that two of the fundamental tenets of Mīmāṃsā philosophy – Halbfass (p. 30) speaks of "the central and symptomatic notions of the 'self-evidence' or 'self-sufficient validity' (*svataḥprāmāṇya*) of valid cognition[1] and of the 'authorlessness' (*apauruṣeyatva*) and 'eternity' (*nityatva*) of the Veda" – have an inherent connection with the Mīmāṃsā method of Vedic exegesis. In order to show this, it will be necessary to leave philosophical questions aside for the time being, and to enter into some of the details of the sometimes complicated exegetical discussions of the school. While doing so, we will confine our attention to the basic text of the school, Śabara's *Mīmāṃsābhāṣya*.

Śabara's exegetical efforts do not infrequently concentrate on comparing two different interpretations of a Vedic statement. One of the two is in the end discarded, the other one is retained. The Mīmāṃsā has formulated a number of criteria meant to be of help in deciding in such situations. These criteria do not interest us in themselves at present. We are more interested in the type of reasoning used to establish those criteria, and to choose between different interpretations in general. Here we find that Śabara sometimes uses the expressions "nearest meaning" (*saṃnikṛṣṭa artha*) and "more remote meaning" (*viprakṛṣṭa artha*). Of these two, Śabara always gives preference to the "nearest meaning." He follows in this respect the *Mīmāṃsāsūtra* on which he comments. *sūtra* 3.3.14[2] enumerates a number of factors that can play a role in the interpretation of a Vedic statement and adds that, in cases where several of these factors apply simultaneously, the ones figuring later in the enumeration are weaker than the earlier ones, *because the meaning obtained with their help is more remote* (*arthaviprakarṣāt*).

Consider, as a concrete example, the injunction "One [must] worship the *gārhapatya* [fire] with the Aindrī."[3] The Aindrī is a sacred formula which begins with the words: *kadā ca na starīr asi nendra saścasi dāśuṣe*.[4] This formula contains the name Indra, which might be taken to indicate that it is to be used in order to worship the god Indra. The injunction, on the other hand, states clearly that the Aindrī must be used to worship the *gārhapatya*, which is a sacrificial fire. In other words, two conflicting interpretations present themselves.

Śabara's *Bhāṣya* discusses this question at length under *sūtra* 3.3.14. The position finally accepted is as follows. The injunction to worship the *gārhapatya* fire is explicit (*pratyakṣa*) and constitutes for this reason the closest interpretation. The formula *kadā ca na* etc., does not state explicitly that Indra is to be worshipped with it; this latter interpretation is therefore more remote and must be discarded.[5]

Consider next the sacred formula: *syonaṃ te sadanaṃ kṛṇomi ghṛtasya dhārayā suśevaṃ kalpayāmi; tasmin sīdāmṛte pratitiṣṭha vrīhīṇāṃ medha sumanasyamānaḥ*. "I make your seat agreeable, with a stream of clarified butter I make it very dear. Sit on it, establish yourself in the nectar of immortality, oh oblation of rice, being favourably disposed."[6] Unlike the formula studied above, there is in this case no injunction which specifies the context in which this formula is to be used. One must therefore be guided by its contents. But here there is a difficulty. The formula has two parts: the first part concerns the preparation of the seat, the second the placing of the sacrificial cake. Should the whole formula be used at both these occasions? Or should one use the first half during the preparation of the seat, the second half while the sacrificial cake is placed on it? Here, too, the answer depends on the relative "proximity" of the different interpretations. The "nearest" interpretation will eliminate the others. Which is the nearest interpretation in this case? For Śabara there is no doubt.[7] The connection between the second half of the formula and the placing of the sacrificial cake is direct, more direct at any rate than the link between the first half of the formula and this activity. The second half refers to the placing of the cake, whereas the first half is syntactically connected with the second half, which in its turn refers to that activity. A similar reasoning applies to the relationship of the two halves to the preparation of the seat.[8]

The *Bhāṣya* under *sūtra* 3.3.14 contains a number of further discussions relating to the relative priority of one out of two possible interpretations of a Vedic statement. This *sūtra* establishes, as a matter of fact, a number of principles of priority which are used throughout the *Bhāṣya*. All these discussions have in common that one of two interpretations is discarded because it is less "near" than its competitor. We shall not here study all these cases. The two examples which we have considered suffice to reveal a general exegetical principle of the Mīmāṃsā: the correct interpretation of a Vedic statement is its most direct interpretation. The direct interpretation, we further learn, follows as far as possible what the text states explicitly, and avoids inferential and multi-layered arguments.

There is an obvious "psychological" or "epistemological" dimension to these discussions, which however rarely becomes explicit. But sometimes Śabara gives a hint that he is aware of it. So at the end of his discussion of *sūtra* 3.3.14. Here we learn that in the case of competing interpretations, different *notions* are in competition. The difference between a correct and an incorrect notion is that the latter is followed by another notion to the extent that it is incorrect, whereas the former is not.

The principle that the most direct interpretation is the correct one pervades many other discussions in Śabara's *Bhāṣya*. For one thing, if we are to find the most direct interpretation of a Vedic statement, it must exist and be unambiguous. This is not however evident in all cases. Take the meanings of individual Sanskrit words. Almost any Sanskrit word, as is testified by the dictionaries, has various meanings.[9] Which is the "direct" interpretation that we must choose? The Mīmāṃsā takes a categorical position in this matter: each word has but one primary sense; the other meanings are derived from this primary sense. The primary sense is known from the word alone; secondary meanings are understood because of some connection with the primary sense which is understood first.[10]

In concrete cases it is not always easy to decide which of two known senses is primary, which one secondary. Where there are Vedic passages that clearly use the term concerned in one of the two meanings, there is no difficulty. The word *yava*, for example, can refer to barley and to long pepper. The Vedic sentence "Where other plants wither, these [*yava* plants] stand up happily, as it were" shows that the meaning "barley" is primary in the Veda.[11] Sometimes the Veda does not help to make the choice. Take the example of the word *parvan*. It is known right from the Himālaya down to Cape Comorin,[12] Śabara reminds us, that this word is used in the sense "time" and "combination." Which of these is the primary sense? Etymological reflections point to "combination" as the primary sense. The meaning "time" can be obtained from this primary sense.[13] Different reasons are adduced to choose between the two meanings of the term *caru*, "vessel" and "oblation of rice," both of them "known from the Himālaya down to Cape Comorin." The details, and the outcome, of this discussion do not interest us at present.[14] The presupposition which expresses itself in them interests us all the more: it is the principle that Vedic statements allow of an unambiguous and direct interpretation.

Śabara's *Bhāṣya* on *MīS* 1.3.30-35 contains an interesting discussion on what exactly is denoted by words. Is it the shape (*ākṛti*) shared in common by all individuals designated by that word? Or is it an individual (*vyakti*) thus designated? Both are understood when a word (and Śabara obviously thinks here in the first place of generic terms, such as "cow") is pronounced, but both cannot be designated (no doubt for the same reason as above, viz., that a word cannot have two "meanings"). Only the shape is directly expressed. Śabara explains why in the following passage: "It is self-evident that an individual is understood when a word is pronounced. The distinction whether [the individual is understood directly] from the word or from the shape is not evident [to everyone]."[15]

Śabara subsequently establishes that the individual is understood from the shape rather than from the word, by showing that an individual is known from the shape, even when no word is uttered; and where a word is uttered but the relevant shape is not understood, there no individual is understood either. In other words, what we understand directly from the word is the shape. This shape, in its turn, can bring to our mind an individual characterized by it. This means that the shape, rather than any individual, comes most immediately to our mind when hearing a word. And this means, in view of the principle under discussion, that words denote shapes rather than individuals.[16]

Elsewhere in Śabara's *Bhāṣya* a different answer is considered to the question as to which is the notion most directly communicated by words. According to an opponent, it is the notion of mere sound devoid of meaning. This position is clearly inspired by the principle we are studying. Words first communicate the notion of sound; the meaning which we understand from a word arises as a result of recognizing the sound first. Ergo, words primarily communicate the notion of sound. It is obvious that this conclusion, though close to the general principle of exegesis of the Mīmāṃsā, cannot be acceptable. Both the *Mīmāṃsāsūtra* (7.2.5) and Śabara's *Bhāṣya* reject it by stating that the connection between words and meanings is natural (*autpattika*). In other words, no extra step is required to get from hearing the sound to understanding its meaning. This way the exegetical principle of the Mīmāṃsā is saved. One could also say that the belief that the words and meanings of the Sanskrit language have an inherent connection, is a consequence of the dogma that Vedic statements can be correctly and unambiguously interpreted by choosing the "most direct" interpretation, that is, the interpretation which involves the minimum of mental or epistemological stages.

This same principle allows us to understand other discussions in Śabara's *Bhāṣya*, too. Some words express a meaning different from the one suggested by their parts. The word *kuśala* is an example. The parts *kuśa* + *la* explain the word as "he who cuts (*lāti*) *kuśa* grass." Yet *kuśala* expresses the meaning "skilful." Śabara admits that the meaning "skilful" can be explained as a derivative of the meaning "who cuts grass." Yet the meaning "skilful" must be preferred, precisely because we understand the word in that sense. In other words, we arrive more directly at the meaning "skilful."[17] This same type of reasoning applies even to words that are only used by barbarians.[18]

Direct interpretation determines what analysis to apply to the compound *niṣādasthapati*. At first sight two interpretations seem possible: "leader (*sthapati*) of the Niṣādas," or "leader who is a Niṣāda." The Niṣādas constitute a non-Aryan tribe, who are not, therefore, allowed to participate in Vedic rites. Yet the *niṣādasthapati* is mentioned in the context of a Vedic sacrifice. The question is unavoidable whether this leader is himself a Niṣāda. The second analysis designates him as one, whereas the first analysis leaves the possibility open that he isn't. Śabara prefers none-the-less the second analysis. His reasoning is as follows: The part *niṣāda-* in *niṣādasthapati* means primarily, and therefore most directly, "Niṣāda." The meaning "of the Niṣādas," which appears in the first interpretation, can only be arrived at secondarily.[19] The exegetical principle that the most direct interpretation is to be accepted, decides therefore in favour of the meaning "leader who is a Niṣāda," and this in spite of the problems this interpretation brings about.

It is easy to see that this same principle can be used to justify the belief that words in the Veda have the same meanings as in ordinary life. The very first sentences of Śabara's *Bhāṣya* present this line of reasoning in connection with the interpretation of *sūtras*, but it is clear that the same applies to the interpretation of Vedic statements. The main weakness of any other position is that it entails superfluous effort (*yatnagaurava*). This argument derives its strength from the principle which we now know, and according to which the best and only acceptable interpretation is the most direct one, which is the one that implies minimal mental effort. Śabara on *MīS* 1.3.30 states simply that there is no difference between words in the Veda and in ordinary life, because we do not notice a difference between them.[20]

Attention has already been drawn to the psychological/epistemological dimension of many of the exegetical arguments. This dimension is rarely made explicit. An exception is the discussion of the injunction "one should perform the Darśa and the Pūrṇamāsa sacrifices" (*darśapūrṇamāsābhyāṃ yajeta*).[21] This injunction is incomplete: it does not specify how these sacrifices are to be performed. Indeed, Śabara calls this injunction "the beginning of an injunction" (*vidhyādi*), which needs an end. The required information is found in the section which prescribes adding fuel to the fire, etc. (*agnyanvādhānādividhānakāṇḍa*). The injunction forms one single statement with this section, which has been put next to it *in the mind*; the resulting single statement is of the form "One should *in this manner* perform the Darśa and the Pūrṇamāsa sacrifices."[22]

This proximity in the mind has to be treated with much caution, as we can learn from Śabara's discussion under *sūtra* 3.1.21. This discussion concerns the sections (*anuvāka*) 7 to 11 of *Taittirīyasaṃhitā* 2.5. Sections 7 and 8 deal with the *mantras* called *Sāmidhenī*; section 9 deals with the *Nivids*; section 10 continues the discussion of certain *Sāmidhenīs*. The question presents itself whether the sections that deal with the *Sāmidhenīs* can be understood together, thus constituting the context (*prakaraṇa*) for section 11. The idea is launched that sections 7, 8 and 10 can be understood "as a single statement" (*ekavākyatā*) because the sections 7 and 8 come together with section 10 *in the mind*. This idea is rejected with the argument that these sections are separated from each other by another section which deals with a different subject. Where another subject is introduced, the earlier subject is no longer present in the mind. Here the opponent persists, and observes that one can recall the earlier subject through mental effort (*dhyāna*), etc. Śabara's reply is important: In that case the result is due to human understanding, and is no longer Vedic.[23]

This last remark is very significant. It identifies the mind as a potential source of error in the correct interpretation of a Vedic statement. The correct interpretation must therefore involve an absolute minimum of participation of the mind. In fact, the most direct interpretation is precisely the one which involves the least participation of the mind. It is of course axiomatic for the Mīmāṃsā that the perfect interpretation of a Vedic statement exists, and can be found. In other words, it is possible to reduce the participation of the mind to an absolute minimum.

It is easy to see how this position can be extended so as to cover all forms of valid cognition. It then states that all forms of cognition are right, unless they have been interfered with. This, of course, is what came to be known under the name *svataḥprāmāṇya*. Schmithausen (1965, pp. 158-159), while presenting the position of the Vṛttikāra (whose comments on *MīS* 1.1.4-5 are included in Śabara's *Bhāṣya*; see Frauwallner 1968, p. 24ff.), observes correctly:

> Die wahre Erkenntnis ist also der *Normalfall*, der Irrtum aber das *Abnorme*, da er durch ein *zusätzliches* Moment, die Störung, bewirkt ist. D.h. alle Erkenntnis ist *grundsätzlich* wahr, kann jedoch ausnahmsweise durch Störungen *verdorben* werden.

These disturbances (*Störungen*; *doṣa*) can very well come from the mind. Correct perception, the Vṛttikāra observes, can fail to come about because the mind is disturbed by hunger etc., or the sense-organ by the eye disease called *timira* etc., or the outer object by minuteness and the like.[24]

It will be clear that the notion of self-sufficient validity of valid cognition (*svataḥprāmāṇya*) and the exegetical principle identified in the preceding pages are closely related. Both try to identify, then to exclude disturbing influences from the process leading to valid cognition, and both start from the assumption that such identification and exclusion are indeed possible. Perception that arises from a causal complex which is free from disturbing factors is necessarily correct. In the same way, Vedic statements naturally (*svataḥ*) (i.e., when there are no disturbances by more than basic human mental activity) give rise to an interpretation (i.e., understanding, cognition) that is as a result necessarily correct. The proclamation that this interpretation of a Vedic statement – i.e., the one in the production of which no disturbances play a role – is necessarily correct serves, no doubt, apologetic concerns. The belief, on the other hand, that an interpretation can – and should – be found that has arisen without disturbances, is a programmatic principle which determines how to interpret Vedic statements. Interpreting the Veda means identifying disturbing factors – such as the more than basic activity of the human mind – and eliminating them. Any interpretation that requires more participation of the mind than is strictly necessary, is no longer Vedic, it is due to human understanding.

The purity of the Veda, then, is endangered by the activity of the human, or any other, mind. This conviction expresses itself in another fundamental dogma of the Mīmāṃsā, too. For mental activity does not only threaten to play a role in the arising of the interpretation of a text; mental activity normally plays a role in its composition, too. The Mīmāṃsā avoids this danger by denying that the Veda has been composed at all. The Veda has no author, and this is possible because it has no beginning in time. Eternality and authorlessness are therefore two sides of the same position. And this position is ultimately based on the belief that the purity of the Veda is endangered by contact with any mind, be it human or divine.

In order to justify this position, the Mīmāṃsā presents a theory of the inherent correctness of the word by itself, which can however be lost on account of the use made of it by human beings. The following passage explains this:

> It is a contradiction to say '[the Vedic word] states' and 'incorrectly.' When one says 'it states,' this means 'it makes known,' that it is the cause that [the thing] is known. ... If, then, it is understood on the basis of an injunction that the Agnihotra results in heaven, how can one say that it is not like that? And if it is not like that, how can it be known? It is contradictory to know a thing that does not exist. ... With regard to a statement made by a human being, on the other hand, if it comes from a person who is trustworthy, or if it refers to the realm of the senses, it is not incorrect. But if it comes from an untrustworthy person, or if it does not refer to the realm of the senses, then it is produced by the human understanding [only] and is not a means of valid knowledge.[25]

It goes without saying that the dogma of the authorlessness of the Veda, too, like the principle of interpretation discussed earlier, influences the way Vedic statements are interpreted. A text without beginning cannot, of course, refer to events that happened at any particular time.[26] Śabara is aware of this, and explicitly refers to it at some places. There is, for example, a Vedic statement which says that the god Prajāpati extracted his omentum.[27] Śabara discusses this statement and observes: "If a historical event were to be referred to, the Veda would be open to the charge of having a beginning."[28] Similarly, the Vedic statement "We grasped your right hand, o Indra,"[29] if taken literally, would be open to the same charge.[30] Elsewhere (1.1.31) Śabara is obliged to give different interpretations to expressions such as *prāvāhaṇi* and *auddālaki*, which normally signify "son of Pravāhaṇa" and "son of Uddālaka."[31]

In cases like these the principle of the most direct interpretation and the dogma of the beginninglessness of the Veda are in conflict. For clearly, the most direct interpretation of the statement "Prajāpati extracted his omentum" is that Prajāpati, at some point of time, extracted his omentum. The principle of the most direct interpretation meets with difficulties in other situations, too. Some Vedic statements do not agree with our experience. Śabara gives the following examples: "The trees sat down for a sacrificial session"; "The snakes sat down for a sacrificial session"; "The old bull sings mad [songs]."[32] Cases like these serve as justification to deviate in numerous cases from the most direct interpretation, and resort to a secondary interpretation instead. Secondary interpretations play a major role in Mīmāṃsā.[33] In the end most of the Veda is interpreted in this way by this school. This does not, however, change the fact that a secondary interpretation is only allowed in cases where the primary interpretation is not possible for one reason or other. The statements that remain for direct interpretation are few indeed. Only Vedic statements that are not, and cannot be, in conflict with other sources of knowledge are in the end retained. Such statements are the injunctions. The injunction, Śabara explains, is a part of the Veda which communicates something which is unknown by other means.[34]

But even if, for practical reasons, only a minority of Vedic statements can be strictly interpreted according to the rule of interpretation expounded above, the general principle remains unaffected, according to which each Vedic statement allows of a most direct interpretation, which is independent of the mental activity of the person who "receives" this interpretation.

The Veda, then, is not produced by a human mind (nor by any other mind for that matter), nor should it be interpreted by a mind. Or rather, only those interpretations which reduce the interference of the mind to a minimum can be accepted as correct. In this way the Veda remains pure, not touched by any mind, both in its composition and in its interpretation. This purity of the Veda, however, is only possible if it is accepted that the Veda is eternal, i.e., without beginning, and secondly, that this corpus allows of a "direct" interpretation. The first consequence became a central tenet in the Mīmāṃsā world view. The second consequence, as I have tried to show, constituted a point of departure for philosophical developments and elaborations within the school.

Seen in this way, the notions of the "self-sufficient validity" of valid cognition and that of the "authorlessness" of the Veda are more than just "motivated by apologetic concerns" (TR, p. 32). They find their basis in a fundamental attitude of the Mīmāṃsā, one that is widely present in Śabara's *Bhāṣya*, and which is also discernible in the earlier *Mīmāṃsāsūtra*. These notions are not, it is true, derived from the Veda itself. But given the central position assigned to Vedic injunctions by this school of exegesis, it is hard to see how the Mīmāṃsā could borrow any theoretical notions from the Veda itself. These notions are, however, closely linked to the no doubt sincere concern of the thinkers of the school to maintain the purity of the Veda and to gain access to its true meaning.

*Université de Lausanne*
*Section de langues et civilisations orientales*
*Lausanne, Switzerland*

# NOTES

[1] Taber (1992, p. 218f.) argues "that *svataḥ prāmāṇya* lies at the very heart of Mīmāṃsā thought."

[2] *MīS* 3.3.14: *śrutiliṅgavākyaprakaraṇasthānasamākhyānāṃ samavāye pāradaurbalyam arthaviprakarṣāt.*

[3] *MS* 3.2.4 (p. 20.13): *aindryā gārhapatyam upatiṣṭhate.*

[4] *MS* 1.3.26; *ṚV(S)* 8.51.7; etc. Geldner (1951, p. 374) translated: "Auch nicht einmal bist du eine unfruchtbare Kuh, nie stehst du für den Opferwilligen trocken." This translation skips the crucial word *indra.*

[5] A similar reasoning is presented under *sūtra* 5.4.1.

[6] *TB* 3.7.5.2-3, which has *karomi* instead of *kṛṇomi.* With *kṛṇomi* this formula is found *MŚS* 1.2.6.19.

[7] On *MīS* 3.3.14 (p. 255f.).

[8] Under *MīS* 2.1.46 Śabara shows that this one sacred formula (*mantra*) consists of two sentences.

[9] One is here reminded of the following observation by Doniger and Smith (1991, p. xxiii): "It has been said that every word in Sanskrit designates its basic meaning, the opposite of that, a word for an elephant, a name of God, and a position in sexual intercourse."

[10] Cf. Śabara on *MīS* 3.2.1: *yaḥ śabdād evāvagamyate, sa prathamo 'rtho mukhyaḥ. mukham iva bhavatīti mukhya ity ucyate. yas tu khalu pratītād arthāt kenacit sambandhena gamyate, sa paścādbhāvāj jaghanam iva bhavatīti jaghanyaḥ. guṇasambandhāc ca gauṇa iti.*

[11] Śabara on *MīS* 1.3.9.

[12] Or "up to the Himālaya and up to Cape Comorin," as Wezler (1992, p. 472) prefers to translate this expression.

[13] Śabara on *MīS* 9.2.51-53.

[14] See Śabara on *MīS* 10.1.34-44.

[15] Śabara on *MīS* 1.3.33: *tad etad ātmapratyakṣaṃ yac chabda uccarite vyaktiḥ pratīyata iti. kiṃ śabdād utākṛter iti vibhāgo na pratyakṣaḥ.*

[16] For an assessment of Śabara's argument see Scharf 1993.

[17] See Śabara on *MīS* 6.7.22.

[18] Śabara on *MīS* 1.3.10.

[19] Śabara on *MīS* 6.1.51.

[20] Śabara on *MīS* 1.3.10: *na teṣām eṣāṃ ca vibhāgam upalabhāmahe.*

[21] The origin of this quotation is obscure. See Garge 1952, pp. 125, 128, 136.

[22] Śabara on *MīS* 8.1.2: ... *vidhyādiḥ* ... *agnyanvādhānādividhānakāṇḍena* ... *buddhau saṃnihitenaikavākyatāṃ yāti darśapūrṇamāsābhyāṃ yajetettham iti.*

[23] Śabara on *MīS* 3.1.21: *avaidikaḥ sa puruṣabuddhipūrvako vākyārtho bhavet.* A parallel situation is discussed under *MīS* 2.1.49. Of a sequence of three *mantras* only the first one has a verbal form; number two requires (but does not have) another verbal form; and number three requires the same verbal form as number one. According to Śabara, this verbal form can be supplied to the third *mantra*, but it is not the Vedic word that is supplied, but the identical secular word.

[24] Frauwallner 1968, p. 26.12-14: *yadā kṣudādibhir upahataṃ mano bhavati, indriyaṃ vā timirādibhiḥ, saukṣmyādibhir vā bāhyo viṣayas, tato mithyājñānam, anupahateṣu samyagjñānam.*

[25] *ŚBh* 1.1.2 (Frauwallner 1968, pp. 16.15-18.5): *vipratiṣiddham idam abhidhīyate 'bravīti ca vitathaṃ ca' iti. bravītīty ucyate 'vabodhayati, budhyamānasya nimittaṃ bhavatīti.* ... *yadi ca codanāyāṃ satyām 'agnihotrāt svargo bhavati' ity avagamyate, katham ucyate 'na tathā bhavati' iti. atha na tathā bhavati, katham avabudhyate. asantam artham avabudhyata iti vipratiṣiddham.* ... *yat tu laukikaṃ vacanaṃ, tac cet pratyayitāt puruṣād indriyaviṣayaṃ vā, avitatham eva tat. athāpratyayitāt puruṣād anindriyaviṣayaṃ vā, tat puruṣabuddhiprabhavam apramāṇam.*

[26] Strangely enough, the rabbinical interpretation of the Hebrew canon does not seem to accept this inference: even though the scriptures are timeless, they do refer to historical events. See Böhl 1991, p. 162.

[27] *TS* 2.1.1.4: *sa ātmano vapām udakkhidat.*

[28] Śabara on *MīS* 1.2.10: *vṛttāntānvākhyāne 'pi vidhīyamāna ādimattādoṣo vedasya prasajyeta.*

[29] *ṚV(S)* 10.47.1 etc.: *jagṛbhmā te dakṣiṇam indra hastam.*

[30] Śabara on *MīS* 9.1.9: *athaivam ucyate, tasyaitad vacanaṃ yo gṛhītavāṃs tasya hastam iti. ucyate - naitad adhyavaseyam. ādimattādoṣo vedasya prasajyate.*

[31] Pollock (1989, p. 608) refers to this passage in an article that draws attention to the non-historical nature of much of Sanskrit literature, possibly in imitation of the Veda.

[32] Śabara on *MīS* 1.1.32: *vanaspatayaḥ sattram āsata; sarpāḥ sattram āsata; jaradgavo gāyati mattakāni.* None of these three citations seems traceable in the Veda as we know it.

[33] Not only in the Mīmāṃsā. Fox (1992, p. 41) observes with regard to Biblical interpretation: "Unerring scripture requires the acceptance of allegory, the belief that a text may appear to say one thing while meaning another."

[34] Śabara on *MīS* 1.4.1: *kaścid asya (= samāmnāyasya) bhāgo vidhir yo 'viditam arthaṃ vedayati yathā somena yajeteti.*

**John Taber**

# THE SIGNIFICANCE OF KUMĀRILA'S PHILOSOPHY

One of Wilhelm Halbfass's most important contributions in *Tradition and Reflection* is the disclosure of the ethical dimension of the thought of the great Mīmāṃsā thinker Kumārilabhaṭṭa. While previous studies of Bhāṭṭa Mīmāṃsā have focussed on epistemology, metaphysics, and philosophy of language, Halbfass opens up a new area of investigation, with his essay "Vedic Apologetics, Ritual Killing, and the Foundations of Ethics,"[1] by discussing Kumārila's views on the sources of our knowledge of right and wrong. This constitutes a welcome and appropriate correction; for, certainly, ethics - more precisely, *dharma* - was the matter of greatest significance for Kumārila, that which his writings are ultimately dedicated to explicating and defending. All other aspects of his system can be seen as subordinate to this topic. Mīmāṃsā is, after all, as the first *sūtra* of the *Mīmāṃsāsūtras* announces, an "inquiry into *dharma*" (*dharmajijñāsā*).

In this essay I wish to reflect on the results of Halbfass's exploration of this aspect of Kumārila's thought from a philosophical perspective. That is to say, I wish to consider what significance Kumārila's views on the nature of *dharma* and its sources might have for us now. To some readers, the suggestion that Kumārila's thought might have any bearing on contemporary philosophical concerns will initially seem implausible, since our historical situation, certainly, must be quite different from Kumārila's (though we do not really know what Kumārila's was); but I hope that what follows will bear it out.

I shall begin by summarizing the most important ideas of Kumārila to which Halbfass draws our attention in his essay.

In the context of discussing the *śyena* ritual, in the *Codanāsūtra-adhikaraṇa* of his *Ślokavārttika*, Kumārila considers the charge raised by heterodox thinkers that any killing, even that which occurs during a Vedic sacrifice, is *adharma*. This he strenuously denies. The Veda itself is the only criterion of right and wrong. What is prescribed by the Veda is right; what is prohibited is wrong (242c-243a); what is neither is neither.[2] There are no other, independent criteria. We cannot *see* at the time a sacrifice is performed that such an act is not beneficial. (*MīS* I.1.2 defines *dharma* as "a [beneficial] purpose (or: thing) (*artha*) indicated by an injunction," *codanālakṣaṇo 'rtho dharmaḥ*.[3]) Certainly, the beneficial nature of an act, which has to do, strictly, with its future effect on the agent, is not something accessible to perception (233). Nor can one reliably *infer* that, because an act causes pain to another being, it will eventually cause pain to oneself (234c-236b). Cause and effect do not always resemble one another. In general, rather, the result of a particular action, also, is whatever the Veda says it is (237c-238a). Principles such as "being helpful or agreeable" (*anugraha*) to another person or being in harmony with one's conscience (*hṛdayakrośana*) are not reliable guides to right and wrong, either. They would not serve to tell us, e.g., that illicit sex is bad or the reciting of *mantras* good (243c-245b), and *mlecchas* could use them to justify their customs as *dharma*, too!

The opponent objects that certainly the Veda intends to teach in general that injury to living beings is bad. Surely, its explicit condemnation in certain cases - most notably, the killing of a Brahmin - is meant to extend to others (249c-250b). But Kumārila denies that scripture asks us to attempt to ascertain the underlying principles of its prescriptions and prohibitions.[4] Everything depends on the details. Does a *śūdra* go to hell by drinking liquor? No; for that is prohibited only for the higher castes. Or would a result accrue to a Brahmin or a *kṣatriya* through the *vaiśyastoma*? No; for that rite is prescribed only for *vaiśyas*. Would one derive any benefit by performing an *iṣṭi* on the fifth day of the month (when it is prescribed for either the new or the full moon), or the *agnihotra* (which is to be carried out at sunrise) in the middle of the day (252c-254b)?! An effect will follow only from the kind of action that scripture indicates as having the capacity to produce it (254c-255b). While, indeed, a general notion of the wrongness of injury to living creatures may be conveyed by prohibitions such as that against killing a Brahmin, it will be set aside by any specific injunction to perform a certain sacrifice that involves killing.

Halbfass summarizes on the basis of this and other passages from the *Ślokavārttika* and *Tantravārttika*:

> Ahiṃsā is not a rule which in itself alone would be "rationally" or "morally" self-evident; it is itself valid only insofar as it is scripturally enjoined. And even in this sense and on this basis, Kumārila does not like to present it as a universal,

> *prima facie* valid rule which would have to be modified by a specific clause such as the traditional *anyatra tīrthebhyaḥ*, "elsewhere than at sacred places," i.e., "if not during rituals" ... In this as well as in other cases, "morality" is derived from "legality." The moral claims of ahiṃsā are rooted in scriptural prohibitions. Such heretics as the Buddhists and the Jainas, who advocate ahiṃsā against the Vedic ritual injunctions, owe the basis and starting point of such anti-Vedic teachings to the Veda itself. Only, they have misused or misunderstood the Veda, have falsely universalized its prohibitions and have disregarded the internal differentiation of its *dharma* ... (TR, p. 95f.)

Thus, we could say, Kumārila attempts to remove *dharma* from a sphere of discourse that is subject to the vicissitudes of human reasoning and feeling. The Veda is the sole, absolute authority in regard to *dharma*. If other principles are recognized alongside it - say, that of providing benefit to others - then even the absurd practices of the so-called Saṃsāramocakas, who claimed to help other people by torturing and killing them and thus liberating them from their bad *karman*, could be defended as *dharma*![5]

> Kumārila is aware of the possibilities of rationalizing hiṃsā as well as ahiṃsā. He knows about the temptations to justify a tradition in terms of its common familiarity (*lokaprasiddhi*), its acceptance by "important" (or numerous) people (*mahājanaparigṛhītatva*), its accordance with ancestral habits (*pitrādyanugama*). But he also knows that others can claim these same criteria, related to other "continents," areas outside India, in support of their own views ... To defend the Vedic *dharma*, including its animal sacrifices, just in these terms would amount to abandoning it. It has to be accepted in its own right, without relying on external, merely human and potentially relative standards. Only the Veda itself can uphold the identity of its *dharma*. Only the Vedic injunction (*codanā*) can save *dharma* from the "jaws of non-being" (*abhāvavaktra*). (TR, p. 111)

In sum, we can say that the means of true knowledge of right and wrong for Kumārila is not reason or conscience or any other human faculty - certainly, not perception! - but only scripture, specifically, the Veda. Right and wrong are not reducible to any more fundamental principle than that of being prescribed or prohibited by the Veda. While the Mīmāṃsā texts suggest that the Veda prescribes acts *because* they are conducive to one's "welfare"[6] - that is to say, the acts are not ends in themselves[7] - nevertheless, it is only the Veda that can tell us what such acts are. For all practical purposes, then, the approval or disapproval of the Veda is the only criterion of right and wrong.

The modern reader will initially find such a view unacceptable, primarily because it would appear to put an end to discourse about good and bad. We may not be confident that we can ever determine with finality what those are, but we feel that our humanity somehow depends on being able to think and talk about them.[8] Are, indeed, human reason and feeling completely unreliable when it comes to matters of right action? Can we not learn to employ reason correctly in matters of morality; can't our intuitions and sentiments be educated and cultured? And can't we, subjecting moral judgements to criticism, correct them? Must we indeed renounce the possibility of basic, interculturally shared principles of moral evaluation, of joint reflection about norms on the level of fundamental principles? Must we resort to an incomprehensible, dictatorial source of ethical judgements, to deliverances *ex cathedra*? For such seems to be Kumārila's proposal.

One must bear in mind, however, that at the basis of Kumārila's insistence on the absolute, exclusive authority of the Veda with regard to *dharma* is the conviction that *humans simply cannot know independently what is right or wrong*. This conviction is based in turn on certain essential epistemological doctrines, first of all, a staunch empiricism. Kumārila - Mīmāṃsā in general - holds that all knowledge other than that gained from scripture is derived from sense perception,[9] while sense perception occurs only when an object stands in contact with a sense organ (*MīS* I.1.4; *ŚV Pratyakṣa* 18, 20). Thus, there is no human knowledge of the supersensible, of things in the future or beyond this physical world. *In particular, there is no direct human knowledge of what effect an action will have at a future time - perhaps after death - hence, of its value for the agent, i.e., whether it is ultimately conducive to heaven or prosperity*. In this connection Kumārila explicitly denies the possibility of supernormal, yogic cognition (*ŚV Pratyakṣa* 26-32). More importantly, he denies the possibility of human omniscience. The Buddhists and Jainas appealed to the latter in grounding the authority of their own scriptures, arguing that we know that they contain true statements about the supersensible, in particular, about *dharma*, because their authors (the Buddha or the Jina, respectively) were omniscient beings. Kumārila's critique of this doctrine, one of the most polemical passages of his entire corpus,[10] is based on a hard-nosed empiricist denial of any human cognitive capacities other than those with which we are familiar in common experience.[11] Kumārila, in fact, is skeptical, even cynical, about human testimony in general. "Men are always for the most part speakers of untruth," he says at one point in this discussion (*ŚV Codanā* 144ab). No human statement can stand on its own but must always be supported by a judgement that the witness is at least in a position to know that of which he speaks (i.e., is in possession of a *mūlapramāṇa*[12]). Such a requirement, certainly, can never be met in the case of testimony about the supersensible.

How, then, can the Veda tell us about the supersensible, about *dharma*, if human testimony cannot? This is where the most well-known epistemological doctrine of Mīmāṃsā, the theory of the intrinsic validity of cognitions, comes in. According to this doctrine a cognition is true unless and until it is in some way shown to be false. Every cognition (and not just true ones - a common misconstrual of the theory) occurs with a sense of conviction, a sense that matters really are as it represents them. If it is not overturned either by a different cognition which declares matters to be in fact otherwise or by an awareness that there exists some "defect" in the circumstances that gave rise to the cognition - the object is very small or far away, the sense organ diseased, the mind distracted or tired, etc. - then it is true for us. Now the Veda conveys definite notions of what actions should and should not be done (with a view to a future result) which are not overturned in either of these two ways. Being about *dharma*, there are no other *valid* cognitions derived from other *pramāṇas* which contradict them. The statements of the Buddha or the Jina may contradict them, but, as we saw, they lack authority. And insofar as the Veda is eternal and authorless (*apauruṣeya*), there is no possibility of a defect in the source of these notions. Hence, they are valid for us in a way that no other statements about right and wrong can be.

This is one of the central ideas, if not the most central idea, of Hindu orthodoxy - that only an eternal, authorless statement can reliably inform us of the transcendent. It also, of course, finds application in Vedānta thought: only the *vedavākya* can convey valid knowledge of the Absolute; it alone, and not any result of reasoning or any teaching originating from a person, no matter how revered or exalted, can evoke enlightenment (cf. TR, pp. 131-204). This idea accounts for aspects of Indian philosophical thought to which many have pointed in distinguishing it from European philosophy, in particular its close connection with religious discourse and its lack of commitment to "pure theory" - matters upon which Halbfass has reflected throughout *India and Europe* (see especially pp. 263-286). It also underlies the rejection of experience as a source of truths about ultimate reality, which, once again, Halbfass has treated as an important orthodox tendency, in contrast to so-called Neo-Hindu thought (IE, pp.

378-402). Above all, however, it is important to see that this idea itself is rationally conceived and defended. It rests on a moderate skepticism, specifically, skepticism about the ability of humans to know the supersensible through their own faculties, which in turn is based on empiricism, as we saw. As a theory of epistemic justification, moreover, the theory of intrinsic validity is quite defensible -- contrary to the judgement of most modern scholars.[13] It resembles in many respects recent proposals in contemporary philosophy, devised by Christian "analytic" philosophers seeking an "anti-evidentialist" theory of knowledge that can serve as the ground of the rationality of religious belief (Alston 1991; Plantinga 1993). In the Mīmāṃsā defense of the exclusive authority of the Veda in regard to *dharma*, rather, it is specifically the premise of the eternality of the Veda that is most questionable and in the end renders the argument unacceptable.

It would seem that the most appropriate characterization of Kumārila's ethics is "traditionalist." It is a version of the view that what is good or bad is what tradition approves or disapproves. To be sure, Kumārila distinguishes the Veda from mere tradition. The Veda is eternal; tradition originates from humans. Simply the fact that an action conforms to what one's forefathers did or is accepted by distinguished people is insufficient to consider it *dharma*. That would be to resort to "mere faith," for in fact everyone everywhere does what one's forefathers did. It would be like saying, "It is valid because it is what *we* do."[14] Moreover, there could be traditions of ignorance as well as of knowledge; there could be a tradition of one blind man telling the next blind man how things look.[15] Nevertheless, the modern reader cannot but feel that Kumārila, in defending the authority of the Veda over against the teachings of Sāṅkhya, Yoga, Pāñcarātra, Śaivism, and Buddhism, is simply insisting – in spite of his claim that the Veda is not a tradition – on the priority of what he considers a more honorable, ancient tradition over newer ones. The Veda is true, in other words, because it is the *authentic* tradition of the Āryas. The other "traditions" represent innovation and independent speculation. They derive from people whose characters and motives can be questioned. They are false simply because they contradict what the culture as a whole has believed and done from time immemorial. The attempt to ground this preference on the claim that the Veda is not, strictly, a tradition at all but an eternal, authorless teaching seems merely a clever gimmick – something which, as Kumārila himself says at one point in his critique of the Buddhist doctrine of omniscience, only a true believer could take seriously (*ŚV Codanā* 138-139). One must also keep in mind that when Kumārila says that the Veda is eternal he does not mean that it exists independently of its transmission by humans. He does not give voice to the belief of Bhartṛhari that the Veda, existing as *śabda* and contained in seed form in the *praṇava*, is ultimately identical with the Absolute (Aklujkar 1991, p. 5). Rather, he means only that it has been forever handed down from one generation to the next. We know that the present generation learned it from the previous generation and the previous generation learned it from the next previous one, and we have no reason to believe that there ever was a beginning to this process (*ŚV Vākya* 365ff.)

Let us consider, then, for the purpose of reflecting philosophically on Kumārila's ideas in a contemporary context, that Kumārila holds right and wrong to be what tradition prescribes and prohibits, "tradition" being any teaching sufficiently ancient not to be identified as originating from a particular source.[16] This is perhaps the most widely held of all ethical theories, but it has rarely been philosophically defended. Philosophical ethics, rather, has always tended in the other direction, away from a traditionalist ethics toward the elucidation of "deeper" principles which can be used to question and critique tradition. Indeed, independence from tradition is often considered to be of the very essence of *philosophical* ethical reflection. Kumārila, therefore, is unique in offering a reasoned justification of tradition as an ethical criterion. He provides a justification, not in the sense of an explanation of why it should be the standard of right and wrong, but in the sense of why it unavoidably is. This justification, as I would reconstruct it, is essentially as follows: the norms handed down by one's culture serve as valid standards of right and wrong simply because they are ineluctable. We cannot but think in terms of them when reflecting on ethical matters; as Kant would say, they appear to us as (synthetic) a priori principles which are the conditions of any possible experience of value. And they have this ineluctable quality, because the sense of conviction with which they are originally received – when they are first taught to us – never diminishes, while all other norms are questionable. They are not negated by judgements deriving from human beings consulting their reason, conscience, sentiments, or whatever; for we know that humans are fallible in the use of these faculties. Moreover, it is not even clear that we can ever discern what one *ought* to do by means of such faculties. The judgements of tradition retain the validity with which they are originally received, we could say, because they have the appearance of impersonal objectivity. They lack the aspect of contingency that attaches to other judgements. They are, simply, "there" as seemingly timeless commands, ascribable to no individual or group of individuals but part of the common property of the culture.

In order to appreciate the force of this theory we must reconsider the doctrine of intrinsic validity upon which it is ultimately grounded. According to that theory,[17] all cognitions have *prima facie* validity; they present themselves as true when they occur. A visual perception of a book on the desk in front of me does not have to be verified in turn by other cognitions in order to be valid for me. It stands on its own as a valid cognition without the support of extrinsic evidence. Such cognitions – cognitions which we are spontaneously inclined to accept as true and which have not in any way been falsified – form the foundation of all that we know.[18] Indeed, knowledge must begin somewhere, with certain cognitions the validity of which is taken for granted. The notion that we are entitled to consider a cognition true only if we have confirmed it by means of another cognition leads inevitably to a regress *ad infinitum*. Now, not only a perceptual cognition, but any cognition of one of the recognized *pramāṇas*, including testimony (*śabda*), can be valid in the suggested way. Just as I am naturally inclined to consider true a visual perception of a book in front of me unless and until it is falsified, so am I naturally inclined to consider true a cognition evoked by a statement made by another person.[19] Of course, we learn through experience to restrict our acceptance of testimony. We learn that certain people, certain circumstances, and certain subject matters are likely to render statements false. As mentioned above, Kumārila holds that in general in order for human testimony to be valid (for us) we must be aware that the witness is in possession of a *mūlapramāṇa*, a means of knowledge which serves as the legitimate basis of his belief – in other words, that he is at least in a position to know that of which he speaks (*ŚV Codanā* 102ff.)

A statement that one ought or ought not do a certain thing that is received, not from a particular person or group of people, but from the culture as a whole – that is, it is not only uttered from time to time by various individuals but is brought home in a hundred other ways by the beliefs and practices of the society in which one lives – such a statement will, like any other, have initial validity for us; for, once again, we are so constituted that if we are told something definitely and unambiguously, we believe it. (Were we not constituted in this way, Thomas Reid claims, we would perish at an early age.[20]) And its validity will not be sublated, first, because no belief deriving from another source will have the power to contradict it. Any counterstatement that one should or shouldn't do something else that has an identifiable human source will be immediately questionable. How, indeed, could he (or they) ever be in a position to know what one should or should not do? What tells *them* that this or that should or should not be done (i.e., what is their *mūlapramāṇa*)? Perception? Inference (reason)? As we saw above, Kumārila stresses that it is not apparent how either of these is capable of apprehending any connection between a particular action and a future benefit. With slightly more sophistication, the Western empiricist tradition (Hume) tells us that these faculties can inform us only of how things *are*, not how they *ought to be*. Is it, then, known by means of sentiment or conscience? But (now contrary to the Western empiricist tradition) our sentiments tell us only what we prefer or do not prefer, not what is right or wrong. And conscience, which would seem to have right or wrong as its object, is so inconsistent that few have ever been seriously inclined to consider it a genuine faculty of knowledge.

Nor will a traditional injunction or prohibition be undermined by the consideration that it, too, must ultimately derive from humans. Perhaps eventually it will - although Kumārila is by no means impressed with the arguments that seek to prove that the fundamental social institution of language is established by convention - but that would be an achievement of speculative, theoretical reason. For the time being, in everyday practice, the injunction of tradition presents itself as anonymous and impersonal. As far as we can determine, it originated from no one, at no time. It is simply given, *as if* it were eternal. And so it remains true - at least subjectively, for us, in everyday practice. As Kumārila says, one doesn't even suspect the invalidity of a Vedic injunction (*ŚV Codanā* 68 cd: *vede ... apramāṇatvaṃ nāśaṅkām api gacchati*).[21]

In sum, the ethical judgements of tradition will be binding for us, because they have in practice the lasting appearance of truth. The interesting corollary of this thesis is that *only* traditional judgements will be binding for us; for we cannot comprehend any other way a genuine "ought" can originate. In this respect, the theory is parallel to the Mīmāṃsā doctrine of the eternality of the denotative power (*śakti*) of words (in fact, it can even be seen as a special case thereof, insofar as the force of an injunction can be traced to the optative ending of the verb): since the ability of words to mean things cannot be explained as originating from some cause – cannot be construed as in any way contingent – it must be eternal. As a further result, any "new" ethical notion that has force for us will in reality be a traditional one, dusted off and renovated, perhaps, after long disuse. That "there is nothing new under the sun" applies especially to ethics. For this reason Kumārila accuses the heterodox critics of Vedic practice of ingratitude; for they refuse to acknowledge that their notions of non-violence, benefitting others, and so forth, come from the Veda itself (TR, p. 96). More generally, any wholesale "trashing" of tradition in the name of other "higher" ideals or "deeper" principles must be seen as an act of bad faith; for tradition provides the resources with which such ideals and principles are ultimately worked out. The opposing of such "new" ideals to tradition has to do, in fact, with the application of already recognized principles to new circumstances, that is, with the proper interpretation of the complex system of values that has been handed down. Ethical discourse, properly conceived, is a hermeneutical project.

The contemporary philosopher who has gone farthest in developing this theme is H.-G. Gadamer. Tradition, Gadamer argues, is inescapable. It forms the context in which any reflection is carried out, even that which opposes and transcends tradition. It provides the "prejudices" (*Vorurteile*) – the motivations and presuppositions – that invariably serve as guidelines of inquiry. "That which has been sanctioned by tradition and custom," Gadamer writes in *Truth and Method*,

> has an authority that is nameless, and our finite historical being is marked by the fact that always the authority of what has been handed down to us – and not just what is clearly grounded – has power over our attitudes and behaviour.[22] All education depends on this, and even though, in the case of education, the educator loses his function when his charge comes of age and sets his own insight and decisions in place of the authority of the educator, becoming mature does not mean that a person becomes his own master in the sense that he is freed from all tradition. The real force of morals, for example, is based on tradition. They are freely taken over but by no means created by a free insight grounded on reasons. This is precisely what we call tradition: the ground of their validity. And in fact it is to romanticism that we owe this correction of the enlightenment, that tradition has a justification that lies beyond rational grounding and in large measure determines our institutions and attitudes. (Gadamer 1989, p. 281)

Gadamer, of course, does not advocate clinging to tradition at all costs, as Kumārila sometimes seems to advocate. These observations, rather, "lead to the question whether in the hermeneutic of the human sciences the element of tradition should not be given its full value"

(1989, p. 282), that is, whether we should not cease pretending to be able to achieve a detached scientific knowledge of history by divorcing ourselves from tradition and its "prejudices" and instead recognize that historical understanding takes place within the horizon of tradition itself. The point is to see tradition as constructively contributing to our understanding of both ourselves and the past, and to respect tradition as a source – perhaps the only source – of values that will enable us to come to terms with new circumstances. Kumārila's thought, I believe, can be seen as contributing to this project by offering a convincing explanation of the binding force of traditional judgements. As we saw, the power of traditional beliefs according to Kumārila has to do simply with the epistemic status they have in the belief systems in which they occur, as defined by a proper theory of epistemic justification, viz., the theory of intrinsic validity. This explanation construes the power of traditional beliefs as epistemically legitimate and not merely the result of such factors as blind obedience or narrow-mindedness.

Another way in which Kumārila's philosophy might be seen as contributing to modern ethical thought is in suggesting a solution to the dilemma about whether value is objective or subjective.[23] Is value a fact that we discover about the world? Or is it something our minds impose on the world? David Hume, for example, suggested that the value we see in actions is simply a projection of our sentiments, of our liking or disliking them. The first alternative, typically championed by rationalist philosophers, accords with the fixed and definite – seemingly, necessary and universal – character of moral judgements. When we consider murder, for example, bad, we consider it so for everyone and everywhere. It would appear to have little to do with sentiment; for surely, even if we all enjoyed killing people, it would still be wrong. Presumably this property of moral judgements is best explained by their being based on cognitions of the real properties of things: seeing actions to be what they really are, we are compelled to judge them in certain ways. The second alternative, on the other hand, which is advocated by empiricist philosophers, accords with the fact that we do not seem to be able to isolate and identify the properties of things that make them good or bad. Value is not a discoverable component of the world. It is not the sort of thing that any scientific inquiry has ever unearthed. When we analyze how things really are, value disappears. As Hume said:

> Take any action allowed to be vicious: Wilful murder, for instance. Examine it in all its light, and see if you can find that matter of fact, or real existence, which

> you call *vice*. In which-ever way you take it, you find only certain passions, motives, volitions, and thoughts. There is no matter of fact in the case. The vice entirely escapes you, as long as you consider the object. (Hume 1958, p. 468)

Kumārila himself says, "... at the time [of the deed], there is no observation of a fault in committing injury" (*na hi hiṃsādyanuṣṭhāne tadānīṃ doṣadarśanam*, *ŚV Codanā* 233cd). Therefore, value must be something our minds impose on things.

A traditionalist ethical theory such as Kumārila's may be able to avoid both horns of this dilemma. On the one hand, it does not consider value to be an objective aspect of the world. For value is merely what is dictated by tradition, not our cognitive faculties apprehending facts; and we may suspend judgement as to how tradition ever in the first place came up with the idea that this or that act is good or bad. That is something that we cannot really conceive; no ethical theory to date has given an adequate account of it. All we know according to this theory is that, for us, in our present situation, the guiding notions of good and bad are handed down to us ready-made. On the other hand, a traditionalist ethical theory does not construe value as a reflection of our sentiments or anything else imposed by the mind, either; for tradition transcends minds. It is received, not invented, by each generation. Whether it originated with people projecting their likes and dislikes onto things, once again, we are unable to tell. We only know that now, in our present situation, it is something given.

In short, a traditionalist ethics might be able to avoid the dilemma about the objectivity of value by abstracting altogether from the issue of how judgements of value originate, for the latter dilemma, strictly speaking, has to do only with that issue. Yet at the same time, as we saw, it can explain how ethical judgements are binding on us, i.e., how they appear universal and necessary - at least in a certain context. A belief can be binding without being based on a cognition of facts and without reflecting an essential component of one's subjectivity. A belief can be binding just by appearing to have a distinctive degree of warrant - as explained by a proper theory of justification. (One need not resort to metaphysics or transcendental psychology to explain the universal and necessary character of certain beliefs; it can be explained, rather, in the context of analytic epistemology.) An ethical judgement, therefore, can have force for us, simply because, regardless how it arose, it appears true. At the same time it can be seen how a traditionalist ethical theory can account for the fact that different ethical judgements have authority in different societies. For an ethical judgement has force insofar as it is traditional; but different judgements will be traditional in different cultures. A traditionalist ethical theory, in other words, will explain how certain ethical judgements can be authoritative - impersonally "objective" and not just expressions of preference or sentiment - in certain societies without being in the fullest sense (for all societies) universal and necessary.

My intention in this paper has been only to provide the barest outline of the essential idea of an ethical theory that can be *extrapolated* from Kumārila's writings. Of course, much of what I have said Kumārila himself would reject. For he does not hold that the Veda is a "mere" tradition, no matter how ancient; it is rather eternal. Otherwise, indeed, it would be on a par with other scriptural writings - a conclusion he would find intolerable. But the modern reader is unable to go along with Kumārila in making such an assumption. If what Kumārila says is to have any relevance for us today we must reconstrue it as pertaining to a Veda that is not really eternal but only apparently so, i.e., a *tradition* that is so ancient as to *seem* eternal and anonymous, in contrast to teachings that have an identifiable, human source. If his ideas are to become viable and interesting for us - if they are to speak at all to the contemporary philosopher - then we must for a moment suspend our concern with historical accuracy.

I have not really begun to develop the ramifications of the traditionalist ethical theory that I see in Kumārila's writings or defend it here; nor am I sure myself that it is ultimately tenable. I hope, however, to have aroused the reader's interest enough for him to consider it worth further investigation. To restate the central insight of the theory: When you walk into a room and see a table, your perception is valid for you until other considerations arise that contradict it. Similarly, when you are told you ought to do this or that, your idea that you ought to do it remains valid for you so long as it is not contradicted. But the things tradition tells us are never effectively contradicted. Therefore, we think, what tradition tells us is what we really should and should not do. Where, after all, do "oughts" come from? Ethics, it seems, has never been able to answer this question. (A moderate skepticism, once again, is an important component of this theory.) It is not entirely incongruous to suggest, therefore, that they in effect come from nowhere. Any valid "ought" for us is one that is already there, which is as good as saying that tradition delivers it. And its validity has to do precisely with the fact that it is traditional, which means that, while conveying a clear sense that something should be done, it is not ascribable to any particular source and so (at least for us in everyday practice) is not questionable.

To recommend such a theory is to go along with Gadamer's suggestion that we "give tradition its due," that is, once again begin to take tradition seriously as a source of insight into right and wrong in dealing with contemporary issues. Perhaps in distancing ourselves, since the Enlightenment, as far as possible from tradition we have not advanced toward a better, more just world at all but simply muddled the tradition of which we are inescapably a part, while ceasing altogether, in certain instances, to be moral.

As a postscript to this discussion I would like to revert from thinking philosophically about Kumārila's thought to thinking about it historically and say a word about its historical significance.

Why is Kumārila so conservative in his treatment of revelation? Why does he accept only the Veda as a valid guide to pious living? Why are other sources of insight into transcendental matters so firmly, even vehemently, rejected by him? Why does he ignore, not only mystical experience, but even a personal intuition of value, of right and wrong? Halbfass, too, has puzzled over this problem in *Tradition and Reflection*, noting that other approaches were taken in the classical period (TR, p. 39). There was, e.g., Bhartṛhari's acknowledgement of all philosophies as the continuing unfoldment of *śabdatattva* and as anticipated in the Veda itself. There was Abhinavagupta's reliance on the Śaivāgamas, Yāmunācārya's defense (in his *Āgamaprāmāṇya*) of the authority of the Pāñcarātrāgamas, and Jayantabhaṭṭa's acknowledgement of various religious traditions on the basis of their "acceptance by great (and/or many) people" (*mahājanaparigṛhītatva*; TR, p. 63). Including Kumārila together with Bhartṛhari, Śaṅkara, and Prabhākara, Halbfass asks:

> Why did they rely on the Veda, and only the Veda? Why not on any other kind of "revelation"? Why did they not simply recognize the need for "revelation," or "objective epiphany," as such and in general? Are there any truly philosophical reasons, apart from cultural, psychological, and ideological motivations? (TR, p. 39)

I believe that we can take a step toward answering this question by regarding a striking Western parallel to Kumārila: Thomas Hobbes. Hobbes is most commonly known as one of the founders of English empiricism and political philosophy, yet his *magnum opus* the *Leviathan* contains in its third and fourth parts a lengthy discussion of religion. There Hobbes attempts to bring Christianity up to date, so to speak, by bringing its teachings as much as possible into harmony with the emerging natural sciences, the epistemological groundwork for which he had laid in the earlier parts of the work. But he is primarily concerned, more broadly, with the problem of religious authority and the legitimacy of scriptural interpretation. He will conclude, extraordinarily enough, that only the sovereign of the commonwealth has the right to determine what is true or false in matters of doctrine and worship.[24] There is no valid, independent source of insight into the meaning of scripture. He even admits that this may in the end cause him to retract his own interpretation of Christianity.

It is in the details of the discussion that the parallels to Kumārila emerge. In restricting religious authority to the sovereign Hobbes adopts a thoroughgoing rationalizing attitude. Such biblical notions as spirit, angel, inspiration, Kingdom of God, heaven, and hell are radically demystified. The spirit of God (frequently mentioned in the Old Testament) is considered variously as wind or breath, insight, violent emotion, etc. Angels are "subtile" or "thin" bodies, made perhaps of air; otherwise they are mental fantasies induced by God. Hobbes insists that nowhere does the Bible require us to believe in an incorporeal substance (which he considered as much an impossibility as Berkeley later considered corporeal substance to be). God Himself is declared incomprehensible in nature. The Kingdom of God is the society of believers in God, between whom and God the Bible records various covenants. The Kingdom of Heaven will be the society of physically resurrected believers presided over by Christ at the end of time. Hobbes denies, once again, that the Bible speaks of an incorporeal soul which might conceivably travel to a heavenly realm; orthodox Christianity, rather, maintains the resurrection *of the body*. Miracles *qua* supernatural events Hobbes grudgingly admits as possible through God's agency. But he holds that much of the time supposed miracles will have a natural explanation. It is the fact that those who witness it are unable to explain it, given the state of their scientific knowledge - that is, its psychological effect - and God's employment of it for his purposes, that makes a certain event a miracle.[25]

None of this, of course, is *exactly* matched in Kumārila. For one thing, Kumārila was hardly a materialist; he argues at length for the existence of an immaterial soul. But the spirit of the discussion is identical. The Mīmāṃsakas, too, and Kumārila foremost among them, attempted to explain away the supernatural content of the Veda. All passages of a mythopoeic nature are – indeed, rather scandalously and frequently without even an honest attempt to reinterpret them, such as Hobbes makes – dismissed as *arthavāda*, hence to be construed, in some way or other, figurately.

The thrust of Hobbes's rationalizing and demystifying of scripture, however – besides to bring it more in line with our understanding of nature through physical science – is to exclude all claims of extraordinary revelation. Here the parallels to Kumārila, specifically, to his polemic against the visionary capacities that were alleged to be possessed by the Buddha and the Jina, are more marked. The prophecy recorded in the Old and New Testaments occurs typically not by means of any direct experience of the Divine, Hobbes observes, but by visions, voices, or dreams induced in the mind of the prophet by God. Only, it seems, in the case of Moses did God address His messenger face to face. Considering, then, that such experiences may occur from natural as well as supernatural causes, there is a special need of the use of reason and judgement in discerning genuine prophecy. Moreover, while the person to whom God speaks, as it were, in this manner may well be convinced that God spoke to him, "how the same may be understood by another, is hard, if not impossible to know." For how could it be proved?

> To say that he [God] hath spoken to him in a Dream, is no more than to say he dreamed that God spake to him; which is not of force to win beleef from any man, that knows dreams are for the most part naturall ... To say that he hath seen a Vision, or heard a Voice, is to say that he hath dreamed between sleeping and waking: for in such manner a man doth many times naturally take his dream for a vision, as not having well observed his own slumbering. To say that he speaks by supernaturall Inspiration, is to say he finds an ardent desire to speak, or some strange opinion of himself, for which he can alledge no naturall or sufficient reason. So that though God Almighty can speak to a man, by Dreams, Visions, Voice, and Inspiration; yet he obliges no man to beleeve he hath so done to him that pretends it; who (being a man), and (which is more) may lie [sic.]. (Hobbes 1985, p. 411)

In general, therefore, we cannot trust those who claim to have direct access to God's word. Even the Bible warns repeatedly against false prophets. Any claim to prophecy must be tested by the criteria mentioned by scripture itself: accompaniment by miracles (themselves difficult to authenticate) and harmony with established doctrine. However, since miracles have ceased to occur in our day, harmony with scripture remains the sole criterion.

> We have no sign left, whereby to acknowledge the pretended Revelations, or Inspirations of any private man; nor obligations to give ear to any Doctrine, farther than it is conformable to the Holy Scriptures, which since the time of our Saviour, supply the place, and sufficiently recompense the want of all other Prophecy; and from which, by wise and learned interpretation, and careful ratiocination, all rules and precepts necessary to the knowledge of our duty both to God and man, without Enthusiasme or supernaturall Inspiration, may easily be deduced (1985, p. 414).

In the end, since the authority to interpret scripture rests with the sovereign power of a Christian commonwealth, to whom its citizens have relinquished most rights for the sake of their own survival and prosperity and whose commands they have agreed to consider law - not, as Hobbes will go on to argue, with one Vicar of Christ constituted over the universal Church, i.e., the Pope - the legitimacy of any religious teaching is ultimately to be decided by the sovereign.

> Every man therefore ought to consider who is the Sovereign Prophet, that is to say, who it is, that is Gods Viceregent on Earth; and hath next under god, the Authority of Governing Christian men; and to observe for a Rule, that Doctrine, which in the name of God, hee command to bee taught; and thereby to examine and try out the truth of those Doctrines, which pretended Prophets, with miracle, or without, shall at any time advance ... (1985, p. 468f.).

Here, of course, Hobbes differs from Kumārila in putting forward a particular human being as the final arbiter in religious disputes. However, that is not because he does not consider scripture as it has been handed down to us the only source of religious truth - indeed he does, though of course he does not go so far as to say that it is eternal. But Hobbes also realizes, unlike Kumārila, that different people will interpret scripture differently. That is where the problem of religious disagreement lies for him, for he lived in a culture in which religion and Christianity were synonymous. Kumārila, on the other hand, often gives the impression that he believes that once the Veda is accepted by all, things will go smoothly - an impression that his own intricately argued interpretations of Vedic passages belie.

Overall, Kumārila and Hobbes are in remarkable agreement about the need to eliminate the influence of "private revelation" on religious life. Both propose theories of prophecy and religious authority - coinciding in some points but diverging in others - which are suited to inhibiting innovation and promoting uniformity of belief and practice. The question remains, why? In Hobbes's case, he himself gives us the answer in the continuation of the last passage cited:

> For when Christian men, take not their Christian Soveraign, for Gods Prophet; they must either take their own Dreams, for the Prophecy they mean to be governed by, and the tumour of their own hearts for the Spirit of God; or they must suffer themselves to bee lead by some strange Prince; or by some of their fellow subjects, that can bewitch them, by slander of the government, into rebellion, without other miracle to confirm their calling, then sometimes an extraordinary success [i.e., a mere coincidence], and Impunity; and by this means destroying all laws, both divine, and humane, reduce all Order, Government, and Society, to the first Chaos of Violence, and Civil warre. (1985, p. 469)

It is well known that Hobbes wrote the *Leviathan* in response to the English Civil War, which he believed to have been caused above all by religious strife. Only by the recognition of a single sovereign who has supreme authority in matters both religious and secular, but who is established and legitimized by a covenant instituted among the citizens of the commonwealth, would peace be restored.

We know virtually nothing about Kumārila's precise historical situation. We can guess, by the usual method of cross-referencing, that he lived in the seventh century. He seems to belong to the same period as Dharmakīrti, Maṇḍana, Śaṅkara, and Prabhākara. His familiarity with South Indian linguistic forms and customs suggests but does not prove that he lived in the South. It seems safe to say, however, that wherever Kumārila might have lived in India in the latter half of the first millennium, he would have been exposed to fierce competition among religious sects, which in turn fed political strife and persecution. Kumārila may not have experienced the turmoil caused by religious dissension in the same form as Hobbes did - civil war - but that he did experience it in some form seems quite likely. It does not seem too farfetched to suggest then, on the basis of an analogy to Hobbes, that Kumārila's extraordinary conservatism with regard to religious practice and belief may have been motivated, not just by the widespread trend toward rationalism - a de-emphasis of the supernatural element and a focus, instead, on logic and epistemology - of his age, but also by specific social and political circumstances.

The above discussion, by the way, can perhaps be seen as a legitimate application of "comparative philosophy" to a historical problem. Halbfass, of course, has also reflected on the nature and value of comparisons in Indian studies and on so-called comparative philosophy in particular (IE, pp. 419-433). Comparative philosophy, I have always felt, can sometimes aid in our understanding of philosophical texts by suggesting possibilities of interpretation. But that is a topic for another essay.[26]

*University of New Mexico*
*Department of Philosophy*
*Albuquerque, New Mexico, USA*

## NOTES

[1] This chapter originally appeared as "Kumārila on Ahiṃsā and Dharma" in Halbfass 1983a.

[2] Kumārila, following Śabara, suggests that the *śyena* sacrifice, which is a means to inflict injury on one's enemy, is not prescribed categorically by the Veda but only hypothetically. As such, it is neither *dharma* nor *adharma* (265a-267b).

[3] Śabara understands *artha* as "that which is conducive to welfare/prosperity (*śreyaskara*)" and also, it seems, as "the highest good" (*yaḥ puruṣaṃ niḥśreyasena saṃyunakti, sa eva dharmaśabdenocyate*). See D'Sa (1980, pp. 49-54) for further discussion of the possible meanings of *artha*.

[4] Specifically, by the method of *āvāpodvāpa*, "addition and subtraction" (250cd), i.e., by discerning the common element in various injunctions or prohibitions to be X, the variable elements to be A, B, C, etc.

[5] The problem of the identity of the Saṃsāramocakas is discussed by Halbfass in this same essay, pp. 99-111.

[6] *Ya eva śreyaskaraḥ, sa eva dharmaśabdenocyate*, *ŚBh* p. 20.4-5. Kumārila offers only a minimal definition of "welfare" as "human happiness," *ŚV Codanā* 191a: *śreyo hi puruṣaprītiḥ*.

[7] The Prābhākara interpretation of *vidhi*, however, tends in this direction. See Maitra (1978, p. 117ff.).

[8] The reverse side of skepticism is nihilism. By telling us that we cannot achieve anything through the exercise of our cognitive faculties, it undermines one of the most important dimensions of human existence. Thus, global skepticism will always be resisted.

Moderate skepticism, on the other hand – the notion that we cannot achieve knowledge of everything – is simply common sense.

[9] *Pratyakṣapūrvakatvāc ca anumānopamānārthāpattīnām apy akāraṇatvam*, *ŚBh*, p. 27.1-2.

[10] The discussion of Kumārila's lost work, the *Bṛhaṭṭīkā*, which is much more extensive than the *ŚV*, is preserved in the *Tattvasaṅgraha* as the *pūrvapakṣa* of the *Atīndriyārthadarśiparīkṣā*.

[11] *ŚV Codanā* 113:

*yajjātīyaiḥ pramāṇais tu yajjātīyārthadarśanam/*
*bhaved idānīṃ lokasya tathā kālāntare 'py abhūt//*

[12] The doctrine of the need for a *mūlapramāṇa* in the case of human testimony is developed by Kumārila's commentators on the basis of his mentioning of *pramāṇāntaramūlatā* at *Codanā* 71b and *mūla* at 103a. See also *Codanā* 136 and 165.

[13] I argue for this in a forthcoming monograph, *Intrinsic Validity and the Philosophy of Kumārilabhaṭṭa*.

[14] Cf. *TV* I.3.4, p. 113:

*mahājanagṛhītatvaṃ pitrādyanugamādi ca/*
*te 'pi dvīpāntarāpekṣaṃ vadanty eva svadarśane//*

*tatra śraddhāmātram evaikaṃ vyavasthānimittaṃ sarveṣāṃ svapitṛpitāmahādicaritānuyāyitvāt.*

[15] This is noted in a *pūrvapakṣa*, *TV* I.3.1, p. 73.

[16] Buddhism and Christianity would be traditions in this sense; for although both in fact originated with historical founders, each is typically transmitted as the "truth" without reference thereto (except insofar as their status is a point of dogma). Kumārila, interestingly enough, considers at *TV* I.3.11-12 (pp. 162-164; cf. *ŚV Codanā* 119-120) attempts by the Buddhists and others to base the authority of their scriptures on their eternality. It would seem, then, that any tradition after a while begins to regard itself as eternal. Often the historical founder of a tradition comes to be viewed as an eternal, metaphysical principle. Buddhism and Jainism specifically teach that their doctrines are re-expounded by enlightened preceptors in every cosmic cycle. Against the appeal to eternality by the Buddhists Kumārila argues that it would contradict other fundamental Buddhist tenets, e.g., the momentariness of entities and the non-eternality of language.

The reader should keep in mind that in considering Kumārila as upholding tradition as an ethical criterion I am reconstruing his statements in a manner with which he would not agree, precisely because it puts the Veda in a class together with all other scriptural writings.

[17] I discuss here only the so-called *svataḥ prāmāṇyaṃ jñaptitaḥ* doctrine, which I believe is the proper interpretation of Kumārila's view of validity in the *Codanāsūtra-adhikaraṇa*. The *svataḥ prāmāṇyam utpattitaḥ* doctrine seems to have originated with Umbeka's interpretation of Kumārila in his *Ślokavārttikavyākhyātātparyaṭīkā*. See Taber 1992.

[18] Thus, the theory is best characterized as a type of "fallible foundationalism." For contemporary discussions see Audi 1993 and Lehrer 1990, p. 63ff.

[19] The eighteenth-century Scottish philosopher Thomas Reid refers to this tendency as "the credulity principle" (1983, pp. 95-97).

[20] See preceding note.

[21] This should not be taken to mean, however, that they are indubitable, but that they appear to us in every way true and there is no basis for considering them false.

[22] Gadamer says elsewhere (1989, p. 272): ". . . the sheer fact that something is being written down [we could also say, transmitted through a formal oral tradition] gives it special authority. It is not altogether easy to realize that what is written down can be untrue."

[23] For a recent treatment of this problem see Stroud 1989.

[24] Within certain obvious limits, that is. He cannot require that his subjects profess anything that contradicts the most basic tenets to which a Christian is committed by conscience, such as that Jesus is the Christ.

[25] Such ideas as these might be taken as support for the thesis put forward by Leo Strauss that Hobbes was really an atheist who feigned piety in order to avoid persecution. His real attitude toward religion was always that "religion must serve the State and is to be esteemed or despised according to the services or disservices rendered to the State" (1936, p. 74). I believe, however, that this view has been decisively refuted by Glover 1965 and others.

[26] I would like to thank the editors of this volume for suggesting various changes and corrections that led to improvements in this paper.

Kunio Harikai

# KUMĀRILA'S ACCEPTANCE AND MODIFICATION OF CATEGORIES OF THE VAIŚEṢIKA SCHOOL

0. In the chapter "The Presence of the Veda in Indian Philosophical Reflection" in *Tradition and Reflection*, Halbfass states that in the field of ontology within the Mīmāṃsā school the different explanations of being (*sattā*) are associated with exegetic positions and refers to Kumārila's adoption and modification of the Vaiśeṣika notion of the highest universal *sattā* (TR, p. 33). In his *On Being and What There Is* he also states:

> Classical Mīmāṃsā, on the other hand, borrows freely from the teachings of early Vaiśeṣika and tries to adjust them to its own systematic needs. We find this process first documented in Śabara's *Mīmāṃsābhāṣya*. In the works of Kumārila, it is much more conspicuous and pervasive. Yet in spite of his free and somewhat eclectic borrowing, Kumārila keeps his critical distance and draws his inspiration from other sources as well, including the Jaina perspectivism. He avoids the additive approach of the Vaiśeṣika and its reification of juxtaposable attributes. For him, all categories, including qualities and universals, remain embedded in the complex and ambiguous unity of the concrete thing (*vastu*, *piṇḍa*), the paradigm of reality. (OB, pp. 121-122)

In this paper I would like to elaborate on these statements in the light of the works of Kumārila Bhaṭṭa, the *Ślokavārttika* and the *Tantravārttika*.

1. Kumārila Bhaṭṭa (ca. 600-660[1]) was the founder of the Bhāṭṭa school, the mainstream school of Pūrva Mīmāṃsā, which was one of the six orthodox schools of brahmanical philosophy and which was established as a school especially concerned with the study of Vedic exegetics. He was, needless to say, one of the most prominent philosophers in the history of Indian philosophy. By his time, the first half of the seventh century A.D., the fundamental philosophical texts already existed, i.e., all the main philosophical *sūtras* and their commentaries, the *bhāṣyas*, of the orthodox schools, and the basic philosophical works of the heterodox schools of Buddhism and Jainism. It was very natural that Kumārila

wrote his main works, *Ślokavārttika* and *Tantravārttika*, using or borrowing the terminology of these earlier works, even though his purpose was to criticize the other philosophical systems from his standpoint as a Mīmāṃsā philosopher. In doing so, he often modified the terminology of the other schools in order to conform to the tenets and exegetics of the Mīmāṃsā school, which inevitably resulted in some distortion of the original usage.

As Halbfass states, we are able to point out some typical cases in Kumārila's use of the ontological terminology of the Vaiśeṣika school. In the *Mīmāṃsāsūtra* we find some terms which also appear in the Vaiśeṣika ontological vocabulary. Terms used for the categories of Vaiśeṣika ontology, i.e., *dravya* (substance), *guṇa* (quality), *karman* (action), *sāmānya* (universal), *viśeṣa* (particular), and *samavāya* (inherence), are employed in the *Mīmāṃsāsūtra* too, but with a different meaning than in Vaiśeṣika. *dravya*, for instance, which, as a Vaiśeṣika category, means "substance," usually denotes in the Mīmāṃsā exegetical *sūtras* either the material offered or the utensils used in the sacrifice. As a matter of course, Kumārila does not distort the Mīmāṃsā usages of these terms when he discusses problems special to Vedic exegetics. However, he follows the usage of the Vaiśeṣika school in the discourse of philosophical topics, especially in his *Ślokavārttika,* and in that of some non-philosophical topics in the *Tantravārttika*. He does not, however, always strictly adhere to the Vaiśeṣika understanding of these ontological terms. Apparently, after having become well-acquainted with Vaiśeṣika ontology, he modifies it in order to accommodate it to Mīmāṃsā theory. As we shall see later on, his originality as a philosopher manifests itself in the way this accommodation is carried out. In his theory of the universal I shall try to point out a typical instance of such an accommodation. Kumārila's method of modification and accommodation will be shown in regard to another case as well where other categories are under consideration. In this paper I intend to clarify his method of manipulating Vaiśeṣika categories and his success in accommodating them to Mīmāṃsā exegetics.

2. The problem of universals in the Mīmāṃsā school originated some centuries before the Christian era in the debate concerning the denotation of words, more precisely, nouns, which are part of the sacrificial injunctions (*vidhi*, *codanā*) in the Veda. According to the testimony of Kātyāyana's *Vārttika* (ca. third c. B.C.), critical notes on Pāṇini's

grammar, a scholar named Vājapyāyana argued that the nouns of the Vedic injunctions denote the universal form or genus (*ākṛti*). Vyāḍi, on the other hand, maintained that the word denotes an individual object (*dravya*).[2] On these *vārttikas*, Patañjali, the author of the *Great Commentary* (*Mahābhāṣya*) (ca. second c. B.C.), introduced long and detailed debates, which suggests that there already existed a Mīmāṃsā text before Patañjali's time in which the question as to the denotation of the word in Vedic injunctions had been discussed.[3] The *Ākṛti-adhikaraṇa*, the section on the topic of the universal form or genus in *MīS* 1.3.30-35, which summarizes the Mīmāṃsā positions on this issue, was apparently compiled on the basis of the debate presented by Kātyāyana and Patañjali. It is a recognized fact that although Kātyāyana supported Vājapyāyana, namely, the position that the universal is the denotation of words, Patañjali took an eclectic standpoint. Jaimini, said to be the author or compiler of the *Mīmāṃsāsūtra*, declared the Mīmāṃsaka position on this issue with the contention that it is the universal (*ākṛti*) which is denoted by the words in a Vedic injunction. The *siddhāntasūtra MīS* 1.3.33 clearly manifests this position: "But [it is] the universal form (or: genus) [that is denoted] because of its use in sacrificial acts" (*ākṛtis tu kriyārthatvāt*). However, the sacrificial acts or rituals enjoined in the Brāhmaṇa portions of the Veda are performed by using concrete materials, e.g., a sheep or a goat in the animal sacrifices (*paśubandha*), and rice, barley, etc., in sacrifices of the *iṣṭi* type.

Samples of Vedic sentences (*codanā, vidhi)* enjoining such sacrificial acts take the following form: "He sprinkles water on rice" (*vrīhīn prokṣati*), "He beats the rice" (*vrīhīn avahanti*), "He should take hold of (or: sacrifice) an animal" (*paśum ālabheta*), etc.[4] The words under consideration in these sentences are *vrīhi* (rice) and *paśu* (animal), i.e., the stems of nouns (*prātipadika*). Sacrificial actions have direct connections with concrete individual objects such as goats or rice. But do not words which denote such materials refer to the universal idea thereof? The *prima facie* view given in Śabara's commentary is that injunctions for such sacrificial acts as *ālambhana* (taking hold of an animal), *prokṣaṇa* (sprinkling water) and *viśasana* (cutting up an animal) cannot be realized if words denote the universal (*ākṛti*), for one cannot perform these sacrificial actions by using some universal form or genus which is an abstract entity.[5] Therefore, one can reasonably summarize the problem faced by the Mīmāṃsaka as follows: How does the universal form or genus, which he declares to be the denotation of the stem of a noun, fulfill its function and establish the relation to concrete individual objects, thereby becoming useful for the accomplishment of the sacrifice? The first problem to be solved is the relationship between the universal (*ākṛti*, *jāti*, *sāmānya*) and the individual, i.e., the concrete particular (*vyakti*). Prior to the elucidation of this problem, however, it is necessary for us to explain briefly the ideas of universal form (*ākṛti*) and individual (*vyakti*) in the Mīmāṃsā philosophy.

3. The word *ākṛti*, as already indicated by my translation, means a universal form belonging to many individuals which can be classified as belonging to one kind or genus. This notion of *ākṛti* in the Mīmāṃsā is opposed to that of other schools, such as the Nyāya, where it means *saṃsthāna*, that is, the external form of each individual which is different in each individual.[6] To be sure, as the word *ākṛti* has as its primary meaning "form," like the word *ākāra* (the form as an idea), we cannot completely eliminate some notion of form from the meaning of this word. However, Mīmāṃsā philosophers defined *ākṛti* as the universal *per se*. For instance, Śabarasvāmin (ca. 500-600) defines it as follows: "*ākṛti* is the universal *per se* of substances, attributes and actions."[7] Further, after refuting the notion of *ākṛti* as *saṃsthāna*, Kumārila declares it to be identical with *jāti* (genus) or *sāmānya* (universal).[8]

Thus, *ākṛti* is identified by Kumārila with the genus and the universal, irrespective of differences among individuals which belong to the same class. This *ākṛti* is considered to be imperishable and eternal (*nitya*), whereas individuals are perishable and therefore non-eternal (*anitya*). Another important point to be noted is that this *ākṛti*, which is a single universal residing in various individuals belonging to one class, is the denotation of the word. For instance, the word *go* (cow) denotes the *gotva* (cow-ness) which all individual cows equally possess. It is unnecessary to explain in detail this nature of *ākṛti*, since many scholars have already discussed the issue.[9] *ākṛti* may naturally be expected as well to denote a concept, i.e., a general idea, but we do not find anywhere in Mīmāṃsā literature such a usage. *ākṛti* is always used in the meaning of "universal" as something real which exists externally and is common to individuals belonging to the same class.

The word *vyakti* stands for the individual. Śabara refers to it as follows: "*vyakti* is that to which no common speciality belongs."[10] "It is said that *vyakti* is what is separated from all universals and specialities."[11]

It is the substrate (*āśraya*) of universal and specialities.[12] Thus, we understand that according to Śabara the concept of *vyakti* (individual) is similar to *hypokeímenon* or *tóde ti* in the philosophy of Aristotle.

4. To return to the main concern of this essay: How did Mīmāṃsā philosophers grasp the relation between *ākṛti* as universal or genus and *vyakti*, the individual? There is no explicit or even implicit reference to this issue in the *Mīmāṃsāsūtra*. However, we encounter the following commentary by Śabara on *MīS* 1.3.33:

> Because the *Universal* (*ākṛti*) is permanently related to the *Individual*; so that when the *Universal* (*ākṛti*), as the one relative, is cognized, the cognition of the other relative (*Individual*) would naturally follow.[13]

Thus Śabarasvāmin refers to the relation between *ākṛti* and *vyakti* as being permanent (*nitya*), but does not specify the kind of relation, i.e., whether it is inherence (*samavāya*), conjunction (*saṃyoga*), or some other relation. We may assume, however, that the relation in this case is inherence, for the relation of two things which are permanently related (*nityasambaddha*) must be inherence (*samavāya*).[14] Even if this would not be the case, we might consider the relation to be *āśrayāśrayibhāva*, the relation between substrate and what depends on this substrate, since according to Śabara, as I have already pointed out, one of the characteristics of the individual (*vyakti*) is to be the substrate (*āśraya*) of universals and specialties. This *āśraya-āśrayin* relation might correspond to the relation of *hypokeímenon* and *eîdos* in Aristotle's philosophy.

Kumārila's position in this question is discussed mainly in two chapters of his *Ślokavārttika*, *Ākṛtivāda* (The Chapter on *ākṛti*) and *Vanavāda* (The Chapter on the Forest).[15] In the third verse of the *Vanavāda*, Kumārila states that many genera beginning with being-ness (*sattā*) inhere in an individual (*piṇḍa*), such as a cow, and that *gotva* (cow-ness), the genus of the cow, is differentiated from the other genera inhering in it by the dewlap, etc.[16] In the light of this explanation it is reasonable to consider the relationship between genus and individual to be that of inherence (*samavāya*). It must, however, be noted here that the relation of *samavāya* in Kumārila's philosophy is not the same as the Vaiśeṣika category *samavāya*. In *ŚV Pratyakṣa* 146-150 Kumārila denies the notion of *samavāya* as involving *ayutasiddhi* (the relation between things which are essentially inseparable), which Vaiśeṣika philosophers consider as a necessary condition for the relation of *samavāya*.

Pārthasārathimiśra (1050-1120)[17], a scholar of the Bhāṭṭa school, defines the *samavāya* relation according to Bhāṭṭa Mīmāṃsā as follows:

> The relation of *samavāya* is that relation by which the *ādheya* (the dependent thing) produces an idea corresponding to itself in respect to the *ādhāra* (substratum), i.e., makes it known by its (the ādheya's) own form.[18]

This definition of *samavāya* by Pārthasārathimiśra would seem to be based on *ŚV Pratyakṣa* 141cd-142:

> *sthitaṃ naiva hi jātyādeḥ paratvaṃ vyaktito hi naḥ//*
> *yadi hy ekāntato bhinnaṃ viśeṣyāt syād viśeṣaṇam/*
> *svānurūpāṃ sadā buddhiṃ viśeṣye janayet katham//*

> We hold that the Universal (*jāti*) etc. are not totally different from the Individual. If the qualification were entirely different from the qualified, then, how could the qualification always produce, in respect to the qualified (object), a cognition precisely similar to itself?[19]

Needless to say, the qualification (*viśeṣaṇa*) and the qualified (*viśeṣya*) in this *kārikā* correspond to the *ādheya* and the *ādhāra* respectively in Pārthasārathi's definition, and they are here the universal and the individual respectively. Kumārila maintains in this *kārikā* that the relation between universal and individual occurs between two things which are *not absolutely different*. This assertion of Kumārila is, perhaps, based on ordinary experience, for instance when one forms a judgement about an individual animal such as "This is a cow," etc. In this judgement, "this" refers to an individual and "cow" to the universal; thus the two words refer to inseparable things which are *not absolutely different*. He further elaborates on this matter in *ŚV Ākṛtivāda* 10-11:

> *nirviśeṣaṃ na sāmānyaṃ bhavec chaśaviṣāṇavat/*
> *sāmānyarahitatvāc ca viśeṣās tadvad eva hi//*
> *tadanātmakarūpeṇa hetū vācyāv imau punaḥ/*
> *tena nātyantabhedo 'pi syāt sāmānyaviśeṣayoḥ//*

> A Universal (*sāmānya*) devoid of Individuals does not exist, (- because of the absence of Individuals) - like the horns of a hare. And in the same manner, because of the absence of Universal (*sāmānya*) there could be no Individuals (without a Universal). Or, these two premises may be mentioned in the forms "because one does not possess the character of the other." By this change, there ceases to exist the slightest difference between the Individual and the Universal (*sāmānya*).[20]

In *Ākṛtivāda* 9, Kumārila also refers to the relation between universal and individuals as a relation between two things which are *dependent on each other* (*anyonyāpekṣin*), inasmuch as one universal belongs to individuals of the same class and individuals of the same class to one universal. Further, in *Ākṛtivāda* 31cd Kumārila maintains that the relation between genus (*jāti*), the universal, and individual is a *relation belonging to their own nature* (*svābhāvikaḥ sambandhaḥ*) and as such is not caused by anything else (*na hetumān*). Thus, Kumārila concludes that the relation between universal and individuals which belong to the class possessing this universal is established by nature and that as such universal and individuals are inseparable and not absolutely different. Because their relation is natural, Kumārila does not ask for the reason as to why they stand inseparable. However, a question may be raised about this relation in terms of the nature of external objective things. Kumārila states in *Ākṛtivāda* 5:

> *sarvavastuṣu buddhiś ca vyāvṛttyanugamātmikā/*
> *jāyate dvyātmatvena vinā sā ca na sidhyati//*

> With regard to all objects there arises a double idea, in the shape of one consisting in its differentiation (as an individual apart from others), and another (a collective idea) consisting of its homogenity (with others resembling it in certain respects). And this double idea is not possible without the double character of the object (as an individual, and as belonging to a universal).[21]

Kumārila maintains here that when we perceive an external object, we recognize two aspects thereof: on the one hand a collective and universal one, and on the other a peculiar and differentiating one. Clearly this double idea corresponds to the cognition of *sāmānyalakṣaṇa* and *svalakṣaṇa* respectively in Dignāga's philosophy.[22] According to the philosophy of the Buddhist Dignāga, *sāmānyalakṣaṇa* is merely a construct (*kalpanā*) of our intellect, and thus not a real external object. The real thing *per se* is just *svalakṣaṇa*, the ultimate particular. Kumārila's position is diametrically opposed to Dignāga's. According to Kumārila, both aspects have real external existence. The point to be noted here is that for Kumārila our ideas must have their counterparts in the external objective world. This concept is common to the realist schools of Indian philosophy as opposed to the idealistic school of Buddhism. Kumārila summarizes in *Ākṛtivāda* 46-47 his concept of the relationship between these two aspects of external objects:

> *sāsnādibhyas tu piṇḍasya bhedo nātyantato yadā/*
> *sāmānyasya ca piṇḍebhyas tadā syād etad uttaram//*

*kasmāt sāsnādimatsv eva gotvaṃ yasmāt tadātmakam/*
*tādātmyam asya kasmāc cet svabhāvād iti gamyatām//*

And when there is no absolute difference between the dewlap, &c., and the individual *cow*, and again between the *Universal* "cow" and the Individuals (composing it), then the reply to the question - "how is it that (the *Universal*) 'cow-ness' applies only to the objects endowed with the dewlap, &c.?" - would be that it does so simply because the Universal consists of the (Individual) (endowed with the dewlap, &c.). Then as for the question - "What is the reason of this fact?"[23] - you must understand that it lies in the very nature (of the Universal and the Individuals composing it).[24]

In verse 46 above, Kumārila refers to two kinds of *atyantabhedābhāva* (non-absolute-difference): on the one hand between a part of a cow (dewlap, etc.,) and the individual cow, and on the other between universal and individual, in spite of the mutual differences between the members composing each set. As previously stated, *ākṛti* or *jāti* is considered by Mīmāṃsā philosophers to be imperishable and permanent (*nitya*) as the meaning of a word (*śabdārtha*), whereas individual things are ephemeral and perishable and thus impermanent (*anitya*). Although they are certainly different entities, Kumārila contends that they are not absolutely different (*atyantabhedābhāva*). Having ascertained his position about the relation between universal and individual, we can also understand why the universal *gotva* (cow-ness) is present just in individual cows which have a dewlap, etc., as the differentiating factors of a genus (verse 47a): it is due to the fact that the genus *gotva* has its existence through individual cows and vice versa (*tadātmaka*) (47b). As to the inquiry regarding the basis for this fact (47c) Kumārila answers that it is due to nature (*svabhāvāt*) (47d). Kumārila thus comes to the conclusion that universal and individual are, despite their differences, in a relation of *atyantabhedābhāva* (non-absolute-difference). In other words, their relation is a relation of *tādātmya*, i.e., each has by nature its existence through the other. This conclusion regarding the relation between universal and individual becomes the starting point of an argument in the *Ākṛti-adhikaraṇa* of the *Tantravārttika*.

5. Before we scrutinize the discussion in the *Ākṛti-adhikaraṇa*, there is another important issue to be examined. It is the problem of the universal on a higher level, in other words, the problem of the existence of such universals as thing-ness (*vastutva*) or being-ness (*sattā*).

As already pointed out, Kumārila mentions in *Vanavāda* 3 that many genera beginning with being-ness (*sattā*) inhere in an individual and that, in the case of a cow, the genus *gotva* (cow-ness) is distinguished by the dewlap, etc., which are the characteristics of the genus *gotva*. Although it may be reasonable, according to this verse, to consider that Kumārila recognises the real existence of *sattā*, etc., the universals on a higher or the highest level, this is problematic for the following reason: Kumārila takes up this question for discussion in *Ākṛtivāda* 19-25 and comes to the conclusion that they are merely denotations of words and therefore just nominally existent. For instance, the highest universal, being-ness (*sattā*), is the denotation of the word *sat* ("being"), and thus does not have real existence in the objective external world (*Ākṛtivāda* 21cd-23).

Although Kumārila often refers to the existence of other universals on a higher level as well, it is just the first-level universal, e.g., the universal *gotva* (cow-ness), that he regards as really existing. This being the case, even the existence of universals of such things as a forest (*vana*), a row (*paṅkti*), and a flock (*yūtha*), which are the denotations of words under consideration in the *Vanavāda* of the *Ślokavārttika*, becomes dubious for Kumārila, because they are merely composites of other real things, e.g., trees in the case of the forest. The fact that he regards just the first-level universal as really existing should be relevant to the question as to how *ākṛti* becomes *kriyārtha* (object of actions) in the *Ākṛti-adhikaraṇa* of the *Tantravārttika*. Kumārila discusses the question of the highest universal *sattā* (being-ness) or *vastutva* (thing-ness) in the *Ākṛti-adhikaraṇa* too, but, unlike in the *Ślokavārttika*, he deals with it in the context of the problem of the denotation of words. In *TV* pp. 239.1-242.18 (= pp. 291.1-300.5) Kumārila adduces negative arguments against *sattā* (being-ness) as the meaning of a word, quoting Bhartṛhari's *VP* 2.119 and referring to *VS* 1.2.7. Although it is unnecessary to go into the details of this argument, the following two points should be noted here:

1. The word *go* (cow) denotes the universal *gotva* (cow-ness), for the denotative power (*vācakaśakti*) of each word is determined to denote a definite object, which is recognized by an inference from circumstances (*arthāpatti*).

2. No other words except the word *sat* (being) denote the universal *sattā* (being-ness). If all words equally denote the highest universal *sattā*,

as the Vedāntin affirms, it is a natural consequence that they become synonyms, which is absurd and contrary to our ordinary experience.

6. Thus we have obtained access to the main theme of this essay: How should we understand the denotation of the noun, more precisely, of the genus-word (*jātiśabda*), in the injunctive sentences of the Veda? The answer of the Mīmāṃsaka is that we should apprehend the universal rice-ness (*vrīhitva*) directly from the word "rice" (*vrīhi*) in injunctions such as "He sprinkles water on rice" (*vrīhīn prokṣati*) or "He beats the rice" (*vrīhīn avahanti*). It denotes neither such higher universals as thing-ness (*vastutva*) or being-ness (*sattā*) nor the individual rice which is pointed out as "this" or "that" (*tóde ti*). The universal rice-ness (*vrīhitva*), however, exists only in the individual rice (*vrīhivyakti*), while at the same time individual instances of rice (*vrīhivyakti*) cannot but have their existence through the universal rice-ness (*vrīhitva*) because, as pointed out above, there is no absolute difference (*atyantabhedābhāva*) between the two or because they are in the relation of *tādātmya*. Consequently, sacrificial actions such as *yāga* (sacrificing), *prokṣaṇa* (sprinkling water), *avahanana* (beating), etc., can be performed by utilizing individual materials such as rice, etc., that bear within themselves particular universals.

Kumārila's assertion that there is no absolute difference between universal and individual (*atyantabhedābhāva*, *anatyantavyatireka*) is further explicated in the context of sacrificial actions:

> And as for the objection that the Universal (*ākṛti*) ("Corn" for instance) being incorporeal, it could not be *washed* or *threshed* (as laid down in Vedic Injunctions), – the Universal is not altogether distinct from the Individual; and as such the said objections are not quite applicable. As a matter of fact, what is denoted by the word is the Universal itself; while in the case of any Actions spoken of with reference to any object, what is denoted is the Universal as impressed by (or contained in) the Individual; and hence the actions of *washing*, &c., cannot be altogether impossible.[25]

Kumārila further explains:

> If the Universal were something totally different from the Individual, it could never form the subject of any Injunction with regard to Dharma; because the Universal "Animal" being incorporeal could never form such a subject. And as for the substance qualified by the Universal "animal," inasmuch as this substance itself could not be cognised without the Universal "substance" (in which the Universal "Animal" also inheres), the substance must be accepted as indicated (by the Universal "Animal"), because both are found to inhere in a single substratum

(the Universal "Substance"), and also because the Universal "Substance" contains within itself the Universal "Animal." But even then, the Universal "substance" also being incorporeal, the aforesaid objection continues to be effective.[26]

As regards the above *Tantravārttika* passage, if one maintains, like the opponent, that universal and individual are absolutely different, a solution must be found for the problem of the relation between the denotation of words and sacrifical actions. The solution the opponent suggests is that the universal which is denoted by the word in the injunctive sentence *indicates* (*upa-√lakṣ*) individuals to be used in the sacrifical action. In other words, he views as problematic the following: The genus animal-ness (*paśutva*), like all universals, is incorporeal (*amūrta*) and cannot become the object of an action, i.e., it cannot be the object of an injunction. However, if a corporeal material (*dravya*) is indicated (*upa-√lakṣ*) by the word *paśu* (animal) in the injunction *paśuṃ viśāsti* ("He cuts up an animal"), the indicated material *paśu* would become the object of the injunction, that is, it would become the material useful for the action of *viśasana* (cutting up an animal for the sacrifice). There would seem to be no inconsistency in the opinion of the opponent. Kumārila, however, rejects this opinion, but without giving any reasons. Someśvara, in his commentary *Nyāyasudhā* on the *Tantravārttika*, explains that there arises the same error in that case too, for the universal *dravyatva* (material-ness), which is also incorporeal (*amūrta)*, must be made understood before the *dravya* (material) is understood as such by the *indication* (*upalakṣaṇa*) through the universal *paśutva*.[27] Therefore the argument adduced by the opponent that the universal denoted by the word indicates the individual cannot be established.

Kumārila describes another difficulty which will be encountered if one supposes an absolute difference between universal and individual. It concerns sentences such as *gauḥ śuklaḥ* ("The cow is white"), which contain the relationship of words bearing the same case ending (*sāmānādhikaraṇya*). He makes the following statement: "And further the *sāmānādhikaraṇya*, etc., comes to be supposed by the indication (*lakṣaṇā*), which is contrary to the general opinion."[28] To explain, the two words *gauḥ* (the nominative "cow") and *śuklaḥ* (the nominative "white") in the sentence *gauḥ śuklaḥ* refer to an individual cow which is white. If universal and individual were absolutely different and words denoted universals, we would have to understand the individual cow (*govyakti*) by way of indication (*lakṣaṇā*) by the universal cow-ness (*gotva*) denoted by the word "cow" (*gauḥ*). In ordinary experience, we certainly recognise such an instance of *sāmānādhikaraṇya*, as in the sentence *gauḥ śuklaḥ,* without any help from an indirect implication, which proves, according to Kumārila, the *atyantabhedābhāva* between universal and individual.[29]

7. Now, in *MīS* 1.3.34, arguments of the opponent are introduced. The entire text of *sūtra* 34 runs thus: *na kriyā syād iti ced arthāntare vidhānaṃ na dravyam iti cet*. This *sūtra* summarizes the opponent's arguments in two parts, i.e., (1) *na kriyā syāt* and (2) *arthāntare vidhānaṃ na dravyam*. The purport of the first argument is apparent from the literal meaning of the text itself: the sacrificial action (which is enjoined by the scripture) would not be realized (*na kriyā syāt*) [if words denoted universals]. Although the purport of the second, on the other hand, is rather vague, it may be understood as follows: when there is an injunction of another object [as a substitute in an emergency, if words denoted universals], there could not be [any word denotative of] the individual material.

Against these arguments of the opponent we read the following *siddhāntasūtra* 1.3.35: *tadarthatvāt prayogasyāvibhāgaḥ*. Explaining the pronoun *tad* in this *sūtra* as *ākṛti* , Śabara interprets it as follows:

> As the word denotes the *ākṛti*, the performance [of the sacrificial action] is [possible] with the individual which is in relation to the *ākṛti*, the universal.[30]

The exact nature of the relation (*sambandha*) between *ākṛti* and *vyakti* according to Śabara remains unclear. After the explanation of this *sūtra*, Śabara refers to the relation between the sacrificial action (*kriyā*) and the individual material (*dravya*), and further to the significance of *ākṛti*, the universal, which is the denotation of the word. First of all, Śabara comments on the sprinkling of water (*prokṣaṇa*) on rice as the material for sacrificial cakes (*puroḍāśa*) as follows:

> For instance, in the case of the sentence "sprinkles water on rice" (*vrīhīn prokṣati*) what is enjoined as to be done is the *sprinkling with water*, of a certain substance; - over which substance? - over that substance which is conducive to the accomplishment of the sacrifice; because the *sprinkling* is for the purpose of bringing about a transcendental result. The *sprinkling* could not be enjoined as to be done over the *Universal*, because no sprinkling of a *Universal* would be possible.[31]

8. Thus arises the next question as to the *significance* (*artha*), that is, the *utility* or *use* of the universal (*ākṛti*, *jāti*) which is the denotation of words. It seems to be a curious and superfluous question for us, but it must have been the most important problem in the exegetical tradition of the Mīmāṃsā. Śabara answers as follows:

> So what happens in this case is that the word "*Vrīhi*," which is really expressive of the *Universal* (*ākṛti*), is used for the purpose of qualifying (indicating) the receptacle of the action of sprinkling water: and the word will naturally denote the *Universal* (*ākṛti*), and this Universal (*ākṛti*), on being cognised, would qualify (and indicate) the receptacle of the action of *sprinkling water*. Thus there would be nothing incongruous in regarding the Word as denoting the *Universal* (*ākṛti*).[32]

Thus Śabara maintains that the function of the universal rice-ness (*vrīhitva*), which is cognized by the word *vrīhīn* in the injunction *vrīhīn prokṣati*, is to qualify (*vi-√śiṣ*) rice (*vrīhi*) as the material (*dravya*) which becomes the receptacle of the action of sprinkling. Śabara finishes his commentary on *sūtra* 35 after pointing out that this function as "the qualification [of the material] as the receptacle of action" (*āśrayaviśeṣaṇa*) of the universal (*ākṛti*) can be applied to instances of the universal denoted by the two words *gāvaḥ* ("cows") and *paśum* in the two injunctions *ṣaḍ deyā gāvo dakṣiṇāḥ* ("Six cows should be given as the sacrificial fee"; i.e., an injunction of the sacrificial fee, *dakṣiṇā*) and *anyam* (*paśum*) *ālabheta* ("One should sacrifice another animal"; i.e., an injunction of a substitute, *pratinidhi*) respectively. These two injunctions have been quoted in the *Śābarabhāṣya* on *MīS* 1.3.31 and 32 (*pūrvapakṣasūtras*) respectively, though not verbatim, as supports for the opponent who maintains that the individual is the denotation of words (*vyaktivādin*).

It can be said that the function of the universal (*ākṛti*), the qualification of the receptacle of action, means nothing but the operation to determine or to restrict the material for the sacricial action to one particular kind. By using the term *niyama* ("restriction"), Kumārila interprets Śabara's words to mean "its (the universal's) denotation is for the sake of the restriction of materials" (*tadabhidhānaṃ tu dravyaniyamārtham*). Kumārila thus specifies the utility of the universal denoted by the word and expounds it further to the effect that the denotation of the universal is not for the sake of the universal itself (*na svārtham*). He adduces three reasons for this:

(1) because a cognition of the Universal by itself is not what is sought after (*jāter anapekṣitatvāt*); (2) because in that case a denotation of the Universal alone would have only a transcendental result (*adṛṣṭārthatvaprasaṅgāt*); and (3) because, being incorporeal, it is not found capable of helping the sacrifice in any way (*sādhanatvāpratīteḥ*).[33]

On the basis of these three reasons Kumārila concludes that the universal itself is not helpful for the action. Further, he denies that the primary function of the universal in the sacrificial action is to be the direct instrument (*karaṇa*) of the sacrifice:

Even in a case when the Universal as signified by a basic noun is recognised as the means of performing a sacrifice (as in "*Somena yajeta*"), it is recognised only as pointing to a definite Substance (*dravyaniyāmaka*), and not to itself independently, as by itself it is of no particular use in the performance of the sacrifice.[34]

It goes without saying that Kumārila's expression (*dravya-)niyāmaka* corresponds to (*āśraya-)viśeṣaka* in *ŚBh*, p. 267.6 (= p. 319.13), which demonstrates Kumārila's meticulous attitude in avoiding careless use of the word *viśeṣaka* which has some ontological connotations.[35]

Unlike Śabara, who interprets the opening word *tad* of the *MīS* 1.3.35 (*tadarthatvāt prayogasyāvibhāgaḥ*) as referring to *ākṛti*, Kumārila takes it as referring to *apūrva* (transcendental result)[36]. He explains the first half of this *sūtra* as follows:

All actions of *washing*, *killing*, &c., being performed for the sake of certain transcendental results, their performance must be taken as part of the means of the accomplishment of such results.[37]

Śabara does not seem to explain the word *avibhāgaḥ* in *sūtra* 35. Kumārila, however, gives five interpretations of this word, together with the preceding word *prayogasya*:

Thus then, the denotation of the Universal (*ākṛti* ) restricting to a definite Substance (*dravyaniyama*), and the Substance being quite capable of being related to the actions of *killing*, *washing*, &c., as also to Genders, Numbers and Cases, - there is nothing that can be urged against our theory. It is with a view to this that the *Sūtra* says - *there is no disjunction*.[38]

Out of the five interpretations of the phrase *prayogasyāvibhāgaḥ* the third and the fourth are the most interesting and important in our context:

... (3) there being no absolute difference between the Universal (*ākṛti*) and the Individual, the Substance is pointed out, at times in the form of the Individual, and at others, in that of the Universal, in accordance with the wish of the speaker; and as such words being found to denote both forms of things, even when the Individual is denoted (by the word), it does not necessitate any multiplicity in the performance of the action; or (4) the Universal (*jāti*) not being totally different from the Individual, the sacrifices performed with reference to the Individual may be accepted as performed with reference to the Universal (*jāti*) also, and *vice versa*; and thus in no case is it necessary to make any difference in the performance of Actions (or Sacrifices).[39]

Thus Kumārila contends that the performance of sacrificial actions can be accomplished only according to the theory that the universal is the denotation of the word. It has become apparent here that behind this theory there has been a scrupulous examination of the relation between universal and individual, undertaken by Kumārila in the *Ślokavārttika*.

9. Thus far I have mainly followed Kumārila's explication of the Mīmāṃsā theory that the universal (*ākṛti*, *jāti*, and *sāmānya*), denoted by the words in injunctive sentences, becomes useful for actions (*kriyārtha*). The core of his interpretation, i.e., that there is no absolute difference (*atyantabhedābhāva* or *anatyantavyatireka*) between universal and individual, is inconsistent with the ontology of the Nyāya and Vaiśeṣika school. Therefore, we are dealing here with a creative application of Vaiśeṣika categories, in this case consisting of fusion between substance (*dravya*) and universal (*sāmānya*).

I would like to point out another instance of such an adaptive manipulation of Vaiśeṣika categories by Kumārila. It is also an instance of confounding categories, at least from the Nyāya and Vaiśeṣika point of view, and in this case of substance (*dravya*) and action (*kriyā*). In his *Tantravārttika* on *MīS* 2.1.5 Kumārila discusses the problem of how a transcendental result (*apūrva*), which is supposed to be a kind of a potency (*śakti*, *yogyatā*) that arises from Vedic sacrifices, continues after the sacrifice:

It may be asked - "How can the potency of that which has been destroyed subsist?" But to this we make the following reply: If the potencies of actions were held to lie within themselves, then on the destruction of these, they could not subsist; but when they inhere in the soul of the performer, there is no reason why they should not subsist.[40]

Kumārila tries in this way to guarantee the continuity of the *apūrva* after the destruction of a sacrifice, interpreting it as inhering in the soul (*ātman*) of the performer of the sacrifice (*kartṛ* = *yajamāna*). Further, he poses the question: "But how can the potency of one thing inhere in another?"[41] The purport of this question is as follows: the potency *apūrva*, which is supposed to originate from sacrificial actions, should naturally be a potency inhering in these actions themselves; therefore it is problematic that the *apūrva* should inhere in the soul (*ātman*) of the performer.[42]

To this question Kumārila gives two answers, the first of which is relevant to the concerns of this paper: "There is no absolute difference between the Action and the Soul of the performer" (*na, kriyātmanor atyantabhedābhāvāt*).[43] Here Kumārila uses the same expression, i.e., *atyantabhedābhāva*, he used in the case of the relation between universal and individual, where he tried to eliminate the rigid partition of Vaiśeṣika categories. Needless to say, action (*kriyā*) and soul (*ātman*) are to be included in the Vaiśeṣika categories *karman* (action) and *dravya* (substance) respectively. According to Vaiśeṣika philosophy, they are absolutely different and should not be confounded. But what is the exact purport of *atyantabhedābhāva* between action and soul? Kumārila does not give any further explanation. I would like, therefore, to venture a conjecture as to his understanding, aided by a clue from Someśvara's commentary.

Someśvara first refers to a principle (*nyāya*), formulated by Kumārila himself[44], to the effect that the denotation of the word "action" (*vyāpāra*) is nothing but the substance (*dravya*) accompanied by a particular potency. He traces Kumārila's assertion of *atyantabhedābhāva* between action and soul back to this *nyāya*.[45] It implies that action (*kriyā*) cannot be absolutely different from substance (*dravya*); consequently, the potency which originates from sacrifical actions would equally be a potency of the soul (*ātman*), which is a substance. Therefore there is no inconsistency in regarding the potency (*apūrva*) produced by a sacrifice as a potency which belongs to the soul (*ātman*) of the performer.

Thus the case of *atyantabhedābhāva* (non-absolute-difference) between action and soul is also a deviation from the rigid use of Vaiśeṣika categories. For Kumārila, however, these deviations are modifications of the Vaiśeṣika ontology which serve to accommodate it to the exegetics of the Mīmāṃsā school.

It has been pointed out that the equivalent expressions *atyantabhedābhāva* or *anatyantavyatireka*, which seem to show the elasticity and flexibility of Kumārila's thinking, are a key to the modification of Vaiśeṣika categories. As I have indicated above in the instance of the relation of inherence (*samavāya*), the theoretical reasons thereof are demonstrated by Kumārila himself in *ŚV Pratyakṣa* 141-150. Kumārila explains in these verses that there is no absolute difference between substance (*dravya*) and universal, etc., (*jātyādi*) which are in the relation of inherence (*samavāya*); but this relation is expounded by him differently than it is within the Vaiśeṣika school. It is probable that etc., (*ādi*) in the word *jātyādi* implies quality (*guṇa*) and action (*kriyā*) which are, like the universal, in the relation of inherence with the substance.[46]

Another point to be noted is the following. It is evident that Kumārila tried to settle the debates of Grammarians and Mīmāṃsakas concerning the denotation of words in the Vedic injunctions which Kātyāyana and Patañjali, about seven hundreds years earlier, had recorded.[47] He must have been convinced of his success in modifying Vaiśeṣika categories. In the history of Mīmāṃsā philosophy after Kumārila, however, his notion of *atyantabhedābhāva* (non-absolute-difference) is modified into *bhedābheda* and gives rise to new discussions. These new developments are evidenced in the *Prakaraṇapañcikā* of Śālikanāthamiśra (between 800-950)[48] and *Śāstradīpikā* of Pārthasārathimiśra.[49] There may be other instances of this notion being used in the attempt to modify Vaiśeṣika categories which remain to be investigated.

*Saga Medical School*
*Saga, Japan*

## NOTES

[1] Cf. Kunjunni Raja 1968, p. 223; Verpoorten (1987, p. 22) settles Kumārila's time between 600-700 A.D.

[2] Cf. *vārttikas* 35 and 45 on *P* 1.2.64.

[3] Cf. Frauwallner 1960, p. 92ff.

[4] Although Śabara and other Mīmāṃsakas quote these sentences as samples of *vidhi*, I cannot identify these sentences either in the Vedic sources, the Saṃhitās and Brāhmaṇas, or in the Śrautasūtras. I think these sentences are inventions by the Mīmāṃsakas as models for *vidhis* of particular sacrificial actions. The indications of sources for these sentences by Agravala (1985) seem to be dubious.

[5] *ŚBh*, p. 242.1-2 on *MīS* 1.3.30 (= p. 300.1-2 in the edition of 1929): *ālambhana-prokṣaṇaviśasanādīnāṃ prayogacodanā ākṛtyarthe na sambhaveyuḥ.*

[6] Cf. *NS* 2.2.66: *ākṛtir jātiliṅgākhyā.* "Die Form nennt man Merkmal des Genus" (Ruben 1928, p. 57).

[7] *ŚBh*, p. 235.2-3 on *MīS* 1.3.30 (= p. 294.2-3): *dravyaguṇakarmaṇāṃ sāmānyamātram ākṛtiḥ.*

[8] *ŚV Ākṛtivāda* 3:

*jātim evākṛtiṃ prāhur vyaktir ākriyate yayā/*
*sāmānyaṃ tac ca piṇḍānām ekabuddhinibandhanam//*

Cf. also *TV*, p. 237.8-24 (= p. 295.20-296.6).

[9] Bhatt 1962, pp. 405-420; Biardeau 1964a, pp. 162ff; D'Sa 1980, p. 80 and *passim.*

[10] *ŚBh*, p. 237.1 on *MīS* 1.3.10 (= p. 296.1): *asādhāraṇaviśeṣā vyaktiḥ.*

[11] *ŚBh*, p. 246.13 on *MīS* 1.3.33 (= p. 303.11): *sarvasāmānyaviśeṣavinirmuktā hi vyaktir ity ucyate.*

[12] *ŚBh*, p. 247.2-3 on *MīS* 1.3.11 (= p. 303.14-15): *yo hy arthaḥ sāmānyasya viśeṣāṇāṃ cāśrayaḥ sā vyaktiḥ.*

[13] *ŚBh*, p. 248,7-8 (= p. 304.14-15): *ākṛtir hi vyaktyā nityasambaddhā, sambandhinyāṃ ca tasyām avagatāyāṃ sambandhyantaram avagamyate.* The translation is taken from Jhā 1973, p. 122. - I utilized translations of *Śābarabhāṣya*, *Ślokavārttika* and *Tantravārttika* by Gangānātha Jhā as far as possible. However, I changed "Class," which Jhā consistently used as a translation for the three Sanskrit words *ākṛti*, *jāti*, and *sāmānya*, into "universal," in which case I placed the original word in parentheses. To my mind "class" signifies the idea of a group or a collection whose members equally possess a certain common trait, the universal (*sāmānya*).

[14] Cf. *Tarkasaṅgraha*, p. 79: *nityasambandhaḥ samavāyaḥ.*

[15] In the following exposition I am greatly indebted to Takenaka 1972.

[16] *ŚV Vanavāda* 3:

*piṇḍe sattādijātīnāṃ bahvīnāṃ samavetatā/*
*tābhyo viśiṣyate gotvaṃ sāsnādibhir asaṃśayam//*

[17] Cf. Verpoorten 1987, p. 41.

[18] *Śāstradīpikā*, p. 100.12-13: *yena sambandhenādheyam ādhāre svānurūpāṃ buddhiṃ janayati, svākāreṇa bodhayatīty arthaḥ, sa sambandhaḥ samavāya iti.*

[19] Jha 1983a, p. 93, partly changed.

[20] Jha 1983a, p. 283.

[21] Jha 1983a, p. 282, partly changed.

[22] Cf. Hattori 1968, p. 76, n. 1.9 (3); *Nyāyabindu* 1.12-17.

[23] Jha translates *tādātmya* as "identity." I think, however, that this translation is misleading. The word *tādātmya* means in this case the fact that the universal consists of individuals; with "this fact" I refer to this situation.

[24] Jha 1983a, p. 289, partly changed.

[25] *TV* on *MīS* 1.3.33, p. 248.22-23 (= p. 304.28-29): *anatyantavyatirekāc cākṛter amūrtatvādyāśrayadoṣāprasaṅgaḥ. sā hi pratīyate niṣkṛṣṭarūpā, kriyāyoginī tu vyaktyupetā bhavaty eveti prokṣaṇādi tu na kathaṃcin na saṃbhavati.* The translation follows Jha 1983b, p. 344.

[26] *TV* on *MīS* 1.3.33, p. 249.8-11 (= 305.9-11): *atyantavyatireke tu naiva dharmavidhiviṣayo vyavatiṣṭheta. na ca paśutvam amūrtatvāt. tadupalakṣitaṃ tu yad dravyaṃ tad dravyatvād ṛte na tādrūpyeṇa gamyata ity ekārthasamavāyād vyāpakatvāc ca dravyaṃ gamayitavyam, tatrāpy amūrtatve doṣaḥ.* The translation follows Jha 1983b, p. 345.

[27] *NSu*, p. 366.4-5: *dravyarūpatāyā dravyatvapratipādanaṃ vinā pratipādayitum aśaktes tad eva pratipādyaṃ syāt tatra ca sa eva doṣa ity arthaḥ.* (I read *śaktes* in the printed text as *aśaktes*.)

[28] *TV*, p. 249.15-16 (= p. 305.15-16): *sāmānādhikaraṇyādi ca prasiddhiviparītaṃ lakṣaṇayā kalpyam.*

[29] Cf. *NSu*, p. 366.29-31: *atyantavyatirekapakṣe ca gauḥ śukla iti sāmānādhikaraṇyaṃ paśuneti liṅgakārakasaṅkhyānvayaś ca lakṣaṇayā syāt sā ca loke mukhyatvaprasiddher ayuktā.*

[30] *ŚBh*, p. 266.13 (= p. 319.7): *ākṛtyarthatvāc chabdasya yasyā vyakter ākṛtyā saṃbandhas tatra prayogaḥ.*

[31] *ŚBh*, p. 267.1-2 (= p. 319.8-9): *prokṣaṇaṃ hi dravyasya kartavyatayā śrūyate. katamasya? yad yajatisādhanam. apūrvaprayuktatvāt tasya nākṛteḥ, aśakyatvāt.* The translation follows Jha 1973, p. 124.

[32] *ŚBh*, p. 267.2-5 (= p. 319.9-12): *tatra vrīhiśabda ākṛtivacanaḥ prayujyate prokṣaṇāśrayaviśeṣaṇāya. sa hy ākṛtiṃ pratyāyayiṣyati, ākṛtiḥ pratītā satī prokṣaṇāśrayaṃ viśekṣyatīti. tenākṛtivacanaṃ na virudhyata iti.* The translation partly modifies Jha 1973, p. 124.

[33] Jha 1983b, p. 371.

[34] *TV*, p. 267.10-12 (= 319.21-22): *yad api jāteḥ prātipadikābhihitāyāḥ karaṇatvaṃ pratīyate tad api dravyaniyāmakatvenaiva na sākṣād ayogyatvāt.* The translation is from Jha 1983b, p. 371.

[35] Someśvara further transforms *dravyaniyāmaka* into *dravyaviśeṣāvacchedaka*, which must be due to Navya-Nyāya influence; cf. *NSu*, p. 388.25.

[36] On *apūrva* see TR, p. 300ff.

[37] *TV*, p. 266.21-267.8 (= p. 319.18-19): *apūrvārthatvād ālambhanaprokṣaṇādyaṅgānām apūrvasādhane prayogena bhavitavyam.* The translation is taken from Jha 1983b, p. 371.

[38] *TV*, p. 267.12-13 (= p. 319.22-24): *tenākṛtyabhidhānasya dravyaniyamārthatvād dravye cālambhanaprokṣaṇasaṅkhyākārakasāmānādhikaraṇyādisaṃbhavād aduṣṭatā. tad āha prayogasyāvibhāga iti.* The translation partly follows Jha 1983b, pp. 371-372.

[39] *TV*, p. 267.15-19 (= p. 319.25-29): *yad vā, ākṛtivyaktyor atyantabhedābhāvāt kadācid vyaktirūpeṇa dravyam abhidhīyate kadācit sāmānyarūpeṇa yathā vivakṣitaṃ tathā śabdasyobhayarūpavastvarthatvād vyaktyabhidhāne 'pi na prayogasya vibhāgo nānārūpateti. jāter vā vyaktito 'tyantabhedābhāvād vyaktau kṛtā dharmā jātau kṛtā eva bhavatīti na prayogasya vibhāgena prayojanam iti.* The translation follows Jha 1983b, p. 372.

[40] *TV*, p. 369.12-15 (= p. 398.2-6): *kathaṃ vinaṣṭasya karmaṇaḥ śaktis tiṣṭhatīti cet, atrābhidhīyate –*

*yadi svasamavetaiva śaktir iṣyeta karmaṇām/*
*tadvināśe tato na syāt kartṛsthā tu na naśyati//*

The translation follows Jha 1983b, p. 511.

[41] *TV*, p. 369.15 (= p. 398.6): *katham anyaśaktir anyatra samavaitīti cet* (Jha 1983b, p. 511).

[42] Cf. TR, p. 304.

[43] The translation follows Jha 1983b, p. 511.

[44] *TV* on *MīS* 2.1.1, p. 341.22-342.2 (= p. 376.29-377.2; the reprint drops one line of the text): "And the word '*vyāpāra*' ('action') signifies only a particular substance, endowed with peculiar potencies, moved in its pristine character, having a mixed nature, having an existence in the past and in the future, – as moved from its former position and not reached the next. And in the case of some Verbs it is the agent himself that is cognised as being in this position,, while in that of others, where the Agent is a well-established entity, it is something else" (*dravyam eva ca viśiṣṭaśaktyupetaṃ pracalitātmatattvaṃ viprakīrṇasvabhāvaṃ pūrvāparībhūtaṃ prathamāvasthātaḥ pracyutaṃ parām avasthām aprāptaṃ vyāpāraśabdavācyaṃ bhavati. tatra kadācit kartaivamavasthaḥ pratīyate, kadācit siddhe kartary anyaḥ*; translation in Jha 1983b, p. 476). See also Frauwallner 1938, p. 226.

[45] *NSu*, p. 605.10-13: *dravyam eva viśiṣṭaśaktyupetaṃ vyāpāraśabdavācyaṃ bhavatīty anenanyāyenakriyātmanoratyantabhedābhāvenātmasamavetasyāpūrvasyakriyāto 'tyantabhedābhāvāt sādhyasādhanasambandhopapādakatvaṃ sambhavatīty āśayena pariharati.* Cf. also *Ajitā*, p. 8.22-23: *kartur avasthā kriyā tasyāḥ śaktiḥ kartur eva bhavati. ato nānyasamavāya iti.*

[46] Cf. *NSu*, p. 554,18-19: *jātiguṇavat kriyāyā 'pi dravyād atyantavyatirekābhāvān na vyatirekānupalambhamātreṇābhāvo bhavati ...* .

[47] *TV*, p. 251.11-12 (= p. 306.27-28):

*prayogasya pratīteś ca tulyatvāc chabdalakṣaṇe/*
*vyaktipakṣābhidhānāc ca saṃśayaḥ pratibhāti naḥ//*

Cf. *NSu*, p.369.32f.: *śabdalakṣaṇe mahābhāṣyakāreṇa kiṃ punar ākṛtiḥ padārtha āho svid dravyam iti pṛṣṭvā ubhayam ity āhety ākṛtipakṣavad vyaktipakṣasyāpy abhidhānān na śāstrasyāpy ubhayatra tulyateti dvedhā sandehahetum āha*. See also *TV*, p. 257.13-14 (= p. 312.2): *śāstrāntare vyaktipakṣābhyupagamāt saṃśayaḥ.*

[48] Cf. Verpoorten 1987, p. 38.

[49] *Prakaraṇapañcikā*, p. 63.4-5: *apare tu bhinnābhinnām icchanti*; p. 93.7-8: *yac ca piṇḍebhyo jāter abhinnatvam ubhayarūpatvañ ca dūṣitam, tad asmākaṃ sāhāyakam evācaritam*. Cf. also *Śāstradīpikā*, pp. 100-101.

Victoria Lysenko

# THE VAIŚEṢIKA NOTIONS OF *ĀKĀŚA* AND *DIŚ* FROM THE PERSPECTIVE OF INDIAN IDEAS OF SPACE

I.1. In "The Vaiśeṣika Concept of Time" (OB, pp. 205-228) Wilhelm Halbfass arrives at the conclusion, among others, that in Vaiśeṣika "time is marginalized and superseded ... by being raised to the status of an eternal and 'timeless' substance" (OB, p. 221). But what is the status of an eternal and "timeless" substance with regard to the other two important entries in the Vaiśeṣika list of substances, that is, *ākāśa* and *diś*, each of which has been rather often associated with "space" in the vocabulary of Western interpretations of Indian thought?

As the Vaiśeṣikas interpreted time (*kāla*), *ākāśa* and *diś* with the help of practically one and the same explanatory scheme, I have considered the three to account for the unitary spatio-temporal framework of the Vaiśeṣika universe (Lysenko 1988). In the *Padārthadharmasaṅgraha* of Praśastapāda, all three are referred to as typologically affined, since they have the same status of omnipresent or all-pervasive (*vibhu, sarvagata*) partless substances characterized by "unity" (*ekatva*), "the absence of the lower genera" (*aparajātyabhāva*), "eternity" (*nityatva*), "non-activity" (*niṣkriyāvattva*)[1], and by having in common five qualities (*guṇa*): number (*saṅkhyā*), size (*parimāṇa*), separateness (*pṛthaktva*), conjunction and disjunction (*saṃyoga, vibhāga*).[2]

In this paper, however, I focus my attention mainly on the concept of space in the *Padārthadharmasaṅgraha* and, to some extent, in the *Vaiśeṣikasūtras* of Kaṇāda, while the concept of time is tacitly kept in mind as closely related to it. What I attempt to do throughout this paper is to look at the Vaiśeṣika notions of space from the more general perspective of Indian ideas of space as they appear in the Vedic literature, especially taking into account the clusters of meanings attached to them in the Upaniṣads.

I.2. We can hardly find in the history of human thought any particular philosophies of space and time drafted independently of general philosophical ideas of existence, of substance, of cause and effect, of the status of consciousness, of cognition, etc. In other words, reasoning about space and time has always been somewhat secondary, dependent upon the solution of more fundamental problems mentioned above.

This statement is quite true with reference to Indian thought. All along its development and especially in the period of the most acute debates between Hindu and Buddhist schools, the treatment of space and time was clearly determined by their respective ideas of causality, world generating principles, and most of all, by their approach to the problem of substance (*dravya*). Since Vaiśeṣika construed its spatio-temporal conceptions primarily according to the paradigm of substance, this paradigm deserves special attention.[3]

One of the most important problems that suggests itself along with the introduction of the idea of substance in Indian thought is that of substance and its qualities - either in cosmological terms of support (*āśraya*) and quality (*guṇa*), or in logical terms of subject (*dharmin*) and predicate (*dharma*). The approach to this problem varies considerably from school to school in consonance with their conception of causality.

Advaita Vedānta holds the changeless bearer-substratum to be something truly real, while qualities remain its illusory modifications (*vivartavāda*). Sāṅkhya and Yoga put to the fore the changeable qualities which are capable of passing from unmanifested to manifested state (*pariṇāmavāda*), and treat the substratum as something almost insignificant, being something like their mere aggregation. Nyāya and Vaiśeṣika set out a concept of substance as the bearer of qualities which is not merely their sum. For the Vaiśeṣikas, both qualities and substance are ontologically independent entities which enter into the relation of inherence (*samavāya*).[4]

In spite of their internal divergences, the "orthodox" Hindu schools still accept, more or less unanimously, the reality of the subject (*dharmin*). The Abhidharma Buddhists were the ones who tended to build their theories on the opposite basis, that is, on postulating the reality of *dharmas* conceived neither as qualities of some substance (*dharmin*), nor as qualities without substance, but as discrete elements of becoming. This "antisubstantialist pathos" appears to be quite natural since the Buddhists zealously rejected the concept of an unchanging substance as a synonym of something they were so eager to avoid, i.e., of a changeless and eternal soul or self (*ātman*).

Another significant distinction also comes to suggest itself here. The accent on *dharma* on the one hand and on *dharmin* on the other, proves to contribute considerably to the sharp distinction between the philosophical methods of the Buddhists and of some Hindu schools. The former developed a more analytical approach which gave rise to an absolutely discontinuous picture of existence in the Abhidharma theories of *dharmas*. The latter, first of all Advaita Vedānta with its principle of identity between *ātman* and *brahman* (subject-object), employed what may be with some reserve glossed as "synthetical" methods aimed at the explanation of all things on the basis of one underlying continuous principle.[5]

The Vaiśeṣika approach, as against these two opposite poles, may be placed, I believe, somewhere in-between. It recognizes the reality of qualities (*guṇas*) and of attributes (*dharmas*) which have, however, a different ontological status. Like the Buddhists the Vaiśeṣikas allow for analytic splitting, the "quantering" of reality in their conception of atoms (*aṇu, paramāṇu*) of matter, as well as in their ideas of the conventional ultimate units of time (*kṣaṇa*), space (*pradeśa*), and motion (*saṃyoga, vibhāga*)[6]. Elsewhere I have called this approach "an atomistic mode of thinking" (cf. Lysenko 1986, 1993, 1994). On the other side, Vaiśeṣika tries to find a way of synthesizing and integrating its otherwise discontinuous reality through the concepts of the eternal all-pervasive substances (*dravya*), of the whole (*avayavin*), of inherence (*samavāya*), of the universals (*sāmānya*), and some others. Halbfass even called the Nyāya-Vaiśeṣikas the "champions of permanence and continuity" (OB, p. 95). However, I believe such an estimation to be justified only if referring to an "ideal self-image," cherished as it were, yet never thoroughly realized by the Vaiśeṣikas. It is evidently not accidental that Śaṅkara labeled them "half-nihilists" (*ardhavaināśikas*) as against the Buddhists, who were, for him, extreme nihilists. On the other hand, Śaṅkara contrasts the Vaiśeṣika position with his own "eternalism." He proves thus to be well aware of the "midway," i.e., discontinuous-continuous, character typical of the Vaiśeṣika idea of substance as the cause of things (cf. Lysenko 1993).

I.3. Some scholars following the famous Dutch Sanskritist Barend Faddegon began to render *ākāśa* as "physical space" and *diś* as "mathematical space."[7] Yet, it seems that the relation of the Sanskrit terms to the European idea of space can scarcely be elucidated by such renderings which but explain away the problem of interpreting the notions belonging to another culture by transferring it into the sphere of our own culture-bound linguistic associations. No more satisfactory, in my opinion, is the point of view, or rather mode of expression, of Erich Frauwallner, the author of the best exposition of the Vaiśeṣika philosophy of nature, who states that in the mythological pattern of the world, *ākāśa* first designated space and later came to mean the bearer of sound (*Träger des Tones*), this new meaning being fixed by Vaiśeṣika while it employed the old term *diś* (which formerly used to denominate the "cardinal points") to designate space:

> Auf diese Vorstellungen griff also das Vaiśeṣika zurück, als es sich als nötig erwies, einer neuen Raumbegriff zu schaffen, und zwar gab man dem alten Wort für Weltgegend (dik) die allgemeine Bedeutung Raum. (Frauwallner 1956, pp. 105-106)

Thus, he uses the term "space" without attempting to bring to light what was, in fact, the Indian thinkers' idea of space. However, in my opinion, it is exactly this very idea that is worth scrutinizing, since *ākāśa* and *diś*, I argue, suggest somewhat different ideas of space.

II.1. I see some prototypical world-arranging schemes – pregnant with the later philosophical developments which result in the Vaiśeṣika conceptions of *ākāśa* and *diś* – in the classical Vedic literature of the Brāhmaṇas, Āraṇyakas and especially Upaniṣads. We can distinguish there at least two types of relevant schemes, replete, of course, with mythological, cosmological and associated ritualistic symbolism. Before making them familiar through concrete examples, I will try to describe them in a more general and speculative way.

First, the symbolic creation and cyclic recreation of the world in the sacrifice, i.e., the creative, organizing and regulating activity, the creation of *ṛta*, the cosmos, from *anṛta*, the chaos. In the process of ritualistic "creation of the world," a certain spatial coordinate system, oriented vertically and also towards the cardinal points, is formed, this being a morphological reproduction of the sun's movement around a mythical mount Meru. Through its rays the sun becomes contiguous with different points of the terrestrial surface and thus is supposed to model the system of cardinal points, zenith and nadir.

Second, a tendency to see the ritual activity as based on a single source furnishing it both with structure and creative energy; a gradually increasing urge to discern the most steadfast and enduring support that might serve as its sole basis and receptacle.[8] The latter is exhibited in one of the most momentous cosmogonic acts, the establishment of the permanent base. There is a variety of symbols for this all-embracing unity as the central focal point in space endowed with supreme sacred power – the tree of the universe, mount Meru, the *skambha* (the world pillar or fulcrum of the universe identified with *puruṣa* and *brahman*), the sacrificial altar, etc. However, this center came gradually to be regarded as localized not in one particular place, but as present everywhere, constituting a core of being as such.

Thus, the second spatial scheme refers to much more abstract space, something surmounting material concreteness of different actions, being a sort of receptacle in which their structural variety is dissolved in a common *subsistence-in-something*. This second scheme presupposes also a certain infinite *substratum* which, while causing dynamical processes, always remains a static one.

The latter is often associated with the sun in the zenith, as in *ChU* III.11.1[9]:

> Henceforth, after having risen in the zenith, he will no more rise nor set. He will stand alone in the middle.

*puruṣa* is located in the disk of the sun and in the eye, as in *BṛĀU* II.5.5[10]:

> This shining immortal person who is in the sun ..., this is Immortal, this is *Brahman*, this is .ll.

Most often it is associated with *ātman* and *brahman*.

II.2. What is, then, the relation of the tendencies mentioned above to our notions of *diś* and *ākāśa*? *diś*, which is certainly of more ancient origin than *ākāśa*,[11] has received in the Vedic literature a more or less uniform rendering as a "direction," "what is pointed at" ("wohin man zeigt," as it is etymologized in the *Sanskrit-Wörterbuch*[12]), "region," "quarter of space," "quarter in the sky," even a "place" in general, but most often it is associated with four, five, six, eight or ten "cardinal points": east, west, south, north, and the intermediate directions (*avāntaradiśaḥ*) – southeast, southwest, northeast, northwest, plus zenith and nadir. This system of cardinal points or directions was indispensable for the organization of sacrificial space, such as the construction of the altar and proper arrangements of the accessories, as well as for ritual action itself (e.g., sacrificial oblations).

But with the development of a more abstract or symbolic ritual, which was gradually transferred to the mental sphere, culminating in the Upaniṣadic teaching about the unity of *ātman* (the individual soul) with *brahman* (the universal spiritual basis), this space so carefully structured seems to have lost its crucial importance. In the *Atharvaveda*[13] we can find the universalization of the manifold spatial directions (the cardinal points, the zenith, the nadir) by bringing them to a single source, such as the sun, *brahman,* and *puruṣa*. In the Upaniṣads this tendency shows itself in a distinct and significant manner, as in *MaiU* VI.17[14]:

> Verily, in the beginning this world was *Brahman*, the infinite one, infinite in the east, infinite in the south, infinite in the west, infinite in the north, above and below, infinite in every direction.

The image of the supreme reality (*ātman, brahman, puruṣa*) devoid of any attributive characteristics required, in its turn, a counterpart notion of space, more universal and all-embracing than that of the cardinal points (*diśaḥ*). The latter were often associated with something somehow restricting space, e.g., *srakti* (a corner, an edge, as in *ChU* II.15.1) or *parśu* (ribs, as in *BṛĀU* I.1.1), or even with the extreme limit of space, as in the expression "the end of the quarters" (*diśām antaḥ*, cf. *BṛĀU* I.3.10). The notion of *ākāśa* proved to be much more suitable for the image of the supreme reality than that of *diś*:

> For him, indeed, east and the other directions exist not, nor across, nor below, nor above. Incomprehensible is that Supreme Self, unlimited, unborn, not to be reasoned about, not to be thought of (unthinkable), he whose self is space (*ākāśātman*). (*MaiU* VI.17)[15]

Thus, we have obtained our first intimations of what *ākāśa* may signify from the description of the supreme self (*ātman*). In the expression "he whose self is *ākāśa*" (*ākāśātman), ākāśa* seems to be comparable to the absolute. Like the latter, it is changeless, eternal, indivisible, invisible, omnipresent, infinite (always exceeding the sum of finite things), homogeneous and incorporeal. Sometimes, in the progressive series of cosmological identifications promoting the deepest insight into the *ātman-brahman* identity, it appears as one of the most appropriate vehicles to the highest knowledge.

> "What is the goal of this world?" He replied: "Space (*ākāśa*), for all these creatures are produced from space." They return back into space. For space is greater than these. Space is their final goal. (*ChU* I.9.1)[16]

In meditation, it is through the realization of the infinity and omnipresence of *ākāśa* as absorbing and superseding the finite things that the mastery of infinity - so essential for the realization of the absolute whatever its name - may be acquired.

> He who meditates on ether (*ākāśa*) as *Brahman*, he verily attains the worlds of ether and of light, unconfined and wide extending. As far as ether goes, so far he who meditates on *ākāśa* as *Brahman*, has unlimited freedom. (*ChU* VII.12.2)[17]

II.3. The term *ākāśa*, as we can easily see, is much richer in its meanings than that of *diś*. *ākāśa* is primarily associated with what can be perceived in a perspective, with openness, wide extension, and perhaps for this reason it comes to be closely connected with light - etymologically *ākāśa* means "light."[18] In the Veda and in later literature the word *ākāśa* is used in the sense of "sky," "aerial atmosphere," "heaven," "extended free space," etc.[19] Besides, as we shall see later on, it is also used in the sense of "empty space," "vacuity," or even "a hole."[20]

As to the commonly accepted translation of *ākāśa* as "ether," in order to have an accurate view of both terms, we should remember that the term "ether" may be used in two senses: as the quintessence, i.e., fifth cosmological element, playing the role of receptacle of the celestial bodies, the sun and the moon, as in ancient Greek cosmology; and as a hypothetical bearer of light, as in nineteenth century physics. The first meaning is clearly attested in some Upaniṣadic statements, as in *ChU* VII.12.1[21]:

> Ether (*ākāśa*) verily is greater than fire, for in the ether exist both sun and moon, lightning, stars, and fire.

As for the second meaning of "ether," it is not light, but sound which became related to ether in ancient India. Nevertheless, in its role as the sound-substratum, *ākāśa* may be well translated as "ether," for the same reason that the light-substratum was thus called in nineteenth century physics. In both cases there was a need for a hypothetical substance to account for some commonly observable phenomena.

II.4. It is plausible that the correlation between *ākāśa* and the sense of hearing has been inherited by *ākāśa* from *diśaḥ*, with which hearing, and its organ, the ear, had been customarily associated, as in *AiU* I.2.4:

> Fire, becoming speech, entered the mouth. Air, becoming breath, entered the nostrils. The sun, becoming sight, entered the eyes. The quarters of space (*diśaḥ*), becoming hearing, entered the ears,

and I.1.4:

> The ears were separated out: from the ears hearing, and from hearing the quarters of space (*diśaḥ*).[22]

It is significant, too, that in the series of macro-microcosmic identifications, where *diśaḥ* and *ākāśa* are mentioned together, the former is always tightly linked with the sense of hearing or the ear, while the latter is associated with a particular sacred inner-body space, or heart-*ākāśa*. According to the "science of *madhu*" ("science of honey"), that is, the idea of something, as Max Müller explains, "which is both cause and effect, things which are mutually dependent on each other like bees and honey," communicated by Dadhyac to the Aśvins in *BṛĀU* II.5.6,

> This space (*diśaḥ*, the quarters) are the honey of all beings, and all beings are the honey of *diśaḥ*. Likewise this bright, immortal person in this space, and that bright immortal person existing as the ear in the body (both are *madhu*). He indeed is the same as that self, that immortal, that *brahman*, that all.[23]

As for *ākāśa*, it is further described in the following way:

> This *ākāśa* is the honey of all beings, and all beings are the honey of this ether (*ākāśa*). Likewise this bright, immortal person in this ether, and that bright, immortal person existing as the heart-ether (*hṛdayākāśa*) in the body (both are *madhu*). He indeed is the same as that Self, that Immortal, that *Brahman*, that All. (*BṛĀU* II.5.10)[24]

Thus, as we can see from the above, *ākāśa* was thought to be closer to the spiritual, immaterial being, as in *TaiU* 1.6.2: "There is *Brahman* whose body is ether (*ākāśa*) ... ," than to the material sense-organs. The heart-*ākāśa*, or the cavity of heart (*hṛdayasyākāśaḥ*), is construed as a sort of space occupied by *ātman* and *brahman* in the body (cf. *BṛĀU* II.5.10). This internal *ākāśa* (*antarātmannākāśaḥ*) is "immaterial" (*amūrta*), "immortal" (*amṛta*), etc. (*ibid.* II.3.5). However, immaterial as it is, the internal *ākāśa* still represents a kind of a "sentient space." In this sense *ākāśa* is often identified with *kha* ("cavity," "hollow," "empty space," "ether," "sky") as in the following passages:

> Breath is *Brahman*, *Ka* (pleasure) is *Brahman*, *Kha* (ether) is *Brahman*. He said: "I understand that breath is *Brahman*, but I do not understand *Ka* or *Kha*." They said: "What is *Ka* is *Kha*, what is *Kha* is *Ka*." They therefore taught him *Brahman* as breath and as the ether (in the heart). (*BṛĀU* IV.10.5)[25]

Max Müller points out that according to the commentator (i.e., Śaṅkara) these two words are to mutually determine each other, and thus to form one idea:

> Ka therefore does not mean ordinary pleasures, but pleasures such as belong to Kha, the ether. And Kha does not signify the ordinary outward ether, but the ether in the heart, which alone is capable of pleasure. What is meant by Ka and Kha is therefore the sentient ether in the heart, and that is Brahman, while Prāṇa, breath, is Brahman, in so far as it is united with the ether in the heart. (Müller 1988, p. 65, n. 2 on *ChU* IV.10.5)[26]

The same "inner" space as a locus of pleasure is also meant in other passages, for example *TaiU* II.7[27]:

> For, truly, on getting the essence, one becomes blissful. For who, indeed, could live, who breathe, if there were not this bliss in space (*ākāśa*)? This, verily, is it that which bestows bliss.

Thus, *ākāśa* is something that is "outside" as well as "inside" man (*bahirdhā puruṣād ākāśaḥ, antaḥ puruṣa ākāśaḥ*). But does it mean that there is one *ākāśa* which simply permeates the human body from outside? This passage, I believe, should be primarily understood as referring to the series of macro-microcosmic identifications so characteristic of the classical ritual, rather than to some more or less independent cosmological speculation. Man as a microcosm contains in himself a counterpart of a macrocosmic spatial infinity and all-pervasiveness:

> Then he should say: "As large as this ether (*ākāśa*) is, so large is that ether within the heart (*antarhṛdaya ākāśaḥ*). Both heaven and earth are contained within it, both fire and air, both sun and moon, both lightning and stars; and whatever there is of him (the Self) here in the world, and whatever is not (whatever has been and will be), all that is contained within it." (*ChU* VIII.1.3)[28]

As is clear from the above, *ākāśa* symbolizes here not only the infinity and omnipresence of "outer" and "inner" space, but also the capacity of both to embrace and to shelter whatever exists in this world. That is why it is not a mere vacuity, or the absence of something, but *a room for* experience of finite and infinite things and, in the final analysis, a room for realizing the identity of *ātman* with *brahman*.[29]

It is not quite clear from the Upaniṣads whether *ākāśa* permeates what it contains, though it is emphatically stated: "In the ether (*ākāśa*) everything is born, and towards the ether everything tends when it is born" (*ChU* VII.12.1)[30]. The second mention of *ākāśa* seems to refer not to the cosmological element, but most probably to the atmosphere. But the question still remains as to why this lofty *ākāśa* came to be treated as the substratum of sound.

In the micro-macrocosmic identifications of hearing, or the ear, with *diś* the main purpose seems to be to underline the ear's ability to apprehend sounds *from all directions*,[31] while the correlation of hearing with *ākāśa* has directly in view the explanation of the *manner of transmission* of sound (*śabda*); cf. *ChU* VII.12.1[32]: "Through ether (*ākāśa*) one calls, through ether one hears, through ether one answers."

I think that the correlation of *ākāśa* with sound and sense of hearing is connected with the interest displayed towards the phenomenon of sound. This interest may be explained by the search for the physical justification of the transmission of the sacred word. This question needs special investigation, but it seems to me that it is owing to its correlation with sound in the role of its milieu that the Upaniṣadic *ākāśa* acquires the features of a physical entity. Thus it becomes a primary element (*mahābhūta*) in the cosmology of the five elements. It is often mentioned side by side with earth, water, fire and air as the most subtle element which emerges first in the process of world origination.[33] Sometimes *ākāśa* is treated as a sort of intercosmic space, an interstice between heaven and earth.[34]

II.5. It is time to gather the results of this brief and limited survey of the meanings of *ākāśa*. Evidently, in pre-philosophical literature these were extremely manifold, divergent, and even contradictory: In some passages eternity is attributed to *ākāśa*, in others it is considered as a created element, etc.[35] But if we try to single out, for our future analysis of the philosophical developments of this term, the most important configurations of ideas arising out of this survey, we must dwell on two of them.

First, *ākāśa* as a common container of all things which at the same time happens to be free space, free in the sense that it has the capacity to be filled with something. Even though mentioned as an object for meditation, *ākāśa* is by no means considered as an absolute void, the entire absence of things and events.[36] The point is that *ākāśa*, unlike mythological space merged with the world of things and events, seems to be estranged from what it contains, indifferent to things, being in no way affected by them.

The only essence which is close to *ākāśa*, as we have seen, is the infinite soul (*ātman*). And being elevated to such a lofty position, the

Upaniṣadic *ākāśa*, like the *ātman*, in the final analysis seems to be more real than the world of things. We may well imagine that things, unlike *ākāśa*, are so insignificant and transient that they may, after all, be ignored. For a *yogin* meditating upon *ākāśa* things subsisting therein become something transparent that allow him to see the infinite space through and beyond them.

In this way, we may suggest that *ākāśa* is somehow responsible for the experience of openness, extension, infinity and homogeneity of "outer" and "inner space" ( the latter associated with the experience of self-realization) on the one hand, and on the other hand for the experience of things as ***being situated in something*** which always exceeds them, a sort of great container.

The second configuration of ideas may be called a "physicalization" of *ākāśa* by its association with sound and sound transmission, and thus by the emphasis of its correlation with one of the sense-organs, as well as by its identification with one of the great elements (*mahābhūta*). In this sense *ākāśa* is rather a milieu or medium, than free space. But as a medium of sound *ākāśa* continues to be a "sentient space," i.e., *ākāśa* in the ear cavity.

As for the general pre-philosophical ideas of space in the Upaniṣads, we suggest to take into account two tendencies of the semantic development of both *ākāśa* and *diś*. The first tendency may be rendered as an attempt of the Upaniṣads to apply these notions to the spiritual endeavor aimed at discovering within one's self (*ātman*) its identity with *brahman* (the universal spirit). For this task, as we saw, *ākāśa* was regarded as a much more pertinent notion since it was associated with the infinity and omnipresence of some higher reality where all spatial distinctions lost their regulative sense.

The second tendency manifests itself in the ascription of a qualitative, foremost physical, concreteness to these two notions. It is quite probable that *diś*, which had primarily been more closely associated with the ritualistic micro-macrocosmic identifications, passed on to *ākāśa* its correlation with sound, and this correlation became a physical addendum, as it were, to the more general role of *ākāśa* as the container of things and the infinite room for the infinite *ātman*. As for *diś*, its concreteness in the role of the directions of space remained intact.

III.1. In religio-philosophical doctrines which can be – directly or indirectly – traced back to the Upaniṣads and the other Vedic texts, *ākāśa* retains all of its main meanings when used both as a term correlative with macro-microcosmic space in the process of self-realization and as a cosmological conception denoting a cosmic primary element and the bearer of sound. The latter is well evidenced in Sāṅkhya. Here *ākāśa* is one of the *mahābhūtas* produced from the subtle element (*tanmātra*) of sound.[37]

In Vedānta the succession of the elements in the process of origination is the same as in the Upaniṣads and Sāṅkhya. In both cases *ākāśa* arises as the first element followed by air, fire, water and earth, according to the principle "From what is more subtle to what is more gross." The main difference between Sāṅkhya and Vedānta is that the latter ascribed the creation of *ākāśa* to *īśvara*, almighty God. Also in Advaita Vedānta, all the ideas referring to the creation or origination of the world, its beginning and end, as well as its evolution, were allocated to the lower, profane level of knowledge (*aparavidyā*), which was to be superseded in the higher-level insights (*paravidyā*). In the light of *paravidyā ākāśa* turns out to be almost identical with *brahman* or quite near to it. In the *Brahmasūtras* it is declared that "*ākāśa* is *brahman* being distinct from 'name and form' (*nāmarūpa*)" (*BS* I.3.41).

Yet, the Vedāntic *ākāśa*, though ever so proximate to the supreme reality, should not be completely identified with it. *ākāśa* does not ascend as far as *brahman* does, since it is "burdened" with various profane cosmogonical and physical associations (with the *mahābhūtas*, with sound, etc.). In his commentary on the *Brahmasūtras*, Śaṅkara holds that contrary to *brahman* ether (*ākāśa*) is not infinite, but only very extended; cf. *BSBh(Th)* on II.3.7: "... such passages as 'It is greater than ether,' prove that the extent of ether is less than that of *Brahman*." Similarly, it is not eternal, but temporal because it has an origin (*ibid.*). Thus, concludes Śaṅkara, "ether is an effect of *Brahman*" (*ibid*).

Although in cosmological speculations *ākāśa* appears as a created, that is, non-eternal, primary element possessing certain features of a physical substance, namely, sound and the correlation with the sense of hearing, it is still one of the most proper vehicles to promote the understanding of the otherwise inconceivable reality of *brahman*. In a famous Vedāntic simile the relation between *brahman* and things is likened to *ākāśa* divided by numerous jars – when the latter are broken, the primary unity of *ākāśa* gets restored. The same holds good for *brahman* which only appears to be split into the multitude of souls and things, but in reality exists everywhere in the state of a self-identical unity. In this simile *ākāśa* is supposed to be a homogeneous space free from inner differences and independent of the things it contains. The meditation on such a space in connection with the highest reality may instruct an adept to keep aloof from the external world as he manages to see as if through concrete things. This approach to *ākāśa* seems to be inspired by attempts to rationalize yogic experience and we can find it not only in Vedānta and Yoga, but also in Buddhism.

In some Buddhist Abhidharma schools *ākāśa* was considered as empty space, in the sense of the absence of any material obstacles (*āvaraṇa*) and limitlessness. In Buddhist meditation *ākāśa* corresponds to the stage of deep meditation (first *arūpidhyāna*) and the realm of infinity of space (*ākāśānantyāyatana*), or the first *arūpabrahmaloka*, so called because in it exist beings who have mastered the idea that space is infinite. In Vaibhaṣika dogmatics it is included in the group of the *asaṃskṛtadharmas*, the "uncompounded," non-conditioned, indestructible and immutable *dharmas*, alongside with *pratisaṅkhyānirodha* and *apratisaṅkhyānirodha*. Only the Sautrāntikas regard *ākāśa* not as a *dharma*, but as the mere absence of obstruction. Other Buddhist schools treated it as a positive entity, all pervading and eternal.[38]

Closest to the Vaiśeṣika concept of *ākāśa* comes the Jaina one to which we can refer only in passing. In classical Jaina texts, and already in Umāsvāti's *Tattvārthādhigamasūtra* (V.1-18), *ākāśa* is considered to be one of the substances (*dravya*), alongside with matter (*pudgala*), *dharma* and *adharma* (conditions of movement and rest respectively), soul (*jīva*) and sometimes time (*kāla*), though its status as a substance is of no special significance to the Jainas. They hold that *ākāśa* remains the same, although passing through different modifications (*paryāya*). Contrary to the material substances earth, water, fire and air, it is a subtle entity. Like other substances, time excepted, *ākāśa* is qualified as *astikāya*, a thing that occupies space and has some pervasiveness, but its pervasiveness is unlimited. The main function (*upakāra*) of *ākāśa* is that of the container of everything that exists in the common world (*loka*) as well as in the world of liberated souls (*aloka*).

In other words, for the Jainas *ākāśa* is an all-pervading and all-embracing subtle substance which serves as a common place for the localization of different things and events. The minutest place that may be occupied by a thing in *ākāśa* is that which is occupied by the minutest particle of matter, an atom (*paramāṇu*). It is called *pradeśa* and is regarded as a purely conventional unit, used merely for convenience in spatial orientations. It is essential that *pradeśa* - due to the extensive character of all *astikāyas* - is a unit not only of *ākāśa*, but also of other substances, in particular of *dharma* and *adharma*. The multitude of such units is infinite, although the common world (*loka*) is finite.

III.2. The meaning of *ākāśa* in Vaiśeṣika, as compared to that of Jainism, Buddhism, Vedānta and Mīmāṃsā, is more evidently associated with physical connotations. The Vaiśeṣikas explicitly stress the correlation of *ākāśa* with the sense of hearing, by proclaiming it the substratum of sound (*śabda*). As the Vaiśeṣikas, contrary to the Mīmāṃsakas, rejected the eternity and omnipresence of sound, they came across a problem: How can a transient sound occurring in one place be perceived at a distance from its source? This was a vital problem because it concerned their principle of *indriyārthasannikarṣa*, the direct contact between the sense-organ and its object. In the case of hearing it is not a conjunction (*saṃyoga*), but the relation of inherence (*samavāya*) between sound and the part of *ākāśa* contained in the ear. As for the conjunction, it is possible only between the atomic "organ of thinking" (*manas*) and *ākāśa* as the auditory sense.[39] Though the problem of sound perception does not concern us here, I would like to point out that Vaiśeṣika somehow inherited from the Upaniṣads the distinction between "outer" and "inner" *ākāśa* - the latter being a kind of "sensory" part of the former contained in the cavity of ear.

To illustrate the process of sound transmission the Vaiśeṣikas, starting with Praśastapāda, used the image of sound-ripples which successively reach the ear.[40] Every moment one sound-wave produces another up to the moment of perception. Nevertheless, the actual vehicle of sound in Vaiśeṣika is not *ākāśa*, but rather air, or more precisely, wind (*vāyu*).[41]

We have already noticed that the Upaniṣadic *ākāśa* is a homogeneous space: although containing various objects, it remains everywhere the same. We can see that Praśastapāda describes the homogeneity of *ākāśa* as something which follows from its being the bearer of sound:

> Because there is no difference as to the mark [of *ākāśa*], [namely] sound, it is established that [it] is one [by number]. From this follows its separateness as one. Because [the *Vaiśeṣikasūtra*][42] states [its] all-pervasiveness, [its] extension is [established as] the greatest. As [it is] said to be the cause of sound, conjunction and disjunction [are established for it].[43]

Hence, we can see that almost all the qualities (*guṇas*) of *ākāśa* are somehow inferred from its being the bearer of sound: *ākāśa* is one and for this reason it is the same everywhere, since sound may be perceived universally; for the same reason, being one it is separated or distinguished from the other substances, extremely extended and all-pervasive. And again, as sound is produced by conjunctions and disjunctions, *ākāśa* is also predicated with these two qualities. It is natural that in the chapter on *ākāśa* (*ākāśaprakaraṇa*) the main stress is laid on its physical character, inasmuch as its existence is justified there only in its role as the substratum of sound[44].

III.3. Still, this "overphysicalization" of *ākāśa* does by no means exhaust the Vaiśeṣika idea of it. One should not neglect the more metaphysical aspect of *ākāśa*, namely, the one connected with its status of a substance. As Praśastapāda puts it: "Being endowed with qualities, and not being located in another substratum, it is a substance."[45] In other words, the substantiality of *ākāśa* consists in its possessing qualities (*guṇas*) and in its self-sufficiency and independence from the other substances.

As for *ākāśa* which corresponds to yogic experience, there is some evidence for a Vaiśeṣika attempt to incorporate this meaning, too. One can adduce the description of yogic perception (*yogipratyakṣa*) given by Praśastapāda (*PDhS*, p. 187), where he states that *ākāśa*, *diś* and time (*kāla*) are the objects of an unerring seeing "assisted by *dharma* arising from *yoga*."[46] On the other hand, one can well agree with Wezler (1982) and Isaacson (1994) that the ideas of *yoga* and *yogipratyakṣa* were introduced by the early Vaiśeṣikas under the influence of other schools with the aim to "secure certain ontological entities against attack" (Isaacson 1994, p. 154).

The early Vaiśeṣikas, unlike the Jainas, Vaibhāṣikas and the adherents of Sāṅkhya-Yoga, do not emphatically associate *ākāśa* with the possibility of free movement and thereby with the absence of things which may be an obstruction to it. Thus, for them *ākāśa* is not an emptiness (empty room) suggestive of some motion either mechanical or mental, but rather a "fullness," because it fills up all the universe.

The position of *ākāśa* among the material and immaterial substances is in a way intermediary. With the former, the first four *mahābhūtas*, it has in common the correlation with the sense-organs, namely, the sense of hearing, with the latter, for example *diś* and time, only the qualities of number, size, separateness, and conjunction and disjunction. With the soul (*ātman*) it has in common the possession of such specific qualities (*viśeṣaguṇa*) which last only for a single moment and exist only over certain "parts" of their substrata, like sound (for *ākāśa*), and the psychological qualities of pleasure, pain, etc. (for the soul).[47]

Thus, *ākāśa* as a medium for sound transmission pertains to the physical universe, whereas as a substance it constitutes a part of a metaphysical framework aimed, in the final analysis, at justifying the continuity and integrity of being. In this sense it is one of the principles, together with *diś*, time (*kāla*) and soul (*ātman*), which accounts for the continuous substantial character of the universe, i.e., it is not a mere mechanical collocation of discrete particles, namely, the atoms. As Praśastapāda observes,

> *ākāśa*, *diś*, *kāla* and *ātman* are all-pervasive (*sarvagatatva*), have the greatest extension (*paramamahattva*) and are the common place or receptacle of all conjoined things (*sarvasaṃyogisamānadeśatva*).[48]

Things are therefore not absolutely distinct essences, like the atoms divided by the void in the physics of Democritus, but part and parcel of one continuum - they are connected not only with each other, but through their conjunctions they also come to be somehow united with *ākāśa* and, as we shall see later on, with the other all-pervasive substances.

III.4. However, the all-pervasiveness of *ākāśa* has been the subject of rather early criticism, as documented in the *Nyāyasūtras* of Gautama. The main problem concerns the incompatibility of this characteristic with the indivisibility of the atoms. The opponent argues that if *ākāśa* is all-pervasive, it will permeate even inside the atom. If that is the case, either the latter could not be indivisible, or the former would not be all-pervasive.[49] According to Gautama and Vātsyāyana, "inside" and "outside" are spoken of with reference only to the constitutive parts of an effect-substance, some of which are hidden by other parts and thus called "inside," while those which hide them are called "outside." As for the atom, it has neither "inside" nor "outside," because it is a cause-substance and as such has no parts.[50] Thus, Gautama is compelled to redefine the notion of pervasiveness. The all-pervasiveness of *ākāśa*, he states, consists in the fact that its qualities sound and conjunction are everywhere.[51]

In this respect we would like to refer briefly to the polemics of the later Nyāya authors Uddyotakara and Vācaspatimiśra on the possibility of conjunction between atoms. The opponent assumes that, as in the case of other conjoined material entities, the conjunction between atoms occurs at different points on their surface, and hence they can be divided according to these points.[52] Uddyotakara argues that conjunction is a quality inhering in things which are in contact, but is not a special link between them.[53]

The relationship between *ākāśa* and the atoms is a rather elusive subject. This is indicative of a somewhat weak point in Vaiśeṣika physics. Unlike the void in Democritus' physics, which serves as an interval between the atoms, the role of *ākāśa* with regard to the atoms is quite obscure. There is no indication in the available sources that *ākāśa*, like the void, assists the motion of the atoms and their combinations as their common milieu or free space.

Some new characteristics of *ākāśa*, as compared to those mentioned by Kaṇāda and Praśastapāda, are introduced by Gautama when he argues:

> The properties of *ākāśa* are as follows: non-separation (*avyūha*), non-obstruction (*aviṣṭambha*) and all-pervasiveness (*vibhutva*).[54]

As Vātsyayāna explains in his commentary to this *sūtra*, there may arise the question as to why *ākāśa*, being all-pervading, does not obstruct objects moving in it and is not sundered by them, like water that obstructs driftwood and is sundered by its movement. He answers that *ākāśa*, unlike water, does not have the quality of touch (*sparśa*), and therefore neither obstructs any movements nor is sundered by the movements of other substances.[55] In this way the Naiyāyikas allude to the idea of *ākāśa* as the absence of obstacles to movement that rather belongs to Buddhism, Jainism and Sāṅkhya, than it does to Vaiśeṣika.

III.5. The significance of *ākāśa* in Vaiśeṣika was briefly characterized by Bhaduri as follows:

> The part played by *ākāśa* in the scheme of reality is therefore extremely limited. Like the luminiferous ether of the nineteenth century physicists, it is a purely hypothetical physical entity, filling all space and permeating all matter ... Thus we see that the very existence of *ākāśa* depends on the establishment of two conclusions, viz., that sound is a quality, and that it cannot belong to any other recognized substance. (Bhaduri 1947, p. 166)

Though one can agree with Bhaduri in what he says about the preoccupation of the Vaiśeṣikas with the idea of a sound-substratum, one should not underestimate the metaphysical function of *ākāśa* as a substance. With the latter notion the Vaiśeṣikas attempted to find a way around the discontinuity characteristic of the atomic structure of the universe. Since all conjunctions and disjunctions (*saṃyoga, vibhāga*), not merely those of sound-transmission, take place in *ākāśa*, the latter may be designated as "communicating space." On the one hand *ākāśa* provides room for all sorts of interconnections between finite corporeal things involved in dynamical processes, but on the other hand it always exceeds the sum of these, being their common receptacle.

III.6. There is another important usage of *ākāśa* which deserves our attention. In the chapters on conjunction and disjunction (*saṃyoga, vibhāga*) in the *PDhS*, we come across expressions like *ākāśādideśāt* and *ākāśādideśebhyaḥ*, which relate to the disjunction of a thing from its place in *ākāśa* etc., and its conjunction with different places in *ākāśa* etc.[56] What is meant here by "etc." (*ādi*)? It certainly alludes to the other intangible, partless and all-pervasive substances, like *diś*, time (*kāla)* and soul (*ātman*). Different things have their "places" not only in *ākāśa*, but also in time, *diś* and soul. Thus "place" is not exclusively a part of space, be it *ākāśa* or *diś*, but of any substance which is capable of coming into conjuction with other substances, starting with earth. This means that the idea of place (*topos*) is in no way connected with the idea of space as in European thought. What, then, is *diś*? What is its relation to *ākāśa* and to the idea of space in Vaiśeṣika?

IV.1. At first glance, Praśastapāda keeps the traditional meaning of *diś* as a cardinal point or quarter of space:

> *diś* is that from which there arise the ten notions of east, southeast, south, southwest, west, northwest, north, northeast, below and above, with regard to a corporeal substance (*mūrtadravya*) after one has made another corporeal substance the point of reference.[57]

Consequently, in what may be considered a definition of *diś*, an element of "relativity" is introduced, inasmuch as the dependence of the system of the ten spatial coordinates upon a certain point of reference (*avadhi*) is emphasized. This point of reference, as it will be explained below, is dependent in its turn on the position of the observer.[58]

Praśastapāda explains the origin of the different designations of the cardinal points as follows:

> Although [*diś*] is rightly one, because there is no difference as to the mark of *diś*, the great *ṛṣis* – for the sake of the activities regarding *śruti* and *smṛti*, and those of everyday life – created [with regard to it] self-understood designations, tenfold according to the division into east etc., for the regions of *diś* occupied by the world protectors [which regions are nothing but] the conjunctions and disjunctions of the venerable sun circling Meru on its right (i.e., clockwise). Therefore the ten directions are established [only] metaphorically. These very directions have additionally ten designations according to the occupation by [respective] deities: Māhendrī, Vaiśvānarī, Yāmyā, Nairṛtī, Vāruṇī, Vāyavyā, Kauberī, Aiśānī, Brāhmī, Nāgī.[59]

As Śrīdhara elaborates, this system of spatial directions was created by the great *ṛṣis* "for the sake of the proper performance of the *śrauta*, *smārta* and ordinary actions." Thus we may conclude that the system was first of all meant for the purpose of ritualistic activity. It was based on the Vedic cosmological model according to which sun, moon, stars and planets revolve around the sacred center of the earth, mount Meru. Each region of space has its guardian.[60] In this model, different regions of space have different sacred and ritualistic meanings. This is further illustrated by Śrīdhara's examples of Vedic and *smārta* prescriptions: "One should not sleep with one's head towards the west," and "For the sake of long life one takes food facing the east". Śrīdhara also refers to everyday practice, that is, to the designations of spatial directions just for the sake of geographical orientation when one says: "Go to the east," "Look to the south," and so on.[61]

IV.2. However, this close association of *diś* with the qualitatively different quarters of space could not satisfy the Vaiśeṣika need for a more abstract and homogeneous substance responsible for the localization, direction and positional relations of all finite things. *ākāśa* could not meet this need as it had already been allocated the function of sound-substratum and common receptacle. For the Vaiśeṣikas, who were especially careful to avoid any confusion of the functions of different substances, the particular role of *diś* in their model of the world was suggested by the "verbal" localization of things.

Kaṇāda asserts that the objective existence of *diś* is confirmed by such expressions as "This is here," etc. (*VS*(*S*) I.2.10). Praśastapāda adds to these examples of adverbial modifiers of place the notions of east, etc. Such a constant reference to linguistic usage, which can be observed also in the case of time, would be surprising if Vaiśeṣika were treated as a mere philosophy of nature. But it is quite appropriate when we take into consideration the particular brand of Vaiśeṣika realism. First, realism in the sense that the world is real and that in principle our language and knowledge correspond to it; second, realism as a doctrine similar to scholastic conceptualism in its tendency to regard common names as due to universals which are as real as common things.

To be able to raise *diś* to the metaphysical position of such a universal source of different spatial loci, Praśastapāda "relativizes" the Vedic model of cardinal points by declaring *diś* to be a single (*eka*) substance having the same qualities of number, size, separateness, conjunction and disjunction as *ākāśa* and time (*kāla*) have.

In the Vaiśeṣika texts *diś* may be associated either with direction and place[62], or with distance ("remote," "near"). On the other hand, size or dimension (*parimāṇa*) and distance (*paratva, aparatva*) are considered by the Vaiśeṣikas not in terms of space, i.e., as characteristics or parts of *diś* or *ākāśa*, but as qualities of the things themselves. "Place," as we shall see later on, is not an independent spatial category in the strict sense of the word; its size or spatial extension is not mentioned at all. The only way of determining it seems be a conjunction (*saṃyoga*) between two substances. This conjunction is restricted in the following manner: either both substances are of limited size and possess form (*mūrti*), like two jars, or one of them is of limited size, like a jar, the other of unlimited (*paramamahat*) extension, like *ākāśa*. The conjunction of two substances of unlimited size is not admitted.[63] Since a place is defined solely in operational terms, that is, through a conjunction, it seems to be possible to ignore its size altogether and to equate it with a spaceless point.

IV.3. In this way we can distinguish hypothetically two primary intuitions of space which appear in different conceptual garbs in Vaiśeṣika: intuition of co-subordination of separate things forming the structure of the universe, related to the crystallization of the ritual arrangement of things, and the intuition of an extremely extended substance which is the receptacle of all material things and their interrelations, related to the striving for a single support. Toporov mentions some cross-cultural intuitive images of space:

> Space has been preordained to accept things, it is receptive and proffers itself to things, gives itself to them, cedes them the form and offers instead its own order, its rules of extending things within space. (Toporov 1983, p. 279).

In Vaiśeṣika these functions are accomplished by different "spaces": the one receives things in itself, the other accounts for their positional relations within this receptacle. The first is *ākāśa*, the second is *diś*. The latter has been comprehensively explained by Bhaduri in his chapter dedicated to *diś*, which he renders as "space":

> The Vaiśeṣika regards space as essentially a relating principle. We are told by Kaṇāda that it is because of space that of two simultaneously existing bodies one is perceived as before or behind another (*VS* II.1.10). Space, in other words, is that which sets up certain positional relations among co-existent bodies ... If space accommodates discrete objects, it does so only to arrange them in a definite order, so that the position of each of them is definable only by reference to that of others. (Bhaduri 1947, p. 214)

In other words, according to Vaiśeṣika space does not "extend itself." It is either arranging or receiving things in its lap. *diś* is space whose structure is determined by things and by the persons who perceive them,[64] while *ākāśa* is a mere undifferentiated reservoir, a kind of absolute space comparable to Newtonian space, which contains both things and their positional relations, but is in no way affected by them. However, this distinction has been merely outlined, and not fully developed into a clear-cut division of spatial functions.

IV.4. We would like to conclude this section with the suggestion that the Vaiśeṣikas never formed a unified notion of space as a homogeneous expanse, one and the same in all its parts. The absence of something comparable to geometrical space, as in European thought, could well be accounted for by the absence of the impact of geometry on the development of philosophy and science in India. There were two terms for "space," and the functions mentioned above were distributed rather vaguely between them. We would also like to point out that various spatial characteristics, such as size, distance, etc., had not been dissociated from things and covered by the category of space, as was the case in the history of European science; places and distances were not measured in terms of spatial units. One could only speculate as to why the Vaiśeṣikas did not create a notion of space which would correspond to our modern demands. Captivated by such speculation alone, we risk missing the importance of the substantialization of space and time in the history of Indian thought.

When the Vaiśesikas assign the status of eternal substances to *ākāśa*, *diś* and time (*kāla*), they reveal an interest in formulating a synthetic basis for their pluralistic scheme of the universe. Taking this tendency into account, it is quite understandable that these three notions were considered later on to constitute different words for a single entity. As Karl Potter puts it:

> Since all of these are ubiquitous substances with different functions, it is tempting to reduce them to one substance with manifold functions. (Potter 1977, p. 93)

Due to this tendency, I believe, later Vaiśeṣika with its idea of a supreme soul (*paramātman*) found its place within the framework of the Advaita Vedānta project of a global synthesis of reality through the notion of a general spiritual basis of existence, i.e., of the identity of *ātman* and *brahman*.

V.1. Next we have to address the problem of the origin of the qualities remoteness and nearness (*paratva*, *aparatva*) produced by *diś* (*dikkṛta*). These qualities are of special interest for our understanding of space since in their analysis we come across what may be called real concrete space, as distinct from abstract and metaphysical "spatial" substances. As a matter of fact, *paratva* and *aparatva* are qualities (*guṇa*) not of *diś*, but of things, and, what is more important, they are qualities dependent on *apekṣābuddhi*, that is, on a "relational cognition." In other words, they are determined by the position of the observer.

Praśastapāda analyzes cognitions of the positional relation of two things situated at different distances from the observer. What interests him here is the process by which the observer conceives that one thing is closer to him than another.

> When of two things situated in one direction [with regard to an observer the number of] conjunctions with the conjoined are large [in the case of one thing], small [in the case of the other], there arises for the observer, who has made the close [thing] the point of reference, the "remote" cognition "This is remoter than that," with regard to that which is the locus of remoteness. Then, depending on this [cognition], because of the conjunction with a remote place in space, [the quality of] remoteness arises. Similarly, [for the observer] who has made the remote [thing] the point of reference, there arises the "close" cognition "This is nearer than that," with regard to the other [thing], which is the locus of nearness; then, depending on this [cognition], because of the conjunction with a close place in space, [the quality of] nearness arises.[65]

Thus, there are two objects situated at points N (near) and M (remote), which lie in the same direction with regard to the observer who occupies the point O. One of these objects (*piṇḍa*) is chosen as a point of reference for the comparison. The situation itself seems to be clear enough, but it is not clear at all by what particular means the observer appraises the distance between himself and the objects. The text contains an enigmatic expression, *saṃyuktasaṃyogabahvalpabhāva* (literally: "numerousness and fewness of conjunctions with the conjoined"). What is "conjoined," and with what? How can we interpret the expression *bahvalpa(bhāva)*, "large and small [number of conjunctions]"?

The only explanation I have been able to find so far is that of Bhaduri:

> When there are two bodies, *M* and *N*, existing simultaneously and occupying positions in the same direction from an observer, represented by *O*, he immediately perceives that one of the two bodies is remoter from (or nearer to) him than another. Now the distance between *O* on the one hand, and *M* or *N* on the other is measured by the number of conjunctions of the bodies that exist in-between them. *O* is conjoined to the next body, *a*, which is the place (*bhūpradeśa*) on which *O* stands; *a* is conjoined to the next body (or place-unit), *b*; and similarly *b* to *c*, *c* to *d*, and so on till *M* is reached. Then, again, *M* is conjoined to the next body, *p*, which is the ground on which *M* is placed; and, as before, *p* is conjoined with the next body (or place-unit), *q*, and *q* to *r*, and so on till *N* is reached. Now, it is the number of intervening bodies or rather of their conjunctions that constitutes remoteness or nearness accordingly as the number is greater or less in relation to a fixed point of reference, which is furnished in the above case by *O*. Since, in the above series starting from *O*, the place of *M* is before that of *N*, the number of conjunctions between *O* and *N* is greater than that between *O* and *M*, and so *N* is judged as comparatively remote from, and *M* as comparatively proximate, to *O*. This results in the emergence of the qualities of priority and posteriority in *N* and *M* respectively. (Bhaduri 1947, p. 216)

There is a presupposition in Bhaduri's explanation which is absent among Praśastapāda's premises - the presence of "intermediate bodies." From my point of view this assumption, which seems rather artificial, is unavoidable, unless we suppose that in the analysis of the concrete cognitive situation the Vaiśeṣika tacitly relies on a discontinuous image of space as consisting in a series of points (*pradeśa*). These points may be hypothetically singled out by conjunctions of the observer's eye-ray with the surface of the ground whereon he and the objects he compares are situated. The observer standing on place O perceives the distance to M and N in the following manner: His eye-ray enters into conjunction with each point on the surface in the same manner as our finger touches successively a number of points when it passes over a surface. This is a punctual series of conjunctions which lasts as long as the eye-ray touches the objects M and N. Thus, the principle of direct contact between sense-organs and their objects *(indriyārthasannikarṣa)* is observed. I quite agree with Preisendanz that

> the starting-point of the theories of vision was the requirement of some physical conjunction between the visual sense and its object in perception, just as there is conjunction between e.g. the tactile and gustatory senses and their objects. (Preisendanz 1989, p. 146)

However, it seems to me that in the case of Vaiśeṣika visual perception was modeled after touch rather than taste, since the former grasps reality more extensively than the latter which is always delimited by the cavity of the mouth. Thus, what seemed unified from an overall metaphysical point of view appears as fragmented when one is analyzing a concrete situation. Hence, the expression "conjunction with the conjoined" may mean that the observer's eye-ray enters into conjunction with the points on a surface, whatever this surface may be and no matter whether it is occupied by or is free from "intermediate bodies." Each of these points has its place in *ākāśa* etc., as the common spatial matrix. Thus, while *ākāśa* may stand for the container of all conjunctions of things, *diś* might be considered as the sole source of positional relations, a sort of universal "continuous" frame of reference for "discontinuous" places.

V.2. Hence, we may suggest the crucial reason as to why one should treat the "atomization" of space in Vaiśeṣika merely as a conditional one, dependent on the observer. If space is viewed only as a cóllocation of distinct places or points, we are unable to compare and appraise different spatial positions since they would be, to use modern terms, positions in different systems of coordinates. Thus, we need a unifying system of coordinates or frame of reference. At first glance the system of cardinal points formulated by the great *ṛṣis* might be the one we are looking for, but we are told that it was also the result of subjective evaluation, though more authoritative than ours. Let us recall that the Vedic seers based this system on the circular movement of the sun around mount Meru. However, it is clear that the existence of anything which is claimed to be a substance cannot be based on motion, since the Vaiśeṣikas hold that motion depends on substance, not vice versa. Thus, the substance *diś* is supposed to be an independent and therefore absolute system of coordinates which makes possible all positional relations between things and between ourselves.

Though the qualities of remoteness and nearness are dependent on a relational cognition, they cannot be claimed to be purely subjective. We cannot assume that another observer placed at the same point O would have different spatial notions, since the source of these ideas as well as of their referents is supposed to be an eternal substance independent of man. Thus, the substantiality of *diś* somehow guarantees that human ideas about spatial relations are true and generally comprehensible. Furthermore, we can conclude that distance in space is determined not by spatial units, but exclusively by the conjunctions of the observer's eye-ray with certain surface points.

V.3. Strictly speaking, conjunction cannot be the standard or measure to determine any quantitative characteristics of things. This is why conjunction is used in Vaiśeṣika not for "arithmetical" evaluation ("How much?"), but rather for "algebraic" appraisal ("more than," less than," as in the formula: $a > b, b < c$ ), which presupposes a situation of comparison including the observer. No matter what the size of the conjoined objects, at the moment of conjunction there is practically no interstice between them, and the place where this conjunction is produced may be equated to a point (*pradeśa*). When conjunction is regarded not only as a type of relation between two substances, but also as the act of entering into this relation, "conjunction" is momentary. By reducing all time and space relations to conjunctions and disjunctions the Vaiśeṣikas introduced a sort of "process atom," comprising the "atoms" of space (*pradeśa*) and of time (*kṣaṇa*).

I would like to suggest that whenever the Vaiśeṣikas deal with the explanation of processes, including that of knowledge, i.e., with the dynamic aspect of being, it is the "atomization" of space, time and motion that comes to be of paramount importance. However, contrary to the "atomicity" of the four elements, the "atomicity" of space (*ākāśa* and *diś*) and time is considered to be only relatively real, as something imposed upon these by the relations between other substances, primarily by their conjunctions and disjunctions. The continuity and indivisibility of the spatio-temporal substances, however, is unconditioned and absolute.

VI.1. Taking the above into consideration, we can distinguish at least three levels of Vaiśeṣika reasoning about spatio-temporal notions. The first one may be called metaphysical. From its heights, space and time appear as eternal and continuous substances. The second one is connected with the Vaiśeṣikas' attempt to solve concrete physical and epistemological problems by explaining all phenomena in a mechanical and atomistic way, that is, by reducing them to a set of indivisible units entering into the relations of conjunction and disjunction. This is the level of logical or discursive thinking, relating to an "atomized" spatio-temporal framework. The third level is that of everyday practical thinking, connected with traditional mythological and ritualistic patterns.

VI.2. To sum up, we stress again that Vaiśeṣika philosophical reasoning about space and time is governed by the paradigm of substance as the locus of attributes. In general, this approach to spatio-temporal conceptions may be treated as a combination of two tendencies in Indian philosophy.

First, the Buddhists' attempt to comprehend the dynamical character of the universe in dynamical categories, i.e., the categories of *dharmas*. Second, the Upaniṣadic tendency, developed to its extremes in Advaita Vedānta, to explain dynamical processes in statical terms by reducing them to the supreme reality (*ātman*, *brahman*, *puruṣa*), foreign to changes and divisions, free from any internal differences.

In the analysis of concrete phenomena, the Vaiśeṣikas, like the Buddhists, fracture reality into indivisible units. However, when the more general metaphysical framework of Vaiśeṣika is concerned, the "atomization" of time and space obtains a relative and conventional character, comparable to *aparavidyā* in Advaita Vedānta. Unlike the Buddhist time instant (*kṣaṇa*) the Vaiśeṣika time instant cannot draw its dynamic force from its union with a process of becoming, similar to the flow of *dharmas*, as there is no such unity. This divests things of their inherent temporality. In order to introduce into this *being-in-time* some source of dynamic change another kind of time proved necessary, time which is identical with eternity and which, while supporting all dynamic processes, remains a changeless and static substance. Such time is in harmony with the substance of undifferentiated space (*diś*), which is devoid of the "positional relativity" of things, but which, on the other hand, constitutes its source.

*Russian Academy of Sciences*
*Institute of Philosophy*
*Moscow, Russia*

## NOTES

[1] Cf., for instance, *VS(S)* V.2.23: "*diś*, time and *ākāśa* are inactive as they differ from what possesses activity" (*dikkālāv ākāśaṃ ca kriyāvadbhyo vaidharmyān niṣkriyāṇi*).

[2] *PDhS*, p. 58.

[3] For a thorough and comprehensive analysis of the idea of substance in the history of Indian thought, see "The Vaiśeṣika Concept of Substance" in OB, pp. 89-112.

[4] For a discussion of the Vaiśeṣika *guṇas*, see *OB*, pp. 113-137.

[5] For the difference between the continualistic strategy of Śaṅkara and the atomistic approach of the Vaiśeṣika, see Lysenko 1993, pp. 31-39.

[6] The motion of an object is regarded as consisting of its disjunction with one point in space and its conjunction with another.

[7] Cf. Faddegon 1969, p. 213.

[8] The literature concerning the different aspects of Vedic literature about ritual is too abundant to be referred to here, but some basic works must be still mentioned: Dandekar 1972, Kuiper 1983, Silburn 1955.

[9] The translation follows Radhakrishnan 1953. Cf. also III.19.1.

[10] The translation follows Radhakrishnan 1953.

[11] *ākāśa* is not attested in the *Ṛgveda,* while *diś* certainly is; see Grassmann 1955.

[12] Cf. Böhtlingk and Roth 1855-75.

[13] Cf. IX.2.21, XIX.54.5, etc.

[14] The translation here follows Radhakrishnan 1953. While following in general the translations by Radhakrishnan and Max Müller, I have inserted the original terms beside the translations of *ākāśa* (ether, space) and *diś* (cardinal point, space).

[15] The translation follows Radhakrishnan 1953.

[16] Translation according to Radhakrishnan 1953.

[17] Translation according to Radhakrishnan 1953.

[18] In this sense, *ākāśa* is close to *uru loka*, "the broad world," as well as to *vyoman*. *loka* is paraphrased by Halbfass as "room to exist freely and without hindrance and obstruction" (cf. OB, p. 30).

[19] See *ākāśa* in Böhtlingk and Roth 1855-75.

[20] Especially in *ŚPB(E)* III.3.2.19: "He then makes a finger-hole in the middle ..." (*madhye 'ṅgulijākāśaṃ karoti*) and IV.6.8.17: "The reason why they have different dhiṣṇyas, is that there may be wider space (*attareṇākāśa*) for moving about."

[21] Translation according to Radhakrishnan 1953. Cf. also V.10.4.

[22] Cf. also *BṛĀU* II.5.6, *MuU* II.1.4, *AiB* 2.6, *ChU* III.18.6, etc.

[23] Translation according to Müller 1988.

[24] Translation according to Müller 1988. Cf. also II.1.5.

[25] The translation follows Müller 1988.

[26] Cf. also *ŚPB* X.5.2.11.

[27] The translation follows Radhakrishnan 1953.

[28] The translation follows Radhakrishnan. Cf. also *ChU* (III.12.7-9): "The *Brahman* which has been thus described (as immortal with three feet in heaven, and as Gāyatrī) is the same as the ether (*ākāśa*) which is around us; (7) And the ether which is around us, is the same as the ether within us. And the ether which is within us, (8) that is the ether within the heart. That ether in the heart (as *Brahman*) is omnipresent and unchanging. He who knows this obtains omnipresent and unchangeable happiness" (9) (translation according to Müller 1988).

[29] As Charles Malamoud notes, "Le *brahman-ātman* est donc un espace, *ākāśa*, un trou, *kha*. La plénitude de l'âme, l'âme comme plénitude se rélève, se déploie dans un espace vide, abrégé de l'espace infini. Elle est cet espace; plus précisément, l'identité de l'*ātman* et du *brahman*, c'est-à-dire la vérité de l'un et de l'autre, de l'un par l'autre, se fonde sur l'identité de ces deux espaces" (Malamoud 1975, p. 220).

[30] Translation according to Müller 1988.

[31] Sometimes the sense organs are enumerated in the sequence of the increase of their perceptivity, and then the sense of hearing precedes all other senses.

[32] Translation according to Radhakrishnan 1953.

[33] Cf. e.g., *ŚvU* VI.2, *TaiU* II.1.1 and *PrU* VI.4.8.

[34] Cf. e.g., *ŚPB* VII.1.2.23 and *TaiU* I.3.1.

[35] Cf. *TaiU* II.1 (translation according to Müller 1988): "From that Self sprang ether (*ākāśa*), from ether air, from air fire, from fire water, from water earth, from earth herbs, from herbs food," and the passages where ether is identified with the eternal *brahman* (cf. *BṛĀU* II.5.1-10 and V.1.1, *MaiU* VI.17, etc.).

[36] See again *ChU* VII.12.1, as well as V.15.1.

[37] For the role of *ākāśa* in Sāṅkhya see Larson 1979 and Shokhin 1986.

[38] See Childers 1894, and Rhys-Davids and Stede 1921.

[39] For a discussion of *indriyārthasannikarṣa* and of the polemics between Mīmāṃsā and Nyāya-Vaiśeṣika about the nature of auditory perception, see Preisendanz 1989, pp. 159-164.

[40] Cf. *PDhS, śabdaprakaraṇa* (pp. 287-288).

[41] This is clear from Praśastapāda's explanation of the origination of articulated sounds (*varṇa*). He argues that the air moving upwards strikes such resonators as the throat etc. (*sa* [= *vāyu*] *cordhvaṃ gacchan kaṇṭhādīn abhihanti*) (*PDhS*, p. 287).

[42] Cf. *VS(S)* VII.1.22.

[43] Cf. *PDhS*, p. 58: *śabdaliṅgāviśeṣād ekatvaṃ siddham. tadanuvidhānād ekapṛthaktvam. vibhavavacanāt paramamahat parimāṇam. śabdakāraṇatvavacanāt saṃyogavibhāgāv iti.*

[44] Praśastapāda observes that sound cannot be the specific quality of tangible substances. It is perceptible, and its production is not preceded by the corresponding quality in the inherent cause of the substance to which it belongs. It does not pervade, and is not co-existant with the substance to which it belongs; it is perceived elsewhere than at the locus where it is produced. It is also not a quality of soul, since it is perceived by an external sense-organ. It cannot be a quality of *diś*, *kāla* and *manas* as well, because it is grasped by hearing and is a specific quality, or *vaiśeṣikaguṇa*, while the former are said to be devoid of any specific qualities (*VS(S)* II.1.26; *PDhS*, p. 58).

[45] Cf. *PDhS*, p. 58: *ato guṇavattvād anāśritatvāc ca dravyam.*

[46] I follow the translation in Isaacson 1994, pp.146-147.

[47] Cf. *PDhS*, p. 25: *ākāśātmanāṃ kṣaṇikaikadeśavṛttiviśeṣaguṇavattvam.*

[48] Cf. *PDhS*, p. 22: *ākāśakāladigātmanāṃ sarvagatatvaṃ paramamahattvaṃ sarvasaṃyogisamānadeśatvaṃ ca.*

[49] Cf. *NS(TNT)* IV.2.18: *ākāśavyatibhedāt*, and Vātsyayāna's commentary thereon: *tasyāṇor niravayavasya nityasyānupapattiḥ. kasmāt? ākāśavyatibhedāt. antar bahiś cāṇur ākāśena samāviṣṭo vyatibhinno, vyatibhedāt sāvayavaḥ; sāvayavatvād anitya iti; NS(TNT)* IV.2.19: *ākāśāsarvagatvaṃ vā*, and the commentary thereon: *athaitan neṣyate – paramāṇor antar nāsty ākāśam iti.*

[50] Cf. *NS(TNT)* IV.2.20: *antar bahiś ca kāryadravyasya kāraṇāntaravacanād akārye tadabhāvaḥ*, and Vātsyāyana' commentary thereon: *antar iti pihitaṃ kāraṇāntaraiḥ kāraṇam ucyate. bahir iti ca vyavadhāyakam avyavahitaṃ kāraṇam evocyate. tad etat kāryadravyasya sambhavati, nāṇor akāryatvāt. akārye hi paramāṇāv antar bahir ity abhāvaḥ. yatra cāsya bhāvo 'ṇukāryaṃ tan na paramāṇuḥ, yato hi nālpataram asti sa paramāṇur iti.*

[51] Cf. *NS(TNT)* IV.2.21: *śabdasaṃyogavibhavāc ca sarvagatam.*

[52] Cf. Shastri 1964, pp. 165-180.

[53] The idea of conjunction was further developed by Śrīdhara, Udayana and others who introduced the distinction between locus-pervading and non-locus-pervading conjunctions; cf. Potter 1979, p. 81, and Shastri 1964, pp. 177-178.

[54] *NS(TNT)* IV.2.22: *avyūhāviṣṭambhavibhutvāni cākāśadharmāḥ.*

[55] Cf. Vātsyāyana on *NS(TNT)* IV.2.22: *saṃsarpatā pratighātinā dravyeṇa na vyuhyate yathā kāṣṭhenodakam. kasmāt? niravayavatvāt. sarpac ca pratighāti na viṣṭabhnāti – nāsya kriyāhetuṃ guṇaṃ pratibadhnāti. kasmāt? asparśatvāt, viparyaye hi viṣṭambho dṛṣṭa iti sa bhavān sāvayave sparśavati dravye dṛṣṭaṃ dharmaṃ viparīte nāśaṅkitum arhati. aṇvavayavasyāṇutaratvaprasaṅgād aṇukāryapratiṣedhaḥ.*

[56] See Bronkhorst and Ramseier 1995, p. 104.

[57] Cf. *PDhS*, p. 66: *mūrtadravyam avadhiṃ kṛtvā mūrteṣv eva dravyeṣv etasmād idaṃ pūrveṇa dakṣiṇena paścimenottareṇa pūrvadakṣiṇena dakṣiṇāpareṇāparottareṇottarapūrveṇa cādhastād upariṣṭāc ceti daśa pratyayā yato bhavanti sā dig iti.*

[58] Compare the common usage of *diś* as "that which is pointed at."

[59] Cf. *PDhS*, p. 67: *digliṅgāviśeṣād añjasaikatve 'pi diśaḥ paramamaharṣibhiḥ śrutismṛti-lokasaṃvyavahārārthaṃ meruṃ pradakṣiṇam āvartamānasya bhagavataḥ savitur ye saṃyogaviśeṣāḥ lokapālaparigṛhītadikpradeśānām anvarthāḥ prācyādibhedena daśavidhāḥ sañjñāḥ kṛtāḥ. ato bhaktyā daśa diśaḥ siddhāḥ. tāsām eva devatāparigrahāt punar daśa sañjñā bhavanti. māhendrī vaiśvānarī yāmyā nairṛtī vāruṇī vāyavyā kauberī aiśānī brāhmī nāgī ceti.*

[60] Indra - the guardian of the east, Vaiśvānara or Agni - of the southeast, Yama, the deity of death - of the south, Nirṛti - of the southwest, Varuṇa, the deity of waters - of the west, Vāyu, the deity of wind - of the northwest, Kubera, the deity of the underworld - of the northeast, Iśāna, a form of Śiva - of the north, Brahmā, the lord of heavens - of what is above, Nāga, the guardian of the underworld - of what is below.

[61] Cf. *NK*, pp. 68-69.

[62] Note that *pradeśa* is a derivative of √*diś*.

[63] See the chapter on *saṃyoga* (*PDhS*, pp. 139-141).

[64] This calls to mind a theory of relativity where space and time depend on the observer.

[65] Cf. *PDhS*, p. 164: *ekasyāṃ diśy avasthitayoḥ piṇḍayoḥ saṃyuktasaṃyogabahvalpabhāve saty ekasya draṣṭuḥ sannikṛṣṭam avadhiṃ kṛtvā etasmād viprakṛṣṭo 'yam iti paratvādhāre 'sannikṛṣṭā buddhir utpadyate. tatas tām apekṣya pareṇa dikpradeśena saṃyogāt paratvasyotpattiḥ . tathā viprakṛṣṭaṃ cāvadhiṃ kṛtvā etasmāt sannikṛṣṭo 'yam ity aparatvādhāra itarasmin sannikṛṣṭā buddhir utpadyate. tatas tām apekṣyāpareṇa dikpradeśena saṃyogād aparatvasyotpattiḥ.*

Bruce M. Perry

# EARLY NYĀYA AND HINDU ORTHODOXY: *ĀNVĪKṢIKĪ* AND *ADHIKĀRA*

In his masterly analysis of the relations between Hindu orthodoxy and the philosophical schools, Wilhelm Halbfass contends that Nyāya is engaged largely in Vedic apologetics rather then exegetics.[1] While this claim is sound, there is a deeper dynamic to how Nyāya views itself in relation to the Veda and to Hindu orthodoxy in general that is more fully explored in this paper. The development and, even more, the articulation of these relations are crucial to an understanding of early Nyāya: orthodoxy casts a long shadow over its avowed rationalism.

One of the collective projects of the four commentators on the first *Nyāyasūtra* is securely to locate *Nyāyaśāstra* among the orthodox, Hindu traditional sciences.[2] Much of the felt need for this endeavor arises from the dual nature of Nyāya itself: it is claimed to be at once a discursive science of reasoning and soteriological in orientation. There is, to be sure, no necessary contradiction between these claims, but the commentators attempt to steer, as it were, a middle course between them. Reasoning and logic are not to invalidate or disprove scriptural revelation (*śruti*), nor does Nyāya either espouse an heterodox liberation or constitute merely another valid path to orthodox liberation. Summarily stated, the commentators equate Nyāya with analytics (*ānvīkṣikī*), a science with some claim to orthodox legitimacy, which establishes the validity of all sciences including the Vedas, which are the source of orthodoxy itself. Since the attainment of liberation as the highest human good is also taught in the Vedas, Nyāya can thus legitimately adopt and promote orthodox, soteriological doctrines. That it is fully consonant with the Vedas conversely proves that it is an orthodox science. Nyāya thus emerges as the most fundamental of the orthodox sciences and one that is soteriological as well. Once it has attained this orthodox legitimacy, an issue that gains ground in the commentators is what (orthodox) qualifications (*adhikāra*) an aspiring Naiyāyika must have to undertake its study. It is with Vācaspati and especially Udayana that this question is fully addressed. In this paper, then, these two aspects of early Nyāya's relation to Hindu orthodoxy are explored.[3]

By way of a simple, working definition, Hindu orthodoxy may be taken to consist of the acceptance of the Vedas (*śruti*) as an authoritative source of knowledge.[4] Given so minimal a requirement, it is not surprising to find within the orthodox camp a bewildering array of divergent schools and institutions. It should also be noted that the Veda is not a monolithic structure: it presents a complex interweaving of seemingly irreconcilable doctrines, and no lack of genuine obscurities. While it does not intrinsically stand in contradiction with rational enquiry, there are clear boundaries beyond which such enquiry cannot safely go and still lay claim to orthodoxy. It is well to consider a few passages in which an overreliance on untrammeled reasoning is censured.[5]

> I was a savant, a logician, a despiser of the Veda, devoted to worthless analytics, the science of reasoning, an utterer of logical doctrines, a speaker with reasons in assemblies, both a reviler and haughty in speech against the twice-born concerning Vedic rituals, heterodox and a doubter of everything, a fool and a self-styled learned man: the full fruition of which is this – my being a jackal, oh twice-born one. (*MBh* 12.173.47-49)[6]

> That twice born man who, out of reliance on the system of reasons, would despise these two bases – he is to be excluded by good men – heterodox, a despiser of the Veda. (*Manu*(B) 2.11)[7]

> While the *dharmaśāstras* are principal, unwise men, fixing their thought on analytics, speak what is worthless. (*R Ayodhyākāṇḍa* 100.36-39)[8]

The arguments for the orthodoxy of Nyāya in the *Nyāyacaturgranthikā* are to be viewed, in part, against this background: they reflect a delicate balancing act between the claims of reasoning and orthodoxy. It is also possible that the explicit rejection of hypothetical reasoning (*tarka*) as an independent, valid means of knowledge is motivated as much by a concern for orthodoxy as by philosophical rigor.[9]

## Nyāya and *ānvīkṣikī*[10]

I) Pakṣilasvāmin introduces analytics by way of answering an objection: since the last fourteen categories of doubt through grounds for defeat are subsumed under the first two, their separate mention in the first *sūtra* is inappropriate.[11] On the contrary, their separate mention points to a different purpose, namely that Nyāya is analytics (*ānvīkṣikī*), one of the four orthodox sciences (*vidyā*).[12] Each orthodox science has a distinct basis, and the fourteen dialectical categories form the basis of analytics, which is Nyāya. If these categories were not so specified, Nyāya would, like the Upaniṣads, be mere soteriology (*adhyātmavidyā*).

While his contention that the separate mention of these categories has, or must have, a motivation is of the stock in trade of commentators, the specific purpose Pakṣilasvāmin posits here is pivotal for Nyāya's claim to orthodoxy.

II) He provides an argument, of sorts, for this identity shortly afterwards, when he defines reasoning (*nyāya*):

> But what is this "reasoning"? The examining of an object through the means of knowledge; and inference depends upon perception and scripture. This is [what is meant by] "analysis." The analyzing of an object [already] observed through perception or scripture is "analysis." Since it operates through analysis, it is "analytics" or the "science of reasoning" or the "Nyāya system." But that inference which is contradicted by perception or scripture is pseudo-reasoning.[13]

The restriction that inference not contradict scripture if it is to qualify as true reasoning is problematic. In *NS* 1.1.5, it is stated that inference presupposes or depends upon perception.[14] Comparison and verbal testimony are introduced after inference,[15] and there is nothing in the *sūtras* that argues for reasoning's being dependent on verbal testimony or scripture. In addition, the restriction threatens to undercut the Nyāya doctrine of the overlapping or merging of the means of knowledge: if perception and scripture are the bases of inference, then how can inference be used to validate or verify either? Further, does Pakṣilasvāmin mean to claim that there is no such thing as false perception or false scripture? He seems perilously close to granting intrinsic validity to both perception and scripture: inference, accordingly, would play a subsidiary role, corroborating perception and scripture or extending their application. Finally, since his successors assent to this claim, how can they coherently argue that inference or analytics actually establishes scripture?

In what appears to be Pakṣilasvāmin's source passage, from the *Arthaśāstra*, the crucial point is that analytics[16] examines or analyzes matters through logical reasons (*hetu*):

> By analyzing (*anvīkṣamāṇa*) merit and demerit in the Vedic science, success and failure in agriculture, good means and bad means in political science, and the relative strength and weakness of these [three sciences] through logical reasons, it [analytics] aids the everyday world, it strengthens one's mind in reversal and in success, and produces facility in understanding, speech, and action.[17]

Explicit here is the supremacy of analytics over scripture, which it is empowered to examine. It is difficult to see how such logical reasons would *a priori* not contradict scripture.

III) Pakṣilasvāmin claims that the four Nyāya means of knowledge (*pramāṇa*) inhere in the first four members of an inference (*anumāna/nyāya*) and that their conclusion in the final member constitutes reasoning in the highest sense. This claim looms large in his successors' remarks.

IV) He is content merely to quote, without further comment, a *śloka* from the *Arthaśāstra*:[18] that analytics is proclaimed in the listing of the sciences as the lamp of all the sciences, the means to all actions, and the basis of all *dharmas*. He also asserts that in every science there is "knowledge of the true-nature" and "attainment of the highest good" and that in Nyāya, which is soteriological science (*adhyātmavidyā*), the true-knowledge is of the soul etc., and the attainment of the highest good is the gaining of liberation.[19]

Pakṣilasvāmin's insistence that Nyāya is soteriological science is important: its subject matter is fundamentally the soul and its goal liberation. However, in an earlier passage, he argued that it was not merely soteriological science, in the way the Upaniṣads are, but soteriology as fused with analytics. How this fusion is achieved is left for his successors to unravel.

Ia) Uddyotakara corroborates the *Bhāṣya*: since mere soteriology is included in the Vedic science, if analytics were no more than this, the four-fold scheme of the orthodox sciences would collapse.

By maintaining the sanctity, as it were, of the four-fold scheme of the sciences, Uddyotakara raises the stakes in ensuring Nyāya its rightful place in the scheme. A failure to identify Nyāya with analytics now results in the actual collapse of the tradition. It would seem to follow, however, that Nyāya must strictly be analytics, not a blending or fusion with soteriology, if the four-fold scheme depends on it. How it can also be soteriology, even in part, is no less puzzling on Uddyotakara's account than on Pakṣilasvāmin's.[20]

IIa) Uddyotakara explains what Pakṣilasvāmin meant by saying that reasoning is the examining of an object through the means of knowledge: that reasoning (*nyāya*) is the apprehension of an object through the operation of all the means of knowledge, and not one taken individually. If perception and scripture corroborate a matter apprehended through inference, then that apprehension becomes all the clearer, whereas the independent, non-corroborative use of these means of knowledge is a travesty of reasoning.

He also provides an example of an inference being contradicted by scripture: a begging bowl made of a human skull is pure, because, like mother-of-pearl in a shell, it is part of a living creature.[21] This inference is false, he asserts, because the notion of purity must have some basis and a determinate character. If that basis is the Vedas, then the inference is patently false, since there are explicit prohibitions in the Vedas about touching a human skull. On the other hand, Uddyotakara implicitly disallows that any heterodox scripture could have validity in this matter, and concludes that, since the proponent of the inference has no coherent account of what is pure or impure, no inference at all is possible for him.

There is, then, on Uddyotakara's view, a complementarity among the means of knowledge. Inference does not intrinsically have independent authority, but is subject to confirmation by the other means of knowledge, especially perception and verbal testimony. His articulation of a principle of scope is insightful, though insufficiently developed.

IIIa) Uddyotakara gives Pakṣilasvāmin's claim an explicitly sentential turn. By "inherence" in one thing is meant fusion in a single sentence, and by "capacity" is meant their dependency on a meaning which they mutually cause to make known. Hence the members of an inference (*anumāna/nyāya*) are concluded or connected with a single, sentential meaning. This conclusion of all the members is what Pakṣilasvāmin termed "reasoning in the highest sense." Reasoning in the highest sense, then, consists in teaching one who is confused. Each means of knowledge, functioning independently, teaches one who is not confused; but when they form a sentence, they teach one who is confused.[22]

IVa) He first explains that analytics, or the science of reasoning, is the lamp of all sciences because it illumines them: the other sciences teach matters which the means of knowledge etc., have previously explained. His next claim is extraordinary: the other sciences do not possess the means of knowledge etc., because they lack the qualification (*adhikāra*) for understanding them. It is not clear wherein this lack of qualification resides, unless he has the distinct bases of the respective sciences in mind. He proceeds to claim that analytics, or Nyāya, is the means to all actions because it is the instrumental cause of the actions the means of knowledge have illumined. Again, the other sciences carry out a matter that the means of knowledge have illumined. It is the basis of all *dharmas* because it assists all the branches of science.

On Uddyotakara's account, Nyāya takes on a third agenda, in addition to those of soteriology and analytics, as science of the means of knowledge (*pramāṇaśāstra*). He clearly subordinates the other sciences to analytics, since it alone, through its means of knowledge etc., establishes their respective subject matters.

The soteriological aspect of Nyāya, which both Pakṣilasvāmin and Uddyotakara claim is its purpose proper, has yet coherently to be reconciled with the analytical.

Ib) Vācaspati adds force to Uddyotakara's claim that the four-fold division of the sciences collapses if analytics is omitted: analytics is necessary because this science alone is the cause of the purification of all the sciences.[23]

IIb) Vācaspati makes explicit Pakṣilasvāmin's implicit argument: that the five members, the thesis etc., which have the means of knowledge as their sources, are means of knowledge. Insofar as inference is endowed with the five members, it relies upon perception and scripture and does not contradict them. When there is a contradiction, there is no mutual synthesis, or single sententiality, among the members, which have the means of knowledge as their sources. If there is a contradiction between the means of knowledge which underlie them, the meanings of the words in the members lack suitability and have no real syntactic connection.

Vācaspati's reinterpretation of the "dependence" of inference upon perception and scripture does not fully square with Pakṣilasvāmin's assertion. There must be concordance among inference, perception, and scripture at the means of knowledge level. There is, however, no compelling reason to grant primacy to any one of the underlying means of knowledge on this interpretation, as Pakṣilasvāmin clearly does for perception and scripture.

Vācaspati sheds light on Uddyotakara's example of an inference contradicted by scripture.[24] The proponent's notion of purity must rest on some authority. It will not do for him to claim that it is based on the performance of an immemorial rite, since the validity of such a rite can only be inferred if the performers of that rite duly observe what is prescribed by orthodox scripture in all other respects. That is, because one is, in fact, inferring the existence of an otherwise lost Veda. Conversely, no inference divorced from scripture can differentiate the pure from the impure. The proponent's inference thus either contradicts scripture, or is simply incoherent, since anything and everything is pure for him.

Vācaspati's argument appeals to a principle on the relation between scripture and inference. There are domains, purity in this instance, which are not accessible to inference but scripture only. So far as inference is employed as a coequal with scripture in such domains, it will generate either an outright contradiction or nonsense. If used as a subordinate to scripture, it can perform a vital function; his argument supports a strong reading of Pakṣilasvāmin's original claim.

IIIb) Since the first member of this special reasoning is the thesis, it is directly the content of the subject matter of scripture and indirectly the content of that reasoning which teaches the validity of the scripture relating to that. The purpose of the figurative usage of "scripture" to the thesis statement, accordingly, is: reasoning is assisted by scripture through agreement with a subject matter and becomes purposive, because it is commonly held that the knowledge of the subject matter of scripture is the cause of the highest good. Therefore, even if the thesis, which is found in all reasoning, is not scripture, nevertheless this has to be understood as the meaning of the specific reasoning under consideration. Further, this relation to scripture rules out imaginary contents. Vācaspati qualifies the general claim made by Pakṣilasvāmin, and its figurative interpretation by Uddyotakara, that the thesis is scripture, and restricts its application proper to two inferences only: one that establishes the objects of knowledge and one that establishes the validity of the scripture on which the (soteriological) objects of knowledge are based.

Vācaspati thus contends that the ultimacy of reasoning consists in its ability to teach someone the validity of the Vedas and the nature of the objects of knowledge. That these cannot be conveyed without reasoning is a bold enough claim. That Nyāya actually establishes the validity of the Vedas is extraordinary. The Vedas, which define orthodoxy, are now dependent upon reasoning. It follows that Nyāya is the most fundamental of the orthodox sciences, since it is the means by which orthodoxy itself is established. Although its teachings about the soul etc., may be found in other works, namely the Upaniṣads, those teachings can have no validity until Nyāya is brought into play. The question of full conformity between scripture and Nyāya has been set on its head.

IVb) Vācaspati first expands on Uddyotakara's assertion that, while Akṣapāda stated that the purpose of the *śāstra* is the attainment of the highest good, Pakṣilasvāmin claims that there is no purpose of which analytics is not the instrumental cause.[25] Even if the other sciences propound a valid subject matter, they operate upon the true-nature they respectively have to explain in dependence upon the means of knowledge etc., which have to be explained by this science. In this way, analytics assists all the sciences.

Vācaspati goes some way towards explaining the qualification (*adhikāra*) Uddyotakara alleged the other sciences lack. Analysis appears to be uniquely qualified to explain both itself (namely, the dialectical categories) and the means of knowledge, which then are applicable to the subject matter of any science.

Vācaspati adds that one should not take the literal statements of the sciences at face value, but rather subject their interpretation to scrutiny. Consequently, the Vedic science and the rest are to entered upon only after one has ascertained the true-nature of what they teach by way of introducing doubt, examination, and the means of knowledge.[26] These other sciences carry out chants etc., which are illumined by the means of knowledge that are purified by analytics.

According to Uddyotakara and Pakṣilasvāmin, the distinctive feature of analytics is its dialectical categories. Both hold that in its soteriological doctrines it does not materially differ from the Vedic science, particularly the Upaniṣads. Vācaspati argues that these soteriological doctrines are actually the distinguishing mark of analytics, while its dialectical and epistemological categories are common to the other sciences. The five-membered reasoning alone can establish both the validity of the Vedas and the soteriological category of object of knowledge. It follows that Nyāya, or analytics, is the supreme science of soteriology.

What stands out in Vācaspati's remarks is that Nyāya is fundamentally soteriological science, mediated through analytics. Neither Pakṣilasvāmin nor Uddyotakara seemed able satisfactorily to harmonize the competing soteriological, epistemological, and analytical claims of Nyāya. The analytical and, by extension, epistemological parts of Nyāya become, as it were, the common property or foundation of all orthodox sciences. It retains as its unique domain the soteriological and, since it uniquely establishes the validity of the Vedas, which are soteriological in a secondary and corroborative way, it is the actual source of orthodoxy. Since Nyāya, however, is thus virtually identical with the Vedic science, its distinct place as analytics among the sciences is undercut.

IIIc) Udayana adds a new dimension to the discussion of an inference contradicted by scripture. He frames Vācaspati's argument with a preliminary objection. There is no direct statement in the Veda that a human-skull begging bowl is impure; on the contrary, there is an exactly opposite statement:

> Rudra indeed performed a mighty vow: he took up a human-skull begging bowl.

Therefore, how can there a contradiction with scripture in this case?[27] According to Udayana, Vācaspati's idea in citing *Manu* and other *smṛti* texts as evidence for the impurity of the skull is this: even if a direct statement (*śruti*) on this matter is not known, nevertheless a clear *smṛti*, which is based on the Vedas, is the means of knowledge for its impurity. On the other hand, such a statement as the objector brings forth is mere *arthavāda,* whose purpose is to reveal the praiseworthiness of man's intellect, and is not a means of knowledge for the purity of a human-skull begging bowl.[28] Since the due performance of other Vedic matters is the logical mark for inferring an underlying Vedic text, which would validate purity, and the proponent both denies the Vedas and does not perform what it enjoins, his tradition can have no basis.[29]

Novel in the passage is the introduction of explanatory statement (*arthavāda*) and its potential for explicating scriptural passages and resolving contradictions between scripture and inference.[30] Further, it provides the litmus-test for orthodox practices in general.

IVc) Udayana is sporadically helpful in the final passage, the role of analytics among the sciences. Following Vācaspati, he states the meaning of the *Bhāṣya* as follows: because every purpose of prudent men is based upon means of knowledge which analytics has to explain, there is no cause for apprehension that liberation, the highest human good, might not be based on the means of knowledge because of the undesirable consequence that it loses its status as a human end if it is not based on them.

Udayana expands on Vācaspati's reply that one should not take the words found in the sciences at face value: a valid means of knowledge does not require another means of knowledge to explain what it has to explain, but it does need hypothetical reasoning, which serves as its proper implementation (*itikartavyatā*). This is to be obtained from analytics. The operation of hypothetical reasoning (*tarka*), which analytics teaches, relates to the appropriate implementation of the means of knowledge. Hence, analytics establishes both the means of knowledge and hypothetical reasoning, which guarantees their proper operation.

The commentators collectively grant a priority to analytics in order to establish the validity of the means of knowledge, the Vedas, and its soteriological teachings, all of which, in turn, are the bases for establishing both the doctrines of Nyāya proper and the orthodoxy of all other sciences. Analytics so conceived is a method of proof or demonstration, and it is hardly distinguishable from hypothetical reasoning.

Yet the soteriological doctrines of Nyāya, which they no less champion and which are the ultimate end of Nyāya, appear to remain ambiguously related to analytics. It is the dialectical categories of doubt through grounds for defeat that constitute or characterize analytics proper and give Nyāya its unique identity among orthodox sciences. Vācaspati, however, essentially equates it with the Vedic science (*trayī*). There is, for all the commentators' arguments, still something of an identity crisis in early Nyāya as to its orthodox status.

There is one final issue briefly to consider. It is common practice in Sanskrit texts so profusely to praise both the importance of the work in question and the benefits that accrue to its study that it seems wholly to eclipse all other works.[31] Nyāya (as analytics) here is portrayed as the science of all sciences, the science that justifies all human purposes, and the supremely orthodox science. Some of these claims, at any rate, are to be viewed in the spirit of *arthavāda*.

## *adhikāra* in Nyāya

Now that the commentators in the *Nyāyacaturgranthikā* have brought Nyāya within the fold of, or even made it the criterion for, orthodoxy, the orthodoxy of students of Nyāya itself seems to be necessitated. Yet there is nothing explicit in the *sūtras* or *Bhāṣya* about specific qualifications for a Naiyāyika. With Vācaspati and especially Udayana, this issue is directly addressed.[32] Since Nyāya purports to be a science of reasoning (*anumāna*/*nyāya*), there is no obvious reason why anyone with the requisite mental capacities should not be eligible to study it. Further, as the first *sūtra* relates, liberation is attained by the true knowledge of the Nyāya categories. There is no stipulation here of ritual activities and the like for knowing them, qualification for which might be restricted. In the balance of this paper, the emergence of *adhikāra* as an issue in early Nyāya will be explored.

The role of *adhikāra* (eligibility, requirement, mandate) is familiar in the realm of ritual.[33] There are clear prescriptions about who is qualified (*adhikārin*) to perform or have performed Vedic rites. Manu, for example, states that the first three orders of society are so qualified, while *śūdras* are not:

> To Brāhmaṇas he [the lord] assigned teaching and studying (the Veda), sacrificing for their own benefit and for others, giving and accepting (of alms).
> The Kṣatriya he commanded to protect the people, to bestow gifts, to offer sacrifices, to study (the Veda), and to abstain from attaching himself to sensual pleasures;
> The Vaiśyas to tend cattle, to bestow gifts, to offer sacrifices, to study (the Veda), to trade, to lend money, and to cultivate land.[34]

The lowest order, the *śūdras*, are debarred from the study of the Veda, which is the source of orthodox rituals, and by extension the rituals proper. They also lack a number of societal qualifications, but, by obedience to the three highest orders, they can attain a higher status in the next life:

> One occupation only the lord prescribed to the Śūdra, to serve meekly even these (other) three castes.[35]
> But to serve Brāhmaṇas (who are) learned in the Vedas, householders, and famous (for virtue) is the highest duty of a Śūdra, which leads to beatitude.
> (A Śūdra who is) pure, the servant of his betters, gentle in speech, and free from pride, and always seeks a refuge with the Brāhmaṇa's, attains (in the next life) a higher caste.[36]

There are two *sūtras* that point to a presumption that Brāhmaṇas are eligible to be students of Nyāya. The first (*NS*(TNT) 4.1.58) is framed as an objection: that there can be no liberation due to one's debts, pain, and activity. Pakṣilasvāmin explains how, when a Brāhmaṇa is born, he incurs three debts: abstinence to the sages, sacrifice to the gods, and offspring to his ancestors.[37] Further, these debts have to be discharged throughout one's life, and it is only with death that one is finally released from them. It may also be that such debts are not restricted to Brāhmaṇas; Pakṣilasvāmin, in fact, speaks of the debt as a connection or a relation to the respective rites. The force of the objection would then hold true for any of the three highest classes of society.

The second (*NS*(TNT)4.2.48) is more revealing:

> For the sake of this [liberation] one should resort to this [discussion] with one's pupils, teacher, fellow students and those seeking the specific good – who are without envy.

Now by the immediately preceding *sūtra*, two measures are recommended for the sake of liberation: practice at grasping knowledge and discussion with those who know it. According to Pakṣilasvāmin, knowledge here means the science of soteriology.[38] The mention of fellow students (*sabrahmacārin*) points unmistakably to Brāhmaṇas: being a *brahmacārin* "student/celibate" is the first stage in the life of a Brāhmaṇa.[39] Vācaspati, however, thinks that besides pupils, teachers, and fellow-students, the *sūtra* allows another discussant, namely one who is learned in the *śāstra* and is seeking the highest good.[40] It is *prima facie* possible that one could be learned in the *śāstra* and lack any specific eligibility otherwise. Thus a presumption that Brāhmaṇas, or failing that, at least the three highest orders, may study Nyāya is fully consistent with the *sūtras*.

Uddyotakara explicitly relates the audience of this *śāstra*: a student (*antevāsin*) who does not already know the true-nature of real objects through inference and perception.[41] He is richly endowed with spiritual powers (*adhyātmaśakti*).[42] There is, again, a presumption here that Brāhmaṇas are eligible to be Naiyāyikas.

In his introductory verse, Uddyotakara states that Akṣapāda proclaimed the *śāstra* for the tranquillity of the world. Vācaspati states that Akṣapāda did so out of his supreme compassion, since he saw the world itself stuck in the morass of pain.[43] If he had not done so, the *śāstra* would not have come into being. He further claims that this treasury of asceticism incurred no sin for teaching those who lacked the qualification (*anadhikṛta*) to receive it. He cites two *exempla*, the sages Viśvāmitra and Vasiṣṭha performing sacrifice and marriage respectively for and with the unqualified Triśaṅku and Akṣamālā.[44] It was by the power of their asceticism that they did not suffer any sin, whereas we who are of weak asceticism should not teach the unqualified.

Vācaspati clearly states that it was sinful for Akṣapāda to have uttered the *śāstra* for the tranquillity of the world. Since later Naiyāyikas would likewise incur sin but lack the required asceticism to destroy it, they should desist from teaching the unqualified. He is content, however, to leave matters thus: he does not explain what qualification the student of Nyāya rightly should have if everyone is not eligible. That the teaching of Nyāya involves sin in any way is, however, a remarkable claim.

Udayana takes up the whole issue with a passion.[45] He introduces his discussion with a lengthy objection and counter-objection.[46] The phrase, "for the tranquillity of the world," in the *Vārttika* is difficult to construe, because it is both inconceivable and impossible. Since no one ever acts out of a desire to save the world, it is inconceivable that even a sage would do so. It is also impossible for those who are bent on enjoyments, nor does the world itself desire liberation. Therefore, the student, whose forms are those of being a Brāhmaṇa etc. and which are grasped from another *śāstra*, must be stated. One who lacks the qualification and acts is no more successful in the *Brahmakāṇḍa* than in the *Karmakāṇḍa*. Udayana now introduces a counter-objector to meet these claims. The concern, he begins, about the qualification does not relate to an end, because this is not the domain of human effort and because there is no prohibition about a thing's merely being desired. Rather, the question of qualification concerns the means, because this is the domain of the *śāstra* and of human activity. In this case, the knowledge of the true-nature, like liberation insofar as it is what is sought, is the end, because it is not established, and the means is the means of knowledge. The teaching of inference and perception is not, like teaching the Veda, prohibited for a *śūdra* and the like, whereby he would lack the qualification for these things also. If this were the case, then, by apprehending fire from smoke or through perception, he would incur sin, as if he were studying the Veda. And inferences and perceptions concerning the soul and the like are not specifically prohibited for *śūdras* etc., because there is no teaching of atonement, as there is for a Brāhmaṇa who sees a *caṇḍāla*. On the contrary, the *Bhagavadgītā*, a *smṛti* text states:

> Women, *vaiśyas*, *śūdras*, and others of low birth.[47]

Therefore, just as that specific heaven is effected by one who lacks the qualification for Vedic sacrifice by another means, namely obedience and so forth to the three highest classes,[48] in the same way if the apprehension of the soul is made by a *śūdra* by some other means, namely inference and the like, then what is the harm?

Udayana at last presents the final view. An inference that is corroborated by scripture ascertains its object, but not one that is contradicted by it. Pakṣilasvāmin stated that an inference that is contradicted by perception or scripture is pseudo-reasoning.[49] The determination of the non-contradiction with scripture depends upon the ascertainment of its meaning. In this the *śūdra* and the like has no qualification at all.[50] By disregarding scripture and taking refuge in mere inference, he could only produce harm, as in using a begging bowl made of a human skull. Therefore, since the *śāstra* operates insofar as it forms a single statement with scripture, only he who is qualified in scripture is qualified in it. Therefore, *śūdras* and the like are, so to speak, unqualified. Consequently, Uddyotakara's use of the word "world" is taken by some to mean, "all those who are qualified."

Udayana's hesitation outright to declare *śūdras* and the like unqualified to study Nyāya is telling. A *śūdra* might, in fact, arrive at an inference fully in accord with scripture, without knowing that scripture. In such a case, it is unclear why his being unqualified in scripture would of itself make him unqualified in inference or make his inference harmful.[51] Secondly, as implicit in the objection to the Vedāntin's position, a *śūdra* is not disqualified in such inference or perception as does not concern scriptural matters. Insofar as scripture and the *Nyāya-śāstra* form a single statement, the *śūdra* would have no way of determining when he had crossed over the line into scriptural matters when employing inference or even perception. Perhaps Udayana's whole intent is that the *śūdra* should not undertake the study of Nyāya at all in order safely to avoid falling afoul of scriptural prohibitions.[52]

Vācaspati spoke of Akṣapāda as being "supremely compassionate."[53] Udayana expands somewhat on this by way of answering the original objector to Uddyotakara's verse. Compassion is the desire for the elimination of another's suffering without any ulterior motive. Since one who sees an individual suffering can be compassionate, why could it not belong to one who sees the world itself suffering? If it does, what is impossible in his operating towards a means to eliminate this pain?

Udayana also frames an objection for Vācaspati's assertion that the *śāstra* would otherwise not have come into being. Even if the sage were compassionate, he should explain it to one eager to have it explained, and not one in the opposite condition: a singer does not sing among the deaf. Vācaspati's reply amounts to this: it is not the case that, because a sick man, to his misfortune, does not act on the medical advice of Caraka, the utility of that advice ceases. Hence, the benefit of the *śāstra* is undiminished if one fails to act upon it.

Udayana again frames an objection, in the form of a dilemma, for Vācaspati's claim that Akṣapāda did not incur any sin by composing the *śāstra* for the benefit of the world. If one does not see that there is only sin in explaining the *śāstra* to those who are unqualified to receive it, how could what he says be taken seriously? Conversely, if he does so see, how could he not desist? Even if he sees and acts out of compassion, he would be deluded. Moreover, who would put his faith in the statements of a man who has no dread of the next world? Udayana restates Vācaspati's claim, that Akṣapāda incurred no sin for having done this, and explains that the activity of one who is free from afflictions does not lead to rebirth.[54] Vācaspati mentions the power of asceticism as able to remove sin, however, since it is otherwise inconceivable how it can be eliminated.

Udayana frames another objection, that it is better not to be involved with what is impure at all, according to the saying:

> Far better not to touch muck than to wash it off.[55]

Udayana cites Vācaspati's reply and explains its meaning: able men, out of pity, and not out of fear of being smeared with muck, rescue cows sunk in the mud. Once they have rescued them, they wash off the muck.

Udayana frames an anticipatory objection to the *exempla* of Triśaṅku and Akṣamālā, in the form of a dilemma: if one is unqualified, how can he enjoy the result, or if he enjoys the result, how can he be unqualified? Vācaspati asserts, in reply, that such is the power of asceticism that such sins vanish. Udayana now explains his reply. Just as these sins vanish due to the power of their asceticism, in the same way by the power of asceticism even those who are unqualified, insofar as their resolve is true, enjoy the result. Further, they do not lack qualification in terms of the end: they lack the qualification in terms of a rite. But a rite, performed by one who is unqualified, being defective, does not lead to its end, because the completion of it is due to the good qualities of the specific sacrificer. The sacrificer alone, by sacrificing what should not be sacrificed, would effect sin. His sin vanishes through his asceticism. Hence the claim is made that those who lack the qualification to undertake a rite could not achieve their end; only the duly qualified sacrificer can produce the desired result. If he improperly sacrifices, he may incur a sin though he will also attain his end. By asceticism, he can clear away his sin. Accordingly, an unqualified man can attain the fruits of such a sacrifice and incur no sin thereby.

Udayana does not entertain the question of whether Akṣapāda's selfless act and subsequent ascetic cleansing of his sin apply open-endedly to everyone, regardless of qualification. In what follows, however, it is argued that subsequent Naiyāyikas should not emulate Akṣapāda.

Udayana now cites a final objection that, according to the maxim,

> That is the path on which the great men go,[56]

even we ought to teach those who are unqualified. The answer, provided by Vācaspati, is that this is not the case. Udayana does not spell out the perhaps obvious sense: since later Naiyāyikas lack Akṣapāda's asceticism, they should not undertake such teaching of the unqualified.

Udayana is the first author in the *Nyāyacaturgranthikā* to make an explicit argument for a qualification to study Nyāya. He does so by combining a claim in the *Bhāṣya*, that inference must not be in contradiction with scripture, with Śaṅkara's description of the qualifications needed to undertake the study of Vedānta. That the fit is imperfect Udayana concedes by hedging on the lack of qualification on the part of *śūdras* and the like: they are only, so to speak, unqualified. Whereas Vedānta is widely held to be derived from the Veda proper, Nyāya's connection to the Veda is more adventitious. With Pakṣilasvāmin, explicit arguments for the orthodoxy of Nyāya begin, and Uddyotakara formulates the more radical thesis that Nyāya is itself the means of establishing the validity of all orthodox sciences. Vācaspati asserts that Akṣapāda taught those who were unqualified, but does not state wherein they were unqualified. It may simply be that Udayana is making good a lacuna in the overall argument of what Nyāya is and who is to study it.[57] In any case, it is sobering to see Akṣapāda's compassionate act, in uttering the *śāstra* for the tranquillity of the whole world, reinterpreted to apply only to the qualified.

*St. John's College*
*Santa Fe, New Mexico, USA*

## NOTES

[1] Cf. TR, pp. 23-29. He succinctly treats of *ānvīkṣikī* and mentions *adhikāra* in Nyāya in passing. See further Chemparathy 1983 on the specific arguments Nyāya adduces to establish the authority of the Veda.

[2] The early school of Nyāya is represented principally by works on the *Nyāyasūtras*, which are attributed to Akṣapāda and date to approximately the second century AD. A set of four (super) commentaries on the *Nyāyasūtras*, called the *Nyāyacaturgranthikā*, effectively forms the *Nyāyaśāstra* proper. These commentaries, in order, are: the *Bhāṣya* of Pakṣilasvāmin (*NBh*), the *Vārttika* of Uddyotakara (*NV*), the *Tātparyaṭīkā* of Vācaspati Miśra (*NVT*), and the *Pariśuddhi* of Udayana (*NVTP*). The works of Jayanta Bhaṭṭa, the *Nyāyamañjarī* (*NM*(Ś)), a synopsis of Nyāya, and Bhāsarvajña, the *Nyāyabhūṣaṇa* (*NBhū*), an auto-commentary on his *Nyāyasāra*, are not commentaries proper on the *Sūtras*. They are treated here only incidentally. Unless indicated by *TNT* (Taranatha Nyaya-Tarkatirtha's *Nyāyadarśanam* edition), all references to the *Nyāyacaturgranthikā*

are to Thakur's *Nyāyadarśana* edition.

[3] This paper is a major reworking of a chapter in Perry 1995.

[4] The normal term for orthodoxy is *āstikya* ("is-ness"): i.e., the Veda *is* or *exists*. (Conversely, heterodoxy is termed *nāstikya*, "not-is-ness": sometimes, however, the adjectival base of this word (*nāstika*) can more broadly mean "nihilistic.") By the "Veda(s)" is here meant the Vedic texts proper (*saṃhitā*) and their closely allied works (Brāhmaṇas, Āraṇyakas, and Upaniṣads). More sweeping but equally valid characterizations are frequently encountered.

An important consequence of accepting the Veda as valid is that the whole orthodox social order (*varṇāśrama*), which derives from the Veda, has to be accepted as valid as well. The notion of qualification (*adhikāra*) is closely bound up with this social order. See TR, pp. 1-130, for an exhaustive treatment of a number of issues relating to Hindu orthodoxy.

[5] See further Thakur 1974. Uddyotakara, not without humor, criticizes a *kāpālika* for using inference, contradicted by scripture, to justify the use of a begging bowl made of a human skull (*NV* p. 15.15-21).

[6] *aham āsaṃ paṇḍitako haituko vedanindakaḥ/*
*ānvīkṣikīṃ tarkavidyām anurakto nirarthakām//*
*hetuvādān pravaditā vaktā samsatsu hetumat/*
*ākroṣṭā cābhivaktā ca brahmayajñeṣu ca dvijān//*
*nāstikaḥ sarvaśaṅkī ca mūrkhaḥ paṇḍitamānikaḥ/*
*tasyeyaṃ phalanivṛttiḥ śṛgālatvaṃ mama dvija//*

[7] *yo avamanyeta te mūle hetuśāstrāśrayād dvijaḥ/*
*sa sādhubhir bahiṣkāryo nāstiko vedanindakaḥ//*

[8] *dharmaśāstreṣu mukhyeṣu vidyamāneṣu durbudhāḥ/*
*buddhim ānvīkṣikīṃ prāpya nirarthaṃ pravadanti te//*

[9] See *NBh* p. 4.15ff. Hypothetical reasoning is not of the same status as are the means of knowledge: it cannot invalidate or overrule them, but instead assists them by determining the proper scope of their operation.

[10] In the following, four passages in the *Bhāṣya* and succeeding commentaries, when illuminating, will be discussed. Full citations for the passages are:

| | |
|---|---|
| I *NBh* p. 2.13-18 | the four *vidyās:* Nyāya is analytics |
| a) *NV* p. 14.5-11 | |
| b) *NVT* p. 47.13-18 | |
| c) *NVTP* p. 126.13-21 | |
| II *NBh* p. 3.5-8 | description of *ānvīkṣikī* |
| a) *NV* p. 15.1-27 | |

b) *NVT* pp. 49.6-20-54.4
c) *NVTP* pp. 128.6-134.12

| | |
|---|---|
| III *NBh* p. 4.8-12 | correlation of the means of knowledge and members |
| a) *NV* p. 17.1-26 | |
| b) *NVT* pp. 57.13-61.13 | |
| c) *NVTP* pp. 136.27-141.4 | |
| IV *NBh* p. 5.13-19 | recapitulation of equation; *śloka* quoted |
| a) *NV* p. 21.1-17 | |
| b) *NVT* pp. 67.6-68.5 | |
| c) *NVTP* pp. 146.13-149.12 | |

[11] Pakṣilasvāmin has shortly above introduced the *arthapadas* (cardinal entities), which are essentially soteriological categories (*NBh* p. 2.9-12) and which, as Uddyotakara relates, are embraced by all teachers in the soteriological sciences (*NV* p. 14.4). He seems to subordinate the Nyāya categories to them. The objection to the inclusion of the dialectical categories thus holds at two levels: these categories are subsumed within the first two categories, which are in turn subsumed within the cardinal entities. It should be noted that these four cardinal entities are not strictly orthodox, since they stem ultimately from the four noble, Buddhist truths: see TR, pp. 243-265, and *NBhū* p. 442.

[12] Jayanta Bhaṭṭa quotes two verses in which fourteen orthodox sciences are listed: *tarka* appears in the first, and the expression *nyāyavistara* in the second (*NM*(Ś) I, p. 4.5ff.).

[13] Cf. *NBh* p. 3.5-8: *kaḥ punar ayaṃ nyāyaḥ? pramāṇair arthaparīkṣaṇam. pratyakṣāgamāśritaṃ cānumānam. sānvīkṣā. pratyakṣāgamābhyām īkṣitasyārthasyānvīkṣaṇam anvīkṣā. tayā pravartata ityānvīkṣikī nyāyavidyā nyāyaśāstram. yat punar anumānaṃ pratyakṣāgamaviruddhaṃ nyāyābhāsaḥ sa iti.*

[14] *NS* 1.1.5: *atha tatpūrvakaṃ trividham anumānaṃ pūrvavac cheṣavat sāmānyatodṛṣṭaṃ ca. tat* here refers to perception (*pratyakṣa*), which is characterized in the preceding *sūtra NS* 1.1.4: *indriyārthasannikarṣotpannaṃ jñānam avyāpadeśyam avyabhicāri vyavasāyātmakaṃ pratyakṣam.*

[15] *NS* 1.1.6: *prasiddhasādharmyāt sādhyasādhanam upamānam*, *NS* 1.1.7: *āptopadeśaḥ śabdaḥ.*

[16] Kangle, among others, incorrectly translates *ānvīkṣikī* by "philosophy," influenced by Kauṭilya's statement that Sāṅkhya, Yoga, and Lokāyata are *ānvīkṣikī* (*AŚ*(K) 1.2.10): see IE, pp. 263-286. Kauṭilya's description, quoted here, speaks more to a logical method than to philosophical enquiry or the like. I have ventured to translate the term by "analytics," which attempts to capture both its etymological meaning (see *NBh* p. 3.6) of "a re-examining" and its status as a methodology.

[17] *AŚ*(K) 1.2: *sāṃkhyaṃ yogo lokāyataṃ cetyänvīkṣikī* (10). *dharmādharmau trayyām arthānarthau nayāpanayau daṇḍanītyāṃ balābale caiteṣāṃ **hetubhir** anvīkṣamāṇā lokasyopakaroti vyasane 'bhyudaye ca buddhim avasthāpayati prajñāvākyakriyāvaiśāradyaṃ ca karoti* (11).

[18] So Thakur, note 10 *ad NBh* p. 5.15. Kauṭilya here asserts, possibly for the first time, that *ānvīkṣikī* is one of the four (orthodox) sciences (*vidyā*) (*AŚ*(K) 1.2.8-11).

[19] *NBh* p. 5.17-19: *NV* p. 21.10-16. See Slaje 1986 for an interpretation *contra* the tradition.

[20] Vācaspati states that the sciences should not have an overlap (*saṅkara*, a term used, incidentally of caste-miscegenation) of end (*NVT* p. 67.7; cf. *NVTP* p. 149.6ff.).

[21] Cf. *NVT* pp. 52.7-53.5.

[22] Cf. *NV* p. 6.10-13, where Uddyotakara divides people into four groups: *pratipanna* (knowing), *apratipanna* (un-knowing), *sandigdha* (in doubt), and *viparyasta* (in error).

[23] *avadātīkaraṇa-* (*NVT* p. 47.17). Vācaspati uses similar, sacral language of the dialectical categories in *NVT* p. 27.8-10: *saṃśayāditattvajñāna**pariśodhita**paramanyāyamargaḥ* ... See also *NVTP* pp. 89.23-90.6.

[24] *NVT* p. 52.7ff. A highly condensed version of his lengthy argument is presented here.

[25] *NVT* p. 67.6ff.

[26] Vācaspati here seems to equate analytics with hypothetical reasoning (*tarka*) as providing the key to the exegesis of texts: Nyāya is thus a sort of organon of Hindu sciences. However, he states that doubt, examination, and the means of knowledge are at issue: how hypothetical reasoning enters in here is hard to make out. Cf. *NVT* p. 62.15ff.

[27] Udayana's objector here is orthodox (later, the *kāpālika* will enter): so the objection is fundamentally the question of how to decide among or between contradictory scriptural statements.

[28] Cf. *NS*(TNT) 2.1.64: "Praise, blame, contradictory injunctions, and ancient practice are what is called explanatory statement (*arthavāda*)" (*stutinindā parakṛtiḥ purākalpa ity arthavādaḥ*).

[29] Udayana, following Vācaspati, here makes a patently circular argument: only the Veda can directly or indirectly teach what is pure, and those who do not follow the Veda can have no coherent notion of purity.

[30] Jayanta Bhaṭṭa notes that the Mīmāṃsakas are incapable of upholding the validity of the Vedas: ... *na ca mīmāṃsakāḥ samyag vedaprāmāṇyarakṣaṇakṣamāṃ saraṇim avalokayituṃ kutarkakaṇṭhanikaraniruddhasañcaramārgābhāsaparibhrāntā khalu te iti vakṣyāmaḥ* (*NM*(Ś) I, pp. 4.27-5.6).

[31] E.g.: "A brahmin who knows the four *Vedas* with their branches and *Upaniṣads*, but does not know this epic, has no learning at all ... Just as the four kingdoms of creatures rise from the five elements, so, ye twiceborn, all Lore ranges in the realm of this epic. Even as all the senses rest on the manifold workings of the mind, so all works and virtues rest upon this narrative. No story is found on earth that does not rest on this epic – nobody endures without living off its food" (*MBh*(VB) p. 43).

[32] Bhāsarvajña holds that the student and the like need not be specified in the first *sūtra*, but rather are to be supplied by a commentator: "In this [first sūtra] there is no mention of the *śāstra*, the pupil, and the teacher because they have to grasped by reasoning, but it must be done by a commentator, whereby, thinking thus that 'This *śāstra* is connected with a purpose and the like,' 'This teacher alone is fit to explain this *śāstra*,' 'I, in turn, am qualified (*adhikārin*) to listen to this,' and supposing that there will be establishment of his desired object, the hearer acts" (*NBhū* pp. 4.6-5.2).

[33] Most notably the sixth *adhyāya* of Jaimini's *Mīmāṃsāsūtra*. *adhikāra* connotes both an eligibility to perform a rite as well as the compulsion or necessity to perform it. See Lariviere 1988 on this distinction: in the case of Nyāya, the second sense is less applicable. See further TR, pp. 66-74.

[34] *Manu*(B) 1.88-90.

[35] *Manu*(B) 1.91; see also *Manu* 8.410.

[36] *Manu*(B) 8.334-335.

[37] *TNT* p. 1013.1ff.

[38] *ātmavidyāśāstra* (*TNT* p. 1097.1); Vācaspati glosses this by *ānvīkṣikī* (*TNT* p. 1097.19).

[39] See *Manu* 3.2, 2.49.

[40] *TNT* p. 1097.23-24.

[41] *NV* p. 6.9-10. The expression *antevāsin* literally applies to a Brāhmaṇa boy dwelling at the house of his guru. Uddyotakara speaks of the audience (*viṣaya*) for this *śāstra* as such a student: he does not mention any eligibility *per se*.

[42] Vācaspati glosses this phrase by "obedience and the like" (*NVT* p. 26.7: *śuśrūṣādi*).

[43] *NV* p. 6.1; *NVT* p. 22.18ff.

[44] *NVT* p. 22.22. On Viśvāmitra and Triśaṅku see *R* I.57-59; on Vasiṣṭha and Akṣamālā, see *Taittirīyāraṇyaka* 3.92 and *Kāṭhakasaṃhitā* 37.10.

[45] *NVTP* pp. 71.21-74.7.

[46] It is certain that the objector is meant to be taken as a Vedāntin: the mention of the *Karmakāṇḍa*, the ritual portion of the Veda, and the *Brahmakāṇḍa*, the knowledge portion of the Veda, are hallmarks of Vedānta. Likewise, the quotation of Śaṅkara's definition of the qualification for an aspiring Vedāntin (*NVTP* p. 72.4-5): *śamadamādisaṃpattir nityānityavivekaḥ, aihikāmuṣmikabhogavairāgyaṃ mumukṣutā ca*. Cf. *Brahmasūtrabhāṣya* ad *BS* 1.1.1 (*BSBh*(N) pp. 71.2-73.1). The counter-objector's identity is hard to make out, other than that he is at some level a champion of *śūdras*, if not simply playing the devil's advocate.

[47] Cf. *BhG* 9.32:

*māṃ hi pārtha vyapāśritya ye/*
*striyo vaiśyās tathā śūdrās te//*

[48] *traivarṇikaśuśrūṣā* (*NVTP* p. 70.16). See note 36 *supra*.

[49] *NBh* p. 3.8 and *supra* p. 451. Cf. *BSBh*(N) p. 89.1-2 on *BS* 1.1.2: *satsu vedāntavākyeṣu jagataḥ janmādikāraṇavādiṣu tadarthagrahaṇadārḍhyāyāpi vedāntavākyāvirodhipramāṇaṃ bhavan na nivāryate, śrutyaiva ca sahāyatvena tarkasyābhyupetatvāt*.

[50] See *BS* 1.3.34-38 (and Śaṅkara's commentary) on the *śūdra*'s lack of qualification to study the Veda. Rāmānuja comments, *à propos* of Śaṅkara: "We must here point out that the non-qualification for Śūdras for the cognition of Brahman can in no way be asserted by those who hold that a Brahman consisting of pure non-differentiated intelligence constitutes the sole reality..." (*BSBhR*(Th) on *BS* 1.3.39, p. 343).

[51] It is true, however, that since he is forbidden from studying the Veda and cannot licitly find out its meaning from any member of the three superior orders (short of encountering an Akṣapāda), he can never be certain that his inference on any soteriological matter is not prohibited. On the other hand, since Nyāya is the means by which one determines the validity of the Veda, a *śūdra* could paradoxically determine that he is unfit to study Nyāya by studying Nyāya.

[52] Though Udayana does not do so, it could here be argued that to study the Veda is *ipso facto* to be a Naiyāyika. He does, however, incidentally assert that Nyāya operates in reference to Vedic matters and not mundane matters (*vaidika vyavahāra/laukika vyavahāra*) (*NVTP* p. 81.5-6; *NVT* p. 24.18).

[53] In the *Bhāṣya* to *NS*(TNT) 2.1.68 (*TNT* pp. 535.4-536.1), Pakṣilasvāmin lists three attributes of a trustworthy authority (*āpta*): 1) that he has directly observed the matter in question, 2) that he has compassion for creatures (*bhūtadayā*), and 3) that he has a desire to speak of matters in accordance with his correct knowledge (see also *NBh* 365.14-15 on *NS* 1.1.7, where he mentions the first and third). Vācaspati here emphasizes that Akṣapāda is indeed a trustworthy authority.

[54] *NS*(TNT) 4.1.63: *na pravṛttiḥ pratisandhānāya hīnakleśasya*: cf. *NS*(TNT) 3.1.24: *vītarāgajanmādarśanāt.*

[55] *MBh* 3.2.47.

[56] *NVTP* p. 73.5, *MBh* Appendix I.32.68. *mahājana* could also mean "the great majority of people," though this sense is inappropriate to the context. See Chemparathy 1983, pp. 58-64, on the ambiguity of this term.

[57] That there are four *anubandhas* or "elements," including *adhikāra*, in śāstraic and other texts was perhaps something of a commonplace by Udayana's time: see, e.g., the introductory remarks in Śaṅkara's commentary on the *Kaṭhopaniṣad*. In his *Nyāyasūtrasūcīnibandha*, Vācaspati gives the title *abhidheyaprayojanasambandhaprakaraṇa* ("section on the content, purpose, and their relation") to the first two *Nyāyasūtras*: *adhikāra* is the missing fourth element.

Wilhelm Halbfass

# RESEARCH AND REFLECTION: RESPONSES TO MY RESPONDENTS

## IV. Topics in Classical Indian Philosophy (Responses to Chapter 3)

1. Explicitly or implicitly, our preceding reflections and responses have already dealt with the question of how to study and "understand" ancient and classical Indian philosophy, whether and how to address it *as* philosophy, and how to approach it as an integral part of the Indian tradition. According to a familiar disjunction, Indian philosophy concerns either historians and philologists or systematically committed philosophers. Supposedly, the first group's primary interest would be in texts as historical, cultural and linguistic formations, while the second group would be committed to the contents of these texts, the bearing they have on contemporary philosophical debate, the significance of the questions they raise, and the veridical status of the answers they propose. Fortunately, this dichotomy is not as clear and simple as it appears at first sight and in the language of those who like to propose it. There is not only much factual overlap in the work of individual scholars. There is also an inevitable continuum of philology, history and philosophical or conceptual commitment, which is part of the process of understanding itself, and in particular of that kind of cross-cultural enterprise which accepts and respects the otherness of the other, but postulates, nonetheless, his or her presence and participation in a realm of shared or shareable meanings and questions. This is, of course, not to deny that there are very significant differences in emphasis. We must also recognize the simple fact that those who study, teach and explore Indian philosophy today, have different types of affiliation, i.e., with Departments of Philosophy, Asian Studies, or Religious Studies. This implies certain inevitable differences in outlook and scholarly orientation.

At this point, I want to raise a simple or even simplistic question: Who in the Western or Westernized world has, up to now, "done more" for the exploration and understanding of Indian philosophical thought – Indologists (i.e., historians and philologists of Indian philosophical texts) or philosophers with systematic commitments? The answer can be just as simple: the (often self-declared) philologists and historians. But is it really that simple? Are they really just that – philologists and historians without philosophical interest and commitment? We should certainly not simply take their word for it.

Erich Frauwallner (1898-1974), one of the pioneers of the historical and philological exploration of Indian philosophy, insisted that he was not interested in any kind of philosophical or comparative assessment of the materials he was dealing with. Moreover, he argued that much more philological and historical work was needed before such philosophical assessment from a European perspective might become meaningful. He wanted to present to his readers the Indian thinkers and their thoughts "as they are" ("wie sie sind"). He never asked the question whether the application of the concept of philosophy as such might imply any kind of European perspective or assessment. However, his use of the concept of philosophy as a device to assess and demarcate Indian materials is not significantly different from the procedure of such advocates of a philosophically committed approach to India as Karl Potter. In fact, Potter seems to be less at ease with the use of "philosophy" as a means of classifying and demarcating Indian texts than Frauwallner himself.[1]

Frauwallner dismisses the Vedic verse collections as philosophically irrelevant and adds, more specifically, that the Ṛgvedic pantheon is as insignificant for the history of Indian philosophy as Homer's pantheon for the history of Greek philosophy. Quite obviously, Frauwallner, the philologist, ceases to be a mere philologist at this point. And we may add that he had little choice. Anybody who wants to write a history of Indian philosophy has to draw the line somewhere, even if it is only for pragmatic reasons. But it would certainly have been appropriate to use the occasion for some questions and reflections not only about the Indian materials, but also about our tools of interpretation and classification (including the term "philosophy" itself). The concept of philosophy, as used in the history of Western thought, is problematic and ambiguous in itself, and it can hardly serve as a clear and well-defined measure to determine equivalents or counterparts in non-Western traditions, such as India. But even if it could be used as such a measure, this would certainly not amount to the pursuit of understanding, which is incompatible with the possession of definitive and unquestionable conceptual achievements, and which *requires* the readiness to return to and to question one's premises. Certainly, dealing with Indian thought philosophically means having questions not only about Indian thought, but also about philosophy itself, its goals and conditions, its roots and presuppositions, its distinction from and interaction with other cultural formations or modes of self-understanding. In this sense, the philosophical study of India need not and should not be restricted to the study of such texts which seem to correspond to any preconceived Western notion of philosophy. We may, indeed, respond philosophically to a text such as the *Ṛgveda* regardless of the question whether we consider it to be a philosophical text *per se* or not.

We have rejected the idea that Indian thought has had a "great beginning" and a persistent character of its own which would be concealed or distorted by the very application of the concept of philosophy. On the other hand, we cannot deal with the history of Indian thought as if it were part of the prehistory of our own thought, or as if it were the inherent telos of its terms and concepts to be aligned with and superseded by European concepts. In dealing with India, we are not dealing with Europe's past, but with a vast tradition, or even a whole cluster of traditions, "which has had its own origins, undergone its own peculiar transformations, and developed its own characteristic tensions between past and present" (OB, p. 13). It has also developed its own complex theoretical and reflective ways of dealing with itself, of correlating its past with its present, and of defining and questioning its meaning and direction. From an early time, India has not simply had a tradition, but a tradition accompanied by reflection. This is hardly a controversial statement. But it may not have received the attention it deserves from those who treat Indian thought as a mere *object* of historical and philological research.

There is not only a vast variety of different views and possibilities of thought in the Indian traditions of Hinduism, Buddhism, Jainism, etc. There are also numerous ways of accommodating such variety, attempts to provide it with a sense of coherence and direction, theoretical frameworks of interpretation and harmonization, conceptions of different levels of meaning and truth. In several chapters of *India and Europe* and *Tradition and Reflection*, I have dealt in more detail with various manifestations of inclusivism, gradualism, perspectivism and eclecticism in Hinduism, Buddhism, and Jainism, and in general with indigenous Indian forms of reflection on the plurality of religious attitudes and philosophical views. There is no need to repeat or even summarize these observations here.

I want to conclude these introductory notes with a brief reminder. Those historians who wanted to exclude India from the historiography of philosophy claimed as one of their reasons that Indian thought remained committed to and restricted by tradition, and that there was no room for a free theoretical commitment to truth. But what does commitment to tradition really mean in the Indian context? There can be no doubt that it provided a framework and horizon of thought which left not much room for sheer relativism, historicism, and positivism. But it is equally clear that it entailed a vast array of choices and possibilities of thought and interpretation. What does, what can "commitment to truth" mean within such a horizon? Is it incompatible with the "commitment to truth" claimed by the Western critics of tradition? Whether or not we are able to answer this question, we should not forget its hermeneutic significance.

2. Jan Houben's careful and erudite contribution relates directly to some of the issues raised in our introductory notes, specifically to the treatment of religious and philosophical pluralism and the accommodation of alternatives in Indian thought. Bhartṛhari is, no doubt, one of the central figures in the history of Indian thinking about the scope and meaning of tradition, specifically the Vedic tradition, and its capacity to accommodate variety and plurality. I am grateful to Dr. Houben for his thorough textual explorations, which supplement and corroborate some of my own observations and question others in a cautious and considerate fashion. There is not much for me to disagree with.

Bhartṛhari is an elusive philosopher, and much of what can be said about him will have to be tentative. Much work remains to be done; but no amount of philological research will be able to eliminate that kind of elusiveness which is a systematic ingredient of Bhartṛhari's own thought.

In his introductory remarks, Houben identifies "a simple principle which pervades the whole of the *Vākyapadīya*": "The principle is that, in a very fundamental way, the validity of different perspectives is accepted." This basic diagnosis leaves, of course, some significant questions unanswered which Houben himself raises in the following sections of his introduction. Is Bhartṛhari's "perspectivism," is his "doctrinal tolerance" simply part of an inclusivistic strategy to uphold and promote his own basic ideas and systematic commitment? If so, what would be the nature of this commitment? Does it relate to "the validity of the Veda, the acceptance of ontological doctrines, or the status of grammar, or a combination of these?" (p. 320) In *India and Europe*, I noted that the "Jaina perspectivism and the Vedāntic form of treating other doctrines" (IE, p. 355) do not imply any "relativizing or abandoning of one's own position." Houben asks: "Does this apply to Bhartṛhari's perspectivism as well?" In his typically cautious and tentative (if not "elusive") manner, he analyzes several specific instances which might suggest that Bhartṛhari's own *kārikās* (perhaps not the *Vṛtti*) somehow transcend the inclusivistic and perspectivistic notions of the Vedāntins or Jainas. They seem to allow for a more radical openness for true alternatives, and a wider, less structured, "more universalistic" (p. 344), although still fundamentally Veda-oriented conception of doctrinal plurality than was apparent in my presentation of Bhartṛhari. In support of his suggestion, Houben cites "three cases of perspectivism in the first *kāṇḍa*" (p. 327). My comments on these three cases will be brief and selective. I will avoid the question whether the author of the *Vṛtti* was identical with the author of the *kārikās* or not. Houben himself believes that "some (often very subtle) evidence can be adduced for either view" (p. 321). For the time being, I do not see any *compelling* argument for either position; nor do I think that my own earlier observations on Bhartṛhari's "perspectivism" were in any way dependent on his identity with the author of the *Vṛtti*.

I will not discuss the first case (*VP* 1.155-157), which deals with the "results of the use of words," in any detail. Houben himself admits that "nothing can be proved" (p. 331). Even if his interpretation were correct (which I do not find entirely plausible), it would not be a strong and compelling case of perspectivism.

The second case (*VP* 1.172-173), which deals with "the eternality of the universe and revealed texts" (pp. 331-336), is more significant. But does it really follow from the words of the *Vākyapadīya* that the "cyclical and non-cyclical view of the universe and revealed texts" were "two acceptable theoretical alternatives" (p. 336) for Bhartṛhari? It is certainly very appropriate that Houben makes us rethink the common view (adopted without hesitation by K. A. Subramania Iyer and Ashok Aklujkar) that Bhartṛhari was an adherent of the "cyclical" view. It may be true that in view of the ultimate timelessness of the absolute *brahman* this was not a major concern for him, and that he did not make any sustained theoretical effort to decide the issue either way. Still, the sequence of the two verses 1.172 and 173 and the general context of his work leave little doubt that the "cyclical" view was the preferable one for him. Such preference was certainly not a merely theoretical matter for him, and it was not primarily based on supposedly stronger arguments. It was, above all, a matter of traditional acceptance (*lokaprasiddhi*), which is in general a very important factor for Bhartṛhari. There can be little doubt that *lokaprasiddhi* in Bhartṛhari's days did not favor the "non-cyclical" view. Incidentally, it might be advisable to use the expression "non-cyclical" somewhat more cautiously than Houben seems to do. I do not think that the Mīmāṃsakas of Bhartṛhari's time held a *completely* non-cyclical view of the world. Certainly, Kumārila, the great classical *philosopher* of the Mīmāṃsā after Bhartṛhari, did not question the theory of recurrent *yugas*. He did, of course, reject the notion of *mahāpralaya*, the utter breakdown of the universe, which he considered to be unnecessarily radical and incompatible with his metaphysical "common sense."

The third case (*VP* 1.175-183) deals with the "relation between correct and incorrect words" (pp. 336-341). The "direct expressiveness of *apabhraṃśa*" may, indeed, be a "theoretical possibility" (p. 341) for Bhartṛhari. But this does not imply that the derivation of Sanskrit from Prakrit, to which he seems to refer in verse 182, would be an equally viable option for him. Once again, this cannot be a matter of mere theory and unguided argumentation; traditional acceptance and respectability are at least equally important. As a matter of fact, one implication of the section under debate seems to be that even such traditions which disregard the true and ultimate source of all traditions, i.e., the Veda and its language, may still function as traditions insofar as they allow for a distinction between (relatively) correct and incorrect forms.

Concerning Houben's discussion of the significance of authoritative tradition and of direct perception in Bhartṛhari and in Indian thought in general, I would like to add some brief supplementary notes. Adherence to an authoritative textual tradition on the one hand and direct perception on the other cannot be construed as a clear disjunction. The Mīmāṃsakas *excluded* perception from the domain of *dharma* alone, although even in the worldly sphere they did not show any enthusiasm for yogic capabilities. On the other hand, such systems as Vaiśeṣika, Nyāya or even Yoga, which do recognize extraordinary forms of "direct perception," do so only in a way which is strictly limited and controlled by tradition. That these systems make room for "direct perception" does not in any way imply that they encourage their followers to practice or invoke it as a source of independent personal verification or critique of the tradition. In general, there seems to be a tendency toward some idealized form of convergence of "tradition" and "perception" or "experience" which amounts in most cases (at least as far as the Hindu schools are concerned) to a subordination of experience to tradition.

We may now return to a question raised by Houben and cited earlier in this response: If it is true that there is, regardless of all perspectivism, a sense of systematic commitment in Bhartṛhari's thought, and that he continues to uphold and promote certain ideas, what is the nature of this commitment and these ideas? It is obvious from Bhartṛhari's own words and Houben's presentation that it is not primarily a matter of upholding certain theoretical doctrines against other doctrines. Bhartṛhari has some undeniable preferences in this respect. But in general, he displays "a certain aloofness towards the different theories" discussed by him, "even towards those theories which seem to be his own construction" (p. 318). He is, in a sense, speaking from a higher semantic and theoretical level. He does not advocate particular doctrines, but a framework for such doctrines, within which they have their legitimacy, but by which they are ultimately superseded. For Bhartṛhari, this framework is not a human construct, but provided by the Veda, its recensions, its subsidiary branches, and the infinite variety of its interpretations. Ultimately, it is rooted in the *praṇava*, the Vedic *om* which is above and beyond all doctrinal dichotomies and incompatibilities. This is the *tattva*, the ultimate truth and essence which Bhartṛhari sometimes invokes after presenting series of doctrinal alternatives (for instance, *VP* 3, *sambandhasamuddeśa* 87 and *sādhanasamuddeśa* 39ff.; see also *VP* 3, *dravyasamuddeśa* 8ff.). Elsewhere, he refers to the *nirṇaya*, the one ultimate "ascertainment" which stands above and beyond the variety of views and conceptual constructs (see, for instance, *VP* 3, *jātisammuddeśa* 22). Although Bhartṛhari does not have an explicitly developed theory of "two truths" (*dve satye*, as in Nāgārjuna's *Madhyamakakārikā* XXIV.8), the "two truths" pattern has certainly left its traces in his work. We may also say that in his own way he has succeeded in filling Nāgārjuna's "absolute truth" (*tattva*; see *kārikā* XV.6; XVIII.9; XXIV.9) of voidness (*śūnyatā*) with Vedic content. In connection with the term *nirṇaya*, we may recall here the significance of this term in the work of the great Digambara Jaina teacher Kundakunda (ca. A.D. 200?), especially in his

*Samayasāra*, which represents a unique combination of traditional Jaina perspectivism with Nāgārjuna's "two truths."

For the most part, I find Dr. Houben's investigations and interpretations entirely compatible with my own understanding of Bhartṛhari. Differences seem to be mostly a matter of emphasis and degree. I am certainly willing to concede that there may be even more room for a genuine coordination and juxtaposition of doctrinal alternatives within Bhartṛhari's Vedic framework than my own statements indicate. I may have overrated the element of hierarchy and subordination, which is certainly not absent in Bhartṛhari, but generally more typical of classical Advaita Vedānta, as represented by the school of Śaṅkara. In connection with Bhartṛhari's procedure, it may not be inappropriate to recall the notion of "option" (*vikalpa*) in Vedic ritualism and exegesis, as well as the factual and unresolved juxtaposition of alternatives in Manu and other *dharma* texts.

3. The following three contributions to this chapter lead us into the area of Mīmāṃsā studies. I have learned from and been stimulated by all three of them. However, references to my own specific views are more casual in this case. Accordingly, my responses to the articles by Johannes Bronkhorst, John Taber and Kunio Harikai can be shorter.

Professor Bronkhorst emphasizes the significance of the idea and ideal of directness and immediacy in Vedic exegesis, i.e., the notion that the Veda should be allowed to speak as directly as possible, and with a minimum of intervening mental and exegetic activities, to those who are committed to its message. He wants to show that the concepts of "self-sufficient validity" (*svataḥprāmāṇya*), "authorlessness" (*apauruṣeyatva*) and "eternity" (*nityatva*) of the Veda have an "inherent connection" with this exegetic principle (p. 359). It is certainly easy to agree that the ideal of directness is an important regulative idea in the Mīmāṃsā approach to the Veda, in Uttaramīmāṃsā no less than in Pūrvamīmāṃsā. After all, the Vedic *śruti* is supposed to operate at the same level of directness and epistemic authority as direct perception (*pratyakṣa*) does among the worldly means of knowledge.

We may also agree that there is a connection between the notion of such authoritative and incontrovertible directness and the concept of "self-sufficient validity" or "self-evidence" (*svataḥprāmānnya*). Moreover, there is at least a potential correlation between the idea of directness and the concepts of authorlessness (*apauruṣeyatva*) and, by implication, eternity (*nityatva*) of the Vedic word. Later authors, such as Vācaspati, have tried to make this connection explicit and to use it as an argument for the incomparable epistemic power and authority of the Veda: Because of its authorlessness, *śruti* is not only more authoritative, it also operates more quickly (*śīghratara*) and immediately than any teaching based on and mediated by personal experience and recollection (IE, p. 392).

Yet there is also much distance between the early exegetic postulate to receive the Vedic message as directly as possible and the later conceptualizations of the authority of the Veda. There is no need to deny that these conceptualizations and philosophical reconstructions have somehow grown out of earlier exegetic attitudes. But there were also pervasive reinterpretations and transformations on the way, as well as an unprecedented objectification of the Veda. These developments occurred when the early exegetic concerns were transferred into the open arena of philosophical argumentation and debate with other schools. Even Kumārila's conceptual efforts may still reflect a sense of genuine and sincere attachment to the Veda. Yet he also treats it as an epistemological device and a philosophical (if not ideological) construct meant to uphold the identity and stability of the Āryan tradition and its way of life against all heterodox challenges.

Finally, Bronkhorst himself notes that the actual occurrence of a direct and immediate access to *śruti* is by no means common in Mīmāṃsā. The mental activity of exegesis, which should be minimal according to the ideal, and the use and refinement of complex exegetic and hermeneutic devices is, in actual practice, most conspicuous and significant in this tradition. The word *mīmāṃsā* itself indicates the intensity of the mental effort involved in the exegetic (and, later on, apologetic) enterprise.

John Taber's contribution is, above all, a challenging and intriguing attempt to bring Kumārila's thought closer to our time and, more specifically, into the context of contemporary ethical debate.

> Let us consider, then, for the purpose of reflecting philosophically on Kumārila's ideas in a contemporary context, that Kumārila holds right and wrong to be what tradition prescribes and prohibits, "tradition" being any teaching sufficiently ancient not to be identified as originating from a particular source. This is perhaps the most widely held of all ethical theories, but it has rarely been philosophically defended. (p. 379)

In his paraphrase of, or extrapolation from, Kumārila, Taber adds:

> The judgments of tradition retain the validity with which they were originally received, we could say, because they have the appearance of impersonal objectivity. (pp. 379-380)

An ethical theory based on such an understanding of tradition might be able to avoid some common problems of ethics, such as the dilemma about the objectivity or subjectivity of values (p. 384).

I am not sure to what extent Taber's reflections are meant as an account of how tradition might have functioned as a provider of ethical rules and directives in traditional societies, or how far he wants to go in suggesting that some sort of traditionalist ethics might be implemented again, or at least theoretically defended, in our "post-traditional" or anti-traditional age. Clearly, Taber, citing Gadamer, accepts and welcomes the inescapable presence of tradition even in our days; and he advocates its inherent values and uses in ethics and elsewhere (see, for instance, p. 382). Contemporary ethicists might, indeed, be well advised to pay greater attention to tradition as a positive factor in ethics, and not only as an obstacle to human responsibility and autonomy. However, instead of speculating on the potential role of tradition in ethical theory and practice, I want to return to Kumārila and to the question whether he is the best possible witness for the sense of tradition which Taber seems to have in mind.

Taber himself concedes:

> Of course, much of what I have said Kumārila himself would reject. For he does not hold that the Veda is a "mere" tradition, no matter how ancient; it is rather eternal. (p. 385)

But he adds that this distinction can and has to be disregarded, if Kumārila's thought "is to have any relevance for us today." Does this concession go far enough? I don't think so. Kumārila does not simply represent a special kind of traditionalism; he is a fundamentalist. For him, traditionalism (which is characterized by the acceptance of ancestral habits, commonly recognized standards, etc.) is nothing more than conventionalism. To be sure, Kumārila did not have to face the modern specter of relativism. Yet he was familiar with numerous mutually incompatible religious traditions and moral codes; and he faced these traditions as well as his own tradition from the outside. He did not simply advocate what he had received from and through his tradition, but he set himself the task of identifying an underlying principle for his tradition, and of defending it in an open arena of philosophical debate.

Of course, this principle, this foundation is not a universal rational norm, but a textual datum, the Veda. But what counts is the sharp and radical distinction he draws between habitual recognition and familiarity (*loka-prasiddhi*) and the postulate of an irrefutable epistemic ground and basis. The latter cannot simply be received from the past. Even if it is, according to Kumārila, not a rational ground in itself, its ascertainment requires, nonetheless, a sustained use of reason and argument, and a certain distance from, and objectification of, tradition as a factual transmission of norms and beliefs. Of course, my disagreement with Taber's reading of Kumārila may, in the end, be reducible to differences in perspective and terminology. In a sense, I can accept his reference to "a reasoned justification of tradition" (p. 379) as a characterization of Kumārila's doctrine of the authority of the Veda. Yet in another sense, I continue to believe that Kumārila's procedure reflects not only his commitment to tradition, but also his awareness of the potential pitfalls of tradition. Perhaps the perspectives can supplement each other in a meaningful manner.

Kunio Harikai's article on Kumārila's use of Vaiśeṣika categories is another welcome contribution to our understanding of this towering figure in the history of Indian philosophy. Kumārila's importance is widely recognized, but he has not yet received the sustained scholarly and hermeneutic attention he deserves. There can be no question that he is a truly great thinker, with a penetrating sense of fundamental problems in epistemology, metaphysics and ethics, in command of formidable intellectual powers and dialectical skills. But he also has an undeniable agenda: He is the champion of the Vedic *dharma*, the identity and stability of the Āryan tradition, the superiority of the brahmins and the social status quo. Philosophy, theory, metaphysics, epistemology are in the service of this goal, although his philosophical temperament will often carry him away in the pursuit of theoretical problems. His primary commitment is to the *dharma* as a set of ritual norms and duties enjoined by the Vedic *vidhis*. Merely theoretical truths and matters of fact are of secondary importance; their role may be compared to that of the *arthavādas* in the Veda. In this area, he practices an undisguised eclecticism, borrowing freely from the conceptual achievements of his time. Professor Harikai examines one particular aspect of this eclecticism.

The "main theme" of Harikai's essay is, in his own words, the following question:

> How should we understand the denotation of the noun, more precisely, of the genus-word (*jātiśabda*), in the injunctive sentences of the Veda? (p. 404)

It is a question which, together with related issues, was also discussed by Peter Scharf in a doctoral dissertation submitted to the University of Pennsylvania in 1990 (see Scharf 1990). However, in connection with this "main theme," Harikai presents a number of very pertinent and valuable observations, which illustrate not only Kumārila's "creative application" or "adaptive manipulation" (p. 409) of Vaiśeṣika categories, but also his style of thought and argumentation in general. In the following, I will focus on one particular, but exemplary issue, which seems to call for further discussion and clarification.

In his opening statements, Harikai cites passages from *Tradition and Reflection* and *On Being and What There Is*, which deal with conceptualizations of being within the Mīmāṃsā tradition, and with Kumārila's use of Vaiśeṣika teachings. I said that "Kumārila adopts and modifies the Vaiśeṣika notion of the highest universal *sattā*," and I contrasted his procedure with Prabhākara's and Śālikanātha's explanation of being as *pramāṇasambandhayogyatā*, "suitability for valid cognition," and Maṇḍana's *vartamānatā*, "being present" (TR, p. 33; OB, p. 153). In this connection, and in response to Harikai's presentation, the following question needs to be addressed: *How* did Kumārila use the Vaiśeṣika concept of *sattā*? How far did his modification (or perhaps transformation) of this concept go? Harikai notes that in the *Vanavāda* chapter of the *Ślokavārttika sattā* appears as one among other universals which inhere in individual things (see pp. 399 and 403), and that we might thus conclude that Kumārila recognizes *sattā* as a real universal. However, he adds immediately that such a conclusion is problematic. He refers to the *Ākṛtivāda* (verse 19-25) and says that here

> the highest universal, being-ness (*sattā*), is the denotation of the word *sat* ("being"), and thus does not have real existence in the objective external world. (p. 403)

He also says that Kumārila regards only "first-level universals," such as cowness (*gotva*), as real and excludes universals "on a higher level," such as *sattā* or *vastutva* ("thingness"). The *Ākṛti-adhikaraṇa* of the *Tantravārttika* is cited for further support. Is this interpretation justified?

Of course, we cannot exclude the possibility that Kumārila's statements on *sattā* are not entirely consistent. There are ambiguities, even discrepancies with regard to other, comparable issues, for instance, the treatment of colors as universals in one place, and their presentation as *instances* of color-universals elsewhere (see OB, p. 126 and p. 136, n. 84f.). But did Kumārila really distinguish between real "first-level universals" and unreal "universals on a higher level," and did he ever exclude *sattā* from the domain of real universals? No doubt, he rejects the reality of *vastutva*, "thingness" or "somethingness". But this is an entirely different case. The concept of *vastutva*, as *mahāsāmānya*, postulates a universal which would be present in all six categories, including the universals. This would entail an infinite regress (*anavasthā*), which is as unacceptable to the Vaiśeṣika teachers as to Kumārila. However, no such regress is associated with *sattā*, which inheres in the first three categories only. The *Ākṛtivāda* itself presupposes this distinction, and the commentaries make it more explicit.

Moreover, the statement that *sattā* is "the denotation of the word *sat*" (p. 403) can hardly count as an argument against its reality; nor is this suggested by Kumārila himself. The debate on whether *sattā* is the meaning of all words (as suggested by Bhartṛhari) or of the word *sat* alone has no direct bearing on the question of the reality of universals. Here, Kumārila continues to follow the lead of Vaiśeṣika, but avoids its tendency to reify the universals and to separate them ontologically from their substrates. In this sense, all universals, including *sattā*, are "less real" for him than for the Vaiśeṣika.

4. With the articles by Victoria Lysenko and Bruce Perry, we move on to the great classical systems of Vaiśeṣika and Nyāya. Both of these articles relate to significant and symptomatic issues with which I have dealt in my publications, and which continue to be of great interest to me. They provide very pertinent and valuable additions to my own observations, and they fill gaps in my own understanding. Once again, my response can be brief, shorter even than what I had to say about the three preceding contributions.

I begin with Victoria Lysenko's observations on a somewhat neglected topic: the meaning of *ākāśa* and *diś* and the understanding of space in classical Vaiśeṣika, as related to other Indian notions of space. She gives numerous citations which illustrate the meaning or meanings of *ākāśa*. Of course, her list cannot be expected (and was not meant) to be exhaustive. Much could be added, in particular from the Buddhist side. Here, Lysenko provides only some vague and general hints, which are based on the Pāli dictionaries of Childers and Rhys Davids/Stede. The ambiguous role of *ākāśa* (*ākāsa*) in relation to the material elements and the development of the distinction between "unconditioned" (*asaṃskṛta*; Pāli *asaṅkhata*) and "elemental" space (*ākāśadhātu*) in the different schools of Buddhist thought pose interesting problems for future research. Y. Karunadasa's *Buddhist Analysis of Matter* (1967) gives some useful references. Likewise, the Jaina understanding of space calls for further study and clarification. But instead of pursuing these issues, I want to ask some more specific questions concerning the Vaiśeṣika conception of space. Although these questions, for which I do not have a clear answer, are specific and somewhat technical, their implications are potentially far-reaching.

How and when did the concepts of "space points" (*dikpradeśa*) and "time points" (*kālapradeśa*) find their way into the Vaiśeṣika teachings? We do not find them in the *Vaiśeṣikasūtra*; but they do emerge in Praśastapāda's work. It does not seem that they are well integrated into the system. May we assume a connection with Jaina terminology, which uses *pradeśa* (Ardhamāgadhī: *paesa*) in the sense of "ultimate unit" or "constituent point"? Likewise, the emergence and development of *kṣaṇa* and *kṣaṇika* in Vaiśeṣika *after* the *sūtras* and the possibility of a tacit interaction with Buddhist notions of momentariness deserves further study (see also OB, p. 215f.).

Also, the identification of the three unitary substances space (*diś*), time (*kāla*) and ether (*ākāśa*) in Śivāditya's *Saptapadārthī* poses some intriguing questions. What is the background of this unusual procedure, which finds no justification in the standard texts of classical Vaiśeṣika? Why did it occur in the work of Śivāditya, an otherwise rather conservative author? Are there connections with Vedāntic ideas or, more specifically, with Śaivite nondualist teachings? Centuries later, Raghunātha Śiromaṇi proposed an even more radical revision, which identified the three substances space, time and ether with God (see OB, p. 217f.).

Bruce Perry's article reminds us of the vicissitudes of reasoning and "analytics" (Perry's translation for *ānvīkṣikī*) in classical Nyāya from Akṣapāda Gautama's *Nyāyasūtra* through the *Pariśuddhi* by Udayana, a period which covers the first millennium CE. Torn between the two poles of pride in argument and commitment to the Vedic tradition, Nyāya was caught in a long-lasting, though largely unacknowledged, "identity crisis" (p. 458). Various attempts to resolve the tension and to find a proper balance remained questionable in the end. Nyāya claims to be *ānvīkṣiky ātmavidyā*, "a discursive science of reasoning" (p. 449) which is at the same time "soteriological in orientation," and which acknowledges the authority of the sacred Vedic texts. Its initial project to pursue analytical reasoning in accordance with, and guided by, the Veda turned out to be ambiguous. The development of thought through the four classical commentaries by Vātsyāyana Pakṣilasvāmin, Uddyotakara, Vācaspati and Udayana led to more pronounced and far-reaching claims concerning the role of reason vis-à-vis the Vedic revelation. The later commentators were not content with accepting the authority of the Veda; they also wanted to verify its teachings and provide rational proof for its validity (something avoided by other schools, especially Mīmāṃsā and Vedānta). In the end, the authority of "the Vedas which define orthodoxy" depends on a validation which only reasoning can provide. Reasoning (or "analytics") itself establishes orthodoxy: "The question of full conformity between scripture and Nyāya has been set on its head" (p. 455). In a sense, analytics itself assumes the role of "supreme science of soteriology" (p. 456). As I observed in *Tradition and Reflection* (p. 27), Udayana claims that only *ānvīkṣikī* can, in the final analysis, validate and legitimize "human goals" (*puruṣārtha*); without it, final liberation (*niḥśreyasa*), the ultimate human goal, might lose its status as a *puruṣārtha*.

Such self-proclamation of reason in Nyāya does not in any way imply a critical distance from the Vedic tradition, nor a readiness to question or turn away from the social norms of the Dharmaśāstras. On the contrary, the commitment to the Vedic *dharma* becomes more pronounced and explicit over the centuries. This is exemplified by the treatment of *adhikāra*, a concept which has had a long and distinctive history in Mīmāṃsā and Vedānta. According to Uddyotakara's introductory verse, Akṣapāda composed the *Nyāyasūtra* for the peace and tranquillity (*śama*) of the world. There is no reference to "eligibility" or "qualification" (*adhikāra*) for the study of Nyāya in this context; this should, of course, not suggest any disregard for the rules of *dharma*. However, the issue of *adhikāra*, and Akṣapāda's failure to refer to it, becomes a problem for Vācaspati and Udayana. In Udayana's *Pariśuddhi*, the question of who should be admitted to the study of Nyāya and who should be excluded is discussed at length. The exclusion of the "unqualified" (*anadhikṛta*, including those who are not qualified in terms of caste membership), which may have been simply taken for granted in the older texts, is now part of the Nyāya *teachings*. In this respect,

Nyāya has, so to speak, finally caught up with Mīmāṃsā and Vedānta and their exemplary level of Vedic "orthodoxy."

## NOTES

[1] See Frauwallner 1973, vol. 1, p. XLIX (German original: 1953, p. 4); for Potter, see the preface to his "Bibliography" (1970).

# 4

# Developments and Attitudes in Neo-Hinduism

Andrew O. Fort

# *JĪVANMUKTI* AND SOCIAL SERVICE IN ADVAITA AND NEO-VEDĀNTA[1]

In both *India and Europe* and *Tradition and Reflection*, Wilhelm Halbfass writes about the pervasive influence of Western (i.e., Euro-American) categories and ways of thinking on many modern Indian thinkers, most of whom were schooled in educational institutions which follow Western models in administration, curriculum, and language of instruction. This influence is apparent on those who write about and see themselves as part of the classical Advaita tradition of Śaṅkara and his followers. These thinkers and/or scholars, whom we shall call "neo-Vedāntins," include such well-known figures as Swami Vivekananda and Sarvepalli Radhakrishnan.

While I will be critical of some neo-Vedāntic appropriation of Western ideas below, I recognize that all traditions are products of a process of assimilation and integration of concepts (and practices) deriving from a variety of sources. All thinkers, when attempting to formulate a coherent worldview, select and interpret from the cultural materials available to them. Neo-Vedāntins, greatly influenced by Anglo-Christian education and ways of thought, can be seen to be at the forefront of creative religio-cultural assimilation, syncretizing and harmonizing past and present. During a time of rapid cultural change, mediating between and trying to integrate two (at least) very different cultures is a difficult and important task.

On the other hand, a number of neo-Vedāntins have made some questionable claims about teachings found in the classical Advaita tradition, generally in response to Western, particularly Christian missionary, criticisms of that tradition. For example, often censured Advaitic teachings about caste exclusivity and devaluation of everyday activity are downplayed or even ignored, while ideas seen as laudable, such as caring for and actively providing humanitarian social service to all persons without distinction are claimed to be present but go without support from the classical texts.[2]

My paper will focus on the attempt of some modern neo-Vedāntic thinkers and scholars of Advaita to demonstrate a relationship between *jīvanmukti* (liberation, while living, from bondage to all desire) and Western-style social service (actively performing "good works" for the welfare of others), and to read this understanding back into traditional Advaitic views. As stated above, all traditions change, and adding social service to the classical model of *jīvanmukti* is legitimate (and one might even say good), yet it is still important to note that this idea is a reinterpretation - or even a distortion - of the views of Śaṅkara and his followers. While it is traditional to claim unity and continuity in Advaitic thought, those of us who are part of (or imbedded in) the Western academic tradition (which emphasizes presupposition-questioning critical reflection) cannot so easily ignore changes from earlier ideas, particularly when unrecognized or unstated. The influence of Western thought and values on these modern neo-Vedāntic thinkers demonstrates that they are, like most in the West, to some degree "other" to the classical Advaita tradition. Neo-Vedāntic scholars often use categories and research methods of Western "critical inquiry," frequently less self-consciously than Western scholars themselves. Their "otherness" to classical Advaita can be seen as part of the ongoing "Europeanization of the earth" (or at least India) mentioned so prominently - and ambivalently - in Halbfass' *India and Europe*. While acknowledging that neo-Vedāntins may have good reasons to "update" Advaitic thought, I also want to argue that accurate representation is one form of respect due to important thinkers, and neo-Vedāntins sometimes fall short of honoring Śaṅkara and classical Advaita in that way.[3]

Liberation (*mukti*, *mokṣa*) in Advaita Vedānta is the cessation of ignorance about the nondual nature of reality and the end of bondage to transmigratory existence (*saṃsāra*). One who attains liberation while living (*jīvanmukti*) realizes the identity of *ātman/brahman* and becomes utterly detached from worldly desires, knowing the body and "ego" are not the self.[4] Many questions relating to social service arise from this view, including: thus detached, does the Advaitic *jīvanmukta* show concern for the welfare of other, ignorant beings, and, if so, how? In particular, does the *jīvanmukta* actively do "good works" or perform social service in ways familiar to the modern West? Will the liberated being at least teach others about his[5] realization? Such questions are particularly significant since most neo-Vedāntic thinkers (including many contemporary Indian scholars of Advaita), assert that *jīvanmukti* and social service are compatible and/or closely related. This view, I will argue, stems from a desire to justify *jīvanmukti*, and Indian "ethical" thought generally, in light of Western and Christian notions that a perfected person looks after the welfare of others. Some also seem to want to establish the relevance of the *jīvanmukti* ideal in contemporary life. Below, we shall see that neo-Vedāntins hold that the *jīvanmukta*, although desireless and knowing that all is ultimately nondual, stays here to teach and serve other (ignorant) beings. Further, social service, while not necessary for one so detached, is seen to be the "natural" outflow of the compassionate love of the liberated being.

To begin, we should look at the central problem with which neo-Vedāntins must contend when asserting their views on social service: the devaluation of everyday existence (*vyavahāra*) in Advaitic thought. If the liberated being realizes the world of duality lacks ultimate reality, this person would not necessarily show any concern for (non)others in this realm, even by teaching them. R. C. Pandeya (1966) has made the case well that Advaitic views on nonduality lead to a "transcendence" of Western-style social ethics.[6] He argues that while the body and social realm persist for a *jīvanmukta*, such a being knows they are not the highest truth. Thus liberation brings a thoroughgoing detachment from everyday existence, with no mandatory duties. Looking out for the welfare of others means attending to the world of duality and the "others" there to care for. Not only is concern for others ultimately based on a delusion, but such concern can itself become an attachment.[7] We might even grant that once one knows nonduality, one will do no evil action, given the extensive training on the path to liberation, but there still is no imperative to do Western- (or *bodhisattva*-) style good. Pandeya concludes that while some modern Indians might be uncomfortable in finding Advaita lacking social concern, they must admit that, from the traditional Advaitic view, such concern is based in ignorance (*avidyā*).[8]

When turning to the actual textual record in classical Advaita, one finds no explicit call to perform social service or to do "good works" for those who suffer. In light of neo-Vedāntic claims to come, we might briefly mention here that Advaitic statements about the metaphysical identity of all being(s) are not linked to statements about helping others, or more generally to social and religious equality in *vyavahāra*. It is well-known that the hierarchical *varṇāśramadharma* (law of caste and life-stage) privileges certain people (especially Brahmin males) by birth. Śaṅkara clearly concurs with this view; in his *BS* I.3.34-8 commentary, he states that low-caste *śūdras*, even if interested and literate, are not entitled to study the Veda or perform Vedic rites (the necessary starting points to gain release). In fact, the commentary on *sūtra* 38 refers to texts indicating a *śūdra* hearing the Veda should have his ears filled with lead and one reciting the Veda should have his tongue chopped off.[9] Women are not even mentioned in this context. Contrary to neo-Vedāntins, who generally ignore this passage, we can agree with Halbfass (TR, p. 385) that classical Advaitins find the highest nondual truth irrelevant to equality in everyday social relations, and that they instead link identity in liberation with "an uncompromising adherence to an unequal, caste-bound access to it." One might add here that while some have argued that Śaṅkara himself, through his activity as debater and teacher, embodied the social action of the *jīvanmukta*, he nowhere demonstrates or advocates the liberated being as egalitarian "social worker."

In fact, the clearest indications of a "proactive" concern for ignorant beings in classical Advaita appear when Śaṅkara and later Advaitins occasionally refer to the knower as a teacher, i.e., one who compassionately remains in a body to share his realization.[10] The classical Advaita thinker Vimuktātman (*Iṣṭasiddhi*, pp. 74-78) makes the liberated being's role as teacher a central issue. He and others claim that a teacher is necessary for liberation, but not that a knower (*jñānin*) is obliged to teach.[11] Śaṅkara expresses concern for ignorant beings in *Upadeśasāhasrī* Prose I.6, in which the teacher's compassion (*dayā*) and concern (*anugraha*) for others are mentioned, but not elaborated. Some refer to Śaṅkara's comments on *BS* III.3.32,[12] which imply that a liberated being could take birth again to fulfill a certain commission (*adhikāra*) arising due to the condition of the world. However, Śaṅkara seems here to be responding to the demands of the text; he does not mention the idea of a commission elsewhere. He also indicates the commission is to promulgate the Veda, which, while keeping the world well-ordered, is not what a reader might immediately think of as the neo-Vedāntic version of social service.

When arguing that Śaṅkara calls for "social service," most neo-Vedāntins make reference to the idea of *lokasaṃgraha*, which is often translated "welfare of the world," and suggest that this is part of the liberated being's orientation to perform service to society. However, in the most important references to *lokasaṃgraha* relevant here, found in *BhG* III.20 and elsewhere, Kṛṣṇa seems to instruct Arjuna to act for the "well-being" of the world (or people in general) by upholding or preserving dharmic order rather than general human or global welfare. In his commentary on this passage, Śaṅkara certainly holds to such an understanding of *lokasaṃgraha*. Sustaining the *dharma* may bring 'well-being, in the cosmos and to (Āryan) people, but will not necessarily provide service or "welfare" for all.

From this view, *BhG* III.20 states that one attains perfection (*samsiddhi*) through (detached) action (*karman*), so one should act considering only *lokasaṃgraha*, that is, the world's well-being, which is brought about by selflessly upholding the dharmic order. In his commentary, Śaṅkara argues that while pursuing or after achieving right insight (*samyagdarśana*), in which one achieves perfection (i. e. *mokṣa*), one continues acting, due to currently manifesting or *prārabdhakarman*. Śaṅkara seems to suggest that the wise person should be a "role model" and world order preserver; he here defines *lokasaṃgraha* as preventing the world's (or people's) activity from going astray (*lokasyonmārgapravṛttinivāraṇam*). The exact nature of this activity, while unspecified, seems to mean not straying from the *dharma*. In accord with the ensuing verses (III.21-25), Śaṅkara points out that since people follow the standard a superior person sets, such a person, despite being (like Kṛṣṇa) utterly detached and needing to do nothing, should and does act only for the sake of others.[13] Here then one may see a call to attend to the well-being of the world (at least the part which includes the Āryan twice-born), but neither Śaṅkara nor the *Bhagavadgītā* prescribe any Western-style "social action" nor do they describe the actions the wise perform for the world's welfare as humanistic service to all.[14]

## Swami Vivekananda on *jīvanmukti* and Social Service

To understand the views of contemporary neo-Vedāntic scholars of Advaita concerning *jīvanmukti* and social service, we must consider some ideas of two modern Indian thinkers who have greatly influenced these scholars on a range of topics, Swami Vivekananda and Sarvepalli Radhakrishnan. Both were trained in English-speaking missionary schools, read widely in Western literature and philosophy, and travelled extensively in the West. Both valued reason, tolerance, and social progress, and claimed that Advaita Vedānta (not Christianity) was the most ethical, scientific, progressive, and universal religion. On the other hand, neither were simply "Western"; both were familiar with, and claimed as authoritative, Vedāntic texts and Indian philosophical thought in Sanskrit. Their writings (and their lives) also became models for the "translation" and to some degree assimilation of Hinduism into terms of Western humanism.

Swami Vivekananda, the most famous disciple of the Bengali master Ramakrishna, additionally participated in both sides of the guru-student system, took the vow of *saṃnyāsa*, and worshipped the Goddess. He organized a Hindu monastic order, but stressed the performance of social service activities rather than retreat and contemplation. Vivekananda also became, following the 1893 Parliament of Religions in Chicago, by far the best-known messenger of Hinduism in the West. He is important here both because of the exemplary nature of his remarks on living liberation and social service and because many present-day Indian scholars of Advaita refer to Vivekananda as a model of modern *jīvanmukti*. Detailing his interpretation of Advaita and "Hinduism" generally is beyond the scope of this paper, though he does call Advaita "the fairest flower of philosophy and religion that any country in any age has produced" (Vivekananda 1962, p. 74).[15] We shall see below that, while a skillful communicator and advocate, Vivekananda gave little attention to scholarly accuracy or to the problems of interpreting and matching categories and concepts across cultures.[16]

Vivekananda often claimed that Vedānta and social service are completely compatible. Reacting in part to criticism of Hindu caste-boundedness by Christian missionaries, he argued strenuously for "spiritual harmony," tolerance and universal brotherhood, and held that such ideas were Vedāntic because Vedānta claims that when we feel oneness in human nature and with the universe, we "rush forth to express it ... . This expression of oneness is what we call love and sympathy, and it is the basis of all our ethics and morality. This is summed up in the Vedānta philosophy by the celebrated aphorism *Tat Tvam Asi*, 'Thou Art That.'"[17] This means your soul and body are one with all others, and "in hurting anyone you hurt yourself; in loving anyone you love yourself (Vivekananda 1962, p. 32)." Although he admits that India has actually been a nonpareil "land of privilege," he goes on to say that "[n]one can be Vedāntists and at the same time admit of privilege to anyone," and that "[t]he work of the Advaita, therefore is to break down all these privileges." His exemplar of one holding to a "Vedāntic ethics" of equality without privileges is the Buddha (pp. 46-47).[18] Such statements are, of course, advocacy rather than description and go far afield from traditional Advaita (and even from the views of his master, Ramakrishna).

Vivekananda only rarely explicitly mentions *jīvanmukti*, and in these passages he generally does not make extravagant claims for the social ethics of the liberated being. For example, he writes that "there are men still living for whom delusion has vanished forever." Although having the highest knowledge, their bodies will continue "until the momentum of past work is exhausted." Further, "[t]he man who has in this life attained to this state ... is called 'free while living.' This is the goal of the Vedantist, to attain freedom in life (Vivekananda 1953, p. 333)." He expands on these ideas elsewhere, comparing the body's continuation after liberation to the unattended potter's wheel temporarily continuing motion. He states that when the liberated being knows the world's unreality, and lives without bondage or pain, in "that state he is called *jīvanmukta*, 'living-free.'" *jīvanmukti* is the "aim and end in this life for the *jnana-yogi*." He "can live in this world without being attached," like the lotus, water-borne but unwet. He is "the highest of all beings; for he has realized his identity with the Absolute" and oneness with God. Vivekananda then specifically asks, after liberation, "[w]hat good shall we do to the world?" Once we know

> there is nothing else but this *Atman*, that everything else is but a dream, with no existence in reality, then this world with its poverties, its miseries, its wickedness, and its goodness will cease to disturb us. If they do not exist, for whom and for what shall we take trouble? This is what the *jnana-yogis* teach. (1962, pp. 84-85)

Here Vivekananda takes seriously the world-devaluation of traditional Advaita, and thus one finds no social responsibility mandated for the *jīvanmukta*.

Yet Vivekananda has a bit more to say about living liberation and action in the world. While the liberated being is utterly free and beyond all moral law, Vivekananda disputes that the *jīvanmukta* would do any evil; "good is the inner coating of the Real Man, the Self." He argues that "what is left attached to the man who has reached the Self and seen Truth is the remnant of the good impressions of his past life, the good momentum." This good manifests in a remarkably Christian-sounding way:

> Even if he lives in the body and works incessantly, he works only to do good; his lips speak only benediction to all; his hands do only good works; his mind can think only good thoughts; his presence is a blessing wherever he goes. He is himself a living blessing. Such a man will, by his very presence, change even the most wicked persons into saints. Even if he does not speak, his very presence will be a blessing to mankind. Can such men do any evil? (1953, pp. 334-335)

Vivekananda concludes that the realized being does good by loving all, thus bringing peace. Neo-Vedānta clearly takes precedence over Śaṅkara's Advaita here.

## Radhakrishnan on *jīvanmukti* and Social Service

After Vivekananda, Sarvepalli Radhakrishnan is probably the best-known champion of neo-Vedānta. Radhakrishnan, born a Telugu Smarta Brahmin, was, like Vivekananda, educated in English in mission schools, and was steeped in Western ways of thinking (valuing "rationality," religious humanism, and "progress" in history). Unlike Vivekananda, however, he saw himself as a university-based scholar/educator, and knew Vedānta and Sanskrit in some depth.[19]

Throughout Radhakrishnan's works, one sees a tension between his desire to be an impartial scholar and his inclination to be an apologist, for a reified "Hinduism" in general, and for Śaṅkara's Advaita in particular. This tension is quite evident in his writings on both *jīvanmukti* and social service. As Robert Minor points out (1987, p. 131ff.), Radhakrishnan constructed his own normative "Hinduism," whose essence was not, as its critics charged, world-denying, fatalistic, polytheistic, caste-bound, or deficient in social concern.[20] Instead, like Vivekananda, Radhakrishnan claims that Hinduism is a progressive, activist, rational, and tolerant "religion of the spirit." The purportedly experience-based "monistic idealism" of Advaita Vedānta is the highest manifestation of this spiritual religion.

Particularly relevant here is the importance that Radhakrishnan, again like Vivekananda, ascribed to social ethics and his sensitivity to Christian missionary criticisms of Advaitic "world-denial." Radhakrishnan argues that Advaita's inclusive, eternal wisdom would bring world community (unlike the exclusivist "dogma" found in much of Christianity). He claims that detachment due to realization of nonduality is not necessarily world-renunciation, and that in fact, Advaita is quite compatible with social service. In his more than 200 page chapter on Śaṅkara's thought in *Indian Philosophy*,[21] Radhakrishnan writes that Śaṅkara's own life "is a standing refutation of the charge that the existent world-order with its institutions is a thing to be escaped from (Radhakrishnan 1931, p. 632)," and that Śaṅkara's emphasis "is not on retirement from the world, but on renunciation of the self (p. 633)." So far, Radhakrishnan's view has merit: according to Advaitic tradition, Śaṅkara was an active teacher and debater. Yet Radhakrishnan goes on to link this activity with a more expansive and questionable claim of selfless world-saving; he continues (and anticipates his description of the *jīvanmukta* elsewhere) that the detached person's attitude is not "world-fleeing, but world-saving. The perfect man lives and dies, not for himself, but for mankind (p. 633)." He makes a similar claim in *Eastern Religions and Western Thought*, where he writes that "[t]he liberated individual works for the welfare of the world (Radhakrishnan 1940, p. 100)," and quotes the *Bhagavadgītā* to that effect. Until their absorption into "the Absolute," he states, "freed individuals share, though in a disinterested spirit, in the work of the world (p. 101)." While words like "freedom" and "welfare of the world" can at times appropriately be linked to the terms "*mokṣa*" and "*lokasaṃgraha*," Radhakrishnan's usages here seem rather different than Śaṅkara's.

The alteration of meanings in shared terminology is made evident when Radhakrishnan goes on to suggest (as Vivekananda does) that "*tat tvam asi*" (you/*ātman* are that/*brahman*) indicates social responsibility as well as metaphysical identity. Responding to Albert Schweitzer's ideas, he claims that *tat tvam asi* "is bound up with an ethic of active service." His support for this assertion comes not from Śaṅkara or another Advaitin, but from Paul Deussen, the German scholar of Advaita, who draws a parallel with the Sermon on the Mount by saying "That art thou" indicates "[y]ou should love your neighbor as yourselves because you are your neighbor (Radhakrishnan 1940, p. 101)."

Radhakrishnan's most extensive comments on *jīvanmukti* specifically are at the end of the introduction to his translation of the *BS* (1960, pp. 215-218, 222). His interpretation is largely in accord with Advaitic tradition: one can be liberated while living, for liberation is based on detachment and knowing *brahman*, not on dropping the body.[22] However, consistent with his desire to deny that Hinduism is world-renouncing, he emphasizes the idea, found in the *Yogavāsiṣṭha*, that the detached knower may act in the world in various ways (he mentions Kṛṣṇa, Śuka, Rāma, and Janaka). He gives a long (unreferenced) quotation from the *Yogavāsiṣṭha* on the detached action of the *jīvanmukta*, and states that "what binds us is not action but the spirit in which it is done (Radhakrishnan 1960, p. 217)." He does not here claim that Advaitins hold that the egoless activity of the liberated being is social service. Still, he clearly presents his own Christian-influenced neo-Vedāntic views by saying he favors the liberated being acting for "*sarva-mukti*," which he calls "corporate salvation (p. 218)" and "world-redemption (p. 220)." For Radhakrishnan, "[t]wo conditions are essential for final salvation, (i) inward perfection attained by intuition of self, (ii) outer perfection possible only with the liberation of all. The liberated souls which attain the first condition continue to work for the second (p. 219)." While he implies that Śaṅkara agrees with this view, he explicitly writes only that "Śaṅkara's view of the *Jīvan-mukti* condition makes out that inner perfection and work in the finite universe can go together (p. 222)." Even this goes without citation, however. One can see here the tension between accurate reporting and apologetic wish.[23]

The activity of the *jīvanmukta* is also mentioned in *Indian Philosophy*: While Śaṅkara first seems to say that the nondual realization of *mokṣa* is not consistent with dualism-accepting work in the world, Radhakrishnan states that "so far as *jīvanmuktas* are concerned, activity is allowed," since they are "above the sense of egoity" and the "law of karma (Radhakrishnan 1931, p. 644)." Again, no textual citation appears, although he does go on to mention the *BSBh* III.3.32 passage on the possibility of a liberated being taking rebirth to fulfill a commission (*adhikāra*), such as teaching the Veda. Further, concerning ethical behavior, Radhakrishnan also claims that Śaṅkara "holds that moral obligation has no meaning for the freed soul" yet "moral virtues are [not] abandoned by him." For the liberated being, "[e]vil action is psychologically impossible," for he has "died to sin (p. 620)."[24] Once again, Radhakrishnan's writing about Śaṅkara's views is filtered through Christian categories of "morality" and "sin." In the next section, we shall see that, as Vivekananda and Western ways of thinking shaped Radhakrishnan, modern scholars of Advaita continue to be shaped by Radhakrishnan and the enduring impact of Western thought on India.

## Modern Advaitic Scholars on *jīvanmukti* and Social Service

Contemporary neo-Vedāntic scholars writing on living liberation follow classical Advaitic thinking in part, yet they also make quite untraditional claims concerning the social ethics of the *jīvanmukta*. While accepting that the *jīvanmukta* is utterly detached from desire and has no duty to act, many of these scholars stress that the liberated being's nature is to "altruistically" love and serve others. For example, N. Veezhinathan and S. K. Ramachandran (1966, p. 127) assert that the *jīvanmukta* has a "mission as teacher and saviour ... to enable men to realize their true self."[25] The liberated being "cannot but help others to attain" liberation (p. 128), for "pure love [is the] spontaneous expression of his very nature (p. 127)." In fact, Veezhinathan and Ramachandran claim that the *jīvanmukta* tells followers to follow their *dharma* "out of sheer love for fellow-beings (p. 129)." In a similar vein, A. G. Krishna Warrier argues that liberated beings postpone "deliverance [for] missions of service to struggling humanity (Krishna Warrier 1961, p. 508)." He elsewhere adds that "these supermen ... furnish the living proof of the validity of the Advaitic claim that the realization of Self delivers one from the clutches of the separatist ego (p. 528)." A. K. Lad (1967, pp. 118-119) claims that the *jīvanmukta* is "Supra-moral, not immoral," and that while doing "spontaneous activity for the welfare of the world," he "overcomes the dualism of 'Is' and 'Ought.'" Few, if any, classical textual references are supplied for any of the above assertions, and one can argue, as Pandeya does, that Advaitic desirelessness in practice has not and in theory will not "naturally" breed love and service.

Contemporary Advaitic scholars such as P. K. Sundaram and R. Balasubramaniam hold similar views. Balasubramaniam (1988, p. 385) writes that the *jīvanmukta* is "engaged in action of his own accord for the sake of *lokasangraha*, i.e., for the preservation of the world-order, for social service, without the sense of 'I' or 'mine.'" One notes here (and will see again below) the explicit linkage of preservation of the world (*lokasaṃgraha*) with social service, a tie never specifically made in traditional Advaita. In conversation, Balasubramaniam added that the *jīvanmukta*, seeing others suffer in the world of duality, serves both as a model for right action and as a teacher due to compassion for the ignorant. He added, "His attachment is not like ours. He acts without any sense of agency," and is not (like us) impelled by desire.[26] P. K. Sundaram also held the view that after knowing oneness, one would naturally altruistically help alleviate the suffering of "others," since with his mental clarity, the *jīvanmukta* sees human unity. For one knowing identity with others, social service is inevitable, since, Sundaram argued, no one wants to hurt oneself (in actuality, a debatable proposition). In response to the view that the liberated being would not act since he knows suffering to be unreal, Sundaram claimed that the *jīvanmukta*'s activity is "not logical but phenomenological" because he knows the ignorant person feels the suffering as real.[27]

I have written elsewhere (Fort 1992) about the clearest recent example of linkage between *jīvanmukti* and a highly Westernized (particularly Christian) notion of social service: L. K. L. Srivastava's *Advaitic Conception of Jīvanmukti* (1990). Srivastava argues that the *mukta* is a "detached saint," rooted "in an all comprehensive love"; further, "his service is rendered to all regardless of caste and class (p. 17)." The liberated being looks from the "viewpoint of the welfare of mankind," an ideal "based on universal brotherhood and love (p. 24)"; he "is not fulfilled if he does not do good to others or does not strive for removing woes and sufferings from the world (p. 25)." This view, which Srivastava calls part of *lokasaṃgraha*, "represents the true spirit of Indian culture" (p. 25).[28] Srivastava praises Buddhist and Jain models of socially concerned liberated beings, while lamenting the lack of such examples found in Śaṅkara's and Vidyāraṇya's writings (p. 80ff.). Unsurprisingly, his model Hindu *jīvanmukta* is Swami Vivekananda.[29] Srivastava approvingly quotes Vivekananda's abovementioned claim that the liberated person "works only to do good, his lips speak only benediction to all, his hands do only good works; his mind can only think good thoughts, his presence is a blessing wherever he goes."[30] While Srivastava argues that Vivekananda is "a burning example of this ideal (p. 284)," the ideal mentioned seems closer to a nineteenth century image of a Christian saint than that of the *jīvanmukta* in traditional Advaita.

Other modern scholars of Advaita argue that while *jīvanmuktas* do not perform or promote Western-style social service, they do assist others by being teachers and "good examples" of liberated living. For example, Chacko Valiaveetil (1980, pp. 162-164) writes that the *jīvanmukta*'s presence and teaching increase the spiritual, versus material, welfare of the world, but that no "social" activity is possible given ultimate nonduality. The modern nondualist Ramana Maharshi, who many claim to be a *jīvanmukta*, can be seen as such a teacher. Many have said that his primary teaching is his peace-giving presence and his comforting and healing look. In his book translating Sarvajñātman's *Saṃkṣepaśārīraka*, N. Veezhinathan (1985, p. 139) also writes that "a preceptor is necessary in order to preserve and propagate the Advaitic tradition." The view that the *jīvanmukta* compassionately teaches can be grounded in the Advaita tradition. Veezhinathan's view on the necessity of a teacher echoes that of the classical Advaitin Vimuktātman, and Veezhinathan (1985, pp. 138-139) points to passages in sacred texts which hold that "one who has a teacher directly experiences Brahman-Atman" (*ChU* VI.14.2) and that truth-seeing sages impart that knowledge to students (*BhG* IV.34). In his commentaries, Śaṅkara concurs that the *brahman* knower will, out of great compassion, teach one blindfolded by ignorance about the true nondual self (*ChU* VI.14.2) and that the truth-seer teaches the supreme knowledge (*BhG* IV.34). One could argue that Śaṅkara himself was an example of such a person.

Finally, the Vedānta pandit at Madras Sanskrit College, R. Krisnamurthi Sastry, gave two additional reasons why a *jīvanmukta* would remain and teach. First, he claimed that since anyone remaining embodied still has *prārabdhakarman*, which includes a unique personality, it might be part of a particular *jīvanmukta*'s disposition to teach or do good. He also suggested the idea that the *jīvanmukta* stays to teach due to the good karmic fruits of the not yet liberated. In this view, we ignorant beings cause the detached liberated one to remain.

It seems apparent that the number and range of the arguments forwarded above by modern neo-Vedāntic thinkers and scholars of Advaita are in part an attempt to counter the view that Advaita is not concerned with being compassionate or doing good in the world (as opposed to the Buddhist *bodhisattva* or some Christian ideals). These scholars seem persuaded that interest in and action to increase social welfare is good, and thus the Advaitic *jīvanmukta* (at least today) must have such concern. In closing, I would argue however that one might better compare the traditional image of a *jīvanmukta* in Advaita to a Theravāda Buddhist *arhat* than to a socially active saint or *bodhisattva*, for the *arhat* assists others primarily by "mere" presence, being a field of merit and modelling detached serenity (as well as teaching). Yet in the end, the *arhat* is not focussed on world-affirming social service, but is waiting to reach *nirupadhiśeṣanirvāṇa* (which Advaitins might say occurs when *prārabdhakarman* ceases).

*Texas Christian University*
*Department of Religion*
*Fort Worth, Texas, USA*

## NOTES

[1] I would here like to thank Mackenzie Brown of Trinity University and Shanti Kumar, graduate student at TCU, for their close readings and helpful suggestions.

[2] On caste in the Hindu tradition, see Chapter 10 in *Tradition and Reflection*.

[3] I recognize that language like "accurate representation" is contested by post-modernists and others. I endorse the possibility of multiple readings of a text, but I am not ready to abandon the idea (and importance) of authorial intent.

[4] Advaitins claim Śaṅkara to be a model *jīvanmukta*; Ramana Maharshi would be a more recent example.

[5] I will generally avoid using the male pronoun, however the Advaita tradition unambiguously privileges males concerning liberation.

[6] When conversing with K. Kunjuṅni Raja of the Adyar Library in Madras, I found he largely agreed with Pandeya's view.

[7] This view is clear in the teachings of the modern Indian nondualist Ramana Maharshi. In this view, the liberated being leads by his example of serene Self-knowledge and by the grace of his presence.

[8] K. Kunjunni Raja added that while one can argue that seeing oneness will lead to helping others, this view is not made explicit in traditional Advaita (Personal interview, 1/22/90).

[9] Neo-Vedantins, of course, claim that Śaṅkara's views were very different. In his biography of Śaṅkara (based on the traditional *Śaṅkaradigvijaya* of Mādhava), the neo-Vedāntin I. S. Madugulu (1985, p. 26) asserts that a *caṇḍāla* (really Śiva in disguise) teaches Śaṅkara a lesson in "practical Vedanta" by pointing out that one should identify only with the nondual Self and not with the body or Brahmin caste. After this instruction, Madugulu writes, Śaṅkara "realized his error which was the result of his social conditioning and his upbringing but entirely contrary to his conviction."

[10] See Śaṅkara's commentaries on *ChU* VI.14.2 and *BhG* IV.34.

[11] Sarvajñātman's *Saṃkṣepaśārīraka* (II.225-227) and Prakāśānanda's *Vedāntasiddhāntamuktāvali* (42) state that there is an imagined teacher who, when thought to be omniscient, brings knowledge to the ignorant in accordance with the *śāstras*.

[12] Ramachandra Rao 1978, p. 61, Radhakrishnan 1931, p. 644, and P. K. Sundaram in conversation.

[13] The idea that despite having no aims of one's own after liberating knowledge, one continues to act to uphold the world order also appears in Śaṅkara's commentary on *BhG* II.10 and IV.20.

[14] The liberated being's concern for others is somewhat of an issue in yoga-influenced Advaita texts like Vidyāraṇya's *Jīvanmuktiviveka* however. See especially his description of austerity (*tapas*), the second purpose of attaining *jīvanmukti*, in Chapter IV.

[15] The best statement of Vivekananda's views on many topics relevant here is probably his four lectures on "Practical Vedanta." See Vivekananda 1953, pp. 338-377.

[16] For example, his usages of "freedom" sometimes suggest Mill more than *mokṣa*, and "evolution" Spencer more than Sāṃkhya.

[17] Halbfass points out (IE, p. 239) that when Paul Hacker surveyed ethical maxims in Sanskrit literature and their links with philosophical teachings, he found no evidence that the metaphysical identity statement "*tat tvam asi*" was ever used to justify "practical" ethical imperatives as Vivekananda attempts to do (Hacker 1978, pp. 531-564).

[18] He also writes that while Śaṅkara made Vedānta "rationalistic," and stressed the "intellectual" side of Vedānta, the Buddha emphasized the "moral" side (1953, p. 249). This notion will reappear in Radhakrishnan's thought.

[19] He held the Spalding chair at Oxford, headed Banaras Hindu University, and eventually became President of India.

[20] Radhakrishnan writes extensively on the caste system, in part defending it, and in part agreeing with its critics. His position is that caste is, *or should be*, based on character and natural capacity, not on birth. However, in his clearest statement on caste, the last lecture in *The Hindu View of Life*, he claims that caste does discourage "indiscriminate racial amalgamation (Radhakrishnan 1927a, p. 98)." He defends castes as customary social groupings which emphasize cooperation, and are "functional" in a complex society. The caste system also gives a feeling of solidarity to a society. Radhakrishnan shows his Brahmin solidarity here, holding that Brahmins are "said to be above class interests and prejudices," being "freed from the cares of existence" to develop and broadcast "spiritual ideals (p. 108)." See also Radhakrishnan 1940, pp. 351-378.

Radhakrishnan (1931, p. 616) distorts Śaṅkara's views on the *varṇāśramadharma*, repeatedly suggesting that Śaṅkara was merely meeting "the common beliefs of his age."

He claims that while "the efficacy of caste institutions has ceased to be vital for Śaṃkara, he allows room for belief in it (p. 616)." He admits that Śaṅkara privileges Brahmins and *saṃnyāsins*, yet argues that overall "Śaṃkara undermined the belief of the exclusive right of the upper classes to salvation (p. 617)." (He passes over the exclusion of women in one sentence). Radhakrishnan's interpretation of the relevant *Brahmasūtra* commentary here demonstrates both his attempt to represent the text accurately and his desire to make the text fit his view of what Hinduism/Vedānta/Śaṅkara *should* say.

[21] He here asserts the common neo-Vedāntic view that Śaṅkara was "rational," a "philosopher," and a "social idealist" aiming to unify earlier "Hindu" thought (Radhakrishnan 1931, pp. 655-658).

[22] He also mentions currently manifesting *karman* and the two moons analogy (in which one knows only one moon exists, but sees two from eye-disease, *BSBh* IV.1.15).

[23] He makes a number of similar, but less focussed, comments on the nature of the liberated being in the introduction to his translation of the principal Upaniṣads (Radhakrishnan 1953, p. 121ff.). Minor writes that Radhakrishnan, when speaking on the *Dhammapada*, called the Buddha a *jīvanmukta* who realized *tat tvam asi* and then returned to the world as a social reformer and prophet of Vedānta (Minor 1987, p. 97). Radhakrishnan was not always quite this "ecumenical."

[24] Other comments on good and evil appear in Radhakrishnan 1940, pp. 102-103.

[25] Their article immediately follows the Pandeya article mentioned earlier, and is also called "*Jīvanmukti* and Social Concerns."

[26] Personal interview, 1/19/90.

[27] Personal interview, 1/10/90.

[28] This statement is true only of an "India" influenced by modern Western ideas. Elsewhere Srivastava (1990, p. 28) recognizes that Śaṅkara and others emphasize *karmasaṃnyāsa* and no obligations to society, including social service.

[29] Vivekananda was also mentioned by Sundaram.

[30] Found in Vivekananda 1987, p. 284.

**Stuart Elkman**

## RELIGIOUS PLURALITY AND SWAMI VIVEKANANDA

Professor Halbfass begins Chapter 3 of *Tradition and Reflection* with some insightful, yet somewhat sweeping, remarks concerning ideas of religious plurality in present-day Hinduism. He asserts that modern proponents of Hinduism often try to demonstrate the superiority of Hinduism by claiming that it is not a religion in the ordinary sense, but rather a "framework, a concordance and unifying totality of sects" (p. 51). They maintain, claims Halbfass, that by declaring Hinduism to be a kind of "meta-religion" (*sanātanadharma*), they seek to set it above "ordinary" religions, which find their respective places within it. According to this view, Hinduism subsumes other religions, reconciles them, shows their common denominator, and is thus superior to them.

There are no doubt champions of Hinduism (some of whom Halbfass quotes directly) who would raise no objections to having their "religion" praised in such terms, despite, of course, the unspoken charges of paternalism and chauvinism implied in his words. Unfortunately, Swami Vivekananda, whom Halbfass cites as his first example, terming him "the most famous apostle of Hinduism in the West," would, in my view, not have been one of them. On the contrary, he most likely would have taken great exception to the above-mentioned remarks for some subtle, yet significant, reasons. In fact, it was exactly this kind of superior attitude held by proponents of different faiths, whether on exclusive or inclusive grounds, that he spent much of his life fighting against.

There is clearly a certain degree of truth in many of the remarks quoted by Halbfass in this chapter, and Swami Vivekananda would be the first to agree with them. Hinduism is unique, or at least different from most religions, in many respects, all of which tend to set it apart from other religions (which Vivekananda never considered "ordinary") without, however, placing it above them. For one thing, Hinduism is undeniably quite different from other religions in a historical sense. It is a simple fact that before the invasion of peoples professing other faiths, the proponents of the various sects which today are collectively known as "Hinduism" had no reason to consider themselves members of a single religion or to even give a name to their religion. This is demonstrated by the well-known fact that even the term "Hindu" was brought to India by outsiders whose inability to understand the religion of the people of India was mirrored in their inability to pronounce the very term they coined to designate them.[1] This is not to say that there was no common basis for the various sects in India. Philosophically they shared many beliefs regarding such ideas as *karman* and reincarnation; they had a common caste system to bind them together; and they recognized themselves as "orthodox," as opposed to the Buddhists and other "heterodox" schools, based on their acceptance of the authority of the Vedas. However, for each point they held in common, there were others on which they differed: their objects of worship, methods of spiritual practice, beliefs in the hereafter, etc. Even their sacred texts were different, though, as mentioned above, all paid homage to the Vedas in varying degrees. Thus, despite the fact that they may have recognized a certain unity among themselves and may have believed that each different sect was a means to the same ultimate goal, they did not feel the need to belong to some kind of super-religion, an umbrella under which they all could sit, with its own name and identity, until foreign invasion gave them a feeling of unity based on their common differences from their new rulers. Other religions had no such identity problems because, unlike Hinduism, they generally had a particular founder and a concrete starting point in history. In this respect, we can say with some objectivity that the different sects within Hinduism, many of which trace their origins to a particular saint or sage at a particular period of history, resemble other religions more than Hinduism does. We can also agree that Hinduism is at the very least a "totality of sects" if not a "unifying totality of sects" (TR, p. 51).

This, then, is the first obvious distinction between Hinduism and other religions, a distinction which is a simple historical fact. There are other differences, such as the emphasis placed in Hinduism on direct experience of spiritual truth, although this is a trait also found in other Eastern religions and in mystical traditions in general. The real question here, however, is whether Hinduism is unique in some higher sense as well. Is it somehow ontologically different? Is it, as claimed by certain so-called "Neo-Hindu" thinkers, different by its very essence from other religions, possessing the power to absorb other religions into itself and thereby render them superfluous through a process of assimilation? This seems to be the charge Halbfass makes when he quotes certain remarks of Swami Vivekananda regarding the fate of Buddhism in India. He cites Vivekananda as saying that Buddhism was India's first sect and that, in the context of Hinduism, it was never more than a sect. According to Vivekananda, " ... in India this gigantic child was absorbed, in the long run, by the mother that gave it birth ..." (Vivekananda 1984, p. 511). There is obvious truth in these statements, not, however, from any metaphysical point of view, but again from a purely historical one. Buddhism *was* a sect of Hinduism in the same sense that Christianity was a sect of Judaism, a comparison which Vivekananda himself makes. Its founder *was* a Hindu, and one who, like Jesus after him, never claimed to belong to any religion other than the one to which he was born. His teachings *were* well within the bounds of Vedic thought (with the important distinction that they did not depend on the authority of the Vedas). Buddhism was eventually absorbed into Hinduism in the sense that its adherents ultimately lost their separate identity as Buddhists (many of them also converting to Islam); the Buddhist temples (those which were not destroyed) were reinstalled with Hindu deities (the Buddhist *Dharma* itself becoming a deity); and Buddha was himself inducted into the pantheon of *avatāras*. This was a historical process based on a unique set of circumstances. It was no doubt aided by the ability of Hinduism to embrace other religions as valid paths to truth, but was primarily the result of historical factors coupled with the fact that Buddhism was an offspring of Hinduism which had never strayed very far from home to begin with. It was not due to some insidious propensity of Hinduism to destroy other faiths through a process of inclusion. Jainism, whose position with regard to Hinduism perfectly parallels that of Buddhism, somehow managed to avoid the same end as Buddhism in India, not because of any measures taken to avoid the death-like embrace of Hinduism, but because many of the historical factors which led to the demise of Buddhism in India were simply not present in Jainism.

It is difficult to understand, therefore, how Halbfass can draw conclusions regarding Hinduism and other religions (notably Christianity) based on the unique relationship between Hinduism and Buddhism. Halbfass writes,

> The implicit references to Christianity can hardly be overlooked when Vivekananda and other modern Indian thinkers speak about Buddhism: Buddhism is a much older and much more universal missionary religion than Christianity; yet it is

> nothing more than a sect in the totality and universality of Hinduism. The other religions are, or will be, ultimately included in Hinduism; Vivekananda speaks about the "infinite arms" of Vedānta, which will be able to embrace and to include all present and future developments in science, religion and philosophy. (TR, p. 52)

How would Vivekananda respond to such charges? How would he react to claims that Hinduism is on some kind of mission to absorb other religions (or, due to its very nature, will inevitably absorb other religions), to wrap its infinite tentacles around other faiths and swallow them whole? What would he say to the idea that the fate of Buddhism in India awaits the other great religions of the world as well? How would he address the fear that the fact that a Hindu can worship Christ with as much reverence as a Christian is a sure sign that Christ will one day be demoted from being the son of God to merely the eleventh *avātara*?

In order to answer these questions, it will be helpful to examine Swami Vivekananda's views regarding the nature of Hinduism, in what sense it is unique or superior to other religions, and how it relates to other religions. Part of the confusion in this entire discussion stems from the fact that Swami Vivekananda makes an important distinction between Hinduism and *sanātanadharma* (the eternal spiritual truths of religion), while Halbfass here identifies the two. The distinction for Vivekananda can clearly be seen in two parables which he learned from his guru, Sri Ramakrishna. The first parable is about a pond with several bathing ghats. At one ghat, Muslims come and draw water in leather pouches. They call the water *pāni*. At another ghat, Hindus come; they draw water in their pitchers and call it *jal*. At a third ghat, Christians come; they also fill their containers, but call it *water*. The second parable concerns a man who has a vat of dye. When someone wants his cloth dyed a certain color, the man dips the cloth in the dye and it comes out the desired color. One man wants a blue cloth, and it comes out blue; another wants a green cloth, and it comes out green, and so on. Now, these two parables can be interpreted in two different, but closely related, ways. On the one hand, the liquid in the vat which has the power to dye the cloth whatever color one desires, as well as the water in the pond, represent the unmanifest, *nirguṇaṃ brahma*, beyond name and form, while the various dyed cloths and the water, with its distinctive names and in its distinctive forms, represent the manifest *saguṇaṃ brahma*. Similarly, these two parables can also be taken to show the distinction between religion in its universal form, the *sanātanadharma*, and the particular, and necessarily incomplete, manifestations of the universal principles of religion. From these two parables, we can clearly see that for Sri Ramakrishna, and equally so for Swami Vivekananda, not only is there a clear distinction between Hinduism and the *sanātanadharma*, but that Hinduism, being one of the many different manifestations of the universal religion, is seen by them to be on an equal footing with other religions. In this sense, Hinduism, along with Buddhism, Islam, Christianity, Judaism, and the other world religions are all sects within the one universal religion, termed by the Hindus *sanātanadharma*. In no sense did Vivekananda consider the other religions to represent sects within Hinduism. When Vivekananda speaks about the ability of Hinduism to embrace other faiths, it is not with menacing arms meant to strangle them, but with open arms and an attitude of acceptance based on a feeling of unity. If Hinduism has the capacity to include the various "ideals of other religions" (Vivekananda's actual phrase, not "other religions," as Halbfass implies) and to worship the saints and sages of other religions it is only because it recognizes its common ground with them: it realizes that they are all drawing water from the same pond.

Many of the claims made by Halbfass regarding Swami Vivekananda's beliefs make sense when we see them in the context of the *sanātanadharma* and not in the context of Hinduism. Vivekananda did believe that there was a common basis of all religions, that there was a unity in diversity, that there was a common goal to which they all aspire, knowingly or unknowingly, and he based his beliefs on the teachings of Vedānta, specifically the Advaita school.[2] This is an important point, because, for him, Vedānta was more than the ancient teachings of the *ṛṣis* of India, embodied in the Upaniṣads; it represented the universal truths of religion which could not be claimed as the exclusive property of any one religion or country, the *sanātanadharma*. These truths no more belonged to India and Hinduism, in his mind, than does the law of gravity belong to Sir Isaac Newton and England. If it was in India that these truths were first discovered and worked out, that was no doubt to the great credit of Hinduism. However, for Vivekananda, this fact conferred no special status on Hinduism and did not prevent him from criticizing his fellow Hindus for not living up to the very teachings they discovered. In a revealing letter written to Mohammed Sarfaraz Husain, Vivekananda said:

> Whether we call it Vedantism or any *ism*, the truth is that Advaitism is the last word of religion and thought and the only position from which one can look upon all religions and sects with love. I believe it is the religion of the future enlightened humanity. The Hindus may get the credit of arriving at it earlier than other races,

> they being an older race than either the Hebrew or the Arab; yet practical Advaitism, which looks upon and behaves to all mankind as one's own soul, was never developed among the Hindus universally. On the other hand, my experience is that if ever any religion approached to this equality in an appreciable manner, it is Islam and Islam alone ... Mankind ought to be taught that religions are but the varied expressions of THE RELIGION, which is Oneness, so that each may chose that path which suits him best. (Vivekananda 1985, p. 415)

The final sentence quoted above of Swami Vivekananda's letter to Mohammed Husain is of special importance because it clearly shows Vivekananda's views regarding other religions. Far from wanting to see other religions absorbed into Hinduism, Vivekananda felt that the greater the number of religions and sects, the better it would be for mankind, the ideal state of affairs coming when each individual represented a sect unto himself. He said,

> I am not against any sect. I am glad that sects exist, and I only wish that they may go on multiplying more and more ... When religions are dead, there will be no more sects; it will be the perfect peace and harmony of the grave. But so long as mankind thinks, there will be sects. Variation is the sign of life, and it must be there. I pray that they may multiply so that at last there will be as many sects as human beings, and each one will have his own method, his individual method of thought in religion. (Vivekananda 1987, pp. 363-364)

Vivekananda felt that each religion had its own original contribution to make, a "soul" of its own without which it could not live. Each religion thus represented a single tile in the mosaic of the universal religion without which it would be incomplete. Each was not only true, but necessary. Each religion was to be not only tolerated, but accepted. No one religion was to impose itself on any other; no one's spiritual attitude was to be tampered with. Vivekananda stated at the Parliament of Religions,

> Do I wish that the Christian would become Hindu? God forbid. Do I wish that the Hindu or Buddhist would become Christian? God forbid ... each must assimilate the spirit of the others and yet preserve his individuality and grow according to his own law of growth. (Vivekananda 1986, p. 24)

This was the "embrace" which Swami Vivekananda envisioned, not an embrace which smothers and destroys, but an embrace of love, based on unity, brotherhood, and spiritual oneness.

*Vedānta Society of Southern California*
*Trabuco Canyon, California, USA*

## NOTES

[1] It is interesting to note that even as late as the 1890's when Swami Vivekananda attended the Parliament of Religions in Chicago, there was a certain amount of confusion regarding the name to use for the religion which he represented. Vivekananda was described by such various terms as a Brahmin Sanyasi (sic), a Brahmin Priest, a Brahman monk, a representative of the Vedic Religion, of Brahmanism, of the Brahman Religion, Hinduism, and even Buddhism. Aside from the difficulties regarding the name of his religion, the mere fact that no representative was formally sent to represent "Hinduism" (there were representatives from splinter groups, such as the Brāhmo Samāj) shows the lack of any formal organization within the religion.

[2] It was one of Swami Vivekananda's keen desires to write a philosophical work showing the reconciliation (*samanvaya*) of the different schools of Vedānta based on the doctrines of *advaita*. He mentioned this several times in letters from the West to India and requested that the *bhāṣyas* of Śaṅkara, Rāmānuja, and Madhva be sent to him. Unfortunately, his desire to accomplish this task was never fulfilled.

It is important to note, also, that such a reconciliation of the dualistic, qualified dualistic, and non-dualistic schools of Vedānta was not meant to show the superiority of Advaita over the other schools, only that it was from the non-dualistic standpoint that the other positions could be shown to be true. Swami Vivekananda recognized the fact that most individuals are better suited for devotional and dualistic paths, and he believed, along with Sri Ramakrishna, that through devotion one could also attain the highest state of oneness. It should also be mentioned that Vivekananda extended this reconciliation to all the religions of the world insofar as each found its place in one of the three schools of Vedānta. He also recognized the fact that the vast majority of Hindus are dualistic in attitude, as are the vast majority of all religions.

# 5

# Indian Religion, Past and Present

**Minoru Hara**

## A NOTE ON *DHARMASYA SŪKṢMĀ GATIḤ*[*]

In his article entitled "Human Reason and Vedic Revelation in Advaita Vedānta" (TR, pp. 131-204), Professor Halbfass discusses the problem of the instability (*apratiṣṭhitatva*) of human reason (*yukti* or *tarka*) as expounded by Advaita Vedāntins (p. 147). According to their philosophy, human reasoning, if unguided by the Vedic revelation, is just a "dried up" (*śuṣka*), i.e., fruitless and groundless activity (p. 146). As a matter of fact, the world is such that the possibility of exceptions or irregularities can never be excluded. Under such circumstances, assumptions produced by human thought alone (*puruṣamatiprabhavāḥ kalpanāḥ*) are inevitably futile (p. 153, cp. also p. 174).

These statements remind us of those found in the Epic literature in relation to the term *dharmasūkṣmatva*. According to this maxim, the course, or unfolding process (*gati*) of *dharma* is too subtle (*sūkṣma*) to be judged solely by human reason (*tarka*), which is almost equal to nothing in face of the Vedic revelation. In an often-quoted passage[1] we read:

*tarko 'pratiṣṭhaḥ śrutayo vibhinnā/*
*naiko ṛṣir yasya matam pramāṇam//*
*dharmasya tattvaṃ nihitaṃ guhāyām/*
*mahājano yena gataḥ sa panthāḥ//*

(*MBh* 3 App. 32.65-68, p. 1089)

"Reasoning is unstable and the Vedic texts differ. There is no single sage whose opinion is authoritative.
The true nature of *dharma* is hidden in a cave [of mystery]. The path [of behaviour complying with *dharma*] is that through which the majority of people[2] proceed."

Curiously enough the statement of this *dharmasūkṣmatva* is often connected to the authoritative character of the Vedic revelation (*śrutipramāṇo dharmaḥ*: *MBh* 3.197.39, 3.200.2; cf. also 8.49.18 and 48).

Being enlightened and, at the same time, much inspired by the illuminating contribution of Professor Halbfass, we would like to study here systematically the sporadic occurrences of the concept of *dharmasūkṣmatva* in the *Mahābhārata*. As will be shown below, this concept is unique, because its contextual atmosphere occasionally suggests the weakness of *dharma*, and consequently its unreliability, despite a general Hindu belief in the sublime concept of *dharma*.[3]

## I Balāka and Kauśika Stories (*MBh* 8.49)

This story was told by Kṛṣṇa to Arjuna when the latter tried to kill Yudhiṣṭhira. This violent decision was made by Arjuna because he had sworn previously that anybody who would disparage him as a warrior unqualified to hold the divine weapon of Gāṇḍīva should be killed mercilessly by him.[4] Even though the person who laid this blame on him happened to be Yudhiṣṭhira, Arjuna wanted to carry out his original vow.[5] On seeing this, Kṛṣṇa put a question to him as to which of the two were more important, to keep one's vow (*pratijñā*) or to kill one's respected brother (*guru*). Arjuna was then in a moral dilemma, but was finally dissuaded by Kṛṣṇa from carrying out his vow and spared instead the life of his brother. On this occasion, Kṛṣṇa suggested to Arjuna to address Yudhiṣṭhira with the word *tvam*, the slighting salutation to the elder, which is as harmful as actual slaughter.[6] By this abuse, which is tantamount to actual killing, Arjuna was theoretically made free from the fault of untruthfulness as well as from killing his brother.[7]

Here, in this situation, breaking one's vow is thought of as a trifle matter when compared to the slaughter of the respected elder. But we note that when two moral precepts are in conflict with each other, one is forced to choose one of them. Here, the breaking of a vow, that is the violation of a general rule of *satya*, is praised from the point of view of *dharma*.[8] This aspect of human affairs, which are not so simply and easily determined, but are subtly entangled with other matters, is reflected in the term *dharmasūkṣmatva*.

The story begins with Kṛṣṇa's critical remarks about Arjuna's rash decision:

*idānīṃ pārtha jānāmi na vṛddhāḥ sevitās tvayā/*
*akāle puruṣavyāghra saṃrambhakriyayānayā/*
*na hi dharmavibhāgajñaḥ kuryād evaṃ dhanaṃjaya//*
(*MBh* 8.49.14)

"Now I know, O Pārtha, that you have not waited upon the elders, since, O tiger among men, you have yielded to wrath at a time when you should not have done so. No one who knows the distinctions among *dharmas* would act in this way, O Dhanaṃjaya."

Then Kṛṣṇa starts his discourse on *dharmarahasya* (25), saying

*na hi kāryam akāryaṃ vā sukhaṃ jñātuṃ kathaṃcana/*
*śrutena jñāyate sarvaṃ tac ca tvaṃ nāvabudhyase//*
(*MBh* 8.49.18)
*sa guruṃ pārtha kasmāt tvaṃ hanyā dharmam anusmaran/*
*asaṃpradhārya dharmāṇāṃ gatiṃ sūkṣmāṃ duranvayām//*
(*MBh* 8.49.24)[9]

"It is by no means easy to distinguish what is right to do and what is not. Everything is known through the Revelation, but you do not realize this.(18)
Keeping *dharma* in your mind, how could you harm the respected elder, without having ascertained the subtle course of *dharmas* which is so difficult to be followed?"(24)

Two stories are introduced here as an illustration of *dharmasūkṣmatva*. The first is a case of moral luck. A hunter Balāka who was devoted to his duty (*svadharmanirata*) and nourished his old parents once killed a ferocious creature called Andha. But this Andha happened to have been a nuisance to all creatures for a long time. It was, therefore, a blessing that he killed it. By this merit of having killed the evil being, he ascended to heaven[10]:

*tad dhatvā sarvabhūtānām abhāvakṛtaniścayam/*
*tato balākaḥ svar agād evaṃ dharmaḥ sudurvidaḥ//*
(*MBh* 8.49.40)

"Having slain that [animal] which had resolved to slay all creatures, Balāka went to heaven. Thus, *dharma* is difficult to be understood."

The second story relates to an undesirable result of telling the truth (*satya*). There was a certain ascetic, not well-versed in the Veda (8.49.41: *tapasvī na bahuśrutaḥ*). His name was Kauśika and he took a vow (*vrata*) to tell the truth throughout his life. One day some bandits (*dasyu*) were chasing a group of travellers with the intention of killing them. Kauśika was sitting nearby at the cross roads. The travellers passed by, and requested him not to show the miscreants which way they had fled. Kauśika did not answer. Soon after that, the bandits arrived and asked him about the travellers; and Kauśika told the truth. As a result, the travellers were all caught and killed:

*tenādharmeṇa mahatā vāgduruktena kauśikaḥ/*
*gataḥ sukaṣṭaṃ narakaṃ sūkṣmadharmeṣv akovidaḥ/*
*aprabhūtaśruto mūḍho dharmāṇām avibhāgavit//* (*MBh* 8.49.46)

"In consequence of that great sin (*adharma*) consisting in words spoken wrongly, Kauśika, ignorant of the subtle *dharmas*, went into a grievous hell, the foolish man, not knowing the distinctions among *dharmas*, and not profoundly learnt in Vedic scriptures."

By killing Balāka attained heaven, and by telling the truth Kauśika went into hell. *hiṃsā* brings about felicity and *satya* brings about hell.

These stories tell us that the ordinary moral precepts in the form of *ahiṃsā* and *satya* should not always be applied blindly. Blind observance of a general rule sometimes brings about misfortune. This is so because there is a certain limit to human reasoning, illustrated by the stories of *dharmasūkṣmatva*. This coincides with the concept of *śuṣkatarka*.[11]

Having heard these stories, Arjuna, following the suggestion of Kṛṣṇa, addressed Yudhiṣṭhira by *tvam*. Yudhiṣṭhira felt greatly humiliated and decided to retreat to the forest. Arjuna, for his part, was also greatly annoyed by this act of dishonouring his elder and resolved to kill himself. Seeing this, Kṛṣṇa spoke to Arjuna as follows:

*tvam ity uktvaiva rājānam evaṃ kaśmalam āviśaḥ/*
*hatvā tu nṛpatiṃ pārtha akariṣyaḥ kim uttaram/*
*evaṃ sudurvido dharmo mandaprajñair viśeṣataḥ//* (*MBh* 8.50.3)

"Having only addressed the king by *tvam*, you are possessed by such cheerlessness. But if you had slain the king, O Pārtha, what would you have done after that? Thus, *dharma* is inscrutable, especially by persons of slow wits."

Attention should be drawn to the fact that in this context the expressions such as *śrutipramāṇo dharmaḥ*, which praise the authority of the Veda, appear together with the concept of *dharmasūkṣmatva*.

II The Story of the Brahmin Kauśika (*MBh* 3.196)

A haughty Brahmin ascetic in anger burnt a bird with an evil glance when the bird dropped feces upon his head. Experiencing remorse because of this cruel act, he then visited the house of a faithful wife, who knew all he had done by clairvoyance. Curious about her supernatural power, he started to talk to her. She, however, kept him waiting, serving her husband first. After pleasing her husband in disregard of the respectable guest, she greeted him and suggested to him to go to Mithilā to see a righteous hunter (*dharmavyādha*) who was working in the market. Thus, he decided to go to Mithilā. The hunter, a Śūdra, welcomed him, and he too surprised the Brahmin by his clairvoyance. He gave the Brahmin instructions on *dharma*.[12]

Here, the ascetic Brahmin is instructed in *dharma* by a woman and a Śūdra, who are both intent on the performance of their own duty, viz., the wife in service of her husband (*pativratā*) and the Śūdra in engagement in his family-tradition of butchery as well as in the service of his old parents (*guruśuśrūṣā*). At the end of the story, the intense performance of *svadharma* at home by a woman and a Śūdra is praised more than asceticism (*tapas*) in the forest by a celibate Brahmin ascetic with no regard to his family.

The story, thus, consists of two parts, *pativratopākhyāna* (*MBh* 3.196-197 = *strīṇāṃ māhātmyam*) and *brāhmaṇavyādhasaṃvāda* (*MBh* 3.198-206). Here, as in the story of Tulādhāra, a Śūdra instructs a Brahmin ascetic on *dharma*. Actually, however, this Śūdra was a Brahmin under the curse of another Brahmin whom he killed unknowingly in the previous life.

Below, we shall list the relevant passages where the concept of *sūkṣmatva* of *dharma*[13] is spoken of.

The woman started to speak:

*durjñeyaḥ śāśvato dharmaḥ sa tu satye pratiṣṭhitaḥ/*
*śrutipramāṇo dharmaḥ syād iti vṛddhānuśāsanam//*
*bahudhā dṛśyate dharmaḥ sūkṣma eva dvijottama/*
*bhavān api ca dharmajñaḥ svādhyāyanirataḥ śuciḥ/*
*na tu tattvena bhagavan dharmān vetsīti me matiḥ//*
(*MBh* 3.197.39-40)

"The eternal *dharma* is hard to know, but it is founded upon truthfulness (*satya*). *dharma* should be authorized by Revelation (*śruti*), thus teach the elders. In many ways the *dharma* is observed as subtle, O great brahmin. Devoted to study and pious, you are also conversant with the *dharma*. Yet, sir, in my opinion in reality you are ignorant of *dharma*."

Following her advice, the Brahmin resolved to go to Mithilā:

*cintayānaḥ sa dharmasya sūkṣmāṃ gatim athābravīt/*
*śraddadhānena bhāvyaṃ vai gacchāmi mithilām aham//*
(*MBh* 3.198.2)

"Pondering on the subtle course of the *dharma*, he then said, 'I must trust you. I shall go to Mithilā.'"

*bahu loke viparyastaṃ dṛśyate dvijasattama/*
*dharmayuktam adharmaṃ ca tatra kiṃ pratibhāti te//*
(*MBh* 3.199.33)

"Much in this world is viewed upside down, O best of Brahmins, and *adharma* is conjoined with *dharma*. What do you think of this?"

*śrutipramāṇo dharmo hi vṛddhānām iti bhāṣitam/*
*sūkṣmā gatir hi dharmasya bahuśākhā hy anantikā//*
*prāṇātyaye vivāhe ca vaktavyam anṛtaṃ bhavet/*
*anṛtaṃ ca bhavet satyaṃ satyaṃ caivānṛtaṃ bhavet//*
*yad bhūtahitam atyantaṃ tat satyam iti dhāraṇā/*
*viparyayakṛto 'dharmaḥ paśya dharmasya sūkṣmatām//*
(*MBh* 3.200.2-4)

"The elders say that *dharma* is authorized by Revelation. For the course of *dharma* is subtle, greatly ramified[14] and boundless. One may voice a lie when about to die, or in marriage; [then] the lie becomes truth and the truth a lie. It is generally held that [the word] that is entirely beneficial to living beings is the truth, and that the opposite [becomes] *adharma*. Notice the subtlety of the *dharma*!"[15]

III Jājali and Tulādhāra Story (*MBh* 12.253-256)

A similar story is told in the *Śāntiparvan* in the form of a dialogue between the Brahmin ascetic Jājali and the Vaiśya Tulādhāra. Not only the philosophical content, but also the setting of the frame-story is notably similar to that of the *dharmavyādha*.[16]

This episode is related by Bhīṣma to Yudhiṣṭhira, who had a notion of the absolute and eternal value attached to *dharma*. The problem of *dharmasūkṣmatva* is first put forward by Yudhiṣṭhira:

> *sūkṣmaṃ sādhu samādiṣṭaṃ bhavatā* ***dharmalakṣaṇam***/
> *pratibhā tv asti me kācit tāṃ brūyām anumānataḥ*//
> (*MBh* 12.252.1)

"Verily you have indicated the subtle characteristic mark of *dharma* [to me]. However, a certain idea occurs to me, [and] with [your] permission I will speak of it." (Proudfoot)

The episode itself runs as follows. Once a Brahmin ascetic Jājali thought that he had attained *siddhi* (12.253.38: *siddho 'smi*; cf. 41: *dharmaḥ prāpto mayā*) and declared that there was nobody equal to him in the world (12.253.6: *na mayā sādṛśo 'stīha loke*). Upon hearing his boastful statement, certain beings (12.253.7-11: *rakṣas*, *piśācas*, or *bhūtas*, 42: simply a divine voice) said to him that even Tulādhāra, a merchant in Vārāṇasī, could not be so proud to speak out as he did. Provoked by this admonition, Jājali then decided to see Tulādhāra in Varanasi, who welcomed him, knowing everything by his clairvoyance. The dialogue between them and Tulādhāra's discourse on *dharma* as given in the Poona critical edition present a textual conglomerate, which contains four segments. These points have now been critically analysed by Proudfoot.[17] The passages which concern us here (12.254.4ff.; *uvāca dharmasūkṣmāṇi vaiśyo dharmārthatattvavit*) apparently belong to the oldest layer (pp. 23-36).[18]

Tulādhāra's discourse on *dharma* is concentrated on its relativity. *dharmas* are after all fabrications of human reasoning, and thus are often motivated by personal interest, applicable only to a particular society under limited conditions. They cannot be universal and are destined to be ephemeral, and even illusory:

*imāni hi prāpayanti sṛjanty uttārayanti ca/*
*na dharmaḥ paripāṭhena śakyo bhārata veditum//*
*anyo dharmaḥ samasthasya viṣamasthasya cāparaḥ/*
*āpadas tu kathaṃ śakyāḥ paripāṭhena veditum//*
(*MBh* 12.252.3-4)
*dṛśyate dharmarūpeṇa adharmaṃ prākṛtaś caran/*
*dharmaṃ cādharmarūpeṇa kaścid aprākṛtaś caran//*
(*MBh* 12.252.6)
*dharmasya hriyamāṇasya balavadbhir durātmabhiḥ/*
*yā yā vikriyate saṃsthā tataḥ sāpi praṇaśyati//* (*MBh* 12.252.11)
*gandharvanagarākāraḥ prathamaṃ saṃpradṛśyate/*
*anvīkṣyamāṇaḥ kavibhiḥ punar gacchaty adarśanam//*
(*MBh* 12.252.13)

"[Men may] proclaim, enunciate and refute these matters, [and] *dharma* cannot be known completely, o Bhārata.(3)
There is one *dharma* for the flourishing [person] and another for the one in difficulty, and still another in case of calamity. How is it possible to know them completely [*paripāṭha*]?(4)
It is a matter of ordinary experience that a vulgar man commits sin (*adharma*) in the form of virtue (*dharma*), while a noble man performs virtue in the form of sin.(6)
Whenever, as *dharma* wanes, a rule (*saṃsthā*) is perverted by the powerful and the wicked, that rule itself vanishes.(11)
At first sight, [*dharma*] appears in the form of the city of the Gandharvas, but when scrutinized by the wise it dissolves again into invisibility."(13)

This elusive and transitory character of *dharma* is due to the fact that it is often confused with *ācāra*:

*pranaṣṭaḥ śāśvato dharmaḥ sadācāreṇa mohitaḥ/*
*tena vaidyas tapasvī vā balavān vā vimohyate//* (*MBh* 12.254.21)

"The eternal *dharma* perishes everytime when confused with good customary behaviour (*sadācāra*). By this everyone is stupefied, no matter whether learned, ascetic or powerful."

An oft-quoted simile of accidentalism is here applied to *ācāra*:

*nadyāṃ yathā ceha kāṣṭham uhyamānaṃ yadṛcchayā/*
*yadṛcchayaiva kāṣṭhena saṃdhiṃ gaccheta kenacit//*
*tatrāparāṇi dārūṇi saṃsṛjyante tatas tataḥ/*
*tṛṇakāṣṭhakarīṣāṇi kadācin na samīkṣayā/*
*evam evāyam ācāraḥ prādurbhūto yatas tataḥ//*

(*MBh* 12.254.23-24)

"In this world, a piece of wood borne along at random in a river may come by chance into contact with another piece of wood.
There again, sometimes other logs from here and there come into contact, straw, wood and cowdung, unexpectedly. Exactly in the same way customary behaviour (*ācāra*) makes its appearence randomly."[19]

According to this pessimistic view of human ethics which sounds to the orthodox Brahmin as the statement of an impious nihilist (*MBh* 12.255.3: *nāstikya*), there is no absolute standard, with the possible exception of *ahiṃsā* (*sanātana*-, or *sādhāraṇadharma*), by which to judge what is good (*dharma*).[20] Tulādhāra continues his instruction:

*akāraṇo hi nehāsti* ***dharmaḥ sūkṣmo*** *'pi jājale/*
*bhūtabhavyārtham eveha dharmapravacanaṃ kṛtam//*
***sūkṣmatvān na sa vijñātuṃ*** *śakyate bahunihnavaḥ/*
*upalabhyāntarā cānyān ācārān avabudhyate//*

(*MBh* 12.254.35-36)

"O Jājali, in this world there is no [code of] *dharma*, however subtle [in conception, which is] unmotivated; [human] formulations of *dharma* are made for the sake of something past or future.
Because of its subtleness, the deeply concealed [true *dharma*] cannot be discerned; only through grasping [the nature of] other [kinds of] conduct [can] it be conceived." (Proudfoot)

Though the song by the king Vicakhnu, which praises *ahiṃsā*, belongs to the second segment of the episode, this concluding song also refers to the subtlety of *dharma*:

*tasmāt pramāṇataḥ kāryo* ***dharmaḥ sūkṣmo*** *vijānatā/*
*ahiṃsaiva hi sarvebhyo dharmebhyo jyāyāsī matā//*

(*MBh* 12.257.6)

"Therefore, the subtle *dharma* should be performed by the discerning [man] according to [that] authority. For non-injury is the best of all *dharmas*."

## IV Fault of *upadeśa* (*MBh* 13.10)

In a story which Bhīṣma related to Yudhiṣṭhira (*MBh* 13.10), we meet twice the phrase *sūkṣmā gatir hi dharmasya*. A Brahmin who imparted the knowledge of the Vedic ritual of *pitṛkārya* to a Śūdra ascetic (*śūdra-tāpasa*) had to suffer the consequences of his fault, namely, teaching (*upadeśa*) to an unqualified person (*varṇāvara*). Though the Brahmin did this out of kindness and friendship, he reaped the fruit of his misdeed in the next life by his being employed as a *purohita* by a king who was that Śūdra in the previous life.

The story begins with Yudhiṣṭhira's request to Bhīṣma:

> *etad icchāmi tattvena vyākhyātuṃ vai pitāmaha/*
> ***sūkṣmā gatir hi dharmasya** yatra muhyanti mānavāḥ//*
> (*MBh* 13.10.2)

"O grandfather, I wish this to be expounded as it is. For the course of *dharma* is subtle. Men are [often] stupefied there."

The story ends with Bhīṣma's remarks praising silence (*mauna*) rather than verbose instruction:

> *tasmāt sadbhir na vaktavyaṃ kasyacit kaṃcid agrataḥ/*
> ***sūkṣmā gatir hi dharmasya** durjñeyā hy akṛtātmabhiḥ//*
> (*MBh* 13.10.64)

"Therefore good men should not speak anything to anybody. For the course of *dharma* is subtle and is hardly comprehensible by persons of uncleansed soul."

## V Miscellanea

Since the absolute judgement of what is right is beyond human apprehension, suspension of definite judgement upon doubtful matters is often accompanied by our phrase.

The best known example may be Bhīṣma's suspension of judgement in the *Dyūtaparvan*. As is well known, Yudhiṣṭhira lost round after round in the game of dice, and finally he bet himself. Śakuni won this game and made him a slave. Next, he bet his wife Draupadī and Śakuni won once again, making her a *dāsī*. Duryodhana ordered Vidura to bring her to the court. Vidura refused to do so, saying,

> *na hi dāsītvam āpannā kṛṣṇā bhavati bhārata/*
> *anīśena hi rājñaiṣā paṇe nyasteti me matiḥ//* (*MBh* 2.59.4)

"O Bhārata, Kṛṣṇā has not become a female slave, for in my opinion she was put at stake by the king who was no longer free."

Forcibly brought to the court, Draupadī raised the question whether she had been staked by Yudhiṣṭhira and lost to Śakuni. She could not approve of Yudhiṣṭhira's action, but nevertheless she had to admit the subtlety of *dharma*. She says:

> *dharme sthito dharmasutaś ca rājā*
> ***dharmaś ca sūkṣmo** nipuṇopalabhyaḥ/*
> *vācāpi bhartuḥ paramāṇumātraṃ*
> *necchāmi doṣaṃ svaguṇān visṛjya//* (*MBh* 2.60.31)

"The king, son of *dharma*, abides by *dharma*, and *dharma* is subtle, apprehensible only by the wise. But even at my husband's behest I do not want [to commit any] fault, no matter how small, by abandoning my virtue."

Despite the opinion of Vidura, Bhīṣma retained final judgement, saying

> *na **dharmasaukṣmyāt** subhage vivaktuṃ*
> *śaknomi te praśnam imaṃ yathāvat/*
> *asvo hy aśaktaḥ paṇituṃ parasvaṃ*
> *striyaś ca bhartur vaśatāṃ samīkṣya//* (*MBh* 2.60.40)

"Since *dharma* is subtle, my dear, I fail to answer this question properly. It is true that a man without property can not stake other's property, yet, seeing that a wife is the husband's chattels ..."[21]

Similarly, in answer to Drupada who could not follow the strange custom of a girl to be married to five husbands and thus was against Draupadī's marriage to five brothers, Yudhiṣṭhira resorted to this maxim. The dialogue between them reads as follows:

*Drupada uvāca -*

*ekasya bahvyo vihitā mahiṣyaḥ kurunandana/*
*naikasyā bahavaḥ puṃso vidhīyante kadācana//*
*lokavedaviruddhaṃ tvaṃ nādharmaṃ dhārmikaḥ śuciḥ/*
*kartum arhasi kaunteya kasmāt te buddhir īdṛśī//*

*Yudhiṣṭhira uvāca -*

***sūkṣmo dharmo** mahārāja nāsya vidmo vayaṃ gatim/*
*pūrveṣām ānupūrvyeṇa yātaṃ vartmānuyāmahe//*

(*MBh* 1.187.26-28)

"Drupada said: 'It is laid down that one man may have many queens, scion of Kuru, but never that one woman may have many men! Righteous and pure as you are, you may not perpetrate such a breach of the Law that runs counter to the world and the Veda, Kaunteya! Whence such a design in you?'
Yudhiṣṭhira said: '*dharma* is subtle, great king, and we do not know its course. We [simply] follow the path that was trodden by the predecessors one after the other.'"[22]

Likewise, an inexperienced youth who is ignorant of the world is sometimes styled as a person unaware of *dharmasūkṣmatva*. When priority was given by Bhīṣma to Kṛṣṇa, the king of Cedi became angry and blamed Bhīṣma as follows:

*bālā yūyaṃ na jānīdhvaṃ **dharmaḥ sūkṣmo** hi pāṇḍavāḥ/*
*ayaṃ tatrādhyatikrānta āpageyo 'lpadarśanaḥ//* (*MBh* 2.34.3)

"You are just boys and you don't know! For *dharma* is subtle, Pāṇḍavas! This short-sighted son of a river has violated (the *dharma*) here (on this occasion)."

By contrast, in a complementary address of the old blind king we read:

*vettha tvaṃ tāta **dharmāṇāṃ gatiṃ sūkṣmāṃ** yudhiṣṭhira/*
*vinīto 'si mahāprājña vṛddhānāṃ paryupāsitā//* (*MBh* 2.65.4)

"Yudhiṣṭhira, my dear son, you know the subtle course of *dharmas*, you are courteous, my wise one, and you attend to your elders."

Likewise, in asking an advice, Dhṛtarāṣṭra approached Vidura:

*prajñā ca te bhārgavasyeva śuddhā*
***dharmaṃ** ca tvaṃ paramaṃ vettha **sūkṣmam**/*
*samaś ca tvaṃ saṃmataḥ kauravāṇām*
*pathyaṃ caiṣāṃ mama caiva bravīhi//* (*MBh* 3.5.2)

"Your insight is as clear as was Bhārgava's. You know *dharma* both supreme and subtle. You are esteemed impartial by the sons of Kuru; so declare what is right for them and for me."

VI From *Indische Sprüche*

Finally, we shall quote the passages from O. Böhtlingk's *Indische Sprüche*. The present writer is here guided by the Index prepared by A. Blau.[23]

(1)

*kānīnasya muneḥ svabāndhavavadhūvaidhavyavidhvaṃsino*
*naptāraḥ khalu golakasya tanayāḥ kuṇḍāḥ svayaṃ pāṇḍavāḥ/*
*te 'mī pañca samānayoniratayas teṣāṃ guṇotkīrtanād*
*akṣayaṃ sukṛtaṃ bhaved avikalaṃ **dharmasya sūkṣmā gatiḥ**//*
(1624)

"The Pāṇḍavas are grandsons of the sage [Vyāsa], who was just a son of an unmarried woman (kānīna), who destroyed the widowhood of the wife of his own relative. They are also sons of a widow's bastard (golaka), and themselves born in adultery (kuṇḍa). These five enjoy one and the same wife. Yet, an unperishable and enormous amount of merit is to be gained by praising their virtue. The course of merit (*dharma*) is subtle."

(2)

*yātaḥ kṣmām akhilāṃ pradāya haraye pātālamūlam baliḥ*
*saktuprasthavisarjanāt sa ca muniḥ svargaṃ samāropitaḥ/*
*ā bālyād asatī satī surapurīṃ kuntī samārohitā*
*hā sītā patidevatāgamad adho **dharmasya sūkṣmā gatiḥ**//* (5439)

"Bali went to the bottom of hell, though he gave the entire earth to Viṣṇu. And this sage was made to ascend to heaven, though what he had given up was a small portion of barley-meal. Kuntī went to heaven, though she was unchaste from childhood. Alas, though true to her husband, Sītā went down [to the nether world]. Indeed, the course of *dharma* (good deeds) is subtle."

(3)

*na tad balaṃ yan mṛdunā virudhyate*
***sūkṣmo hi dharmas** tarasā sevitavyaḥ/*
*pradhvaṃsinī krūrasamāhitā śrīr*
*mṛdupraudhā gacchati putrapautram//* (3263)
(*Vikramacarita* 81)

"It is not power that stands in contrast to the weak. *dharma* is subtle and should be served with zeal. Good luck, when attended upon with harshness, ruins, but driven on with mildness, it goes up to the generation of son and grandson."

(4)

***sūkṣmaḥ** paramavijñeyaḥ satāṃ **dharmaḥ** plavaṃgama/*
*hṛdisthaḥ sarvabhūtānām ātmā veda śubhāśubham//* (7155)
(*R* 4.18.15, Gor. 17.6)

"O Monkey, *dharma* of the good people is subtle and to be known only by the highest person. Yet, the soul which resides in the heart of all creatures knows the good and bad."

The following two verses speak of the same, not about *dharma*, but about *karman* and *kāla*:

(5)

*vasor vīryotpannām abhajata munir matsyatanayām*
*tathā jāto vyāsaḥ śataguṇanivāsaḥ kim aparam/*
*svayaṃ vedān vyasyac chamitakuruvaṃśaprasavitā*
*sa evābhūc chrīmān ahaha **viṣamāḥ karmagatayaḥ**//* (6004)
(*Pañcatantra*, ed. Bombay, 4.50)

"The sage (Parāśara) loved the daughter of fish, born of the seed of Vasu. Thus born was Vyāsa, the receptable of hundred virtues. This is not all. He compiled the Vedas and became the founder of the Kuru race, though now ruined. Yet, he himself became so successful. O, the course of *karman* is uneven."

(6)

*apsu lavanti pāṣāṇā mānuṣā ghnanti rākṣasān/*
*kapayaḥ karma kurvanti* ***kālasya kuṭilā gatiḥ****//* (7451)

"Stones swim on water and men kill the demons. Monkeys make a [wonderful] work. The course of destiny (*kāla*) is crooked."[24]

The subtlety of *dharma* is beyond human reasoning. Its unpredictability results in despair for the righteous Karṇa. We may conclude this essay with his words. When his chariot was out of control, Karṇa blamed *dharma* as follows:

*amṛṣyamāṇo vyasanāni tāni*
*hastau vidhunvan sa vigarhamāṇaḥ/*
*dharmapradhānān abhipāti dharma*
*ity abruvan dharmavidaḥ sadaiva/*
*mamāpi nimno 'dya na pāti bhaktān*
*manye na nityaṃ paripāti dharmaḥ//* (*MBh* 8.66.43)

"Unable to endure all those calamities, he waved about his arms and began to rail [against *dharma*], saying, 'Those who are conversant with *dharma* always say that *dharma* protects those that are righteous. Yet, now it has declined even for me. It does not protect its devotees (*bhakta*). It seems to me that the *dharma* does not always protect.'"[25] [26] [27]

*University of Tokyo*
*Department of Sanskrit Literature and Indian Languages*
*Tokyo, Japan*

## NOTES

* This study was made possible by the Mitsubishi Foundation Subsidy for the Human Sciences.

[1] Cf. Matilal 1989 p. 17; Kane 1973, p. 860, and 1962, p. 1469. One may compare this subtlety of *dharma* with *MBh* 3.32.33-34:

*karmaṇām uta puṇyānāṃ pāpānāṃ ca phalodayaḥ/*
*prabhavaś cāpyayaś caiva devaguhyāni bhāmini//* (33)
*naitāni veda yaḥ kaś cin muhyanty atra prajā imāḥ/*

*rakṣyāṇy etāni devānāṃ gūḍhamāyā hi devatāḥ//* (34)

[2] For *mahājana*, cf. TR, p. 25 and p. 43, n. 11; cf. also Proudfoot 1987, p. 220, n. 17 and p. 222, n. 4.

[3] To the best of my knowledge there does not yet exist any systematic and comprehensive study on this subject. James W. Laine in his book entitled *Visions of God* repeatedly says that the subtlety of *dharma* is one of the central issues of the *MBh* ("characteristically epic"), in addition to the problem of human struggles (*puruṣakāra*) and destiny (*daiva*), and uncertainty of human existence (see index p. 298; one may add also p. 246), but no relevant passages are given there. Furthermore, though he mentions the *MBh* passages 1.187-91, 3.28-36, 3.198-206, 8.49, and 9.59 as relevant to the subject (p. 251), there is no mention of *dharmasūkṣmatva* in 3.28-36, nor in 9.59! For other sporadic references to the concept, see Schomer 1989, p. 153, Sullivan 1990, pp. 43 and 56, and Ramanujan 1991, p. 435. I owe these references to Koskikallio 1994, p. 259.

[4] *MBh* 8.48.14, 8.49.9, 8.49.61 and 62, 108.

[5] Cf.

*pratijñāṃ pālayiṣyāmi hatvemaṃ narasattamam//*
*so 'haṃ yudhiṣṭhiraṃ hatvā satye 'py ānṛṇyatāṃ gataḥ/*
(*MBh* 8.49.11cd-12ab)

[6] Cf.

*tvam ity atrabhavantaṃ tvaṃ brūhi pārtha yudhiṣṭhiram/*
*tvam ity ukto hi nihato gurur bhavati bhārata//* (*MBh* 8.49.67)

Cf. Hopkins 1930-32, pp. 375-376. Cf. also Hopkins 1969, p. 26, n. 1.

[7] *mukto 'nṛtād bhrātṛvadhāc ca pārtha* (*MBh* 8.49.71c).

[8] Cf.

*prāṇātyaye vivāhe vā sarvajñātidhanakṣaye/*
*narmaṇy abhipravṛtte vā pravaktavyaṃ mṛṣā bhavet/*
*adharmaṃ nātra paśyanti* **dharmatattvārthadarśinaḥ**// (*MBh* 8.49.53)

Cf. *MBh* 12.35.20, 3.200.3, 8.49.29, 12.110.18, 1.77.16, and further, Derrett 1980-81, pp. 286-292.

[9] Cf. Matilal 1989, p. 12.

[10] Cf.

*satyasya vacanaṃ sādhu na satyād vidyate param/*
*tattvenaitat sudurjñeyaṃ yasya satyam anuṣṭhitam//* (*MBh* 8.49.27)
*duṣkaraṃ paramajñānaṃ tarkeṇātra vyavasyati/*
*śrutir dharma iti hy eke vadanti bahavo janāḥ//* (*MBh* 8.49.48)

[11] For *tarka* in general cf. Kane 1962, p. 1468ff.

[12] For this story of the *dharmavyādha* cf. Alsdorf 1961, pp. 30-32. Cf. also Śaṅkara ad *BS* 1.3.38.

[13] To begin with, Yudhiṣṭhira asked Bhīṣma to teach *sūkṣmadharma*:

*śrotum icchāmi bhagavan strīṇāṃ māhātmyam uttamam/*
*kathyamānaṃ tvayā vipra sūkṣmaṃ dharmaṃ ca tattvataḥ//*(*MBh* 3.196.2)

[14] Cf. *MBh* 12.154.3 (*mahān ayaṃ dharmapatho bahuśākhaś ca*) and 12.154.4 (*dharmasya mahato ... bahuśākhasya*).

[15] Cf.

*evaṃ tu sūkṣme kathite dharmavyādhena bhārata/*
*brāhmaṇaḥ sa punaḥ sūkṣmaṃ papraccha susamāhitaḥ//* (*MBh* 3.203.1)

[16] Cf. Proudfoot 1987, p. 156 and pp. 243-244.

[17] Proudfoot 1987. This is the first attempt of higher textual criticism of the *Mahābhārata* on variations of text-order (cf. p. 40ff.)

[18] Cf. Proudfoot 1987, p. 101ff.

[19] Cf. *MBh* 12.28.36, 12.168.15; *R* 2.98.25; *Hitopadeśa* 4.74.

[20] Cf. Proudfoot 1987, pp. 101-102.

[21] Cf. Kulkarni 1989, pp. 150-156.

[22] Cf. Sullivan 1990, p. 56.

[23] Blau 1966, p. 68 (*Moralisches Verdienst ist fein, schwer zu erfassen*).

[24] The same is said of the work of Nārāyaṇa: *kāmaṃ tasya gatiḥ sūkṣmā devair api durānugā* (*Harivaṃśa* 39.8).

[25] Cf. Hopkins 1972, p. 176.

[26] One may compare this idea of *dharmasya sūkṣmā gatiḥ* with the following passage of the *Manusmṛti*:

*nādharmaś carito loke sadyaḥ phalati gaur iva/*
*śanair āvartamānas tu kartur mūlāni kṛntati//* (4.172)

For this passage, a reference has to be made to Lüders 1940, p. 185.

[27] The weakness of *dharma* is also indicated by the story of *Dharma* (personified) who incurred a curse from the Brahmin ascetic Aṇī Māṇḍavya and consequently was born in the human form of Vidura, as related in *MBh* 1.101.25-27 (cf. the contribution by Albrecht Wezler in the present volume).

Albrecht Wezler

# THE STORY OF AṆĪ-MĀṆḌAVYA AS TOLD IN THE MAHĀBHĀRATA:

## Its Significance for Indian Legal and Religious History

0. Wilhelm Halbfass' two earlier books, viz. *India and Europe: An Essay in Understanding* and *Tradition and Reflection: Explorations in Indian Thought*, would certainly offer me ample opportunity for entering into a discussion with him: I could then not only examine, and at least in some cases also refute, his criticism of some views expressed by me, but also consider the correctness and appropriateness of some of his own views, not to mention additions to his books I have in mind since quite some time, e.g., regarding the modern "neo-hinduistic" reception of the Veda and the origin or early history of Indian doxography. The conditions under which I have to work are however such that I do not have the time absolutely necessary in order to be able to deal with these questions in a satisfactory manner. Therefore, it is only a small and modest contribution which I can make this time. It refers to and, I think, it is also of some significance for the conception of *karman* – our understanding of which has been furthered most remarkably by Halbfass[1] who will, however, deal with it in a comprehensive manner only in a book still to be written.

1. The story of Aṇī-Māṇḍavya is first of all of importance for Indian literary history as it belongs to the vast mass of narrative material which has been repeatedly worked upon by various authors at different points of time and in many languages. Most of the Sanskrit and Buddhist sources in which it has come down to us, have been thoroughly examined and carefully compared by N. B. Utgikar in an article[2] which an Indologist at the end of our century cannot but find quite remarkable for a number of reasons: the command of English, the familiarity with the relevant (European) secondary literature, the manner of arguing, the polite, but confident critique of a scholar like Jacobi, the lucid exposition

- all this is clearly impressive, nay in fact exemplary to such an extent that a modern reader will most probably say to himself that many a younger and by no means only Indian colleague of Utgikar's could take a leaf out of his book, almost literally so to say. Nevertheless, Utgikar too did not intend to, and could not, exhaust the topic entirely; hence there is room for improvement and addition, i.e., a kind of re-examination. My own attempt at continuing Utgikar's work will, however, be limited mainly to the version of the story as found in the *Mahābhārata* (I 101),[3] and in particular to its significance for Indian history of ideas; for, in my view it is precisely in this regard that Utgikar's article is really deficient in substance.

2. According to Utgikar[4] "the story in the *Ādiparvan* remains ... as the original form of the story from which the other versions might be reasonably supposed to have borrowed." I do not want to dispute the second part of his conclusion, but I am in doubt as regards its first part, i.e., the contention that the Mahābhārata version is the original one in an absolute sense of the word. Utgikar of course, is aware of the fact that "this Epic version ... comes only as an *upākhyāna*, an episode," and adds "very probably not existing in the original *Bhārata* Epic ... but only added to this during the period when this was being evolved to the great (*Mahā*)*Bhārata*, the repository of all ancient legends and stories";[5] but to admit an independent pre-existence of this story is, it need hardly be said, not tantamount to excluding the possibility that it was altered in some manner when it was incorporated in the Great Epic. It is true, Utgikar expresses himself in a way, that leaves his readers in doubt as to what precisely he had in mind; but the fact that he does not make any explicit remark, nay not even alludes to this possibility, is, I think, not pure chance.

2.1. But before I may pursue this problem further, I should, of course, first acquaint my readers with the contents of this story, and this can be done best by simply quoting Utgikar's summary,[6] Jacobi's[7] being definitely too short:

"There was a certain Brahmin by name Māṇḍavya, devoted to truth and asceticism. He stood[8] at the door of his hermitage practising austerities with a vow of silence (v. 3).[9] After a long while *dasyus* carrying stolen property came there, pursued by guards. Before they (the latter) could arrive the thieves hid the stolen property and themselves in the sage's hermitage.[10] The guards arrived and asked of the sage which way the thieves had gone (v. 8). The sage made no reply (9). Wherefore they searched his hermitage and found the thieves and the stolen wealth (10). They suspect the sage, seize him and the thieves and carry them all to the king (11). The kind orders the sage and the thieves to be hanged[11] and the sage is impaled on a stake (*śūle protaḥ*) but even after a long while, and though without food, he does not die (14) but keeps himself alive[12] and brings around to where he was impaled the *Ṛṣis* by the force of his penance (15). The *Ṛṣis* are extremely dejected and having assumed the form of birds fly round him[13] and disclosing themselves as best as they could,[14] ask him as to what sin it was because of which he was having that terrible misery on the stake. Aṇī-Māṇḍavya replies in the first v. of the next *adhyāya* - that he has no one else to blame (*doṣataḥ kaṃ gamiṣyāmi* (v.l. *doṣasyāntaṃ ga-*) and that none has offended him (*na hi me 'nyo 'parādhyati*).[15] Curiously enough these are the only words put into the mouth of A. M. in reply to the laborious query of the *Ṛṣis*. When the servants of the king see him thus situated for a long while they report the fact to the king. He takes counsel with his ministers (approaches and) appeases the sage on the stake (3). He orders the sage to be taken down and takes out the stake but is unable to extract the whole of it[16] and he leaves the end of the stake in his body (6). The sage moved about with the end of the stake fixed inside (his body)[17] and by the great endurance involved therein conquered heaven unattainable to other men (7) and because of this is he known as A. M.[18] in the world. A. M. now goes to the abode of Dharma (Yama) and censures him, "What sin was committed by me unknowingly in expiation of which such misery was ordained to me?" (10). Yama replied that A. M. had fixed a blade of grass (*iṣikā*) in the wings of flies[19] and his present misery was in retaliation for this offence (11). An offence howsoever small meets with a great punishment (12). Being asked as to when that sin was committed by him, A. M. is told that it was in his boyhood (13). A. M. then ordains that whatever a boy might do till he reaches twelve years from his birth will not be a sin (14). And inasmuch as Yama has made him and a Brahmin too, suffer a punishment out of proportion to his offence, Yama would be born as a human being in the Śūdra caste (15a). And finally, he (re-?)promulgates[20] that no action committed by a human being till he is fourteen years of age shall be regarded as a sin which it would thereafter (as against the twelve years limit set up above) (17). The last two vv. (18 and 19) sum up the story in Vaiśampāyana's words by saying that it was because of this curse that Yama was born as a Śūdra in the person of Vidura."[21]

2.2. This is Utgikar's rather detailed summary of the story to which I shall return after a short while. First attention has to be drawn to his report on and critical examination of the "allusion to" this story in "the *Kauṭilīya Arthaśāstra*,"[22] and again, the best way of achieving my goal is to quote *in extenso* Utgikar himself:

"The *Kauṭilīya Arthaśāstra* ... does not indeed give the whole of our story but only a part at page 220 where the author says: –[23]

> *dṛśyate hy acoro 'pi coramārge yadṛcchayā; sannipāne[24] coraveṣaśastrabhāṇḍasāmānyena gṛhyamāṇo dṛṣṭaḥ corabhāṇḍasyopavāsena vā yathā hi[25] māṇḍavyaḥ karmakleśabhayād acoraḥ coro 'smīti bruvāṇaḥ|*
>
> Kauṭilīya Arthaśāstra – Shamashastri's 2nd Edn.

Mr. Shamasastri thus translates the last sentence[26] – Māṇḍavya ... under the fear of torture, admitted himself to be a thief ...

The Māṇḍavya referred to here is evidently the A. M. It was Jacobi who first pointed out this reference in the *K.A.S.* to the A. M. story (in the *SBPAW*, Phil.-Hist. Classe 1911, p. 970);[27] but he and after him, J. Charpentier (*W.Z.K.M.*, 28 (1914) p. 238) are inclined to hold that the incident of the A. M. story, as referred to in this work, viz. his saying that he was the thief, though innocent, because he feared the torture (of punishment) is in direct conflict with the Mbh. story, where the sage is represented as making no reply whatever the watchman's enquiry about the way the thieves had gone. A further conclusion is drawn from this divergence (among certain other ones between the *Mahābhārata* and *Arthaśāstra* versions) that at the time of the *K.A.S.* 'there did not still exist a redaction of the Mbh. ascribed to the Vyāsa Kṛṣṇa Dvaipāyana, at least, it had not as yet received a canonic authority in Brahmanic circles' (Jacobi, *L.C.* p. 971; Charpentier, *L.C.* pp. 213, 238). With due deference to the view of so high an authority as Jacobi, it must be said that the reference by Kauṭilya to the story of A. M. cannot be made to support the weighty arguments based thereon: nor can it be argued that the reference itself shows a divergent version of the A. M. story. As we are not at present concerned with the date of the Mbh., this question need not be treated here at great length, but it may be pointed out that our ancient writers were scarcely at great pains to be exact in their quotations or to verify them or to indicate their sources. It is quite possible to imagine that with the story already existing as in our present version Kauṭilya might have used the story (we might even say adapted the story) to illustrate the points he had in mind, viz., that at times it is possible to come by a case where a person in order to avoid all bother of the police custody and the proverbial torture it involves, makes a false admission. It may also be that the way in which Kauṭilya refers to the story is a rationalistic way of interpreting an old story, - an old *Itihāsa* or *Ākhyāna*. Given the story, the question would arise as why the sage did not speak out that he had no hand whatsoever in the theft. Of this there is no answer in the Mbh., or the Buddhist version. A man with an intensely practical and inductive turn of mind may say that the purpose was the ascetic's desire to avoid all torture, or to offer himself in the place of the thieves. And it is to be noted that the original reply which is given by A. M. in the story of the Mbh. as we have it and which Jacobi regards as opposed to the *K.A.S.* statement, viz. A. M.'s words *na kiṃcid vacanaṃ rājann abravīt sādhv asādhu vā* in Mbh (I.107.9) and Cāṇakya's words *acoraś coro 'smīti bruvāṇaḥ* (*K.A.S.*), - this reply is not made to the watchman's question whether A. M. had committed theft - but is made to the question as to what way the thieves have gone. It looks therefore more probable that Kauṭilya is to be regarded more as theorizing on the A. M. story than quoting therefrom either verbatim or in substance. I am even inclined to hold that, if anything, Kauṭilya's reference points to an inferable familiarity with the Mbh. story. After getting no reply from the sage, which way the thieves had gone the king's servants search the hermitage of the sage. There they find according to the Epic story both the thieves and the stolen articles (*corabhāṇḍam* of *K.A.S.* = *corāṃs tad dravyam eva ca* of the Epic). We must now imagine A. M.'s position. He realises that he is now undone. The stolen property and the thieves are discovered hidden in his hut and howmuchsoever he might now protest he was sure to be seized as a thief (or an accomplice). He therefore hands himself over to the king's men without offering any resistance, because even if he resisted he was sure to be seized - and so *karmakleśabhayāt*, though he was not a thief (*acoraḥ*) he admits *coro 'smīti bruvāṇaḥ.*"[28]

It was necessary to quote this passage in full in spite of its length, because it is only when this background is known that my own remarks can be made without in each case first having to explain what they refer to, and it is only thus that they are also easier to follow.

1. Utgikar has evidently made a convincing point when he emphasizes that A. M.[29]'s keeping silent, in the *MBh*, forms part of a quite different situation, viz. the king's men's asking him about the way the thieves have taken. That he observes his vow of silence even at this moment is quite understandable in terms of Indian asceticism, – at least as understandable as his speaking, i.e., not observing this vow when he is entreated by the *ṛṣis* to disclose the reason for his suffering impalement.

2. Utgikar is equally to be followed in his criticism directed against Jacobi, and Charpentier, at least in principle: Evidently these two scholars have taken the easy way out of one of the problems posed by the divergence between the Epic and the *AŚ* version of the story and have not taken into consideration also the still more basic problem of the extraordinary difficulties one is confronted with when dealing with various versions of a narrative and determining which of them is the "original" one.[30]

3. On the other hand, Utgikar does not seem to clearly distinguish between A. M.'s fear of torture as a means of obtaining a confession and his fear of "the torture of punishment." It is of course possible that an innocent suspect out of fear of the punishment to be expected confesses to a crime and due to the mere confession receives precisely the punishment he was so much afraid of, but such irrational a behaviour is hardly what the *Arthaśāstra* (= *AŚ*) has in mind; besides the wording (at *AŚ* 4.8.12) is entirely unequivocal: *karmakleśabhayāt* cannot but mean "because of the fear of the pain of torture," as rightly translated by R. P. Kangle,[31] – as is also clear from the wider context as I am going to show a little later.

4. As for this particular feature of the story, I think one can easily agree with Utgikar if what he ultimately wants to say is that it may have been important for the "author" of the *AŚ*, but not for the author of the Epic version, i.e., that it may well have formed a part of the "original" story. For there is no likelihood at all that the "author" of the *AŚ* deliberately changed the story, i.e., introduced a feature "originally" alien to it: After all what he does here, and in general agreement with *AŚ* 1.5.13f.[32] at that, is to refer to an *itihāsa* by way of giving a suitable example; and this device by its very nature and purpose implies that the contents of this *itihāsa* are regarded as

something known to the reader/ hearer and hence as something which cannot be altered: what is the use of an example if everybody knows that it does in fact not illustrate what it is said to illustrate?

In this regard I disagree with J. J. Meyer who speaks[33] of a "little change," which he believes the "author" of the *AŚ* capable of having introduced and of which he expressly states that it does not prove that the "author" of the *AŚ* did not know the Epic version of the story. First of all Utgikar is quite evidently right when he – though in the context of his critical examination of Jacobi's and Charpentier's interpretation – expresses the opinion that the phrase *"coro 'smi" iti bruvāṇaḥ* cannot by any means refer to a confession made by keeping silent, – no matter how many times and clearly the idea may be attested in Dharmaśāstra literature that "he who keeps silent, confesses";[34] and, secondly, what can at best be admitted regarding the relation between the *AŚ*'s reference to the story of A. M. and its Epic version, is – not that it was in any way substantially changed, but only – that an immediately plausible interpretation of a particular element of the story was added which was, or could have been, simply passed over in the *MBh*, viz. the question why A. M. was put on the stake, too.[35] In passing only I should like to mention here that the "author" of the *AŚ* could have referred to this story in connection with 4.8.6 as well,[36] where he states among other things that the punishment "for one hiding a thief" shall be that for a thief.

To sum up, it can be said that for a number of reasons it is Utgikar who should be followed if, or insofar as, he arrives at the conclusion that what is said in the *AŚ* about A. M. does not by any means stand in contradiction with the story as told in the Mbh., but can in one way or other convincingly be shown to be in accordance with it.

But one cannot return from the *AŚ* to the *MBh* without at least a brief appreciation of the context of this chapter. For it deals with investigation through interrogation and through torture,[37] and torture as a means of obtaining admission is, to be sure, neither a specific "invention" of Indian criminal law[38] nor unfortunately just an inhumane cruelty of the past. It is, however, some comfort, though still a pretty cold one, that the passage under discussion takes into account the possibility that a suspect may under torture or rather out of fear of imminent torture make a wrong confession and that hence precautions have to be taken to ensure that the truth is nevertheless found out with the help of additional means of quite different a character.[39] To which extent this - juridically sensible - insight was observed in the actual administration of law in India, however, is another question, and one which I cannot address for obvious reasons.

3. Returning now to the Epic version, the first question to be re-examined is Utgikar's opinion that it is "the original form of the story" though it is an *upākhyāna* only, "an episode, very probably not existing in the original *Bhārata* Epic ... but only added to this during the period when this was being evolved to be the great *(Mahā)Bhārata* ... ."[40] This conclusion is a bit amazing, not of course as regards the relation between the other versions and the Epic one, but if attention is focussed on the latter alone; for in complete accordance with the Sanskrit original Utgikar's own summary points to a kind of rupture in the narrative. Does not the verse (1.101.21)

> *sa tathāntargatenaiva śūlena vyacaran muniḥ/*
> *sa tena tapasā*[41] *lokān vijigye durlabhān paraiḥ/*
> *aṇīmāṇḍavya iti ca tato lokeṣu kathyate//*

form a quite natural ending of the story and is it not rather surprising that the story is continued after it at all? And to be sure, the fact that the part which follows upon this ending and which may be called "the visit paid to Dharma," is referred to at other places in the *MBh*[42] cannot by any means be regarded as proving that it formed an original part of the story right from the beginning, i.e., the period when it was incorporated in the "Great Epic." On the other hand, it is also possible that the verse quoted just now forms but a remark concluding only the first part of the story. In addition what has to be taken into account is the connection between the story of A. M. and the Epic as such, which is formed by his curse and Vidura's *śūdra* descent. Therefore it is perhaps advisable not to press this point, but rather leave this problem of higher textual criticism undecided for the time being.

4. In any case what really matters - and what has apparently been overlooked by all scholars who have dealt with this story - is the fact, stated as clearly in the text itself as one can wish, that it has a "moral": quite evidently the second part - in either sense of the word - is meant to convey a most significant message, viz. that human beings are responsible, in terms of Hindu *dharma*, for their actions only when they have reached a particular age.

4.1. Neither A. M. himself nor the *ṛṣis*[43] are able to recognize[44] the reason for the - seemingly - innocent ascetic's impalement. It is God Dharma who, coerced by A. M.,[45] solves the riddle: Māṇḍavya has in his boyhood[46] done an act of cruelty to animals - as it is unfortunately not uncommon for children in general -: he pierced[47] small birds[48] with stalks of grass or reed, i.e., practically impaled and thus killed them. A. M.'s own impalement hence turns out to be nothing but the retribution for a similar act of his own, yet in accordance with the *lex talionis* which is expressed in the *Old Testament*[49] by the oft quoted formula "an eye for an eye and a tooth for a tooth," i.e., which means that the culprit should suffer exactly the same evil he has caused somebody else, or another living being, as one has to say with regard to the Indian tradition. For, this principle of "retaliation"[50] is in India, I think, for the first time attested in the story of "Bhṛgu in the next world"[51] as found in the *Śatapatha-* and the *Jaiminīya-Brāhmaṇas*,[52] or perhaps I should be a bit more cautious and say that this story can be interpreted as testifying among others to this idea.[53] In any case there is no doubt that the principle expressed in the *lex talionis* has exercized a palpable influence on Dharmaśāstra, especially on the ideas about rebirth and hell, although the relevant material has unfortunately not yet been studied comprehensively, not to mention the still more deplorable fact that not all scholars using the term *lex talionis* seem to know what it really means.[54]

Seen against this historical background the possibility has at least to be considered that the story of A. M., of the *MBh*, forms a criticism, or even protest, against this "legal"[55] principle. Yet even if this possibility cannot indeed be entirely excluded, this much is certain: the emphasis is here not on the principle as such, but on the disproportion between offence and punishment (1.101.25ab: *alpe 'parādhe vipulo mama daṇḍas tvayā kṛtaḥ*)! Yet what the story ultimately aims at is not the almost unbelievable severity of the punishment[56] - in form of the impalement of a grown up man, and an ascetic at that, who had happened to kill a number of birds in his boyhood - *but that what A. M. has done as a boy without recognizing, or even being able to recognize, it to be wrong is punished at all*!

4.2. This is stated in the text itself with all necessary clarity, for after cursing Dharma A. M. goes on to say (1.101.26):

> *maryādāṃ sthāpayāmy adya loke dharmaphalodayām/*
> *ā caturdaśamād varṣān na bhaviṣyati pātakam/*
> *pareṇa kurvatām evaṃ doṣa eva bhaviṣyati//*

Today/now I [hereby] lay down a limit for[57] the arising of consequences of an action: [Anything done by a human being] until his fourteenth year will not be (i.e., represent) an offence to be punished by death.[58] For those who commit such [a deed] afterwards (i.e., after this age limit), it will be [regarded as] constituting a mistake (i.e., an offence).[59]

There is some uncertainty regarding the age: *ā caturdāśamād varṣān* could mean "before the completion of the fourteenth" or of "the fifteenth year of one's life."[60] In a verse rejected in the critical edition[61] it is the "twelfth year" that is given as limit, but it seems that this is found only in Mss. from South India,[62] and that the tendency to lower the limit is indeed a later development.[63]

Be that as it may, none of the three figures is easy to understand, i.e., to interpret in the context in Indian culture. The date of the relevant texts, i.e., first of all the Gṛhyasūtras, about the appropriate age for the *upanayana*, the ceremony of initiation into the group of the "twice-born" and hence the beginning of the study of the Veda, do not only vary as regards the *varṇa*, the "class," of the boys, and do not only distinguish a minimal and maximal age, but they do not at all agree, if one text is compared with another.[64] Therefore one will definitely hesitate to draw any conclusion if one of the three ages is met with again among the many non-uniform ones mentioned in the Gṛhyasūtras and similar texts. In addition what has to be taken into account is that A. M., though a Brahmin himself, does not have in view any particular of the three upper *varṇas* when laying down this limit: what he says, in fact looks very much like a general statement which might even extend to the *śūdras*.

4.3. A further problem is posed by the fact that A. M. seems to refer to a particular category of offences, the most heinous ones, viz. those called *pātaka*. But this problem can be resolved by assuming either that quite understandably he still has in mind the punishment he himself had had to suffer (though not up to the end it is ultimately meant for, i.e., death), or that the expression *pātaka* is used in its wider sense of "crime, offence." Thus what is said in the verse rejected in the critical edition, viz.

> *bālo hi dvādaśād varṣāj janmano yat kariṣyati/*
> *na bhaviṣyaty adharmo 'tra atra na prajñāsyati vai doṣaḥ//,*

could be accepted as a basically correct interpretation of what A. M. in fact wants to say, of course apart from the particular age mentioned here. And this is tantamount to stating that the second part of the story of A. M. as told in the *MBh* is *about the age of criminal responsibility*.

Now, there is a passage in the *AŚ* which refers to the same legal point, viz. 3.3.1-2:

> *dvādaśavarṣā strī prāptavyavahārā bhavati, ṣoḍaśavarṣaḥ pumān/ ata ūrdhvam aśuśrūṣāyāṃ dvādaśapaṇaḥ striyā daṇḍaḥ, puṃso dviguṇaḥ,*[65]

rendered by Kangle[66] as follows:

> A woman twelve years of age attains majority, a man when sixteen years of age. If after this there is a failure to carry out marital duties, there shall be a fine of twelve *paṇas* for the woman, twice that for a man.

It is true that this passage cannot be totally dislinked from 3.2.1 *vivāhapūrvo vyavahāraḥ*,[67] "(all) transactions begin with marriage,"[68] but the evident connection between the two passages is duly recognized also if the compound *prāptavyavahāra-* of 3.3.1 is interpreted to mean "attains majority *if* she/he is already married" or "*insofar* as she/he is already married." And there is no need whatsoever[69] to assume that the expression *śuśrūṣā*, literally "obedience," refers to "marital duties." Not only is *śuśrūṣaka*, i.e., person bound to obey, said[70] to comprehend five persons, viz. a pupil, a religious pupil, a hired servant, an officer and a slave, but it is also simply absurd to suppose that a recently married girl complains to a judge about her husband's failure to have sexual intercourse with her after her menses and that the husband is thereupon fined 24 *paṇas*. There are hence good reasons to follow in this case J. J. Meyer who by way of explaining "in case of disobedience" adds within brackets "to such people to whose commands one has to submit."[71]

Therefore I feel justified to contend that what the passage *AŚ* 3.3.1-2 is really about is *the age of majority and of criminal responsibility*, though the latter perhaps only in a limited sense.[72] That women and men[73] are distinguished in this regard is little wonder, just as the fact that the age of majority is the same as that of criminal responsibility or that the *AŚ* does not like modern law differentiate in addition between complete and limited legal competence (of a person), etc.

Nevertheless if this passage of the *AŚ* should all the same form no parallel to the "moral" of the story of A. M., by following a reference of J. J. Meyer in the "Addenda" to his translation of the *AŚ*,[74] a parallel from a Dharmaśāstra text is to be found, viz. *Nāradasmṛti* 1 (= *ṛṇādāna*) 31.32ab:[75]

> *garbhasthaiḥ sadṛśo jñeya ā varṣād aṣṭamāc chiśuḥ/*[76]
> *bāla ā ṣoḍaśāj jñeyaḥ pogaṇḍaś cāpi śabdyate//*
> *parato vyavahārajñaḥ svatantraḥ pitarau vinā/,*

which has been rendered by R. Lariviere[77] thus:

> Until his eighth year a child is considered the same as an embryo and until the sixteenth year he is a youth, also called a *pogaṇḍa*.[78] After that, he is competent in commerce and independent,[79] provided his parents are dead ... .[80]

Already J. Jolly observes in a footnote[81] that "this rule of Nārada has become the foundation of the modern law regarding minority," and this development is outlined in greater detail by Lariviere,[82] who also summarizes Asahāya's explanation according to which

> a child is incompetent with regard to matters such as purity, study, etc., until his eighth year. He is then competent with regard to matters of purity, study, etc., but not until his sixteenth year is he competent in matters of commerce.[83]

This parallel is interesting not only because of the age, 16, but also because of the subdivision of this first stage of life into two parts, "childhood" and "boyhood," the reason evidently being the age at which the *upanayana* is performed on - Brahmin - boys. Yet *Nāradasmṛti* 1.31f. is also somewhat disappointing in that it does not, at least not explicitly, say anything about criminal responsibility. According to P. V. Kane,[84] however,

> Angiras quoted by the Mit. (on Yāj III.243) states that[85] an old man over eighty, a boy below sixteen, women and persons suffering from diseases are to be given half prāyaścitta and Śaṅkha quoted by Mit. (on the same verses)[86] that a child less than five commits no crime nor sin by any act and is not to suffer any punishment nor to undergo a prāyaścitta.

4.4. If seen within this framework of more or less completely parallel passages from the *AŚ* and certain Dharmaśāstra texts, the story of A. M. as told in the *MBh* stands out by a number of features that deserve our full attention.

1. The *upanayana* - and the consequences it has in marking the end of childhood with its famous *kāmacāra*, "following one's own pleasure,"[87] and the beginning of a new period in life,[88] viz. *brahmacarya*, which is characterized by not a few observances (*vrata*) - the ceremony of *upanayana* is simply ignored in the *MBh*.

2. The establishing of the age of criminal responsibility is not described as an element, an integral part, of *dharma*. Rather it is presented here as something A. M. has to wrest from God Dharma: *Criminal responsibility is laid down by a human being as a result of a clash with Dharma* - who is described as a person in this part of the story which has rather the character of a myth.

3. And the human being who does this is a man, an ascetic of rare unwaveringness who has experienced for himself to which abominably cruel consequences the law of *karman* can lead if it is applied even to children who don't know anything about *dharma*[89] and *adharma* and cannot hence be held responsible for what they do.

The ultimate meaning[90] of the story of A. M., its "message," thus turns out in the end to be that the law of *karman* is, contrary to its very nature, not universally valid, but for human beings limited to that age of life during which a man, or woman[91] is in principle regarded to be responsible for his actions. And when this age begins - and ends - is something to be agreed upon by the members of a society, something that has to be laid down by a "law-maker." Therefore it is not a *prauḍhokti* on my part to state in concluding this essay that the story of A. M. as told in the *MBh* evidently reflects the awareness of the friction between the intrinsic claim of universal validity in principle of the law of *karman*, on the one hand, and the morally well-founded and humane insight, on the other, that there are natural limits to man's criminal responsibility; and as the particular solution found seems in itself to be in agreement with historical facts as attested in other texts, one is tempted to assume that the story is a literary transformation of, and reaction to, a historical process of discussing this friction and finding an adequate solution to it. The impact this cannot but have on the conception of *karman*, and of *dharma*, however, is not even touched upon[92] by the unknown "author" who used[93] the story of A. M. just to emphasize, though in an impressive manner, that prior to a certain age of his life, i.e., majority, man is not "morally" responsible even for an act of *hiṃsā*.

*Ceterum censeo terram Tibetanam*
*in veterem dignitatem ac libertatem*
*esse vindicandam.*

*Universität Hamburg*
*Institut für Kultur und Geschichte Indiens und Tibets*
*Hamburg, Germany*

## NOTES

[1] What I have in mind is first of all Halbfass 1980a and TR (see "Index").

[2] Utgikar 1922. – For parallels not discussed by Utgikar see Grey 1990, p. 53 (to which my attention has kindly been drawn by my friend Oskar von Hinüber). On the identification of Jesus with Aṇī-Māṇḍavya and its – more than justified – rejection see Keny 1942-43.

[3] In the critical edition, Poona 1933-1959. The edition used by Utgikar is apparently that published in Bombay 1868-1888.

[4] Utgikar 1922, p. 238.

[5] Utgikar 1922, l.c.

[6] Utgikar 1922, p. 222f.

[7] Jacobi 1903, p. 13f.

[8] In this and some of the subsequent notes I make some additions to and corrections of Utgikar's summary or give some additional explanations, all of which are based on the text as constituted by V. S. Sukthankar in his edition of the *Ādiparvan* (cf. n. 3); for obvious reasons I don't enter into a discussion of the textcritical and philological problems involved. – Māṇḍavya is characterized as *ūrdhvabāhur* here (I 101.3c).

[9] As for Utgikar's references see n. 3.

[10] Note that nowhere in this part of the story – nor later – is it expressly stated that Māṇḍavya actually saw the thieves and what they did. This is, however, most probably suggested by stating that "he stood at the door/gate/entrance of his hermitage" (*sa*

*āśramapadadvāri ... tasthau*: 1.101.3), an element of the story that would otherwise seem a bit strange.

[11] Actually the king's command is "he is to be killed" (*anvaśād vadhyatām iti*: 1.101. 11b), but because of the preceding *pāda*, viz. *taṃ rājā saha taiś corair*, [note that I don't reproduce the wavy line used by Sukthankar to indicate that the constitution of a word or part of the text is regarded by him as not certain] it is I think evident that the punishment for the thieves and the ascetic too is the same, viz. impalement which is the "normal" method of executing *coras* (see Wezler 1996). That the thieves are here mentioned for the last time is quite understandable in terms of the logic of the narrative: they are not important any longer. As for Utgikar's "hanged," my surmise is that he uses the word in the sense of "executed."

[12] The miracle, if this is the right word, consists not in not being killed instantaneously after being put on the stake, but in the *length* of the period of surviving the torture; cf. also Wezler 1996. Evidently it is because of this miracle that Māṇḍavya was later regarded also as characterized by particular longevity, and is mentioned by Vācaspatimiśra in his *Tattvavaiśāradī* (on *YS* 4.1).

[13] At the level of reality these are, of course, the species of birds typical of places of execution, gallows, etc.; cf. also Wezler 1996. – Regarding the interpretation of the expression *ṛṣi* as used here see below n. 14 and n. 43.

[14] The original reads here *(te ... śakunā bhūtvā) darśayanto yathāśakti (tam apṛcchan dvijottamam)*. Van Buitenen 1973, p. 237, decided in favour of translating this as "after showing their powers, as far as they were capable," but his not following Nīlakaṇṭha – who explains *svāni rūpāṇi prakāśayantaḥ* – is not convincing at all. If *ṛṣi* means "seer" here, and, I think, there can hardly be any doubt that it does (cf. n. 43 below), and if *yathāśakti* is to be connected with *darśayanto*, preference should be given to Nīlakaṇṭha – and Utgikar –, but a more literal translation chosen, viz. "making [him] see [them] to the best of their capacity," the *avyayībhāva* most probably amounting to something like "completely/clearly."

[15] On this sentence see Wezler 1996.

[16] Utgikar seems to have misunderstood the text here. In reality the stake cannot be extracted at all and has therefore to be cut "at its root," i.e., Māṇḍavya's anus.

[17] In reality it is its "top" (*aṇī*!) which keeps sticking out of his body.

[18] Note that I take over this and other abbreviations from Utgikar.

[19] Van Buitenen 1973, p. 28, too, takes *pataṃgaka* to mean "little flies"; the expression *puccha* (1.101.24ab: *pataṃgakānāṃ puccheṣu tvayeṣīkā praveśitā*), however, rather speaks in favour of the other meaning of *pataṃgaka*, viz. "(little) bird," although it is

admittedly but an euphemism, or a taboo word, for what is evidently meant, viz. that Māṇḍavya inserts the stalk of some grass or reed into the birds' anus and thus *de facto* impales them. This interpretation is strikingly confirmed by the reference to the story of Aṇī-Māṇḍavya at *MBh* 1.57.77ff. where in spite of the manifest intention of the author to make disproportion even larger (see n. 56 below) the unequivocal expression *śakuntikā* is used.

[20] On this verse, rejected in the critical edition, and the problem of determining the exact age intended see below § 4.2 and n. 46.

[21] Utgikar 1922, p. 223, rightly, states (in the immediately following paragraph): "The setting in which this story of A. M. is placed in the Epic deserves some notice," and he continues: "The story occurs in the *Sambhavaparva* section of the *Ādiparvan*. This *Sambhavaparva* describes the birth and other antecedents of the Epic characters, and as such that of Vidura, who is described as being Yamadharma undergoing as mortal Vidura an expiation of his offence against the sage A. M. ... ."

[22] This, and the subsequent passages, are quoted from Utgikar 1922, p. 232ff.

[23] This is *AŚ(K)* 4.8.11-12, p. 140.

[24] Read, of course, *saṃnipāte*.

[25] Note that Kangle (*AŚ(K)*, p. 140) has rightly decided in favour of the reading *yathā-ṇimāṇḍavyaḥ*.

[26] Shamasastry 1929, p. 248 (but with "the thief" instead of "a thief").

[27] Cf. Jacobi 1970, pp. 502-521. Only Jacobi is referred to by Sten Konow 1945, p. 11.

[28] The passages in Sanskrit quoted here and in the preceding are printed in Devanāgarī in Utgikar 1922.

[29] See above n. 18. Instead of "Mbh." and "*K.A.S.*," however, I use "*MBh*" and "*AŚ*."

[30] I should, however, like to underscore that I very much doubt that the term "original" or "*Ur-Version*" makes really sense when applied to at least a particular type of narrative literature; because what has come down to us are but "written" versions which as a rule don't even give us the faintest idea about the "life," and also earlier "life," of a particular story as element of an oral, and perhaps popular, tradition. Of course, in theory any story, or at least a part of it or its kernel, must have been told sometime "for the first time," but recognizing this doesn't help much.

[31] Kangle 1963, p. 318. – I fully agree with Kangle 1963, p. 317, note on 4.8 – and Kane 1973, p. 254f., n 332 – that *karman* in this particular passage of the *AŚ* cannot but mean "torture," though I am also not able to give a further example for this meaning from this or another text; in this connection it is, however, noteworthy that in Pali, especially of course in Vinaya texts, *kamma* is used to denote "proceedings, ceremony, performed by a lawfully constituted chapter of bhikkhus" (PTS Dictionary). In a special context, viz. that of the investigations of an "examining magistrate," torture is just one of the types of "acts" performed, especially if *karman* stands in opposition to *vākya-anuyoga*, "(simple) verbal examination"; cf. also below n. 37.

[32] Which reads as follows (*AŚ(K)*, p. 7): *paścimam* (scil. *aharbhāgam*) *itihāsaśravaṇe* (scil. *vinayaṃ gacchet*) /13/ *purāṇam itivṛttam ākhyāyikodāharaṇaṃ dharmaśāstram arthaśāstraṃ cetītihāsaḥ* /14/. – In passing I should like to state that I regard the latter sentence as formally so close a parallel to the famous one of *AŚ* 1.2.10 (*sāṃkhyaṃ yogo lokāyataṃ cety ānvīkṣikī*) that for this very reason I hesitate to accept Hacker's (Hacker 1958, p. 12f.) interpretation of the *iti* (in *AŚ* 1.2.10); I should rather propose to start from the assumption that *iti* means in *both* cases "when [the designations/terms ABC ...] are mentioned [what comes to one's mind] is x" > "x is associated with the designations/terms A, B, C ... ." – As for the first examples of such *itihāsas* see *AŚ* 1.6.4ff.

[33] Meyer 1926, p. 343, n. 2.

[34] Meyer 1926, l.c.; cf. also Henry Fielding, *Tom Jones*, London 1966, p. 98 (= Book Two, chapter 4): "and this silence being interpreted to be a confession of the charge, by the whole court, they all began at once, *una voce*, to rebuke and revile him, repeating often, that none but a coward ever struck a woman." – Meyer 1926, p. 819, rightly refers to "N(āradasmṛti), Einl(eitung) I, 42," but I am not fully convinced that here "the same is taught by the same warning example" as by Kauṭilya, because Nārada expresses himself in such a way (*acauraś cauratāṃ prāpto māṇḍavyo vyavahārataḥ*: 1.36, Lariviere 1989 [edition], p. 19) that it is not at all clear whether what he has in mind is the *AŚ* version, or – as Asahāya thinks – that of the *MBh*. The two verses quoted by Aparārka (p. 599) from Bṛhaspati – to which Kane 1973, l.c., draws attention in addition to the *Nāradasmṛti* passage – are even less unambiguous.

[35] That the thieves share his fate is clear from the context and because of general considerations; see n. 11 above.

[36] *AŚ(K)*, p. 140: *acoraṃ coram ity abhivyāharataś corasamo daṇḍaḥ, coraṃ pracchādayataś ca*, "for one calling another, who is not a thief, a thief, the punishment shall be that for a thief, also for one hiding a thief" (Kangle 1963, p. 318).

[37] Cf. the heading of this *prakaraṇa* (no. 83), viz. *vākyakarmānuyogaḥ*, and the *Śrīmūla* commentary on it: *vākyakarmānuyoga iti sūtram. vākyena karmaṇā ca śaṅkābhigṛhītasya anuyogo 'bhidhīyata iti sūtrārthaḥ. śaṅkādiliṅgānāṃ vyabhicārasambhavād vastuto 'corasyāpi daṇḍabhayādinānṛtavāditvadarśanāc ca coratvanirṇayāya vākyakarmānuyogaḥ*

*prastūyate*.

[38] Therefore apologetic remarks like those of Kane 1973, l.c., are quite unnecessary – though they are typical, and not only of this Indian scholar working on Dharmaśāstra: whenever they come to speak of an element of Indian tradition of which they feel that it could provoke the frown of a modern enlightened Westerner they more often than not point out that a similar or even worse practise or idea is attested in the European etc., tradition too. These remarks are annoying not so much because they are made at all, but because the intention for making them lacks all subtlety.

[39] See e.g., – as rightly pointed out by Meyer 1926, p. 819 – *Nāradasmṛti* 1.59-65 (Lariviere 1989 [edition], pp. 27-29).

[40] Utgikar 1922, p. 238; cf. also above § 2.

[41] Though Māṇḍavya is called among others a *mahāyogin* in 1.101.3, there cannot be any doubt that he practises *tapas*, not *yoga*, and that it is the extraordinary power accumulated by ascetisicm that enables him to survive the impalement, and not "through *yoga*" as Jacobi 1903, p. 14, writes.

[42] Viz. 1.57.77ff. and 15.35-14.

[43] According to the first interpretation of two alternative (?) ones, given by Nīlakaṇṭha, *ṛṣīn* at 1.101.13 means *vedān*, and the statement that Māṇḍavya "led" them "towards himself, i.e., made [them] dependent on himself" (*samupānayat [=] svādhīnān akarot*), has to be understood as amounting to "did not forget the Vedas in spite of being tortured for a long time" (*ciraṃ vedanārto 'pi vedān na vismṛtavān ity arthaḥ*). Though there are a number of good reasons to reject this interpretation, it is, I think, interesting to note that even at the time of Nīlakaṇṭha the Veda was still easily associated with the expression *ṛṣi*. – Note that A. M. himself is also classed among the *ṛṣis*, e.g., at 1.101.17.

[44] This follows from the fact that A. M. as well as the *ṛṣis* enquire what the reason for his being punished in so cruel a manner is. *ajānatā* (in 1.101.23ab: *kiṃ nu tad duṣkṛtaṃ karma mayā kṛtam ajānatā*) rather expresses that A. M. was not aware that what he did was wrong, i.e., that whichever deed may have caused his misery, it was something done by him unknowingly. – Note, however, that according to the parallel 1.58.78ff. it is Māṇḍavya himself who remembers what he did as a boy, but takes Dharma to task for the fact that his accumulated ascetic power was not sufficient to make good his deed.

[45] See 1.101.23ed: *śīghram ācakṣva me tat tvaṃ* (or: *tattvam*?) *paśya me tapaso balam*.

[46] This is, however, stated so clearly only in a verse rejected by Sukthankar (see below n. 89), viz. 1.1101*:

*bālo hi dvādaśavarṣāj janmano yat kariṣyati/*
*na bhaviṣyaty adharmo 'tra na prajñāsyati vai diśaḥ//*,

in which the lack of the preposition *ā* (or should we read *hy ā dvā°*?) is noteworthy as also the use of *diś* f. in the sense of "that whatever is right" (a survival of one of the meanings this word has in Vedic Sanskrit or a new semantic development similar to that of *mārga* and synonyms?).

[47] Note that in the parallel passage 1.57.78d the expression *viddhā* is used.

[48] Cf. above n. 19.

[49] Cf. *Moses* 2.21.23-25.

[50] Kant uses the expression "*Wiedervergeltung.*"

[51] Cf. Lommel 1950.

[52] Viz. at 11.6.1 and 1.42 respectively.

[53] Lommel's own interpretation, however, differs: for him "the significance of this legend lies in its showing ... that in yonder world, among the dead, everything is the reverse of our world" (Lommel 1950, p. 101; cf. also Lommel 1951, p. 201f.). I am of the opinion that this interpretation does not exclude that this story also shows, even if this is not at its centre, a particular idea about "retaliation" – just as much of the parallel material from the Indian and other cultures drawn upon by Lommel.

[54] Cf. Wezler 1995.

[55] Originally, however, it seems to have formed part of taking the law in one's own hands.

[56] Note that the disproportion is quantified at 1.57.79c (*sahasrasaṃmitam*) and deliberately made larger by diminishing the number of the victims of little Māṇḍavya to one bird only (*ekā ... śakuntikā*: 1.78.c).

[57] Note the peculiar compound *dharmaphalodayām*.

[58] That is to say, I here start from the assumption that *pātaka* is used in a particular terminological sense; see below § 4.3.

[59] Van Buitenen's (1973, p. 238) translation of this verse reads thus: "Now I lay down the limit on the fruition of the Law: nothing shall be a sin up to the age of fourteen years; but if they do it beyond that age it shall be counted an offence."

[60] On the "inclusive" and "exclusive" meaning of *ā* see *P* 2.1.13 etc.; cf. Wezler 1992, p. 468.

[61] Cf. above n. 46 for the text.

[62] As for the two Devanāgarī Mss. (Dn3 and D4) in which the verse is also found, one should remember Sukthankar's remark (1933, "Prolegomena," p. LXII) that "a Devanāgarī manuscript of the Mahābhārata may, in fact, contain practically any version or combination of versions." On D4, in particular, see "Prolegomena," p. XVIII.

[63] And Nīlakaṇṭha's remark on 1.101.26, viz. *vastutas tūktahetoḥ* (viz. *bālo hi* ... of the rejected verse, see n. 46 above) *puṇyapāpavibhāgajñānaparyantam eva pāpānutpattiḥ. tena pañcavarṣādyantara eva doṣo nāstītyādi vacanaṃ vidvadabhiprāyam. anyathā kaliśeṣe alpāyuṣṭvena pāpābhāvaprasaṅgaḥ syāt*, is quite evidently an attempt to reconcile the statement of the *MBh* with the age of the *upanayana* and at the same time to avoid the theologically highly problematic consequences that at the end of the *kaliyuga* human beings could not commit any *pāpa*, i.e., *adharma*, at all, because the span of their life is not longer than the period of 14 years during which, if the *MBh* is taken literally, no *pāpa* is possible.

[64] Cf. e.g., Gonda 1980, p. 379.

[65] *AŚ(K)*, p. 100.

[66] Kangle 1963, p. 232.

[67] *AŚ(K)*, p. 98.

[68] Kangle 1963, p. 227. – Note that the *Śrīmūla* commentary on the heading of the 59th "chapter" (*prakaraṇa*) of the *AŚ*, viz. *vivāhasaṃyuktam*, contains interesting information on the views of various authorities about the relative rank of the various *vyavahāras*, and that according to Kauṭilya *vivāhasaṃyuktavyavahāra* is the most important one because marriage is the cause of the *gārhasthya*. Therefore *vivāhapūrvo vyavahāra* is explained as follows: *vivāha ity jātāv ekavacanaṃ, sarve vyavahārāḥ vivāhamūlāḥ. vivāhapūrvatvaṃ copapāditam.*

[69] It seems that just the opposite is true: insofar the *AŚ* is going to deal in this "chapter" with "marriage," or rather "what is connected with marriage," it comes also to speak of the age of majority.

[70] See Monier-Williams 1960, s.v. He refers to "W." (i.e., Wilson 1819) only, but in fact this enumeration is found in the *Mitākṣarā* on *Yājñavalkyasmṛti* 2.181, and this in its turn seems to go back to *Nāradasmṛti* 5.2-3 (Lariviere 1989 [edition], p. 149). Thus the first four are the *śiṣya*, the *antevāsin*, the *bhṛtaka* and the *adhikarmakṛt*.

[71] Meyer 1923, p. 246; cf. also the *Śrīmūla* commentary on this passage: ... *aśuśrūṣāyām* [=] *aparicaryāyām* ..., ... *prāptavyavahārā* [=] *paricaraṇakarmaniyojanārhā bhavati.*

[72] I.e., if *śuśrūṣā* denotes only "obedience" of those 5 types of people who owe it to their "master"; cf. above n. 70.

[73] Note that according to *AŚ* 1.5.9 (*brahmacaryaṃ cā ṣoḍaśād varṣāt*) this coincides with the end of the *brahmacarya* of a *kṣatriya*.

[74] Meyer 1923, p. 755.

[75] The numbering according to Lariviere 1989 (edition), p. 67f.

[76] Lariviere's ed. has a printing mistake here (*chiṣuḥ*).

[77] Lariviere 1989 (translation), p. 40.

[78] For the etymology or explanation of this word cf. Mayrhofer 1963, p. 344, and Turner 1966, pp. 476 (no. 8394) and 477 (no. 8399).

[79] Cf. also Schetelich 1977.

[80] Cf. 32cd: *jīvator asvatantraḥ syāj jarayāpi samanvitaḥ*.

[81] Jolly 1889, p. 51, n. on verse 35.

[82] Lariviere 1989 (translation), p. 41.

[83] I fail to understand Asahāya's remark (*tāvat putro 'pi vṛddhatvam api prāpto 'vibhaktabhāg asvatantra eveti*). *kāryakāraṇayogyatvāpekṣayaitad ucyate*. Apart from the question if this is really the right place, I wonder whether one should not rather read: *kāryakaraṇa°*; cf. 1.35: *yad bālaḥ kurute kāryam* etc. – Regarding the age limit of sixteen cf. also the verse

*lālayet pañca varṣāṇi daśa varśāṇi tāḍayet/*
*prāpte tu śoḍaśe varṣe putraṃ mitravad ācaret//*

(Vṛddha-Cāṇakya 3.18, also quoted in anthologies and Sanskrit textbooks).

[84] Kane 1973, p. 394f.

[85] *aśītir yasya varṣāṇi bālo vāpy ūnaśoḍaṣaḥ/*
*prāyaścittārdham arhanti striyo vyādhita eva ca//*;

the reading attested in the *Mitākṣarā* in fact is *rogiṇa eva ca*.

[86] Kane 1973, l.c.:

*ūnaikādaśavarṣasya pañcavarṣāt parasya ca/*
*prāyaścittaṃ cared bhrātā pitā vānyaḥ suhṛjjanaḥ//*,

the last two *pādas* however as quoted by Kane (from Haradatta on *GautDhS* 1.2.6) reading thus:

*cared guruḥ suhṛc caiva prāyaścittaṃ viśuddhaye//*;

the continuation is:

*ato bālatarasyāsya nāparādho na pātakam/*
*rājadaṇḍo na tasyāsti prāyaścittaṃ na vidyate//*;

note that in this case Haradatta actually attests the reading *tasyātaḥ prāyaścittaṃ ca neṣyate* (it seems that Kane has mixed up the quotations from Haradatta and Vijñāneśvara). It should also be noted that according to Haradatta all three verses are found in "another Smṛti" (*smṛtyantare*), and that Vijñāneśvara in addition quotes a verse from Sumantu, viz.

*arvāk tu dvādaśād varṣād aśīter ūrdhvam eva vā/*
*ardham eva bhavet puṃsāṃ turīyaṃ tatra yoṣitām//*,

and another one from the *Viṣṇupurāṇa*, viz.

*strīṇām ardhaṃ pradātavyaṃ vṛddhānāṃ rogiṇāṃ tathā/*
*pādo bāleṣu dātavyaḥ sarvapāpeṣv ayaṃ vidhiḥ//*.

[87] Cf. e.g., *GautDhS* 1.21: *prāg upanayanāt kāmacāraḥ kāmavādaḥ kāmabhakṣaḥ*; see also *BaudhDhS* 1.2.3.6, *VāsDhS* 2.6 and *ĀpDhS* 2.6.15.18-25.

[88] As an initiation rite the *upanayana* should contribute to the formation of the roles of the sexes and of the grown up people, as anthropologists would say, but in the Indian context it first of all marks the beginning of the study of the sacred texts of the Veda, and to some extent of the ritual life of the sacrificer. To say as Smith 1989, p. 150, does that it "constitutes the child into a responsible being and member of the society" means to grossly simplify the actual data found in the relevant text material (e.g., the verses quoted above in n. 86).

[89] Cf. 1.1101*d, quoted above n. 46, and Nīlakaṇṭha, quoted above n. 63.

[90] Regarding the interpretation of culture as a "historically transmitted pattern of meanings embodied in symbols" etc., I refer to "Religion As a Cultural System," p. 89, in Geertz 1973.

[91] In spite of what is said about women in the verses quoted above in n. 86, it is not likely, or rather there is reason to believe, that they were not regarded as (entirely) not responsible for their actions.

[92] Though the questions one cannot help asking oneself in this connection are numerous, such as: If this phase of the "non-production of negative *karman* substance" is limited to human beings, or even male human beings only, how is this to be explained in terms of the theory of liberation? Is it nevertheless possible to produce positive *karman* substance during this stage of life? How can this idea (of the "non-production") be regarded as compatible with the conception of the law of *karman* as valid by necessity and automatically as it were? Etc., etc. – A first attempt though has already been made by Goldman 1985 (particularly pp. 418-419) – an article upon which I chanced only after finishing the present essay, viz. when I happened to look into von Stietencron 1992

(where, however, the Goldman reference is not found s.v. Aṇī-Māṇḍavya, but strangely enough only in the "Index of quoted passages"). R. Goldman has indeed recognized that "if ... we are to read this story in part as a dramatic and personalized illustration of the operations of the law of *karma* ..., then it would seem that at least one element of the tradition regards this law, this system of cause and effect, to operate differently, or not at all, in the case of minors." As for the rest, I cannot but state that had I known his article earlier, I would, of course, have expressed myself at some points in a slightly different manner; but this does not mean that the foregoing considerations are superfluous.

To another relevant article my attention was kindly drawn much later (May 1995) by my friend Thomas Oberlies, viz. Patil 1987. Though Patil does not quote any secondary literature on the story, he cannot be denied to have himself recognized its significance, and has to be given credit for rightly emphasizing the role of the personified Dharma and for following up the legal problem involved into modern times.

[93] After all that has been said in this essay, it is highly probable that this is in fact what the "author" of the *MBh* version did.

Yohanan Grinshpon

# EXPERIENCE AND OBSERVATION IN TRADITIONAL AND MODERN PĀTAÑJALA YOGA

The following presentation takes clues from Wilhelm Halbfass' discussion of "The Concept of Experience in the Encounter between India and the West" (IE, chapter 21). It applies his analysis of the different roles of experience in traditional and modern Indian thought to the situation in classical and modern Yoga.

Classical Yoga, a textual tradition based upon Patañjali's *Yogasūtra*, is primarily an "intellectual," verbalized tradition. The explication of concepts and ideas used in the *Yogasūtra* is evidently the major purpose of the commentaries. However, there does seem to be much potential in classical Yoga for drawing upon experience and observation. Many of Patañjali's *sūtras* refer to various dimensions of "observable reality." Particularly significant in this context are the consequences of the *yogin*'s behavior and his application of practices of Yoga. While many of the *sūtras* are comfortably understood as definitions or as – even if expressed by indicative sentences – prescriptions, numerous other *sūtras* refer to the results of the yogic practice and way of life. Such *sūtras* are best understood to relate to observable reality and they imply an obvious sense of factual description. References to first-hand experience or to observations made by others could thus be conducive to the understanding of such *sūtras*.

For example, in *YS* 2.35 Patañjali describes the *yogin* who has become proficient in non-violence (*ahiṃsā*) as one in whose immediate environment violence ceases (*ahiṃsāpratiṣṭhāyāṃ tatsannidhau vairatyāgaḥ*). *YS* 2.35 seems to consist of an indicative, descriptive sentence. Its exact import is that consequent upon the successful observance of *ahiṃsā* a certain result (stopping of violence) is to be expected. Obviously, there are many questions pertinent to the precise meaning of the *sūtra*. What counts as being "well-established in *ahiṃsā*"? Do the *yogin*'s enemies become more friendly to him? What is the dynamics involved in disarming one's enemies' hostility? Does the *yogin* improve the very nature of beings in his environment? Once the meaning of the *sūtra* has become clear, there could arise the question as to its "correspondence with reality." Is it really the case that the *yogin* who exercises *ahiṃsā* controls his environment? Since the result of observing *ahiṃsā* as described in *YS* 2.35 is somewhat unusual and ambiguous, references to experience and observation might clarify as well as corroborate Patañjali's statement. In particular, if the truth-value of the *sūtra* were the focus of attention for the commentator, observation would become crucially important. However, while first-hand familiarity with relevant phenomena might be highly significant in terms of *sūtra*-corroboration, it is not as strictly necessary toward the clarification of the meaning of the *sūtra*. In the case of *YS* 2.35 Vācaspati suggests that the observance of *ahiṃsā* on the part of the *yogin* changes for the better the natural behavior of the animals. Even eternal foes such as the horse and the buffalo, the rat and the cat, the snake and the *nakula*, in the vicinity of an Elevated one (the *yogin*) who is established in the observance of *ahiṃsā*, follow his peaceful mind and forgo violence.[1] Vācaspati's interpretation follows Vyāsa's brief comment to the effect that the renunciation of violence (*vairatyāga*) mentioned in *YS* 2.35 becomes an aspect of the behavior of all the creatures (*sarvaprāṇināṃ bhavati*).

Does Vācaspati's commentary on Vyāsa's *Bhāṣya* express first-hand familiarity with the phenomena consequent upon the practice of *ahiṃsā*? Does he suggest that the cessation of hostility in the *yogin*'s immediate environment does actually occur? On the one hand, Vācaspati uses a straightforward indicative sentence to say that the animals such as the horse etc., forgo their hostility (*vairaṃ parityajanti*). The proposition that under certain circumstances violence among eternal foes ceases appears as an empirical, factual statement. On the other hand, the "factuality" suggested by the indicative sentence is already embodied in the *sūtra* or the *Bhāṣya*. The commentator may elaborate on Patañjali's *sūtra* or on Vyāsa's *Bhāṣya* without addressing the truth-value of the statements he comments upon. However, even in this case the commentator's enterprise is not without value. In *TVai* on *YS* 2.35 Vācaspati creates the conditions for evaluating the truth-value of *YS* (and *YSBh*) 2.35. Once the exact meanings of *YS* (and *YSBh)* 2.35 are clarified by Vācaspati, the question of truth could be addressed. In other words, as the theoretical proposition underlying *YS* 2.35 becomes specific enough, observations become relevant. Did anybody see the behavior of horses etc., in the vicinity of the *yogin*? Is there any other kind of evidence for it? But Vācaspati stops short of such questions. Likewise, Vyāsa does not refer to the truth-value of Patañjali's *sūtras* and the thinkers following Vyāsa do not consider the truth-value of his propositions.

The lack of openness to experience in classical Yoga shows also in the absence of intellectual opponents, *pūrvapakṣins*, who would deny the truth of propositions raised by the *sūtrakāra* or the various commentators. There are, to be sure, *pūrvapakṣins* invoked in the commentaries on the *sūtras* or on Vyāsa's *Bhaṣya*. However, they challenge the *siddhāntin* on logical grounds rather than from observation.[2] None of the *pūrvapakṣins* invoked by Vyāsa, Vācaspati, Bhoja, the author of the *Vivaraṇa*, Vijñānabhikṣu, Nāgeśa etc., ever says that a certain proposition is not seen to be true. This is most conspicuous in the commentaries on the Vibhūtipāda section of the *Yogasūtra* which appears most susceptible to observation and (consequently) to refutation. In this section the *Yogasūtra* describes in detail the various powers and unusual attainments (*siddhi*, *vibhūti*) of the proficient *yogin*. Once the *yogin* has finished his training in the "eightfold yoga" (*aṣṭāṅgayoga*) he attains many powers. He can know his previous lives and experiences,[3] predict the time of his death,[4] and understands the sounds of all the creatures.[5] He can overcome through meditation the pangs of hunger and thirst,[6] move freely in the air,[7] etc. Most of these attainments are evidently observable in principle. If the truth-value of the respective propositions were significant for the commentators, one might expect references to observation, made either by *pūrvapakṣins* or by the *siddhāntin*. But there are none. One could suggest, of course, that the truth-value of the propositions of Yoga capable in principle to be refuted or corroborated was taken for granted. While this is not impossible, yet in this case observation or experience would also be irrelevant.

L. Schmithausen, in his tracing of the conceptualization of early Buddhist meditation,[8] defines a continuum of "description" and "theory." Description is "primary verbalization of actual experience," and theory is "secondary transformation of such a primary verbalization."[9] If the examples brought forth above are characteristic of Yoga – as we suggest – then the tradition of classical Yoga is essentially a theoretical tradition, being devoid of "primary verbalization."

Among the great commentators of classical Yoga, Vācaspati is considered to have been the least concerned with "practice." He was a "pundit through and through"; "his knowledge was theoretical rather than practical," and "he tends to expand on philological and epistemological matters while leaving important practical considerations unexplained."[10] However, in terms of drawing upon either experience or observation, there is no significant difference between Vācaspati and Vyāsa. A statement claiming that "Vyāsa was in all likelihood a *yogin* of considerable attainment, since he writes with great authority about rather esoteric matters"[11] disregards the complete absence of references - direct as well as indirect - to observation or experience in Vyāsa's work.

T. S. Rukmani, who translated Vijñānabhikṣu's 16th century Yoga-commentary, the *Yogavārttika*, into English, suggests that Vijñānabhikṣu was a real *yogin*, i.e., a practitioner of *yoga*. She suggests that experience and observations play a significant part in his commentary. In her introduction to the second volume of her translation of the *Yogavārttika*, she says: "Bhikṣu's detailed analysis of *prajñā* (*YS* 2.27) and the five external aids to *yoga* (2.29), with a minute description of the four varieties of *prāṇāyāma* (2.50-51) lends weight to the belief that he was a practising yogi and was describing the different kinds of *prāṇāyāma* from personal experience." Rukmani compares Vijñānabhikṣu favorably with Vācaspati in this respect. "Thus, while Bhikṣu goes through great pains to describe the *sthambhaka-deśa-prāṇāyāma*, Miśra does not even comment on it."[12]

She responds similarly to his presentation of the *siddhis*. In her introduction to the *Yogavārttika* on the Vibhūtipāda, Rukmani thinks of Vijñānabhikṣu as being acquainted first-hand with such phenomena. "In conclusion one could say that the detailed description of the powers acquired by a yogi as given in this *pāda* again confirms the opinion that Vijñānabhikṣu was either a great yogi and siddha himself, or else was very familiar with the *siddhis* acquired by great yogis."[13]

The suggestion that Vijñānabhikṣu's "minute description" of *prāṇāyāma* in *YV* on *YS* 2.50-51 expresses some kind of "personal experience" on his part is worthwhile of examination. Indeed, control of breathing, *prāṇāyāma*, is a field of yogic practice in relation to which the concrete knowledge and expertise of the commentator could have been of much help. Many issues with respect to various aspects of the practices of *prāṇāyāma* could be raised and clarified by *yogins* who are proficient in breath control. Such *yogins* could elaborate on the respective length of the three stages of breathing (inhalation - *pūraka*, exhalation - *recaka*, and holding the breath - *kumbhaka*), on the psychological and physical benefits of the practice, on the difficulties bound to occur during *prāṇāyāma*, etc. With regard to such phenomena, much use could also be made of testimonies of others. Considering the "impersonal style of Indian Śāstra literature,"[14] others' testimony or the observations of *yogins* in action could serve as a substitute for personal experience in matters such as the practice of *prāṇāyāma*.

Vijñānabhikṣu's comments on *YS* 2.50-51 are indeed lengthy. He does refer to various dimensions of the practice of *prāṇāyāma*. However, there is no evidence that he considers his own experience or his observations of other *yogins* as a useful and legitimate source in the interpretation of the *Yogasūtra*. Vijñānabhikṣu rather refers to texts such as the Purāṇas as his source of knowledge. Concerning the proper sequence of the three stages of *prāṇāyāma* he says that it is mentioned in the Purāṇas etc., many times (*purāṇādiṣu bāhulyena darśanāt*).[15] He quotes a long section from the *Vasiṣṭhasaṃhitā* with respect to the practice of filling in the air (*pūraka*), holding the breath (*kumbhaka*) and exhaling the air (*recaka*).[16] About the length of the different breathing-motions - measured by units of *mātra* - Vijñānabhikṣu mentions as his source the *Mārkaṇḍeyapurāṇa*.[17] Elsewhere in his commentary on *YS* 2.50, where levels of intensity of *prāṇāyāma* are discussed, he quotes the *Kūrmapurāṇa*.[18] In the description of *kevalakumbhaka* in *YV* on *YS* 2.51 he includes a section from the *Vasiṣṭhasaṃhitā* in which different methods of *prāṇāyāma* are compared. The method which induces sweat is said to be inferior, and is also associated with shivering. The best method of yogic breathing (*kevalakumbhaka*) is said in the *Vasiṣṭhasaṃhitā* to involve rising up, or levitation (*utthānaṃ cottame bhavet*).[19] When the *yogin* becomes fully proficient in the practice of *kevalakumbhaka* and in the control of natural breathing there is nothing too difficult for him to achieve in the three worlds.[20] Vijñānabhikṣu chooses to elaborate on this latter aspect of the practice of *prāṇāyāma*. He suggests that the *prāṇāyāma* called *kevalakumbhaka* (which is, as seen above, a total arrest of normal breathing) can last indefinitely, even for a month or a year, according to the *yogin*'s desire (*nāpi kālasaṅkhyābhyāṃ paricchinnaḥ svecchayā māsasaṃvatsarādikālasthāyitvāt*). Vijñānabhikṣu adds in this context that this *prāṇāyāma* is described in the *Viṣṇupurāṇa* (*sa ca prāṇāyāmo dhruvasya viṣṇupurāṇe śrūyate*).[21] The more detailed description of Vijñānabhikṣu's in this context contributes nothing to the factuality of the statements from the *Vasiṣṭhasaṃhitā*. Very much like Vācaspati's contribution of details in *TVai* on *YS* 2.35, Vijñānabhikṣu does not resort to experience or observation by making the truth-value of the text he comments upon (the *Vasiṣṭhasaṃhitā*) the topic of his commentary. Thus, Vijñānabhikṣu's commentary cannot be considered as a "primary verbalization of actual experience." It is rather a "secondary transformation of such a primary verbalization."

The irrelevance of experience and observation in the commentaries of classical Yoga stands in contrast to their role in "Neo-Yoga." The distinction between "classical Hinduism" and Neo-Hinduism is most appropriately transposed to the domain of Yoga. This distinction is drawn by Halbfass as anchored in the concept of "experience."[22] Following some casual remarks of P. Hacker, Halbfass suggests that major features of Neo-Hinduism, and primarily the insistence on personal experience as the quintessential basis of religion, were developed by Radhakrishnan, Debendranath Tagore, Keshab Chandra Sen, Vivekananda, Aurobindo and others very much as a response to the thirst for experience in the West.[23] Unlike classical Hinduism as it is represented in the six orthodox *darśanas*, where the partial correlates of the concept of experience (*anubhava*, *sākṣātkāra*, *pratyakṣa*) were treated with much care and caution, even with a certain dose of suspicion, Neo-Hinduism treats experience as a primary, unconditional clue for the veracity and value of faith and religion. Likewise, Neo-Yoga emphasizes the interpretation of the *Yogasūtra* in the light of the concepts of experience and observation. In general, says Vivekananda, "Man wants truth, wants to experience truth for himself."[24] As to the role of *yoga*, Vivekananda says that "the science of Rāja-Yoga proposes to put before humanity a practical and scientifically worked out method of reaching this truth.." More specifically, Yoga is the method of "observing the internal states."[25]

The scientific, observational approach to Yoga is incorporated in treatises of Neo-Yoga otherwise very close to classical Yoga. Hariharānanda Āraṇya (1869-1947) is in style and spirit a classical Yoga commentator, who founded a Yoga-Sāṅkhya school in Bihar. Essentially, he seeks support from the classical texts. He does not refrain, however, from referring to observations such as of *siddhis*. In his commentary on *YS* 3.42, he refers to a "famous medium (D. D. Home) [who] used to go up in the air."[26] In his commentary on *YS* 4.1, Āraṇya speaks of the various causes of the *siddhis* mentioned in the *sūtra* with much faith in the reality of the *siddhis* produced by the respective causes. He mentions that "powers of clairvoyance or of thought-reading have been found to be produced by particular dispositions."[27] He also says that "herbs also induce supernormal powers. Some (people) in a state of stupor through the application of anaesthetics like chloroform etc., acquire the power of going out of the body."[28] He says that "it is certain that supernormal powers on a small scale can be acquired by the application of drugs."[29] Such statements reflect an openness to observation and experience which is absent in classical Yoga.

Is the openness to observation in classical Yoga completely absent? In general, as suggested above, this is the case.[30] The "reality status" of the propositions of Yoga is a topic avoided by the classical Yoga commentators from Vyāsa on. *siddhāntins* and *pūrvapakṣins* alike avoid the reflection on the "mode of being" of the *yoga*-related phenomena. Thus, classical Yoga is exclusively a tradition of "secondary transformation of primary verbalizations." Though most valuable in terms of meaning-clarification, the various commentaries of classical Yoga are highly repetitive.[31] Major questions which arise in the context of the *Yogasūtra* remain unanswered by the tradition of classical Yoga. Above all, the relationship of Sāṅkhya theory and yogic practice, which was certainly a crucial issue for the compilers of the *Yogasūtra*, is not addressed by the tradition following the composition of the *Yogasūtra*. Indeed, Patañjali's *Yogasūtra* might be considered as the end of a long and vital tradition rather than as its beginning.

*Tel-Aviv University*
*Department of East-Asian Studies*
*Tel-Aviv, Israel*

## NOTES

[1] Cf. *TVai* on *YS* 2.35: *śāśvatikavirodhā apy aśvamahiṣamūṣakamārjārāhinakulādayo 'pi bhagavataḥ pratiṣṭhitāhiṃsasya sannidhānāt taccittānukāriṇo vairaṃ parityajantīti.*

[2] A good example is the way Vācaspati and Vijñānabhikṣu invoke *pūrvapakṣins* in the course of their commentary on *YSBh* on *YS* 3.6. The discussion focuses on the order of the stages of meditation (*saṃyama*). Vācaspati's *pūrvapakṣin* raises the question about the source of knowledge concerning the order of the stages implied by the statement of the *sūtra*. Suppose, he says, that the subdivisions of the various stages be known from the tradition. Wherefrom (would arise) the knowledge as to the priority and posteriority (of the stages)? (*syād etad āgamataḥ sāmānyato 'vagatānām apy avāntarabhūmibhedānāṃ, kutaḥ paurvāparyāvāgatir iti*).

Vijñānabhikṣu's *pūrvapakṣin* sees a contradiction between the statement that the *yogin* should practise *saṃyama* according to the prescribed order and the proposition concerning the need to skip some stages if spiritual progress has been achieved by other means. If skipping over the established order is not allowed, and if applying *saṃyama* to higher stages (once the *yogin* has been capable of applying it to higher objects) is not appropriate, how could their mastery be possible in the beginning? (*nanūtsargāt siddhaṃ kramam ullaṅghya prathamam uttarabhūmikāsu saṃyamārambha eva na yuktaḥ, tat katham ādau tajjayo ghaṭeteti cet*).

When illustrating, in his *TVai* on *YS* 3.6, the practical need to meditate upon simpler, more gross objects before one contemplates more complex or subtle ones, Vācaspati brings forth the example of a person walking from Śilāhrada to the Ganges who must pass through Meghavana on his way. This illustration is logical rather than experiential. Vācaspati does not adduce any example from the domain of meditation, the practical structuring of which he tries to elucidate in *TVai* on *YS* 3.6. And when he describes the process of meditation as involving the increased abstraction of an object, he gives an example taken from the *Viṣṇupurāṇa* and the *Nāradīyapurāṇa*.

[3] *YS* 3.18.

[4] *YS* 3.22.

[5] *YS* 3.17.

[6] *YS* 3.31.

[7] *YS* 3.42.

[8] Cf. Schmithausen 1981.

[9] Schmithausen 1981, p. 200.

[10] Cf. Feuerstein 1989, p. 174.

[11] Cf. Feuerstein, loc. cit.

[12] Cf. Rukmani 1983, p. xi.

[13] Rukmani 1987, p. xi.

[14] Cf. IE, p. 390.

[15] Cf. *YV*, p. 227.

[16] Cf. *YV*, p. 225.

[17] Ibid., p. 225.

[18] Ibid., p. 227.

[19] The *Vasiṣṭhasaṃhitā* adds here that this superior method of *prāṇāyāma* comes about as the natural motions of inhalation and exhalation cease; cf. *YV*, p. 230: *tayor nāśe samarthaḥ syāt kartuṃ kevalakumbhakam//*.

[20] *kevale kumbhake siddhe recakapūrakavijite/*
*na tasya durlabhaṃ kiñcit triṣu lokeṣu vidyate//* (loc. cit.)

[21] Ibid., p. 229. We leave open the question whether one can actually remain in the condition of *kevalakumbhaka* for a year.

[22] Cf. IE, ch. 21 ("The Concept of Experience in the Encounter Between India and the West"), pp. 378-402.

[23] Cf. IE, p. 399: "The concept of experience has thus become one of the most significant devices for presenting and interpreting the Hindu tradition to a world dominated by science and technology."

[24] Cf. Vivekānanda 1982, p. 5.

[25] Ibid., pp. 5-6. However open Neo-Yoga may be to "consciousness research," many works characteristic of Neo-Yoga, such as Vivekananda's *Rāja-Yoga* (1982), Taimni's *The Science of Yoga* (1986) and Rajneesh's *Yoga, the Science of the Soul* (1984), express caution in their references to the domain of experience and observation. The essential tendency is to shift the import of the *Yogasūtra* into "inner space" and interpret the *Yogasūtra* in the light of modern traditions such as physics, psychoanalysis, humanistic psychology, etc. Thus, powers such as of an elephant, which are the *siddhi* following yogic meditation applied to "strengths" according to *YS* 3.24 (*baleṣu hastibalādīni*), are construed in Neo-Yoga in terms of inner energy. Rohit Mehta asserts, that the *sūtra* "does not mean that man comes in possession of animal strength or that the spiritual aspirant gets the strength of the elephant. To interpret the *sūtra* thus is to misunderstand it completely. It means that one discovers in oneself a tremendous source of energy" (Mehta 1990, p. 328). Hariharānanda Āraṇya, however, understands this *sūtra* in a more straightforward sense. He says, that "all physical culturists know that by consciously

applying the will-power on particular muscles, their strength can be developed. *saṃyama* on strength is only the highest form of the same process" (Āraṇya 1983, p. 296).

[26] Cf. Āraṇya 1983, p. 319.

[27] Ibid., p. 346. Āraṇya means here the powers which come about as a result of a certain "birth" (*janma*).

[28] Ibid. Āraṇya adds, that "it has also been reported that by the application of hemlock all over the body similar power is acquired. Witches were supposed to practise this method." Apparently, however, Āraṇya did not go as far as experimenting with these possibilities.

[29] Ibid., p. 347.

[30] Rarely, however, there seem to be traces of indirect reference to the issue of observation applicable to the fruits of *yoga*. Thus, for example, Vyāsa seems to address the issue of the visibility of the *siddhis* by apparently answering a question such as: Why don't we see the *siddhis*? In his commentary on *YS* 3.45 he deals with the possibility that the *yogin* capable of the *siddhis* would interfere with the ordinary course of the world. Vyāsa denies the *yogin*'s wish to do so. He explains that the order of the world as we know it is essentially sanctioned by Īśvara. Wishing to comply with the will of the *pūrvasiddha*, the *yogin* does not disrupt the order of things, though he is capable to do so (*na ca śakto 'pi padārthaviparyāsaṃ karoti*). Even if the *siddhis* are not to be seen because their production is willingly inhibited, the powers must nevertheless be there. Otherwise Vyāsa's suggestion as to the reason of their invisibility would be meaningless. The potentially observable reality of the *siddhis* is thus implied according to *YSBh* on *YS* 3.45.

[31] It is somewhat difficult to dissociate the reading of the *Yogasūtra* from Vyāsa's *Bhāsya*. One wonders, however, about the extent of Vyāsa's contribution to the clarification of the main philosophical and practical problems raised in the *Yogasūtra*.

**Frank J. Korom**

# LANGUAGE, BELIEF, AND EXPERIENCE IN BENGALI FOLK RELIGION*

Religious discourse in the Judeo-Christian context has been a theological concern since the days of Augustine. The contemporary study of religious language in the West arose to a great extent from the fifth and sixth theses of Wittgenstein's *Tractatus Logico-Philosophicus* (1961), in which he holds that since theological propositions are not univocal (i.e., empirical facts) and cannot be properly articulated, we cannot discuss them. The silent attitude taken in this treatise was later refuted by the author himself in the posthumous publication of *Philosophical Investigations* (1968). There we find a new idea based on a contextual understanding of utterance. In this illuminating work Wittgenstein suggested that the meaning of a word is bound up with its use in speech. This meaningless/meaningful controversy caused by Wittgenstein's musings led to a number of approaches in the study of religious language which fall into a continuum between the aforementioned extremes. Inspired by the early Wittgenstein, the logical positivists, perhaps best represented by A. J. Ayer's *Language, Truth and Logic* (1936), held that all utterances of a religious nature were void of meaning since they were non-verifiable. In reaction to this position theologians - especially those interested in what is now known as "story theology" - maintained that religious utterance was indeed meaningful. The gap between these two extremes has, to some degree, been bridged by the functional-situational philosophers who follow Wittgenstein's thought as presented in *Philosophical Investigations*. Dallas High's *Language, Person and Belief* (1967) is perhaps the best representative of the latter position. The emphasis taken is on "depth grammar" as opposed to "surface grammar" and a close scrutiny of the variety of modes in speech (i.e., how things are said). These same issues have, of course, been pursued by philosophically-minded anthropologists such as Rodney Needham, who even refutes the term "belief" in non-

Western contexts in his classic work *Belief, Language and Experience* ([1972] cf. also Southwold 1979; Tooker 1992).

These approaches, among others, serve their own purpose in relation to philosophical theology and analytic philosophy in that they attempt to prove or disprove the truth claims of a given tradition (with the exception of the functional-situationalists whose *epoché* presumably guards them against this), yet their lofty language and focus on epistemological propositions does obfuscate our understanding of just what is said and how it is said by focusing on the normative opinions and positions of the traditions in question at the expense of the everyday statements and personal convictions of the believers, the folk.

Religious language certainly encompasses a broader gamut of speech beyond the philosophical terminology of the philosopher and theologian. The data which I present below, for example, are aspects of "plain speech" or "ordinary language," yet show a distinct religious quality in that they deal with fundamental questions concerning mankind's ontological status and purpose in the universe by describing personal experiences pertaining to encounters with the Divine. I do not wish to grapple with the problem of defining "religion" or "religious" here (this in itself is a murky domain that has not been fully explored to date), but I do wish to point out that the way things are said, regardless of their intellectual import, can play an important role in deciding what is "god talk." It may also serve as groundwork for placing personal experience narratives at the center of academic discourse about "folk" religion. Sociolinguistics offers an appropriate medium for the investigation of such narratives in that it demands a close look at the text without sacrificing context (cf. Ferguson 1973; Samarin 1973). In what follows, I intend to ask the question: "Are there any unique features of personal experience narratives which could serve as defining qualities for a distinct genre?" But before pursuing my own ethnographic data, let me begin reflexively by providing an account of an experience that I had while doing fieldwork in West Bengal in 1990.

## A *Personal* Personal Experience Narrative

Early on in my fieldwork in the village of Goalpara, an all-Hindu community located in the Birbhum District of West Bengal, I set out to visit the shrines of some of the multiforms (*bahurūps*) of Dharmaraj, a local, aniconic deity of obscure origins who is worshipped annually as a *grāmya debatā* (village deity).[1] One hot, sunny afternoon, I left the veranda of Bandana and Kshudu Lohar's dwelling along with their adolescent son Kalyan and another boy who lived next door to see and photograph Megh Ray (Cloud King), an important manifestation of Dharmaraj. We walked west on the main dirt path leading out of the enclave and stopped in front of one of the numerous small, inconspicuous ponds dotting the landscape. Kalyan pointed with his chin in the direction of a thorny bush on the bank of the pond. Somewhat puzzled by this, I asked him what he was doing. He responded simply by saying that Megh Ray lived within the brambles. Excited at having my first encounter with a manifestation of the deity that I traveled so far to study, I took off my shoes and proceeded through the mud towards the bush. Once I was near it I lowered my eyes to remove the lens cap of my camera when I suddenly felt a sharp pain in my left forearm. Glancing in the direction of the deity's abode, I noticed that a few fishing hook-like thorns jutting out from a branch of the bush had pierced my skin. The more I attempted to remove them, the firmer they became embedded in my flesh. I looked over my shoulder and saw Kalyan and his companion frozen in the same spot where I had left them. They looked horrified, but I could see slight hints of smiles on their faces. I called out to them for assistance but they would not approach. Finally, I managed to remove the thorns, took my pictures, and we headed back to Kalyan's house. The boys were hesitant to talk about the incident, but later on in the evening I recounted the event to Shashthi Sutradhar, a carpenter and image maker in the village, over a cup of tea. His response? "*E rakam hai*!" ("It happens like this!"). What the carpenter implied was that my experience was nothing extraordinary or unusual. Events such as the one experienced by me are part of everyday life in Goalpara, as they are in many places where Dharmaraj is said to reside.

I begin my paper with this story to illustrate the obvious fact that telling stories about personal experience is an innate human trait, most certainly making it the oldest form of narrative tradition in the world (Neumann 1991, p. 10). Indeed, it is probably as ancient as speech itself, for people can (and do) talk best and most authoritatively about things that have happened to them in the past. Being a genre drawing on reality, embellished, perhaps, by elements of the fantastic,[2] personal experience narratives offer the possibility for every individual to "break through into performance" (Hymes 1981) by drawing on events that leave indelible impressions on the contours of an individual's mentalscape.[3] Through recapitulation in story form the original event also becomes a part of the listener's repertoire.[4] Hearers, however, do not always remember all of the details discussed by the raconteur, and may not be able to recount the event in the same manner described by the experiencer.

What I have found in Goalpara is that the identity of the key actor(s) and the place of encounter remain most vivid in the memories of audience members. So long after the contents of this article recede into the inner recesses of the reader's mind, it is likely that certain features of the above narrative will leave a lasting impression, namely the identity of the narrator and the place of occurrence. These aspects - especially the latter - are central markers in the narrative tradition discussed below. For this reason, I will emphasize the notion of place throughout the presentation of my data in order to get "beyond etiology" (Simpson 1984).

## Locating the Personal Experience Narrative

Because personal experience is the language of autobiography (Titon 1980, p. 278) it is safe to say that the kind of narrative I am concerned with here is a portion of the life story (*ātma kāhinī*) or life history (*jībaner ithihās*), a more all-encompassing biographical genre that gained much anthropological speculation some three to four decades ago in America (Langness 1965). This ethnographic trend toward fictionalizing the subject led to some landmark studies in South Asia, most notably James Freeman's *Untouchable: An Indian Life History* (1979). Yet because of the tendency to focus on the big picture, episodic themes such as "a day in the life" were not emphasized (but see Jacobson 1978). In Europe, however, a distinct form of first-person accounts pertaining to encounters with other-worldly figures was already proposed by Carl Wilhelm von Sydow in 1948. It is unfortunate that American social scientists were slow to act upon von Sydow's cue, and it was only after the publication of William Labov's influential work on *Language in the Inner City* (1972) that accounts of personal experience were taken seriously into account by sociolinguists and narratologists.[5] In short, personal experience narratives have only recently become the object of much discussion in discourse analysis (cf. Langellier 1989).[6]

Even with all of the academic interest now being shown in narratives of this sort, one would be hard-pressed to cite studies of this phenomenon in South Asia (but see Grima 1991, 1992; Hancock 1991; Obeyesekere 1981). Perhaps this is due in part to a classical Indian philosophical reticence on the issue. Wilhelm Halbfass' essay titled "The Concept of Experience in the Encounter Between India and the West" (1988) raises a number of important issues that relate to the theme of why there is such a paucity of personal experience narratives in the classical philosphical texts of India. As he states with regard to the impersonal nature of the *śāstra* literature: "... actual 'reports' about personal experiences in the first person singular are not very common ... ." He goes on to say that "if it [personal experience narrative] occurs, it is usually expressed in poetry and not in prose discourses" (IE, p. 393). Yet Halbfass also admits that *anubhava* (experience) plays a significant role in what Paul Hacker has termed "Neo-Hinduism" (IE, p. 381), even though few thinkers writing from this point of view utilize their own experiences to elucidate philosophical arguments (IE, p. 383). Halbfass may have overlooked some Vedic, Upanishadic and Vedantic sources by generalizing about the paucity of personal experience accounts, as John Taber (1991) points out in his review of the work cited above, but the fact remains that such accounts appear less frequently in Hindu philosophical literature than they do in later accounts.

The picture is somewhat different in the vernacular *bhakti* (devotional) traditions where we find experience being used as an emotional basis for poetic expression. However, in the medieval Bengali *maṅgalkābya* (auspicious poetry) literature we find an abundance of prose accounts about personal experience which closely parallel the contemporary oral narratives that I discuss below. *maṅgalkābyas* are lengthy panegyric texts that thematically resemble epics but structurally seem more like *purāṇas*. They were written for the propagation of a specific deity in whose honor the text was named; hence, *dharmamaṅgal*, *manasāmaṅgal*, etc. These weighty texts usually contain tales having to do with a writer's conversion to the worship of the deity being glorified in the text. Take, for instance, the following autobiographical account of the eighteenth century Dharmamangal writer Rajaram Das. Like so many other stories of conversion in this genre (Smith 1980, p. 180), the writer is walking along a road when he encounters Dharmaraj (Kilpatrick 1983, p. 2):

> 13. I was not able to see the way due to the dense darkness. I thought meaningless thoughts and sat down in the middle of the road.
> 14. Distress rose immediately in (my) mind so I sat down. A compassionate (*dayada*) sannyasi came face to face with me.

> 15. He had a golden trident in his hand that glistened. He was clad in a tiger skin. His two eyes were red.
> 16. When I saw the matted hair on his head, I became afraid. I had it in mind to flee, but I did not possess the strength.
> ...
> 23. When the stars fell to earth, they twinkled. In a flash of lightning, I saw the earth.
> 24. The one who had bathed after the rite pervaded the Cosmic Emptiness and vanished. Before one's eyes the stars rose in the sky.
> ...
> 26. When I no longer saw the sannyasi, I cried "Alas, alas!" He had descended in the middle of a field almost as in a dream.
> 27. I felt much distress and struck a blow to my head with my hand.

This account, which exemplifies what I have termed elsewhere the "Saul of Tarsus syndrome,"[7] is strikingly similar to oral accounts of numinous encounters with Dharmaraj recorded in Goalpara.

Keshto *mājhi* is a Santali youth in his mid twenties who works as a bonded laborer (*māhindār*) for a wealthy Brahman landlord in Goalpara. Although other people in the village were quite willing to relate their encounters to me, Keshto was not very forthcoming. In fact, he was absolutely terrified to talk about his experience due to fear of retribution from the deity.[8] He was also very concerned about relating his story to a foreigner, but had no objection to eyewitnesses telling me about it. I first heard about Keshto's experience from Ram Bilas Mishra, whose narrative will follow shortly. I did not record it at the time, but had the opportunity to do so at a later date when one of my research assistants, Abhijit Bhattacharjya, told me the story one day while transcribing tapes. The following extract is taken from his retelling:[9]

> ... It had slightly become night. So he's returning. ... It was the hot season. [There] also wasn't paddy in the fields, there wasn't even anything. [There] not a bit. So when he is returning, then he sees light at that, that very place. When he came up close, there was light. And there weren't any other dwellings at that place. There was no dwelling!
>
> So suddenly [he] sees light. And arriving at such a place, there wasn't any path behind him to return on. He saw that and advances a bit further. So he went. Then he sees a tall *sādhu* (mendicant) [with] a huge body ... I mean whom we call *sant* (saint), wearing red cloth, wearing the dress of a *sādhu* -- he is standing there. So then he didn't say anything at all. So he grabbed him. But in some way, he shook his hand loose and got away. And returning back, he didn't glance [in his direction]. He says that he had gone straight. And the road then ... we didn't have any of this [light]. Going straight, [he] was going on the road. ...

In both textual and oral account, we notice that the encounter with Dharmaraj in the guise of a renunciant occurs in the dark as the individual is engaged in the act of walking. Other themes, such as a strong bolt of light marking the deity's hierophany are implicated, as is the fear (*bhaẏ*) brought on by the numinous encounter.[10] Clearly, writers of Dharmamangals experienced something very similar to descriptions given by people in Goalpara. There seems to be a remarkable regularity on the experiential level; very similar phenomena seem to be occurring. What I suspect is that these features are not formulaic utterances around which to weave a good tale, but rather the careful formulation of canonical statements based on a transformation of experiential knowledge into narrative form.[11]

The stories included above exemplify one type of personal experience narrative, namely, a physical encounter with a manifestation of the deity. But there is also another sort of narrative that arises out of encounters in dreams.[12] The medieval literature is filled with such accounts of dream commands (*svapnādeś*). This pattern dates back to 1510 CE, to what is believed to be the oldest Dharmamangal text, Khelaram's *Gauṛkābya*. In it Dharmaraj visits the Brahman Khelaram in a dream and commands him to compose the text (Sen 1975, p. 159).[13] Dreams for the purpose of performing some task on behalf of the deity, as one might suspect from the foregoing argument, are also quite common in contemporary Bengali society. One brief example will suffice here before moving into a presentation of an extended example of each type.

Ador Hari (also known as *hājrā paṇḍit*) is a low caste toddy tapper in his mid-fifties who performs an hereditary pig beheading each year at sunset on the last day of the annual Dharma *pūjā* held during the Bengali month of Caitra (April-May). According to Ador, he must perform the blood sacrifice because the responsibility was given by *bābā* (Dharmaraj) to one of his ancestors in a dream:

> My ancestor Jiban Hajra had a dream in which Dharmaraj himself said "You, the Hajras, will sacrifice a pig for me." People objected, saying "there are goats, rams, and chickens, so why a pig?" Well Kalu Ray[14] likes pig meat, but Baharadihi[15] likes goats. That's why we have both. Dharma explained this to Jiban Hajra himself. I have myself been doing it for thirty-five or thirty-six years. My father did it before me. He died at the age of ninety-six.[16]

Stories such as this, then, play an important role not only in legitimating individual experiences but also in creating an authoritative canon of oral texts used as the foundation of Dharmaraj's local theology (cf. Korom

1993). In the absence of a corpus of written texts to serve this purpose, Goalpara residents have utilized in the past, and continue to utilize creatively in the present, their own narrative sensibilities to demonstrate the deity's central role in the village's system of religious praxis. By doing so the identity of humankind as *homo narrans* merges with the notion of *homo religiosus*; that is, telling stories becomes an essential part of religious identity. Let us now turn to a few lengthier examples to exemplify each of the two types of personal experience narratives described above.

## Dreamt Realities and Wondrous Animals[17]

The first narrative that I present below exemplifies the *svapnādeś* or dream command type, and was collected from a Brahman resident of Goalpara named Ram Bilas Mishra. Ram is originally from Bihar, but his family settled in Birbhum when he was a child. He has adopted Bengali as his family language, although he speaks Bhojpuri with his wife and children on occasion. Ram is a watchman at the local primary school located on the eastern side of the main road just outside of the village. He also owns a small plot of land, and was overseeing the tilling of a rice paddy along with some of his relatives on the afternoon that I asked him to relate his experience to me. At first, he was reluctant to tell me the story, wondering why I should be interested in his personal life. When I explained that I was not interested in disproving his experience, but rather in knowing what he heard, saw, and felt, he agreed to speak, breaking into the following narrative:

> When I was sleeping at night ... while I was sleeping, it could be said that the sound of [ankle] bells arose, going jingle, jingle, jingle, jingle, jingle, jingle ... . Then my sleep was broken. Then, when I woke and came outside, I see nothing. I don't manage to see anything. Then I go and fall asleep again. After I went to sleep, again a little while later, it seems that a horse, horse, horse who is striking its hooves - tap, tap, tap, tapping - is striking its hooves.
>
> After that, when I came outside, I see that ... no ... there's nothing at all. So what's the matter? Then I had a suspicion that indeed it was the *ṭhākur*[18] himself. Indeed, *bābā ṭhākur* was frightening me himself in this way. Then I went into the house and slept. But I couldn't get to sleep anymore all night.

> I came out and see that a swine came and went along this side. A swine, a swine ... *pig*. [Frank: I know.] ... *pig* went by. A *pig* went by along the side. Then I thought to myself and called "*hei hei*." After a while, I saw that the swine was gone. [Frank: Uh huh.] It was as if the swine became supernatural. I mean it couldn't be seen any more. Then I became really afraid. What happened to that bastard? This, though, is a really difficult situation. A few days after that, my Baba possessed me. He sat on my shoulders and [said] that "I am not being *menśen* (mentioned) properly ... that people are pissing on me, doing this and doing that. They are harassing me a lot. Why aren't you watching out for me?"
>
> Then I let the people know that this is how it is. He gave me a dream in the night that ... that "People are committing many atrocities to me. The boys and girls that go by my road to Shantiniketan." Those boys supposedly piss away at that place where *bābā* Dharam is. [Frank: I see] [On] that bush ... [Frank: Yes?] They supposedly piss there. [Frank: I see] That's why *bābā* got very angry and told me that "It's this kind of situation. You should look into it, so that my *pūjā* is done well." After all this, I told the people of the village. After being told, they started to offer a little better *pūjā* and according to the rules. They started offering. From that day on, I don't manage to see anything. [Frank: I see.] It's almost ... say ... twelve or thirteen years from today.

Ram Bilas describes what David Hufford has termed the "sensation of presence" (1978, p. 18), which is not visually oriented, but draws on other senses to validate the feeling. In other words, it is an interiorization of emotion, rather than an external projection of an embodied manifestation. The sensation of presence seems to be a more common feature in dream visitations where an individual is given a command to perform some duty for the deity. This seems to be true of the textual tradition as well (W.L. Smith 1982, p. 77), as I mentioned above. But in other dreams where the individual has to interpret the nature of the dream in order to act upon it, there is an actual visualization of the deity or his agent.[19]

Ram's narrative, like virtually all of the ones I heard in Goalpara and elsewhere in Bengal, focuses primarily on place (lines 25-27) and only secondarily on time (lines 32-33). This is demonstrated linguistically by the employment of deixis (i.e., *oikhāne* = there; line 27) and physically through the use of bodily gestures such as nose, chin and finger pointing.[20] It is also instructive to mention that the locative emphasis in personal experience narratives also pertains to aetiological tales and legends (*kiṅgbadantī*) in Goalpara (cf. Nicolaisen 1988; Simpson 1984), whereas it does not apply to the fairy tale (*rūpkathā* ; cf. Lüthi 1982). This is most probably associated with belief in the Bengali context, for the former two genres are told as if true, while the latter is generally considered to be fictitious.[21] In other words, the important point here is that personal experience narratives are not liminal in any sense of the word; they are firmly grounded in specific places precisely because they are believed to be true.[22] But by using the word "belief" here I do not wish to imply its occidental sense as something opposed to knowledge (Kopytoff 1981), for this is not intended in the Bengali usage of the multivocalic term *bisvās* (belief, faith, trust) as I have come to understand it in Goalpara. For example, when I systematically asked people during a census if they "believed" in Dharmaraj, they always stated "of course" (*niścaẏi*). Further discussion usually led to the same quasi-Cartesian conclusion: "We know that Dharmaraj exists, therefore we place our faith (belief, trust) in him." There is a parity here between belief and knowledge that we often tend to overlook in academic discussions of belief.

The special place referred to in Ram Bilas Mishra's narrative is a small grove on the southwestern border of the village known as *buṛodharamtalā* (The Place of the Old Dharma). Along with the small earthen temple in the village, this place is the site of worship for Dharmaraj, and is venerated by residents. It is a small open grove marked by a number of bo trees, with a sacred pond called *muktadhar pukur* (the liberation enhanced pond) located to the northwest. Locals consider it a pretty place (*sundar jāẏgā*), but residents are also aware that it is not just physical beauty that attracts passersby to this spot. It is also the intense (*prabal*) force emanating from the place in the grove where a circle of seven stones representing the autochthonous multiforms of the deity are located that constantly draws people towards it. One story of origin describes this mystical tug as a "downward pulling attraction" (*nimnabhi mukhī ākarṣaṇ*; Mitra 1972, p. 127). Thus the power of the place itself is understood to be transforming (Eck 1981, p. 337). People who have not personally experienced the soteriological force of the *talā*, however, are not normally aware of its transformative potential, and there is even a story of a drunken village boy, home on leave from the military, who stepped on the circle of stones with his army boots on and died of gangrene as a result. In order to avoid such events, and in accord with

Dharmaraj's command to Ram, a number of signboards handwritten in formal Bengali (*sādhu bhāṣā*) were nailed to trees in the grove proclaiming that anyone walking through it should remove their shoes. Place, then, is the pivotal point around which personal experience narratives revolve, for the ontological need for situatedness is central to our experience of being human, as Heidegger (1958) was well aware (cf. also Casey 1993). And narratives of this sort describing numinous encounters tend to occur at the *buṛodharamtalā*. My final example also occurs at this spot, describing an encounter between an elderly Brahman and a strange, mysterious animal.

When I had acquired a fair amount of narrative data, I was very eager to transcribe the materials so that I could follow up on the contents of the stories. To this end, I asked Abhijit Bhattacharjya to assist me. One day, as we were listening to Ram Bilas Mishra's story together, Abhijit mentioned that his uncle, Cittaranjan Bhattacharjya, had a similar experience, albeit not in a dream. I was not aware of this, and asked him if it would be possible to visit his uncle so that I might record the story. We made arrangements to visit him the following evening. Cittaranjan is in his early sixties. He often serves as a *bhaktyā* or devotee of Dharmaraj during the annual *pūjā*, especially when a calamity of some sort has occurred in his household. His own faith in Dharmaraj was greatly enhanced by the encounter he described, and suggests one of the reasons for Dharmaraj's recurrent appearances in the village. After dinner, Cittaranjan told me the following story in the presence of his extended family. The male members had already eaten, while the women and girls were just sitting down for their food when he began.

OK. I was coming from Shantiniketan. On the road I see a cat. While watching me, the cat became a horse, greater than a usual horse! One uhh ... a dangerous thing! After that I got some fear [in me]. I saw that because of seeing this I felt bad. After screaming, I began to shout to *īśvar* (god). Then, while yelling to *īśvar*, I came up to your Dharam *talā*. After coming there, I screamed again. Then again a horse. While acting in that very way for a while, he showed me various kinds of things. Then I had a bit of fear in my mind.

So after that, after a lot of screaming, I slowly sat down there for a few moments. After that, after sitting down, I performed *bābā* Dharmaraj's obeisance. [... Please drink some tea.] After performing *praṇām* and whatnot, I scream again. A lot of people came running. After that

I came to the village. And there, I see them: various kinds of horses, cats had come.

After that, that *bābā* Dharmaraj's showing whatever gradually became a lot less. After that, your many people [going], all went to see what the matter is, what's the matter. Then absolutely nothing else. So for this, that *ṭhākur*'s whatever ... Have you understood?

So the road ... while coming I saw two kinds, three kinds on the road. One kind of horse, one kind of cat, one kind of big dog. Various kinds of imaginings occurred to me. After that I got extremely scared. I got more and more scared, more and more scared. After that, "What will I do?" I call out to that *īśvar*, to *ṭhākur*, to Dharmaraj and scream. After doing like this for a long while, I felt a bit better. After that, while calling out to *bābā*, this happened, [due to] that very *bābā* Dharmaraj.

After seeing a horse, and your many kinds of things, much more favorable circumstances came about. A lot of people gathered. Then I stopped. Then - stop - I came home. A lot of our village's people came. [They] came and asked questions. I said "This, this is the matter." Within this [time] whatever happened. This and this, I saw." So many people said, "That happens man! *ṭhākur* is there. *ṭhākur* is there. Those kinds of things happen. We have also heard [and] seen." They were conversing amongst themselves. So then I said "So what else?" I saw this for the first time, though. After that I didn't see anything else." After doing this for a while, much of your time passed. A lot of people came, [they] inquired after [me]. After that, your fear left. Performing obeisance to *ṭhākur*, I finished.

[Frank: After that nothing happened?] No, after that nothing else happened. And afterwards, I didn't see any ... nothing else. So sometimes I get dreams. My children were lame. I became *bābā* Dharmaraj's devotee. Gradually, becoming a devotee, those children's legs got better. Our Haren *bābu* was a *ḍāktār* (doctor). He used to say that, "Your children won't survive." I used to say that "*Ḍāktār bābu*, if they don't survive, what will you do? What will I do? Please give me whatever prescription exists. However little [you can] cure. So due to *bābā* Dharmaraj's mercy, my children got better. Now they are studying [for] BA [and] MA. You understand, right? [It's] going fine. There aren't any inconveniences. And due to that, I am always a devotee of Dharmaraj. As long as I am able, I will do it. While doing this, I now see what *ṭhākur* does.

Then, I don't know what intentions my children now have. I will go on doing my job. Now, exactly knowing Dharmaraj and whatnot, I will do the work. I have [lots of] faith in that very *bābā*. Based on that very faith, I keep on doing [work]. Now let's see what *ṭhākur* will do. The responsibility is with *ṭhākur*. From my doing, so to say, nothing will happen. Whatever *ṭhākur* will have done, that will happen. What does *ṭhākur* do? So let us see what *ṭhākur* does. Then I continue to do like this for your *bābā* Dharmaraj. Now, I do each whatever for *bābā* Dharmaraj.

I perform, travel, I perform obeisance, whenever I go I do [it]. People even say it! For that, each time when I become *bābā* Dharmaraj's devotee, [I] go to Udharanpur for *gaṅgāsnān* [Ganges bath] at my own expense. From there, I bathe the bath in the name of *bābā* Dharmaraj. I vow to perform *pūjā* in whatever way I know. I perform the *gāyatrī pāṭh* (recitation of the *gāyatrī mantra*). Whatever [I] know, whatever knowledge [I] have, in that way I do [it].

Now, I have done this continuously. Coming and going, I perform obeisance to *bābā* again. After coming and doing *praṇām*, I perform meditation at *bābā* 's side. Now, after that *bābu*, like this, whatever *bābā* has [me] do, I do exactly that. Since I will do a bit myself, nothing will happen. Now whatever *bābā* will have [me] do, that I will have to do. Or in that way it will go on. This was the matter. You understand, right? So saying this, as long as it goes ... I will call *īśvar*, I [take] the *pūjā* vow, I call *ṭhākur*. Now all of my children have become fine.

I also have deep faith in *bābā* Dharmaraj. That *bābā* really does offer reprisals to my prayers. So now let us perform as long as one can. Doing so for all my life, I recite and worship in *bābā*'s name. Now after worshipping him, only *bābā* will know what will happen or not. But I don't have any need to know anything. So now, continuously knowing this and doing this, whatever little happens ... goes on.

In the end what will happen? You understand, right? This is the matter. Then the *pūjā* vow happens, *hom* happens. After that we get water. At night, on the day of *muktasnān*,[23] Dharmaraj goes around the whole village. After going around, the devotees fill up by drinking water and whatnot. Then, continuously doing that, your whatever happens. Then around sunset *balidān* (animal sacrifice) happens. Then around evening *caṛak* and whatnot happens. Continuously doing all this, many kinds of things happen. But you have seen a lot, or are seeing. While doing all this, and going on in a small manner, my work is finished.

[Frank: What is your age?] Now my age is *sikrṭi-ṭhri*. [Frank: sixty-three, sixty-three years young.]

Cittaranjan's use of the Bengali slang word *iẏe* (in lines 12, 52, 84, 86), which I translate as "whatnot," is a common occurrence in the colloquial dialect of Birbhum, and is found in a number of other similar narratives. In all of the cases, the use of the term should not suggest offhandedness or irreverence, for it simply implies a way of speaking Bengali. In fact, the term is used as a filler when the narrator is not certain exactly what was heard, felt, or seen. In this way, the use of *iẏe* reinforces the notion of numinous experience by suggesting that the event was so existentially overwhelming that specific details have been relegated to a minor role vis-à-vis the indelible overall effect the encounter had on the individual. This is similar to a nightmare, for example, when we do not remember the details of the dream, but feel the impact that it has on us. The experience is what counts, not necessarily the details. The fear and uncertainty during the numinous encounter often lead to "irrational" thinking in Rudolf Otto's sense, for the experience seems unreal, and leads to self-doubt. As Cittaranjan's use of the word *parikalpanā* (imagination) in line 21 suggests, he thought that he was imagining the things he saw. But the seriousness of such encounters does not preclude the cordial atmosphere in which the narratives are told, or the matter-of-factness with which the narrator recounts the experience. As I have already suggested above with reference to Keshto's encounter, such stories are often not told because of a latent fear that the telling might bring about negative repercussions. However, once the person begins to tell the story, it is told in a plain, yet animated, way.

Cittaranjan's performance for his kin and me was certainly animated. Like Ram, he used deixis (i.e., line 6) as a rhetorical strategy, but relied much more on body movement for conveying extra-textual meanings. When he described the encounter, for instance, his body shook violently in fear, as if he were re-living the original incident. Voice tremor also heightened the sense of holy terror that he initially felt, while providing comical relief for the children in the audience. All in all, his performance was more successful as an attention grabber and emerging storytelling event (Georges 1969), even though Ram's was more concise and coherent. This fact should not only provide us insight into the idiosyncratic style of personal narration, but it should also tell us something about the context of telling personal experience narratives.

Recall that Ram was engaged in work activity when he told me his account, while Cittaranjan had reached a point of leisure in his daily routine: a perfect time for storytelling. Variables such as these account somewhat for depth of character and descriptive detail, but that is not the whole story. As I mentioned above, some people do not discuss their own experiences in detail out of fear, yet listeners recount other people's stories constantly as public gossip (*āḍḍā*), be it in the tea stall, on the temple veranda, at the market, or in the workplace. Even private tellings in the home to exemplify the oscillating ferocious and magnanimous qualities of *bābā* perpetuate the need to reinforce past religious experience by making it present. Moreover, narrative elicits exegesis, as was always the case after an oral telling or a recorded playback. Through a complex communicative system of continuous telling, hearing, and commenting, the community's local theology is always in the process of becoming. Religious experiences are thus verbally shaped into axioms that accomodate and explain new phenomena, while constantly reifying items of the tradition which have become parts of the oral canon. Through doing so, Dharmaraj, the village deity (*grāmya debatā*), remains active (*jāgrata*) and unpredictable, not docile and otiose, as one investigator has suggested (Robinson 1980).

## Conclusion

In the above discussion, I have been attempting to show but a fraction of the religious dynamics of a small Hindu community by presenting a neglected dimension of local story theology. I began by drawing some textual parallels from medieval sources not to show that modern-day accounts of encounter with the deity consciously draw on these sources, but rather to illustrate that experienced-centered notions of religion are deep-rooted in Bengali culture.[24] Such experiences are "numinous" in Otto's (1982) way of thinking, for as he describes, it is an "emotion of a creature submerged and overwhelmed by its own nothingness in contrast to that which is supreme above all creatures" (Ibid. 10). For Otto the experiencing of the numinous is summed up as *mysterium tremendum*, which, through various descriptions of the term, can best be understood as an intense sense of ecstasy. This feeling includes, among other things, awe (*die Scheu*), a mixed emotion of reverence, fear, and wonder stimulated by something majestic and/or sublime. The Bengali word *bhaẏ* (fear), used in many of the narratives that I have accumulated, provides a viable counterpart to Otto's usage of "awe." Awe, as Otto suggests, most aptly depicts *mysterium tremendum* in the English language, and the term certainly embodies the mixed sense of sublime fear and wonder that suggests itself in the narratives presented above. While Otto's overall thesis has been questioned in the context of Eastern religions (Lopez 1979) and proven to be highly problematic as a comparative principle for the general study of religion (cf. Poland 1992), his terminology seems retainable here for heuristic value alone, so long as we realize the obvious limitations of his theological agenda.[25]

The locus of numinous experience is not found to occur unequivocally at some archetypal *axis mundi*, however. Yet for some reason many of the narratives that I have heard in Goalpara set the stage at the *buṛodharamtalā*. To be sure, encounters do take place at other locations, but the *ākarṣaṇ* (attraction) of the place continues to lure people back to that spot, or unsuspectingly engrosses them while there. This latter point, the sudden nature and unpredictability of when a numinous encounter might occur, contrasts to some extent with the idea of the gradual accrual of experience through the sorts of disciplined practice associated with *yoga* and meditation.[26] As we have seen, enounters with Dharmaraj are not predicated upon practice. On the contrary, encounters with the deity's multiple forms themselves engender religious praxis. Recall that Dharmaraj chooses when, where, and whom he wishes to affect. So unlike some philosophical Hindu notions about the internal and disciplinary nature of practice leading to the gradual inducement of religious experience, encounters with Dharmaraj are, with the exception of encounters in dreams, external and immediate.[27] Here it is appropriate to draw on one dimension of Halbfass' analysis of experience as something that "overcomes, overwhelms ..., something that escapes and transcends all methods and frameworks of human planning" (IE, p. 379). This is consonant with Otto's statement that the numinous is a "primary reference to an object outside of the self" (1982, p. 11). Having made this claim, however, we must also keep in mind that all experiences are ultimately psychological states, born within and projected outwards. From this point of view, religious encounters may be the exteriorization of the object of one's experience. The ambiguous nature of such encounters suggests the interpretive difficulty one faces when attempting to construct a generic dichotomy between internal and external types of experience. Perhaps the veridical power of experience is to be found in the dialogue or tension between the two, as Halbfass hints at (IE, p. 379).

Lastly, I wish to conclude by returning to the concept of narrative and place.[28] As Belden C. Lane (1988, p. 11) has pointed out, "Above all else, sacred place is 'storied place.' Particular locales come to be recognized as sacred because of the stories that are told about them" (cf. also Griffith 1992). Here is where we must take into account Yi-Fu Tuan's reminder that "... words alone, used in an appropriate situation, can have the power to render objects, formerly invisible because unattended, visible, and impart on them a certain character" (1991, p. 684).[29] These statements concerning the power of narrative and words in general certainly ring true in the Indian context where a host of genres such as the *sthala purāṇa* and the *māhātmya* serve as panegyric tract for the propogation of a particular site. These written genres, of course, are not often told in the first person, but they do occasionally draw on experiential anecdotes provided by deities and humans alike to weave an aura of mystique around the place in question. By doing so, people residing in the area of the sacred spot develop a special relationship to the place, a unique existential sense of "being there." This is best exemplified in the city of Banaras, one of India's *saptamahātīrthas* (seven great pilgrimage sites), where the term *kāśīvāsī* or "resident of Kashi" (an alternate name for the city) takes on a very distinct sense of place: someone who constantly partakes in the daily exigencies of life in the sacred city. This holds true for the people of Goalpara as well. Residents are very quick to point out that their village, even though very tiny, is a special place.[30]

The uniqueness of Goalpara is not to be found in any book, but rather in the stories people tell about themselves and about the place in which they live. Through the continuous telling and retelling of accounts concerning encounters with the Divine, residents construct an experiential story theology to serve as a basis for religious action and belief. Whether or not the narrative features discussed above can be used as a basis for establishing personal experience narratives as a discrete category or genre of discourse remains to be argued, but such accounts do provide inquisitive outsiders with rich and detailed stories of how individuals create a distinct sense of sacred place and community (Johnstone 1990, p. 5).

*Museum of New Mexico's*
*Museum of International Folk Art*
*Santa Fe, New Mexico, USA*

## NOTES

* Various versions of this paper were read at the University of Pennsylvania, Wesleyan University and the University of New Mexico. I thank all of the numerous people who attended those talks and made comments. I am also grateful to the editors for their insightful remarks on the final revision. This paper is dedicated to the memory of Günther-Dietz Sontheimer, whose work on folk religion and narrative in South Asia continues to provide inspiration to many of us.

[1] For a brief history of the various theories concerning the deity's origin and identity, see Korom (1992a, pp. 14-26).

[2] As William F.H. Nicolaisen (1990, p. 6) states: "Even in our autobiographical recollections we continually invent ourselves, and the stories of our personal pasts are therefore as much intoxicated fabulation as sober memory, however genuinely portrayed as nothing but the truth."

[3] I use the suffix "scape" here, in the sense defined by Appadurai (1990, p. 7). He suggests that the use of the suffix allows for the positing of fluid interactions: "These terms with the common suffix -scape also indicate that these are not objectively given relations which look the same from every angle of vision, but rather they are deeply perspectival constructs inflected by historical, linguistic and political situatedness of different sorts of actors ..."

[4] Thus, someone else's first-person account of numinous encounter has the potential to be transformed into a second-person narrative told by a narrator who heard the account from a primary, secondary, or even tertiary source. In this way, a story of numinous encounter eventually flows into the slipstream of the community's sacred lore.

[5] The emerging interest actually goes back five years earlier to an article co-published by Labov and Waletzky (1967).

[6] Von Sydow (1948, pp. 60-88) first coined the German term *memorat* as a taxonomic designation for accounts of a non-profane nature. However heuristic this designation may be, more recent research (Stahl 1989, p. 19) has made it clear that the distinction between sacred and profane in the study of personal experience narratives may be an academic prejudice. On the general inappropriateness of separating sacred and profane, see Iteanu (1990).

[7] See Korom (1992a, p. 141).

[8] This is only a partial explanation. I take his silence as an indicator of a Santali way of speaking. It is evident that Santalis are generally not very willing to discuss their religious experiences with outsiders.

[9] For the full text, see Korom (1992a, p. 140).

[10] Although I do not include the relevant sections here due to length, both accounts also contain the theme of personal suffering and affliction.

[11] On the translation of knowledge into narrative see White 1980.

[12] This phenomenon is an understudied aspect of Bengali religion which needs more careful attention. But see Morinis 1982.

[13] There is some controversy about this early date. Sukumar Sen suggests that because the extant lines of the text are in *payār* meter it must be quite recent in origin. See Sen (1975, p. 161).

[14] Kalu Ray is a multiform of Dharmaraj, and is known from the Dharmamangal literature as the hero Lausen's Dom general. See Korom (1992a, pp. 67-72).

[15] The name of the administrative block in which Goalpara is situated and the collective name of Dharmaraj's seven multiforms in the village. See Korom (1992a, pp. 66-67).

[16] A similar story is told by drummers in the nearby village of Sukhbazaar, about why they have to perform special rhythms for the duration of the annual Dharmaraj festival in Goalpara.

[17] The following two narratives have been selected from a body of lore contained in chapter three of my doctoral dissertation. See Korom (1992a, pp. 83-149). I have attempted to provide literal translations of the Bengali texts in order to give the reader a sense of the spoken discourse. For the Bengali transcriptions, see ibid., pp. 305-306; 307-309.

[18] A generic term for any deity or Brahman, but here used as an appellation for Dharmaraj.

[19] As in the dream narrative of Kshudu Lohar. He sees a gocse floating by on the nearby Kopai River while he is washing clothes. Later he interprets this dream to be a signal from Dharmaraj to perform a special worship service for the deity.

[20] On the importance of deixis in the study of narrative and the contextual usage of language in general, see Hanks 1992.

[21] There is evidence of the truth/fiction dichotomy from other parts of West Bengal. Chatterji (1985, pp. 50-125), for example, analyzes this distinction based on narratives from Purulia District with some success.

[22] This distinction is not absolute, however, since Lūthi himself states that "No single narrative will rigidly follow all the rules of the genre" (1982, p. 108). The notion of "fairy tale" also needs to be distinguished from "fairy lore" because the latter deals with belief systems as well. As such, "fairy lore" also emphasizes place. As has recently been stated, "... specific folkloric mechanisms ... established proxemic boundaries on the cognitive maps of community residents, boundaries which demarcated geographic areas of purity, liminality, and danger" (Narváez 1991, p. 337).

[23] Literally, "the liberating bath." Refers to the second day of the annual rites. See Korom (1992a, pp. 211-225).

[24] The concept of rootedness, as in Victor Turner's "root metaphor," incipiently hints at the fact that narratives of this sort are grounded in spatial interpretations.

[25] Just as Eliade's term *axis mundi* has become a phenomenological trope, even in the light of the inadequacy of his overall theory. See Korom 1992b.

[26] It is in this sense that we have to understand the Bengali vernacular rendering of *anubhava*. Although the term should be more literally translated as emotion, a permanent and subjective apprehension of feeling, it is also imbued with the sense of sudden experience in common parlance.

[27] Even the famous Bengali mystic Ramakrishna, whose experiences of *bhor* (possession) were sudden and unpredictable, trained to achieve that state of unity with the Goddess. See, for instance, Sarkar (1985, pp. 6-49).

[28] The notion of place has recently been problematized and revitalized in the social sciences. For a recent summary of the literature, see Rodman 1992.

[29] Schegloff's discussion of the practice of "formulating place" in conversation is also worth noting in this regard; see Schegloff 1972.

[30] For a general introduction to the community, see Rohner and Chaki-Sircar 1988. Korom (1992a, pp. 37-82) deals more specifically with the special relationship between individual and place in Goalpara.

**Wilhelm Halbfass**

# RESEARCH AND REFLECTION: RESPONSES TO MY RESPONDENTS

## V. Developments and Attitudes in Neo-Hinduism; Indian Religion, Past and Present (Responses to Chapters 4 and 5)

1. The terms "Neo-Hinduism" and "Neo-Vedānta," which emerge in the titles of chapter 4 and the article by Andrew Fort, have been discussed in my response to Jitendra Nath Mohanty (see above). As we have seen, these terms seem to have been used in India first. Nonetheless, their adoption by Western scholars such as Paul Hacker reflects Christian and European claims and perspectives which continue to be an irritant to Indians today. For Hacker, the "Neo" in "Neo-Hinduism" implies a lack of authenticity, an apologetic accommodation of Western ideas, and a hybridization of the tradition. His critique of Neo-Hinduism found its most intense and poignant expression in his article "Schopenhauer und die Ethik des Hinduismus" (1961), which is now available in an English translation by Dermot Killingley (see Hacker 1995, pp. 273-318). The central theme of this article is the development of ethical thought in traditional and modern Vedānta (which he finds exemplified in the work of Vivekananda) and the possibility of an "applied nondualism," or a "*tat tvam asi* ethics." Andrew Fort's exploration of the role of "social service" and its connection with the idea of *jīvanmukti*, "liberation while alive," in traditional and modern Vedānta supplements Hacker's observations, as well as my own comments on the issue in *India and Europe*. The discrepancies between classical texts and some of their modern interpretations and applications which Fort points out are, indeed, obvious and do not require much further elaboration. We may add that even Vivekananda's master Ramakrishna, who was glorified both as a

*jīvanmukta* and as an *avatāra*, showed very little interest in (or even explicit opposition to) social service (see also Jackson 1994, pp. 75-80).

In his article of 1961, Hacker speaks as a "historian and philologist" who sees it as his responsibility to uncover discrepancies and questionable reinterpretations with reference to the *tat tvam asi* and its potential application as a principle of ethics and a metaphysical foundation of brotherly love. His historical diagnosis that traditional Indian (in particular, Hindu) thought did not draw any ethical conclusions from the metaphysics of strict nondualism may have to be questioned and scrutinized; still, the contrast with Vivekananda's "practical Vedānta" is undeniable. However, Hacker goes further than this. He speaks not only of a factual historical absence of "applied nondualism" or "*tat tvam asi* ethics," but also of its logical impossibility; in his view, the *tat tvam asi* would not leave any room for the concept of the person, which he considers to be the condition of the possibility of ethics and morality. Impersonal ethics would simply be an absurdity and "monstrosity." Here, I disagree, and have done so in an increasingly explicit manner. In fact, in my most recent statement on the issue (Halbfass 1995b), I have tried to come to the defense of Vivekananda and to argue that Hacker's radical critique reflects above all, a typically Christian and European obsession with the concept of the individual person. Regardless of the actual presence or absence of "nondualistic" and "impersonal" ethics in the tradition, it is inappropriate to simply deny the conceptual legitimacy of such ethics, and to reject *a priori* all attempts to interpret and extrapolate nondualism in an ethical direction.

We have referred to Vivekananda. His views are at the center of Stuart Elkman's article on "religious plurality." May we apply the distinction between legitimate extrapolation and historical-philological analysis to Elkman's reading of Vivekananda? Perhaps. And if so, I would have no problem with the first alternative; but I would hardly be able to accept this reading as a "historian and philologist" in Hacker's sense.

I can easily agree with Elkman's observation (see, for instance, p. 508) that Vivekananda did not advocate the actual historical absorption of Christianity and other religions by Hinduism; nor did he preach proselytization and conversion. But this is not the point, and it is not what I said (besides TR, see also IE, pp. 231ff., 235ff. and especially 238). What Vivekananda does say or imply is that no actual absorption or conversion is necessary. Not only the various groups and sects within

Hinduism (among them the Buddhist schools) are, and have always been, included in and superseded by the supreme truth of Advaita Vedānta; the same principle of transhistorical inclusion applies also to the other religious traditions in the world. On p. 508, Elkman refers to "the fact that a Hindu can worship Christ with as much reverence as a Christian." Certainly, this makes sense from the vantage point of Advaita Vedānta. But would it be acceptable to the Christian?

Dr. Elkman states that "Vivekananda makes an important distinction between Hinduism and *sanātanadharma*," i.e., "religion in its universal form" (p. 508), and that he sees Hinduism "to be on an equal footing with other religions" (p. 509). The two parables (i.e., the water and its many names and the vat of dye) cited in this connection and the subsequent reference to *śaguṇa* and *nirguṇa brahman* are hardly sufficient to support this interpretation. On the contrary, they leave little doubt that the standpoint of *sanātanadharma* from which Vivekananda assesses all other "religions" (including the religious "sects" of Hinduism) is still a standpoint within Hinduism: It is the "ultimate truth" of Advaita Vedānta which, according to Vivekananda, fulfills and transcends the ideals of all other (Indian or non-Indian) religions. Moreover, we should not forget that the concept of *sanātanadharma*, as used by Elkman, is a modern creation and a Hindu response to the claims of foreign religions (see IE, p. 343ff.). It is a concept which has not only served as an expression of tolerance and reconciliation; it has also inspired fundamentalists and nationalists. In Vivekananda's own thought and rhetoric, ideas of national identity and revival are often associated with his notion of Hindu spirituality. The letter to Mohammed Sarfaraz Husain and the statements at the Parliament of Religions in Chicago, which Elkman quotes at the end of his article, do not tell us the whole story.

All this is not meant to deny the legitimacy of Elkman's defense of Vivekananda. In fact, my own respect for Vivekananda has grown over the years. We just have to be cautious and alert to the possibility of different interpretations. And we should not overlook the distinction between apologetics and historical analysis.

2. Yohanan Grinshpon and Frank Korom both deal with questions concerning the role of "personal experience" in Indian thought and literature; in different ways, they supplement or qualify my observations in chapter 21 of *India and Europe* (pp. 378-402). Frank Korom's contribution is the only one in this volume which is primarily based on

field work. Its observations on "personal experience narratives" come from sources conspicuously different from those with which most of the other contributors (including myself) are used to work. It serves as a convincing reminder of the vast variety of forms and levels of thought and expression *within* the Indian cultural tradition; it should caution us against extrapolating and generalizing observations which may be true for specific areas of the tradition, such as the absence or paucity of personal experience narratives in Indian philosophy or other branches of theoretical and formal literature. The situation in the vernaculars is, of course, in general somewhat different from that in Sanskrit, the prime vehicle of the impersonal *śāstra* tradition.

Yohanan Grinshpon's article takes us back to the impersonal style of philosophical Sanskrit literature, in which personal statements or even the first person singular itself are very rare. In particular, Grinshpon deals with the commentarial tradition of the classical Yoga system of Patañjali. In a system which puts so much emphasis on the inner world of awareness and on mental events and transformations, the absence not only of records of, but even of brief references to personal experiences (including the experiences of others) must appear surprising and intriguing.

Moreover (and this is the main focus of Grinshpon's article), references to observation and experience are also conspicuously absent when it comes to certain remarkable claims and teachings relating to the external, physical and empirical world. In particular, Grinshpon refers to the supernormal Yogic achievements (*siddhi*), which are discussed at length in the literature of classical Yoga. Most of these should, at least in principle, be observable occurrences in time and space. But empirical observation is neither invoked to support the factuality of such occurrences, nor to dispute it. Neither the Yoga commentators themselves nor the opponents (*pūrvapakṣin*) whom they cite offer arguments based on experience and observation. Does this mean that they were no longer committed to or interested in the truth of the statements with which they are dealing, and that they were content with verbal and conceptual clarifications? This is, indeed, Grinshpon's suggestion, and it deserves very careful consideration. He contrasts the procedure of the traditional commentators with that of such modern exponents of Pātañjala Yoga as Hariharānanda Āraṇya (1869-1947), who accepts the authority of the classical texts, but tries to support it by referring to actual observations.

In a somewhat casual manner, Grinshpon also considers the possibility that the classical commentators saw no need for raising the issue of truth or factuality because they took it simply for granted (p. 557). But even then, we might want to ask: In what sense? Did they believe in a literal sense that Yogins can learn how to fly in the air, change the shape and size of their bodies, etc.? Or could it be that the physical reality of such phenomena was not a major concern for the practicing Yogins as well as the scholastic commentators, and that the mental realization (*bhāvanā*) of such occurrences and the capacity to *produce* their experience at will was more important for them? This would mean that we are dealing, above all, with the mental power to *generate* or *summon* certain images and experiences; this would leave little room for epistemological concerns or for the application of the ordinary standards of truth (*pramāṇa*). *Yogasūtra* IV.1, which lists alternative ways of inducing *siddhi* experiences (apparently including hallucinogenic substances), could suggest such an interpretation. We should, however, note that it is not pursued in any explicit fashion by the commentators.

Traditionally, Yoga scholars have tried to avoid the *Vibhūtipāda* and the syndrome of "supernormal powers," which appeared to them as an embarrassment within an otherwise respectable tradition. Yohanan Grinshpon deserves our recognition for facing the "embarrassment" (not only in his contribution to this volume, but also in his Ph.D. dissertation submitted to the University of Pennsylvania in 1995), and for asking some very simple, yet pertinent questions about it.

To conclude this section, I would like to add a postscript both to Dr. Grinshpon's article and to my own chapter on "experience" in *India and Europe* (pp. 378-402). In this chapter, I tried to clarify the role of personal experience in traditional and orthodox Hinduism and to describe some of the systematic efforts to domesticate it and to assure its compliance with the authority of the sacred tradition. We find such efforts epitomized in the theory of the "authorlessness" (*apauruṣeyatva*) of the Veda and its depiction as an eternal and objective structure of words and meanings. The Veda in this sense may lead to experience and realization, but it is in no way based on personal experience. However, the confinement and domestication of experience can also be observed in numerous theistic movements, for instance, in Rāmānuja's orthodox and Sanskritic transformation of the tradition of the *ālvārs*.

The situation is, of course, different in the case of Buddhism and other movements which trace themselves back to the discoveries and enlightenment experiences of personal founders. But even here, we have to be cautious.

> Following the experiential path of the Buddha does not mean to continue a process of open-ended experimentation and inquiry. There is no "empiricist" openness for future additions or corrections; there is nothing to be added to the discoveries of the Buddha and other "omniscient" founders of soteriological traditions. In the understanding of their followers, their experiences provide objective standards and frameworks and anticipate all future experiences of their followers. (IE, p. 393)

Dharmakīrti, the greatest representative of Buddhist logic and epistemology, articulates his misgivings about unguided personal experiences and "yogic perceptions" in six memorable verses of his *Pramāṇavārttika* (III/*Pratyakṣa*, v. 281-286). In his view, all yogic perceptions and visualizations are potentially deceptive, regardless of their clarity, vividness, and apparent self-evidence. Therefore, only such truths or objects should become contents of experiential realization (*bhāvanā*) which have been scrutinized beforehand and sanctioned by reasoning and authoritative tradition. And in general, the Buddhist progression from obedient listening and learning to theoretical reflection and meditative realization (*śruta/suta*, *cintā*, *bhāvanā*) is, in its didactic structure, not fundamentally different from the Vedāntic scheme of *śravaṇa, manana* and *nididhyāsana*.

3. The contributions by Minoru Hara and Albrecht Wezler deal with the vicissitudes of theoretical norms, rules and principles, as they occur within the infinite variety of human life and the ambiguity of actual situations. They deal with problems concerning the application and applicability of *dharma* and *karman*, with grey areas in which right and wrong, *dharma* and *adharma* seem to overlap or lose their meaning, with special cases and circumstances in which general laws and rules seem to call for modifications and exceptions. Such considerations and reflections come more naturally in the form of narratives than systematic treatises. And no source is richer and more rewarding in this respect than that most massive and complex of all narrative structures, the *Mahābhārata*. Professor Hara's citations from this text illustrate, indeed, the "subtlety" and elusiveness of *dharma* and its precarious interpenetration with *adharma*. *dharma* as that which ought to be done in a particular situation cannot be rationalized once and for all, and it cannot be put into clear, simple, and rigid rules. Human reason would be at a loss without the guidance provided by the sacred Vedic tradition, or even by sheer precedent and convention. But even then, ambiguities and uncertainties remain.

In its own impressive way, Wezler's article also illustrates the problematic relationship between the general principles of *dharma* and *karman* and the variety of individual human situations. According to Wezler, the story of Aṇī-Māṇḍavya, as told in the *Mahābhārata*,

> reflects the awareness of the friction between the intrinsic claim of universal validity in principle of the law of *karman*, on the one hand, and the morally well-founded and humane insight, on the other, that there are natural limits to man's criminal responsibility. (p. 545)

This may be true, and it may, indeed, have been the main concern of the unknown author of this section in the *Mahābhārata*. However, we should not forget that fully universalized versions of the karma theory, which assume a strictly uniform and inflexible "law" of retribution, are rare (in spite of the legalistic manner in which certain texts correlate acts and their results). The expression "law of karma" is, of course, a modern one, without clearly identifiable precedent in the tradition. In Buddhism, the role of judgment and intention (*cetanā*) and, by implication, of responsibility has always been very significant. In Hinduism, on the other hand, the complexities of the *varṇāśramadharma*, which stipulates that (depending on the status of the agent) the same type of act may have very different moral implications and karmic consequences, stand in the way of a strictly uniform interpretation of karma. In general, the "course" or "operation" of karma (*karmagati*) is as "difficult to understand" (*durvijñeya*, *durvijñāna*; see Uddyotakara, *Nyāyavārttika* on III.2.60, and Vyāsa, *Yogasūtrabhāṣya* on II.13) as the "course" of *dharma* according to the passages cited by Minoru Hara. Here, the philosophers agree with the story-tellers.

In conclusion, I want to thank Professors Hara and Wezler and all the other contributors to this volume for their insightful and stimulating essays. I feel honored by the attention they have paid to my work. At this point, I would like to add a word of appreciation for the authors of numerous earlier reviews and review articles on the publications discussed in this book. I owe a very special gratitude to my friends Eli Franco and Karin Preisendanz for the many hours of work they invested in the book, and for their truly heroic efforts to ensure its overall quality. I also want to thank Professor Leszek Nowak who initiated this entire project when we met at the Wissenschaftskolleg/Institute for Advanced Study in Berlin during the academic year 1989/90. Loriliai Biernacki helped prepare the final manuscript of my "Responses." Her work was supported by a generous grant from the Research Foundation of the University of Pennsylvania.

Participating in this scholarly and intellectual exchange has been one of the most gratifying experiences of my academic life.

## ABBREVIATIONS

ABORI Annals of the Bhandarkar Oriental Research Institute
AiU Aitareyopaniṣad
AKM Abhandlungen zur Kunde des Morgenlandes
ĀpDhS Āpastambadharmasūtra
AŚ Arthaśāstra
AŚ(K) Arthaśāstra (Kangle's edition)
AS/ÉA Asiatische Studien/Études Asiatiques
ASS Ānandāśrama Sanskrit Series
BaudhDhS Baudhāyanadharmasūtra
BhG Bhagavadgītā
BṛĀU Bṛhadāraṇyakopaniṣad
BS Brahmasūtra
BSBh Brahmasūtrabhāṣya (Śaṅkara)
BSBh(N) Brahmasūtraśāṅkarabhāṣya (Nirṇaya Sāgar Press)
BSBh(Th) Brahmasūtrabhāṣya (Śaṅkara), in Thibaut 1988
BSBhR(Th) Brahmasūtrabhāṣya (Rāmānuja), in Thibaut 1971
ChU Chāndogyopaniṣad
CSS Chowkhamba Sanskrit Series
EB *The Encyclopaedia Britannica*. Editor in Chief J[ames] L. Garvin. 14th ed. London/New York: The Encyclopaedia Britannica Company Ltd/ Encyclopaedia Britannica INC, 1929.
EW *English Works of Raja Rammohun Roy*. Cf. Ghose and Bose 1906.
GA Heidegger, *Gesamtausgabe*
GautDhS Gautamadharmasūtra
GOS Gaekwad's Oriental Series
HOS Harvard Oriental Series
IE *India and Europe*. Cf. Halbfass 1988a.
IIJ Indo-Iranian Journal
IPA Indian Philosophical Annual
JAOS Journal of the American Oriental Society
JIP Journal of Indian Philosophy
KSS Kashi Sanskrit Series
MaiU Maitrāyaṇyupaniṣad
Manu Manusmṛti
Manu(B) Manusmṛti, in Bühler 1970
MBh Mahābhārata (critical edition)
Mbh. Mahābhārata (1863ff. edition)
MBh(VB) Mahābhārata, in Van Buitenen 1973

MBhD Mahābhāṣyadīpikā
MīS Mīmāṃsāsūtra
MS Maitrāyaṇī Saṃhitā
MŚS Mānavaśrautasūtra
MuU Muṇḍakopaniṣad
NBh Nyāyabhāṣya, for Adhyāya I in Nyāyadarśana, for Adhyāyas II-V in Nyāyadarśanam
NBhū Nyāyabhūṣaṇa
NK Nyāyakandalī
NKaṇ Nyāyakaṇikā
NKaṇ(G) Nyāyakaṇikā (Goswami's edition)
NM Nyāyamañjarī
NM(Ś) Nyāyamañjarī (Śukla's edition)
NS Nyāyasūtra. Cf. Ruben 1928.
NS(TNT) Nyāyasūtra, in Nyāyadarśanam
NSu Nyāyasudhā
NV Nyāyavārttika, in Nyāyadarśana
NVT Nyāyavārttikatātparyaṭīkā, in Nyāyədarśana
NVTP Nyāyavārttikatātparyapariśuddhi, in Nyāyadarśana
OB *On Being and What There Is*. Cf. Halbfass 1992a.
OED *A New English Dictionary*. 10 vols. Oxford: Clarendon Press, 1884-1928, reissued as *The Oxford English Dictionary*. 12 vols. Oxford: Clarendon Press, 1933.
P Aṣṭādhyāyī
PDhS Padārthadharmasaṅgraha
PDhS(J) Padārthadharmasaṅgraha (Jetly's edition)
PEW Philosophy East and West
PrU Praśnopaniṣad
R Rāmāyaṇa
RG *Rāmamohana Granthāvali*. Cf. Banerji and Das 1952, cited by volume and page number.
ṚV Ṛgveda
ṚV(S) Ṛgveda with the commentary of Sāyaṇācārya
SBE Sacred Books of the East
ŚBh Śābarabhāṣya; cf. Mīmāṃsāsūtrabhāṣya
ŚPB Śatapathabrāhmaṇa
ŚPB(E) Śatapathabrāhmaṇa in Eggeling 1988-89
StII Studien zur Indologie und Iranistik
ŚV Ślokavārttika

ŚvU Śvetāśvataropaniṣad
TaiU Taittirīyopaniṣad
TB Taittirīyabrāhmaṇa
TNT Nyāyabhāṣya, Nyāyavārttika and Nyāyavārttikatātparyaṭīkā in Nyāyadarśanam
TR Tradition and Reflection. Cf. Halbfass 1991.
TS Taittirīyasaṃhitā
TSaṅ Tattvasaṅgraha
TV Tantravārttika
TVai Tattvavaiśāradī
VāsDhS Vāsiṣṭhadharmasūtra
ViS Vijñaptimātratāsiddhi
VP Vākyapadīya (Rau's edition)
VP I Vākyapadīya I
VP II Vākyapadīya II
VP IIIa Vākyapadīya IIIa
VS Vaiśeṣikasūtra
VS(S) Vaiśeṣikasūtra, in Nandalal Sinha 1986
WZKM Wiener Zeitschrift für die Kunde des Morgenlandes
WZKS(O) Wiener Zeitschrift für die Kunde Süd(- und Ost)asiens
YD Yuktidīpikā
YV Yogavārttika
YS Yogasūtra
YSBh Yogasūtrabhāṣya

# REFERENCES

## 1. Texts in Sanskrit and Pali

Ajitā. In: Kunio Harikai (Ed.) (1991). *Ajitā* and *Vijayā* on the Apūrva and Two Other Adhikaraṇas (Mīmāṃsāsūtra 2.1.5-12). *Acta Eruditiorum* (Annual Report of the General Education, Saga Medical School), **10**, 1-24.

Atharvaveda. Cf. Bloomfield 1897.

Arthaśāstra. *The Arthaśāstra of Kauṭalya with the Commentary "Srīmūla" of Mahāmahopādhyāya T. Gaṇapati Sāstrī*. Ed. N. P. Kuni. Pt. II. Delhi/Varanasi: Bharatiya Vidya Prakashan, 1984.

Arthaśāstra. In: R. P. Kangle. *The Kauṭilīya Arthaśāstra*. Part I. *A Critical edition with a Glossary*. Bombay: University of Bombay, 1960. (University of Bombay Studies: Sanskrit, Prakrit and Pali 1)

Aṣṭādhyāyī. *Pāṇini's Grammatik*. Ed. and tr. Otto Böhtlingk. 2nd ed. Leipzig: Hermann Haessel, 1887.

Āpastambadharmasūtra. *Āpastambīyadharmasūtram. Āpastamba's Aphorisms on the Sacred Law of the Hindus*. Ed. George Bühler. 3rd ed. Bombay: Government Central Book Depot, 1932. (Bombay Sanskrit Series **44, 50**)

Iṣṭasiddhi. *Iṣṭa Siddhi of Vimuktātman*. Ed. P. K. Sundaram. Madras: Swadharma Swaarajya Sangha, 1980.

Upadeśasāhasrī. *Upadeśasāhasrī of Śrī Śaṅkarācārya*. Ed. and tr. Swami Jagadananda. 7th ed. Madras: Sri Ramakrishna Math, 1984.

Ṛgveda. *The Hymns of the Rig-Veda*. Ed. Friedrich Max Müller. 2 vols. 2nd ed. London: Trübner & Co., 1877. [repr. Varanasi: Chowkhamba Sanskrit Series Office, 1965. KSS **167**]

Ṛgveda. *Ṛgveda-Saṃhitā with the commentary of Sāyaṇāchārya*. Eds. N[arayan] S[hripad] Sontakke et al. Vol. 3 (Maṇḍalas 6-8) and 4 (Maṇḍalas 9-10). Poona: Vaidika Saṃśodhana Maṇḍala, 1978, 1983.

Aitareyopaniṣad. In: *Eighteen Principal Upaniṣads*. Vol. I. Eds. V[ishnu] P[rabhakar] Limaye and R[anganath] D[attatraya] Vadekar. Poona: Vaidika Saṃśodhana Maṇḍala, 1958.

Kaṭhopaniṣad. *Kāṭhakopaniṣat saṭīkādvayaśaṅkarabhāṣyopetā*. Ed. Vaijanatha Sarma Rajavade. 8th ed. Poona: Ānandāśrama Press, 1977. (ASS 7)

Kāṭhakasaṃhitā. *Yajurvedīyaṃ Kāṭhakasaṃhitam*. Ed. Śrīpāda Dāmodara Sātavalekara. 4th ed. Pāraḍī: Svādhyāyamaṇḍala, 1983.

Kāvyālaṅkāra. *Kāvyālaṅkāra (A treatise on Rhetoric) of Rudraṭa with the Sanskrit commentary of Namisādhu*. Ed. Rāmadeva Śukla. Varanasi: Chowkhamba Vidya Bhawan, 1966.

Gautamadharmasūtra. *The Gautama-dharma-sūtra with the 'Mitākṣarā' Sanskrit Commentary of Haradatta*. Ed. Umesh Chandra Pandey. Varanasi: Chowkhamba Sanskrit Series Office, 1966. (KSS 172)

Carakasaṃhitā. *The Charakasaṃhitā by Agniveśa, Revised by Charaka and Dṛidhabala with the Āyurveda-Dīpikā commentary of Chakrapāṇidatta*. Ed. Vaidya Jādavji Trikaṃji Āchārya. 3rd ed. Bombay: Satyabhāmābhāī Pāndurang, for the Nirṇaya Sāgar Press, 1941 [4th ed. = repr. Delhi: Munshiram Manoharlal, 1981]

Chāndogyopaniṣad. Cf. Chāndogyopaniṣadbhāṣya.

Chāndogyopaniṣadbhāṣya. In: *Īśādidaśopaniṣad with Śaṅkarabhāṣya*. Delhi: Motilal Banarsidass, 1978.

Jaiminīyabrāhmaṇa. *Jaiminiya-Brahmana of the Samaveda*. Eds. Raghu Vira and Lokesh Chandra. Nagpur: International Academy of Indian Culture, 1954. (Sarasvati-Vihara Series 31)

Tattvavaiśāradī. In: *Pātañjalayogadarśanam* (cf. Yogasūtra).

Tattvasaṅgraha. *Tattvasaṃgraha of Śāntarakṣita, with the commentary Pañjikā of Kamalaśīla*. Vol. 1. Ed. Embar Krishnamacharya. Baroda: Oriental Institute, 1926. (GOS 30) [repr. 1984]

Tattvārthādhigamasūtra. *Tattvarthadhigama Sutra by Sri Umasvami Acharya*. Ed. and tr. J[agomandar] L[al] Jaini. Arrah: The Central Jaina Publishing House, 1920. (Sacred Books of the Jainas 2)

Tantravārttika of Kumārilabhaṭṭa. In: *Mīmāṃsādarśanam* (cf. Mīmāṃsāsūtra).

Tarkasaṅgraha. *Tarka-Saṃgraha of Annambhaṭṭa*. Ed. Yashwant Vasudev Athalye. 3rd ed. Poona: Bhandarkar Oriental Research Institute, 1930. (Bombay Sanskrit and Prakrit Series 55)

Taittirīyabrāhmaṇa. *Taittirīya-brāhmaṇam*. Ed. Nārāyaṇa Goḍbole Śāstrī. Vol. 2. Poona: Ānandāśrama Press, 1979. (ASS 37)

Taittirīyasaṃhitā. *Taittirīya Saṃhitā, with the Padapāṭha and the commentaries of Bhaṭṭa Bhāskara Miśra and Sāyaṇācārya*. Vol. 2, part 1 (Kāṇḍa 2). Ed. T[rivikram] N[arayan] Dharmadhikari. Poona: Vaidika Saṃśodhana Maṇḍala, 1981.

Taittirīyāraṇyaka. *The Taittiriya Aranyaka of the Black Yajur Veda: With the commentary of Sayanacharya*. Ed. Rajendralal Mitra. 2 Vols. Calcutta: Asiatic Society of Bengal, 1864-1872. [repr. Osnabrück: Biblio Verlag, 1982]

Taittirīyopaniṣad. Cf. Aitareyopaniṣad.

Nāradasmṛti. Cf. Lariviere 1989.

Nirukta. *The Nighaṇṭu and the Nirukta*. Ed. Lakshman Sarup. London/Lahore: University of Punjab, 1920-1927. [repr. Delhi: Motilal Banarsidass, 1984]

Nyāyakaṇikā. Vācaspati Miśra's Nyāyakaṇikā in: *Vidhiviveka of Maṇḍana Miśra*. Ed. Rāma Śāstri. Benares, 1907.

Nyāyakaṇikā. In: *Vidhiviveka of Maṇḍana Miśra with the commentary Nyāyakaṇikā of Vāchaspati Miśra*. Ed. Mahaprabhu Lal Goswami. Varanasi: Tara Publications, 1978.

Nyāyakandalī. Cf. Padārthadharmasaṅgraha.

*Nyāyadarśana of Gautama with the Bhāṣya of Vātsyāyana, the Vārttika of Uddyotakara, the Tātparyaṭīkā of Vācaspati and the Pariśuddhi of Udayana* [*Volume I Chapter I*]. Ed. Anantalal Thakur. Darbhanga: Mithila Institute of Post-Graduate Studies and Research in Sanskrit Learning, 1967. (Mithilā Institute Ancient Text Series 20)

*Nyāyadarśanam: with Vātsyāyana's Bhāṣya, Uddyotakara's Vārttika, Vācaspati Miśra's Tātparyaṭīkā, and Viśvanātha's Vṛtti*. Eds. Taranatha Nyaya-Tarkatirtha and Amarendramohan Tarkatirtha. 2nd ed. New Delhi: Munshiram Manoharlal, 1985.

Nyāyabindu. In: *Paṇḍita Durveka Miśra's Dharmottarapradīpa [Being a sub-commentary on Dharmottara's Nyāyabinduṭīkā, a commentary on Dharmakīrti's Nyāyabindu]*. Ed. Dalsukhbhai Malvania. 2nd ed. Patna: Kashi Prasad Jayaswal Research Institute, 1971. (Tibetan Sanskrit Works Series **2**)

Nyāyabhūṣaṇa. *Nyāyabhūṣaṇa of Bhāsarvajña on his Nyāyasāra with Pādaṭippaṇa of editor*. Ed. Svāmi Yogīndrānanda. Varanasi: Ṣaḍdarśana Prakāśana Pratiṣṭhāna, 1968. (Ṣaḍdarśanaprakāśanapratiṣṭhānagranthamālā **1**)

Nyāyamañjarī. *Nyāyamañjarī of Jayanta Bhaṭṭa. With Ṭippaṇī Nyāyasaurabha by the editor*. Ed. K. S. Varadacharya. 2 vols. Mysore: Oriental Research Institute, 1969, 1983. (University of Mysore Oriental Research Institute Series **116**, **139**)

Nyāyamañjarī. *Nyāyamañjarī of Jayanta Bhaṭṭa*. Part I. Ed. Surya Nārāyana Śukla. 2nd ed. Varanasi: Chowkhamba Sanskrit Series Office, 1971 (KSS **106**)

Nyāyavārttika. Cf. *Nyāyadarśanam*.

Nyāyasudhā. *Nyāyasudhā Tantravārtika-Ṭīkā Bhaṭṭasomeśvaraviracitā*. Ed. Mukunda Sastri: Benares: Chowkhambha Sanskrit Series Office, 1901ff. (CSS **14**)

Nyāyasūcīnibandha. In: *Nyāyasūtras with Vātsyāyana's Bhāṣya and Vācaspati Miśra I's Nyāyasūcīnibandha*. Ed. and tr. Ganganatha Jha. Poona: Oriental Book Agency, 1939. (Poona Oriental Series **58**)

Padārthadharmasaṅgraha. *The Praśastapāda Bhāshya with Commentary Nyāyakandali of Sridhara*. Ed. Vindhyesvari Prasad Dvivedin. Delhi: Sri Satguru Publications, 1984. (Sri Garib Dass Oriental Series **13**) [repr. of 1895]

Padārthadharmasaṅgraha. *Praśastapādabhāṣyam with the Commentary Kiraṇāvalī of Udayanācārya*. Ed. Jitendra S. Jetly. Baroda: Oriental Institute, 1971. (GOS **154**)

Prakaraṇapañcikā. *Prakaraṇa Pañcikā of Śālikanātha Miśra with Nyāya-Siddhi of Jaipuri Nārāyaṇa Bhaṭṭa*. Ed. A. Subrahmanya Sastri. Varanasi: Banaras Hindu University. (Banaras Hindu University Darśana Series **4**)

Pramāṇavārttika. *Pramāṇavārttika of Acharya Dharmakirtti with the commentary 'Vritti' of Acharya Manorathanandin*. Ed. Swami Dwarikadas Shastri. Varanasi: Bauddha Bharati. (Bauddha Bharati Series **3**; Dharmakirtti Nibandhawali **1**)

Praśnopaniṣad. Cf. Aitareyopaniṣad.

Bṛhadāraṇyakopaniṣad. Cf. Aitareyopaniṣad.

Baudhāyanadharmasūtra. *Śrīmaharṣibaudhāyanapraṇītaṃ Baudhāyanadharmasūtraṃ Śrīgovindasvāmipraṇītavivaraṇasametam*. Ed. Jayakṛṣṇadāsa Haridāsa Gupta. Benares: Chowkhamba Sanskrit Series Office, 1992. (KSS **104**)

Baudhāyanadharmasūtra. *Das Baudhāyana-Dharmasūtra*. Ed. E[ugen] Hultzsch. 2nd ed. Leipzig: Deutsche Morgenländische Gesellschaft, 1922. (AKM **16**,2)

Brahmasūtra. In: Brahmasūtrabhāṣya.

Brahmasūtrabhāṣya. *Brahmasūtra-śaṅkarabhāṣya*. Ed. Jagdish Lal Shastri. Delhi: Motilal Banarsidass, 1980.

Brahmasūtrabhāṣya. *Brahmasūtraśāṅkarabhāṣya with the Commentaries Bhāmatī of Vācaspatimiśra, Kalpataru of Amalānandasarasvatī, and Parimala of Appayadīkṣita, and with Index etc.* Eds. Anantakrishna Śāstri and Vasudev Laxman Shāstri Paṇsikar. Varanasi: Krishnadas Academy, 1982. (Krishnadas Sanskrit Series **25**) [repr. of Bombay: Nirṇaya Sāgar Press, 1915, 1917, 1938, 1948]

Bhagavadgītā. Cf. Bhagavadgītābhāṣya.

Bhagavadgītābhāṣya. In: *Śrīmad-bhagavadgītā with Śaṅkarabhāṣya*. Ed. Wasudev Laxman Sastri Pansikar. New Delhi: Munshiram Manoharlal, 1978.

Madhyamakakārikā. *Mūlamadhyamakakārikās (Mādhyamikasūtras) de Nāgārjuna, avec la Prasannapadā commentaire de Candrakīrti.* Ed. Louis de La Valleé Poussin. St. Petersburg: Kaiserliche Akademie der Wissenschaften. (Bibliotheca Buddhica 4).

Manusmṛti. *The Manusmṛti with the commentary Manvarthamuktāvali of Kullūka.* Ed. Nārāyaṇ Rām Ācārya. 10th ed. Bombay: Nirṇaya Sāgar Press, 1946.

Mahābhārata. *The Mahābhārata.* Eds. Vishnu S. Sukthankar et al. Poona: Bhandarkar Oriental Research Institute, 1933-1966. (Critical Edition)

Mahābhārata. Bombay: Ganapat Krishnaji, 1863ff. (Bombay edition)

Mahābhārata. *The Mahābhāratam with Bharata Bhawadeepa Commentary of Nīlakaṇṭha.* Ed. Pandit Ramchandrashastri Kinjawadekar. 1. *Adi Parvan.* Repr. Delhi: Oriental Books Reprint Corporation, 1979.

Mahābhāṣya. *The Vyâkaraṇa-Mahâbhâshya of Patanjali.* Ed. Franz Kielhorn. 3 vols. Bombay: Government Central Book Depot, 1880, 1883, 1885. [repr. Osnabrück: Otto Zeller, 1970]

Mahābhāṣya (A). *The Vyākaraṇa-Mahābhāṣya of Patañjali.* Ed. Franz Kielhorn. 3rd rev. ed. by K[ashinath] V[asudev] Abhyankar. 3 vols. Poona: Bhandarkar Oriental Research Institute, 1962, 1965, 1972.

Mahābhāṣyadīpikā. *Mahābhāṣyadīpikā of Bhartṛhari.* (Edited by a team of scholars.) Poona: Bhandarkar Oriental Research Institute, 1985-1991. (Quoted according to *āhnika*)

Āhnika 1: Johannes Bronkhorst, 1987.

Āhnika 2: G[ajanan] B[alkrishna] Palsule, 1988.

Āhnika 3: G[ajanan] B[alkrishna] Palsule, 1985.

Āhnika 4: G[ovind] V[inayak] Devasthali and G[ajanan] B[alkrishna] Palsule, 1989.

Āhnika 5: V[ishnu] P[rabhakar] Limaye, G[ajanan] B[alkrishna] Palsule, V[amanashastri] B. Bhagavat, 1985.

Āhnika 6a: V[amanashastri] B. Bhagavat, Saroja Bhate, 1986.

Āhnika 6b: V[amanashastri] B. Bhagavat, Saroja Bhate, 1990.

Āhnika 7: G[ajanan] B[alkrishna] Palsule, V[amanashastri] B. Bhagavat, 1991.

Mānavaśrautasūtra. *Mānava-Śrautasūtra*. Ed. Jeanette M. van Gelder. Vol. 1. New Delhi: International Academy of Indian Culture, 1961. (Śata-Piṭaka Series, Indo-Asian Literatures 17) [repr. Delhi: Sri Satguru Publications, 1985. Sri Garib Dass Oriental Series 31]

Mitākṣarā. In: *The Yājñavalkya Smṛti With Viramitrodaya the Commentary of Mitra Misra and Mitaksara the Commentary of Vijnanesvara*. Eds. Nārāyaṇa Śāstrī Khiste and Jagannātha Śāstrī Hośiṅga. Benares: Chowkhambha Sanskrit Series Office, 1930. (CSS 62)

Milindapañha. Cf. Rhys Davids 1890, 1894.

Mīmāṃsāsūtra. In: *Mīmāṃsādarśanam*. Eds. Kāśīnātha Vāsudevaśāstrī Abhyaṃkara and Gaṇeśaśāstrī Jośī. 7 vols. 2nd ed. Poona: Ānandāśrama Press, 1970ff. (ASS 97) (1st ed. 1929).

Mīmāṃsāsūtrabhāṣya (Śābarabhāṣya). For Mīmāṃsāsūtra I.1.1-5 in Frauwallner 1968, otherwise in *Mīmāṃsādarśanam* (cf. Mīmāṃsāsūtra).

Muṇḍakopaniṣad. Cf. Aitareyopaniṣad.

Maitrāyaṇī Saṃhitā. *Die Saṃhitā der Maitrāyaṇīya-Śākhā*. Ed. Leopold von Schroeder. 4 vols. Leipzig: F. A. Brockhaus, 1881-1886. [repr. Wiesbaden: Franz Steiner, 1971-1972]

Maitrāyaṇyupaniṣad. Cf. Aitareyopaniṣad.

Rāmāyaṇa. *The Vālmīki Rāmāyaṇa: Critical Edition*. Eds. G[ovindlal] H[argovind] Bhatt et al. Baroda: Oriental Institute, 1960-1975.

Yājñavalkyasmṛti. Cf. Mitākṣarā.

Yuktidīpikā. *Yuktidīpikā, an ancient Commentary on the Sāṃkhya-kārikā of Īśvarakṛṣṇa*. Ed. Ram Chandra Pandeya. Delhi: Motilal Banarsidass, 1967.

Yogavārttika. Cf. Rukmani 1983 and 1987.

Yogasūtra. In: *Pātañjalayogadarśanam vācaspatimiśraviracitatattvavaiśāradīvijñānabhikṣukṛtayogavārtikavibhūṣitavyāsabhāṣyesametam*. Ed. Nārāyaṇa Miśra. Vārāṇasi: Bhāratīya Vidyā Prakāśan, 1981.

Yogasūtrabhāṣya. In: *Pātañjalayogadarśanam* (cf. Yogasūtra).

Vākyapadīya. In: Wilhelm Rau: *Bhartṛharis Vākyapadīya: Die* mūlakārikās *nach den Handschriften herausgegeben und mit einem* pada-*Index versehen*. Wiesbaden: Franz Steiner, 1977. (AKM 42,4)

Vākyapadīya. *Vākyapadīya of Śrī Bhartṛhari*. Eds. K[ashinath] V[asudev] Abhyankar and V[ishnu] P[rabhakar] Limaye. Poona: Poone University, 1965. (University of Poona Sanskrit and Prakrit Series 2)

Vākyapadīya I. *Vākyapadīya of Bhartṛhari with the Commentaries Vṛtti and Paddhati of Vṛṣabhadeva*. Kāṇḍa I. Ed. K. A. Subramania Iyer. Poona: Deccan College Postgraduate and Research Institute, 1966. (Deccan College Monograph Series 32).

Vākyapadīya II. *The Vākyapadīya of Bhartṛhari. Containing the Ṭīkā of Puṇyarāja and the Ancient Vṛtti [the latter as far as available]*. With a Foreword by Ashok Aklujkar. Kāṇḍa II. Ed. K. A. Subramania Iyer. Delhi: Motilal Banarsidass, 1983.

Vākyapadīya IIIa. *Vākyapadīya of Bhartṛhari with the commentary of Helārāja*. Kāṇḍa III, part 1. Ed. K. A. Subramania Iyer. Poona: Deccan College Postgraduate and Research Institute, 1963. (Deccan College Monograph Series 21)

Vāyupurāṇa. Cf. Tagare 1987, 1988.

Vāsiṣṭhadharmasūtra. *Śrīvāsiṣṭhadharmaśāstram. Aphorisms on the Sacred Law of the Âryas, as taught in the School of Vasishṭha*. Ed. Alois Anton Führer. Bombay: Government Central Book Depot, 1883. (Bombay Sanskrit Series 23)

Vijñaptimātratāsiddhi. *Vijñaptimātratāsiddhi: deux traités de Vasubandhu: Viṃśatikā (la vingtaine) accompagnée d'une explication en prose, et Triṃśatikā (la trentaine) avec le commentaire de Sthiramati*. Ed. Sylvain Lévi. Paris: Librairie ancienne Honoré Champion, 1925. Corrections in Lévi 1932.

Vedāntasiddhāntamuktāvali of Prakāśānanda. Ed. and tr. Arthur Venis. Varanasi: Chaukhamba Orientalia, 1975.

Vaiśeṣikasūtra. *Vaiśeṣikasūtra of Kaṇāda with the Commentary of Candrānanda*. Ed. Muni Śrī Jambuvijayaji. Baroda: Oriental Institute, 1961. (GOS **136**) [repr. 1982]

Śatapathabrāhmaṇa. *The Śatapatha-Brāhmaṇa*. Ed. Albrecht Weber. Berlin/London: Ferd. Dümmler's Buchhandlung/Williams and Norgate, 1849, 1855. [repr. Varanasi: Chowkhamba Sanskrit Series Office, 1964]

Śābarabhāṣya. Cf. Mīmāṃsāsūtrabhāṣya.

Śāstradīpikā. *Shāstradīpikā of Pārthasārathi Miśra with the Commentary Mayūkhamālikā*. Ed. Dharmadatta Jha. Varanasi: Krishnadas Academy, 1988. (Krishnadas Sanskrit Series **103**)

Śuklayajuḥprātiśākhya. *The Śuklayajuḥ-prātiśākhya of Kātyāyana*. Ed. and tr. Shrimati Indu Rastogi. Varanasi: Chowkhamba Sanskrit Series Office, 1967. (KSS **179**)

Ślokavārttika. *Ślokavārttika of Śrī Kumārila Bhaṭṭa with the Commentary Nyāyaratnākara of Śrī Pārthasārathi Miśra*. Ed. Svāmī Dvārikādāsa Śāstrī. Varanasi: Tārā Publications. (Prāchyabhāratī Series **10**)

Śvetāśvataropaniṣad. Cf. Aitareyopaniṣad.

Saṃkṣepaśārīraka of Sarvajñātman. Cf. Veezhinathan 1985.

*Harivaṃśa*. Ed. Parashuram Lakshman Vidya (Critical Edition). Poona: Bhandarkar Oriental Research Institute, 1969.

Hitopadeśa. *The Hitopadeśa of Nārāyaṇa*. Ed. and tr. M[oreshwar] R[amchandra] Kale. Bombay: Gopal Narayan & Co., 1924.

## 2. Modern Authors and Translations


Abdel-Malek, Anouar (Anwar) (1963). Orientalism in Crisis. *Diogenes*, **44**, 103-140.

Abhyankar, K[ashinath] V[asudev] and V[ishnu] P[rabhakar] Limaye (1965). Appendices. In: *Vākyapadīya of Śrī Bhartṛhari* (cf. Texts in Sanskrit and Pali).

Abid Husain, S[yed] (1985). *The National Culture of India*. New Delhi: National Book Trust.

Agravala, Dharmalala Javaharalala (Ed.) (1985). *Mīmāṃsā Uddharaṇa Kośa*. Poona: Vaidika Saṃśodhana Maṇḍala.

Ahmad, Aziz (1964). *Studies in Islamic Culture in the Indian Environment*. Oxford: Oxford University Press.

Aklujkar, Ashok (1991). Bhartṛ-hari's Concept of the Veda. In: Madhav Deshpande (Ed.), *Panels of the VIIth World Sanskrit Conference*. Vol. 5. *Pāṇini and the Veda*. Leiden: E. J. Brill, pp. 1-18.

— (1989a). The Number of Pramāṇas According to Bhartṛ-hari. *WZKS*, **33**, 151-158.

— (1989b). Prāmāṇya in the Philosophy of the Grammarians. In: Avanindra Kumar et al. (Eds.), *Studies in Indology: Prof. Rasik Vihari Joshi Felicitation Volume*. New Delhi: Shree Publishing House, pp. 15-28.

— (1978). The Concluding Verses of Bhartṛ-hari's Vākya-kāṇḍa. *ABORI*, **58/59**, 9-26.

— (1972). The Authorship of the Vākyapadīya-vṛtti. *WZKS*, **16**, 181-198.

— (1971a). The Number of Kārikās in Trikāṇḍī, Book I. *JAOS*, **91**, 510-513.

— (1971b). Nakamura on Bhartṛhari. *IIJ*, **13**, 161-175.

al-'Azm, Sadik Jalal (1981). Orientalism and Orientalism in Reverse. *Khamsin*, **8**, 5-26.

Allinson, Robert E. (Ed.) (1989). *Understanding the Chinese Mind*. Hong Kong: Oxford University Press.

Almond, Philip (1988). *The British Discovery of India*. Cambridge: Cambridge University Press.

Alper, Harvey P. (1983). Feature Book Review of *Indien und Europa*. *PEW*, **33**, 189-196.

Alsdorf, Ludwig (1962). *Beiträge zur Geschichte von Vegetarismus und Rinderverehrung in Indien*. Wiesbaden: Franz Steiner. (Akademie der Wissenschaften und der Literatur Mainz. Abhandlungen der geistes- und sozialwissenschaftlichen Klasse, Jahrgang 1961, Nr. 6)

Alston, William (1991). *Perceiving God: The Epistemology of Religious Experience*. Ithaca, New York: Cornell University Press.

Appadurai, Arjun (1990). Disjuncture and Difference in the Global Cultural Economy. *Public Culture*, 2/2, 1-24.

Āraṇya, Hariharānanda (Tr.) (1983[1963]). *Yoga Philosophy of Patañjali*. Albany: State University of New York Press.

Arora, Uday Prakash (1983). Greek Attitude Towards the Indians. *Journal of the Ganganatha Jha Research Institute*, **37** (= Prof. Baldeva Upadhyaya Felicitation Volume), 97-109.

— (1982). Greek Image of the Indian Society. *Μακεδονικά*, **12**, 470-482.

Ashcroft, Bill, Gareth Griffiths and Helen Tiffin (Eds.) (1995). *The Post-Colonial Studies Reader*. London/New York: Routledge.

Assmann, Jan (1989). *Maat, l'Egypte pharaonique et l'idée de justice sociale*. Paris: Julliard.

Aubenque, Pierre (1991). *Le problème de l'être chez Aristote*. Paris: Presses Universitaires de France. (Collection "Quadriges")

Audi, Robert (1993). Fallibilist Foundationalism and Holistic Coherentism. In: Louis Pojman (Ed.), *The Theory of Knowledge: Classic and Contemporary Readings*. Belmont, California: Wadsworth, Inc., pp. 263-279.

Avineri, Shlomo (1970). *The Social and Political Thought of Karl Marx*. Cambridge: Cambridge University Press.

Ayer, A[lfred] J. (1936). *Language, Truth and Logic*. New York: Dover Publications.

Babinger, F[ranz] (1920). Isaak Jacob Schmidt, 1779-1847. *Ostasiatische Zeitschrift*, **8** (= Festschrift für Friedrich Hirth), 7-21.

Bagchi, S[itansusekhar] (1933). *Inductive Reasoning*. Calcutta (no publisher recorded)

Balagangadhara, S. N. (1990). Understanding and Imagination: A Critical Notice of Halbfass and Inden. *Cultural Dynamics*, **3/4**, 387-405.

Balasubramaniam, R. (1988). *The Naiṣkarmyasiddhi of Sureśvara*. Madras: Radhakrishnan Institute for Advanced Study in Philosophy, University of Madras. (Madras University Philosophical Series **47**)

Balazs, Etienne (1964). *Chinese Civilization and Bureaucracy*. New Haven: Yale University Press.

Balslev, Anindita N. (1983). *A Study of Time in Indian Philosophy*. Wiesbaden: Otto Harrassowitz.

Balthasar, Hans Urs von (1988). *Kosmische Liturgie: Das Weltbild Maximus' des Bekenners*. Einsiedeln/Trier: Johannes-Verlag.

Banerji, Brajendranath and Sajanikanta Das (Eds.) (1952). *Rāmamohana Granthāvali*. Calcutta: Baṅgīya Sāhitya Pariṣat.

Barnes, Jonathan (Ed.) (1984). *Aristotle: Complete Works*. 2 vols. Princeton: Princeton University Press.

Baron, Jonathan (1985). *Rationality and Intelligence*. Cambridge: Cambridge University Press.

Bartlett, Robert (1993). *The Making of Europe*. Princeton: Princeton University Press.

Bascom, William (1972). African Dilemma Tales: An Introduction. In: Richard M. Dorson (Ed.), *African Folklore*. New York: Anchor Books (Doubleday), pp. 143-155.

Basham, A[rthur] L. (1976). *La civilisation de l'Inde ancienne*. Tr. Claude Carme et al. Paris: Arthaud.

— (Ed.) (1975). *A Cultural History of India*. Oxford: Oxford University Press.

— (1967). *The Wonder that was India: A Survey of the History and Culture of the Indian Sub-Continent before the Coming of the Muslims*. 3rd rev. ed. London: Sidgwick and Jackson.

— (1954). *The Wonder that was India: A Survey of the Culture of the Indian Sub-Continent before the Coming of the Muslims*. London: Sidgwick and Jackson.

— (1951). *History and Doctrines of the Ājīvikas*. London: Luzac.

Bennett, J[ohn] G. (1976). *Gurdjieff: Making a New World*. New York etc.: Harper Colophon Books.

Bennett, Jonathan (1984). *A Study of Spinoza's Ethics*. Cambridge: Cambridge University Press.

Bhaduri, Sadananda (1947). *Studies in Nyāya-Vaiśeṣika Metaphysics*. Poona: Bhandarkar Oriental Research Institute. (Bhandarkar Oriental Series 5)

Bharati, Agehananda (1982). *Hindu Views and Ways and the Hindu-Muslim Interface*. Santa Barbara: Ross-Erikson.

— (1978). *Great Traditions and Little Traditions*. Varanasi: Chowkhamba.

— (1970). The Hindu Renaissance and Its Apologetic Patterns. *Journal of Asian Studies* 29/2, 267-287.

Bhatt, Govardhan P. (1989). *The Basic Ways of Knowing: An In-depth Study of Kumārila's Contribution to Indian Epistemology*. 2nd rev. ed. of Bhatt 1962. Delhi: Motilal Banarsidass.

— (1962). *Epistemology of the Bhāṭṭa School of Pūrva Mīmānsā*. Varanasi: Chaukhamba Amarabharati Prakashan. (Chowkhamba Sanskrit Studies **17**)

Bhattacharyya, Sibajiban (Tr.) (1990). *Gadhāra's Theory of Objectivity*. 2 vols. Delhi: Indian Council of Philosophical Research in association with Motilal Banarsidass.

Biardeau, Madeleine (1964a). *Théorie de la connaissance et philosophie de la parole dans le brahmanisme classique*. Paris/La Haye: Mouton & Co. (École Pratique des Hautes Études - Sorbonne. Sixième section: sciences économiques et sociales. Le monde d'outre-mer, passé et présent. Première série: études **XXIII**)

— (Tr.) (1964b). *Bhartṛhari, Vākyapadīya Brahmakāṇḍa, avec la Vṛtti de Harivṛṣabha*. Paris: Éditions E. de Boccard. (Publications de l'Institut de Civilisation Indienne, Série In-8, Fasc. **24**)

— (1957). La définition dans la pensée indienne. *Journal Asiatique*, **245**, 371-384.

Bidari, T. F. (1992). Review of *India and Europe*. *Path Way to God*, **26**/2, 49-52.

Biderman, Shlomo and Ben-Ami Scharfstein (Eds.) (1989). *Rationality in Question: On Eastern and Western View of Rationality*. Leiden: E. J. Brill.

Binion, R[udolph] (1968). *Frau Lou: Nietzsche's Wayward Disciple*. Princeton: Princeton University Press.

Biswas, Dilip Kumar (1973). Rammohun Roy and Horace Hayman Wilson. *Bengal Past and Present*, **92**, 125-147.

Biswas, Dilip Kumar and Prabhat Chandra Ganguli (1962). Notes and other editorial material in Collet 1962.

Blau, August (1966 [1893]). *Index zu Otto Böhtlingks Indischen Sprüchen*. Liechtenstein: Kraus. [repr. of Leipzig: Deutsche Morgenländische Gesellschaft] (AKM **9**,4)

Bloomfield, Maurice (Tr.) (1897). *Hymns of the Atharvaveda*. Oxford: Clarendon Press. (SBE **42**)

Bodde, Derk (1991). *Chinese Thought, Society, and Language*. Honolulu: University of Hawaii Press.

Böhl, Felix (1991). Die etymologische Namensdeutung in der rabbinischen Literatur. In: *Discours étymologique*. Actes du Colloque international organisé à l'occasion du centenaire de la naissance de Walther von Wartburg. Edités par Jean-Pierre Chambon et Georges Lüdi, avec la collaboration de Hans-Martin Gauger, Frank Lestringant, Georges Pinault. Tübingen: Max Niemeyer Verlag, pp. 161-172.

Böhtlingk, Otto [von] and Rudolf [von] Roth (1879-89). *Sanskrit-Wörterbuch in kürzerer Fassung*. Bearbeitet von Otto Böhtlingk. 7 vols. St. Petersburg: Kaiserliche Akademie der Wissenschaften.

— (1855-75). *Sanskrit-Wörterbuch*. 7 vols. St. Petersburg: Kaiserliche Akademie der Wssenschaften.

Bongard-Levin, G[rigory] and A[lexei] Vigasin (1984). *The Image of India: The Study of Ancient Indian Civilisation in the USSR*. Moscow: Progress.

Bosworth, C[lifford] E. (Ed.) (1971). *Iran and Islam: In Memory of the Late Vladimir Minorsky*. Edinburgh: Edinburgh University Press.

Bottéro, Jean (1992). *Mesopotamia: Writing, Reasoning, and the Gods*. Tr. Zainab Bahrani and Marc van de Mieroop. Chicago: University of Chicago Press.

Braun, Lucien (1973). *Histoire de l'histoire de la philosophie*. Paris: Ophrys.

Breckenridge, Carol A. and Peter van der Veer (Eds.) (1993). *Orientalism and the Post-Colonial Predicament*. Philadelphia: University of Pennsylvania Press.

Brière, O. (1965). *Fifty Years of Chinese Philosophy: 1898-1948*. Tr. Laurence G. Thompson. New York: Praeger.

Bronkhorst, Johannes (1993). Buddhist Hybrid Sanskrit. In: Kameshwar Nath Mishra (Ed.), *Aspects of Buddhist Sanskrit. Proceedings of the International Symposium on the Language of Sanskrit Buddhist Texts, Oct. 1-5, 1991*. Sarnath, Varanasi: Central Institute of Higher Tibetan Studies, pp. 396-414.

— (1991a). Studies on Bhartṛhari, 3: Bhartṛhari on Sphoṭa and Universals. *AS/ÉA*, **45**/1, 5-18.

— (1991b). Two Literary Conventions and Their Consequences. *AS/ÉA*, **45**/2, 210-227.

— (1990). Vārttika. *WZKS*, **34**, 123-146.

— (1989). Studies on Bhartṛhari, 2: Bhartṛhari and Mīmāṃsā. *StII*, **15**, 101-117.

— (1988) Études sur Bhartṛhari, 1: L'auteur et la date de la Vṛtti. *Bulletin d'Études Indiennes*, **6**, 105-143.

Bronkhorst, Johannes and Yves Ramseier (1995). *Complete Word Index to the Printed Editions of the Praśastapādabhāṣya*. Delhi: Motilal Banarsidass.

Brown, Truesdell Sparhawk (1949). *Onesicritus: A Study in Hellenistic Historiography*. Berkeley, Los Angeles: University of California Press. (University of California Publications in History **39**)

Brown, W[illiam] Norman (1978). *India and Indology: Selected Articles*. Ed. Rosane Rocher. Delhi: Motilal Banarsidass.

Brüll, Lydia (1989). *Die japanische Philosophie*. Darmstadt: Wissenschaftliche Buchgesellschaft.

Brunner, Hellmut (1970). Die Lehren. In: B[ertold] Spuler (Ed.), *Handbuch der Orientalistik: Der Nahe und der Mittlere Osten*. Vol. 1.1: *Ägyptologie: Literatur*. Leiden: E. J. Brill, pp. 113-139.

Bühler, Georg (Tr.) (1970 [1886]). *The Laws of Manu: Translated with Extracts from Seven Commentaries*. Delhi: Motilal Banarsidass. [reprint of Oxford: Clarendon Press] (SBE **25**)

— (1882). Über die Erklärung des Wortes *āgama* im Vākyapadīya 2.1-6 [= 2.485-490 in Rau's edition]. *Zeitschrift der Deutschen Morgenländischen Gesellschaft*, **36**, 653-654.

Burlingame, Eugene Watson (1991 [1922]). *Buddhist Parables*. Delhi: Motilal Banarsidass.

Casey, Edward S. (1993). *Getting Back into Place: Toward a Renewed Understanding of the Place-World*. Bloomington: Indiana Univer sity Press.

Caṭṭopādhyāẏa, Nagendranātha (1972 [1881]). *Mahātmā Rāmamohana Rāẏer jīvanacarita*. Calcutta: De's Publishing.

Chan, Wing-tsit (1963). *A Source Book in Chinese Philosophy*. Princeton: Princeton University Press.

Charpentier, Jarl (1914). Sagengeschichtliches aus dem Arthaśāstra des Kauṭilya. *WZKM*, 28, 211-240.

— (1909). Über Rudra-Śiva. *WZKM*, 23, 151-179.

Chatterjee, K[rishna] N[ath] (Tr.) (1980). *Vasubandhu's Vijñaptimātratā-siddhi*. Benares: Kishor Vidyā Niketan.

Chatterjee, Partha (1986). *Nationalist Thought and the Colonial World*. Tokyo: U. N. University.

Chatterji, Roma (1985). *Folklore and the Formation of Popular Consciousness in a Village in the Purulia District of West Bengal*. Ph.D. Dissertation, University of Delhi.

Chattopadhyay, Rampada (1992). *A Vaiṣṇava Interpretation of the Brahmasūtras: Vedānta and Theism*. Leiden: E. J. Brill.

Chattopadhyaya, Deviprasad and Mrinalkant Gangopadhyaya (Eds.) (1990). *Cārvāka/Lokāyata*. New Delhi: Indian Council of Philosophical Research, in collaboration with Rddhi-India, Calcutta.

Chemparathy, George (1983). *L'autorité du Veda selon les Nyāya-Vaiśeṣikas*. Louvain-La-Neuve: Centre d'histoire des religions. (Conférences et Travaux 2)

Ch'en, Kenneth K. S. (1973). *The Chinese Transformation of Buddhism*. Princeton: Princeton University Press.

— (1964). *Buddhism in China: A Historical Survey*. Princeton: Princeton University Press.

Childers, Robert C. (1874). *A Dictionary of the Pāli Language*. London.

Chimpa, Lama and Alaka Chattopadhyaya (Trs.) (1970). *Tāranātha's History of Buddhism in India*. Delhi: Motilal Banarsidass.

Ching, Julia and Willard Oxtoby (Eds.) (1992). *Discovering China: European Interpretations in the Enlightenment*. Rochester: University of Rochester Press.

Coedès, G[eorge]. (1948 [1900]). *Les états hindouisés d'Indochine et d'Indonésie*. Paris: de Boccard.

Collet, Sophia Dobson (1962). *The Life and Letters of Raja Rammohun Roy*. Ed. Dilip Kumar Biswas and Prabhat Chandra Ganguli. 3rd ed. Calcutta: Sadharan Brahmo Samaj.

Coward, Harold (1990). *Derrida and Indian Philosophy*. Albany: State University of New York Press.

Cua, Antonio S. (1985). *Ethical Argumentation: A Study in Hsün Tzu's Moral Epistemology*. Honolulu: University of Hawaii Press.

Curley, Edwin (1988). *Behind the Geometrical Method: A Reading of Spinoza's Ethics*. Princeton: Princeton University Press.

Dale, Stephen (1994). *Indian Merchants and Eurasian Trade, 1600-1750*. Cambridge: Cambridge University Press.

Dalley, Stephanie (1989). *Myths from Mesopotamia*. Oxford: Oxford University Press.

Dalmia, Vasudha and Heinrich von Stieṭencron (Eds.) (1995). *Representing Hinduism: The Construction of Religious Traditions and National Identity*. New Delhi: Sage Publications.

Dandekar, R[amchandra] N[arayan] (1972). *Universe in Hindu Thought*. Bangalore: Vikas.

Dargyay, Eva (1989). Review of *India and Europe*. *Hindu-Christian Studies Bulletin*, 2, 7-8.

Dascal, Marcelo (Ed.) (1991). *Cultural Relativism and Philosophy*. Leiden: E. J. Brill.

Dasgupta, Surendranath (1933). *Indian Idealism*. Cambridge: Cambridge University Press.

— (1922). *A History of Indian Philosophy*. Vol. 1. Cambridge; Cambridge University Press.

Dawood, N. J. (Tr.) (1990). *The Koran*. Harmondsworth: Penguin Books.

De Bary, Wm. Theodore, Wing-tsit Chan and Burton Watson (Eds.) (1960). *Sources of Chinese Tradition*. New York: Columbia University Press.

De Crespigny, Anthony (1975). F. A. Hayek: Freedom for Progress. In: Anthony de Crespigny and Kenneth Minogue (Eds.), *Contemporary Political Philosophers*. London: Methuen, pp. 49-66.

De Jong, J[an] W. (1987). *A Brief History of Buddhist Studies in Europe and America*. Delhi: Sri Satguru Publications.

Demiéville, Paul (1986). Philosophy and Religion from Han to Sui. In: Twitchett and Loewe 1986, pp. 808-872.

Derrett, J[ohn] Duncan M. (1980-81). Privileged Lies. *The Adyar Library Bulletin*, **44/45** (= Kunjunni Raja Felicitation Volume), 286-292.

Derrida, Jacques (1993). *Aporias*. Tr. Thomas Dutoit. Stanford: Stanford University Press.

— (1992). *The Other Heading*. Tr. Pascale-Anne Brault and Michael B. Naas. Bloomington: Indiana University Press. (Studies in Continental Thought)

— (1991). *L'autre cap*. Paris: Minuit.

Deshpande, Madhav M. (1993). The Changing Notion of *śiṣṭa* from Patañjali to Bhartṛhari. *AS/ÉA*, **47**/1, 95-115.

De Smet, R. V. (1982). Review of *Indien und Europa*. *Indian Theological Studies*, 183-188.

Deutsch, Eliot (Ed.) (1991). *Culture and Modernity: East-West Philosophical Perspectives*. Honolulu: University of Hawaii Press.

Dharampal-Frick, Gita (1994). *Indien im Spiegel deutscher Quellen der Frühen Neuzeit*. Tübingen: Max Niemeyer Verlag.

Dirks, Nicholas (1989). The Invention of Caste. *Social Analysis*, 25, 42-52.

Doniger, Wendy and Brian K. Smith (Trs.) (1991). *The Laws of Manu*. Harmondsworth: Penguin Books.

Droit, Roger-Pol (1986). *L'oubli de l'Inde: Une amnésie philosophique*. Paris: Galilée. (Collection Perspectives philosophiques)

D'Sa, Francis X. (1994). The Re-Membering of Text and Tradition. Some Reflections on Gerhard Oberhammer's Hermeneutics of Encounter. in: Francis X. D'Sa and Roque Mesquita (Eds.), *Hermeneutics of Encounter: Essays in Honour of Gerhard Oberhammer on the Occasion of his 65th Birthday*. Vienna: Institute for Indology, University of Vienna, pp. IX-L. (Publications of the De Nobili Research Library 20)

— (1980). *Śabdaprāmāṇyam in Śabara and Kumārila*. Vienna: Indological Institute, University of Vienna. (Publications of the De Nobili Research Library 7)

Dunbar, Sir George (1939). *A History of India from the Earliest Times to the Present Day*. London: Nicholson & Watson.

Eck, Diana (1981). India's Tīrthas: "Crossings" in Sacred Geography. *History of Religions*, 20/4, 323-344.

Edwards, Paul (Ed.) (1972). *The Encyclopedia of Philosophy*. Vol 4. New York: Macmillan and Free Press.

Eggeling, Julius (Tr.) (1988-89 [1882-1900]). *The Śatapatha Brāhmaṇa*. Delhi: Motilal Banarsidass. [repr. of Oxford: Clarendon Press] (SBE **12**, **26**, **41**, **43-44**)

Eisenstadt, Samuel N. (Ed.) (1986). *The Origins and Diversity of Axial Age Civilization*. Buffalo: State University of New York Press.

Elman, Benjamin A. (1984). *From Philosophy to Philology: Intellectual and Social Aspects of Change in Late Imperial China*. Cambridge, Massachusetts: Council on East Asian Studies, Harvard University.

Embree, Ainslie T. (1989). *Imagining India*. Delhi: Oxford University Press.

— (Ed.) (1988). *Sources of Indian Tradition*. Vol. 1. 2nd ed. New York: Columbia University Press.

Eno, Robert (1990). *The Confucian Creation of Heaven*. Albany: State University of New York Press.

Faddegon, B[arend] (1969 [1918]). *The Vaiśeshika System*. Wiesbaden: Dr. Martin Sändig. [repr. of Amsterdam: J. Müller]

Fairbank, John K. (1992). *China: A New History*. Cambridge, Massachusetts: Harvard University Press.

Ferguson, Charles A. (1973). Some Forms of Religious Discourse. *International Yearbook for the Sociology of Religion*, **8**, 224-235.

Feuerstein, Georg (1989). *Yoga: The Technology of Ecstasy*. Los Angeles: Jeremy P. Tarcher, Inc.

Fløistad, Guttorm (Ed.) (1993). *Contemporary Philosophy*. Vol. 7: *Asiatic Philosophy*. Dordrecht: Kluwer.

Fohrer, Georg (1972). *History of Israelite Religion*. London: S.P.C.K.

Fort, Andrew O. (1992). Neither East nor West: A Case of Neo-Vedānta in Modern Indian Thought. *Religious Studies Review*, **18**, 95-100.

Fox, Robin Lane (1992 [1991]). *The Unauthorized Version: Truth and Fiction in the Bible*. Harmondsworth: Penguin Books.

Franco, Eli (Ed./Tr.) (1988). Keṭ'a mitokh reayon 'im Prof. Wilhelm Halbfass, mitokh reayon sheshudar beKol Israel, Mai 1987; Eropa, Hodu, veha"Eropeizatsia shel kadur ha'arets" (Extract from an Interview with Prof. Wilhelm Halbfass, from an Interview Broadcasted by the Voice of Israel, May 1987; India, Europe and the "Europeanization of the Earth"). *Proza*, **101/102**, 80-88.

Frauwallner, Erich (1982). *Kleine Schriften*. Ed. Gerhard Oberhammer and Ernst Steinkellner. Wiesbaden: Franz Steiner. (Glasenapp-Stiftung 22)

— (1973). *History of Indian Philosophy*. 2 vols. Delhi: Motilal Banarsidass.

— (1968). *Materialien zur ältesten Erkenntnislehre der Karmamīmāṃsā*. Wien: Hermann Böhlaus Nachf. (Österreichische Akademie der Wissenschaften. Philosophisch-historische Klasse. Sitzungsberichte, 259. Band, 2. Abhandlung. Veröffentlichungen der Kommission für Sprachen und Kulturen Süd- und Ostasiens, Heft 6)

— (1960). Sprachtheorie und Philosophie im Mahābhāṣyam des Patañjaliḥ. *WZKSO*, 4, 92-118. (= Frauwallner 1982, pp. 284-310)

— (1959). Dignāga, sein Werk und seine Entwicklung. *WZKSO*, 3, 83-164. ( = Frauwallner 1982, pp. 759-841)

— (1958). Die Erkenntnislehre des klassischen Sāṃkhya-Systems. *WZKSO*, 2, 84-139. ( = Frauwallner 1982, pp. 223-278)

— (1956). *Geschichte der indischen Philosophie*. Bd. II. Salzburg: Otto Müller.

— (1953). *Geschichte der indischen Philosophie*. Bd. I. Salzburg: Otto Müller.

— (1938). Bhāvanā und Vidhiḥ bei Maṇḍanamiśra. *WZKM*, 45, 212-252. ( = Frauwallner 1982, pp. 161-201)

Freeman, James M. (1979). *Untouchable: An Indian Life History*. London: George Allen and Unwin.

Fung, Yu-lan (1953). *A History of Chinese Philosophy*. Vol. 2. 2nd ed. Princeton: Princeton University Press.

— (1952). *A History of Chinese Philosophy*. Vol. 1. 2nd ed. Princeton: Princeton University Press.

— (1948). *A Short History of Chinese Philosophy*. New York: Macmillan and Co.

Gadamer, Hans-Georg (1989). *Truth and Method*. 2nd revised edition. Rev. Joel Weinsheimer and Donald G. Marshall. New York: Crossroad Publishing.

— (1988). *Truth and Method*. Tr. Garrett Barden and John Cumming. 3rd impression. London: Sheed and Ward.

Gandhi, Virchand Raghavji (1964). *Selected Speeches*. Bombay: Shri Vallabhsuri Smarak Nidhi.

Garelli, Paul (1969). La pensée préphilosophique en Mésopotamie. In Parain 1969, pp. 24-49.

Garge, Damodar Vishnu (1952). *Citations in Śabara-Bhāṣya*. Poona: Deccan College. (Deccan College Dissertation Series **8**)

Gasché, Rodolphe (1994). *Inventions of Difference: On Jacques Derrida*. Cambridge, Massachusetts: Harvard University Press.

Geertz, Clifford (1973). *The Interpretation of Cultures: Selected Essays*. New York: Basic Books, Inc.

Geldner, Karl Friedrich (Tr.) (1951). *Der Rig-Veda, aus dem Sanskrit ins Deutsche übersetzt und mit einem laufenden Kommentar versehen*. Zweiter Teil, fünfter bis achter Liederkreis. Cambridge, Massachusetts: Harvard University Press. (HOS **34**)

Geldsetzer, Lutz (1968). *Die Philosophie der Philosophiegeschichte im 19. Jahrhundert*. Meisenheim am Glan: A. Hain.

Georges, Robert (1969). Toward an Understanding of Storytelling Events. *Journal of American Folklore*, **82**, 313-328.

Gernet, Jacques (1982). *China and the Christian Impact*. Tr. Janet Lloyd. Cambridge: Cambridge University Press.

Ghose, Jogendra Chunder and Eshan Chunder Bose (Eds.) (1906). *The English Works of Raja Rammohun Roy with an English Translation of "Tuhfatul Muwahhidin."* Allahabad: Panini Office.

Ghosh, Jajneswar (1926). *Higher Education in Bengal under British Rule*. Calcutta: The Book Company.

Glasenapp, Helmuth von (1960). *Das Indienbild deutscher Denker*. Stuttgart: Koehler.

Glover, Willis B. (1965). God and Thomas Hobbes. In: K[eith] C. Brown (Ed.), *Hobbes Studies*. Cambridge, Massachusetts: Harvard University Press, pp. 141-168.

Gluck, Carol (1986). *Japan's Modern Myths: Ideology in the Late Meiji Period*. Princeton: Princeton University Press.

Goekoop, C. (1967). *The Logic of Invariable Concomitance in the Tattvacintāmaṇi*. Dordrecht: D. Reidel.

Goethe, Johann Wolfgang von (1972). *West-östlicher Divan*. Gesamtausgabe. Ed. Hans-J. Weitz. Frankfurt: Insel.

Goldman, Robert P. (1985). Karma, Guilt and Buried Memories: Public Fantasy and Private Reality in Traditional India. *JAOS*, **103**/3, 413-425.

Goldschmidt, Hermann Levin (1981). Review of *Indien und Europa*. *Zürichsee-Zeitung*, **192**.

Gonda, Jan (1980). *Vedic Ritual: The Non-Solemn Rites*. Leiden: E. J. Brill.

— (1963). *The Vision of the Vedic Poets*. The Hague: Mouton & Co.

Gould, Stephen J. (1987). *Time's Arrow, Time's Cycle*. Cambridge, Massachusetts: Harvard University Press.

Graham, Angus C. (1991). Reflections and Replies. In: Rosemont 1991, pp. 267-322.

— (1989). *Disputers of the Tao: Philosophical Argument in Ancient China*. La Salle: Open Court.

— (1986). *Studies in Chinese Philosophy and Philosophical Literature*. Buffalo: State University of New York Press.

— (1978). *Later Mohist Logic, Ethics and Science*. Hong Kong/London: Chinese University of Hong Kong/School of Oriental and African Studies.

Gran, Peter (1980). Review of Said, *Orientalism*. *JAOS*, **100**, 328-331.

Grassmann, H[ermann] (1955 [1872]). *Wörterbuch zum Rig-Veda*. Wiesbaden: Otto Harrassowitz.

Grey, Leslie (1990). *A Concordance of Buddhist Birth Stories*. Oxford: The Pali Text Society.

Griffith, James S. (1992). *Beliefs and Holy Places: A Spiritual Geography of the Pimería Alta*. Tucson: The University of Arizona Press.

Grima, Benedicte (1992). *The Performance of Emotion among Paxtun Women*. Austin: University of Texas Press.

— (1991). The Role of Suffering in Women's Performance of *Paxto*. In: Arjun Appadurai, Frank J. Korom and Margaret Mills (Eds.), *Gender, Genre, and Power in South Asian Expressive Traditions*. Philadelphia: University of Pennsylvania Press, pp. 81-101.

Grimm, Tilemann (1981). *Sinologische Anmerkungen zum europäischen Philosophiebegriff*. Heidelberg: Carl Winter Universitätsverlag.

Grinshpon, Yohanan (1995). *The Place and Meaning of the Siddhis and Saṃyama in the Yogasūtra Tradition*. Ph.D. Dissertation, University of Pennsylvania, Philadelphia.

Gunderson, Lloyd L. (1980). *Alexander's Letter to Aristotle about India*. Meisenheim am Glan: A. Hain. (Beiträge zur klassischen Philologie **110**)

Gupta, Sisir Kumar (Tr.) (1977). *Madhusūdhana Sarasvatī on the Bhagavad Gītā*. Delhi: Motilal Banarsidass.

Guthrie, W[illiam] K. C. (1981). *A History of Greek Philosophy*. Vol. 6: *Aristotle*. Cambridge: Cambridge University Press.

Gyekye, Kwame (1987). *An Essay on African Philosophical Thought*. Cambridge: Cambridge University Press.

Hacker, Paul (1995). *Philology and Confrontation: Paul Hacker on Traditional and Modern Vedānta*. Ed. Wilhelm Halbfass. Albany: State University of New York Press.

— (1983). Inklusivismus. Posthumously published in Oberhammer 1983, pp. 11-28.

— (1978). *Kleine Schriften*. Ed. Lambert Schmithausen. Wiesbaden: Franz Steiner. (Glasenapp-Stiftung **15**)

— (1967/1968). Die Indologie zwischen Vergangenheit und Zukunft. *Hochland*, **60**, 150-157. ( = Hacker 1978, pp. 33-40)

— (1958). Ānvīkṣikī. *WZKSO*, **2**, 54-83 ( = Hacker 1978, pp. 137-166).

— (1957). Religiöse Toleranz und Intoleranz im Hinduismus. *Saeculum*, **8**, 167-179. ( = Hacker 1978, pp. 376-388)

— (1953). *Vivarta. Studien zur Geschichte der illusionistischen Kosmologie und Erkenntnistheorie der Inder*. Mainz: Akademie der Wissenschaften und Literatur. (Abhandlung der Geistes- und sozialwissenschaftlichen Klasse, Jahrgang 1953, Nr. 5)

Halbfass, Wilhelm (1995a). An Uncommon Orientalist: Paul Hacker's Passage to India. In: Hacker 1995, pp. 1-23 (Introduction).

— (1995b). Practical Vedānta. In: Dalmia and von Stietencron 1995, pp. 211-223.

— (1992a). *On Being and What There Is: Classical Vaiśeṣika and the History of Indian Ontology*. Albany: State University of New York Press.

— (1992b). Foreword to Mehta 1992, pp. IX-XIII.

— (1991). *Tradition and Reflection: Explorations in Indian Thought*. Albany: State University of New York Press.

— (1989). Philosophy, Comparative. In: Joachim Ritter and Karlfried Gründer (Eds.), *Historisches Wörterbuch der Philosophie*. Band 7 (P-Q). Basel: Schwabe, col. 922-924.

— (1988a). *India and Europe: An Essay in Understanding*. Albany: State University of New York Press. (Indian edition: Delhi: Motilal Banarsidass, 1990)

— (1988b). Europa, Indien und die Europäisierung der Erde. In: Michalski 1988, pp. 230-252.

— (1988c). Cf. Franco 1988.

— (1985). India and the Comparative Method. *PEW*, 35/1, 3-15.

— (1984). Indian Philosophers on the Plurality of Religious Traditions. In: Peter Gaeffke and David A. Utz (Eds.), *Identity and Division in Cults and Sects in South Asia (Proceedings of the South Asia Seminar 1980/81)*. Philadelphia: South Asia Regional Studies, pp. 58-64.

— (1983a). *Studies in Kumārila and Śaṅkara*. Reinbek: Dr. Inge Wezler Verlag für orientalistische Fachpublikationen.

— (1983b). "Inklusivismus" und "Toleranz" im Kontext der indoeuropäischen Begegnung. In: Oberhammer 1983, pp. 29-60.

— (1981). *Indien und Europa: Perspektiven ihrer geistigen Begegnung*. Basel/Stuttgart: Schwabe.

— (1980a). Karma, *Apūrva*, and "Natural" Causes: Observations on the Growth and Limits of the Theory of Saṃsāra. In: Wendy Doniger O'Flaherty (Ed.), *Karma and Rebirth in Classical Indian Tradition*. Berkeley/Los Angeles/London: University of California Press, pp. 268-302.

— (1980b). Review of: *Indian Metaphysics and Epistemology: The Tradition of Nyāya-Vaiśeṣika up to Gaṅgeśa*. Ed. by K. H. Potter. *JAOS*, **100**, 45-48.

— (1979a). Observations on *darśana*. *WZKS*, **23**, 195-203.

— (1979b). Philosophie. In: Heinz Bechert und Georg von Simson (Eds.), *Einführung in die Indologie: Stand, Methoden, Aufgaben*. Darmstadt: Wissenschaftliche Buchgesellschaft, pp. 138-158.

— (1978). On Being and What There Is: Indian Perspectives on the Question of Being. In: Mervyn Sprung (Ed.), *The Question of Being*. University Park/London: Pennsylvania University Press, pp. 95-109.

— (1977). Anthropological Problems in Classical Indian Philosophy. In: *Beiträge zur Indienforschung: Ernst Waldschmidt zum 80. Geburtstag gewidmet*. Berlin: Museum für indische Kunst, pp. 225-236.

— (1976a). *Zur Theorie der Kastenordnung in der indischen Philosophie*. Göttingen: Vandenhoeck & Ruprecht. (Nachrichten der Akademie der Wissenschaften in Göttingen. I. Philologisch-historische Klasse, Jahrgang 1975, Nr. 9)

— (1976b). Zum Begriff der Substanz *(dravya)* im Vaiśeṣika. *WZKS*, **20**, 141-166.

— (1976c). Indien und die Geschichtsschreibung der Philosophie. *Philosophische Rundschau*, **23**, 104-141.

— (1975). Conceptualizations of 'Being' in Classical Vaiśeṣika. *WZKS*, **19**, 183-198.

— (1974). Reden des Buddha. In: Wolfgang von Einsiedel et al. (Eds.), *Kindlers Literatur Lexikon im dtv in 25 Bänden*. Band 19. *Werke Red - Scr*. München: Deutscher Taschenbuchverlag, pp. 8059-8062. [repr. of Zürich: Kindler Verlag, 1965-1974]

— (1973). Hegel on the Philosophy of the Hindus. In: Cultural Department of the Embassy of the Federal Republic of Germany, New Delhi (Ed.), *German Scholars on India: Contributions to Indian Studies*. Vol. 1. Varanasi: Chowkhamba, pp. 107-122.

— (1970). Remarks on the Vaiśeṣika Concept of *sāmānya*. In: J[ayadeva] Tilakasiri (Ed.), *Añjali, Papers on Indology and Buddhism: A Felicitation Volume Presented to O. H. de A. Wijesekera on his 60th Birthday*. Paradeniya: University of Ceylon, pp. 137-151.

— (1968a). *Descartes' Frage nach der Existenz der Welt: Untersuchungen über die cartesianische Denkpraxis und Metaphysik*. Meisenheim am Glan: A. Hain.

— (1968b). Indian and Western Philosophy: Preliminary Remarks on a Method of Comparison. *Journal of the Bihar Research Society (Patna)*, **54**, 359-364.

— (1965). Review of Gregor Sebba, *Bibliographia cartesiana*. *Erasmus: Speculum Scientiarum*, **17**, col. 72-75.

Hall, David L. and Roger T. Ames (1987). *Thinking Through Confucius*. Albany: State University of New York Press.

Hamada, Junko (1994). *Japanische Philosophie nach 1868*. Leiden: E. J. Brill.

Hamblin, C[harles] L. (1970). *Fallacies*. London: Methuen.

Hampson, Norman (1968). *The Enlightenment*. Harmondsworth: Penguin Books. (Pelican History of European Thought **4**)

Hancock, Mary E. (1991). Saintly Careers among South India's Urban Middle Classes. *Man* (NS), **25**, 505-520.

Hanks, William F. (1992). The Indexical Ground of Deictic Reference. In: Alessandro Duranti and Charles Goodwin (Eds.), *Rethinking Context: Language as an Interactive Phenomenon*. Cambridge: Cambridge University Press, pp. 43-76.

Hansen, Chad (1993). Term-Belief in Action: Sentences and Terms in Early Chinese Philosophy. In: Lenk and Paul 1993, pp. 45-68.

— (1992). *A Daoist Theory of Chinese Thought*. New York: Oxford University Press.

— (1991). Should the Ancient Masters Value Reason? In: Rosemont 1991, pp. 179-207.

— (1989). Language in the Heart-Mind. In: Allinson 1989, pp. 75-123.

— (1983). *Language and Logic in Ancient China*. Ann Arbor: University of Michigan Press.

Harbsmeier, Christian (1993). Conceptions of Knowledge in Ancient China. In: Lenk and Paul 1993, pp. 11-30.

— (1991). The Mass Noun Hypothesis and the Part-Whole Analysis of the White Horse Dialogue. In: Rosemont 1991, pp. 49-66.

— (1989). Marginalia Sino-Logica. In: Allinson 1989, pp. 125-166.

Hattori, Masaaki (1968). *Dignāga, On Perception: Being the Pratyakṣapariccheda of Dignāga's Pramāṇasamuccaya from the Sanskrit Fragments and the Tibetan Versions*. Cambridge, Massachusetts: Harvard University Press. (HOS 47)

Hay, Denys (1968). *Europe: The Emergence of an Idea*. 2nd ed. Edinburgh: Edinburgh University Press.

Hay, Stephen N. (Ed.) (1988). *Sources of Indian Tradition*. Vol. 2. 2nd ed. New York: Columbia University Press.

Hayes, Richard (1988). *Dignāga on the Interpretation of Signs*. Dordrecht: Kluwer.

Hegel, Georg Wilhelm Friedrich (1966). *The Phenomenology of Mind*. Tr. J[ames] B. Baillie. 2nd ed. New York: Humanities Press. (The Muirhead Library of Philosophy)

Heidegger, Martin (1988). *Gelassenheit*. Pfullingen: Neske.

— (1982). *Nietzsche*. Volume IV: *Nihilism*. Tr. Frank A. Capuzzi, ed. David Farrell Krell. San Francisco: Harper and Row.

— (1975). *Gesamtausgabe*. Frankfurt: Klostermann.

— (1963). *Sein und Zeit*. Tübingen: Max Niemeyer.

— (1961). *Nietzsche*. Pfullingen: Neske.

— (1958). An Ontological Consideration of Place. In: *The Question of Being*. Tr. William Kluback and Jean T. Wilde. New York: Twayne Publishers, pp. 18-30.

— (1957a). *Der Satz vom Grund*. Pfullingen: Neske.

— (1957b). *Identität und Differenz*. Pfullingen: Neske.

— (1956). *Was ist das - die Philosophie?* Pfullingen: Neske.

— (1954). *Was heisst Denken?* Tübingen: Max Niemeyer.

Heinze, Hartmut (1991). Das war des Pudels Kern. *Goethe-Jahrbuch*, **109**, 159-161.

Henricks, Guy Richard (1983). *Philosophy and Argumentation in Third-Century China*. Princeton: Princeton University Press.

Herzberger, Hans and Radhika Herzberger (1981a). Bhartṛhari's Paradox. *JIP*, **9**, 1-17 (slightly revised version of Herzberger and Herzberger 1981b)

— (1981b) Bhartṛhari's Paradox. In: Dalsukh Malvania et al. (Eds.), *Studies in Indian Philosophy: A Memorial Volume in Honour of Pandit Sukhlalji Sanghvi*. Ahmedabad: L. D. Institute of Indology, pp. 279-299. (L. D. Series **84**)

High, Dallas (1967). *Language, Person and Belief: Studies in Wittgenstein's Philosophical Investigations and Religious Uses of Language*. New York: Oxford University Press.

Hintikka, Jaakko (1989). The Role of Logic in Argumentation. *The Monist*, **72**/1.

Hinüber, Oskar von (1983). Notice of *Indien und Europa*. *ZDMG*, **133**, 227.

Hobbes, Thomas (1985). *Leviathan*. Harmondsworth: Penguin Books.

Hobsbawm, Eric and Terence Ranger (Eds.) (1983). *The Invention of Tradition*. Cambridge: Cambridge University Press.

Holzman, Donald (1976). *Poetry and Politics: The Life and Works of Juan Chi (A.D. 210-263)*. Cambridge: Cambridge University Press.

Hopkins, Edward Washburn (1972 [1889]). *The Social and Military Position of the Ruling Caste in Ancient India*. Varanasi: Bharat-Bharati. [repr. of *JAOS*, **1**, 357-376]

— (1969 [1920]). *The Great Epic of India: Its Character and Origin*. Calcutta: Punthi Pustak. [repr. of 2nd ed. New Haven: Yale University Press]

— (1930-32). Hindu Salutations. *Bulletin of the School of Oriental Studies*, **6**, 369-383.

Hornung, Erik (1983). *Conceptions of God in Ancient Egypt*. Tr. John Baines. London: Routledge and Kegan Paul.

Houben, Jan E. M. (forthcoming). Bhartṛhari's *Vākyapadīya* and the Ancient *Vṛtti*.

— (1994a). Bhartṛhari's Familiarity with Jainism. *ABORI*, **75**/1-4, 1-24.

— (1994b). Early Indian Authors and Linguistic Change. Postscript to "Bhartṛhari's Familiarity with Jainism." *ABORI*, **75**/1-4, 255-256.

— (1993). Who are Bhartṛhari's *padadarśins*? On the Development of Bhartṛhari's Philosophy of Language. *AS/ÉA*, **47**/1, 155-169.

— (1992a). Bhartṛhari's *samaya*/Helārāja's *saṃketa*. A Contribution to the Reconstruction of the Grammarian's Discussion with the Vaiśeṣikas on the Relation between *śabda* and *artha*. *JIP*, **20**, 219-242.

— (1992b). *The Saṃbandha-samuddeśa and Bhartṛhari's Philosophy of Language*. Thesis, Utrecht University, 1992. (A revised version appeared in 1995 as vol. 2 of Gonda Indological Studies, Egbert Forsten Publishing, Groningen.)

— (1990). The Sequencelessness of the Signifier in Bhartṛhari's Theory of Language. *Indologica Taurinensia*, **15/16**, 119-129. (Proceedings of the VIIth World Sanskrit Conference, Leiden, August 23rd-29th, 1987)

How, W[alter] W. and J[oseph] Wells (1964 [1912]). *A Commentary on Herodotus*. 2 vols. Oxford: Clarendon Press.

Hufford, David (1978). Ambiguity and the Rhetoric of Belief. *Keystone Folklore*, **21**/1, 11-24.

Hume, David (1958). *A Treatise of Human Nature*. Ed. L[ewis] A. Selby-Bigge. Oxford: Clarendon Press.

Husserl, Edmund (1981). *The Origin of Geometry*. Tr. David Carr. In: Peter McCormick and Frederick A. Elliston (Eds.), *Husserl: Shorter Works*. Indiana: The Harvester Press.

Hymes, Dell (1981). Breakthrough into Performance. In: *In Vain I Tried To Tell You: Essays in Native American Poetics*. Philadelphia: University of Pennsylvania Press, pp. 79-141. (Studies in Native American Literature **1**)

Inden, Ronald (1991). Notice of *India and Europe*. *History of Religions*, **31**/1, 95.

— (1990). *Imagining India*. Oxford: Basil Blackwell.

— (1986). Orientalist Constructions of India. *Modern Asian Studies*, **29**, 401-446

Ingalls, Daniel Henry Holmes (1951). *Materials for the Study of Navya-Nyāya Logic*. Cambridge, Massachusetts: Harvard University Press. (HOS **40**)

Isaacson, Harunaga (1994). Yogic Perception (*yogipratyakṣa*) in Early Vaiśeṣika. *StII*, **18**, 139-160.

Iteanu, André (1990). Sacred and Profane Revisited: Durkheim and Dumont Considered in the Orokaiva Context. *Ethnos*, **13**/3-4, 169-183.

Iveković, Rada (1992). *Orients: Critique de la raison postmoderne.* Paris: Noël Blandin. (Collection Le Diwan occidental/oriental)

Iyer, K. A. Subramania (1969). *Bhartṛhari: A Study of the Vākyapadīya in the Light of the Ancient Commentaries*. Poona: Deccan College Postgraduate and Research Institute. (Deccan College Building Centenary and Silver Jubilee Series 68)

— (1966). Cf. Vākyapadīya I (Texts in Sanskrit and Pali)

— (Tr.) (1965) *The Vākyapadīya of Bhartṛhari with the Vṛtti*. Chapter I. Poona: Deccan College Postgraduate and Research Institute. (Deccan College Building Centenary and Silver Jubilee Series 26)

— (1964). Bhartṛhari on Apabhraṃśa. *Vishveshwaranand Indological Journal* (Hoshiarpur), 2, 242-246.

Jackson, Carl T. (1994). *Vedanta for the West: The Ramakrishna Movement in the United States*. Bloomington: Indiana University Press.

Jacobi, Hermann (1970). *Kleine Schriften.* Ed. Bernhard Kölver. Wiesbaden: Franz Steiner.

— (1911). Kultur-, Sprach- und Literaturhistorisches aus dem Kauṭilīya. Sitzungsberichte der Kgl. Preußischen Akademie der Wissenschaften, pp. 954-973 (= Jacobi 1970, pp. 502-521).

— (1903). *Mahābhārata. Inhaltsangabe, Index und Concordanz der Calcuttaer und Bombayer Ausgaben*. Bonn: Friedrich Cohen.

Jacobsen, Thorkild (1976). *The Treasures of Darkness*. New Haven: Yale University Press.

Jacobson, Doranne (1978). The Chaste Wife: Cultural Norm and Individual Experience. In: Sylvia Vatuk (Ed.), *American Studies in the Anthropology of India*. New Delhi: Manohar, pp. 95-138.

Jacoby, Felix (1958). *Die Fragmente der griechischen Historiker (FGrHist).* Dritter Teil: *Geschichte der Städte und Völker (Horographie und Ethnographie).* C. *Autoren über einzelne Länder Nr. 608a-856.* Erster Band: *Ägypten - Geten Nr. 608a-708*. Leiden: E. J. Brill.

Jaspers, Karl (1949a). *Einführung in die Philosophie*. Zürich: Artemis.

— (1949b). *Vom Ursprung and Ziel der Geschichte*. München: Piper.

Jha, Ganganath (Tr.) (1983a [1900-1908]). *Ślokavārttika*. Delhi: Sri Satguru Publications. (Sri Garib Das Oriental Series **8**) [repr. of *Çlokavārttika*. Calcutta: Asiatic Society. Bibliotheca Indica **146**]

— (Tr.) (1983b [1903-1924]). *Tantravārttika*. Delhi: Sri Satguru Publications. (Sri Garib Das Oriental Series **9**) [repr. of *Tantravārtika*. Calcutta: Asiatic Society. Bibliotheca Indica **161**]

— (Tr.) (1973 [1933]). *Shabara-Bhāṣya*. Baroda: Oriental Institute. (GOS **56**, **70**, **73**)

Johnstone, Barbara (1990). *Stories, Community, and Place: Narratives from Middle America*. Bloomington: Indiana University Press.

Jolly, Julius (1889). *The Minor Law Books*. Pt. 1: *Nārada. Brihaspati*. London: Clarendon Press. (SBE **33**)

Jonas, Hans (1959). The Practical Uses of Theory. *Social Research*, **26**, 127-166

Jones, Kenneth W. (1989). *Socio-Religious Reform Movements in British India*. Cambridge: Cambridge University Press.

Kahrs, Eivind G. (1992). What is a *tadbhava* Word? *IIJ*, **35**, 225-249.

Kane, Pandurang Varman (1973). *History of Dharmaśāstra* (*Ancient and Medieval Religious and Civil Law*). Vol. III. 2nd ed. Poona: Bhandarkar Oriental Research Institute. (Government Oriental Series Class B., No. **6**)

— (1962) *History of Dharmaśāstra*. Vol. V. Poona: Bhandarkar Oriental Research Institute.

Kangle, R. P. (Tr.) (1963). *The Kauṭilīya Arthaśāstra*. Part II. *An English Translation with Critical and Explanatory Notes*. Bombay: University of Bombay.

Kannu Peeru, S. (1992). *The Critical Study of Praśastapādabhāṣya*. Delhi: Kanishka Publishing House.

Kant, Immanuel (1974). *Anthropology from a Pragmatic Point of View*. Tr. Mary J. Gregor. The Hague: Nijhoff.

— (1933). *Immanuel Kant's Critique of Pure Reason*. Tr. Norman Kemp Smith. London: Macmillan and Co.

Kapp, Robert A. (Ed.) (1980). Review Symposium: Edward Said's *Orientalism*. *Journal of Asian Studies*, **39**, 481-517.

Karttunen, Klaus (1989). *India in Early Greek Literature*. Helsinki: Finnish Oriental Society. (*Studia Orientalia* **65**)

— (1988). Expedition to the End of the World - An Ethnographic *τόπος* in Herodotus. *Studia Orientalia*, **64**, 177-181.

Karunadasa, Y. (1967). *Buddhist Analysis of Matter*. Colombo: Department of Cultural Affairs.

Kaviraj, Gopinath (1924). The Doctrine of *pratibhā* in Indian Philosophy. *ABORI*, **5**, 1-18; 113-132.

Keith, Arthur Berriedale (1978). *The Karma-Mīmāṃsā*. New Delhi: Oriental Books Reprint Corporation.

Kejariwal, O[m] P[rakash] (1988) *The Asiatic Society of Bengal and the Discovery of India's Past: 1784-1838*. Delhi: Oxford University Press.

Keny, Liladhara B. (1942-43). Jesus Christ in the Mahābhārata. *Quarterly Journal of the Mythic Society*, N.S., **33**, 22-28.

Killingley, Dermot (1995). Rammohun Roy and Bishop Heber's View of the Trinity. In: Jon Davies, Graham Harvey and Wilfred G. E. Watson (Eds.), *Words Remembered, Texts Renewed: Essays in Honour of J. F. A. Sawyer*. Sheffield: Sheffield Academic Press, pp. 480-496. (Journal for the Study of the Old Testament Supplement Series **195**)

— (1993). *Rammohun Roy in Hindu and Christian Tradition*. Newcastle upon Tyne: Grevatt and Grevatt.

— (1991). Varṇa and Caste in Hindu Apologetic. In: Dermot Killingley (Ed.), *Hindu Ritual and Society*. Newcastle upon Tyne: S. Y. Killingley, pp. 7-31.

— (1982). *The Only True God: Works on Religion by Rammohun Roy, Selected and Translated from Bengali and Sanskrit*. Newcastle upon Tyne: Grevatt and Grevatt.

— (1978). *Rammohun Roy's Interpretation of the Vedānta*. Ph.D. thesis, University of London.

Kilpatrick, G. Wayne (1983). Rajaram Das' Middle Bengali Account of His Conversion to the Dharma Cult. In: Ray Langsten (Ed.), *Research on Bengal: Proceedings of the 1981 Bengal Studies Conference*. East Lansing, Michigan: Asian Studies Center, Michigan State University, pp. 1-6.

Kimmerle, Heinz (1993). Afrikanische Philosophie als Weisheitslehre? In: R[am] A. Mall and D[ieter] Lohmar (Eds.), *Philosophische Grundlagen der Interkulturalität*. Amsterdam: Editions Rodopi, pp. 159-180. (Studien zur interkulturellen Philosophie/Studies in Intercultural Philosophy **1**)

Kimmig, Rainer (1985). Indien und Europa: Ein ungleicher Dialog. Anmerkungen zu Wilhelm Halbfass (Review paper of *Indien und Europa*). *Internationales Asienforum*, **16**/3-4, 349-361.

Kisiel, Theodore (1993). *The Genesis of Heidegger's* Being and Time. Berkeley/Los Angeles/London: University of California Press.

Kneale, William and Martha Kneale (1962). *The Development of Logic*. London: Oxford University Press.

Kohler, Lotte and Hans Sauer (Eds.) (1992). *Hannah Arendt - Karl Jaspers Correspondence*. Tr. Robert and Rita Kimber. New York: Harcourt Brace.

König, G[ert] (1989). Perspektive, Perspektivismus, perspektivisch I. *Philosophie; Theologie; Geistes- und Naturwissenschaften*. In: Joachim Ritter and Karlfried Gründer (Eds.), *Historisches Wörterbuch der Philosophie*. Darmstadt: Wissenschaftliche Buchgesellschaft. Band 7 (P-Q), col. 363-375.

Konow, Sten (1945). *Kautalya Studies*. Oslo: Jacob Dybwad.

Kopf, David (1969). *British Orientalism and the Bengal Renaissance: The Dynamics of Indian Modernization 1773-1835*. Berkeley: University of California Press.

Kopytoff, Igor (1981). Knowledge and Belief in Suku Thought. *Africa*, **51**/3, 709-723.

Korom, Frank J. (1993). Oral Canon Formation in a Bengali Religious Community. Paper read at the Annual Meeting of the *American Academy of Religion*, Washington, D.C.

— (1992a). *"To Be Happy": Narrative, Ritual Play and Leisure in an Annual Bengali Religious Festival*. Ph.D. Dissertation, University of Pennsylvania, Philadelphia.

— (1992b). Of Navels and Mountains: A Further Inquiry into the History of an Idea. *Asian Folklore Studies*, **51**/1, 103-125.

Koskikallio, Petteri (1994). When Time Turns: Yugas, Ideologies, Sacrifices. *Studia Orientalia*, **73**, 253-271.

Kotovsky, G[rigory] G[rigoryevich] and N[ina] N[ikolayevna] Sosina (Eds.) (1976). *Bibliografiya Indii* (Bibliography of India). Moscow: Nauka.

Kripalani, Krishna (1962). *Rabindranath Tagore: A Biography*. New York: Grove Press.

Krishna, Daya (1993). Emerging New Approaches in the Study of Classical Indian Philosophy. In: Fløistad 1993, pp. 69-82.

Krishna, Daya, M[eghasyama] P[undalika] Rege, R. C. Dwivedi, and Mukund Lath (Eds.) (1991). *Samvāda*. Delhi: Indian Council of Philosophical Research, in association with Motilal Banarsidass.

Krishnamoorthy, K. (1983). Bhartṛhari's Idea of Grammar. *Journal of the Oriental Institute* (Baroda), **33**, 11-16.

Krishna Warrier, A. G. (1961). *The Concept of Mukti in Advaita Vedānta*. Madras: University of Madras Press.

Kuhn, Thomas S. (1977). Second Thoughts on Paradigms. In: Thomas S. Kuhn. *The Essential Tension: Selected Studies*. Chicago: Chicago University Press, pp. 293-319.

— (1970). *The Structure of Scientific Revolutions*. 2nd enlarged ed. Chicago: Chicago University Press.

Kuiper, F[ranciscus] B. J. (1983). *Ancient Indian Cosmogony*. Ed. John Irwin. Delhi: Vikas.

Kulkarni, S. M. (1989). An Unresolved Dilemma in Dyūtaparvan: A Question Raised by Draupadī. In: Matilal 1989, pp. 150-156.

Kunjunni Raja, K. (1991). Notice of *India and Europe*. *ALB*, **55**, 165.

— (Ed.) (1968). *New Catalogus Catalogorum*. Vol. 4. Madras: University of Madras.

Labov, William (1972). *Language in the Inner City*. Philadelphia: University of Pennsylvania Press.

Labov, William and Joshua Waletzky (1967). Narrative Analysis: Oral Versions of Personal Experience. In: June Helm (Ed.), *Essays on the Verbal and Visual Arts*. Seattle: University of Washington Press, pp. 12-44.

Laclau, Ernesto and Chantal Mouffe (1985). *Hegemony and Socialist Strategy: Towards a Radical Democratic Politics*. London: Verso.

Lad, Ashok Kumar (1967). *A Comparative Study of the Concept of Liberation in Indian Philosophy*. Burhanpur: Gindharlal Keshavdas.

Laine, James W. (1989). *Visions of God: Narratives of Theophany in the Mahābhārata*. Vienna: Institute for Indology, University of Vienna. (Publications of the De Nobili Research Library 16)

Lakatos, Imre (1978). *The Methodology of Scientific Research Programmes: Philosophical Papers Volume I*. Ed. John Worral and Gregory Currie. Cambridge University Press.

Lane, Belden C. (1988). *Landscapes of the Sacred: Geography and Narrative in American Spirituality*. New York: Paulist Press.

Langellier, Kristin (1989). Personal Experience Narratives: Perspectives on Theory and Research. *Text and Performance Quarterly*, 9/4, 243-276.

Langness, L[ewis] L. (1965). *The Life History in Anthropological Science*. New York: Holt, Rinehart and Winston.

Lao, Sze-kwang (Lao Yung-wei) (1989). On Understanding Chinese Philosophy. In: Allinson 1989 pp. 265-293.

Lariviere, Richard W. (Ed./Tr.) (1989). *The Nāradasmṛti*. Critically edited with an introduction, annotated translation, and appendices.

Part I: Text, Part II: Translation. Philadelphia: University of Pennsylvania.

— (1988). Adhikāra - Right and Responsibility. In: Mohammed Ali Jazayery and Werner Winter (Ed.), *Languages and Cultures: Studies in Honor of E. C. Polomé*. Berlin/New York: Mouton de Gruyter, pp. 359-364.

Larson, Gerald James (1979). *Classical Sāṃkhya: An Interpretation of its History and Meaning*. Delhi: Motilal Banarsidass.

Larson, Gerald James and Ram Shankar Bhattacharya (Eds.) (1987). *Sāṃkhya: A Dualist Tradition in Indian Philosophy*. Princeton/Delhi: Princeton University Press/Motilal Banarsidass. (Encyclopedia of Indian Philosophies 4)

Larson, Gerald James and Eliot Deutsch (Eds.) (1988). *Interpreting across Boundaries*. Princeton: Princeton University Press.

Lassen, Christian (1852). *Indische Alterthumskunde*. Theil II. Leipzig: Verlag L. A. Kittel.

Lau, D. C. (1982). *Tao Te Ching*. Hong Kong: Chinese University Press.

Laurens, Henry (1978). *Aux sources de l'orientalisme: La Bibliothèque Orientale de Barthélemi d'Herbelot*. Paris: G.-P. Maisonneuve et Larose.

Lavine, Thelma Z. and Victorino Tejera (Eds.) (1989). *History and Anti-History in Philosophy*. Dordrecht: Kluwer.

Leff, Gordon (1968). *Paris and Oxford in the Thirteenth and Fourteenth Centuries*. New York: Wiley.

Lehrer, Keith (1990). *Theory of Knowledge*. San Francisco: Westview Press.

Lele, Jayant (1993). Orientalism and the Social Sciences. In: Breckenridge and van der Veer 1993, pp. 45-75.

Lenhoff, Gail (1979). Bèyond Three Seas: Afanasij Nikitin's Journey from Orthodoxy to Apostasy. *East European Quarterly*, 13/4, 432-447.

Lenk, Hans and Gregor Paul (Eds.) (1993). *Epistemological Issues in Classical Chinese Philosophy*. Buffalo: State University of New York Press.

Leslau, Charlotte and Wolf Leslau (1962). *African Proverbs*. Mount Vernon, N. Y.: Peter Pauper Press.

Levenson, J[oseph] R. (1968). *Confucian China and Its Modern Fate: A Trilogy*. Berkeley: University of California Press.

Lévi, Sylvain (1932). *Matériaux pour l'étude du système Vijñaptimātra*. Paris: Librairie ancienne Honoré Champion.

Lewis, Bernard (1993). *Islam and the West*. Oxford/New York: Oxford University Press.

— (1983). The Question of Orientalism. *New York Review of Books*, **30** (June 30, 1983), 35-38.

— (1982a). The Question of Orientalism. *New York Review of Books*, **29** (June 24, 1982), 49-56.

— (1982b). The Question of Orientalism. *New York Review of Books*, **29** (August 12, 1982), 44-48.

Lewis, Bernard, Edmund Leites and Margaret Case (Eds.) (1985). *As Others See Us: Mutual Perception, East and West*. New York: International Society for the Comparative Study of Civilizations.

Lindtner, Christian (1993). Linking up Bhartṛhari and the Bauddhas. *AS/ÉA*, **47**/1, 195-213.

Lipsey, Roger (1977). *Coomaraswamy: His Life and Work*. Princeton: Princeton University Press.

Lloyd, G[eoffrey] E. R. (1979). *Magic, Reason and Experience*. Cambridge: Cambridge University Press.

Loewe, Michael (1986). The Concept of Sovereignty. In: Twitchett and Loewe 1986, pp. 726-746.

Lohner, Edgar (Ed.) (1971). *Studien zum West-östlichen Divan Goethes*. Darmstadt: Wissenschaftliche Buchgesellschaft.

Lommel, Hermann (1978). *Kleine Schriften*. Ed. Klaus Ludwig Janert. Wiesbaden: Franz Steiner. (Glasenapp-Stiftung 16)

— (1951). Nachtrag zu "Bhṛgu im Jenseits" (*Paideuma* IV. (1950) S. 93ff.). *Paideuma*, 5 (1950-54), 201-202. (= Lommel 1978, pp. 290-291)

— (1950). Bhṛgu im Jenseits. *Paideuma*, 4, 93-109. (= Lommel 1978, pp. 209-227)

Lopez, Donald S. (1979). Approaching the Numinous: Rudolf Otto and Tibetan Tantra. *PEW*, 29/4, 467-476.

Lott, Eric (1950). *Vedantic Approaches to God*. London: Macmillan and Co.

Lowe, Lisa (1992). *Critical Terrains: British and French Orientalisms*. Ithaca: Cornell University Press.

Loy, David (1992). The Deconstruction of Buddhism. In: Harold Coward and Toby Foshay (Eds.), *Derrida and Negative Theology*. Albany: State University of New York Press, pp. 227-253.

Ludden, David (1993). Orientalist Empiricism: Transformations of Colonial Knowledge. In: Breckenridge and van der Veer 1993, pp. 250-278.

Lüders, Heinrich (1940). *Philologica Indica*. Göttingen: Vandenhoeck & Ruprecht.

Lundbæk, Knud (1986). *T. S. Bayer (1694-1738): Pioneer Sinologist*. London/Malmö: Curzon Press.

Lüthi, Max (1982). *The European Folktale: Form and Nature*. Tr. John D. Niles. Bloomington: Indiana University Press.

Lützeler, Paul Michael (Ed.) (1982). *Europa: Analysen und Visionen der Romantiker*. Frankfurt: Insel.

Lyotard, Jean-François (1991). Aller et retour. In: John Rajchman and Cornel West (Eds.), *La pensée américaine contemporaine*. Paris: PUF, pp. 5-30. (Collection Philosophie d'aujourd'hui)

— (1983). *Le Différend*. Paris: Minuit. (Collection "Critique")

Lysenko, Victoria (1994). "Atomistic Mode of Thinking" as Exemplified by the Vaiśeṣika Philosophy of Number. *AS/ÉA*, **48/2**, 781-806.

— (1993). Śaṅkara's Critique of the Vaiśeṣika Atomism. In: Serebriany 1993b, pp. 31-40.

— (1988). Filosofiya prostranstva i vremeni v Indii: shkola Vaisheshika (Philosophy of Space and Time in India: The Vaiśeṣika School). In: Marietta Stepanyants (Ed.), *Ratsionalisticheskaya traditsiya i sovremennost. Indiya* (Rationalistic Tradition and Modernity. India). Moscow: Nauka (Vostochnaya Literatura), pp. 75-102.

— (1986). *Filosofiya prirody v Indii. Atomism shkoly Vaisheshika* (Philosophy of Nature in India. Atomism of the Vaiśeṣika School). Moscow: Nauka (Vostochnaya Literatura).

Macdonell, Arthur A. (1960 [1917]). *A Vedic Reader for Students*. Madras: Oxford University Press.

Madugulu, Indusekhara Sastri (1985). *The Ācārya: Śaṅkara of Kālaḍī*. Delhi: Motilal Banarsidass.

Maitra, Sushil Kumar (1978). *The Ethics of the Hindus*. New Delhi: Asian Publication Services.

Majumdar, R[amesh Chandra], H[emchandra] Raychaudhuri and Kalikinkar Datta (1946). *An Advanced History of India*. London: Macmillan and Co.

Malamoud, Charles (1975). La brique percée. Sur le jeu du vide et du plein dans l'Inde brāhmaṇique. *Figure du vide. Nouvelle revue de psychanalyse*, **11** (Printemps), 205-222.

Marion, Jean-Luc (1994). Metaphysics and Phenomenology: A Relief for Theology. *Critical Inquiry*, **20/4** (summer), 572-591.

Marshall, Peter J. (1987). *Bengal: The British Bridgehead*. Cambridge: Cambridge University Press. (New Cambridge History of India 2,2)

Marshman, Joshua (1822). *A Defence of the Deity and Atonement of Christ, in Reply to Ram Mohun Roy of Calcutta*. London: Kingsbury, Parbury and Allen.

Masson-Oursel, Paul (1926). *Comparative Philosophy*. Tr. F[rancis] G. Crookshank. London: Kegan Paul.

— (1923). *La philosophie comparée*. Paris: Félix Alcan.

Masson-Oursel, Paul, Helena de Willman-Grabowska and Philippe Stern (1934). *Ancient India and Indian Civilization*. [Tr. M. R. Dobie] London: Kegan Paul, Trench, Trübner & Co.

Matilal, Bimal Krishna (1990). *The Word and the World: India's Contribution to the Study of Language*. Delhi: Oxford University Press.

— (Ed.) (1989). *Moral Dilemmas in the Mahābhārata*. Delhi: Indian Institute of Advanced Study, Shimla, in association with Motilal Banarsidass.

— (1986). *Perception: An Essay on Classical Indian Theories of Knowledge*. Oxford: Oxford University Press.

— (1985). *Logic, Language and Reality*. Delhi: Motilal Banarsidass.

— (1982). *Logical and Ethical Issues of Religious Belief*. Calcutta: University of Calcutta.

— (1968). *The Navya-Nyāya Doctrine of Negation*. Cambridge, Massachusetts: Harvard University Press. (HOS 46)

May, Herbert G. and Bruce M. Metzger (Eds.) (1973). *The Holy Bible*. Rev. ed. New York: Oxford University Press.

Mayrhofer, Manfred (1963). *Kurzgefasstes etymologisches Wörterbuch des Altindischen*. Heidelberg: Carl Winter Universitätsverlag (1956-1980).

McCall, Henrietta (1990). *Mesopotamian Myths*. London/Austin: British Museum Publications/University of Texas Press.

Mehta, J[arava] L[al] (1992). *J. L. Mehta on Heidegger, Hermeneutics and Indian Tradition*. Ed. William J. Jackson. Leiden: E. J. Brill.

— (1987). Heidegger and Vedānta: Reflections on a Questionable Theme. In: Graham Parkes (Ed.), *Heidegger and Asian Thought*. Honolulu: University of Hawaii Press, pp. 15-45.

— (1985). *India and the West: The Problem of Understanding*. Chico, California: Scholars Press.

— (1970). Heidegger and the Comparison of Indian and Western Philosophy. *PEW*, 20, 303-317.

Mehta, Rohit (1990). *Yoga: The Art of Integration*. Adyar, Madras: The Theosophical Publishing House.

Melman, Billie (1992). *Women's Orients*. London: Macmillan.

Meyer, Johann Jacob (Tr.) (1926). *Das altindische Buch vom Welt- und Staatsleben: Das Arthaśāstra des Kauṭilya aus dem Sanskrit übersetzt und mit Einleitung und Anmerkungen versehen*. Leipzig: Otto Harrassowitz.

Meyer, Urs W. (1994). *Europäische Rezeption indischer Philosophie und Religion: Dargestellt am Beispiel von Arthur Schopenhauer*. Bern: Peter Lang.

Michalski, Krzysztof (Ed.) (1988). *Europa und die Folgen*. Stuttgart: Klett-Cotta. (Castelgandolfo-Gespräche 1987)

Michelfelder, Diane and Richard Palmer (Eds.) (1989). *Dialogue and Deconstruction: The Gadamer-Derrida Encounter*. Albany: State University of New York Press.

Minor, Robert (1987). *Radhakrishnan: A Religious Biography*. Albany: State University of New York Press.

Misch, Georg (1950a). *Der Weg in die Philosophy*. Zweite, stark erweiterte Auflage. München/Bern: Leo Lehnen/A. Francke.

— (1950b). *The Dawn of Philosophy*. Ed. R[ichard] F. C. Hull. London: Kegan Paul.

Mitter, Partha (1977). *Much Maligned Monsters*. Oxford: Clarendon Press.

Mitra, Amalendu (1972). *Rāṛher Saṅgskṛiti o Dharmaṭhākur* (The Culture of Rāṛh and Dharma Ṭhākur). Kālikātā: Pharma Ke. El. Mukhopādhyāẏ.

Mohanty, Jitendra Nath (1994). *Theory and Practice*. Calcutta: Allied Publishers.

— (1992). *Reason and Tradition in Indian Thought*. Oxford: Oxford University Press.

Mommsen, Katharina (1988). *Goethe und die arabische Welt*. Frankfurt: Insel.

Monier-Williams, Sir Monier (1960 [1899]). *A Sanskrit-English Dictionary*. Oxford: Clarendon Press.

Moreland, W[illiam] H. and Atul Chandra Chatterjee (1953). *A Short History of India*. 3rd ed. London etc.: Longmans, Green and Co.

Morin, Edgar (1991). *La méthode. 4. Les idées. Leur habitat, leur vie, leurs moeurs, leur organisation*. Paris: Éditions du Seuil.

Morinis, E. Alan (1982). Levels of Culture in Hinduism: A Case Study of Dream Incubation at a Bengali Pilgrimage Centre. *Contributions to Indian Sociology* (NS), **16**/2, 255-270.

Mote, Frederick W. (1989). *Intellectual Foundations of China*. 2nd ed. New York: Knopf.

Mudimbe, V[alentin] Y. (1988). *The Invention of Africa*. Bloomington: Indiana University Press.

Mukherjee, S[oumyendra] N[ath] (1974). *Sir William Jones: A Study in Eighteenth-century British Attitudes to India*. Cambridge: Cambridge University Press.

Müller, Friedrich Max (Tr.) (1988 [1879, 1884]). *The Upaniṣads*. Delhi: Motilal Banarsidass. [repr. of Oxford: Clarendon Press] (SBE **1**, **15**)

Muller-Ortega, Paul Eduardo (1989). *The Triadic Heart of Śiva*. Albany: State University of New York Press.

Mungello, David E. (1989). *Curious Land: Jesuit Accomodation and the Origins of Sinology*. Honolulu: University of Hawaii Press.

Murray, Michael (Ed.) (1978). *Heidegger & Modern Philosophy*. New Haven/London: Yale University Press.

Nagley, Winfield E. (1970). Introduction to the Symposium and Reading of a Letter from Martin Heidegger. *PEW*, **20**, 221.

Nakamoto, Tominaga (1990). *Emerging from Meditation*. Tr. Michael Pye. Honolulu: University of Hawaii Press.

Nakamura, Hajime (1988). The Meaning of the Terms "Philosophy" and "Religion" in Various Traditions. In: Larson and Deutsch 1988, pp. 137-151.

— (1960). Bhartṛhari the Scholar. *IIJ*, 4, 282-305.

Ñāṇajīvako, Bhikkhu (Čedomil Veljačić) (1992). *A Buddhist Philosophy of Religion*. Burlingame: The International Translation Institute, Dharma Realm Buddhist Association.

— (1987). Hegel in Indian Philosophy. *Synthesis Philosophica*, **3**, 203-224.

— (1983). *Studies in Comparative Philosophy*. Vol. 1. Colombo: Lake House.

— (1973). Aniccam - The Buddhist Theory of Impermanence. In: *The Basic Facts of Existence*. Kandy: Buddhist Publication Society, pp. 13-38. (The Wheel Publications **186/187**)

— (1972). Karma and the Ripening Fruit. *Main Currents in Modern Thought*, **29**/1, 28-36.

— (1965). Dependence of Punar-bhava on Karma in Buddhist Philosophy. *IPA*, **6**, 32-37.

Narváez, Peter (1991). Newfoundaland Berry Pickers "In the Fairies": Maintaining Spatial, Temporal, and Moral Boundaries Through Legendry. In: Peter Narváez (Ed.), *The Good People: New Fairylore Essays*. New York: Garland Press, pp. 336-368.

Needham, Joseph (1956). *Science and Civilisation in China*. Vol. 2. Cambridge: Cambridge University Press.

— (1954-85). *Science and Civilisation in China*. 6 vols. Cambridge: Cambridge University Press.

Needham, Rodney (1972). *Belief, Language and Experience*. Chicago: University of Chicago Press.

Nehru, Jawaharlal (1964). *The Discovery of India*. Bombay etc.: Asia Publishing House.

Neumann, Siegfried (1991). Ich-Erzählung. In: Kurt Ranke et al. (Eds.), *Enzyklopädie des Märchens: Handwörterbuch zur historischen und vergleichenden Erzählforschung*. 7.1. Berlin: Walter de Gruyter, pp. 10-15.

Neusner, Jacob (1994). *Introduction to Rabbinic Literature*. New York: Doubleday.

Nicolaisen, William F. H. (1990). Why Tell Stories? *Fabula*, 31/1-2, 5-10.

— (1988). Once upon a Place, or Where is the World of the Folktale? In: Albrecht Lehmann and Andreas Kuntz (Eds.), *Sichtweisen der Volkskunde: Lebensformen* 3. Berlin: D. Reimer.

Nikitin, Afanasy (1986). *Khozheniye za tri morya* (The Journey beyond Three Seas). Ed. Yakov Solomonovich Lurye and Leonid Sergeyevich Semyonov. Leningrad: Nauka.

Oberhammer, Gerhard (1992). Der frühe Nyāya: Bemerkungen zur inneren Gestalt seines Denkens. In: A. W. van den Hoek, D[irk] H. A. Kolff, and M[arianne] S. Oort (Eds.), *Ritual, State and History in South Asia. Essays in Honour of J. C. Heesterman*. Leiden: E. J. Brill, pp. 244-258.

— (1991). "Begegnung" als "Kategorie" der Hermeneutik altindischer Heilssysteme. In: Gerhard Oberhammer (Ed.), *Beiträge zur Hermeneutik indischer und abendländischer Religionstraditionen*. Wien: Verlag der österreichischen Akademie der Wissenschaften, pp. 193-211. (Österreichische Akademie der Wissenschaften. Philosophisch-historische Klasse. Sitzungsberichte, 573. Band. Beiträge zur Kultur- und Geistesgeschichte Asiens 6)

— (1989). *"Begegnung" als Kategorie der Religionshermeneutik*. Wien: Institut für Indologie der Universität Wien. (Publications of the De Nobili Research Library. Occasional Papers 4)

— (1987) *Versuch einer transzendentalen Hermeneutik religiöser Traditionen*. Wien: Institut für Indologie der Universität Wien. (Publications of the De Nobili Research Library. Occasional Papers 3)

— (Ed.) (1983). *Inklusivismus: Eine indische Denkform*. Wien: Institut für Indologie der Universität Wien. (Publications of the De Nobili Research Library. Occasional Papers 2)

Obeyesekere, Gananath (1981). *Medusa's Hair: An Essay on Personal Symbols and Religious Experience*. Chicago: University of Chicago Press.

O'Flaherty, Wendy D. (Ed.) (1980). *Karma and Rebirth in Classical Indian Traditions*. Berkeley: University of California Press.

O'Leary, Joseph Stephen (1994). *La vérité chrétienne à l'âge du pluralisme religieux*. Paris: Editions du Cerf. (Collection "Cogitatio Fidei")

— (1992). Theological Resonances of *Der Satz vom Grund*. In: Christopher Macann (Ed.), *Critical Assessments: Martin Heidegger*. Vol. I. London: Routledge, pp. 213-256.

— (1985). *Questioning Back: The Overcoming of Metaphysics in Christian Tradition*. Minneapolis, San Fransciso: Winston Press, Harper & Row.

— (1980). Topologie de l'être et topographie de la révélation. In: Richard Kearney and Joseph S. O'Leary (Eds.), *Heidegger et la question de Dieu*. Paris: Grasset, pp. 194-237.

O'Meara, Dominic J. (1989). *Pythagoras Revived: Mathematics and Philosophy in Late Antiquity*. Oxford: Oxford University Press.

Organ, Troy (1989). *Radhakrishnan and the Ways of Oneness of East and West*. Athens (Ohio): Ohio University Press.

Otto, Rudolf (1982 [1950]). *The Idea of the Holy*. Tr. John W. Harvey. 2nd ed. New York: Oxford University Press.

Pandeya, R. C. (1966). *Jīvanmukti* and Social Concerns. *IPA*, 2, 119-124.

Pappu, S. S. Rama Rao and R[amakrishna] Puligandla (Eds.) (1983). *Indian Philosophy: Past and Future*. Columbia/Delhi: South Asia Books/Motilal Banarsidass.

Parain, Brice (Ed.) (1969). *Histoire de la philosophie*. Vol. 1. Paris: Gallimard.

Parasher, Aloka (1991). *Mlecchas in Early India: A Study in Attitudes towards Outsiders up to AD 600*. Delhi: Munshiram Manoharlal.

Parker, W[illiam] H. (1960). Europe: How Far? *The Geographical Journal*, 126, 278-297.

Parkinson, G[eorge] H. R. (1954). *Spinoza's Theory of Knowledge*. Oxford: Oxford University Press.

Patil, Narendranath B. (1987). Aṇī Māṇḍavya and Criminal Liability. *Vishveshvaranand Indological Journal*, 25/1-2, 150-154.

Patzig, Günther (1969). *Aristotle's Theory of Syllogism*. Tr. Jonathan Barnes. Dordrecht: D. Reidel. (Tr. of *Die aristotelische Syllogistik. Logisch-philologische Untersuchungen über das Buch A der "Ersten Analytiken."* Göttingen, 1959).

Paul, Gregor (1993). Equivalent Axioms of Aristotelian, or Traditional European, and Later Mohist Logic: An Argument in Favor of the Universality of Logic and Rationality. In Lenk and Paul 1993, pp. 119-135.

Peerenboom, R[andall] P. (1993). *Law and Morality in Ancient China*. Buffalo: State University of New York Press.

Peri, Sarveswara Sharma (1981). The Idea of Power (*śakti*) in the Vākyapadīya. *Bhāratīya Vidyā*, 41, 75-79.

Perry, Bruce M. (1995). *An Introduction to the Nyāyacaturgranthikā, with English Translations*. Ph.D. Dissertation, University of Pennsylvania, Philadelphia.

Peters, F[rancis] E. (1967). *Greek Philosophical Terms: A Historical Lexicon*. New York/London: New York University Press/University of London Press.

Peters, Heinz Frederick (1962). *My Sister, My Spouse. A Biography of Lou Andreas-Salomé*. New York: W. W. Norton and Company.

Piovesana, Gino K. (1968). *Recent Japanese Philosophical Thought 1862-1962*. Rev. ed. Tokyo: Enderle Bookstore.

Plantinga, Alvin (1993). *Warrant and Proper Function*. Oxford: Oxford University Press.

Poland, Lynn (1992). The Idea of the Holy and the History of the Sublime. *Journal of Religion*, 72/2, 175-197.

Poliakov, Léon (1974). *The Aryan Myth: A History of Racist and Nationalist Ideas in Europe*. Tr. Edmund Howard. London: Chatto Heinemann.

Pollock, Sheldon (1993). Deep Orientalism? Notes on Sanskrit and Power Beyond the Raj. In: Breckenridge and van der Veer 1993, pp. 76-133.

— (1989). Mīmāṃsā and the Problem of History in Traditional India. *JAOS*, **109**, 603-610.

Potter, Karl H. (Ed.) (1977). *Indian Metaphysics and Epistemology: The Tradition of Nyāya-Vaiśeṣika up to Gaṅgeśa*. Delhi: Motilal Banarsidass. (Encyclopedia of Indian Philosophies **2**)

— (1970). *Encyclopedia of Indian Philosophies: Bibliography*. Princeton: Princeton University Press. (Encyclopedia of Indian Philosophies **1**)

— (1965). *Presuppositions of India's Philosophy*. New Delhi: Prentice-Hall.

Potter, Karl H. and Sibajiban Bhattacharyya (Eds.) (1993). *Indian Philosophical Analysis: Navya-Nyāya from Gaṅgeśa to Raghunātha Śiromaṇi*. Delhi: Motilal Banarsidass. (Encyclopedia of Indian Philosophies **6**)

Preisendanz, K[arin] (1989). On *ātmendriyamanorthasannikarṣa* and the Nyāya-Vaiśeṣika Theory of Vision. *Berliner Indologische Studien*, **4/5**, 141-213.

Pritchard, James B. (Ed.) (1955). *Ancient Near Eastern Texts Relating to the Old Testament*. 2nd ed. Princeton: Princeton University Press.

Probyn, Elspeth (1993). *Sexing the Self: Gendered Positions in Cultural Studies*. New York: Routledge.

Proudfoot, Ian (1987). *Ahiṃsā and a Mahābhārata Story: The Development of the Story of Tulādhāra in the Mahābhārata in Connection with Non-Violence, Cow protection and Sacrifice*. Canberra: Faculty of Asian Studies, Australian National University. (Asian Studies Monographs, New Series **9**)

Puskás, Ildikó (1983). Herodotus and India. *Oikumene*, **4**, 201-207.

Qi, Gong (1991). The Relationships between Poetry, Calligraphy, and Painting. In: Alfreda Murck and Wen C. Fong (Eds.), *Words and Images: Chinese Poetry, Calligraphy, and Painting*. New York/Princeton: Metropolitan Museum of Art/Princeton University Press, pp. 11-20.

Radhakrishnan, Sarvepalli (1960). *The Brahma Sūtra: The Philosophy of Spiritual Life*. London: George Allen and Unwin.

— (1953). *The Principal Upanishads*. London: George Allen and Unwin.

— (1948). *The Bhagavadgītā*. London: George Allen and Unwin.

— (1940). *Eastern Religions and Western Thought*. London: Oxford University Press.

— (1931). *Indian Philosophy*. Vol. 2. Rev. 2nd ed. London: George Allen and Unwin.

— (1927a). *The Hindu View of Life*. London: George Allen and Unwin.

— (1927b). *Indian Philosophy*. Vol. 2. London: George Allen and Unwin.

— (1923). *Indian Philosophy*. Vol. 1. London George Allen and Unwin.

Radhakrishnan, Sarvepalli and Charles A. Moore (Eds.) (1957). *A Source Book in Indian Philosophy*. Princeton: Princeton University Press.

Raghavan, V[enkatarama] (1945-46). Dara Shikoh's Majma-ul-Bahrain (*Samudra-Saṃgama-Grantha*). *Journal of Oriental Research* (Madras), **15**, 150-157.

Rajneesh, Bhagavan Shree (1984). *Yoga: The Science of the Soul*. Rajneeshpuram, Oregon: Rajneesh Foundation International.

Raju, P[oolla] T[irupati] (1983). The Western and the Indian Philosophical Traditions. In: Pappu and Puligandla 1983, pp. 61-100.

— (1970 [1962]). *Introduction to Comparative Philosophy*. Carbondale/Edwardsville: University of Southern Illinois Press.

Ramachandra Rao, S[aligrama] K[rishna] (1978). *Jīvanmukti in Advaita*. Bangalore: IBH Prakashana.

Ramachandran, S. K. and N. Veezinathan (1966). *Jīvanmukti* and Social Concerns. *IPA*, **2**, 125-130.

Ramanujan, A. K. (1991). Repetition in the Mahābhārata. In: Arvind Sharma (Ed.), *Essays on the Mahābhārata*. Leiden: E. J. Brill, pp. 419-443. (Brill's Indological Library **1**)

Rapson, E[dward] J. (Ed.) (1922). *The Cambridge History of India*. Vol. I. *Ancient India*. Cambridge: Cambridge University Press.

Rasmussen, Knud (1929). *Intellectual Culture of the Iglulik Eskimos*. Copenhagen: Gyldendalske Boghandel. (Report of the Fifth Thule Expedition 1921-24)

Rawlinson, George (Ed./Tr.) (1862). *History of Herodotus: A New English Version*. Vol. 2. London: Murray.

Ray, Prafulla Chandra (1956 [1902]). *A History of Hindu Chemistry*. Calcutta: Indian Chemical Society. [repr. of London: Williams and Norgate]

Raychaudhuri, Tapan (1988). *Europe Reconsidered: Perceptions of the West in Nineteenth Century Bengal*. Delhi: Oxford University Press.

Rawlinson, Hugh George (1926). *Intercourse between India and the Western World*. 2nd ed. Cambridge: Cambridge University Press.

Reding, Jean-Paul (1993). La pensée rationelle en Chine ancienne. In: Fløistad 1993, pp. 165-193.

— (1985). *Les fondements philosophiques de la rhétorique chez les sophistes grecs et chez les sophistes chinois*. Bern: Lang.

Reese, Wilhelm (1914). *Die griechischen Nachrichten über Indien bis zum Feldzuge Alexanders des Grossen*. Dissertation, Leipzig.

Reichenbach, Bruce R. (1990). *The Law of Karma: A Philosophical Study*. Honolulu: University of Hawaii Press.

Reid, Thomas (1983). Inquiry into the Human Mind on the Principles of Common Sense. In: Ronald Beanblossom and Keith Lehrer (Eds.), *Thomas Reid's Inquiry and Essays*. Indianapolis: Hackett Publishing.

Rhys Davids, Th[omas] W. (Tr.) (1890, 1894). *The Questions of King Milinda*. 2 vols. Oxford: Clarendon Press.

Rhys Davids, Th[omas] W. and William Stede (1921). *The Pali Text Society's Pali-English Dictionary*. London: Luzac.

Ricoeur, Paul (1978). The Task of Hermeneutics. In Murray 1978, pp. 141-160.

Rizvi, S[aiyid] A[thar] A[bbas] (1993). *The Wonder that was India*. Vol. II. *A Survey of the History and Culture of the Indian Sub-Continent from the Coming of the Muslims to the British Conquest. 1200-1700*. New Delhi: Rupa.

Robinson, Sandra P. (1980). *The Dharmapuja: A Study of Rites and Symbols Associated with the Bengali Deity Dharmaraj*. Ph.D. Dissertation, University of Chicago.

Rodman, Margaret C. (1992). Empowering Place: Multilocality and Multivocality. *American Ethnologist*, 94/3, 640-656.

Roerich, G[eorge] (Yury) N[ikolayevich] (1945). Indology in Russia. *Journal of the Greater India Society*, 19/2, 69-98.

Rohner, Ronald P. and Manjusri Chaki-Sirkar (1988). *Women and Children in a Bengali Village*. Hanover, Connecticut: University of New England Press.

Romm, James S. (1992). *The Edges of the Earth in Ancient Thought*. Princeton: Princeton University Press.

Rorty, Richard, J[erome] B. Schneewind and Quentin Skinner (Eds.) (1981). *Philosophy in History*. Cambridge: Cambridge University Press.

Rosemont, Henry (Ed.) (1991). *Chinese Texts and Philosophical Contexts*. La Salle: Open Court.

Rossellini, Michèle and Suzanne Saïd (1978). Usages de femmes et autres nomoi chez les "sauvages" d'Hérodote: essai de lecture structurale. *Annali della Scuola Normale Superiore di Pisa, Classe di Lettere e Filosofia* Serie III, 8, 949-1005.

Roy, Priyada Ranjan (1978). *Vijñān, Darśan o Dharma* (Science, Philosophy & Religion). Calcutta: Jijñāsā.

Ruben, Walter (1928). *Die Nyāyasūtra's*. Text, Übersetzung, Einleitung und Glossar. Leipzig: Deutsche Morgenländische Gesellschaft. (AKM **18**,2)

Ruegg, D[avid] Seyfort (1994). *Pramāṇabhūta*, **pramāṇa(bhūta)-puruṣa*, *pratyakṣadharman* and *sākṣātkṛtadharman* as Epithets of the *ṛṣi*, *ācārya*, and *tathāgata* in Grammatical, Epistemological and Madhyamaka texts. *Bulletin of the School of Oriental and African Studies*, **57**/2, 203-320.

Rukmani, T[richur] S[ubramaniam] (Tr.) (1987). *Yogavārttika of Vijñānabhikṣu*. Vol. 3. *Vibhūtipāda*. New Delhi: Munṣhiram Manoharlal.

— (Tr.) (1983). *Yogavārttika of Vijñānabhikṣu*. Vol. 2. *Sādhanapāda*. New Delhi: Munshiram Manoharlal.

Russell, Bertrand (1966). *Sceptical Essays*. London: Unwin Books.

Said, Edward W. (1994). Afterword. In: Edward Said, *Orientalism*. New ed. New York: Vintage Books, pp. 329-352.

— (1989). Representing the Colonized: Anthropology's Interlocutors. *Critical Inquiry*, **15**, 205-225.

— (1978). *Orientalism*. London/New York: Routledge and Kegan Paul/Pantheon Books.

— (1976). Raymond Schwab and the Romance of Ideas. *Daedalus*, **105**/1, 151-167. [repr. as "Foreword" in Schwab 1984]

Saltykov, A[lexei] D[mitriyevich] (1985). *Pisma ob Indii* (Letters on India). Moscow: Nauka.

Samarin, William (1973). Sociolinguistics and Religion. *Georgetown University Monograph Series on Languages and Linguistics*, **25**, 335-337.

Sarkar, Sumit (1985). *The Kathamrita as a Text: Towards an Understanding of Ramakrishna Paramahamsa*. New Delhi: Nehru Memorial Museum and Library. (Occasional Papers on History and Society **22**)

Sastri, Gaurinath (1991). *Philosophy of Bhartṛhari*. Delhi/Varanasi: Bharatiya Vidya Prakashan.

— (1959). *The Philosophy of Word and Meaning: Some Indian Approaches with Special Reference to the Philosophy of Bhartṛhari*. Calcutta: Sanskrit College Research. (Calcutta Sanskrit College Series 5, Studies **2**)

Scharf, Peter M. (1993). Assessing Śabara's Arguments for the Conclusion that a Generic Term denotes just a Class Property. *JIP*, **21**, 1-10.

— (1990). *The Denotation of Generic Terms in Ancient Indian Grammar, Nyāya, and Mīmāṃsā*. Ph.D. Dissertation, University of Pennsylvania, Philadelphia.

Scharfstein, Ben-Ami (1989). *The Dilemma of Context*. New York: New York University Press.

— (Ed.) (1978). *Philosophy East/Philosophy West*. Oxford/New York: Basil Blackwell/Oxford University Press.

Schegloff, Emanuel A. (1972). Notes on a Conversational Practice: Formulating Place. In: David Sudnow (Ed.), *Studies in Social Interaction*. New York: The Free Press, pp. 75-119.

Schetelich, Maria (1977). *asvatantra* in der altindischen Rechtsliteratur. *Alt-Orientalische Forschungen*, **5**, 22-33.

Schimmel, Annemarie (1973). *Islamic Literatures of India*. Wiesbaden: Otto Harrassowitz.

Schmithausen, Lambert (1981). On Some Aspects of Descriptions or Theories of "Liberating Insight" and "Enlightenment" in Early Buddhism. In: Klaus Bruhn and Albrecht Wezler (Eds.), *Studien zum Jainismus und Buddhismus: Gedenkschrift für Ludwig Alsdorf*. Wiesbaden: Franz Steiner, pp. 199-250. (Alt- und Neu-Indische Studien **23**)

— (1965). *Maṇḍanamiśra's Vibhramavivekaḥ. Mit einer Studie zur Entwicklung der indischen Irrtumslehre*. Wien: Hermann Böhlaus Nachf. (Österreichische Akademie der Wissenschaften. Philosophisch-historische Klasse. Sitzungsberichte, **247**. Band, 1. Abhandlung. Veröffentlichungen der Kommission für Sprachen und Kulturen Süd- und Ostasiens, Heft 2)

Schneider, Ulrich Johannes (1990). *Die Vergangenheit des Geistes: Eine Archäologie der Philosophiegeschichte*. Frankfurt: Suhrkamp.

Schomer, Karine (1989). Paradigms for the Kali Yuga: The Heroes of the Ālhā Epic and Their Fate. In: Stuart H. Blackburn, Peter J. Claus, Joyce B. Flueckiger and Susan S. Wadley (Eds.), *Oral Epics in India*. Berkeley/Los Angeles/London: University of California Press, pp. 140-154.

Schüling, Hermann (1969). *Die Geschichte der axiomatischen Methode im 16. und beginnenden 17. Jahrhundert*. Hildesheim: Olms.

Schwab, Raymond (1984). *The Oriental Renaissance*. Tr. Gene Patterson-Black and Victor Reinking. New York: Columbia University Press.

— (1950). *La renaissance orientale*. Paris: Payot.

Schwartz, Benjamin (1985). *The World of Thought in Ancient China*. Cambridge, Massachusetts: Harvard University Press.

Schweer, Thomas (1990). Review of *Indien und Europa*. *Spirita*, **4**/1, 59-60.

Seal, Brajendra Nath (1958 [1915]). *The Positive Sciences of the Ancient Hindus*. Delhi: Motilal Banarsidass.

Seignobos, Charles (1939). *The Rise of European Civilization*. Tr. Catherine Alison Phillips. London: Jonathan Cape.

Sen (née Mookerjee), Reena (1992). Heidegger und die indische Perspektive: Heidegger und Sri Aurobindo. In: Dietrich Papenfuss and Otto Pöggeler (Eds.), *Zur philosophischen Aktualität Heideggers*. Band 3. Frankfurt: Vittorio Klostermann, pp. 273-291.

Sen, Sukumār (1975 [1963]). *Bāṅglā Sāhityer Itihās* 1 (The History of Bengali Literature, Volume 1). Barddhamān: Sāhitya Sabhā.

Serebriany, Sergei Dmitriyevich (1993a). The *Bhagavadgītā* in Russia (Notes towards the *Rezeptionsgeschichte*). In: Serebriany 1993b, pp. 50-71.

— (Ed.) (1993b). *The IXth World Sanskrit Conference (January 10-16 1994, Melbourne, Australia). Contributions of Russian Scholars*. Moscow: The Institute for Advanced Studies in the Humanities, Russian State University for the Humanities

— (1987). *Leo Tolstoy and Sri Ramakrishna*. Calcutta: The Ramakrishna Mission Institute of Culture.

Serres, Michel (1991). *Le tiers instruit*. Paris: F. Bourin.

Shamasastry, R[udrapatna] (Tr.) (1929). *Kauṭilya's Arthaśāstra*. 3rd ed. Mysore: Weseleyan Mission Press.

Sharma, Arvind (Ed.) (1988). *Neo-Hindu Views of Christianity*. Leiden: E. J. Brill.

Sharma, Virendra (1977). *Vākyapadīya-Sambandhasamuddeśa: Helārājīya vyākhyā ke prakāś meṃ ek vivecanātmak adhyayan* (Vākyapadīya - Saṃbandhasamuddeśa: A Critical Study with Special Reference to the Commentary of Helārāja). Hoshiarpur: Vishveshvaranand Vishva Bandhu Institute of Sanskrit and Indological Studies, Panjab University. (Panjab University Indological Series 9)

Sharpe, Eric J. (1985). *The Universal Gītā: Western Images of the Bhagavadgītā*. London: Duckworth.

Shastri, Dharmendra Nath (1964). *Critique of Indian Realism*. Agra: Agra University.

Shifman, Alexander (1978). *Tolstoy and India*. Tr. Alexander Vladimirovich Esaulov. New Delhi: Sahitya Akademi.

Shokhin, Vladimir (1986). Classical Sāṃkhya about the Ultimate Elements of the Material World. In: Wolfgang Morgenroth (Ed.), *Sanskrit and World Culture: Proceedings of the 4th World Sanskrit Conference of the International Association of Sanskrit Studies*. Berlin: Akademie-Verlag, pp. 556-559.

Silburn, Liliane (1955). *Instant et cause: Le discontinu dans la pensée philosophique de l'Inde*. Paris: Vrin.

Simpson, Jacqueline (1984). Beyond Etiology: Interpreting Local Legends. *Fabula*, **24**, 223-232.

Sinha, Jadunath (1961). *Indian Psychology*. Vol 2. Calcutta: Sinha Publishing House.

— (1958). *Indian Psychology*. Vol. 1. Calcutta: Sinha Publishing House.

— (1956). *A History of Indian Philosophy*. Vol. 1. Calcutta: Sinha Publishing House.

Sinha, Nandalal (Tr.) (1986 [1911]). *The Vaiśeṣika Sûtras of Kaṇâda with the Commentary of Śaṅkara Miśra and Extracts from the Gloss of Jayanârâyaṇa Together with Notes from the Commentary of Chandrakânta and an Introduction by the Translator*. Delhi: S. N. Publications. [repr. of Allahabad: Panini Office] (Sacred Books of the Hindus 20)

Sinha, Pradip (1978). *Calcutta in Urban History*. Calcutta: Firma KLM.

Sivin, Nathan (1992). Ruminations on the Tao and Its Disputers. *PEW*, **42**/1, 21-29.

Slaje, Walter (1992). Sarvasiddhāntasiddhānta. On "Tolerance" and "Syncretism" in the Yogavāsiṣṭha. *WZKS*, **36**, Supplementband, 307-322.

— (1986). Niḥśreyasam im alten Nyāya. *WZKS* **30**, 163-178.

Sloterdijk, Peter (1989). *Eurotaoismus: Zur Kritik der politischen Kinetik*. Frankfurt: Suhrkamp. (Edition Suhrkamp - Neue Folge)

— (1988). *Zur Welt kommen – Zur Sprache kommen*. Frankfurter Vorlesungen. Frankfurt: Suhrkamp. (Edition Suhrkamp - Neue Folge)

Smith, Brian K. (1994). *Classifying the Universe: The Ancient Indian Varṇa System and the Origins of Caste*. New York: Oxford University Press.

— (1989). *Reflections on Resemblance, Ritual and Religion*. New York/Oxford: Oxford University Press.

Smith, William L. (1982). The Celestial Village: The Divine Order in Bengali Myth. *Temenos*, **18**, 69-81.

— (1980). *The One-Eyed Goddess: A Study of the Manasā Maṅgal*. Stockholm: Almqvist and Wiskell International.

Snellgrove, David (1987). *Indo-Tibetan Buddhism*. 2 vols. Boston: Shambala.

Solbrig, Ingeborg H. (1973). *Hammer-Purgstall und Goethe*. Bern/Frankfurt: Herbert Lang.

Solomon, Esther A. (1978). *Indian Dialectics*. Vol. 2. Ahmedabad: B. J. Institute of Learning and Research.

— (1976). *Indian Dialectics*. Vol. 1. Ahmedabad: B. J. Institute of Learning and Research.

Sommerfeld, Susanne (1943). *Indienschau und Indiendeutung romantischer Philosophen*. Zürich: Rascher.

Southwold, Martin (1979). Religious Belief. *Man*, **14/4**, 628-644.

Spear, Percival (1963). *The Nabobs: A Study of the Social Life of the English in 18th Century India*. London: Oxford University Press.

Spivak, Gayatri Chakravorty (1994). Can the Subaltern Speak? In: Williams and Chrisman 1994, pp. 66-111.

— (1987). *In Other Worlds: Essays in Cultural Politics*. New York: Methuen.

Sprinker, Michal (Ed.) (1992). *Edward Said: A Critical Reader*. Oxford: Basil Blackwell.

Srivastava, Lalit Kishore Lal (1990). *Advaitic Conception of Jīvanmukti*. Delhi: Bharatiya Vidya Bhavan.

Staal, Frits (1988). *Universals: Studies in Indian Logic and Linguistics*. Chicago: University of Chicago Press.

Stacy, Robert H. (1985). *India in Russian Literature*. Delhi: Motilal Banarsidass.

Stahl, Sandra (1989). *Literary Folkloristics and the Personal Narrative*. Bloomington: Indiana University Press.

Stephenson, Gunther (1983). Review of *Indien und Europa*. *Philosophischer Literaturanzeiger*, **36**/1, 31-37.

Stietencron, Heinrich von (Ed.) (1992). *Epic and Purāṇic Bibliography* (upto 1985) annotated and with indexes. Compiled under the chairmanship of Heinrich von Stietencron by P. Flamm ... et al. Pt. II. Wiesbaden: Otto Harrassowitz.

Strauss, Leo (1936). *The Political Philosophy of Thomas Hobbes*. Oxford: Clarendon Press.

Stroud, Barry (1989). The Study of Human Nature and the Subjectivity of Value. In: Grethe Peterson (Ed.), *The Tanner Lectures on Human Values*. Vol. 10. Salt Lake City: University of Utah Press, pp. 211-259.

Sukale, Michael (1976). *Comparative Studies in Phenomenology*. The Hague: Martinus Nijhoff.

Sukthankar, Vishnu S. (1933). Prolegomena. In: *Mahābhārata* (cf. Texts in Sanskrit and Pali).

Sullivan, Bruce M. (1990). *Kṛṣṇa Dvaipāyana Vyāsa and the Mahābhārata: A New Interpretation*. Leiden: E. J. Brill.

Swarup, Ram (1991). Indo-European Encounter: An Indian Perspective. Review paper of *India and Europa*. *Journal of Indian Council of Philosophical Research*, 8/2, 75-96.

Sydow, Carl Wilhelm von (1948). Kategorien der Prosa-Volksdichtung. In: *Selected Papers on Folklore*. Kopenhagen: Rosenkilde and Bagger, pp. 60-88.

Taber, John (1992). What did Kumārila Bhaṭṭa mean by *svataḥ prāmāṇya*? *JAOS*, **112**/2, 204-221.

— (1991). Review of *India and Europe: An Essay in Understanding*. *PEW*, **41**/2, 229-240.

Tagare, Ganesh Vasudeo (Tr.) (1987, 1988). *The Vāyu Purāṇa*. 2 vols. Delhi: Motilal Banarsidass.

Tagore, Rabindranath (1988 [1931]). *The Religion of Man*. London etc.: Unwin Paperbacks. [repr. of London: George Allen and Unwin]

— (1969). *Towards Universal Man*. Bombay etc.: Asia Publishing House.

— (1917). *Nationalism*. London: Macmillan and Co.

— (1912). *Geetanjali: Song Offerings*. London: India Society.

Taimni, I. K. (1986 [1961]). *The Science of Yoga*. Wheaton: The Theosophical Publishing House.

Takenaka, Tomoyasu (1972). Fuhen to Kobutsu no Kankei no Ichi-Danmen - Bhāṭṭa Ha no bhedābheda Ronshō to Nyāya-Vaiśeṣika Hihan (The Relationship between "Universal" and "Individual"). *Journal of Indian and Buddhist Studies*, **20**/2, 122-126.

Tanaka, Stefan (1993). *Japan's Orient: Rendering Pasts into History*. Berkeley: University of California Press.

Thakur, Anantalal (1974). The Mahābhārata and the Nyāyaśāstra. *Proceedings of the All-India Oriental Conference*, 403-408.

Thapar, Romila (1966). *A History of India*. Vol. 1. Harmondsworth: Penguin Books.

Thibaut, G[eorge] (Tr.) (1988 [1904]). *The Vedânta-Sûtras with the Commentary by Śaṅkarācārya*. Delhi: Motilal Banarsidass. [repr. of Oxford: Clarendon Press] (SBE **34**, **38**)

— (Tr.) (1971 [1904]). *The Vedânta-Sûtras with the Commentary by Rāmānuja*. New Delhi: Motilal Banarsidass. [repr. of Oxford: Clarendon Press] (SBE **48**)

Thieme, Paul (1982-83). Meaning and Form of the "Grammar" of Pāṇini. *StII*, **8/9**, 3-24.

Titon, Jeff (1980). The Life Story. *Journal of American Folklore*, **93**/369, 276-292.

Tiwari, Kapil N. (1986). *Suffering: Indian Perspectives*. Delhi: Motilal Banarsidass.

Tooker, Deborah E. (1992). Identity Systems of Highland Burma: "Belief," *Akha zan*, and a Critique of Interiorized Notions of Ethno-Religious Identity. *Man*, **27**/4, 799-820.

Toporov, Vladimir (1985). Sanskrit i yego uroki (Sanskrit and Its Lessons). In: Grigory Bongard-Levin, Victoria Vertogradova and Sergei Kullanda (Eds.), *Drevnyaya Indiya: yazyk, kultura, tekst (*Ancient India: Language, Culture, Text). Moscow: Nauka (Vostochnaya literatura), pp. 5-29.

— (1983). Prostranstvo i tekst (Space and Text). In: Tatyana Tsivyan (Ed.), *Tekst: semantika i struktura (*Text: Semantics and Structure). Moscow: Nauka, pp. 227-285.

Tripathi, Dipti S. (1986). Apabhraṃśa in Sanskrit Grammar. An Appraisal of Bhartṛhari's View. *Aligarh Journal of Oriental Studies*, **3**, 81-92.

Tsalka, Dan (1993). Ko amar Kumarila (Thus Spake Kumārila). In: Dan Tsalka, *Dapim Mehudakim be'Eṭev* (Pages Held by a Peg). Tel Aviv: Zmora Bitan, pp. 138-140. [repr. of *Ha'ir*, December 16th, 1988]

Tsunoda, Ryusaku, Wm. Theodore de Bary and Donald Keene (Eds.) (1958). *Sources of Japanese Tradition*. New York: Columbia University Press.

Tuan, Yi-Fu (1991). Language and the Making of Place: A Narrative-Descriptive Approach. *Annals of the Association of American Geographers*, **81**/4, 684-696.

Turner, Ralph L. (1966). *A Comparative Dictionary of the Indo-Aryan Languages*. London: Oxford University Press.

Twitchett, Denis and Michael Loewe (Eds.) (1986). *The Cambridge History of China*. Vol. 1. Cambridge: Cambridge University Press.

Utgikar, N[arayan] B[apuji] (1922). The Story of the Ṛṣi Aṇī-Māṇḍavya in Its Sanskrit and Buddhistic Sources. In: *Proceedings and Transactions of the Second Oriental Conference*. Calcutta: Calcutta University Press, pp. 231-238.

Valiaveetil, Chacko (1980). *Liberated Life*. Madurai: Dialogue Series.

Van Buitenen, J[ohannes] A. B. (Tr.) (1973). *The Mahābhārata*. Vol. 1. *1. The Book of Beginning*. Chicago/London: The University of Chicago Press.

Van der Veer, Peter (1993). The Foreign Hand. In: Breckenridge and van der Veer 1993, pp. 23-44.

Vázquez, Adolfo Sánchez (1977). *The Philosophy of Praxis*. Tr. Mike Gonzalez. London: Merlin Press.

Veezhinathan, N. (Tr.) (1985). *The Saṃkṣepa-śārīraka of Sarvajñātman*. Madras: University of Madras.

Verpoorten, Jean-Marie (1987). *Mīmāṃsā Literature*. Wiesbaden: Otto Harrassowitz. (*History of Indian Literature*, ed. Jan Gonda, 6,5)

Versluis, Arthur (1993). *American Transcendentalism and Asian Religions*. London/New York: Oxford University Press.

Vivekananda, Swami (1987). *The Complete Works of Swami Vivekananda*. Vol. II. Calcutta: Advaita Ashrama.

— (1986). *The Complete Works of Swami Vivekananda*. Vol. I. Calcutta: Advaita Ashrama.

— (1985). *The Complete Works of Swami Vivekananda*. Vol. VI. Calcutta: Advaita Ashrama.

— (1984). *The Complete Works of Swami Vivekananda*. Vol. III. Calcutta: Advaita Ashrama.

— (1982). *Rāja-Yoga*. Calcutta: Advaita Ashrama.

— (1962). *What Religion is in the Words of Swami Vivekananda*. Ed. J. Yale. London: Phoenix House.

— (1953). *The Yogas and Other Works*. New York: Ramakrishna-Vivekananda Center.

Vofchuk, Rosalía C. (1982a). Costumbres y creencias de los indios según Ctesias de Cnido. *Papeles de la India*, **10-11** (1981-82), 59-76.

— (1982b). Las costumbres y creencias filosófico-religiosas de la India según Herodoto de Halicarnaso. *Argos*, **6**, 85-97.

Wada, Toshihiro (1990). *Invariable Comcomitance in Navya-Nyāya*. Delhi: Sri Satguru Publications (Indian Books Centre).

Walicki, Andrzej (1979). *A History of Russian Thought from the Enlightenment to Marxism*. Tr. Hilda Andrews-Rusiecka. Stanford, California: Stanford University Press.

Waligora, Melitta (1984). Review of *Indien und Europa*. *Deutsche Zeitschrift für Philosophie*, **32**/4, 393-396.

Warder, A[nthony] K. (1971). *Outline of Indian Philosophy*. Delhi: Motilal Banarsidass.

Watson, Burton (Tr.) (1968). *The Complete Works of Chuang Tzu*. New York: Columbia University Press.

— (Tr.) (1963). *Hsün Tzu: Basic Writings*. New York: Columbia University Press.

Wezler, Albrecht (1996). An Internal Contradiction in the Mṛcchakaṭika? Some Remarks on Impalement in Ancient and Mediaeval India. *StII*, **20** (= Friedrich Wilhelm (Ed.), *Festschrift Dieter Schlingloff*), 287-306.

— (1995) Der Tod als Mittel der Entsühnung (gemäß dem Dharmaśāstra). In: Gerhard Oberhammer (Ed.), *Im Tod gewinnt der Mensch sein Selbst: Das Phänomen des Todes in asiatischer und abendländischer Religionstradition*. Wien: Verlag der österreichischen Akademie der Wissenschaften, pp. 97-140. (Österreichische Akademie der Wissenschaften. Philosophisch-historische Klasse. Sitzungsberichte, **624**. Band. Beiträge zur Kultur- und Geistesgeschichte Asiens **14**)

— (1992). How Far did Pāṇini's Fame really extend in Patañjali's View? In: Anantalal Thakur (Ed.), *Corpus of Indological Studies. Professor Ramaranjan Mukherji Felicitation Volume*. Delhi: Sharada Publishing House, pp. 468-478.

— (1982). Remarks on the Definition of "yoga"' in the Vaiśeṣikasūtra. In: Louise A. Hercus et al., *Indological and Buddhist Studies: Volume in Honour of Professor J. W. de Jong on his Sixtieth Birthday*. Canberra: Faculty of Asian Studies, pp. 643-686.

Wheatley, Paul (1961). *The Golden Chersonese*. Kuala Lumpur: University of Malaya Press.

White, Hayden (1980). The Value of Narrativity in the Representation of Reality. *Critical Inquiry*, 7, 5-27.

Wiener, Philip P. (Ed.) (1973). *Dictionary of the History of Ideas*. New York: Scribners.

Williams, Patrick and Laura Chrisman (Eds.) (1994). *Colonial Discourse and Post-Colonial Theory: A Reader*. New York: Columbia University Press.

Williams, Paul (1989). *Mahāyāna Buddhism: The Doctrinal Foundations*. London/New York: Routledge.

Wilson, Horace Hayman (1979 [1819]). *A Dictionary, Sanscrit and English*. Delhi: Nag Publishers. [repr. of Calcutta: P. Pereira]

Wink, André (1991). *Al-Hind: The Making of the Indo-Islamic World*. Vol. I. Leiden: E. J. Brill.

Wittgenstein, Ludwig (1968). *Philosophical Investigations*. Tr. G[ertrude] E. M. Anscombe. Oxford: Basil Blackwell.

— (1961). *Tractatus Logico-Philosophicus*. Tr. D[avid] F. Pears and B[rian] F. McGuinness. London: Routledge and Kegan Paul.

Wolf, Larry (1994). *Inventing Eastern Europe*. Stanford, California: Stanford University Press.

Wolfson, Harry A. (1934). *The Philosophy of Spinoza: Unfolding the Latent Processes of His Reasoning*. 2 vols. Cambridge, Massachusetts: Harvard University Press.

Wright, Arthur F. (1959). *Buddhism in Chinese History*. Stanford: Stanford University Press.

Yoyotte, Jean (1969). La pensée préphilosophique en Egypt. In Parin 1969, pp. 1-23.

Zürcher, Erik (1972). *The Buddhist Conquest of China*. 2 vols. Leiden: E. J. Brill.

## ABOUT THE CONTRIBUTORS

*Johannes BRONKHORST* is Professor of Sanskrit and Indian Studies at the University of Lausanne, Switzerland. Having initially opted for a middle-of-the-road career as a mathematician, he realized just in time that this would not give him optimal satisfaction. He then disappeared to India, only to re-emerge a number of years later with an insatiable passion for classical Indian studies, in particular for the question how Indians of that period tried to make sense of the world. His publications are in the realm of traditional Sanskrit grammar, Indian philosophy and its various manifestations, ascetic practices, the impact of Buddhism, etc.

*Francis X. CLOONEY*, SJ, is Professor of Comparative Theology at Boston College, where he has taught since 1984. After teaching high school in Kathmandu, Nepal, during 1973-1975 and completing theological studies for ordination as a Jesuit priest in 1978, he pursued Ph.D. studies in the Department of South Asian Languages and Civilizations at the University of Chicago, specializing in classical India in the Sanskrit and Tamil language traditions. His dissertation, on the early Pūrva Mīmāṃsā ritual school of theology, was published in 1990 as *Thinking Ritually: Rediscovering the Pūrva Mīmāṃsā of Jaimini* (De Nobili Research Series XVII, University of Vienna, 1990). Consequent study on the Mīmāṃsā roots of Vedānta theology, coupled with comparative theological interests, led to *Theology after Vedānta: An Experiment in Comparative Theology* (Albany: State University of New York Press, 1993). He has recently completed *Seeing through Texts: Doing Theology among the Śrīvaiṣṇavas of South India* (Albany: State University of New York Press, 1996) on the Tamil devotional classic *Tiruvaimoli*, its traditional commentaries, and implications of both for Christian theology. Current projects include the comparative study of scholasticism, and the development of systematic theology in the Hindu and Christian traditions.

*Fred DALLMAYR* is Packey Dee Professor of Political Theory in the Department of Government and International Studies at the University of Notre Dame. He holds a doctor of law degree from the University of Munich and a Ph.D. in political science from Duke University. He has been a visiting professor at Hamburg University and at the New School for Social Research in New York, and a fellow at Nuffield College in Oxford. He has been teaching at Notre Dame since 1978. During fall of

1991 he was in India on a Fullbright research grant. Among his publications are: *Beyond Dogma and Despair* (1981), *Twilight of Subjectivity* (1981), *Language and Politics: Why Does Language Matter to Political Philosophy?* (1984), *Polis and Praxis: Exercises in Contemporary Political Theory* (1984), *Critical Encounters between Philosophy and Politics* (1987), *Margins of Political Discourse* (1989), *Life-World, Modernity and Critique* (1991; British edition), *Between Freiburg and Frankfurt: Toward a Critical Ontology* (1991; American edition), *G.W.F. Hegel: Modernity and Politics* (1993), *The Other Heidegger* (1993), and *Beyond Orientalism: Essays on Cross-Cultural Encounter* (1996).

*Stuart ELKMAN*, also known as Brahmachari Veda Chaitanya, is a monastic member of the Ramakrishna Order and resident of the Ramakrishna Monastery in Trabuco Canyon, California, a branch of the Vedanta Society of Southern California. He received his B.A. in philosophy from Northwestern University in 1970 and his Ph.D. from the University of Pennsylvania in 1981. It was at the University of Pennsylvania that he had the privilege of studying with Professor Halbfass under whom he wrote his dissertation on Jīva Gosvāmin's *Tattvasandarbha*.

*Andrew O. FORT* is Associate Professor of Religion at Texas Christian University. He studied Indian thought with Wilhelm Halbfass at the University of Pennsylvania, where he received his Ph.D. in 1982. He is the author of *The Self and Its States: A States of Consciousness Doctrine in Advaita Vedānta* (Delhi: Motilal Banarsidass, 1990) and co-editor (with Patricia Mumme) of the forthcoming *Living Liberation in Hindu Thought* (Albany: State University of New York Press). His articles have appeared in *Journal of Indian Philosophy, Philosophy East and West, Religious Studies Review*, and other journals. His research interests include classical Advaita Vedānta and modern "neo-Vedānta" interpretations of Advaita.

*Yohanan GRINSHPON* grew up in Kibbutz Yagur, Israel. He studied philosophy and sociology at the Hebrew University, Jerusalem, during the years 1969-1973. After a break of eight years he started studies in comparative religion and Sanskrit under Professor David Shulman. His M.A. thesis focused on Śaṅkara's theory of language and liberation. In 1987, as a Lady Davis Fellow, he commenced his Ph.D. program at the

University of Pennsylvania, under the guidance of Professor Wilhelm Halbfass. The dissertation, completed in 1995, deals with the meaning and the status of the supra-normal powers (*siddhis*) in the tradition of Pātañjala Yoga. At present he teaches Indian philosophy in the Department of East-Asian Studies at Tel-Aviv University and in the Department of Indian, Iranic and Armenian Studies at the Hebrew University.

*Minoru HARA* is Emeritus Professor of Sanskrit at the University of Tokyo. Born in 1930 in Tokyo, he was primarily trained in Indian philosophy at the University of Tokyo (1950-53) and studied at Harvard under D.H.H. Ingalls (1955-60). From 1960-1991 he has taught in Tokyo. His dissertation at Harvard dealt with Pāśupata Śaivism, but later on his interest turned to Epic and Classical Sanskrit literature. His second dissertation in Tokyo dealt with the concept of *tapas* in the *Mahābhārata*. In numerous articles he has studied the semantic field of Sanskrit terms (e.g., *bhakti* and *śraddhā*, *guru* and *ācārya*, *bāṣpa* and *aśru*, *jana*, *tapas*, *śīla*, *garbha*). Recently he has become interested in the comparative study of Epic and Pāli Buddhist texts. - At Harvard he was of course influenced by Ingalls, who especially admired five Indologists of the past: A. Weber, H. Oldenberg, G. Bühler, H. Lüders and S. Lévi. During his 31 years of teaching in Tokyo, his main effort was concentrated on internationalizing Japanese Indology in cooperation with his colleagues Ojihara and Hattori in Kyoto, by inviting scholars of eminence from the West (Wilhelm Halbfass included, of course), contributing papers to publications abroad, and sending able young students to the West.

*Kunio HARIKAI* is Associate Professor at the Saga Medical School, Saga City, on Kyūshū, Japan. He studied Indian philosophy and Buddhism under the guidance of Dr. Shoren Ihara of Kyūshū University, and chose Mīmāṃsā philosophy as his special field. His Ph.D. thesis (1987), *Hermeneutics in Classical India: The Mīmāṃsaka Conception of arthavāda and mantra*, was published by Kyūshū University Press in 1990. He is also a naturalist and a member of the Saga Entomological Society. In three issues of *Saga no Konchū* (*Insect of Saga*) he has elucidated the scientific names of Sanskrit origin of more than five hundred tropical butterflies, found in India, Taiwan and Japan.

*Jan E.M. HOUBEN* was born in 1960 in the Netherlands. Since 1978 he studied psychology, linguistics, and classical and Vedic Sanskrit at the

University of Utrecht, where he obtained his M.A. degree in 1987 with a study and translation of *Taittirīya-Āraṇyaka* chapter 5, an ancient commentary on the *pravargya* ritual (published in Delhi, 1991). After carrying out research on Bhartṛhari's philosophy of language in Utrecht, Vancouver and Lausanne, he obtained his Ph.D. in Utrecht in 1992 with a thesis on the *Sambandhasamuddeśa* of the *Vākyapadīya* (published in 1995 in the Gonda Indological Series, Groningen). At present he is affiliated with the International Institute for Asian Studies, Leiden, and the Kern Institute of Leiden University as a NWO fellow. His main interests are Vedic, classical and modern Sanskrit, philosophy of language, ancient Indian philosophy, and Vedic ritual.

*Rada IVEKOVIĆ*, philosopher, Indologist, writer, was born in Zagreb, Yugoslavia, in 1945. She left Zagreb, Croatia, where she had been Chair of Asian Philosophies at the Philosophy Department of the local university, in 1992. She now lives and works in Paris. She has published a dozen or so books as well as many articles in Serbocroat, concerning philosophy (mostly Indian and comparative, including some translations from Sanskrit and Pāli, textbooks and essays), feminist philosophy, literary criticism, essays. Recent books in foreign languages are *Orients: Critique de la raison postmoderne* (Paris: Noël Blandin, 1992), *Benares: Ein Essay aus Indien* (Graz: Literaturverlag Droschl, 1993), *Jugoslawischer Salat* (Graz: Literaturverlag Droschl, 1993), co-authored with Biljana Jovanović, Maruša Krese, Radmila Lazić and Duška Perišić-Osti: *Briefe von Frauen über Krieg und Nationalismus* (Frankfurt a.M./Berlin: Suhrkamp, 1993), and *La balcanizzazione della ragione: Il caso jugoslawo* (Roma: Manifesto libri, 1995). She has edited, together with Jacques Poulain, *Europe-Inde-Postmodernité* (Paris: Noël Blandin, 1993), and *La Croatie depuis l'effondrement de la Yougoslavie: L'opposition non-nationaliste* (Paris: L'Harmattan, 1994).

*Klaus KARTTUNEN* was born in 1951 in Helsinki. He began studies in Sanskrit, Greek and Latin at Helsinki University in 1971 and completed his M.A. in 1977. Unable to make a final choice between two interesting fields, he has tried to go in with a combination of both. After a Licentiate degree in 1985 in Indology, he obtained his Ph.D. in Indology and classical philology (Greek) in 1989. Since 1977 he is teaching at the Departments of Asian Studies (Indology), History (South Asian History), and Classical Philology at Helsinki University. In 1990 he became a docent of Indology and classical ethnography at Helsinki. During 1991-1992 and 1994-1995 he conducted research as an Alexander von Humboldt-fellow at the University of Freiburg, Germany. In addition to *India in Early Greek Literature* (Studia Orientalia 65, Helsinki 1989) and to several books and translations in Finnish, he has published numerous articles on Graeco-Indian relations and the history of Indian and Oriental studies, and also some contributions in the field of Indology.

*Dermot KILLINGLEY* is Senior Lecturer in the Department of Religious Studies, University of Newcastle upon Tyne, where he runs an annual seminar on The Sanskrit Tradition in the Modern World. He has studied in Oxford and London, and was Lecturer in the Department of Indian Studies, University of Malaya, Kuala Lumpur. In 1990 he gave the Westcott Memorial Lectures (also known as the Teape Lectures) in Bangalore, Calcutta and Delhi. He is interested in the Sanskrit tradition and its interaction with modern India and the modern world, and his publications in this field include *Rammohun Roy in Hindu and Christian Tradition* (The Teape Lectures, 1990; Newcastle upon Tyne: Grevatt & Grevatt, 1993) and *Hindu Ritual and Society* (with Werner Menski and Shirley Firth; Newcastle upon Tyne: Grevatt & Grevatt, 1991). He is also interested in the presentation of Hinduism in religious education, and has written a book for teachers, *Approaches to Hinduism* (with Robert Jackson; London: John Murray, 1988). He has written a descriptive sketch for linguists, *Sanskrit* (with Siew-Yue Killingley; Munich: Lincom Europa, 1995), and is completing work on a Sanskrit teaching book.

*Frank J. KOROM* is a Curator of Asian and Middle Eastern Collections at the Museum of International Folk Art in Santa Fe. Trained in folkloristics, anthropology and religious studies, he is interested in a number of ethnographic and philosophical problems related to the study of South Asia. In addition to his indological interests, his research has focussed on the theoretical implications of diasporas originating in India and Tibet. His articles have appeared in such journals as *Asian Folklore Studies*, *Diaspora*, *The Tisch Drama Review*, *The World of Music*, and many others. Among his books are a co-edited volume titled *Gender, Genre and Power in South Asian Expressive Traditions* (Philadelphia: University of Pennsylvania Press, 1991) and a co-authored textbook titled *Folkloristics and Indian Folklore* (Udupi: Regional Resources Centre for the Folk

Performing Arts, 1991). He is currently completing a book-length manuscript on the Islamic *muḥarram* observance as practiced in Trinidad.

*Victoria LYSENKO*, born in 1953 in Prjevalski, Kirghizia, graduated from the Department of Philosophy at Moscow State University in 1976 and from the post-graduate courses at the Institute for History of Science and Technology in 1979. Afterwards she worked as a scholar–editor at the publishing house "Soviet Encyclopaedia." Since 1990 she is a Senior Research Fellow at the Institute of Philosophy of the Russian Academy of Science. She has published, in Russian, *Indian Philosophy of Nature: The Atomism of the Vaiśeṣika School* (Moscow: Nauka Publishers, 1986), *An Introduction to Buddhism: Early Buddhist Philosophy. A Manual for High Schools* (Moscow: Nauka Publishers, 1994), and *Early Buddhist Philosophy* in the series *History of Indian Philosophy*, edited by Marietta Stepanyants (Vol. II, Moscow: Nauka Publishers, 1995). At present she works on a translation into Russian of Praśastapāda's *Padārthadharmasaṅgraha*, along with extracts from Śrīdhara's commentary and historico-philosophical annotation. She also lectures on the history of Indian philosophy at Moscow State University.

*Jitendra Nath MOHANTY* is Professor of Philosophy at Temple University, Philadelphia. He studied in Calcutta and Göttingen where he earned his Ph.D. in 1954. Returning to India, he joined Vinoba Bhave's "Land-gift" movement, and after a year's walk across the state of Orissa, joined the faculty of the University of Calcutta's graduate school while continuing to study Navya-Nyāya under Pandit Ananta Kumar Tarkatirtha of the Sanskrit College, Calcutta. Main works on phenomenology include *Edmund Husserl's Theory of Meaning* (1964), *Husserl and Frege* (1982), *The Possibility of Transcendental Philosophy* (1985), and *Transcendental Phenomenology: An Analytic Account* (1989). Works on Indian philosophy include *Gaṅgeśa's Theory of Truth* (1964), *Reason and Tradition in Indian Thought* (1992), and *Essays on Indian Philosophy, Traditional and Modern* (1993). A past president of the Indian Philosophical Congress, he is also a Humboldt-Forschungspreisträger for 1992, Visiting Fellow of All Souls College, Oxford and member of the Institut Internationale de Philosophie, Paris, and was awarded the Sir William Jones Memorial Gold Medal by the Asiatic Society, Calcutta, in 1993.

*Joseph S. O'LEARY* lectures in English literature at Sophia University, Tokyo. Born in Cork, Ireland in 1949, he studied literature, theology, and philosophy in Maynooth, Rome and Paris, and has taught these subjects in the US, the Philippines and Japan. He has drawn on Heidegger and Derrida for a re-examination of the Athens/Jerusalem tension in Christian tradition (especially in Origen and Augustine). In *La verité chrétienne à l'âge du pluralisme religieux* (1994) he reassesses Christian language and doctrine in the light of the Buddhist two truths-theory. He has also pursued a theological dialogue with literature in essays on Joyce, Beckett and Yeats.

*Bruce M. PERRY* received a Ph.D. in Classics at the University of Washington in 1983: his dissertation was a study of Simplicius' quotations and interpretations of Parmenides. Currently he is preparing a translation of the first half of the first book of Simplicius' commentary on Aristotle's *Physics*. His second Ph.D., from the Department of Asian and Middle Eastern Studies at the University of Pennsylvania, was earned with a translation and study of the four oldest commentaries on the first *sūtra* of the *Nyāyasūtra*. He is a Tutor at St. John's College in Santa Fe since 1990, and was Visiting Lecturer (in Sanskrit) in the Department of South Asian Languages and Civilization at the University of Chicago in 1993-1994. His next Indological project is to prepare a critical edition of Book V of Udayana's *Pariśuddhi* as a preliminary to a study of the *Nyāyapariśiṣṭa*, by the same author: he would like to explore the topic of philosophical dialectic in India. His areas of interest are, then, Greek and Indian philosophy, and the Indian grammatical tradition.

*Srinivasa RAO*, born in 1939, obtained his M.A. and Ph.D. degrees in philosophy from the University of Mysore, India. He became a Lecturer in the Department of Philosophy at the University of Mysore in 1968 and later on moved over to Bangalore University as Reader in 1977 where he became Professor of Philosophy in 1986. He has worked in the areas of logic, philosophy of science, epistemology and Indian philosophy. Outside of philosophy, his serious interests extend to photography and computers. He has published *Advaita: A Critical Investigation*, and his second book, *Perceptual Error: The Indian Theories*, is under publication. He has visited Germany as a fellow of the German Academy, and also some universities in the USA.

*Ben-Ami SCHARFSTEIN* was born in 1919, in New York City. After teaching at Brooklyn College and the University of Utah, he moved in 1955 to Israel, where he founded the Department of Philosophy of Tel-Aviv University, then in its inception. Interested in art, literature, psychology, and the social sciences, he tends to disregard disciplinary and cultural boundaries and the resulting danger of error. His recent books include *The Philosophers: Their Lives and the Nature of Their Thought* (1980), *Of Birds, Beasts, and Other Artists: An Essay on the Universality of Art* (1988), *The Dilemma of Context* (1989), and *Ineffability: The Failure of Words in Philosophy and Religion* (1993). *Amoral Politics: The Persistent Truth of Machiavellism*, a cross-cultural study, has been published in 1995.

*Reena SEN* (née Mookerjee), born in 1936, is Professor of Philosophy at the University of Calcutta. Having received her M.A. degree from the same university, she was an Alexander von Humboldt-fellow at the University of Göttingen from 1961 to 1964, where she earnt her Dr. phil. degree in 1965 for a thesis entitled *Der Begriff der Imagination in der theoretischen Philosophie David Humes*. Kant-studies, phenomenology and existentialism form some of her present areas of interest, and she has published several papers on these topics. Her career as a teacher extends over a period of thirty years covering two universities – Visva-Bharati (Santiniketan, India) and Calcutta University. Her latest paper is included in *Zur philosophischen Aktualität Heideggers*, Band 3 (1992).

*Sergei Dimitriyevich SEREBRIANY* was born in 1946 in Moscow and graduated in 1968 from the Institute of Oriental Languages at Moscow State University, majoring in Hindi and Indian literature. The academic year 1967-68 he spent in India, at the Benares Hindu University and the Deccan College, Poona. From 1970 to 1992 he was a Research Fellow at the Gorky Institute of World Literature in Moscow. Since 1992 he works as a Research Fellow at the Institute for Advanced Studies in the Humanities at the Russian State University for the Humanities. His research and publications have been mostly in the field of Indian (South Asian) and comparative literature, but recently he tries to move into what may be called comparative studies of cultures or comparative cultural history.

*John TABER* is Associate Professor of Philosophy at the University of New Mexico. His dissertation, *Transformative Philosophy: A Study of Śaṅkara, Fichte, and Heidegger* (Universität Hamburg), was published by the University of Hawaii Press in 1983. He has written articles on Indian philosophy, especially Mīmāṃsā, for a variety of anthologies and journals. He is currently working on a longer, systematic study of the thought of Kumārilabhaṭṭa. The question that has motivated much of his work is: what is revelation; in particular, is it the same *logos* that finds expression in both revelation and philosophy? He has found the investigation of Mīmāṃsā philosophy to be an especially apt way to pursue this question.

*Albrecht WEZLER*, born at the beginning of World War II, decided to study Indology (as main subject) after leaving school in 1958. His father, a professor of physiology, who had expected him to become a physician, too, was accordingly deeply worried by this decision; for he thought that there was no money in Indology, and that it is no real science. In order to teach his father better, A.W., after studying with his *guru* Paul Thieme for four years, had to write a doctoral dissertation (1965) and in addition a second thesis (*Habilitationsschrift*) (1972). Much to his surprise he was appointed Professor of Indology at the University of Hamburg the same year. Since then he has continued his studies, letting himself be fascinated by various aspects of Indian culture. His unsteadiness, documented mainly in a number of articles, is interpreted by some of his colleagues as testifying to his breadth - a view which he finds amusing (but quite understandably he does not want this to be disclosed).